Ethics and Medical Decision-Making

The International Library of Medicine, Ethics and Law
Series Editor: Michael D. Freeman

Titles in the Series

Death, Dying and the Ending of Life
Margaret P. Battin, Leslie Francis and Bruce Landesman

Abortion
Belinda Bennett

Ethics and Medical Decision-Making
Michael Freeman

Children, Medicine and the Law
Michael Freeman

Health and Human Rights
Lawrence O. Gostin and James G. Hodge Jr.

Mental Illness, Medicine and Law
Martin Lyon Levine

The Elderly
Martin Lyon Levine

The Genome Project and Gene Therapy
Sheila A.M. McLean

Rights and Resources
Frances H. Miller

AIDS: Society, Ethics and Law
Udo Schüklenk

Women, Medicine, Ethics and the Law
Susan Sherwin and Barbara Parish

Legal and Ethical Issues in Human Reproduction
Bonnie Steinbock

Medical Practice and Malpractice
Harvey Teff

Human Experimentation and Research
David N. Weisstub and George F. Tomossy

Ethics and Medical Decision-Making

Edited by

Michael Freeman

University College London, UK

LONDON AND NEW YORK

First published 2001 by Dartmouth Publishing Company and Ashgate Publishing

Reissued 2018 by Routledge
2 Park Square, Milton Park, Abingdon, Oxon OX14 4RN
605 Third Avenue, New York, NY 10017

Routledge is an imprint of the Taylor & Francis Group, an informa business

Copyright © Michael Freeman 2001.
For copyright of individual articles please refer to the Acknowledgements.

All rights reserved. No part of this book may be reprinted or reproduced or utilised in any form or by any electronic, mechanical, or other means, now known or hereafter invented, including photocopying and recording, or in any information storage or retrieval system, without permission in writing from the publishers.

Notice:
Product or corporate names may be trademarks or registered trademarks, and are used only for identification and explanation without intent to infringe.

Publisher's Note
The publisher has gone to great lengths to ensure the quality of this reprint but points out that some imperfections in the original copies may be apparent.

Disclaimer
The publisher has made every effort to trace copyright holders and welcomes correspondence from those they have been unable to contact.

A Library of Congress record exists under LC control number: 00069961

ISBN 13: 978-1-138-70255-4 (hbk)
ISBN 13: 978-1-138-62942-4 (pbk)
ISBN 13: 978-1-315-20969-2 (ebk)

DOI: 10.4324/9781315209692

Contents

Acknowledgements ix
Series Preface xiii
Introduction xv

PART I   WHAT IS BIOETHICS?

1 Henry K. Beecher (1966), 'Ethics and Clinical Research', *New England Journal of Medicine*, **274**, pp. 1354–60. 3
2 Loren C. MacKinney (1952), 'Medical Ethics and Etiquette in the Early Middle Ages: The Persistence of Hippocratic Ideals', *Bulletin of the History of Medicine*, **26**, pp. 1–31. 11

PART II   BIOETHICS AND LAW

3 Wibren Van der Burg (1997), 'Bioethics and Law: A Developmental Perspective', *Bioethics*, **11**, pp. 91–114. 45

PART III   BIOETHICS AND RELIGION

4 Daniel Callahan (1990), 'Religion and the Secularization of Bioethics', *Hastings Center Report*, **20** (Supplement), pp. 2–4. 71
5 Courtney S. Campbell (1990), 'Religion and Moral Meaning in Bioethics', *Hastings Center Report*, **20** (Supplement), pp. 4–10. 75
6 Lisa Sowle Cahill (1990), 'Can Theology Have a Role in "Public" Bioethical Discourse?', *Hastings Center Report*, **20** (Supplement), pp. 10–14. 83
7 David Novak (1990), 'Bioethics and the Contemporary Jewish Community', *Hastings Center Report*, **20** (Supplement), pp. 14–17. 89
8 James P. Wind (1990), 'What Can Religion Offer Bioethics?', *Hastings Center Report*, **20** (Supplement), pp. 18–20. 93

PART IV   THE PRINCIPLE-BASED APPROACH

9 John D. Arras (1994), 'Principles and Particularity: The Roles of Cases in Bioethics', *Indiana Law Journal*, **69**, pp. 983–1014. 99

10 David DeGrazia (1992), 'Moving Forward in Bioethical Theory: Theories, Cases, and Specified Principlism', *Journal of Medicine and Philosophy*, **17**, pp. 511–39. 131

11 Henry S. Richardson (1990), 'Specifying Norms as a Way to Resolve Concrete Ethical Problems', *Philosophy and Public Affairs*, **19**, pp. 279–310. 161

12 Stephen Toulmin (1981), 'The Tyranny of Principles', *Hastings Center Report*, **11**, pp. 31–39. 193

13 K. Danner Clouser and Bernard Gert (1990), 'A Critique of Principlism', *Journal of Medicine and Philosophy*, **15**, pp. 219–36. 203

PART V THE ABSOLUTE RULE APPROACH

14 G.E.M. Anscombe (1982), 'Medalist's Address: Action, Intention and "Double Effect"', *Proceedings of the American Catholic Philosophical Association*, **54**, pp. 12–25. 223

15 Joseph Boyle (1991), 'Who is Entitled to Double Effect?', *Journal of Medicine and Philosophy*, **16**, pp. 475–94. 237

16 Alan Donagan (1991), 'Moral Absolutism and the Double-Effect Exception: Reflections on Joseph Boyle's *Who is Entitled to Double Effect?*', *Journal of Medicine and Philosophy*, **16**, pp. 495–509. 257

PART VI UTILITARIANISM AND BIOETHICS

17 Julian Savulescu (1998), 'Consequentialism, Reasons, Value and Justice', *Bioethics*, **12**, pp. 212–35. 275

18 John Harris (1999), 'Justice and Equal Opportunities in Health Care', *Bioethics*, **13**, pp. 392–404. 299

PART VII VIRTUE ETHICS

19 Justin Oakley (1996), 'Varieties of Virtue Ethics', *Ratio*, **9**, pp. 128–52. 315

20 Philippa Foot (1977), 'Euthanasia', *Philosophy and Public Affairs*, **6**, pp. 85–112. 341

21 Rosalind Hursthouse (1991), 'Virtue Theory and Abortion', *Philosophy and Public Affairs*, **20**, pp. 223–46. 369

22 R.M. Hare (1994), 'Methods of Bioethics: Some Defective Proposals', *Monash Bioethics Review*, **13**, pp 34–47. 393

PART VIII   THE ETHICS OF CARE

23 Nona Plessner Lyons (1983), 'Two Perspectives: On Self, Relationships, and Morality', *Harvard Educational Review*, **53**, pp. 125–45. 409
24 Sara T. Fry (1989), 'The Role of Caring in a Theory of Nursing Ethics', *Hypatia*, **4**, pp. 88–103. 431
25 Helga Kuhse (1995), 'Clinical Ethics and Nursing: "Yes" to Caring, but "No" to a Female Ethics of Care', *Bioethics*, **9**, pp. 207–19. 447

PART IX   THE CASE APPROACH

26 John D. Arras (1991), 'Getting Down to Cases: The Revival of Casuistry in Bioethics', *Journal of Medicine and Philosophy*, **16**, pp. 29–51. 463
27 Albert R. Jonsen (1995), 'Casuistry: An Alternative or Complement to Principles?', *Kennedy Institute of Ethics Journal*, **5**, pp. 237–51. 487
28 Kevin Wm. Wildes (1993), 'The Priesthood of Bioethics and the Return of Casuistry', *Journal of Medicine and Philosophy*, **18**, pp. 33–49. 503

PART X   CULTURAL DIVERSITY AND BIOETHICS

29 Barry Hoffmaster (1992), 'Can Ethnography Save the Life of Medical Ethics?', *Social Science and Medicine*, **35**, pp. 1421–31. 523
30 Edmund D. Pellegrino (1992), 'Intersections of Western Biomedical Ethics and World Culture: Problematic and Possibility', *Cambridge Quarterly of Healthcare Ethics*, **3**, pp. 191–96. 535
31 Sandra D. Lane and Robert A. Rubinstein (1996), 'Judging the Other: Responding to Traditional Female Genital Surgeries', *Hastings Center Report*, **26**, pp. 31–40. 541

PART XI   SOCIOLOGY AND MEDICAL ETHICS

32 Robert Zussman (2000), 'The Contributions of Sociology to Medical Ethics', *Hastings Center Report*, **30**, pp. 7–11. 553
33 James Lindemann Nelson (2000), 'Moral Teachings from Unexpected Quarters: Lessons for Bioethics from the Social Sciences and Managed Care', *Hastings Center Report*, **30**, pp. 12–17. 559

Name Index 565

Acknowledgements

The editor and publishers wish to thank the following for permission to use copyright material.

American Catholic Philosophical Association for the essay: G.E.M. Anscombe (1982), 'Medalist's Address: Action, Intention and "Double Effect"', *Proceedings of the American Catholic Philosophical Association*, **54**, pp. 12–25.

Baylor College of Medicine for the essay: Kevin Wm. Wildes (1993), 'The Priesthood of Bioethics and the Return of Casuistry', *Journal of Medicine and Philosophy*, **18**, pp. 33–49. Copyright © The Journal of Medicine and Philosophy, Inc. Reprinted by permission.

Blackwell Publishers Limited for the essays: Wibren Van der Burg (1997), 'Bioethics and Law: A Developmental Perspective', *Bioethics*, **11**, pp. 91–114. Copyright © 1997 Blackwell Publishers Limited; Julian Savulescu (1998), 'Consequentialism, Reasons, Value and Justice', *Bioethics*, **12**, pp. 212–35. Copyright © 1998 Blackwell Publishers Limited; John Harris (1999), 'Justice and Equal Opportunities in Health Care', *Bioethics*, **13**, pp. 392–404. Copyright © 1999 Blackwell Publishers Limited; Justin Oakley (1996), 'Varieties of Virtue Ethics', *Ratio*, **9**, pp. 128–52. Copyright © 1996 Blackwell Publishers Limited; Helga Kuhse (1995), 'Clinical Ethics and Nursing: "Yes" to Caring, but "No" to a Female Ethics of Care', *Bioethics*, **9**, pp. 207–19. Copyright © 1995 Blackwell Publishers Limited.

Cambridge University Press for the essay: Edmund D. Pellegrino (1992), 'Intersections of Western Biomedical Ethics and World Culture: Problematic and Possibility', *Cambridge Quarterly of Healthcare Ethics*, **3**, pp. 191–96. Copyright © 1992 Cambridge University Press.

Elsevier Science for the essay: Barry Hoffmaster (1992), 'Can Ethnography Save the Life of Medical Ethics?', *Social Science and Medicine*, **35**, pp. 1421–31. Copyright © 1992 Pergamon Press Limited.

R.M. Hare (1994), 'Methods of Bioethics: Some Defective Proposals', *Monash Bioethics Review*, **13**, pp. 34–47. Copyright © 1994 R.M. Hare.

Harvard Educational Review for the essay: Nona Plessner Lyons (1983), 'Two Perspectives: On Self, Relationships, and Morality', *Harvard Educational Review*, **53**, pp. 125–45. Copyright © 1983 President and Fellows of Harvard College, Appendices B and C Nona Plessner Lyons or the *Harvard Educational Review*. All rights reserved.

Hastings Center for the essays: Daniel Callahan (1990), 'Religion and the Secularization of Bioethics', *Hastings Center Report*, **20** (Supplement), pp. 2–4. Copyright © 1990 The

Hastings Center; Courtney S. Campbell (1990), 'Religion and Moral Meaning in Bioethics', *Hastings Center Report*, **20** (Supplement), pp. 4–10. Copyright © 1990 The Hastings Center; David Novak (1990), 'Bioethics and the Contemporary Jewish Community', *Hastings Center Report*, **20** (Supplement), pp. 14–17. Copyright © 1990 The Hastings Center; James P. Wind (1990), 'What Can Religion Offer Bioethics?', *Hastings Center Report*, **20** (Supplement), pp. 18–20. Copyright © The Hastings Center; Stephen Toulmin (1981), 'The Tyranny of Principles', *Hastings Center Report*, **11**, pp. 31–39. Copyright © 1981 The Hastings Center; Sandra D. Lane and Robert A. Rubinstein (1996), 'Judging the Other: Responding to Traditional Female Genital Surgeries', *Hastings Center Report*, **26**, pp. 31–40. Copyright © 1996 The Hastings Center; Robert Zussman (2000), 'The Contributions of Sociology to Medical Ethics', *Hastings Center Report*, **30**, pp. 7–11. Copyright © 2000 The Hastings Center; James Lindemann Nelson (2000), 'Moral Teachings from Unexpected Quarters: Lessons for Bioethics from the Social Sciences and Managed Care', *Hastings Center Report*, **30**, pp. 12–17. Copyright © 2000 The Hastings Center; Lisa Sowle Cahill (1990), 'Can Theology Have a Role in "Public" Bioethical Discourse?', *Hastings Center Report*, **20** (Supplement), pp. 10–14. Copyright © 1990 The Hastings Center. All reproduced by permission.

Indiana Law Journal and William S. Hein for the essay: John D. Arras (1994), 'Principles and Particularity: The Role of Cases in Bioethics', *Indiana Law Journal*, **69**, pp. 983–1014.

Indiana University Press for the essay: Sara T. Fry (1989), 'The Role of Caring in a Theory of Nursing Ethics', *Hypatia*, **4**, pp. 88–103. Copyright © 1989 Sara T. Fry.

Johns Hopkins University Press for the essays: Loren C. MacKinney (1952), 'Medical Ethics and Etiquette in the Early Middle Ages: The Persistence of Hippocratic Ideals', *Bulletin of the History of Medicine*, **26**, pp. 1–31. Copyright © 1952 The Johns Hopkins University Press; Albert R. Jonsen (1995), 'Casuistry: An Alternative or Complement to Principles?', *Kennedy Institute of Ethics Journal*, **5**, pp. 237–51. Copyright © 1995 The Johns Hopkins University Press.

Massachusetts Medical Society for the essay: Henry K. Beecher (1966), 'Ethics and Clinical Research', *New England Journal of Medicine*, **274**, pp. 1354–60. Copyright © 1966 Massachusetts Medical Society. All rights reserved.

Princeton University Press for the essays: Henry S. Richardson (1990), 'Specifying Norms as a Way to Resolve Concrete Ethical Problems', *Philosophy and Public Affairs*, **19**, pp. 279–310. Copyright © 1990 Princeton University Press. Reprinted by permission of Princeton University Press; Philippa Foot (1977), 'Euthanasia', *Philosophy and Public Affairs*, **6**, pp. 85–112. Copyright © 1977 Philippa Foot. Reprinted by permission of Princeton University Press; Rosalind Hursthouse (1991), 'Virtue Theory and Abortion', *Philosophy and Public Affairs*, **20**, pp. 223–46. Copyright © 1991 PAPA. Reprinted by permission of Princeton University Press.

Swets & Zeitlinger Publishers for the essays: David DeGrazia (1992), 'Moving Forward in Bioethical Theory: Theories, Cases, and Specified Principlism', *Journal of Medicine and Philosophy*, **17**, pp. 511–39. Copyright © 1992 Kluwer Academic Publishers; K. Danner Clouser and Bernard Gert (1990), 'A Critique of Principlism', *Journal of Medicine and Philosophy*, **15**, pp. 219–36. Copyright © 1990 Kluwer Academic Publishers; Joseph Boyle (1991), 'Who is Entitled to Double Effect?', *Journal of Medicine and Philosophy*, **16**, pp. 475–94. Copyright © 1991 Kluwer Academic Publishers; John D. Arras (1991), 'Getting Down to Cases: The Revival of Casuistry in Bioethics', *Journal of Medicine and Philosophy*, **16**, pp. 29–51. Copyright © 1991 Kluwer Academic Publishers; Alan Donagan (1991), 'Moral Absolutism and the Double-Effect Exception: Reflections on Joseph Boyle's *Who is Entitled to Double Effect?*', *Journal of Medicine and Philosophy*, **16**, pp. 495–509. Copyright © 1991 Kluwer Academic Publishers.

Every effort has been made to trace all the copyright holders, but if any have been inadvertently overlooked the publishers will be pleased to make the necessary arrangement at the first opportunity.

Series Preface

Few academic disciplines have developed with such pace in recent years as bioethics. And because the subject crosses so many disciplines important writing is to be found in a range of books and journals, access to the whole of which is likely to elude all but the most committed of scholars. The International Library of Medicine, Ethics and Law is designed to assist the scholarly endeavour by providing in accessible volumes a compendium of basic materials drawn from the most significant periodical literature. Each volume contains essays of central theoretical importance in its subject area, and each throws light on important bioethical questions in the world today. The series as a whole – there will be fifteen volumes – makes available an extensive range of valuable material (the standard 'classics' and the not-so-standard) and should prove of inestimable value to those involved in the research, teaching and study of medicine, ethics and law. The fifteen volumes together – each with introductions and bibliographies – are a library in themselves – an indispensable resource in a world in which even the best-stocked library is unlikely to cover the range of materials contained within these volumes.

It remains for me to thank the editors who have pursued their task with commitment, insight and enthusiasm, to thank also the hard-working staff at Ashgate – theirs is a mammoth enterprise – and to thank my secretary, Anita Garfoot for the enormous assistance she has given me in bringing the series from idea to reality.

MICHAEL FREEMAN
Series Editor
Faculty of Laws
University College London

Introduction

Ethical thinking about medical decision-making has roots deep in history. Tradition pursues this to Hippocrates whose Oath dates from between the fifth and third centuries BCE, but the origins are more than a millennium older.[1] Rules about the payment of fees to physicians are found as early as the Code of Hammurabi (who ruled Babylon between 1728 and 1686 BCE). 'If a physician has performed a major operation on a lord with a bronze lancet and has saved the lord's life ... he shall receive ten shekels of silver'.[2] If, however, he caused his death, his hand should be chopped off. A number of early statements of medical ethics have their foundations in pagan religion. Etziony quotes a monument in a sanctuary of Asclepius which tells doctors to be like God, saviours 'equally of slaves, of paupers, of rich men, of princes, and to all a brother'.[3]

Early ethical codes often took the form of oaths. The Oath of Hippocrates is, of course, the most famous and is reproduced in MacKinney's essay (Chapter 2).[4] The physician is to abjure abuse of his position and to keep professional confidences. He is to use his power to help the sick to the best of his ability and judgement (perhaps the earliest statement of the principle of beneficence) and to abstain from harming or wronging any man when using his medical expertise (the foundation perhaps of the principle of non-maleficence). There is also a prohibition on active euthanasia and one on abortion.

The impact of religion on ethical thinking about medicine remains an important undercurrent – and Part III of this collection examines its influence today.[5] Its influence on the origins of bioethics is considerable. Jewish, Christian and Muslim scholarship of the twelfth century and earlier attests to this. The Jewish polymath, Moses Maimonides (1135–1204), in his *Medical Aphorisms*, emphasized the duties of physicians: 'may I never see in the patient anything but a fellow creature in pain'.[6] Islamic scholars such as al-Razi (865–925) emphasized the importance of reason (*al-'aql*), although this did not deflect him from a view that noblemen were entitled to special consideration when it came to the prescribing of drugs.[7] But, Porter informs us,[8] he did not neglect the poor for whom his treatise *Man la yahduruh al-tabib* (Who Has No Physician To Attend Him) was written. Meanwhile, Christianity was modifying the Hippocratic Oath to make it acceptable to Christians. There is a version (tenth- or eleventh-century) entitled 'From The Oath According to Hippocrates Insofar as a Christian May Swear It'. No longer are physicians required to swear to Greek gods and goddesses. Instead, they address themselves to 'God the Father of our Lord Jesus Christ'.[9]

Christianity's emphasis on loving one's neighbour as oneself[10] was reflected in the establishment of 'hospitals' by religious institutions such as monasteries. Crusading orders – though they had a strange concept of love for one's neighbour[11] – also built hospitals throughout the Mediterranean and German-speaking lands.[12] The Benedictine rule emphasized that the care of the sick was to be placed above and before every other duty 'as if indeed Christ were being directly served by waiting on them'.[13] Moreover, Christian teaching stressed that doctors were to cultivate the virtues of compassion and charity. A treatise (reproduced in MacKinney's essay), thought to date from the early twelfth century, urges doctors not to heal 'for the sake of gain, nor to give more consideration to the wealthy than to the poor, or to the noble than the ignoble' (p. 37). The demanding of an excessive fee by a doctor, even the refusal to give free treatment to a patient who would die without it, was condemned by Aquinas.[14]

Like St Augustine before him,[15] Aquinas also condemned suicide.[16] A leading sixteenth-century canonist, Navarrus,[17] condemned euthanasia, whatever its motive. On abortion there was greater equivocation than we are often led to believe. Thus, Aquinas's position, following Aristotle, was that it was only homicide to abort an animated foetus (animation occurred at 40 days in the case of male foetuses and 90 days with female ones).[18] It was another six centuries before Pope Pius IX outlawed all abortions, regardless of the stage reached by the foetus.[19]

The birth of modern medical ethics can be traced to the Enlightenment and in particular to John Gregory (1725–1773)[20] and Thomas Percival (1740–1804).[21] The publication (in 1772) of Gregory's *Lectures on the Duties and Qualifications of a Physician* is pivotal. Gregory stressed that doctors had a duty to be humane: 'It is as much the business of a physician to alleviate pain, and to smooth the avenues of death, when unavoidable, as to cure diseases'. Percival published *Medical Jurisprudence* (in 1794) and in 1803 expanded this into *Medical Ethics*. He stressed that 'Every case, committed to the charge of a physician or surgeon, should be treated with attention, steadiness and humanity'. The book also presented 'practical advice on how doctors could reinforce paternalism, frankly admitting that charity patients in hospitals could be treated with a degree of authority impractical with wealthy private patients whose foibles had to be humoured'.[22]

The nineteenth century saw the birth of professional nursing[23] and by 1901 the first book on nursing ethics had appeared.[24] However, prior to the resurgence of feminist thinking, the nurse's primary obligation was perceived as the carrying out of the doctor's orders.[25] Reformulated in 1973, her or his primary responsibility is now to those who require nursing care.[26]

By the 1970s modern bioethics had emerged, partly as a response to developments in medicine – in particular, the first heart transplant carried out in 1967 by Christiaan Barnard in Cape Town.[27] The ability to harvest organs from cadavers to save lives necessitated thinking about the definition of death[28] and, although this has almost universally centred on the cessation of brain stem functions,[29] the debate continues.[30] The development of the contraceptive pill in the 1960s and the growth of laws permitting safe abortions (in the UK the 1967 Abortion Act;[31] in the USA the watershed decision of *Roe v. Wade* in 1973[32]) and their interaction with the women's movement challenged the medical profession to confront the issue of women's reproductive rights.[33] Biomedical technology helped spawn the reproduction revolution:[34] in vitro fertilization (the first 'test-tube' baby, Louise Brown, was born in 1978) produced (and continues to stimulate) innumerable ethical issues and led to the establishment of commissions of inquiry, the best known of which, the Warnock commission in the UK, produced its report in 1984.[35] Although essentially a liberal statement endorsing a range of autonomy, its stand on surrogacy – that it was 'totally ethically unacceptable'[36] – reflected a paternalistic moralism.[37] While the report can be criticized on the grounds of its incoherence, perhaps surrogacy (or contract pregnancy as many now label it) is different, and a case, rather than a blanket, approach is called for. Although surrogacy took on a very high profile – with cases such as Baby Cotton[38] in England and Baby M[39] in the USA ensuring that the issue dominated the headlines –other consequences of the reproduction revolution such as embryo research[40] and the possibility of human cloning[41] (and not just for therapeutic reasons) raise more troubling ethical concerns. The literature on cloning (post-Dolly[42]) has burgeoned, much as that on surrogacy did in the 1980s.

At the other end of the spectrum, medicine's ability to preserve life for those who cannot or no longer can live in any meaningful sense (at one extreme the anencephalic baby, at the other the person in a persistent vegetative state) opened up an important debate which pitted absolutist 'sanctity of life' principles against 'quality of life' considerations.[43] In 1973 two paediatricians, Duff and Campbell, questioned whether severely ill or disabled neonates should receive life-sustaining treatment.[44] This raised the further question whether, if treatment were withheld, did we have to wait for them to die or could we assist/accelerate their deaths and in what manner? Thus, the active/passive euthanasia debate was born.[45] England had had the John Bodkin Adams case in the mid-1950s[46] and Glanville Williams,[47] and subsequently Lord Devlin,[48] had addressed some of the ethical issues. But it wasn't until the Karen Quinlan case (in New Jersey in 1976)[49] and in the United Kingdom in 1981 in the context of disabled newborns[50] that any sustained legal and ethical thinking on end-of-life decisions took place. The issues of double effect (addressed in a number of contributions to this collection[51]), the ordinary/extraordinary treatment distinction, killing (and physician-assisted suicide) and allowing to die emerged as central questions within medical ethics.

Ethical thinking about medical decision-making thus has deep roots but is also characterized by ambiguities (MacKinney's essay (Chapter 2)). However, prior to the 1970s, there are few examples of what we would nowadays regard as bioethical thinking. Henry Beecher's essay (Chapter 1), a classic published in 1966[52] and provoked by profoundly unethical research and medical experimentation is an early foray into the field. Journals on the subject were to emerge later – the establishment in the USA of the Hastings Center leading to the first (the *Hastings Center Report*). This was followed in 1974 by the *Journal of Medical Ethics* in the UK and there are now six or more major journals in the English-speaking world, including *Bioethics*, established in 1987 and the *Journal of Medicine and Philosophy*, first published in 1975. There are now so many monographs and collections of essays that no one can possibly have read them all.

This volume offers a selection of some of the more seminal and/or perceptive essays. It sets out a framework for ethical thinking about medical decision-making. Other volumes in the series focus on specific problem areas.

Parts II and III focus on the insights which law and religion respectively can offer bioethics. There are few, if any, areas in which there is a closer interface between law and ethics than in the area of medicine – consider, for example, issues such as patient autonomy, informed consent, privacy and confidentiality. Law and ethics (and bioethics) employ many of the same conceptual categories: rules, principles, right. In addition, they use the same normative language (though not, or not necessarily, the same sources). In Chapter 3 Wibren Van der Burg traces the relationship between law and bioethics through two staged models, a moralistic–paternalistic model and what he perceives to be a flawed liberal model. His own preference (and he uses ideal-types, of course) is a post-liberal model in which the relationship will be more loose than it is within liberalism. When this phase is envisaged (Van der Burg's essay was published in 1997) is not clear. Whether he has read the tea leaves correctly is also questionable: the growth of conventions and human rights legislation keeps faith with the liberal model. But he is right to draw attention to the limits of law. As Carl Schneider noted, there are limits to the extent to which 'the language of the law may safely be imported into bioethical discourse and to which bioethical ideas may be effectively translated into law'.[53]

Many of the founders of contemporary bioethics were theologians (for example, Joseph Fletcher[54] and Paul Ramsey[55]). Not surprisingly in an era of increasing secularization, this is less prevalent today. But there are still theological voices in medical ethics and these are not unique to any one religion. The former Chief Rabbi (Lord) Immanuel Jakobovits situated medical ethics within Judaism,[56] a tradition continued in David Bleich's recent *Bioethical Dilemmas: A Jewish Perspective*.[57] Religious ethical discussion is often conducted by reference to moral rules which either proscribe or prescribe the performance of certain types of action. Religious bioethics imposes rule-based constraints on actions: that on not killing the innocent, even if they request it, is a paradigm example. While this rule could be adopted within a secular tradition, it is more commonly found in religious traditions. On the other hand, the prohibition against separating the sexual and procreative acts, which leads some religious communities to oppose in vitro fertilization (or at least some forms of IVF), would rarely be situated within secular moral norms. Religious ethicists who invoke the sort of rule-based constraint referred to above often insist that the constraints (or certain of them at least) can be justified in secular terms (for example, rule-utilitarianism). Thus, for example, violation of the rule against killing the innocent can be justified by demonstrating what would happen if this constraint was not adhered to – that is, the effect on the sanctity of life, on the norms of the medical profession and so on.

What religion has to contribute to bioethics was explored in a series of essays in a *Hastings Center* Special Supplement in 1990.[58] A number of these essays form the basis of Part III of this volume. As Daniel Callahan points out in Chapter 4, and has been emphasized earlier in this Introduction, religion played a major part in the early history of bioethics. The secularization of bioethics has, Callahan argues, left us 'too heavily dependent upon the law as a working source of morality'.[59] This may be true in today's secular and pluralistic societies; could it be otherwise? His warning that pluralism can become a form of oppression if 'we are told to shut up in public about our private lives and beliefs and talk ... moral esperanto'[60] draws attention to a danger to which it is all too easy to succumb. On the other hand, in a pluralistic society it is also important to recognize 'a wall of separation between religious and public concerns',[61] and this is particularly so where public policy is being articulated by public commissions. In part, religion's contribution to bioethics may lie in insights into questions which now concern bioethics and have long troubled theologians. Courtney Campbell (Chapter 5) points to the example of 'suffering', at the root of discussions about euthanasia and animal rights.[62] Religious thinking too, Campbell reminds us, may broaden our horizons 'beyond our current fixation with problem-solving, for some problems cannot be solved but must still be faced'.[63] But are these insights, as Cahill argues in Chapter 6,[64] that which could have been arrived at without an appeal to the lessons of religious thinking? Certainly, as she indicates, leading Christian thinkers (she cites Ramsey and McCormick) have avoided 'directly religious appeals in the interest of expanding their audience and hence influence'.[65] That this is not the case with minority religions' thinkers may reflect their narrower audience and marginality to public policy debates.

Part IV of this volume concerns principle-based approaches to bioethics. Principle-based approaches may be – and usually are – deontological but may also be consequentialist (utilitarianism appeals to the principle of utility in evaluating actions or rules). In their highly influential *Principles of Biomedical Ethics*,[66] Beauchamp and Childress identify four primary principles: respect for autonomy, non-maleficence, beneficence (including utility) and justice. In addition, there are, according to them, a number of derivative rules mandating the keeping of promises, the protection of privacy, and the preservation of confidences. These rules are derivative because they are founded in the principles. Critics – for example, Clouser and Gert, in Chapter 13 of this collection[67]) have dubbed this approach 'principlism'. Other principle-based approaches are in Veatch's *A Theory Of Medical Ethics*[68] and Engelhardt's *Foundations of Bioethics*.[69] Veatch's list is similar to that of Beauchamp and Childress (beneficence, contract-keeping, autonomy, honesty, avoiding killing and justice); Engelhardt accepts as principles only autonomy and beneficence. Beauchamp and Childress have modified their philosophy in their latest edition, so much so that one reviewer (Emanuel) thought it might 'herald the end of "principlism"'.[70] Whether this happens, and it seems unlikely, the approach will remain a source of bioethical thinking and must be considered as such.

Principles must be connected to particular judgements about cases. And principles can obviously conflict. Henry Richardson, whose essay[71] is reproduced as Chapter 11, identifies three ways in which principles can be connected to case judgements: first, by application (this deduces the right course of action from general principles and rules); secondly, by balancing (this weighs conflicting principles to decide which has priority in the particular situation); and, thirdly, by specification (this specifies circumstances – in particular who, what and when).

As far as application is concerned, most principle-based approaches would consider that this overemphasizes the role of deduction and can lead to results that are mechanical rather than nuanced to the particular problem. The case judgement should be a test for the principles – which may need reinterpretation as a result.

Critical to balancing is the decision as to what to weight and how. Which moral considerations should have weight, and how much should they have? There are a number of distinct approaches to this. First, there are absolutists. Thus, for example, Fletcher's situation ethics[72] took cognisance of only one absolute principle, neighbour-love (or utility). For Fletcher, the only value in principles and rules, other than utility, was in calling upon the experiences of the past to establish the tendencies of particular actions (what was their likely effect). Some principles and rules are doubtless absolute. For example, can there be any exceptions to those against torture[73] or rape? Would it be difficult to construct an absolute principle that the medical profession should never prioritize profit to themselves over the interests of patients? A contrasting approach is that of Beauchamp and Childress who see principles as *prima facie* binding: the agent would have to justify departure from any of the principles upon which they rely. However, Childress himself has now conceded that this approach is 'excessively intuitive'.[74] That is why Beauchamp and Childress in later editions of their text propose a procedure to reduce the reliance on intuition. Deviation from a *prima facie* duty requires on this account a realistic prospect of achieving the moral objective that appears to justify the breach. Additionally, the infringement must not only be necessary in the circumstances, it must also be the least possible commensurate with achieving the primary goal of the action, and the agent must seek to minimize the negative effects of the infringement. A third approach is exemplified by Veatch[75] who would prioritize deontological principles (such as promise-keeping and honesty) over consequentialist ones (beneficence), and, where deontological principles themselves conflict, would employ a balancing strategy when considerations are lexically co-equal – although this inevitably raises questions of how to achieve a balance as surely more is required than an appeal to intuition?

Specification is obviously important. We cannot give content to a principle without specifying its meaning and its scope. It may be that so-called conflicts between principles will evaporate when the principles themselves are clearly spelt out. But can principles be specified with sufficient precision or should we agree with Clouser and Gert (Chapter 13) that more specific rules are required? Gert has offered ten rules in place of the lists of principles described above.[76] These are: do not kill; do not cause pain; do not disable; do not deprive of freedom; do not deprive of pleasure (future as well as present); do not deceive; keep your promise; do not cheat; obey the law; and do your duty (that is what is required by one's role in society). All the rules (except 'promise keeping', obeying the law and doing one's duty) are negative. And, despite their objections to a principle-based approach, the principle of beneficence is clearly in evidence in several (and certainly in the first three) of the rule-prescriptions. Critics would argue that much is also missing: at the root of medical ethics is respect for the patient's self-determination (or autonomy), but it is difficult to see how this can be incorporated into any of these rules.

David DeGrazia (Chapter 10), in a response to Clouser and Gert's criticism that the principles identified by Beauchamp and Childress (and presumably also Veatch and Engelhardt) are overgeneral and too vague, has attempted to inject more content into the principles by means of an interpretation he calls 'specified principlism'.[77] Partly in response to this, the latest edition of Beauchamp and Childress has explicitly developed specifications alongside balancing to connect principles to particular judgements. Childress himself, in *Practical Reasoning in Bioethics*, says that he remains to be convinced that 'specification can be developed as the exclusive model for relating principles and particular judgements',[78] in part because of his sense of 'the inevitability of moral conflict, not only between people but also within the moral universe'.[79] In Chapter 9 John Arras too wonders whether specification is an answer, seeing in attempts to do so similar problems to those encountered when principlists carry out balancing exercises.

Principle-based approaches have been subjected to a number of criticisms. To Clouser and Gert (Chapter 13) principlism is mistaken about the nature of morality and is misleading as to the foundations of ethics. At best, they argue, its proponents offer 'checklists' of considerations, chapter headings which are 'surrogates for theories'.[80] In Chapter 9 Arras also criticizes the almost mechanical recitation of principles. Stephen Toulmin (Chapter 12) attacks what he calls, the 'tyranny of principles'.[81] But is he attacking the principle-based approach as such or just the absolutist variety of this? Others – Downie for example,[82] are critical of the principles actually posited. According to him, utility, which is (at least) a principle of distribution, ought to be included as one of the principles. But is it not embraced within beneficence, which, as we have seen, features in the lists of all the main proponents of a principle-based approach (Beauchamp and Childress, Veatch, Engelhardt)? There are feminist critics, too, who work within Carol Gilligan's ethics of care[83] – an approach explored in Part VIII of this volume. Childress acknowledges that the care perspective is an 'important corrective to some principle-based approaches because it attends to context, narrative, relationships, emotion, compassion and the like'.[84] Women's experiences generally, and as carers within and without the medical profession, cannot be ignored by anyone developing a theory of bioethics.[85]

The absolute rule approach is the subject of Part V of this volume. It has roots in Kantianism and in the Catholic natural law tradition. It is found today within secularist rights literature (where rights cannot be 'trumped' by other considerations),[86] and in the new natural law thinking associated with Grisez[87] and Finnis.[88] An absolute rule has no exceptions – killing the innocent is the most cited example – and so cannot be overridden by other considerations – for example, by appeals to consequentialism. So, to take an example drawn from one of the twentieth century's most famous medical law cases, if non-therapeutic sterilization of the learning disabled is absolutely wrong[89] – which is, of course, contestable – it cannot be justified by eugenic considerations, as has frequently been the case.[90] As G. E. M. Anscombe points out in Chapter 14, the functioning of moral absolutes imposes a 'block' to the introduction of consequentialist considerations into a moral approach which includes them.[91] To Donagan in *The Theory of Morality*[92] (but see also Chapter 16) precepts without exceptions are not to be violated in order to achieve mandatory goals. Referring to the Pauline principle (that evil is not to be done that good may come of it) he argues that it is 'not an external stipulation, like the serial ordering adopted by contractarian theorists ... but a general statement of a condition implicit in every precept of imperfect duty that is validly derivable from the fundamental principle of morality itself. It is structurally necessary'.[93]

Perhaps the most controversial feature of moral absolutism is the doctrine of double effect.[94] The contributions in Part V of this volume concentrate on this. At root the problem lies in defining the absolute prohibition. There are clear cases and penumbral ones. The latter are obviously more difficult to decide and, within both Kantian and Catholic natural law forms of moral absolutism, there is accordingly a resort to casuistry to determine whether or not a particular kind of action falls within that which is prohibited by an absolute rule. Definition and conceptual clarification often, therefore, assume overwhelming importance. The Kantian principle that each rational person must be treated as an end in himself and not as a means to someone else's end is clear enough, but needs to be tested by reference to cases to see which are, and which are not, included within it.[95] The methodology is familiar to lawyers forced to question whether, for example, killing in self-defence or under duress or out of necessity is murder or is wrong or not (because these are justifiable excuses).[96]

This doctrine of double effect presupposes that there is a distinction between an intentional act (say, a lethal injection to kill a terminally ill patient) and a voluntary act which has the same effect although this consequence is not intended (for example, a morphine drip inserted into a terminally ill patient to relieve pain but which will also accelerate death). It is argued that this distinction has moral significance: although there is an absolute prohibition on killing – hence the refusal to contemplate active euthanasia or physician-assisted suicide – the prohibition does not extend to actions which lead to death where this is not the intention.[97] As Anscombe puts it in Chapter 14, the absolute prohibition extends only to the intentional action.[98]

Although Joseph Boyle claims that the doctrine is not an 'ad hoc device to avoid the disagreeable consequences of Catholic absolutism',[99] this is certainly how it appears to many bioethicists. Nor are its distinctions easy to accept. It permits a hysterectomy on a pregnant woman with cancer (the intention being not to kill the foetus which is only a side effect) but not the abortion of a grossly deformed foetus (because the intention would be to kill a potential child). And, as Boyle acknowledges (see Chapter 15), not all harms brought out as side effects can be prohibited since, whatever a person's intention, harmful side effects may occur.[100]

Absolute rule approaches may not be central to bioethical thinking today but they have left an imprint on contemporary debates, on concepts (such as sanctity of life) and on thinking, and they therefore cannot be overlooked.

Part VI of this volume examines utilitarianism, and does so through the prism of a debate between Savulescu and Harris.[101] The classic formulation of utilitarianism can be found in the works of Jeremy Bentham,[102] but utilitarianism has taken many forms since. The main elements of any utilitarian theory are consequentialism (the view that it is the consequences of an act that make it right or wrong);[103] welfarism (in which the consequences that are relevant to the morality of an action are those which maximize the welfare of those who are affected);[104] and, third, aggregationism (where, in choosing between actions, that which promotes the interests of all in sum is to be preferred;[105] Sen and Williams refer to this as 'sum-ranking').[106]

Savulescu's essay (Chapter 17) is a response to an earlier one by Harris,[107] and the debate between them continued into further essays[108] (space did not permit the inclusion of all four essays). In Savulescu's second essay (not reproduced in this volume) he poses the following dilemma. There is one bed in the Intensive Care Unit and three patients who need it.

> Mrs Wobbly is a 68 year old woman who has been in a nursing home in a persistent vegetative state for five years. She has pneumonia. She will never recover any cognitive function. But she and her family are deeply religious and believe in the sanctity of life. 'Besides', her lawyer son says, 'if you don't treat her, we'll sue you. People have recovered from a "permanent" vegetative state. You can't say there is *no* chance that she will recover from her vegetative state. And her pneumonia is treatable.'
>
> Mr Wong is an Asian student who attempted suicide. When he first arrived in Emergency Department, he was conscious and was examined by a psychiatrist. She judged him to be competent and not suffering from a mental illness. Mr Wong refused any treatment. He attempted suicide because he failed his examinations. He could not face the shame.
>
> Mrs Jones is a single mother of two children, her husband having recently left her. She has had an allergic reaction to a peanut.
>
> Both Wong and Jones will recover completely if treated.[109]

Which of the three should be admitted? Harris and Savulescu are both consequentialists. Where they differ is on what constitutes a reason for action. Harris believes that reasons for action are based on desires. But this would suggest that Mrs Wobbly should be treated rather than Mr Wong. If instead one offers, as Savulescu does, a value-based account of what constitutes a reason, one would certainly prefer Mr Wong to Mrs Wobbly. But would we also prioritize him over Mrs Jones? And this in turn would depend on which values were valued. To argue, as Harris does, that each person is entitled to an equal opportunity to benefit from a public health system upholds the principle of non-discrimination but hardly assists the doctor's dilemma. Would it be so very difficult to justify treating Mrs Jones, which our intuition would tell us is the right course of action, and which (crude) utilitarianism might also confirm?

Part VII of this volume is about virtue ethics, the rebirth of which is usually attributed to an essay by G. E. M. Anscombe published in 1958.[110] It is a response to consequentialist and deontological theories which are said to have placed too much emphasis on what we ought to do, rather than concentrating on what sort of person we ought to be and what sort of life we ought to lead. The language used by virtue ethics is richer than that found in consequentialism and Kantianism (it uses words like 'honest', 'just' and 'courageous' when evaluating actions) and the scope is also broader, stressing the ethical importance of personal relationships (such as friendship).

From the extensive virtue ethics literature in bioethics I have selected essays by Philippa Foot on euthanasia (Chapter 20) and Rosalind Hursthouse on abortion (Chapter 21). Those interested in virtue ethics – particularly in relation to abortion – should read back from Hursthouse's essay to her important book, *Beginning Lives*.[111] Hursthouse argues that debating abortion in terms of the competing rights of mother and foetus is irrelevant to the morality of abortion. Instead, the morality of a woman's decision to terminate her pregnancy depends on the sort of character she manifests (in particular, why she is having an abortion, since there is a big difference between having an abortion because carrying a child will interfere with one's holiday plans and being young and unready for motherhood). A virtue ethics approach to abortion brings out reasons why, in some circumstances, a woman would be acting wrongly in exercising her privilege to terminate her pregnancy.

Foot's essay on euthanasia is an early classic on the subject, and a fine example of the application of virtue ethics to a number of end-of-life questions. Among the issues Foot tackles are when death is a good for a person. Wanting to die is not enough: death can be a good only when life lacks a minimum of basic human goods, such as autonomy, friendship and moral support. But when such goods are absent, the virtues of justice and charity allow one to accede to a person's request to be allowed to die. She also argues that analysing end-of-life decisions in terms of these virtues enables a distinction to be drawn between killing and letting die. Killing – active euthanasia – is acceptable within the moral parameters of virtue ethics when a person lacks a minimum of basic human goods and requests death. Only currently in the Netherlands is such an expression regarded as acceptable,[112] and only then when prescribed procedures are carried out. And the issue remains controversial in the Netherlands.[113] Foot also points to the difficult situation where a person *in extremis* wishes to continue to live (in effect to die in agony). In such circumstances the virtues conflict: justice forbids killing and charity countenances it.

Virtue ethics has its defenders (see Justin Oakley in Chapter 19) and its critics, such as R. M. Hare (Chapter 22). To Hare (and others) virtue ethics is incomplete and needs the underpinning of another ethical theory (whether this be deontological or utilitarian). Veatch's concern is about 'well-intentioned, bungling do-gooders' who, he assures us, 'exist with unusual frequency in health care, law and other professions with a strong history of stressing the virtue of benevolence with an elitist stance'.[114] Is reference to what a virtuous agent would have done sufficient to justify a particular action? A further criticism of virtue ethics questions whether the concept of virtue is clear enough to provide the foundation of a criterion of what is right.[115] It is, it is said, too vague to act as a justification for moral action. It has to be said that it is difficult to state what a virtuous agent would be like without first knowing what actions are right: in this sense, virtue ethics presupposes an ethical source outside of itself. Can it therefore stand alone as an ethical theory?

Part VIII examines the ethics of care. The most obvious sources of this are Carol Gilligan's *In A Different Voice*[116] and Nel Noddings' book *Caring: A Feminine Approach To Ethics and Moral Education*.[117] In an important essay (which could not be reproduced in this volume because it is in an edited collection), Joan Tronto and Berenice Fisher defined care as 'a species activity that includes everything that we do to maintain, continue and repair "our" world so that we can live in it as well as possible. That world includes our bodies, our selves and our environment, all of which we seek to interweave in a complex, life-sustaining web.'[118] Thus conceived, care is not 'a marginal activity of life but one of the central procedures of human existence'.[119]

It was Gilligan who showed that there was a difference between an ethics of care and one of justice. Her research demonstrated that there were two different moral languages – a language of 'justice' and a relational language of 'care'. They 'encode disparate experiences of self and social relationships'.[120] And the 'different voice' (that of care), she found, was mostly associated with women. But the different voice is characterized 'not by gender but theme', although its association with women is 'an empirical observation'.[121] So, when Gilligan put an ethical dilemma – what should a man do whose wife needs a drug without which she will die but who cannot afford it – to an 11–year-old boy and an 11–year-old girl, the boy says that he should steal it (life is more important than property), while the girl is much more circumspect. She doesn't think that theft is the answer: 'If he stole the drug, he might save his wife then, but if he did, he might have to go to jail, and then his wife might get sicker again, and he couldn't get more of the drug, and it might not be good. So, they should really just talk it out and find some other way to make the money.'[122] Gilligan characterizes the boy's response as rooted in the ethics of justice and the girl's as mediated by an ethics of care. But one could respond that the girl put a universal principle of justice (not stealing) above care for a particular person, and the boy rejected principled thinking for the sake of care. And, asks Helga Kuhse in her *Caring: Nurses, Women and Ethics*, 'how would we classify the responses of Nigel Cox and Roisin Hart, when the first deliberately ended the life of his patient Lilian Boyes, and the second blew the whistle on Dr Cox? Who acted from a perspective of justice and who from a perspective of care? Can we be entirely confident about the answer we might want to give?'[123]

Whether or not the two ethics can be so definitively gender-related, it is clear that there are two different voices. What differentiates the care voice is its recognition of special obligations (those imposed by relationships, actual and potential and by those imposed by roles). And, as Manning points out, 'since it understands communities as more than mere aggregates of individuals, and relationships as more than properties of individual persons, it is committed to saying that communities and relationships have moral standing'.[124]

A variant on this way of thinking is found in the essay by Nona Lyons (Chapter 23). She links the two moral perspectives of *In A Different Voice* to two notions of the self. In Tronto's account of Lyons:

> Those who viewed the self as 'separated' from others, and therefore 'objective', were more likely to voice a morality of justice, while those who viewed the self as 'connected' to others were more likely to express a morality of care. Since men are usually 'separate/objective' in their self/other perceptions, and women more often view themselves in terms of a 'connected' self, the differences between expressing moralities of justice and care is thus gender related. ... In the separate/objective view of the self, relationships are experienced in terms of reciprocity, mediated through

rules, and grounded in roles. For the connected self, relationships are experienced in response to others on their terms, mediated through the activity of care and grounded in interdependence.[125]

Separate/objective selves see moral dilemmas as involving a conflict between their principles and the needs or desires of someone else. Connected selves perceive as moral dilemmas those which involve the breakdown of relationships with others. Separate/objective selves must appeal to the voice of justice, but connected selves can mediate moral dilemmas through the voice of care.

The ethics of care has clear implications in bioethics. The development of the hospice movement where 'care of the sick is primary; disease *per se* is untreated, and physicians are ... ancillary to nurses'[126] is a model of the ethics of care in action. In hospitals, disagreements between medical and nursing staff over end-of-life decisions concerns nurses rather more it seems than doctors. As Kuhse notes:

> ... disagreement arises because the nurse believes that the doctor's decision to sustain a patient's life (and, occasionally, the doctor's failure to do so) is not in the patient's best interest, does not respect the patient's wishes or the patient's 'right to die'. In other words, nurses may often feel that doctors act from principle, whereas nurses respond from a perspective of care.[127]

Yet critics will point to the situations where justice (patients' rights) and care will be in conflict. Justice demands acknowledgement of self-determination, and the patient as consumer; the care model will see the patient as someone in need for whom paternalism/ maternalism is appropriate intervention. On a justice model there is no room for 'doctor knows best' or the therapeutic privilege;[128] the patient's informed consent is fundamental.[129] One resolution of this conflict is to adapt the model to suit the patient: does she or he want justice or care? But whose would the decision be? Another answer (Manning's)[130] is that respecting rights is the 'moral minimum' (in Fuller's language 'a morality of duty') but the treatment of patients in a genuinely caring way is the goal (Fuller's 'morality of aspiration' is an analogy).[131]

The case approach, the subject of Part IX of this volume, has an obvious appeal both to common lawyers and the medical profession. Like the common lawyer and, in most cases, the doctor, the casuist reasons from the paradigmatic case to find the 'right' result in the new, perhaps perplexing, situation. This is done by means of analogical reasoning. The case at hand is compared with the paradigm case (or cases) and similarities and differences focused upon. So, where the question is whether a grossly disabled newborn baby should be allowed to die the paradigmatic cases would be, on the one hand, a case such as 'Baby Alexandra' (a Down's syndrome child with an intestinal blockage who, of course, must be treated)[132] and, on the other, a child for whom any treatment is futile and who will die. anyway in a matter of months.[133] What, then, of the many cases in between these paradigms – for example, the child who is not dying and can be easily resuscitated but who can experience little else but pain'.[134] The casuist will try to find arguments to categorize the case in terms of its proximity to one or other paradigm. Perhaps the busy doctor does this anyway. Certainly, it is an approach used within common law reasoning.[135] It is, as John Arras describes it (in Chapter 26) a bottom-up, as opposed to a top-down, approach. It is inductive and particularist, and it would appear dismissive of principles. Certainly, in the views of some casuists (Stephen Toulmin offers an example in Chapter 12) principles would be seen as nothing more than what we have learnt from our intuitive responses to a series of cases. But this is not the view of Albert Jonsen (see Chapter 27), who argues that principles can guide actions. To John Arras (Chapter 26) as well, casuistry can be regarded as complementary to the development and use of principles, emphasizing the importance of details of cases. Casuists differ from those who espouse a principle-based approach in arguing about where principles come from. It is the contention of casuists that principles do not emerge from some 'celestial vault',[136] as Arras puts it, but rather develop out of the methodology of a case-based approach over a period of time. And, casuists argue, principles cannot just be applied; they need fine-tuning to tackle the individual case. Thus, for example, the principle of patient autonomy may have greater or lesser weight depending upon the circumstances. It may have less pulling power when the patient is a child[137] (where it may be thought to have a differential impact on decisions to consent or refuse treatment)[138] or where the interests of others are threatened (as in the case of the pregnant woman who refuses a medically recommended caesarean section).[139]

The case-based approach has its critics. One major criticism is bias. Kopelman explains this:

> The potential for bias arises at each stage of a case method of reasoning, including in describing, framing, selecting and comparing of cases and paradigms. A problem of bias occurs because, to identify the relevant features for such purposes, we must use general views about what is relevant; but some of our general views are biased, both in the sense of being unwarranted inclinations and in the sense that they are one of many viable perspectives.[140]

In short, is casuistry committed to the thinking of the past and therefore wedded to unjust social practices and prejudices? Does it have the ability to challenge the inherent biases in the paradigm cases to which it must return? Similar criticisms have been made of common law methodology by critical legal theories,[141] within feminist jurisprudence[142] and critical race theory.[143] Any philosophy which is backward-looking (as casuistry is) is likely to be conservative. But it does not have to be. Analogical reasoning is a tool and, like all tools, it depends on who handles it.

The other major criticism indicts the indeterminacy of casuistry. This shortcoming is addressed by Kevin Wildes in Chapter 28. As a methodology, casuistry depends on the mind-set of its practitioners. When there was consensus (in the days of common Christian belief), casuistry was workable. But, the argument goes, can it work in pluralistic societies? The common law works, but it has clearly defined authorities to which it can appeal (judges, a hierarchy of courts, a system of precedent, well-established methods of interpreting statutes). Casuistry may work within the bounds of a particular religion (Roman Catholicism or Judaism, for example) but its appeal to a secular, pluralistic, post-modern society may be limited by the difficulties it has in surmounting this hurdle.[144]

The final Part of this volume takes up issues of pluralism. Most writing in bioethics emanates from Western (and liberal) societies and is strongly ethnocentric. As Elliott has pointed out:

> Ethics does not stand apart. It is one thread in the fabric of a society, and it is intertwined with others. Ethical concepts are tied to a society's customs, manners, traditions, institutions – all of the concepts that structure and inform the ways in which a member of that society deals with the

world. When we forget this, we are in danger of leaving the world of genuine moral experience for the world of moral fiction – a simplified, hypothetical creation suited less for practical difficulties than for intellectual convenience.[145]

Despite this understanding there has been a thrust towards universalism and away from particularism. Thus, in a recent essay, Callahan can argue that it conveys a moral perspective that is 'valid under most circumstances for most people most of the time'.[146]

Western bioethics is challenged both by non-Western practices[147] and by the operation of different principles and ethical perspectives. Different understandings of the meaning of death (for example, in Japan) can lead to different policies on the removal of organs from cadavers.[148] Female genital mutilation, practised (in different ways) in vast swathes of the world (and in Western societies by African immigrants) is now widely discussed (see, for instance, Lane and Rubinstein, Chapter 31). Universalists, relativists and pluralists[149] take different positions on it: Western legislatures increasingly outlaw it, even where adult women consent to such surgical interventions – a difficult tightrope to tread when breast implants and gender reassignments are lawful. Fundamental Western concepts also cannot necessarily be found in non-Western thinking. The liberal West takes the principle of individual autonomy for granted, but the non-Western value system is more likely to value cultural, communal or family autonomy.[150] Is this understanding to be taken cognisance of by Western doctors treating patients from such cultures? In England, in 1993, an elderly patient of Caribbean origin in a criminal asylum refused to agree to the amputation of a gangrenous leg. As it happens, he suffered from paranoid schizophrenia and thought he knew more about gangrene than the doctors treating him. The English Court of Appeal upheld his refusal to submit to an amputation.[151] Did the doctors and the courts situate his attitudes within his culture? Was evidence adduced of this? Certainly, in Africa, death is thought preferable to the loss of dignity.[152]

Western bioethics needs to gain insights into non-Western practices and beliefs (as it has done with non-standard practices and beliefs, such as those of Jehovah's Witnesses in relation to blood transfusions). One way it can do this is by focusing on bioethical problems which concern the non-Western world. This is already beginning to happen as Western bioethicists (Schüklenk, Harris) grapple with the ethical dilemmas of the HIV/AIDS pandemic in sub-Saharan Africa.[153] But the most difficult challenge is at the level of fundamental ethical values. It may be that the answer lies neither with universalism (in effect, cultural imperialism) nor with particularism (cultural pluralism at best or, at its most crude, cultural relativism) but in transcultural bioethics (based on values and principles which transcend cultures).[154] This is, of course, a mammoth task – but it offers a worthwhile challenge.

And perhaps it is here that the social sciences have an input. The final part of this volume addresses the possible contribution, continuing and engaging with (in Zussman's case) Hoffmaster's essay in Part X. Robert Zussman (Chapter 32) rejects Hoffmaster's 'manifesto for a sociology of medical ethics'.[155] For Zussman the social sciences may lend a bit of reality to the 'flights of fancy'[156] that can characterize medical ethics, and may also lead to new issues being raised. For James Nelson (Chapter 33) the social sciences offer a challenge to bioethics. Ethics requires an understanding of social life. Without it, there are dangers of its losing its way.

Notes

1   See, generally, Roy Porter, *The Greatest Benefit To Mankind* (London: Harper Collins, 1997).
2   See J. B. Pritchard, *Ancient Near Eastern Texts Relating To The Old Testament* (Princeton, NJ: Princeton University Press, 1969), p. 27.
3   M. B. Etziony, *The Physician's Creed: An Anthology of Medical Prayers, Oaths and Codes of Ethics Written and Recited By Medical Practitioners Throughout The Ages* (Springfield, Ill.: Charles C. Thomas, 1973).
4   See below, p. 11. On Hippocrates see Jacques Jouanna, *Hippocrates* (Baltimore; Johns Hopkins University Press, 1999).
5   See R. L. Numbers and D. W. Amundsen (eds.), *Caring and Curing: Health and Medicine in the Western Religious Traditions* (New York: Macmillan, 1987); L. E. Sullivan (ed.), *Healing and Restoring: Health and Medicine in the World's Religious Traditions* (New York: Macmillan, 1989); Joseph Shatzmiller, *Jews, Medicine and Medieval Society* (Berkeley, University of California Press, 1994) offers a valuable historical context.
6   Quoted in Porter, *op cit.*, note 1, p. 101. See also Julius Preuss, *Biblical and Talmudic Medicine* (New York: Sanhedrin Press, 1978).
7   See Porter, *op cit.*, note 1, p. 97, noting that, in this, he echoed Galen.
8   Ibid.
9   See W. H. S. Jones, *The Doctor's Oath: An Essay In The History of Medicine* (New York: Cambridge University Press, 1924).
10 First found in Leviticus 19:18.
11 Consider, for example, the Crusades, on which see S. Runciman, *A History of the Crusades* (3 vols) (Cambridge: Cambridge University Press, 1951–54).
12 See Nancy G. Siraisi, *Medieval and Early Renaissance Medicine: An Introduction To Knowledge and Practice* (Chicago: University of Chicago Press, 1990); Charles H. Talbot, *Medicine In Medieval England* (London: Oldbourne, 1967).
13 Quoted in Porter, *op cit.*, note 1, p. 111.
14 See MacKinney, below, p. 37.
15 See Georges Minois, *History of Suicide* (Baltimore: Johns Hopkins University Press, 1999), pp. 27–28.
16 *Summa Theologica*, part II-II, q. 64, art. 5.
17 See Philippe Ariès, *The Hour of Our Death* (London: Allen Lane, 1981).
18 See, more generally, John M. Riddle, *Eve's Herbs* (Cambridge, Mass.: Harvard University Press, 1997).
19 See Angus McLaren, 'Policing Pregnancies: Changes in Nineteenth-Century Criminal and Canon Law' in G. R. Dunstan and Mary J. Seller (eds), *The Human Embryo: Aristotle and the Arabic and European Traditions* (Exeter: Exeter University Press, 1990), p. 187; John T. Noonan, 'Abortion and the Catholic Church: A Summary History' (1967) 12 *Natural Law Forum*, p. 105.
20 See, generally, Thomas Hankins, *Science And the Enlightenment* (Cambridge: Cambridge University Press, 1985) and Guenter B. Risse, 'Medicine In The Age of Enlightenment' in A. Wear (ed.), *Medicine In Society: Historical Essays* (Cambridge: Cambridge University Press, 1992), p. 149. On Gregory see Laurence B. McCullough, *John Gregory's Writings on Medical Ethics and Philosophy of Medicine* (Dordrecht: Kluwer, 1998).
21 See T. Percival, *Medical Ethics* (Manchester: J. Johnson and R. Bickerstaff, 1803).
22 Quoted by Porter, *op cit.*, note 1, p. 287.
23 Brian Abel-Smith, *A History of The Nursing Profession* (London: Heinemann, 1960).
24 Isabel Hampton Robb, *Nursing Ethics For Hospital and Private Use* (Cleveland, Ohio: Kieckert, 2nd edition, 1928) (first edition published by J. B. Savage, 1901).
25 See Helga Kuhse, *Caring: Nurses, Women and Ethics* (Oxford: Blackwell, 1997), ch. 2.
26 Ibid., p. 32.
27 Porter, *op cit.*, note 1, p. 621 remarks: 'It may be no accident that South Africa got in first; the land of apartheid had fewer ethical rules hedging what doctors could do.'

28 See Ad Hoc Committee, 'A Definition of Irreversible Coma Report of the Ad Hoc Committee of the Harvard Medical School to Examine the Definition of Brain Death' (1968) 205 *JAMA*, p. 337. French neurologists had coined the term *coma dépassé* in 1959.
29 Alexander M. Capron and Leon M. Kass, 'A Statutory Definition of the Standards for Determining Human Death: An Appraisal and A Proposal' (1978) 121 *University of Pennsylvania Law Review*, p. 87; Julius Korein, 'The Problem of Brain Death: Development and History' (1978) 315 *Annals of the New York Academy of Sciences*, p. 19.
30 For example, Robert D. Truog, 'Is It Time To Abandon Brain Death?' (1997) 27(1) *Hastings Center Report*, p. 29. But compare James L. Bernat, 'A Defense of the Whole-Brain Concept of Death' (1998) 28(2) *Hastings Center Report*, p. 14.
31 On which see Sally Sheldon, *Beyond Control: Medical Power And Abortion Law* (London: Pluto Press, 1997).
32 410 US 113 (1973). A recent challenging book is Georgia Warnke, *Legitimate Differences* (Berkeley, California: University of California Press, 1999).
33 For example, Susan Sherwin, *No Longer Patient: Feminist Ethics and Health Care* (Philadelphia: Temple University Press, 1992); Helen Bequaert Holmes and Laura M. Purdy, *Feminist Perspectives In Medical Ethics* (Bloomington, Indiana: Indiana University Press, 1992); Anne Donchin and Laura M. Purdy, *Embodying Bioethics* (Lanham, Maryland: Rowman and Littlefield, 1999); Lynn M. Morgan and Meredith W. Michaels, *Fetal Subjects, Feminist Positions* (Philadelphia: University of Pennsylvania Press, 1999).
34 See Peter Singer and Deane Wells, *The Reproduction Revolution* (Oxford: Oxford University Press, 1984).
35 See Mary Warnock, *A Question of Life* (Oxford: Blackwell, 1985).
36 Ibid., 8.17.
37 I argue this in 'After *Warnock*: Whither The Law?' (1986) 39 *Current Legal Problems*, p. 33.
38 *Re C* [1985] FLR 846. The surrogate's story is told in Kim Cotton and Denise Winn, *Baby Cotton– For Love and Money* (London: Dorling Kindersley, 1985).
39 *In The Matter of Baby M* 537 A. 2d 1227. And see Dianne M. Bartels, Reinhard Priester, Dorothy E. Vawter and Arthur L. Caplan, *Beyond Baby M: Ethical Issues in New Reproductive Technologies* (Clifton, NJ: Humana Press, 1990).
40 See Warnock, *op cit.*, note 35, ch. 11.
41 Glenn McGee, *The Human Cloning Debate* (Berkeley, California: Berkeley Hills Books, 1998); James M. Humber and Robert F. Almeder, *Human Cloning* (Totowa, NJ: Humana Press, 1998).
42 On Dolly and her aftermath see Gina Kolata, *Clone: The Road to Dolly and the Path Ahead* (London: Penguin Press, 1997).
43 Dan W. Brock, *Life and Death: Philosophical Essays In Biomedical Ethics* (Cambridge: Cambridge University Press, 1993); Bonnie Steinbock, *Killing and Letting Die* (Englewood Cliffs, N.J.: Prentice-Hall, 2nd edn, 1990); Helga Kuhse, *The Sanctity of Life Doctrine In Medicine* (Oxford: Oxford University Press, 1987).
44 R. S. Duff and A. G. M. Campbell, 'Moral and Ethical Problems in the Special-Care Nursery' (1973) 279 *New England Journal of Medicine*, p. 890.
45 Initiated by James Rachels, 'Active And Passive Euthanasia' (1975) 292 *New England Journal of Medicine*, p. 78.
46 Unreported, 1957. See H. Palmer, 'Trial For Murder' (1957) *Criminal Law Review*, p. 365.
47 Glanville Williams, *The Sanctity of Life and the Criminal Law* (London: Faber and Faber, 1958).
48 Patrick Devlin, *Easing the Passing* (London: Bodley Head, 1985).
49 *In The Matter of Karen Quinlan* 355 A. 2d 647 (1976).
50 The 'Baby Alexandra' case: *Re B* [1981] 1 WLR 1421. This coincided with the prosecution of Dr Arthur for attempted murder: see *R v. Arthur* (1981) 12 BMLR 1.
51 See, below, G. E. M. Anscombe, p. 223; Joseph Boyle, p. 237; and Alan Donagan, p. 257.
52 Henry Beecher, 'Ethics and Clinical Research' (1966) 274 *New England Journal of Medicine*, p. 1354, and, below, p. 3.

53 Carl Schneider, 'Bioethics in the Language of The Law' (1994) 24(4) *Hastings Center Report*, p. 16.
54 See his *Morals and Medicine: The Moral Problems of the Patient's Right To Know The Truth, Contraception, Artificial Insemination, Sterilization, Euthanasia* (Boston: Beacon Press, 1954).
55 Paul Ramsey, *The Patient as Person* (New Haven, Conn: Yale University Press, 1970).
56 Immanuel Jakobovits, *Jewish Medical Ethics* (New York: Bloch, enlarged edition, 1975). On Jakobovits see Y. Jacobovits in F. Rosner (ed.), *Pioneers In Jewish Medical Ethics* (Northvale, NJ: Aronson, 1997), p. 127.
57 J. David Bleich, *Bioethical Dilemmas – A Jewish Perspective* (Hoboken, NJ: Ktav Publishing House, 1998). See also Fred Rosner and J. David Bleich (eds), *Jewish Bioethics* (Brooklyn, NY: Hebrew Publishing Co., 1979).
58 'Theology, Religious Traditions and Bioethics', eds. Daniel Callahan and Courtney S. Campbell, *Hastings Center Report* (Special Supplement), July/August 1990, pp. 1–24.
59 'Religion and the Secularization of Bioethics', *ibid.*, p. 2 at p. 4 and, below, at p. 73.
60 Ibid., quoting Jeffrey Stout, *Ethics After Babel: The Languages of Morals And Their Discontents* (Boston: Beacon Press, 1988) p. 294.
61 Courtney S. Campbell, 'Religion and Moral Meaning In Bioethics', *Hastings Center Report* (Special Supplement), July/August 1990, p. 4 at p. 6. And, below, at p. 77.
62 Ibid.
63 Ibid., p. 7 and p. 78 below.
64 Lisa Sowle Cahill, 'Can Theology Have A Role In "Public" Bioethical Discourse?' *Hastings Center Report* (Special Supplement) July/August 1990, p. 10 and, below, p. 83.
65 Ibid.
66 Tom L. Beauchamp and James F. Childress, *Principles of Biomedical Ethics* (New York: Oxford University Press, 4th edn, 1994). The first edition was in 1979.
67 K. Donner Clouser and Bernard Gert, 'A Critique of Principlism' (1990) 15 *Journal of Medicine and Philosophy*, p. 219 and, below, p. 203.
68 R. M. Veatch, *A Theory of Medical Ethics* (New York: Basic Books, 1981).
69 H. Tristam Engelhardt, *Foundations of Bioethics* (New York: Oxford University Press, 2nd edn, 1995).
70 Ezekiel J. Emanuel, 'The Beginning of the End of Principlism' (1995) 25(4) *Hastings Center Report*, p. 37.
71 H. Richardson, 'Specifying Norms as a Way To Resolve Concrete Ethical Problems', (1990) 19 *Philosophy and Public Affairs*, p. 279, and below, p. 161.
72 Joseph Fletcher, *Situation Ethics: The New Morality* (Philadelphia: Westminster Press, 1966).
73 See Alan Gewirth, 'The Epistemology of Human Rights' (1984) 1 *Social Philosophy and Policy*, p. 1.
74 James F. Childress, *Practical Reasoning in Bioethics* (Bloomington, Indiana: Indiana University Press, 1997), p. 112.
75 See Veatch, op cit., note 68.
76 Bernard Gert, *Morality: A New Justification of the Moral Rules* (New York: Oxford University Press, 1989).
77 David DeGrazia, 'Moving Forward in Bioethical Theory: Theories, Cases and Specified Principlism' (1992) 17 *Journal of Medicine and Philosophy*, p. 511, and below, p. 131.
78 Childress, op cit., note 74, p. 38.
79 Ibid.
80 Clouser and Gert, op cit., note 67, p. 223 and, below, p. 207.
81 Stephen Toulmin, 'The Tyranny of Principles' (1981) 11(6) *Hastings Center Report*, p. 31 and below, p. 193. See also Albert Jonsen and Stephen Toulmin, *The Abuse of Casuistry* (Berkeley, California: University of California Press, 1988).
82 R. S. Downie, *Medical Ethics* (Aldershot, Dartmouth, 1996).
83 Carol Gilligan, *In A Different Voice: Psychological Theory and Women's Development* (Cambridge, Mass.: Harvard University Press, 1982).

84 James F. Childress, 'A Principle-Based Approach' in H. Kuhse and P. Singer (eds), *A Companion To Bioethics* (Oxford, Blackwell, 1998), p. 61 at p. 70.
85 Alisa L. Carse, 'The "Voice of Care": Implications for Bioethical Education' (1991) 16 *Journal of Medicine and Philosophy*, p. 5.
86 For example, Ronald Dworkin, *Taking Rights Seriously* (London: Duckworth, 1977); idem, *Life's Dominion: An Argument about Abortion and Euthanasia* (London: Harper Collins, 1993).
87 Germain Grisez, *The Way Of The Lord Jesus*, Vol. 1: *Christian Moral Principles* (Chicago: Franciscan Herald Press, 1983).
88 John M. Finnis, *Moral Absolutes: Tradition, Revision and Truth* (Washington, DC: Catholic University of America Press, 1991).
89 I argue this in 'Sterilising The Mentally Handicapped' in M. D. A. Freeman, *Medicine, Ethics and the Law* (London: Stevens, 1988), p. 55.
90 As in *Buck v. Bell* 274 US 200 (1927).
91 G. E. M. Anscombe, 'Medalist's Address: Action, Intention and "Double Effect"' (1982) 54 *Proceedings of the American Catholic Philosophical Association*, p. 12 at p. 14 and, below at p. 223.
92 Alan Donagan, *The Theory of Morality* (Chicago: University of Chicago Press, 1977).
93 Ibid., p. 155.
94 See T. J. Bole (ed.), 'Double Effect: Theoretical Function and Bioethical Implications' (1991) 16 *Journal of Medicine and Philosophy* (Special Issue), pp. 467–585.
95 See Immanuel Kant, *Groundwork of the Metaphysic of Morals* (1785) (see H. J. Paton's translation, *The Moral Law* (London: Hutchinson, 1948).
96 For a lively discussion in terms of a concrete case (*R v. Dudley and Stephens*) see A. W. B. Simpson, *Cannibalism and the Common Law* (Chicago: University of Chicago Press, 1984).
97 And see Raanan Gillon, 'Killing and Letting Die' (1988) 14 *Journal of Medical Ethics*, p. 115.
98 Anscombe, op. cit., note 91, p. 21, and, below, p. 232.
99 Joseph Boyle, 'An Absolute Rule Approach' in Helga Kuhse and Peter Singer (eds), *A Companion To Bioethics* (Oxford: Blackwell, 1998), p. 72 at p. 78.
100 Joseph Boyle, 'Who Is Entitled To "Double Effect"?' (1991) 16 *Journal of Medicine and Philosophy*, p. 475 at pp. 486–8, and, below, at pp. 248–50.
101 John Harris, 'What is the Good of Health Care?' (1996) 10 *Bioethics*, p. 269; Julian Savulescu, 'Consequentialism, Reasons, Value and Justice' (1998) 12 *Bioethics*, p. 212; John Harris, 'Justice and Equal Opportunities in Health Care' (1999) 13 *Bioethics*, p. 392; Julian Savulescu, 'Desire-Based and Value-Based Normative Reasons' (1999) 13 *Bioethics*, p. 405.
102 Jeremy Bentham, *Introduction to the Principles of Morals and Legislation*, eds. J. H. Burns and H. L. A. Hart (London, Athlone Press, 1970).
103 On which see Samuel Scheffler, *Consequentialism and its Critics* (Oxford: Oxford University Press, 1988).
104 See Amartya Sen, *Choice, Welfare, Measurement* (Oxford: Blackwell, 1982).
105 See R. M. Hare, 'A Utilitarian Approach' in Kuhse and Singer, op cit., note 99, p. 80 at pp. 82–83.
106 See Amartya Sen and Bernard Williams, 'Introduction' in A. Sen and B. Williams (eds), *Utilitarianism and Beyond* (Cambridge: Cambridge University Press, 1982) p. 4.
107 Harris, op cit. (1996) note 101.
108 Op cit. (1999) note 101.
109 Savulescu, op. cit. (1999) pp. 405–406.
110 G. E. M. Anscombe, 'Modern Moral Philosophy' (1958) 33 *Philosophy*, pp. 1–19.
111 Rosalind Hursthouse, *Beginning Lives* (Oxford: Blackwell, 1987). See also Rosalind Hursthouse, 'Normative Virtue Ethics' in R. Crisp (ed.), *How Should One Live? Essays on the Virtues* (Oxford: Clarendon Press, 1996), p. 19.
112 See John Griffiths, Alex Bood and Helen Weyers, *Euthanasia and the Law in The Netherlands* (Amsterdam: Amsterdam University Press, 1998).
113 See John Keown, 'The Law And Practice of Euthanasia in the Netherlands' (1992) 108 *Law Quarterly Review*, p. 51.

114 Robert Veatch, 'The Danger of Virtue' (1988) 13 *Journal of Medicine and Philosophy*, p. 445.
115 Robert Louden, 'On Some Vices of Virtue Ethics' (1984) 21 *American Philosophical Quarterly*, p. 227.
116 Gilligan op. cit., note 83.
117 Nel Noddings, *Caring: A Feminine Approach to Ethics and Moral Education* (Berkeley, California: University of California Press, 1984).
118 Joan Tronto and Berenice Fisher, 'Toward A Feminist Theory of Caring' in E. K. Abel and M. Nelson (eds), *Circles of Care: Work and Identity in Women's Lives* (Albany, NY: State University of New York Press, 1990), p. 8, at p. 40. See also Joan Tronto, *Moral Boundaries: A Political Argument for an Ethic of Care* (New York: Routledge, 1993), p. 103.
119 *Per* Selma Sevenhuijsen, *Citizenship and the Ethics of Care* (London: Routledge, 1998), p. 137 (originally published in Dutch in 1996).
120 Gilligan, op cit., note 83, p. 38.
121 Ibid., p. 2.
122 Ibid., p. 28.
123 Kuhse, *op cit.*, note 25, p. 104.
124 Rita C. Manning, 'A Care Approach' in Kuhse and Singer, *op. cit.*, note 99, p. 98 at p. 101.
125 Tronto, *op cit.*, (1993), note 119, p. 79.
126 Rita C. Manning, *Speaking From The Heart: A Feminist Perspective on Ethics* (Lanham, Maryland, Rowman and Littlefield, 1992), p. 116.
127 Kuhse, *op cit.*, note 25, p. 170.
128 On which see *Canterbury* v. *Spence* 464 F. 2d 772 (DC Cir. 1972). See also G. Dworkin, *The Theory and Practice of Autonomy* (New York: Cambridge University Press, 1988) and S. Wear, *Informed Consent: Patient Autonomy and Physician Beneficence within Clinical Medicine* (Dordrecht: Kluwer, 1993).
129 But see *Sidaway* v. *Bethlehem Royal Hospital* [1985] AC 871. More generally, see P. Appelbaum, C. Lidz and A. Meisel (eds), *Informed Consent: Legal Theory and Clinical Practice* (New York: Oxford University Press, 1987).
130 Lansing, *op cit.*, note 125, p. 104.
131 Lon L. Fuller, *The Morality of Law* (New Haven, Conn.: Yale University Press, 1964).
132 *Re B* [1981] 1 WLR 1421.
133 *Re C* [1990] Fam. 26.
134 *Re J* [1991] Fam. 33.
135 Benjamin Cardozo, *The Nature of The Judicial Process* (New Haven, Conn.: Yale University Press, 1921).
136 J. D. Arras, 'Getting Down To Cases: The Revival of Casuistry in Bioethics', (1991) 16 *Journal of Medicine and Philosophy*, p. 29 and, below, p. 463.
137 See Lainie Ross Friedman, *Children, Families and Health Care Decision-Making* (Oxford: Clarendon Press, 1998). See also her article, 'Health Care Decision-Making by Children: Is it in their Best Interest?' (1997) 27(6) *Hastings Center Report*, p. 41.
138 See *Re R* [1992] Fam. 11; *Re W* [1993] Fam. 64.
139 *Re AC* 573 A 2d 1253 (DC CA); *St George's Healthcare NHS Trust* v. *S* [1999] Fam. 26.
140 Loretta Kopelman, 'Case Method and Casuistry: The Problem of Bias' (1994) 15 *Theoretical Medicine*, p. 21.
141 For example, Peter Gabel, 'Reification in Legal Reasoning' in *Research in Law and Sociology*, vol. 3, 1980, p. 25.
142 For example, Lucinda M. Finley, 'Breaking Women's Silence in Law: The Dilemma of the Gendered Nature of Legal Reasoning' (1989) 64 *Notre Dame Law Review*, p. 886.
143 See Kimberlé Crenshaw, Neil Gotanda, Gary Peller and Kendall Thomas, *Critical Race Theory* (New York: New Press, 1995), Part 4.
144 See K. W. Wildes, 'The Priesthood of Bioethics and the Return of Casuistry', (1993) 18 *Journal of Medicine and Philosophy*, p. 33, and, below, p. 503.
145 Carl Elliott, 'Where Ethics Comes From, and What to do about it' (1992) 22(4) *Hastings Center Report*, p. 28 at p. 29.

146 Daniel Callahan, 'Universalism and Particularism: Fighting to a Draw' (2000) 30(1) *Hastings Center Report*, p. 37.
147 Female circumcision (or genital mutilation) is the most discussed example. See, below, Sandra D. Lane and Robert A. Rubinstein, p. 541.
148 N. Tanida, '"Bioethics" is Subordinate to Morality in Japan' (1996) 10 *Bioethics*, p. 201; and K. Hoshino, 'Why Many Japanese Do Not Accept "Braindeath" as a Definition of Death' (1993) 7 *Bioethics*, pp. 234–238.
149 See Michael Freeman, 'The Morality of Cultural Pluralism' (1995) 3 *International Journal of Children's Rights*, p. 1.
150 See E. Pellegrino *et al.*, *Transcultural Dimensions in Medical Ethics* (Frederick, Maryland, University Publishing Group, 1992).
151 *Re C* [1994] 1 FLR 31.
152 This is explained by Segun Gbadegesin, 'Bioethics and Cultural Diversity' Kuhse and Singer, *op. cit.*, note 99, p. 24, 30. See also Patricia Marshall, David Thomasma and Jurrit Bergsma, 'International Reasoning: The Challenge for International Bioethics' (1994) 3 *Cambridge Quarterly Journal of Healthcare Ethics*, p. 321. See also G. B. Tangwa, 'Bioethics: An African Perspective' (1996) 10 *Bioethics*, p. 183.
153 Udo Schüklenk, *Access To Experimental Drugs in Terminal Illness: Ethical Issues* (New York: Haworth, 1998); John Harris, 'Research on Human Subjects, Exploitation and Global Principles of Ethics' in M. Freeman and A. D. E. Lewis (eds), *Law And Medicine* (Oxford: Oxford University Press, 2000), pp. 379–398. See also 'Symposium', (1998) 12 *Bioethics*, pp. 286–331.
154 And see Barry Hoffmaster 'Can Ethnography Save the Life of Medical Ethics?' (1992) 35 *Social Science and Medicine*, p. 1421, and, below, p. 523. See also Alastair V. Campbell, 'Global Bioethics – Dream or Nightmare?' (1999) 13 *Bioethics*, p. 183 and Hyakudai Sakamoto, 'Towards A New "Global Bioethics"' (1999) 13 *Bioethics*, p. 191.
155 Robert Zussman, 'The Contributions of Sociology to Medical Ethics' (2000) 30(1) *Hastings Center Report*, p. 7, at p. 10 and below, at p. 556.
156 Ibid.

Bibliography

History of Bioethics

Baker, R. B., Caplan, A. L., Emanuel, L. L. and Latham, S. R. (1999), *The American Medical Ethics Revolution*, Baltimore: Johns Hopkins University Press.
Jones, W. H. S. (1924), *The Doctor's Oath: An Essay In the History of Medicine*, Cambridge, Cambridge University Press.
Jonsen, A. R. (1998), *The Birth of Bioethics*, New York: Oxford University Press.
Lloyd, G. E. R. (1978), *Hippocratic Writings*, Harmondsworth: Penguin.
Porter, R. (1997), *The Greatest Benefit To Mankind*, London, Harper Collins.
Temkin, O. (1992), *Hippocrates in a World of Pagans and Christians*, Baltimore: Johns Hopkins University Press.
Wear, A (1992), *Medicine in Society: Historical Essays*, Cambridge: Cambridge University Press.

Some Standard Texts

Beauchamp, T. L. and Childress, J. F. (1994), *Principles of Biomedical Ethics*, (4th edn), New York: Oxford University Press.
Beauchamp, T. L. and Walters, Le Roy (1994), *Contemporary Issues in Bioethics* (4th edn), Belmont, Calif.: Wadsworth.

Childress, J. (1997), *Practical Reasoning in Bioethics*, Bloomington: Indiana University Press.
Downie, R. S. (1996), *Medical Ethics*, Aldershot: Dartmouth.
Fletcher, J. (1954), *Morals and Medicine*, Boston: Beacon Press.
Gillon, R. (1994), *Principles of Health Care Ethics*, Chichester: John Wiley.
Gert, B., Culver, C. M. and Danner Clouser, K. (1997), *Bioethics: A Return to Fundamentals*, New York: Oxford University Press.
Glover, J. (1977), *Causing Death and Saving Lives*, Harmondsworth: Penguin.
Journal of Medicine and Philosophy (2000), **25**, pp. 653-764, 'Bioethics at the Threshold of the Millennium'.
Kuhse, H. and Singer, P. (1998), *A Companion to Bioethics*, Oxford: Blackwell.
Nelson, H. L. (1997), *Stories and their Limits – Narrative Approaches to Bioethics*, New York: Oxford University Press.
Pence, G. E. (1998), *Classic Works in Medical Ethics*, Boston: McGraw Hill.
Sherwin, S. (1992), *No Longer Patient*, Philadelphia: Temple University Press.
Sumner, W. L. and Boyle, J. (1996) *Philosophical Perspectives on Bioethics*, Toronto: University of Toronto Press.
Veatch, R. M. (1989), *Medical Ethics*, Boston: Jones and Bartlett.

Religion and Bioethics

Bleich, J. O. (1998), *Bioethical Dilemmas: A Jewish Perspective*, Hoboken, NJ: Ktav.
Breck, J. (1998), *The Sacred Gift of Life: Orthodox Christianity and Bioethics*, Crestwood, NY: St Vladimir's Seminary Press.
Camenish, P. F. (ed.) (1994), *Religious Methods and Resources in Bioethics*, Dordrecht: Kluwer.
Cohen, C. B. *et al.* (2000), 'Prayer as Therapy', *Hastings Center Report*, **30**(3), pp. 40-47.
Journal of Medicine and Philosophy (2000), **25**, pp. 367-513, 'Bioethics at the Threshold of the Millennium'.
Lammers, S. E. and Verhey, A. (eds) (1987), *On Moral Medicine: Theological Perspectives in Medical Ethics*, Grand Rapids, Mich.: Wm. Eerdmans.
MacCormick, R. and Ramsey, P. (eds) (1987), *Doing Evil to Achieve Good*, Chicago: Loyola University Press.
O'Rourke, K. D. and Boyle, P. (eds) (1999), *Medical Ethics: Sources of Catholic Teachings*, (3rd edn), Washington, DC: Georgetown University Press.
Rahman, F. (1987), *Health and Medicine in the Islamic Tradition: Change and Identity*, New York: Crossroads.
Verhey, A. and Lammers, S. E. (eds) (1993), *Theological Voices in Medical Ethics*, Grand Rapids, Mich.: Wm. Eerdmans.

Law and Bioethics

Capron, A. M. (1988), 'A "Bioethics" Approach to Teaching Health Law', *Journal of Legal Education*, **38**, pp. 505-9.
Capron, A. M. and Michel, V. (1993), 'Law and Bioethics', *Loyola of Los Angeles Law Review*, **27**, pp. 25-40.
Dickens, B. M. (1994), 'Legal Approaches to Health Care Ethics and the Four Principles' in R. Gillon (ed.), *Principles of Health Care Ethics*, Chichester: John Wiley, pp. 305-17.
Feinberg, J. (1984-86 and 1990), *The Moral Limits of the Criminal Law*, 4 vols, New York: Oxford University Press.
Fletcher, J. C. (1997), 'Bioethics in a Legal Forum: Confessions of an Expert Witness', *Journal of Medicine and Philosophy*, **22**, pp. 297-324.
Freeman, M. and Lewis, A. D. E. (2000), *Law And Medicine*, Oxford: Oxford University Press.
Freeman, M. D. A. (1988), *Medicine, Ethics and Law*, London: Stevens.

Kennedy, I. (1992), *Treat Me Right*, Oxford: Clarendon Press.
Mason, J. K. and McCall Smith, R. A. (1994), *Law and Medical Ethics*, London: Butterworths.
Schneider, C. E. S. (1994), 'Bioethics in the Language of the Law', *Hastings Center Report*, **24**(4), pp. 16–22.

Principlism

Beauchamp, T. and Childress, J. (1994), *Principles of Biomedical Ethics*, (4th edn), New York: Oxford University Press – earlier editions may also be consulted.
Engelhardt, H. T. (1995), *Foundations of Bioethics*, (2nd edn), New York: Oxford University Press.
Evans, J. H. (2000), 'A Sociological Account of the Growth of Principlism', *Hastings Center Report*, **30**(5), pp. 31–38.
Gillon, R. (1994), 'Medical Ethics: Four Principles Plus Attention to Scope', *British Medical Journal*, **309**, pp. 184–88.
Gustafson, J. M. (1965), 'Context Versus Principles: A Misplaced Debate In Christian Ethics', *Harvard Theological Review*, **58**, pp. 171–202.
Meslin E. *et al.* (1995), 'Principlism and the Ethical Appraisal of Clinical Trials', *Bioethics*, **9**, pp. 399–418.
Richardson, H. S. (2000), 'Specifying, Balancing, and Interpreting Bioethical Principles', *Journal of Medicine and Philosophy*, **25**, pp. 285–307.
Special Issue (1995), *Kennedy Institute of Ethics Journal*, **5**, pp. 181–286.
Special Issue (2000), 'Specification, Specified Principlism and Casuistry', *Journal of Medicine and Philosophy*, **25**, pp. 271–360.
Symposium (1994), 'Emerging Paradigms in Bioethics', *Indiana Law Journal*, **69**, pp. 945–1122.
Veatch, R. M. (1981), *A Theory of Medical Ethics*, New York: Basic Books.

The Absolute Rule Approach

Dworkin, R. (1977), *Taking Rights Seriously*, London: Duckworth.
Eberl, J. T. (2000), 'The Beginning of Personhood: A Thomistic Biological Analysis', *Bioethics*, **14**, pp. 134–57.
Finnis, J. (1991), *Moral Absolutes: Tradition, Revision and Truth*, Washington, DC: Catholic University of America Press.
Grisez, G. (1983), *The Way of The Lord Jesus. Vol. 1: Christian Moral Principles*, Chicago, Franciscan Herald Press.
Haber, J. (1994), *Absolutism and its Consequentialist Critics*, Lanham, Maryland, Rowman and Littlefield.

Utilitarianism

Brandt, R. B. (1992), *Morality, Utilitarianism and Rights*, Cambridge: Cambridge University Press.
Frey, R. G. (1984), *Utility and Rights*, Minneapolis: University of Minnesota Press.
Glover, J. (1977), *Causing Deaths and Saving Lives*, Harmondsworth: Penguin.
Griffin, J. (1986), *Well Being*, Oxford: Clarendon Press.
Henson, R. G. (1980), 'Utilitarianism and Wrongfulness of Killing', *Philosophical Review*, lxxx, pp. 320–37.
Kagan, S. (1989), *The Limits of Morality*, Oxford: Clarendon Press.
Sen, A. and Williams, B. (1982), *Utilitarianism and Beyond*, Cambridge: Cambridge University Press.
Smart, J. J. C. and Williams, B. (1973), *Utilitarianism: For and Against*, Cambridge: Cambridge University Press.
Sprigge, T. L. S. (1989), 'Utilitarianism and Respect for Human Life', *Utilities*, pp. 1–21.

Virtue Ethics

Baron, M., Pettit P. and Slote, M. (1997), *The Methods of Ethics: A Debate*, Oxford: Blackwell.
Foot, P. (1978), *Virtues and Vices*, Berkeley, University of California Press.
Hauerwas, S. (1981), *Vision and Virtue*, Notre Dame, Indiana: University of Notre Dame Press.
Hursthouse, R. (1995), 'Applying Virtue Ethics' in R. Hursthouse, G. Lawrence and W. Quinn (eds), *Virtues and Reasons: Philippa Foot and Moral Theory – Essays In Honour of Philippa Foot*, Oxford: Clarendon Press, pp. 57–75.
Kihlbom, U. (2000), 'Guidance and Justification in Particularistic Ethics', *Bioethics*, **14**, pp. 287–309.
Pence, G. (1984), 'Recent Work on the Virtues', *American Philosophical Quarterly*, **21**, pp. 281–97.
Shelp, E. E. (1985), *Virtue And Medicine*, Dordrecht: Reidel.
Slote, M. (1992), *From Morality to Virtue*, New York, Oxford University Press.

The Ethics of Care

Carse, A. L. and Nelson, H. L. (1999), 'Rehabilitating Care' in A. Donchin and L. M. Purdy (eds), *Embodying Bioethics*, Lanham, Maryland, Rowman and Littlefield, pp. 17–31.
Gilligan, C. (1982), *In A Different Voice*, Cambridge, Mass.: Harvard University Press.
Holmes, H. B. and Purdy, L. (eds) (1992), *Feminist Perspectives in Medical Ethics*, Bloomington: Indiana University Press.
Kuhse, H. (1997), *Caring: Nurses, Women and Ethics*, Oxford: Blackwell.
Kuhse, H. (1995), 'Clinical Ethics and Nursing: "Yes" to Caring, But "No" to a Female Ethics of Care', *Bioethics*, **9**, pp. 207–219.
Manning, R. (1992), *Speaking from the Heart: A Feminist Perspective on Ethics*, Lanham, Maryland: Rowman and Littlefield.
Noddings, N. (1984), *Caring: A Feminine Approach to Ethics and Moral Education*, Berkeley: University of California Press.
Veatch, R. M. (1998), 'The Place of Care in Ethical Theory', *Journal of Medicine and Philosophy*, **23**, pp. 210–24.
Wolf, S. (ed.) (1996), *Feminism and Bioethics: Beyond Reproduction*, New York: Oxford University Press.

The Case Approach

Brody, B. (1988), *Life and Death Decision Making*, New York: Oxford University Press.
Keenan, J. F. and Shannon, T. (1995), *The Context of Casuistry*, Washington, DC: Georgetown University Press.
Kuczewski, M. G. (1997), *Fragmentation and Consensus: Communitarian and Casuist Bioethics*, Washington, DC: Georgetown University Press.
Miller, R. B. (1996), *Casuistry and Modern Ethics: A Poetics of Practical Reason*, Chicago: University of Chicago Press.
Strong, C. (1997), *Ethics in Reproductive and Perinatal Medicine: A New Framework*, New Haven, Conn.: Yale University Press, ch. 4.
Strong, C. (2000), 'Specified Principlism: What Is It, and Does It Really Resolve Cases Better Than Casuistry?', *Journal of Medicine and Philosophy*, **25**, pp. 323–41.
Tomlinson, T. (1994), 'Casuistry In Medical Ethics: Rehabilitated, or Repeat Offender?', *Theoretical Medicine*, **15**, pp. 5–20.
Wallace, J. (1996), *Authoritative Practice: The Case for Particularism in Ethics*, Ithaca, NY: Cornell University Press.

Bioethics and Cultural Pluralism

Callahan, D. (2000), 'Universalism and Particularism', *Hastings Center Report*, **30**(1), pp. 37–44.
Flack, H. and Pellegrino, E. (eds) (1992), *African American Perspectives on Biomedical Ethics*, Washington, DC: Georgetown University Press.
Ingstad, B. and Whyte, S. R. (1995), *Disability and Culture*, Berkeley: University of California Press.
James, S. A. (1994), 'Reconciling International Human Rights and Cultural Relativism: The Case of Female Circumcision', *Bioethics*, **8**, 1–26.
Jecker, N. S., Carrese, J. A. and Pearlman, R. A. (1995), 'Caring For Patients in Cross-Cultural Settings', *Hastings Center Report*, **25**(1), pp. 6–14.
Macklin, R. (1995), 'Reproductive Technologies in Developing Countries', *Bioethics*, **9**, pp. 276–82.
Macklin, R. (2000), *Against Relativism*, New York: Oxford University Press.
Marshall, P., Thomasna, D. and Bergsma, J. (1994), 'Intercultural Reasoning: The Challenge for International Bioethics', *Cambridge Quarterly Journal of Healthcare Ethics*, **3**, pp. 321–28.
Nicholas, B. (1996), 'Community and Justice: The Challenges of Bicultural Partnership to Policy on Assisted Reproductive Technology', *Bioethics*, **10**, pp. 212–21.
Pellegrino, E. (ed.) (1992), *Transcultural Dimensions in Medical Ethics*, Frederick, Maryland: University Publishing Group.
Sherwin, S. (2001), 'Moral Perception and Global Visions', *Bioethics*, **15**, pp. 176–88.
Tangwa, G. B. (1996), 'Bioethics: An African Perspective', *Bioethics*, **10**, pp. 183–200.
Tangwa, G. B. (2000), 'The Traditional African Perception of a Person: Some Implications for Bioethics', *Hastings Center Report*, **30**(5), pp. 39–43.
Veatch, R. M. (1989), *Cross Cultural Perspectives in Medical Ethics: Readings*, Boston: Jones and Bartlett.

Social Sciences and Medical Ethics

Addleson, K. P. (1994), *Moral Passages*, New York: Routledge.
De Vries, R. and Conrad, P. (1998), 'Why Bioethics Needs Sociology' in R. De Vries and J. Subedi (eds), *Bioethics and Society*, Upper Saddle River, NJ: Prentice Hall.
Dingwall, R. (2000), 'Law, Society and the New Genetics' in M. Freeman and A. D. E. Lewis (eds), *Law and Medicine*, Oxford: Oxford University Press, pp. 159–76.
Elliott, C. (1999), *Bioethics, Culture and Identity – A Philosophical Disease*, Routledge: New York.
Fox, R. (1989), *The Sociology of Medicine*, Englewood Cliffs, NJ: Prentice Hall.
Fox, R. (1990), 'The Evolution of American Bioethics: A Sociological Perspective' in G. Weisz (ed.), *Social Science Perspectives in Medical Ethics*, The Hague: Kluwer.
Joralemon, D. (1999), *Exploring Medical Anthropology*, Boston: Allyn and Bacon.
Marshall, P. (1992), 'Anthropology and Bioethics', *Medical Anthropology Quarterly*, **6**, pp. 49–73.
Walker, M. U. (1998), *Moral Understandings: A Feminist Study in Ethics*, New York: Routledge.

Part I
What is Bioethics?

ETHICS AND CLINICAL RESEARCH*

Henry K. Beecher, M.D.†

BOSTON

HUMAN experimentation since World War II has created some difficult problems with the increasing employment of patients as experimental subjects when it must be apparent that they would not have been available if they had been truly aware of the uses that would be made of them. Evidence is at hand that many of the patients in the examples to follow never had the risk satisfactorily explained to them, and it seems obvious that further hundreds have not known that they were the subjects of an experiment although grave consequences have been suffered as a direct result of experiments described here. There is a belief prevalent in some sophisticated circles that attention to these matters would "block progress." But, according to Pope Pius XII,[1] ". . . science is not the highest value to which all other orders of values . . . should be subordinated."

I am aware that these are troubling charges. They have grown out of troubling practices. They can be documented, as I propose to do, by examples from leading medical schools, university hospitals, private hospitals, governmental military departments (the Army, the Navy and the Air Force), governmental institutes (the National Institutes of Health), Veterans Administration hospitals and industry. The basis for the charges is broad.‡

I should like to affirm that American medicine is sound, and most progress in it soundly attained. There is, however, a reason for concern in certain areas, and I believe the type of activities to be mentioned will do great harm to medicine unless soon corrected. It will certainly be charged that any mention of these matters does a disservice to medicine, but not one so great, I believe, as a continuation of the practices to be cited.

Experimentation in man takes place in several areas: in self-experimentation; in patient volunteers and normal subjects; in therapy; and in the different areas of *experimentation on a patient not for his benefit but for that, at least in theory, of patients in general*. The present study is limited to this last category.

REASONS FOR URGENCY OF STUDY

Ethical errors are increasing not only in numbers but in variety — for example, in the recently added problems arising in transplantation of organs.

---

*From the Anaesthesia Laboratory of the Harvard Medical School at the Massachusetts General Hospital.

†Dorr Professor of Research in Anaesthesia, Harvard Medical School.

‡At the Brook Lodge Conference on "Problems and Complexities of Clinical Research" I commented that "what seem to be breaches of ethical conduct in experimentation are by no means rare, but are almost, one fears, universal." I thought it was obvious that I was by "universal" referring to the fact that examples could easily be found in *all* categories where research in man takes place to any significant extent. Judging by press comments, that was not obvious; hence, this note.

There are a number of reasons why serious attention to the general problem is urgent.

Of transcendent importance is the enormous and continuing increase in available funds, as shown below.

MONEY AVAILABLE FOR RESEARCH EACH YEAR

	MASSACHUSETTS GENERAL HOSPITAL	NATIONAL INSTITUTES OF HEALTH*
1945	$ 500,000†	$ 701,800
1955	2,222,816	36,063,200
1965	8,384,342	436,600,000

*National Institutes of Health figures based upon decade averages, excluding funds for construction, kindly supplied by Dr. John Sherman, of National Institutes of Health.
†Approximation, supplied by Mr. David C. Crockett, of Massachusetts General Hospital.

Since World War II the annual expenditure for research (in large part in man) in the Massachusetts General Hospital has increased a remarkable 17-fold. At the National Institutes of Health, the increase has been a gigantic 624-fold. This "national" rate of increase is over 36 times that of the Massachusetts General Hospital. These data, rough as they are, illustrate vast opportunities and concomitantly expanded responsibilities.

Taking into account the sound and increasing emphasis of recent years that experimentation in man must precede general application of new procedures in therapy, plus the great sums of money available, there is reason to fear that these requirements and these resources may be greater than the supply of responsible investigators. All this heightens the problems under discussion.

Medical schools and university hospitals are increasingly dominated by investigators. Every young man knows that he will never be promoted to a tenure post, to a professorship in a major medical school, unless he has proved himself as an investigator. If the ready availability of money for conducting research is added to this fact, one can see how great the pressures are on ambitious young physicians.

Implementation of the recommendations of the President's Commission on Heart Disease, Cancer and Stroke means that further astronomical sums of money will become available for research in man.

In addition to the foregoing three practical points there are others that Sir Robert Platt[2] has pointed out: a general awakening of social conscience; greater power for good or harm in new remedies, new operations and new investigative procedures than was formerly the case; new methods of preventive treatment with their advantages and dangers that are now applied to communities as a whole as well as to individuals, with multiplication of the possibilities for injury; medical science has shown how valuable human experimentation can be in solving problems of disease and its treatment; one can therefore anticipate an increase in experimentation; and the newly developed concept of clinical research as a profession (for example, clinical pharmacology) — and this, of course, can lead to unfortunate separation between the interests of science and the interests of the patient.

FREQUENCY OF UNETHICAL OR QUESTIONABLY ETHICAL PROCEDURES

Nearly everyone agrees that ethical violations do occur. The practical question is, how often? A preliminary examination of the matter was based on 17 examples, which were easily increased to 50. These 50 studies contained references to 186 further likely examples, on the average 3.7 leads per study; they at times overlapped from paper to paper, but this figure indicates how conveniently one can proceed in a search for such material. The data are suggestive of widespread problems, but there is need for another kind of information, which was obtained by examination of 100 consecutive human studies published in 1964, in an excellent journal; 12 of these seemed to be unethical. If only one quarter of them is truly unethical, this still indicates the existence of a serious situation. Pappworth,[3] in England, has collected, he says, more than 500 papers based upon unethical experimentation. It is evident from such observations that unethical or questionably ethical procedures are not uncommon.

THE PROBLEM OF CONSENT

All so-called codes are based on the bland assumption that meaningful or informed consent is readily available for the asking. As pointed out elsewhere,[4] this is very often not the case. Consent in any fully informed sense may not be obtainable. Nevertheless, except, possibly, in the most trivial situations, it remains a goal toward which one must strive for sociologic, ethical and clear-cut legal reasons. There is no choice in the matter.

If suitably approached, patients will accede, on the basis of trust, to about any request their physician may make. At the same time, every experienced clinician investigator knows that patients will often submit to inconvenience and some discomfort, if they do not last very long, but the usual patient will never agree to jeopardize seriously his health or his life for the sake of "science."

In only 2 of the 50* examples originally compiled for this study was consent mentioned. Actually, it should be emphasized in all cases for obvious moral and legal reasons, but it would be unrealistic to place much dependence on it. In any precise sense statements regarding consent are meaningless unless one knows how fully the patient was informed of all risks, and if these are not known, that fact should also be made clear. A far more dependable safeguard than consent is the presence of a truly *responsible* investigator.

EXAMPLES OF UNETHICAL OR QUESTIONABLY ETHICAL STUDIES

These examples are not cited for the condemna-

*Reduced here to 22 for reasons of space.

tion of individuals; they are recorded to call attention to a variety of ethical problems found in experimental medicine, for it is hoped that calling attention to them will help to correct abuses present. During ten years of study of these matters it has become apparent that thoughtlessness and carelessness, not a willful disregard of the patient's rights, account for most of the cases encountered. Nonetheless, it is evident that in many of the examples presented, the investigators have risked the health or the life of their subjects. No attempt has been made to present the "worst" possible examples; rather, the aim has been to show the variety of problems encountered.

References to the examples presented are not given, for there is no intention of pointing to individuals, but rather, a wish to call attention to widespread practices. All, however, are documented to the satisfaction of the editors of the *Journal*.

Known Effective Treatment Withheld

Example 1. It is known that rheumatic fever can usually be prevented by adequate treatment of streptococcal respiratory infections by the parenteral administration of penicillin. Nevertheless, definitive treatment was withheld, and placebos were given to a group of 109 men in service, while benzathine penicillin G was given to others.

The therapy that each patient received was determined automatically by his military serial number arranged so that more men received penicillin than received placebo. In the small group of patients studied 2 cases of acute rheumatic fever and 1 of acute nephritis developed in the control patients, whereas these complications did not occur among those who received the benzathine penicillin G.

Example 2. The sulfonamides were for many years the only antibacterial drugs effective in shortening the duration of acute streptococcal pharyngitis and in reducing its suppurative complications. The investigators in this study undertook to determine if the occurrence of the serious nonsuppurative complications, rheumatic fever and acute glomerulonephritis, would be reduced by this treatment. This study was made despite the general experience that certain antibiotics, including penicillin, will prevent the development of rheumatic fever.

The subjects were a large group of hospital patients; a control group of approximately the same size, also with exudative Group A streptococcus, was included. The latter group received only nonspecific therapy (no sulfadiazine). The total group denied the effective penicillin comprised over 500 men.

Rheumatic fever was diagnosed in 5.4 per cent of those treated with sulfadiazine. In the control group rheumatic fever developed in 4.2 per cent.

In reference to this study a medical officer stated in writing that the subjects were not informed, did not consent and were not aware that they had been involved in an experiment, and yet admittedly 25 acquired rheumatic fever. According to this same medical officer *more than 70* who had had known definitive treatment withheld were on the wards with rheumatic fever when he was there.

Example 3. This involved a study of the relapse rate in typhoid fever treated in two ways. In an earlier study by the present investigators chloramphenicol had been recognized as an effective treatment for typhoid fever, being attended by half the mortality that was experienced when this agent was not used. Others had made the same observations, indicating that to withhold this effective remedy can be a life-or-death decision. The present study was carried out to determine the relapse rate under the two methods of treatment; of 408 charity patients 251 were treated with chloramphenicol, of whom 20, or 7.97 per cent, died. Symptomatic treatment was given, but chloramphenicol was withheld in 157, of whom 36, or 22.9 per cent, died. According to the data presented, 23 patients died in the course of this study who would not have been expected to succumb if they had received specific therapy.

Study of Therapy

Example 4. TriA (triacetyloleandomycin) was originally introduced for the treatment of infection with gram-positive organisms. Spotty evidence of hepatic dysfunction emerged, especially in children, and so the present study was undertaken on 50 patients, including mental defectives or juvenile delinquents who were inmates of a children's center. No disease other than acne was present; the drug was given for treatment of this. The ages of the subjects ranged from thirteen to thirty-nine years. "By the time half the patients had received the drug for four weeks, the high incidence of significant hepatic dysfunction . . . led to the discontinuation of administration to the remainder of the group at three weeks." (However, only two weeks after the start of the administration of the drug, 54 per cent of the patients showed abnormal excretion of bromsulfalein.) Eight patients with marked hepatic dysfunction were transferred to the hospital "for more intensive study." Liver biopsy was carried out in these 8 patients and repeated in 4 of them. Liver damage was evident. Four of these hospitalized patients, after their liver-function tests returned to normal limits, received a "challenge" dose of the drug. Within two days hepatic dysfunction was evident in 3 of the 4 patients. In 1 patient a second challenge dose was given after the first challenge and again led to evidence of abnormal liver function. Flocculation tests remained abnormal in some patients as long as five weeks after discontinuance of the drug.

Physiologic Studies

Example 5. In this controlled, double-blind study of the hematologic toxicity of chloramphenicol, it was recognized that chloramphenicol is "well known as a cause of aplastic anemia" and that there is a "prolonged morbidity and high mortality of aplastic anemia" and that ". . . chloramphenicol-induced aplastic anemia can be related to dose . . ." The aim of the study was "further definition of the toxicology of the drug. . . ."

Forty-one randomly chosen patients were given either 2 or 6 gm. of chloramphenicol per day; 12 control patients were used. "Toxic bone-marrow depression, predominantly affecting erythropoiesis, developed in 2 of 20 patients given 2.0 gm. and in 18 of 21 given 6 gm. of chloramphenicol daily." The smaller dose is recommended for routine use.

Example 6. In a study of the effect of thymectomy on the survival of skin homografts 18 children, three and a half months to eighteen years of age, about to undergo surgery for congenital heart disease, were selected. Eleven were to have total thymectomy as part of the operation, and 7 were to serve as controls. As part of the experiment, full-thickness skin homografts from an unrelated adult donor were sutured to the chest wall in each case. (Total thymectomy is occasionally, although not usually part of the primary cardiovascular surgery involved, and whereas it may not greatly add to the hazards of the necessary operation, its eventual effects in children are not known.) This work was proposed as part of a long-range study of "the growth and development of these children over the years." No difference in the survival of the skin homograft was observed in the 2 groups.

Example 7. This study of cyclopropane anesthesia and cardiac arrhythmias consisted of 31 patients. The average duration of the study was three hours, ranging from two to four and a half hours. "Minor surgical procedures" were carried out in all but 1 subject. Moderate to deep anesthesia, with endotracheal intubation and controlled respiration, was used. Carbon dioxide was injected into the closed respiratory system until cardiac arrhythmias appeared. Toxic levels of carbon dioxide were achieved and maintained for considerable periods. During the cyclopropane anesthesia a variety of pathologic cardiac arrhythmias occurred. When the carbon dioxide tension was elevated above normal, ventricular extrasystoles were more numerous than when the carbon dioxide tension was normal, ventricular arrhythmias being continuous in 1 subject for ninety minutes. (This can lead to fatal fibrillation.)

Example 8. Since the minimum blood-flow requirements of the cerebral circulation are not accurately known, this study was carried out to determine "cerebral hemodynamic and metabolic changes . . . before and during acute reductions in arterial pressure induced by drug administration and/or postural adjustments." Forty-four patients whose ages varied from the second to the tenth decade were involved. They included normotensive subjects, those with essential hypertension and finally a group with malignant hypertension. Fifteen had abnormal electrocardiograms. Few details about the reasons for hospitalization are given.

Signs of cerebral circulatory insufficiency, which were easily recognized, included confusion and in some cases a nonresponsive state. By alteration in the tilt of the patient "the clinical state of the subject could be changed in a matter of seconds from one of alertness to confusion, and for the remainder of the flow, the subject was maintained in the latter state." The femoral arteries were cannulated in all subjects, and the internal jugular veins in 14.

The mean arterial pressure fell in 37 subjects from 109 to 48 mm. of mercury, with signs of cerebral ischemia. "With the onset of collapse, cardiac output and right ventricular pressures decreased sharply."

Since signs of cerebral insufficiency developed without evidence of coronary insufficiency the authors concluded that "the brain may be more sensitive to acute hypotension than is the heart."

Example 9. This is a study of the adverse circulatory responses elicited by intra-abdominal maneuvers:

> When the peritoneal cavity was entered, a deliberate series of maneuvers was carried out [in 68 patients] to ascertain the effective stimuli and the areas responsible for development of the expected circulatory changes. Accordingly, the surgeon rubbed localized areas of the parietal and visceral peritoneum with a small ball sponge as discretely as possible. Traction on the mesenteries, pressure in the area of the celiac plexus, traction on the gallbladder and stomach, and occlusion of the portal and caval veins were the other stimuli applied.

Thirty-four of the patients were sixty years of age or older; 11 were seventy or older. In 44 patients the hypotension produced by the deliberate stimulation was "moderate to marked." The maximum fall produced by manipulation was from 200 systolic, 105 diastolic, to 42 systolic, 20 diastolic; the average fall in mean pressure in 26 patients was 53 mm. of mercury.

Of the 50 patients studied, 17 showed either atrioventricular dissociation with nodal rhythm or nodal rhythm alone. A decrease in the amplitude of the T wave and elevation or depression of the ST segment were noted in 25 cases in association with manipulation and hypotension or, at other times, in the course of anesthesia and operation. In only 1 case was the change pronounced enough to suggest myocardial ischemia. No case of myocardial infarction was noted in the group studied although routine electrocardiograms were not taken after operation to detect silent infarcts. Two cases in which electrocardiograms were taken after operation showed T-wave and ST-segment changes that had not been present before.

These authors refer to a similar study in which more alarming electrocardiographic changes were observed. Four patients in the series sustained silent myocardial infarctions; most of their patients were undergoing gallbladder surgery because of associated heart disease. It can be added further that in the 34 patients referred to above as being sixty years of age or older, some doubtless had heart disease that could have made risky the maneuvers carried out. In any event, this possibility might have been a deterrent.

Example 10. Starling's law — "that the heart output per beat is directly proportional to the diastolic filling" — was studied in 30 adult patients with atrial fibrillation and mitral stenosis sufficiently severe to require valvulotomy. "Continuous alterations of the length of a segment of left ventricular muscle were recorded simultaneously in 13 of these patients by means of a mercury-filled resistance gauge sutured to the surface of the left ventricle." Pressures in the left ventricle were determined by direct puncture simultaneously with the segment length in 13 patients and without the segment length in an additional 13 patients. Four similar unanesthetized patients were studied through catheterization of the left side of the heart transeptally. In all 30 patients arterial pressure was measured through the catheterized brachial artery.

Example 11. To study the sequence of ventricular contraction in human bundle-branch block, simultaneous catheterization of both ventricles was performed in 22 subjects; catheterization of the right side of the heart was carried out in the usual manner; the left side was catheterized transbronchially. Extrasystoles were produced by tapping on the epicardium in subjects with normal myocardium while they were undergoing thoracotomy. Simultaneous pressures were measured in both ventricles through needle puncture in this group.

The purpose of this study was to gain increased insight into the physiology involved.

Example 12. This investigation was carried out to examine the possible effect of vagal stimulation on cardiac arrest. The authors had in recent years transected the homolateral vagus nerve immediately below the origin of the recurrent laryngeal nerve as palliation against cough and pain in bronchogenic carcinoma. Having been impressed with the number of reports of cardiac arrest that seemed to follow vagal stimulation, they tested the effects of intrathoracic vagal stimulation during 30 of their surgical procedures, concluding, from these observations in patients under satisfactory anesthesia, that cardiac irregularities and cardiac arrest due to vagovagal reflex were less common than had previously been supposed.

Example 13. This study presented a technic for determining portal circulation time and hepatic blood flow. It involved the transcutaneous injection of the spleen and catheterization of the hepatic vein. This was carried out in 43 subjects, of whom 14 were normal; 16 had cirrhosis (varying degrees), 9 acute hepatitis, and 4 hemolytic anemia.

No mention is made of what information was divulged to the subjects, some of whom were seriously ill. This study consisted in the development of a technic, not of therapy, in the 14 normal subjects.

Studies to Improve the Understanding of Disease

Example 14. In this study of the syndrome of impending hepatic coma in patients with cirrhosis of the liver certain nitrogenous substances were administered to 9 patients with chronic alcoholism and advanced cirrhosis: ammonium chloride, di-ammonium citrate, urea or dietary protein. In all patients a reaction that included mental disturbances, a "flapping tremor" and electroencephalographic changes developed. Similar signs had occurred in only 1 of the patients before these substances were administered:

> The first sign noted was usually clouding of the consciousness. Three patients had a second or a third course of administration of a nitrogenous substance with the same results. It was concluded that marked resemblance between this reaction and impending hepatic coma, implied that the administration of these [nitrogenous] substances to patients with cirrhosis may be hazardous.

Example 15. The relation of the effects of ingested ammonia to liver disease was investigated in 11 normal subjects, 6 with acute virus hepatitis, 26 with cirrhosis, and 8 miscellaneous patients. Ten of these patients had neurologic changes associated with either hepatitis or cirrhosis.

The hepatic and renal veins were cannulated. Ammonium chloride was administered by mouth. After this, a tremor that lasted for three days developed in 1 patient. When ammonium chloride was ingested by 4 cirrhotic patients with tremor and mental confusion the symptoms were exaggerated during the test. The same thing was true of a fifth patient in another group.

Example 16. This study was directed toward determining the period of infectivity of infectious hepatitis. Artificial induction of hepatitis was carried out in an institution for mentally defective children in which a mild form of hepatitis was endemic. The parents gave consent for the intramuscular injection or oral administration of the virus, but nothing is said regarding what was told them concerning the appreciable hazards involved.

A resolution adopted by the World Medical Association states explicitly: "Under no circumstances is a doctor permitted to do anything which would weaken the physical or mental resistance of a human being except from strictly therapeutic or prophylactic indications imposed in the interest of the patient." There is no right to risk an injury to 1 person for the benefit of others.

Example 17. Live cancer cells were injected into 22 human subjects as part of a study of immunity to cancer. According to a recent review, the subjects (hospitalized patients) were "merely told they would be receiving 'some cells' " — ". . . the word cancer was entirely omitted. . . ."

Example 18. Melanoma was transplanted from a

daughter to her volunteering and informed mother, "in the hope of gaining a little better understanding of cancer immunity and in the hope that the production of tumor antibodies might be helpful in the treatment of the cancer patient." Since the daughter died on the day after the transplantation of the tumor into her mother, the hope expressed seems to have been more theoretical than practical, and the daughter's condition was described as "terminal" at the time the mother volunteered to be a recipient. The primary implant was widely excised on the twenty-fourth day after it had been placed in the mother. She died from metastatic melanoma on the four hundred and fifty-first day after transplantation. The evidence that this patient died of diffuse melanoma that metastasized from a small piece of transplanted tumor was considered conclusive.

Technical Study of Disease

Example 19. During bronchoscopy a special needle was inserted through a bronchus into the left atrium of the heart. This was done in an unspecified number of subjects, both with cardiac disease and with normal hearts.

The technic was a new approach whose hazards were at the beginning quite unknown. The subjects with normal hearts were used, not for their possible benefit but for that of patients in general.

Example 20. The percutaneous method of catheterization of the left side of the heart has, it is reported, led to 8 deaths (1.09 per cent death rate) and other serious accidents in 732 cases. There was, therefore, need for another method, the trans-bronchial approach, which was carried out in the present study in more than 500 cases, with no deaths.

Granted that a delicate problem arises regarding how much should be discussed with the patients involved in the use of a new method, nevertheless where the method is employed in a given patient for *his* benefit, the ethical problems are far less than when this potentially extremely dangerous method is used "in 15 patients with normal hearts, undergoing bronchoscopy for other reasons." Nothing was said about what was told any of the subjects, and nothing was said about the granting of permission, which was certainly indicated in the 15 normal subjects used.

Example 21. This was a study of the effect of exercise on cardiac output and pulmonary-artery pressure in 8 "normal" persons (that is, patients whose diseases were not related to the cardiovascular system), in 8 with congestive heart failure severe enough to have recently required complete bed rest, in 6 with hypertension, in 2 with aortic insufficiency, in 7 with mitral stenosis and in 5 with pulmonary emphysema.

Intracardiac catheterization was carried out, and the catheter then inserted into the right or left main branch of the pulmonary artery. The brachial artery was usually catheterized; sometimes, the radial or femoral arteries were catheterized. The subjects exercised in a supine position by pushing their feet against weighted pedals. "The ability of these patients to carry on sustained work was severely limited by weakness and dyspnea." Several were in severe failure. This was not a therapeutic attempt but rather a physiologic study.

Bizarre Study

Example 22. There is a question whether ureteral reflux can occur in the normal bladder. With this in mind, vesicourethrography was carried out on 26 normal babies less than forty-eight hours old. The infants were exposed to x-rays while the bladder was filling and during voiding. Multiple spot films were made to record the presence or absence of ureteral reflux. None was found in this group, and fortunately no infection followed the catheterization. What the results of the extensive x-ray exposure may be, no one can yet say.

COMMENT ON DEATH RATES

In the foregoing examples a number of procedures, some with their own demonstrated death rates, were carried out. The following data were provided by 3 distinguished investigators in the field and represent widely held views.

Cardiac catheterization: right side of the heart, about 1 death per 1000 cases; left side, 5 deaths per 1000 cases. "Probably considerably higher in some places, depending on the portal of entry." (One investigator had 15 deaths in his first 150 cases.) It is possible that catheterization of a hepatic vein or the renal vein would have a lower death rate than that of catheterization of the right side of the heart, for if it is properly carried out, only the atrium is entered en route to the liver or the kidney, not the right ventricle, which can lead to serious cardiac irregularities. There is always the possibility, however, that the ventricle will be entered inadvertently. This occurs in at least half the cases, according to 1 expert — "but if properly done is too transient to be of importance."

Liver biopsy: the death rate here is estimated at 2 to 3 per 1000, depending in considerable part on the condition of the subject.

Anesthesia: the anesthesia death rate can be placed in general at about 1 death per 2000 cases. The hazard is doubtless higher when certain practices such as deliberate evocation of ventricular extrasystoles under cyclopropane are involved.

PUBLICATION

In the view of the British Medical Research Council[5] it is not enough to ensure that all investigation is carried out in an ethical manner: it must be made unmistakably clear in the publications that the proprieties have been observed. This implies editorial responsibility in addition to the investigator's. The question rises, then, about valuable data that have been improperly obtained.* It is my view that such material should not be published.⁵ There is a practical aspect to the matter: failure to obtain publication would discourage unethical experimentation. How many would carry out such experimentation if they *knew* its results would never be published? Even though suppression of such data (by not publishing it) would constitute a loss to medicine, in a specific localized sense, this loss, it seems, would be less important than the far reaching moral loss to medicine if the data thus obtained were to be published. Admittedly, there is room for debate. Others believe that such data, because of their intrinsic value, obtained at a cost of great risk or damage to the subjects, should not be wasted but should be published with stern editorial comment. This would have to be done with exceptional skill, to avoid an odor of hypocrisy.

SUMMARY AND CONCLUSIONS

The ethical approach to experimentation in man has several components; two are more important than the others, the first being informed consent. The difficulty of obtaining this is discussed in detail. But it is absolutely essential to *strive* for it for moral, sociologic and legal reasons. The statement that consent has been obtained has little meaning unless the subject or his guardian is capable of understanding what is to be undertaken and unless all

*As far as principle goes, a parallel can be seen in the recent Mapp decision by the United States Supreme Court. It was stated there that evidence unconstitutionally obtained cannot be used in any judicial decision, no matter how important the evidence is to the ends of justice.

hazards are made clear. If these are not known this, too, should be stated. In such a situation the subject at least knows that he is to be a participant in an experiment. Secondly, there is the more reliable safeguard provided by the presence of an intelligent, informed, conscientious, compassionate, responsible investigator.

Ordinary patients will not knowingly risk their health or their life for the sake of "science." Every experienced clinician investigator knows this. When such risks are taken and a considerable number of patients are involved, it may be assumed that informed consent has not been obtained in all cases.

The gain anticipated from an experiment must be commensurate with the risk involved.

An experiment is ethical or not at its inception; it does not become ethical *post hoc* — ends do not justify means. There is no ethical distinction between ends and means.

In the publication of experimental results it must be made unmistakably clear that the proprieties have been observed. It is debatable whether data obtained unethically should be published even with stern editorial comment.

REFERENCES

1. Pope Pius XII. Address. Presented at First International Congress on Histopathology of Nervous System, Rome, Italy, September 14, 1952.
2. Platt (Sir Robert), 1st bart. *Doctor and Patient: Ethics, morals, government*. 87 pp. London: Nuffield provincial hospitals trust, 1963. Pp. 62 and 63.
3. Pappworth, M. H. Personal communication.
4. Beecher, H. K. Consent in clinical experimentation: myth and reality. *J.A.M.A.* 195:34, 1966.
5. Great Britain, Medical Research Council. *Memorandum*, 1953.

BULLETIN OF THE HISTORY OF MEDICINE

ORGAN OF THE AMERICAN ASSOCIATION OF THE HISTORY OF MEDICINE
AND THE JOHNS HOPKINS INSTITUTE OF THE HISTORY OF MEDICINE

Founded by HENRY E. SIGERIST

Editor—OWSEI TEMKIN

MEDICAL ETHICS AND ETIQUETTE IN THE EARLY MIDDLE AGES: THE PERSISTENCE OF HIPPOCRATIC IDEALS *

LOREN C. MACKINNEY

A prevailing tendency of the reading public is its ready acceptance of derogatory generalizations concerning medieval civilization. There is, for example, the traditional generalization that tends to degrade the medieval physician to the position of quack, charlatan, faith healer, medicine man, barber surgeon. Often he is contrasted with the ancient Greek physician, to whom there have been attributed the superlative ideals which the modern age associates with the Hippocratic Oath.

As a result of the historical researches of twentieth-century scholarship, we are beginning to recognize the inaccuracies and exaggerations imbedded in such generalizations concerning the high medical standards of the ancient Greeks and the degradation of the profession during the Middle Ages. So far as the Greek world is concerned, W. H. S. Jones' *The Doctor's Oath* (Cambridge University, 1924) and the introductions

---

* Much of the research on this topic, in distant libraries, was made possible by grants from the Smith Fund of the University of North Carolina, and from the Carnegie Foundation. Valuable suggestions and assistance on problems of paleography and translation were generously given by Professor Elias Lowe of the Princeton University Institute of Advanced Studies, Miss Dorothy Schullian and William Jerome Wilson of the Cleveland Branch of the Army Medical Library, and Professor B. L. Ullman of the University of North Carolina.

2   LOREN C. MACKINNEY

(especially in vol. II) to his *Hippocrates* (New York, 1923 ff.), and Ludwig Edelstein's *The Hippocratic Oath; Text, Translation and Interpretation* (Baltimore, 1943) indicate the necessity of drastic modifications of the traditionally optimistic picture of the Greek medical profession as a band of high minded healers dedicated to the holy ideals of the Sacred Oath.

With regard to the Middle Ages, much has been done to correct the historical astigmatism of tradition,[1] but it has been confined almost entirely to the later medieval centuries, and especially to the supposed influence of Salerno, reputed center of a revived Hippocratic idealism and scientific Greek practice.[2] It is our purpose to show that the preceding period, from about 400 to 1100 A. D., comprising the so-called Dark Ages, had medical ideals that are worthy of a place in the historical record alongside the Hippocratic and Salernitan " codes." Like most of the institutions of Western Civilization, the regulated conduct of physicians in the early Middle Ages seems to have evolved in normally diverse fashion; also without benefit of Salerno, and with much more borrowing from Hippocrates than from Biblical or clerical authorities.

We present a number of treatises, based for the most part on the original manuscript texts. In general, we propose to let them speak for themselves as to the prevailing medieval ideals concerning the training, character, qualifications, dress, and deportment of physicians. Marked resemblances to passages from Hippocratic works, as well as from the Bible and the Church Fathers, indicate a fusion of classical antiquity with Christianity during these early centuries. Equally impressive are the

---

[1] Especially Mary Welborn's "The Long Tradition: A Study in Fourteenth-Century Medical Deontology" in *Medieval and Historiographical Essays in Honor of James Westfall Thompson*, edited by James Cate and Eugene Anderson (Chicago, 1938). See also Henry Sigerist's "Sidelights on the Practice of Medieval Surgeons" (Henri de Mondeville), in *Proceedings of the Annual Congress on Medical Education, Hospitals and Licensure* (Chicago, Feb. 18-19, 1935); Pearl Kibre's "Hippocratic Writings in the Middle Ages" (*Bull. Hist. Med.*, 1945, 18, 371-412, especially 402); Owsei Temkin's "Geschichte des Hippokratismus im ausgehenden Altertum" (*Kyklos*, 1932, vol. 4); and Paul Diepgen, *Die Theologie und der ärztliche Stand* (Berlin, 1922).

[2] S. De Renzi, *Collectio Salernitana* (Naples, 1852 ff.), II, 73 ff., V, 102 f., 333 ff., gives descriptions of MSS and of the Latin texts. Paul Meyer in *Romania* (1903, 32, 86 f. and 1915-1917, 44, 196 f.) describes similar texts in French from MSS in England. Leopold Delisle, *Le Cabinet des Manuscripts de la Bibliothèque Nationale* (Paris, 1874), II, 533; and M. R. James, *The Ancient Libraries of Canterbury and Dover* (Cambridge, 1903), p. 333, cite MSS. R. Cantarella, in *Archeion* (1933, 15, 305-320) cites a few evidences of the Hippocratic Oath in a " civitas Hippocratica " at Salerno before Frederick II. P. Kristeller's " The School of Salerno " (*Bull. Hist. Med.*, 1945, 17, 138-194) presents a broader and more reliable picture of early Salernitan history.

variations and miscellaneous inclusions, factors that show the constant influence of contemporary conditions and of practical experience. It should be remembered that most of these medieval ideals, like the earlier Hippocratic dicta, reflect merely the highest standards of the medical profession. We trust that the evidence presented will not only serve to correct the extremes of generalization now prevalent concerning Greek and Medieval physicians, but also will help fill a gap in modern knowledge of the development of medical ideals.

From the non-medical viewpoint of lay historians who are interested in pre-Renaissance classicism, the evidence presented is noteworthy. It corroborates the thesis of the persistence of Hippocratic ideas in an unbroken line through the early, as well as late, Middle Ages, and in non-Salernitan centers. This factor has been ably discussed in Owsei Temkin's " Geschichte des Hippokratismus im ausgehenden Altertum " and Pearl Kibre's " Hippocratic Writings in the Middle Ages " (cited in footnote 1).

Original source material for the early Middle Ages is scanty, especially for the period prior to the ninth century. However, from these early Christian centuries come three bits of evidence concerned especially with medical ethics and etiquette. A letter of advice written by St. Jerome (late in the fourth century) to a priest in Northern Italy named Nepotian reveals a vague familiarity with the Hippocratic Oath. The young clergyman was cautioned, among other things, to observe secrecy and chastity with regard to the households in which he visited the sick. He also was reminded of certain qualifications which Hippocrates had laid down for secular physicians.

A. [JEROME], TO NEPOTIAN, PRIEST. [A CLERGYMAN'S DUTIES].

It is a part of your [clerical] duty to visit the sick, to be acquainted with people's households, with matrons, and with their children, and to be entrusted with the secrets of the great. Let it therefore be your duty to keep your tongue chaste as well as your eyes. Never discuss a woman's looks, nor let one house know what is going on in another. Hippocrates, before he will instruct his pupils, makes them take an oath and compells them to swear obedience to him. That oath exacts from them silence, and prescribes for them their language, gait, dress, and manners. How much greater an obligation is laid on us [clergymen]. . . .[3]

Jerome's reference to the Hippocratic Oath as a rule prescribing " language, gait, dress, and manners " indicates either that he was not aware of

---

[3] F. A. Wright's translation, in *Select Letters of St. Jerome* (London and New York, 1933), Letter 52, p. 225. Nepotian, an ex-soldier and nephew of a bishop in Venetia, had asked Jerome for advice as to a young cleric's duties.

the contents of the actual Oath (which has nothing concerning these matters, with the exception of *sex*-manners), or that he interpreted the Oath very loosely to include precepts found in other Hippocratic works such as *Physician, Law,* and *Decorum.* On the other hand, his warning against immorality and the revealing of household secrets corresponds to the last two admonitions of the Hippocratic Oath. Apparently, Christians of Jerome's day had a rather vague idea of Hippocratic ideals, but had considerable respect for them.

Within a century after Jerome, the Germanic law codes of the Visigoths were taking shape in Spain. In these, and later revisions thereof, there is a regulation concerning women patients that reflects the same age-old sex problem of which the Hippocratic Oath and Jerome's letter gave warning. The Visigothic code reads as follows:

B. No physician shall presume to bleed a [freeborn] woman in the absence of [some of] her relatives . . .; the father, mother, brother, son, uncle or some neighbor. . . . X solidi [penalty]. . . . On such occasions scandals multiply. . . .[4]

About two centuries after Jerome, in the Ostrogothic kingdom of Italy, Cassiodorus in writing to the supervising physician of the royal household referred to "certain sacred oaths of a priestly nature" by which medical students were obligated, and also to the standards of practice set up for a governmentally regulated profession.

C. [He stressed the merits of the healing art as a worthy calling in that it concerns both the present and future well being of patients and aids them when other (i. e., spiritual) means fail. He warned physicians to avoid quarrels, envy, all forms of wickedness, and artifices of healing. He exhorted them to ever seek knowledge, to read the works of the ancients and to manifest zeal and cheerfulness in treating the sick, and also purity in their personal lives. For an effective bedside manner, the following advice was given]: Let your visits bring healing to the sick, new strength to the weak, certain hope to the weary. Leave it to clumsy [practicioners] to ask the patients they are visiting whether the pain has ceased and if they have slept well. Let the patient ask you about his ailment and hear from you the truth about it. Use the surest possible informants. To a skillful physician the pulsing of the veins [*venarum*] reveals the patient's ailment while the urine analysis indicates it to his eye. To make things easier, do not tell the clamoring inquirer what these symptoms signify. . . .[5]

Somewhat different from the governmental regulations of Visigothic

---

[4] Visigothic code, book XI, 1 (*MGH, Leges,* Sect. I, vol. I, 400).

[5] The original Latin text can be found in *MGH, Auct. Antiq.,* XII, 191 f.; also in M. Neuburger, *Geschichte der Medizin* (Stuttgart, 1911), II, part i, 246 f.; and L. MacKinney, *Early Medieval Medicine* (Baltimore, 1937), p. 163 ff. There is a free translation into English in T. Hodgkin, *Letters of Cassiodorus* (London, 1886), p. 313 f.

Spain and Ostrogothic Italy are the medical ideals expressed in numerous epistolary treatises that appear in the earliest medical manuscripts of the Middle Ages. Most of these manuscripts were written in North-European monasteries during the eight, ninth, and tenth centuries, an era that is often referred to derogatorily as the age of monastic medicine. To be sure, the monastic spirit dominated the compiling of the medical handbooks of the period, but as we shall see, the result was classical as well as pious, and secular as well as ascetic.

Very few of these monastic treatises subordinated Hippocrates and classical medicine to Christ and clerical ministrations in a manner as marked as that manifested in Jerome's letter, or in the sixth-century writings of Cassiodorus, notably the chapter "Concerning Monks Entrusted with the Care of the Sick" in his *De Institutione Divinarum Litterarum* (chapter 31).

One of the most pious expressions of the monastic ideal of medicine is found in the introduction to a manuscript handbook that was compiled probably in a German monastery, late in the eighth century, was recopied about a century later in its present manuscript form (Bamberg MS L III 8), only to be taken to Bamberg Cathedral somewhere around the year 1000 and kept there even to the present day. The author of the introduction was intent on reconciling the late classical medical works, which comprised most of the manuscript, with Christian monastic ideals. In even more detailed and pious fashion than either Jerome or Cassiodorus, he cited the Holy Scriptures, Pope Gregory I, Isidore of Seville, Bede, etc., to show the divine purpose in human medicine.[6]

D. . . . Wherefore one ought not to spurn earthly medicine since he knows it is advantageous rather than harmful and since it has not been held in contempt by holy men. . . . [St. Luke, St. Cosmas, and St. Damian were physicians]. Wherefore let us honor the physicians so that they will help us when sick, remembering [the word of] that wise one [Ecclesiasticus 38:1. Vulgate]: "Honor the physician of necessity for the Most High created him." And do not hesitate to take what potions he gives you. That same wise one [Ecclesiasticus 38:4] said "The Most High created medicine from the earth, and the prudent man will not reject it." Therefore he who does not seek medicine in time of necessity deserves the name stupid and imprudent. I say that it is wise to do well by the physician while you are well so that you will have his services in time of illness. . . . God wishes to be honored by his miracles performed through man. According to Isaiah [26:12] whatever good is done by man is effected by God; he said "The Lord does all of our works through us." [Christ] himself in the Gospel [Luke 18:27 ?] said

---

[6] The text was described and edited by Sudhoff in *Archiv Gesch. Med.*, 1914, 7, 223-237.

6

"Without me you can do nothing." . . . [The treatise closes with a lengthy exhortation for physicians to serve ailing humans, whether rich or poor, and with a view to eternal rather than earthly rewards.[7] This admonition, derived from the above mentioned passage of Cassiodorus' "Concerning Monks Entrusted with the Care of the Sick," is accompanied by his list of recommended readings and his warning that monastic healers should put their trust in the Lord rather than in herbs and human counsels. The exhortation ends on the following note of Christian idealism:] Aid the sick, your reward coming from Christ, for whoever gives a cup of cold water in His name is assured of the eternal kingdom where with Father and Holy Spirit He lives and reigns for eternity. Amen.

The remainder of the Bamberg manuscript, which is our earliest manuscript source, exemplifies the more practically secular and classical aspects of monastic medicine. Like most early medical manuscripts it contains Latin translations or condensations of Graeco-Roman works on remedies, diet, monthly regimen, substitute medicines, and other miscellaneous bits of information. Among the last mentioned items is a fragment of treatise K(a) (quoted below) which reiterates the chief points in the Hippocratic Oath. This manuscript with its combination of Christian piety and classical idealism typifies the more conservative aspects of monastic medical literature during the early Middle Ages. So far as medical ethics and etiquette are concerned, there are more important manuscript sources.

Somewhat later than the Bamberg manuscript, in Central France a much more detailed medical handbook was compiled (Paris, Bibliothèque Nationale, MS 11219).[8] In it are found many treatises, including a commentary on Hippocrates' Aphorisms (in Latin), a book (attributed to him) on various medical topics, another on diseases and cures, gynecology and herbs, also an antidotary and a miscellany of epistolary treatises attributed to Hippocrates and Galen. The epistolary treatises appear immediately after Hippocrates' Aphorisms, under the title *Liber Epistolarum*. The first seven, which are actually brief treatises concerning medical training, ethics, and etiquette, constitute one of the most complete cover-

---

[7] Similar warnings are given elsewhere in the manuscript, on a folio (5) of verses entitled "Cosmas, Damian, Hippocrates, Galen." They read in part as follows: "Sick one, pay the physician what you owe lest when ills return no one will visit you. Physician, care for the poor as well as the powerful. If the patient is rich you have a just occasion for profit; if poor, let one reward [spiritual] suffice. . . ."

[8] A few scholars have dated the manuscript 9-10th century. Professor Lowe was so kind as to check it recently and assures me as to the 9th century dating. It once belonged to a monastery in Luxemburg. Professor Lowe believes that it originated in the Loire region and that it may have been one of the manuscripts used by the humanistic cleric, Lupus of Ferrieres.

ages of these subjects in early manuscript literature. Strange to say, this part of the manuscript has been neglected, even by specialists in medieval medical history.[9] The collection is especially important in that, in combination with similar treatises in other early manuscripts, it reveals a North-European literature which, amidst monastic influences, reflected the classical ideology of Hippocrates. A parallel collection, also strangely neglected, is found in a slightly later manuscript at Chartres (MS 62). This literature, stemming from transalpine monasteries, antedates the earliest examples from Salerno, the much publicized center of Hippocratic ideas, once referred to by Fielding Garrison as "the isolated outpost of Greek medical tradition in the Middle Ages."

The chronological list (below) of manuscripts which contain the treatises under consideration serves to indicate the importance of non-Salernitan, North-European centers. Obviously the present location of manuscripts (almost all of them in the North) and their datings (all subsequent to 800 A.D) do not eliminate the possibility of pre-ninth-century, Italian, sources for the material found therein. In fact, scholars are convinced that most of the classical element in early Medieval medical literature was derived from compilations and translations (from the Greek) that antedate the ninth-century activities in Northern Europe commonly referred to as the Carolingian Renaissance. The earliest centers of translating are thought to have been in Byzantine Italy, in and about Ravenna, during the fifth, sixth and seventh centuries. Medical works in both Greek and Latin were also current in Southern Italy in Cassiodorus' day (ca. 550). It is possible therefore that we are concerned with a Graeco-Latin medical literature that was originally a product of the Byzantine classicism of Ravenna and the monasticism stemming from the Vivarium and Monte Cassino.

---

[9] Hirschfeld's otherwise excellent survey of "Deontologische Texte des frühen Mittelalters" (*Archiv. Gesch. Med.*, 1928, 20, 353-371) fails even to cite the manuscript, though he presents the texts of some of the treatises contained therein, from later manuscripts. He also omits (perforce) treatises that are unique to this manuscript. The manuscript is likewise unmentioned in Laux's article on "Ars medicinae" (*Kyklos*, 1930, 3, 417-434) save for the citation of a list of surgical instruments, contained therein. The manuscript is cited, but not for the texts with which we are concerned, in H. Diels, *Die Handschriften der antiken Aerzte* (Berlin, 1905) I, 53.

8   LOREN C. MACKINNEY

Manuscripts and Editions of the Treatises.[10]

Bamberg, L III 8, 9th century, folios 1-6 (Sudhoff, Hirschfeld, Laux)
Paris, BN, 11219, 9th century, folios 12-15
St. Gall, 751, 9-10th century, pp. 337-339, 354-359 (Hirschfeld, Laux)
Glasgow, Hunter, V. 3. 2, early 10th century, folio 27
Karlsruhe, 120, 10th century, folios 182-184 (Rose)
Chartres, 62, 10th century folios 1-2
Brussels, 3701-15, 10th century, folios 5-7
Monte Cassino, 97, 10th century, p. 4 (De Renzi, II, 73)
Rome, Vat. Barberini, 160, 11th century, folio 286
Montpellier, 185, 11th century, folio 100 (Sigerist)
Copenhagen, 1653, 11th century, folio 72 (Laux)
Zurich, C 128/32, 11th century, folios 103-104 (Hirschfeld, Laux)
Brussels, 1342-50, 12th century, folios 1-2 (Hirschfeld, Laux)
Rome, Angelica, 1502, 12th century, folio 1 (Giacosa, Hirschfeld)
Breslau, 1302, 12th century, folio 184 (De Renzi, II, 74)
Edinburgh, A. 5. 42, 12th century, last folio
Rome, Vat. Regina, 1443, 12-13th century, folio 39
Rome, Vat. 2376 folio 209 (cited by Diels, I, 123)
Rome, Vat. 2417 folio 275 (cited by Diels, I, 123)
Carpentras, 318, 13th century, folio 79 (Sigerist)
Paris, BN, 15456, 13th century, folio 186
Paris, BN, 7091, 14th century, folio 1 (De Renzi, V, 333)
London, BM, Cotton, Galba, E. IV, 14th century, folio 238 (Rose)
Escorial, a IV 6, 14-15th century, folio 197 (Hirschfeld)
Paris, BN, 6988A, 15th century, folio 121

Using the ninth-century Paris manuscript (BN 11219) as a sort of master copy, we present the translated texts in topical groups; first the more idealistic ones concerning Spiritual Aspects of Medicine and Qualifi-

[10] In practically all cases the dating of the listed manuscripts is based on personal examination (either of the original or of photoreproductions), and also on the opinions of specialists such as Elias Lowe and B. L. Ullman. Where there are printed versions of the manuscript text, the editor's name appears in parenthesis after the manuscript listing; viz., (Sudhoff) for Sudhoff's article cited above in note 6; (Hirschfeld) for Hirschfeld's article cited above in note 9; (Laux) for Laux's article cited above in note 9; (De Renzi) for De Renzi's *Collectio* cited above in note 2; (Sigerist) for Sigerist's article "Early Mediaeval Medical Texts in Manuscripts of Montpellier" (*Bull. Hist. Med.*, 1941, 10, 31 f.); (Giacosa) for P. Giacosa's *Magistri Salernitani nondum editi* (Turin, 1901), p. 360; (Diels) for Diels' *Die Handschriften* cited above in note 9; and (Rose) for V. Rose's *Anecdota Graeca et Graecolatina* (Berlin, 1870), II, 275 f.

cations and Training of the Physician; then those of a more practical nature concerning Etiquette, Women Patients, Pulse Taking, Sick Calls, and other aspects of the "Bedside Manner."[11]

I. SPIRITUAL ASPECTS OF MEDICINE

The first treatise to be presented is similar to the Bamberg introduction (above, treatise D), in that it is predominantly religious in its approach to the subject. Although the Paris treatise is the briefer of the two, it is more emphatic with regard to the divine aspects of healing. From beginning to end the healing of the body is subordinated to the healing of the soul.

E. FOR ALL HEALING DIVINE MEDICATIONS ARE TO BE USED.[12]

For all healing divine medications are to be used because divine power is the proper agent for restoring mortal bodies. It is proper to call such an one physician who is responsible for the health of the soul and the well being of the body . . . [the text continues concerning Christ's ordaining of illness for man's good, also food and drink for his bodily welfare, and ointments, herbs, and medical practitioners for his bodily ills. It ends on a spiritual note, viz.,] He who provides for the healing of soul and body, being made immortal by every divine potentiality, merits pristine health and also security from his own guilt.

In addition to treatises of this sort, occasionally one finds brief passages of an other-worldly nature in otherwise secularly-minded treatises. For example, in a minor, anonymous text which Sigerist edited from the eleventh-century Montpellier manuscript (185), and which exists in at least three other manuscripts (Glasgow, Hunter V. 3. 2, folio 27; Rome, Vat. Barberini, 160, folio 286; Codex Fritz Paneth, folio 175) there is the following: " Medicine was created by the Most High [Ecclesiasticus, 38: 1, 4. Vulgate]. He who fears not God will seek out the physician and not find healing, whereas many of whom physicians have despaired, have been healed by God."

[11] In some cases we have checked or amplified the Paris master text by collation with later manuscripts or editions, notably Chartres MS 62, Rose's version (*op. cit.*, p. 243 ff.) and a late B. M. MS. Furthermore, a few of the treatises presented do not appear in the Paris manuscript. All such variations are indicated in the footnotes. Brackets are used throughout the translations to enclose words or phrases (not in the original text) which have been added in order to clarify the meaning. However, we have not pressed this procedure meticulously since the translations are somewhat free renderings of the original Latin texts; this is not only for purposes of clarification, but also because of numerous variants and uncertainties in the manuscript versions.

[12] This treatise is also found in Brussels MS 3701-15, in similar but not identical wording.

The same Biblical text was cited in support of physicians by other monastic compilers. We have already noted (above, treatise D) that as early as the eighth century this, and other Scriptural passages were quoted to prove that those who refused the God-given ministrations of physicians were "stupid and improvident." A century later, Rabanus Maurus, in the medical section of his *De Universo* (xviii, 5), followed the same line of thought. It seems likely that his section entitled "Medical Healing is not to be Spurned" was borrowed from the eighth-century, Bamberg treatise, though in condensed form.[13]

A briefer, but similarly pious, defense of physicians occurs in a Brussels manuscript (3701-15, f. 5). The author, after a brief discussion of the four parts of the body and the four humors, added the following postscript: "Now let us speak of the minister of nature; the physician, the minister of nature who fights against illness. The physician ought to know the past, to perceive the present, to recognize the future.[14] Luke said in the Bible that it is given to physicians to be the Lord's workers.[15] Like-

---

[13] This pious factor in much of Rabanus *De Universo,* both in the medical and non-medical portions, was brought to my attention years ago by Edward K. Graham in the course of his graduate research. The point is noteworthy in connection with the generalization frequently made, to the effect that Rabanus Maurus' treatment of medicine is more extensive than that of his chief source, Isidore of Seville's *Etymologies.* Rabanus' work, as a matter of fact, is much *less* extensive in actual medical information. As stated by Mr. Graham in his thesis on Rabanus Maurus: "By far the greater part of Rabanus . . . is made up of fragmentary portions of Isidore's material supplemented by exegesis. . . . Rabanus copies part of Isidore, omits part, and substitutes exegesis for the part omitted." Mr. Graham's dictum applies to the passage in question, "Medical Healing is not to be Spurned." Up to this point Rabanus seems to have copied his medical data from Isidore's *Etymologies* (iv. ch. 1 ff.). Omitting chapters 6 (last part), 7-8 of Isidore, he copied only the title of chapter 9, S. 1 ("Medical Healing is not to be Spurned"). In place of Isidore's text he substituted a highly moralistic and Scripture-laden treatment of the topic. This material is so similar to the Bamberg introduction (above, treatise D) that one is tempted to assume that Rabanus, realizing that his Isidorean borrowings were conspicuously un-Christian, decided to shift the emphasis to the religious aspects of healing. For this, the Bamberg treatise was an ideal source.

[14] This past-present-future theme, which appears in modified form in treatises C (above) and F (below), stems from chapter I of the Hippocratic *Book of Prognostics,* of which there were Latin versions in Italy as early as the fifth century, and of which there are extant copies in ninth-tenth century manuscripts (See Kibre, "Hippocratic Writings . . ." p. 387 f.). The theme was repeated in Galen's commentaries on the Hippocratic *Epidemics* (Kühn edition, XVII, part I, 147), in Isidore's *Etymologies* (iv, 10) and in pseudo-Soranus *Quaestiones Medicinales,* alias *Horus Ysagoge* (Chartres MS 62, folio 1; also edited from late-medieval MSS by Rose, *op. cit.,* II, 243 ff., see esp. 246).

[15] Although the sense of the Biblical quotation vaguely resembles several passages in Luke, the Latin wording (*datur medicis ubi operatus dominus*) is closer to the text of

wise, Hippocrates said that the physician achieves just as much as God permits."[16]

The second of the Paris treatises is all-inclusive in scope and highly idealistic in tone. The absence of any reference to classical medicine is noteworthy. On the other hand, when compared with the Bamberg Introduction (treatise D, above) and the first Paris treatise (E, above), it is decidedly mundane in that it reflects little or no concern for the monastic ideal of spiritual healing. It is an excellent expression of the secular qualifications of early medieval physicians.

II. QUALIFICATIONS AND TRAINING OF THE PHYSICIAN

F. Arsenius to Nepotian,[17] his sweetest son, greeting . . . [several lines of polite, inconsequential matter]. I shall point out what you earnestly desire to know as to what sort of person a physician ought to be. First, he should test his personality to see that he is of a gracious and innately good character, apt and inclined to learn, sober and modest; a good conversationalist, charming, conscientious, intelligent, vigilant and affable, in all detailed affairs adept and skillful. Our art also requires that one be amiable, humble, and benevolent. Humility ever seeks knowledge, ever accumulates, and never goes to excess or offends. Good will restores sweetness, inspires sagacity, maintains remembrances in the heart, love in the soul, discipline in obeying, wisdom imbued with fear and diligence, and respect, for he who loves not honors not and will not be skillful or sure in his work. [The physician should] not be hesitant or timid, turbulent or proud, scornful or lascivious, or garrulous, a publican, or a woman-lover; but rather full of counsel, learned, and chaste. He should not be drunken or lewd, fraudulent, vulgar, criminal or disgraceful; it is not right for a physician to be taken in a fault or to blush for shame in the presence of his people. Even as love of wisdom reveals itself in manners, so let him be irreproachable for he is chosen to a higher honor. Medicine is not to be scorned, but invoked. Inasmuch as the physician has high honors he should not have faults, but instead discretion, taciturnity, patience, tranquility, and refinement; not greed but more of restraint and subtilty, rationality, diligence, and dignity. One of the virtues of this art is zeal in the acquisition of wisdom, long

---

Isaiah 26: 12 (*omnia opera nostra operatus est nobis dominus*), as it is cited in treatise D above).

[16] The Hippocratic *Decorum* (ch. vi) reads as follows: "The Gods are the real physicians. . . ."

[17] There is no means of surely identifying either Arsenius or Nepotian, though both names appear in records from the early Christian centuries (e. g., note Jerome's correspondent, above, treatise A; and see Hirschfeld's suggestions *op. cit.*, p. 358 f.). Medieval writers were very free in their attribution of epistolary treatises to various authors, famous or otherwise. The letter in question appears in three early manuscripts; the Paris master manuscript and also Brussels MS 3701-15 and St. Gall MS 751. Hirschfeld's edition is based on the Brussels and St. Gall MSS; our translation is based on all three. There are frequent variants in the readings.

sufferance, and mildness. [The physician should strive for] a cheerful pleasant approach; for even as light illuminates a home and makes men see in dark shadows, so a cheerful physician turns sorrow and sadness into joy, and comforts all of the members of his patient, and restores his spirits. According to the secret teachings which should be pursued in medical instruction, let the physician be cheerful because he is the gentle helper [of his patients]. Enlivening the body, checking illnesses, drying up humors, he prescribes diet, eliminates fevers, warms the marrow, gives remedies, recreates the vital power. He notes the symptoms of ailments and applies beneficial medicines. He shows himself an expert in the varieties of herbs and a healing practitioner who prepares intelligent remedies for the reviving of men's strength. He clarifies the present, reveals the eternal future and senses inner factors. The physician is said to be the preceptor of healing, the liberator, the opportune worker who renders aid in time of need.

The opening lines of still another Paris epistle indicate the existence of an additional letter on the same subject, with however a somewhat more practical approach. Although the folio of the Paris manuscript is badly mutilated, a Chartres manuscript of slightly later date (MS 62, 10th century), along with a fourteenth-century London manuscript (BM, Cotton, Galba, F. IV, folio 239) provides the complete text.

G. WHAT SORT OF PERSON A PHYSICIAN SHOULD BE

Let us now explain what sort of person a physician should be. He should be gentle in manners and modest, with the proper amount of reliability.[18] He should be neither lacking in knowledge, nor proud; he should take care of rich and poor, slave and free, equally for among all such people medicines are needed. Moreover, if certain compensation is offered, let him accept rather than refuse. If however it is not offered, do not demand it because, however much each one pays, the compensation for medical services cannot be equated with the benefits. Moreover, enter the homes you visit in such a manner as to have eyes only for the healing of the sick. Be mindful of the Hippocratic Oath, and abstain from all guilt and especially from immorality and acts of seduction. Keep secret everything that goes on or is spoken in the home. Thus the physician himself, and the art, will acquire greater praise. The physician should have slender, fine fingers so as to be agreeable to all and to be subtle in his touch. Hippocrates himself [*Physician*, ch. I] said this. The physician should be no less agreeable in conversation, and not wanting in philosophy. He should be unassuming in manners so that both perfection in the art and good manners may be harmonized insofar as is possible.

Still another of the Paris epistles (found in the Chartres and London, MSS, also in Edinburgh MS A. 5.42) deals at greater length with the practical aspects of the subject, introducing the question of the specific qualifications necessary for those who plan to study medicine. The im-

---

[18] This and the four succeeding sentences, are also found in a garbled treatise in St. Gall MS 571 (edited by Hirschfeld, p. 363).

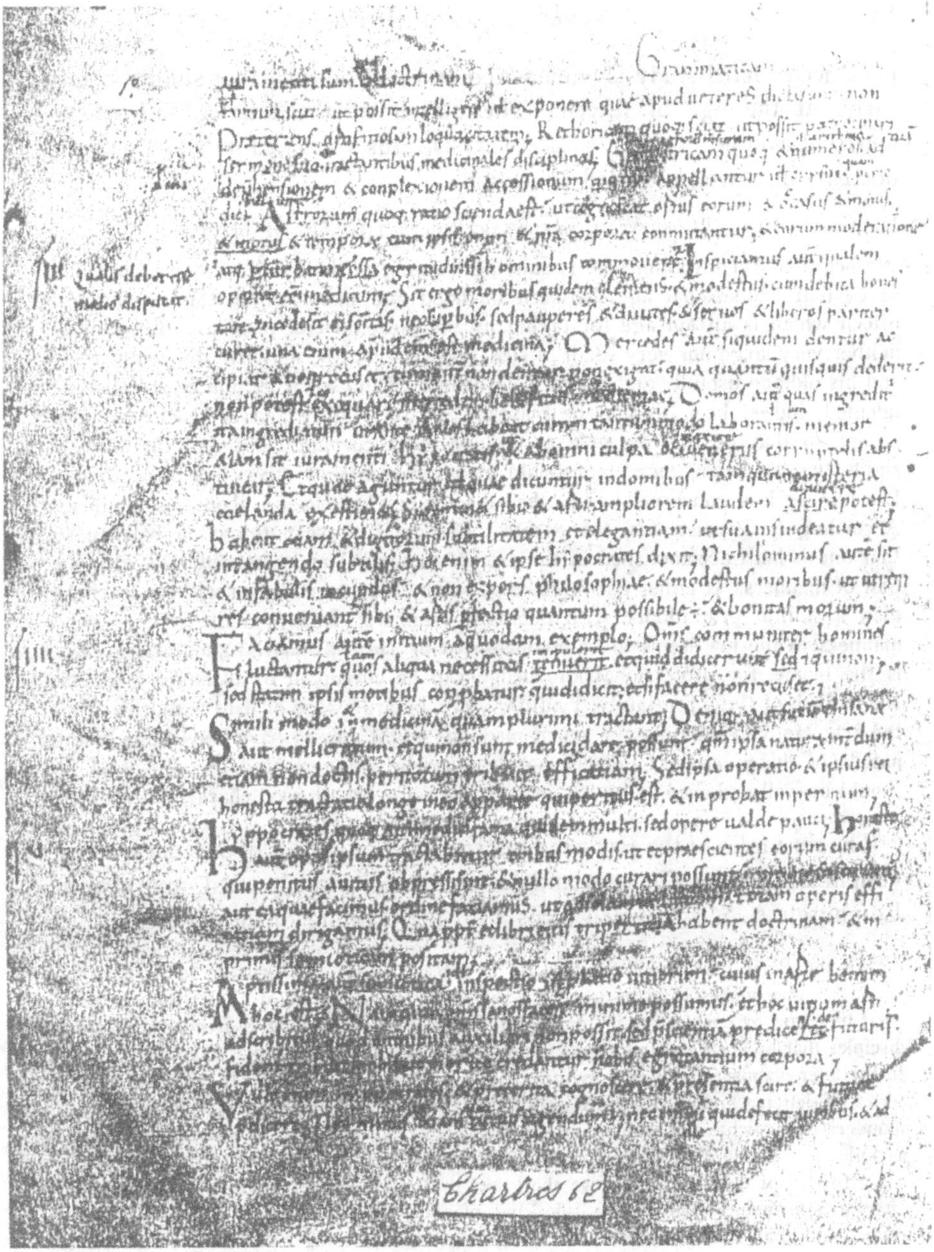

Fig. 1

Chartres MS 62, 10th century, folio 1v.

Portion of a series of letters including the text of treatises G and I which occur in mutilated form in Paris BN MS 11219.

portance of hard study is emphasized and it is advised that students start early, at the age of fifteen. The author of the treatise showed no apparent aversion to the classics; Erasistratus was cited in support of the doctrine of a well balanced education.

H. Concerning Those Who are Starting in the Art of Medicine.[19]

We begin concerning him who is starting training in the art of medicine. Let him be of that transitional age, between boyhood and manhood, that is a youth of fifteen which is an apt age for taking up the sacred art of medicine. Let him be neither very large nor very small in size, and such that he may live his youth freely and his old age usefully and easily.[20] In character and spirit let him be zealous and talented, indeed keen so that he may understand readily and be teachable; also strong so that he may be able to endure the recurring labor and the terrible sights that he encounters. He should make the cases of others his own sorrow. Let him be less concerned with other disciplines, but careful about his manners. According to Erasistratus, the greatest felicity is to keep things in balance so that one is both accomplished in the art [of medicine] and also endowed with the best of manners. If either one is lacking, better to be a good man without learning than a skillful practitioner with depraved manners. If indeed the lack of good manners in the art seems to be compensated by [professional] reputation, greater is the blame, for professional knowledge can be corrupted by blameful manners. But if both of these are faulty, I adjure you who are aware of it to withdraw from the art. He who takes up the art of medicine ought also to have knowledge of the nature of things so that he will not seem to be inexperienced therein. And he should be well endowed and wise, indeed adorned with all good characteristics.

The torn folio of the Paris manuscript has a fragment of another treatise (duplicated in the Chartres and London MSS already cited, and also in Edinburgh A. 5. 42) which deals with the training of the physician, but

---

[19] In the Paris manuscript the treatise is preceded by an exhortation to hard study, viz.: "If one wishes to acquire a knowledge of medicine, first of all let him preserve what he learns by committing it to memory. Then he will be able more frequently to warn disciples that by such gradual acquisition of knowledge they may acquire skill in the art." In the later manuscripts (Chartres, Edinburgh, London) the treatise (H) is the first of a series of letters, and is preceded by an introduction concerning the traditional Greek founders of medicine and methods of training young physicians. The latter section reads as follows: " I begin to tell of the best teaching method for those who are beginning to study the art of medicine. First we shall take up the physician himself, then the art, and afterward medicine itself. Plato, speaking of everything that comes into a course of study, said that the one who has a knowledge of the thing concerning which he is questioned is best able to talk. Since in all things which come under consideration it is necessary to be obliging and helpful to attentive listeners, the following proceedure is best. A middle ground is necessary because of the double problem, concerning him who is beginning the art and concerning him who has already done so. [continues as in treatise H] We begin. . . ."

[20] For further details as to the physical qualifications of the student, see below, treatise K.

in somewhat more academic fashion, reminiscent of Isidore of Seville's *Etymologies* (iv, 13).

I. ON GIVING THE SACRED OATH AND WHAT SORT OF BOOKS ONE SHOULD READ.

He who wishes to begin the art of medicine and the science of nature ought to take the oath and not shrink in any way whatsoever from the consequences. And then by this process of oath taking let him take up the teachings. Let him learn the art of grammar to the point where he can understand and expound the sayings of the ancients, omitting all artificialities of speech. Also let him learn rhetoric so as to be able to defend with his own words those who are carrying on medical teaching; also geometry so that, just as one knows the measuring and numbering of fields, so also he may recognize the ailments called *typi* [fevers] and the crises which are produced by *periodici* [fevers]. He must also know the science of the stars so as to recognize their rising, setting, and other movements, and the seasons of the year, since our bodies change along with these, and since human illnesses are affected by their normality and abnormality.

The above quotations make it clear that a wide range of material concerning the qualifications and training of physicians was available to the North-French compilers of the Paris and Chartres manuscripts. There are also two additional treatises, not found in these manuscripts, but occurring in four later manuscripts (only one of which is earlier than the eleventh century): St. Gall, 751; Zurich 128/32; Copenhagen 1653; and Brussels 1342-50. The Copenhagen manuscript (late eleventh century), of South-Italian origin, is one of our three earliest traces of Salernitan influence. The subject matter of the two treatises contained in the four manuscripts is much like that already presented; a mingling of high ideals with practical advice, apparently descriptive of secular physicians.

J.[21] Before the physician takes the Hippocratic Oath, and before he attempts surgery, he ought to heed words of wisdom. If he is apt at learning he will heed what his preceptor says. By its very nature this oath is an acceptable work. Even as the entire earth is not suitable for growing seed, but only that part which receives it and brings forth fruit, so also not all of the earth is suitable to receive teaching, but only that part which by a good determination is able fully to retain it. Once there was an ancient. He was not very chaste. When in due order he instituted the canon of medicine, everything he contributed was good.[22] Certain of his disciples who surrendered themselves wholeheartedly to their teachers, remained there and persisted to the end in the art which they wished to learn. Those

---

[21] The treatise appears, with many variants, in all except the Zurich manuscript. The Latin text has been edited by both Laux and Hirschfeld (cited above, note 9).

[22] The Brussels manuscript (1342-50) amplifies the passage concerning "the ancient" with references to Hippocrates, the Empiricists, Julius alias Ceron, and "the citizen of Larissa" who "instituted all philosophy and dialectic and geometry and music."

who changed from one teacher to another, when new ones appeared, not only acquired nothing, but even went unenlightened. To the wise this seemed useful, but to the foolish a joke and a laughing matter.

K.[23] Therefore, before expounding the Hippocratic Oath it is necessary to explain what sort of person a student of medicine should be. First he should be a freeman by birth, noble in character, youthful in age,[24] of medium size, sturdy, apt in all things; indeed, as in body, so in spirit; cognizant of good counsel, benign, virile, benevolent, chaste, endowed with unusual diligence of mind, audacious without being wrathful, not hardheaded, quick to perceive and understand what is taught, one who knows how to speak with brevity, elegant, with a good memory and not indolent. First of all he should be taught grammar, dialectic, astronomy, arithmetic, geometry and music. He should avoid rhetoric lest he become talkative. He should be taught philosophy along with medicine . . . [to be continued below as treatise K(a), on dress and deportment].

The last of our treatises on Qualifications and Training, is another of the Paris epistles; so far as I know, the only extant copy. It is probably the most important of the collection in that manuscript. Outstandingly practical and classical in tone, at the outset it purports to be " Admonitions of Hippocrates " and references are made to other classical authors such as Epicurus. It is broadly all-inclusive in subject matter, taking up successively the qualifications of the physician, medical training, dress and the bedside manner, even to such matters as the method of taking the pulse and the necessity of making three calls each day. Due to its wide scope the treatise serves as a recapitulation of most of the topics already presented, and as an introduction to various aspects of medical etiquette.

L. LETTER ESPECIALLY TO BE READ CONCERNING THE LEARNING OF THE ART OF MEDICINE.

[Qualifications and Training]

Let us begin to expound the admonitions of Hippocrates. Whoever wishes to become proficient in this art ought to be capable of unbounded literary effort, so that by longstanding perusal of various volumes his perception and discernment

---

[23] The treatise appears in all except the Brussels manuscript (1342-50). The title and text vary considerably in the three manuscripts.

[24] The expression " youthful in age " occurs in only two of the manuscripts (Zurich C 128/32, and Copenhagen 1653). The Latin term used, *puerum*, usually applies to boys up to the age of about 16. An earlier example of emphasis on youthfulness is found in section 7 of Charlemagne's Thionville Capitulary (805), where it was urged " that *infantes* be sent to learn [medicine]." (*MGH, Leges,* Sect. II, I, 121). " Instruction from childhood " is also stressed in the Hippocratic *Oath* and *Law* (ch. II). See also treatise H (above) for a reference to youthful students of medicine.

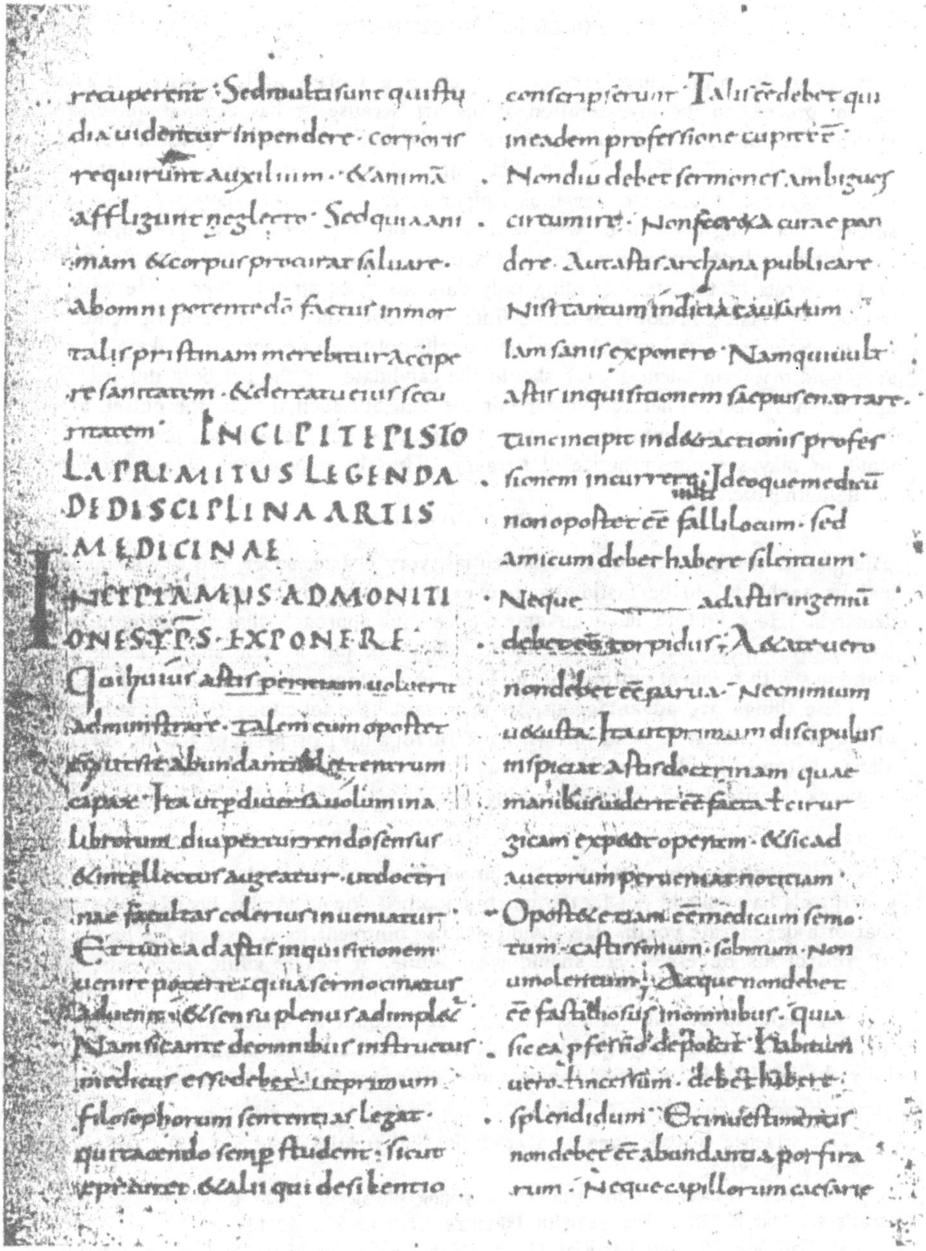

recuperent. Sed multa sunt quibus conspicerunt. Talis ē debet qui dia uidentur inpendere corporis in eadem professione cupit ē requirunt auxilium. & animā Nondiu debet sermones ambiguos affligunt neglecto. Sed qui nani circumire. Non secreta curae pan mam & corpus procurat saluare. dere. Aut astri arcana publicare Ab omni peremedō factus in mor Nisi tantum indicia causarum talis pristinam merebitur accipe sanis exponere. Namq uiuult re sanitatem. & derelatu eius secu a stri inquisitionem saepius enarrare. ritatem. INCIPIT EPISTO Tunc incipit in degractionis profes LA PRIMITUS LEGENDA sionem incurrere. Ideoque medicū DE DISCIPLINA ARTIS non oportet ē ē fallilocum. sed MEDICINAE amicum debet habere silentium.
INCIPIAMUS ADMONITI Neque adstringenti
ONES IPSE EXPONERE. debet ē torpidus. A catu uero
Qui huius astri peritiam uoluerit non debet ē ē parius. Nec nimium
administrare. Talem eum oportet uocusta. It aut primum discipulus
ē ē abundantia litterarum inspicat a stri doctrinam quae
capax. Ita ut p diuersa uolumina manibus uideret ē ē facta t cirur
librorum diu percurrendo sensus gicam expectopem. & sic ad
& intellectus augeatur. ut docen auctorum peruenia noticia.
nae facultas celerius inueniatur. Oportet ē ē ē medicum semo
Et tunc ad astri inquisitionem rum. castum. sobrium. non
uenire poterit. quia sermocinatur umolentum. Atque non debet
adluens. & sensu plenus adimplē ē ē fastidiosus in omnibus. quia
Nam sic ante de omnibus instruitur sic ea p ferro depolat. Habitum
medicus et sic debet ut primum uero. sincerum. debet habere
filosophorum sententias legat. splendidum. Ei ni festimamur
qui tacendo semper student. sicut non debet ē ē abundantia porfira
hyppocrates. & alii qui de silentio rum. Neque capillorum caesarie

FIG. 2
Paris, Bibliothèque Nationale, MS 11219, 9th century, folio 12v.
Text of treatise I, "Admonitions of Hippocrates. . . ."

increase to the point where facility in teaching is more readily acquired.[25] Then he can proceed to the investigation of the art because he has become conversant with it and understands it fully. Before [studying medicine] the physician should be instructed in all subjects.[26] First let him read the opinions of the philosophers, who always study in silence, even as Epicurus and others who have written about silence. Such ought he to be who wishes to enter this profession. He ought not to indulge in long ambiguous discourses, nor to spread abroad his private cures or the secrets of the art, excepting only data on cases already cured. He who is willing to repeat constantly what he finds out about the art of medicine tends to the profession of detractor. A physician ought not to be a deceiver. Like a friend he should maintain silence. Nor should the candidate for the art be a dullard. In age he should be neither too young nor too old, but such that at the outset, as a learner, he may look into the theories of the art which he will see performed by hand, or may seek the practice of surgery. Thus he may arrive at a knowledge of the authorities.

[Medical Etiquette]

The physician ought also to be confidential, very chaste, sober, not a winebibber, and he ought not to be fastidious in everything, for this is what the profession demands. He ought to have an appearance and approach that is distinguished. In his dress there should not be an abundance of purple, nor should he be too fastidious with frequent cuttings of the hair. Everything ought to be in moderation, for these things are advantageous, so it is said. Be solicitous in your approach to the patient, not with head thrown back [arrogantly] or hesitantly with lowered glance, but with head inclined slightly as the art demands. . . . [27] [to be continued below as treatise L(a), on pulse taking, etc.,].

K(a). [continuation of treatise K, above] He ought to hold his head humbly and evenly; his hair should not be too much smoothed down, nor his beard curled like that of a degenerate youth. He should not use ointment to excess on his hands or the tips of his fingers.[28] He should wear white, or nearly white, garments. He should be lightly clad, and walk evenly without disturbance and not too slowly. Gravity signifies breadth of experience. He should approach the patient with moderate steps, not noisily, gazing calmly at the sick bed. He should endure peacefully the insults of the patient since those suffering from melancholic or frenetic

---

[25] This sentence is also found in a brief St. Gall treatise from MS 751. (edited by Hirschfeld, p. 363).

[26] For details concerning the subjects a young physician ought to study, see above, treatises I and K, and compare with Isidore's *Etymologies*, iv, 13.

[27] St. Gall MS 751 and Escorial MS a IV 6 (edited by Hirschfeld, p. 363) have a somewhat condensed version of the subject matter of the entire paragraph on Medical Etiquette. The same topic is treated in great detail (with suggestions as to the physician's clothing, jewels, and horses) in the *Flos Medicinae Scholae Salerni*, written in the later Middle Ages (De Renzi, I, 513 ff.; V, 102 f.).

[28] The material on dress, hair, etc., may have been derived from Galen's *Commentary on Hippocrates' Epidemics* (Kühn edition, XVII, part II, 149 ff.).

ailments are likely to hurl evil words at physicians; these should be ignored for they are not deliberate but rather a result of the harsh annoyance suffered by the patient.

[Etiquette with regard to Women Patients]

Such [as the following] constituted the sacred medical oath according to the precepts of Hippocrates.[29] Enter a home without injuring or corrupting it. Beware lest your medicines bring death to anyone. Do not allow women to persuade you to give abortives, and do not be a part to any such counsel, but keep yourself immaculate and sacred.[30] Abstain from fornication, from [relations with] maidservants, children, married women, and virgins or widows. Keep secret whatever you hear or see in the course of healing, or otherwise, unless it be something that ought to be reported or judged.

[The Taking of the Pulse]

L(a). [continuation of treatise L above]. When a female lies before you and you are about to take her pulse, look neither at the top of her head nor at the bottom of her feet, but at the hand you are holding. By taking the pulse you determine the inner ailment. Learn how to take the pulse so that you can do it standing or seated. Sit on a stool that is neither too high nor too low, but so adjusted that you can take the pulse. If you are holding the right hand below the wrist with your right hand, let the fingers be uppermost so that your thumb may be in the middle in a position outside [i. e., the outer side of the wrist]. Moreover let two fingers, namely the index and middle finger, be placed together inside on the upper part of the vein [venae].[31] Hold the pulse for a long time so that you may detect the up and down

---

[29] Of the five manuscripts that contain this treatise (St. Gall 751, Copenhagen 1653, Bamberg L III 8, Zurich C 128/32, and Brussels 1342-50) the last mentioned has, in addition to the name Hippocrates, those of Apollo and Aesculapius. The reference to the Hippocratic Oath and "precepts" is noteworthy. Contrast this with the false citations from the Oath in Jerome's letter (above, treatise A), and the vague references to an oath in treatises C and I. It is obvious from the references to the Oath in treatises G, J and K (appearing in manuscripts dating from the ninth to the twelfth centuries) that the Oath was known in the early Middle Ages. It may be that it was known at second hand since it is not found in any of the medical manuscripts of this period. The earliest manuscript version cited by Diels is from the thirteenth century. R. Cantarella's "Una Tradizione Ippocratica nella Scuola Salernitana: Il Giuramento de' Medici" (*Archeion*, 1933, 15, 305 ff.) cites references to the Oath in the thirteenth-century regulations of Frederick II and infers that there was an uninterrupted tradition through the earlier centuries, but presents no definite evidence thereof.

[30] The Zurich mansucript has, immediately after "Sacred," the phrase "a custodian of the faith." The Brussels manuscript is fragmentary.

[31] Here apparently "vena" means artery; "arteria" is used in treatise M, below This somewhat incoherent passage on the position of the fingers, etc., defies complete clarification. In the effort to make sense out of it I followed several helpful suggestions from William Jerome Wilson of the Cleveland Branch of the Army Medical Library. It is my intention eventually to publish an article on the mechanics of pulse taking, with numerous quotations from Medieval texts and with several illustrations from Medieval manuscripts. Usually, it seems, the four fingers were placed on the inner (palm) side of the wrist to register the pulse beat.

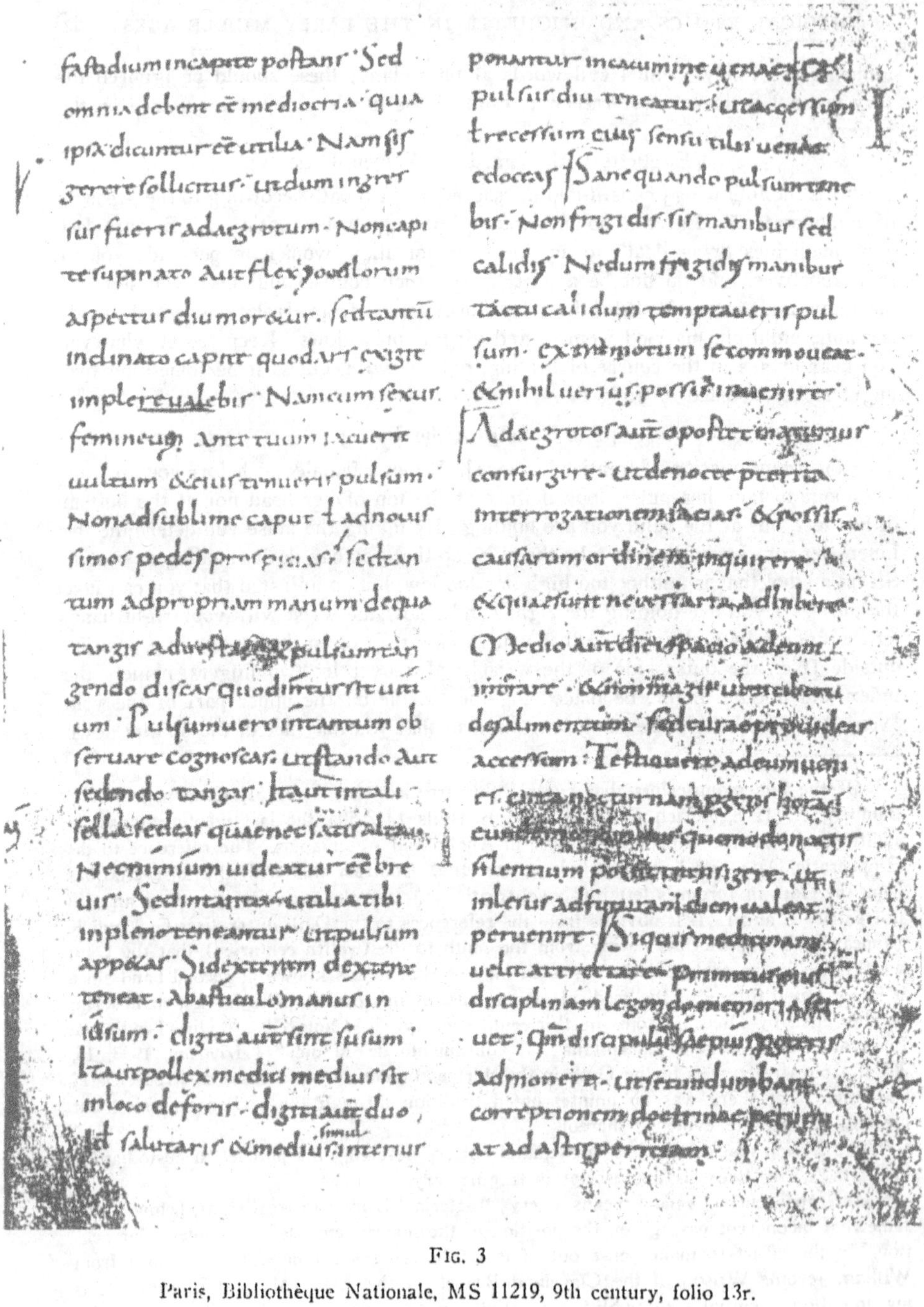

Fig. 3

Paris, Bibliothèque Nationale, MS 11219, 9th century, folio 13r.
Text of treatise L(a), "On taking a Woman's Pulse" (continuation of treatise L).

MEDICAL ETHICS AND ETIQUETTE IN THE EARLY MIDDLE AGES 21

beat by the feeling of the vein. By all means when taking the pulse have your hands warm rather than cold, lest the touch of cold hands upset the warm pulse and make it impossible to determine the true condition.[32] [to be continued below as treatise L(b), concerning sick calls].

The foregoing passage on pulse taking has an almost contemporary parallel in the introduction to a treatise "Concerning the Pulse" (*Peri Sfigmon*) attributed to Soranus. It is found in the tenth-century portion of a manuscript which was written at about the year 900 in the Swiss monastery of Reichenau (it is now at Karlsruhe, MS 120).[33]

M. CONCERNING THE PULSE. Soranus, to his most loved son, greeting. There are many who do not know how long they ought to hold the hand of a patient, and mistakenly think that they have made a true examination. Therefore I urge you, most loved son, to learn early the following method of inspection so that you will never be mistaken. When you visit a patient you should seat yourself in such a position that you may easily see his face, that is, on a stool near the foot of the bed, facing him. In case you are visiting a frenetic patient who would be excited by your facing him, sit near the head whence you can easily see him without being seen. Moreover, if you sit on the bed [do so with a mind to] the conditions of his health, for a slight movement of the person seated there may provoke worse ills, such as a flow of blood or a pernicious reaction or an abundance of sweating or some upset which by lessening in any way the helpfulness of quiet, just that much endangers health by promoting trouble.

Therefore, if this is your first inspection, when you sit down you ought to ask what the bodily affliction is, and how long it has lasted. If it is not your first visit, omit these matters and inquire as to any new ills. Ask if he is sleeping, and

---

[32] A condensed, and apparently garbled, version of the section on pulse taking appears in St. Gall MS 751 and Escorial a IV 6 (edited by Hirschfeld, p. 363). The Paris text and the Karlsruhe treatise (below, treatise M) constitute the most detailed account of the subject that I know of in early Medieval literature. The later Salernitan treatise (below, treatise P) is briefer, and has no additional items. As to the Classical sources for the material, Galen's numerous pulse treatises (Kühn edition, vols. VIII-IX and XIX; especially VIII, 803 ff.) contain no passages exactly like those from the early Middle Ages. It is possible that the Medieval material was taken from the corpus of pulse lore that was transmitted from Classical times to the later Middle Ages under the names of Theophilus, Joannes Philoponos, Meletius, Actuarius and Philaretus (see Temkin's article cited above in note 1, especially p. 54 ff.; also A. Hesse, *Ein Pulstraktat* . . ., Leipzig, 1922).

[33] The text was edited by Rose (*op. cit.*, II, 275 ff.) from A. Torinus' edition in *De Re Medica* (Basel, 1528) and Karlsruhe MS 120. Diels (*op. cit.*, II, 94) cites the Karlsruhe MS and also Chartres MS 62. As a matter of fact the Chartres MS contains only the first few lines of the treatise, after which the text shifts to another pseudo-Soranic treatise which ends with the misleading explicit, *Explicit Peri Sfigmon Ysagogus*. With the exception of the first few lines of *Peri Sfigmon*, this text is the *Ysagogus* or *Horus Ysagoge* mentioned above in note 14; in Thorndike and Kibre's *Incipits* it is listed as *Morus Ysago*.

how often and how much; also if bowels and bladder are functioning normally. After this questioning pause a little, lest the patient has been terrified through timidity or awe at the presence of the physician, or lest he has been upset by his suffering or wakened from sleep. [Give him an opportunity] to compose himself; you might take time for repose by walking about. Then prepare your hand for the pulse taking. Have it moderately warm so that nothing in the hand itself will mislead you; not too warm, not too cold, not sweaty. Such conditions prevail if the hands have been warmed at a fire or heated vessel, or in hot water. It is better to prepare the hands by friction or by placing them next to the chest and under the armpits.

Know which hand to hold; if the patient is lying down, the right hand is better for inspection, or the hand closer to the physician. But it should be on the patient's upper side since the weight of the body from above, pressing on the part underneath, is likely to dominate a normal pulse. Hold the patient's hand with three or four fingers in contact with the artery (*arteria*); with the tips of the fingers press down lightly holding the hand immobile so as to detect the strength, order, and every difference in the movement of the pulse. [treatise continues with a discussion of various types of pulses].

[Sick Calls]

L(a). [continuation of treatise L(a), above]. For those who are ill, you ought to get up early so as to inquire about the preceding night, finding out the order of the causes [of the ailment] and the necessary treatment. At midday pay another visit, not so much to see about the patient's food as to plan for the beginning of a cure. For a third time, visit at about nightfall, staying for an hour in order to make arrangements for him to pass the night [comfortably] so as to be fortified to meet the next day unimpaired. . . . [Treatise ends with an unrelated postscript concerning the study of medicine; apparently it belongs with the succeeding letter: see above, note 19.]

We conclude our series of translations with four treatises, of which the last three are outstandingly practical, being concerned with the bedside manner in particular, and in general with those practices that might be called "tricks of the trade." Although traceable to the age of monastic medicine, these practices seem to have been derived originally from the later Hippocratic treatises, such as *Decorum* and *Precepts*.[34] Apparently it was the late and declining age of Greek medicine that stressed such superficial aspects of medical practice. It is noteworthy that it also was the late, but not declining, age of Medieval medicine that stressed these same factors, which had been known but neglected during the age of monastic medicine. Suffice it to say that this type of late Classical (and also late Medieval) etiquette is distinctly secular in character. In fact,

---

[34] It seems likely that there were Latin translations of these works as early as the fifth and sixth centuries, and presumably there were copies in the ninth and tenth centuries. I have, however, found no evidence of extant manuscripts in any European collections.

it has a distinctly modern flavor, even though it came out of a declining classicism and was nurtured by a "dark age" of ascetic piety. It is also significant that, when the monastic compilers of these late treatises cited authorities, they were Christian rather than Classical. At the same time there is evident a broader, more detailed and increasingly secular expression of the early medieval ethics and etiquette. The last two treatises (from the twelfth century) exemplify the final transition from monastic to Salernitan domination.

The first of the four treatises is so brief and condensed that it might have constituted a code for medieval physicians. It is a noteworthy synthesis of Christian and Hippocratic ideals, despite the fact that the sole authority invoked is the God of Christianity. The treatise seems to have been popular; it appears in at least eleven manuscripts, dating from as early as the ninth, and as late as the fifteenth, century.[35]

N. [Epistle of Hippocrates. Epistle of Galen].[36]

Meanwhile I warn you, Physician, even as I was warned by my master. You ought always to read, and to shun indolence. Visit with care those whom you accept for treatment, and safeguard them. (Hold fast to the cures that you know. Never become involved knowingly with any who are about to die or who are incurable. Do not take up with the daughter or wife of your patient).[37] Cherish modesty, follow chastity, guard the secrets of the homes [you visit]. If you know anything derogatory concerning a patient, keep quiet about it. Do not detract from other [physicians]; if you praise the character and cures of others you yourself will have a better reputation. (At the outset, accept at least half of the

---

[35] Paris BN 11219, Brussels 3701-15, Glasgow Hunter V, 3. 2, Zurich C 128/32, Rome Angelica 1502, Rome Vat. Regina 1443, Rome Vat. 2376, and 2417 (according to Diels, *op. cit.*, I, 123), Carpentras 318, Paris BN 15456, and Paris BN 6988A. In the textual analysis of certain manuscripts of this treatise, and also in the translation, I am indebted to my colleague Professor B. L. Ullman for generous assistance.

[36] Although four of the eleven manuscripts have no author caption, the treatise is attributed to Hippocrates in three (Brussels 3701-15, Rome Vat. Regina 1443, and Paris BN 6988A) and to Galen in three (Paris BN 15456, Rome Vat. 2376 and 2417). The attribution to Isidore of Seville by Hirschfeld (p. 361), Sigerist (p. 32) and Thorndike-Kibre (*Catalogue of Incipits*, under "Interea") is doubtless due to the fact that in Rome Angelica MS 1502 the treatise is preceeded by "*Incipit Liber Ysidori.*" This caption is incorrect both for this treatise and for those that follow it (see Wlaschky's edition in *Kyklos*, 1928, 1, 103 ff.). In BN MS 15456 the treatise begins as follows: "I urge you, O Physician, and with exhortation I warn, and with warning I enjoin you even as I was warned. . . ."

[37] Neither of the passages in parentheses occurs in the pre-eleventh-century manuscripts, excepting the second passage (concerning fees), which is in the tenth-century, South-Italian, version from the Glasgow MS. Was this brutally practical factor in medieval medical ethics Salerno's first contribution to the de-spiritualization of "the Art"?

remuneration without hesitation, for he who wishes to buy [your services] is disposed to pay and to beg [for treatment]. Get it while he is suffering, for when the pain ceases, your services also cease).[37] You will win more thanks if you do all these things, and no physician will be greater than you [in reputation]. Read felicitously, be progressive, fare well, and God's grace be with you, in the practice of medicine and [your other] undertakings. Let healing come from God, who alone is the physician. Amen.[38]

Of a more practical trend is the second treatise, which is concerned solely with the bedside manner. It occurs in at least five manuscripts, dating from as early as the tenth, and as late as the fifteenth, century.[39] It is our only treatise on medical ethics and etiquette that appears earliest in a South-Italian manuscript from the Salernitan region.

O. IN WHAT MANNER YOU SHOULD VISIT A PATIENT.

You do not visit every patient in the same manner. If you wish to learn all, heed [the following]. As soon as you approach the patient ask him if he has any pain. If he says he has, then ask if the pain is severe and constant. After this take his pulse and see if he has fever. If he is in pain you will find the pulse rapid and fluid. Ask if the pain comes when he is cold; also if he is wakeful, and if his bowels and urine are normal. Inspect both parts and see if there is perchance any serious danger. If the ailment is acute inquire as to the beginning of the illness. If it is chronic you will not recognize it at all, for the beginning of such illness is at a time when the patient begins to feel a lesion when performing accustomed functions, as if he could not perform them. After this ask what former physicians said when they visited him, whether all of them said the same. Inquire concerning the condition of the body, whether it is cold or otherwise, whether the bowels are loose, sleep interrupted, the ailment constant, and if he has ever had such ailments before. Having made these inquiries you will easily recognize the causes of the illness and the cure will not be difficult.[40]

Our third treatise comprises a twelfth-century text from a famous Salernitan manuscript (Breslau 1302),[41] and its fourteenth-century amplification attributed to a certain Archimathaeus (ca. 1100 ?). In De Renzi's edition (*op. cit.*, II, 35) the treatise was lauded for its uniqueness among medieval treatises on the relations of physician and patient.

---

[38] Carpentras MS 318 has a more pious ending: "Amen, and He lives and reigns and rules through eternity."

[39] Monte Cassino 97, Montpellier 185, Rome Vat. Barberini 160, Carpentras 318, and Paris BN 6988A. The text is found in De Renzi, II, 73; Neuburger, *op. cit.*, II, pt. I, 257; and Sigerist, p. 31 f.

[40] The Carpentras manuscript has a slightly different ending.

[41] Concerning this manuscript, see De Renzi, II, 74 ff.; Sudhoff, "Die Salernitaner Handschrift in Breslau" (*Archiv Gesch. Med.*, 1920, 12, 101 ff.); and Henschel, "Die Salernitanische Handschrift" (*Janus*, 1846, 1, 40 ff.).

MEDICAL ETHICS AND ETIQUETTE IN THE EARLY MIDDLE AGES

Factual evidences, such as the pre-Salernitan treatises already quoted, indicate that it was merely a link, though an important one, in the development of medieval medical ethics and etiquette. It is clear that this treatise in particular, and Salerno in general, mark neither the beginning nor the revival of highmindedness and intelligence in medical practice. They do illustrate the late-medieval shift of emphasis from ideals to practical considerations.

The Salernitan treatise repeats some of the early medieval idealism that stemmed from both Christian and Classical sources; notably the invoking of God's aid and the Hippocratic warning against immorality. But the treatise is more concerned with a hitherto unimportant factor, the materialistic side of medical practice. Even though it treats of the age old topics, it treats them in a spirit of unrestrained ambition and selfcentered individualism. For the most part, professional cleverness overshadows Hippocratic and Christian idealism. This new secular emphasis, often designated nowadays as modern-mindedness, did not originate at Salerno. It evolved out of earlier practices, during the late-medieval era of rapid urbanization. It was widely prevalent in Italy and elsewhere, meeting with the approval of leaders in the profession: Arnold of Villanova, Henry of Mondeville, Guy of Chauliac, Albert of Bologna, Jan Yperman, and John Arderne.[42] This trend might be said to mark the despiritualization of the medieval physician.

Inasmuch as the Salernitan treatise has appeared in English translations that are readily available,[43] we present the subject matter thereof in condensed form with a few quoted excerpts that are of unusual significance.[44]

P. CONCERNING THE PHYSICIAN'S APPROACH TO THE PATIENT.
Therefore, O physician, when you call on a patient, be a helper in God's name. Let the angel who accompanied Tobias [Tobias 3:25. Vulgate] be your spiritual and physical companion. On entering the home try to find out through the messenger [from the household] how sick the patient is and what sort of an ailment he has. This is necessary so that you will not seem to be entirely ignorant of the ailment when you approach him. . . . [Detailed instructions follow: e. g., ask whether

---

[42] Excerpts from the works of these men (quoted in Miss Welborn's article cited above in note 1) show a marked resemblance to the Salernitan treatise (P, below), which in turn resembles treatises L, M, N, and O (above).

[43] Francis Packard, in *The School of Salernum* (New York, 1920) p. 18 ff.; and George Corner, in "The Rise of Medicine at Salerno," (*Annals Medical Hist.*, 1931, 3, 14 f.).

[44] The text is in De Renzi, II, 74 ff.

the patient has confessed to a priest; pretend that the case is serious; thus, whether he survives or dies, your reputation is safe; in the sick room greet those present and pay compliments concerning the household before turning to the patient]. Make him feel secure and quiet his spirit before you take the pulse. Take care lest he lie on his side or have his fingers over-extended or drawn back into his palm. Support his arm with your left [hand] and consider the pulse beat at least to a hundred. Also take note of the different kinds of pulses. . . . [Inspect the urine for color, subtance, and quantity; on leaving tell the patient that he will get well but tell the servants that he is very sick; do not look with lecherous eyes on women of the household; if invited to dine, do not be officious or overly fastidious; during the meal, enquire about the patient; on leaving, show your appreciation; etc., followed by advice concerning diet, cupping, digestion, etc.; on later visits during the patient's convalescence, the physician is advised to be cheerful and to promise the patient a speedy recovery. Finally] with as much as possible of honest promises go in peace, Christ your guide.

The expanded version of the Salernitan treatise appears in a fourteenth-century manuscript (Paris BN MS Lat. 7091). The final paragraph serves as an excellent expression of the increasingly secular and materialistic spirit of late Medieval medical practice. This tendency, which is seldom emphasized by those optimistic modern commentators who sing the praises of Salernitan medicine, was marked by a strong emphasis on the importance of good public relations. The following quotation (with which the treatise ends) seems very modern, and somewhat reprehensible, by reason of the clever psychological approach, with its hint that the physician should assume a hypocritically cheerful attitude in the interests not only of the patient's health, but also of his own purse.[45]

[It is advised that the convalescing patient be encouraged by having congenial friends visit him; boy-friends for young convalescents, old man for senile patients, and for noblemen, friends who will chat concerning dogs, horses, and falcons. The physician himself, when he calls, should enter the room] with a hilarious countenance and a joyful voice saying: " Hey there, what do you say? What sort of fun are you having? " . . . With such words the patient is encouraged. Finally, accept your remuneration graciously, and with a full purse and with joy and delight for one and all (if that be possible), by their leave go in peace.
Explicit. Book of Instruction for the Physician, according to Alquimathaeus [i. e., Archimathaeus].

In all fairness to the Salernitans, it should be noted that they also had treatises expressing the higher ideals of the profession. This is exemplified in our last treatise, taken from a work attributed to Constantine the African who lived and wrote at about 1100. In late Medieval

---

[45] The text is in De Renzi, V, 348 f.; see also I, 513 and V, 102 for verses from the *Flos Medicinae Scholae Salerni* concerning fees, dress, etc.

manuscripts (of the thirteenth and fourteenth centuries) and in early printed editions (the 1515 Lyons edition of Isaac contains the earliest version), the treatise appears as the prologue to Book I of Constantine's *Liber Pantegni*; Theorica, De Communibus Medico Cognitu Necessariis Locis. I know of no manuscript prior to the thirteenth century, but it is possible that the treatise was compiled by Constantine at about 1100 from Arabic material or from works such as we have noted in the early medieval compilations. At any rate it resembles treatises G and N, quoted above, and appears to be a synthesis of materials long in circulation and originally derived in large measure from Hippocratic sources such as the Oath.

Q. WHAT SORT OF PERSON A STUDENT OF MEDICINE SHOULD BE.[46]

He who wishes to obtain the mantle of medicine ought [so to act] that he is an honor to his master, is praised [by him] and is subject to him just as to his own parents. . . . The master should be honored so that [his disciples] may learn how to handle difficult situations. Whomsoever the master takes for instruction should see to it that he is a worthy disciple. He should teach [only] worthy disciples, without pay or expectation of future emolument; and he should be sure to keep unworthy persons from entering this learned profession. The physician should work for the healing of the sick. He should not heal for the sake of gain, nor give more consideration to the wealthy than to the poor, or to the noble than the ignoble. He should neither teach, nor aquiesce in teaching anyone how to give a harmful potion, lest some ignorant person should hear of it and on his authority mix a death potion. He should not teach anyone to bring about abortion. Moreover, when he visits patients, he should not set his heart on the patient's wife, maidservant, or daughter; they blind the heart of man. He ought to keep to himself confidential information concerning the ailment, for at times the patient makes known to the physician things that he would blush to tell his parents. The physician should flee luxury and avoid worldly pleasures and drunkenness. These things upset the spirit and encourage the vices of the flesh. He should devote himself with assiduous zeal to the healing of the body and should not neglect reading, so that his memory may aid him when books are not at hand. He should never refuse to visit the sick for thus, by experience, he may become more efficient. He should be pious, humble, gentle, likeable, and should seek divine assistance. [In chapter 2 the author discusses " Six Things which it is Well to Know," among them dialectic and " the entire quadrivium." Incidentally it is suggested that the author's book " is useful above all others."].

---

[46] The text in Migne *Patrologia Latina*, vol. 150, 1563, is similar to the sixteenth-century versions.

CONCLUSIONS

In summarizing the possible sources of the above examples of medical ethics and etiquette, we note that many of them bear a marked resemblance to the dicta in certain Hippocratic writings.[47] Neither in Greek nor in medieval times, however, did these dicta constitute an enforced code of conduct; they were merely a set of ideals which the high minded physician was urged to follow. Jones' remarks in the introduction to his translation of the Hippocratic *Law,* to the effect that Greek physicians were subject to neither legal penalties nor a universal guild organization, could be applied equally to medical practice in the Early Middle Ages. The only hint of legal controls is found in the above mentioned Visigothic Spanish laws concerning women patients (treatise B) and in the form letter for the instruction of the governmentally supervised physicians in Ostrogothic Italy (treatise C).

Our second conclusion is that both Greek and Medieval physicians were subjected to two somewhat divergent influences, one of which was idealistic, the other practical; in other words, ethics and etiquette. So far as ethics are concerned, the early Medieval writers seem to have combined Hippocratic and Christian ideals without any apparent feeling of conflict or inconsistency. They repeated much of the ideology of the Hippocratic Oath, notably the moral injunctions against giving poisons or abortives, and against violating the patient's confidence or the virtue of his womenfolk.[48] The Medieval exhortation that the physician keep himself " immaculate and sacred " (treatise K[a]), may be a reflection of the " pure and holy " clause of the Hippocratic Oath. Furthermore, the array of virtues recommended for members of the medieval medical profession (especially in treatises F, G. H and K) reads much like the standard set for Greek physicians in the Hippocratic works concerning the *Physician* (Chapter I) and *Decorum* (Chapter V; also III, VII and

---

[47] See W. H. S. Jones, "Greek Medical Etiquette (*Royal Soc. Med., Proc.,* 1922-23, 16, Hist. pp. 11-17); *The Doctor's Oath* (Cambridge University, 1924); and the introductory essays in his *Hippocrates,* II, pp. xxxiii ff. and 257 ff., also I, 295 where he describes travesties of medical ethics such as the practice of abortion (described in *Nature of the Child*), which was a startling contrast to the anti-abortion pledge of the Oath. See also Edelstein *The Hippocratic Oath,* p. 63.

[48] These ideals, plus those from the *Decorum* and *Precepts* concerning fee collecting, were widely prevalent in Ancient and Medieval times. Exigencies of space prevent our citation of the extensive modern literature on Hippocratic ideals among Medieval Jewish physicians, the Arabs, and in China, etc.

XII).⁴⁹ In like fashion the Medieval analogy concerning seed planting and medical education (treatise J) is similar to chapter III of the Hippocratic *Law*. The importance of starting medical education early in life is found in both Ancient and Medieval works (treatises H and K, and note 24). One factor not found in Hippocratic writings is the Medieval emphasis on a broad background of liberal-arts education (treatises I, K, L, and Q).

Turning to the realm of everyday medical etiquette, one finds even more noteworthy parallels between the Hippocratic and the Medieval writings; for example, (1) admonitions for the physician to avoid the use of wine to excess (compare treatises F, L, and Q with Hippocratic *Decorum*, chap. XV), (2) to avoid excessive use of ointments (compare treatise K[a] with *Precepts*, chap. X and *Physician*, chap. I) and (3) to avoid ostentation in dress and manners (compare treatises G, L and K[a] with *Precepts*, chap. X and *Decorum*, chap. II-III, VII); also (4) the bedside manner, especially the exercise of patience with difficult patients (compare treatise K[a] with *Decorum*, chap. XII), (5) the withholding of information from the patient (compare treatises C and P with *Decorum*, chap. XVI), and (6) restraint in pressing for payment of fees (compare treatises N and P with *Decorum*, chap. II and *Precepts*, chap. IV).⁵⁰ Finally, (7) in both literatures there is evidence of the contrast between the high ideals of physicians for their own profession (compare treatises A, C ff. with *Decorum*, chaps. V-VI, XVIII) and its low moral repute among the general public (compare treatises B, J and K[a] with *Art*, chaps. I, IV-V; *Law*, chap. I; and *Decorum*, chaps. II, VII). It seems that the inefficiency and waywardness of medical practitioners has been condemned by lay critics in all ages.⁵¹

Perhaps the chief surprise that comes to the student of early Medieval medical manuscripts is the rarity of instances of that pious other-worldly spirit which is supposed to have hung like a cloud over the Middle Ages. To be sure this spirit is the dominant element in two of our seventeen treatises (D and E), and in two others (A and N) it is combined with an approximately equal amount of classical or contemporary pragmatism.

---

⁴⁹ The Hippocratic works cited here and in the succeeding sentences are found in Jones, *Hippocrates*, vol. II, except for *Precepts*, which is in vol. I.

⁵⁰ With regard to fees, medieval writers, especially in the later centuries, recommended more drastic measures than those found in Greek writings. See the articles by Welborn and Sigerist, cited above in note 1; also Diepgen's chapter (IV) on the subject.

⁵¹ This can be seen in the works of Pliny the Elder, Seneca, Sidonius, John of Salisbury, Petrarch, and Molière.

In most of the treatises, however (to be specific, in thirteen out of seventeen), it is almost completely eclipsed by the viewpoints of secular medicine.

Our explanation of this paradox is the obvious fact that "everybody who talks about Heaven" is not intent on it at all times. Medieval *religious* literature to the contrary notwithstanding, during the Middle Ages most people lived in *this* world. The public utterances of the monastic writers who monopolized early Medieval literature were likely to be piously religious when concerned with ideals; though in writing of *medical* ideals they often used Hippocratic substitutes. Practical activities, medical or otherwise, were discussed in a more earthly manner. Thus it is that, whereas the treatises on medical *ethics* often manifest a highly Christian ideology, those on *etiquette* are more secular. When one passes from the era of our survey to the later Medieval centuries, he finds still less of otherworldliness and more of those characteristics which seem to be widely prevalent among medical men of all civilized ages.

It might be enlightening for modern folk to think of the early Middle Ages in somewhat the same perspective in which we think of our primitive and rather pious pioneer ancestors of frontier days. The otherworldly utterances of their preachers reflect only one aspect of their civilization. Their medical practices, like other aspects of their everyday lives, were highly practical and secular. So it was in the early Middle Ages. The progressive, secular trend that is exemplified in the Salernitan treatises evolved out of the monastic-Hippocratic environment of the preceding centuries,[52] long before Salerno's rise to prominence in the twelfth century. This trend is to be attributed, not to an Italian Renaissance of Hippocratic classicism, but to the Christian "Hippokratismus" which persisted through the disintegration of the Western Empire and the early Middle Ages, then expanded as the gradual secularization of Medieval life, under the influence of industry, commerce, and other phases of urban civilization, turned men's minds more and more to this-worldly affairs.

---

[52] A noteworthy point in the transmission of Hippocratic ethics and etiquette to the monastic West is the lack of Galenic influence. Galen's commentaries on various Hippocratic works existed in early Medieval Latin versions, but (as has been indicated above in several footnotes) the Medieval texts on ethics and etiquette seldom show as close relationships to Galenic works as they do to late Hippocratic treatises such as the *Oath, Decorum,* etc.

APPENDIX

THE HIPPOCRATIC OATH (Fourth-Century B. C.).[53]

I swear by Apollo Physician and Asclepius and Hygieia and Panaceia and all the gods and godesses, making them my witnesses, that I will fulfil according to my ability and judgment this oath and this covenant:

To hold him who has taught me this art as equal to my parents and to live my life in partnership with him, and if he is in need of money to give him a share of mine, and to regard his offspring as equal to my brothers in male lineage and to teach them this art—if they desire to learn it—without fee and covenant; to give a share of precepts and oral instruction and all other learning to my sons and to the sons of him who has instructed me and to pupils who have signed the covenant and have taken an oath according to the medical law, but to no one else.

I will apply dietetic measures for the benefit of the sick according to my ability and judgment; I will keep them from harm and injustice.

I will neither give a deadly drug to anybody if asked for it, nor will I make a suggestion to this effect. Similarly I will not give to a woman an abortive remedy. In purity and holiness I will guard my life and my art.

I will not use the knife, not even on sufferers from stone, but will withdraw in favor of such men as are engaged in this work.

Whatever houses I may visit, I will come for the benefit of the sick, remaining free of all intentional injustice, of all mischief and in particular of sexual relations with both female and male persons, be they free or slaves.

What I may see or hear in the course of the treatment or even outside of the treatment in regard to the life of men, which on no account one must spread abroad, I will keep to myself holding such things shameful to be spoken about.

If I fulfil this oath and do not violate it, may it be granted to me to enjoy life and art, being honored with fame among all men for all time to come; if I transgress it and swear falsely, may the opposite of all this be my lot.

---

[53] The following translation is reprinted from Ludwig Edelstein, *The Hippocratic Oath*, Baltimore, 1943, p. 3.

Part II
Bioethics and Law

BIOETHICS AND LAW: A DEVELOPMENTAL PERSPECTIVE[1]

WIBREN VAN DER BURG

ABSTRACT

In most Western countries, health law bioethics are strongly intertwined. This strong connection is the result of some specific factors that, in the early years of these disciplines, facilitated a rapid development of both. In this paper, I analyse these factors and construe a development theory existing of three phases, or ideal-typical models.

In the moralistic-paternalistic model, there is almost no health law of explicit medical ethics and the little law there is is usually based on traditional morality, combined with paternalist motives, the objections to this modal are that its paternalism and moralism are unacceptable, that it is too static and knows no external control mechanisms.

In the liberal model, which is now dominant on most Western countries, law and ethics closely cooperate and converge, both disciplines use the same framework for analysis: they are product-oriented rather than practice-oriented; they use the same conceptual categories, they focus on the minimally decent rather than the ideal, and they are committed to the same substantive normative theory in which patient autonomy and patient rights are central. However, each of these four characteristics also result in a certain one-sidedness.

In some countries, a third model is emerging. In this postliberal model, health law is more modest and acknowledges its inherent and normative limits, whereas ethics takes a richer and most ambitious self image. As a result health law and ethics will partly diverge again.

---

[1] This article is partly the result of a common research project on Ethics and Law at the Center for Bioethics and Health Law, Utrecht University, the Netherlands, and has profited from many discussions with my colleagues participating in that research group. I had the opportunity to present the basic ideas of this paper on various occasions: at a conference organized by the Center for Bioethics and Health Law and at seminars at the University of Copenhagen, Denmark and at the Ersta Institute for Health Care Ethics, Stockholm, Sweden. I am grateful to many colleagues who presented helpful suggestions on these occasions, as well as to the two readers of *Bioethics*.

92 WIBREN VAN DER BURG

1 INTRODUCTION

In most Western countries, health and law and bioethics are strongly intertwined.[2] This situation can be found in various spheres. In the public debate, legal and moral issues are connected in many ways. Legal and ethical discussions influence each other so strongly that they can sometimes hardly be distinguished. Ethicists discuss and criticise the law on abortion or on euthanasia. Government-installed committees chaired by moral philosophers present recommendations on legislation on embryo research that are largely based on ethical analysis. Conversely, lawyers openly discuss ethical questions and intervene in the public moral debate. Legal categories (like doctrines of self-determination and patient rights) sometimes strongly determine and even structure the public debate concerning organ transplants and medical experiments.[3]

In law and legal practice, there are many references to ethics and to moral norms. The Council of Europe has even drafted a 'Bioethics Convention' (which has recently been renamed as 'Convention on Human Rights and Biomedicine'). In statutory provisions we find references to open norms, like 'the care of a good caregiver', which can only be substantiated by an appeal to morality.[4] In judicial decisions, we may find explicit reference to standards of medical ethics, for instance, in cases concerning euthanasia.[5] Acting according to the standards of medical ethics is regarded in the Netherlands as one of the criteria for a justified appeal to *force majeure* in cases of euthanasia.[6] Consequently, ethicists act as expert witnesses in courts

---

[2] My analysis in this article is primarily based on the Dutch and American situations, because I know them best and because they seem to be the two countries in which the liberal model (as sketched below) has gained most support and in which the postliberal tendencies are most clearly to be seen. Yet, the intertwinement of bioethics and health law is a broader phenomenon, which can be found in most of the Anglophone countries and many European countries as well. For the US, see Schneider, C.E. 1994, 'Bioethics in the Language of the Law', *Hastings Center Report*, July–August 1994, 24, no. 4 p. 16–22.

[3] Trappenburg, M., *Soorten van gelijk. Medisch-ethische discussies in Nederland* (diss. Leiden), Zwolle: W.E.J. Tjeenk Willink, 1993 argued that, in the Netherlands, these two topics are a 'legally structured territory', which means that it has been impossible to introduce other problem definitions and normative notions in the public debate than those dictated by legal doctrine. Cf. also Schneider op. cit.

[4] Cf. Burg, W. van der, P. Ippel, et al., 'The care of a good caregiver. Legal and ethical reflections on the good health care professional', *Cambridge Quarterly of Health Care Ethics*, Vol. 3, nr. 1 Winter 1994, p. 38–48.

[5] Cf. the two court decisions mentioned in Davis, D. 1995, 'Legal trends in Bioethics', *Journal of Clinical Ethics*, 6 1995 p. 187–192, one in the US and one in the Netherlands.

[6] For the Dutch situation on euthanasia, see Battin, M. *The Least Worst Death: Essays in Bioethics on the End of Life*, New York: Oxford University Press, 1994. 130ff.

© Blackwell Publishers Ltd. 1997

on criminal cases concerning euthanasia.[7] A very interesting phenomenon is the institutionalised character of ethics committees and ethical review boards. In many countries such committees and boards are acquiring a legal basis and their positive advice is (or is expected to be in the near future) a precondition for official permission for medical experiments and animal experiments. Thus, paradoxically, they have to make judgements on ethical rather than legal grounds, yet these judgements have legal status. This semi-judicial role for ethics committees seems to blur the distinction between morality and law quite radically.

Finally, the academic disciplines closely co-operate. Doctrines of euthanasia and abortion, of informed consent and the right to privacy, of restrictions on experiments with embryos have all been developed in close co-operation between ethicists and lawyers. In ethics textbooks, legal cases are used as examples.[8] Legal textbooks refer to writings by moral philosophers to support legal doctrines, or even have ethics in their book titles.[9]

This strong connection between law and ethics is rather unique. There is probably no other field of law — with the exception perhaps of animal law and animal ethics, which may be regarded as a subfield of bioethics in a broad sense — where the connection is so strong and explicit. It is remarkable that this phenomenon can be found in many Western countries, though not in all (France and Sweden seem to be important exceptions here[10]) and not everywhere with the same intensity.[11]

and Griffiths, J. 1995 'Recent Developments in the Netherlands Concerning Euthanasia and other Medical Behavior that Shortens Life', *Medical Law International*, 1 1995 p. 347–386.

[7] In some court cases on euthanasia and other issues, Dutch ethicists have acted as expert witnesses; in many other cases, lawyers and judges have explicitly quoted ethical opinions. For instance, in the Dutch case referred to in note 5 above (the case at the Court in Alkmaar concerning a severely handicapped neonate), a professor in medical ethics, Inez de Beaufort, submitted an elaborate expert opinion on the ethical issues involved. It should be added that, in the Netherlands, expert witnesses are considered to be fully impartial, their expenses being paid by the courts, rather than to be witnesses on behalf of and paid by one of the parties. For a critical reflection on the latter role in the US legal system, see Caplan, A.L. 1991, 'Bioethics on Trial', *Hastings Center Report* 1991 p. 19–20.

[8] For example, most of the case material in Beauchamp, T.L. and J.F. Childress, *Principles of Biomedical Ethics* New York: Oxford University Press, 1994: 509f. is based on court cases.

[9] Cf. Mason, J.K. and R.A. McCall Smith, *Law and Medical Ethics*, London: Butterworths, 1994.

[10] In France, the idea that bioethics should be the subject of a specialised (philosophical or theological) discipline has met strong resistance. In Sweden, both health law and bioethics are still in a premature stage and, partly as a result of its legal positivist tradition, the relation between the two is rather weak.

© Blackwell Publishers Ltd. 1997

How should we explain this? A superficial explanation may be that the field of biomedicine is extremely morally sensitive. Though there is a core of truth in this in the sense that, more than in other fields, we perceive normative problems explicitly as moral problems, it is not the only explanation. Environmental issues also have a strong moral dimension — they concern literally matters of life and death, especially for future generations; yet, environmental law usually has a much more instrumental character and is not, or only slightly, connected to the discipline of environmental ethics. The structure of the welfare and social security system and the basic tax structure are of great moral importance, yet ethicists seldom discuss them — and if they do, their work is considered to be of no legal relevance at all.[12] So there must be some other explanation.

A historical perspective may be illuminating here. The strong connection between health law and bioethics is only of a relatively recent date; it seems to be the result of a set of very specific factors that, in the early years of these disciplines, facilitated a rapid development of both.

In this paper I will analyse these factors and, on the basis of that analysis, construct a developmental theory existing of three phases or ideal-typical models of relationships between bioethics and law. First, I will sketch the older phase, which we may call the moralistic-paternalistic model. In this phase, there is almost no health law or explicit medical ethics, and the little law there is is usually based on traditional morality, combined with paternalist motives. The second phase, which is now dominant in most Western countries, may be called the liberal model. In this model, law and ethics closely co-operate and converge. In some countries, we can see a third model emerging, a post-liberal one, in which law and ethics partly diverge again.

2 THE MORALISTIC-PATERNALISTIC MODEL[13]

Until the sixties, bioethics or health law did not yet exist as independent disciplines in most Western countries. This does not

---

[11] Moreover, the connection exists only in a specific part of health law; the part that is concerned with the bureaucratic organisation of the health care system usually has little connection to ethics.

[12] For other examples of how fields of law are connected to morality, see Lee, S. *Law and Morals*, Oxford University Press, 1986, 18–21.

[13] The models developed here are ideal-types. Though the essentials can be recognised in reality as characteristic ways of ordering the normative dimensions of health care practice, reality is more nuanced, and usually combines elements of various models.

mean, of course, that the medical profession was amoral, but normativity was implicit in medical practice rather than being extensively elaborated by lawyers and ethicists.[14] Medical ethics was the ethics of good medical practice, of being a good doctor. For this there was no elaborate body of guidelines and rules, neither in moral philosophy, nor in law. Theoretical or philosophical reflection on medical issues usually did not address the public at large.

Professional practice was strongly paternalistic. Doctors were expected to act for the good of the patient and to know what this good was, both in the moral and in the non-moral sense of the word. Patients were often not given full information about the diagnoses of their illnesses, especially if the prognosis was dim. Insofar as the determination of the patient's good demanded moral evaluation, this was seldom explicitly acknowledged, nor need it be, because the moral norms were considered non-controversial, being based on a traditional (usually religious) morality that was largely accepted by all in society, or by all in the subgroup to which both doctor and patient belonged.[15] In a sense, we might even say that moralism and paternalism were not clearly distinguished, simply because the moral evaluations, involved in judgements about the patient's good, were so uncontroversial that they largely remained implicit.[16]

Specific rules of health law were virtually non-existent, though in many countries some form of disciplinary law existed. The law largely upheld and respected professional autonomy, and only marginally interfered with medical practice. It upheld a great deal of discretionary power for doctors. Especially in the field of psychiatry, both the law and the medical profession were strongly paternalistic; the patient's best interest, as judged by the psychiatrist, was the basic criterion for non-voluntary treatments and institutionalisation. Of course, there were some rules in criminal law, prohibiting abortion, euthanasia, (assisted) suicide and various sexual practices like adultery,[17] prostitution and homosexuality. The justification for these

[14] This sketch is partly based on Kuitert, H.M. *Mag alles wat kan? Ethiek en medisch handelen*, Baarn: ten Have, 1989.

[15] The latter addition is essential because in strongly segmented societies like the US or the Netherlands, on some issues no broad, social consensus existed, but only a group consensus within the group of Roman Catholics or within the group of orthodox Protestants.

[16] Kuitert, op. cit.: 66 expressed this by saying that, from the profession's point of view, the technically necessary and the morally obligatory are 'interfolded' as it were and often cannot be distinguished.

[17] When artificial insemination by donors was introduced, many countries discussed whether this should be regarded as a form of adultery and, hence, as a criminal offence. Cf. Mason and McCall Smith op. cit.: 53.

prohibitions was often directly moralistic: they were considered immoral by traditional morality.

This brief and much too simplified sketch suffices to illustrate the relationships between law and morality in this model. Insofar as law dealt with moral issues involved in medical practice rather than leaving them to the medical profession, it was directly moralistic and paternalistic. Insofar as it gave discretionary powers to the autonomous profession, it sanctioned paternalism and moralism of that practice, and thus was indirectly moralistic and paternalistic.

The model has clear advantages. It works efficiently because external legal and bureaucratic interference is marginal and doctors can simply make their own decisions, without having to discuss them extensively with patients or staff. As long as their decisions and actions are embedded in a morally decent traditional practice and are accepted by all as authoritative, good medical treatment is guaranteed.

However, it may be clear that many of the implicit presuppositions of this model are no longer acceptable or valid in modern societies.[18] Firstly, the idea of medical and legal paternalism has come under attack. The general emancipation process in which citizens claim their own rights and freedom, has not left medicine untouched. The simple confidence in psychiatrists, knowing what is good for their patients, has been shattered. Withholding information about the true nature of a disease is no longer deemed acceptable. Both as a result of the general trend towards emancipation which started in the sixties and as a result of specific factors in the field of biomedicine, patients claim their rights and want to control their own lives. Secondly, and partly connected to the criticisms of paternalism, the moralism of doctors and of the law has come under attack. Traditional morality has changed rapidly, resulting in a more pluralist character of modern societies. The sexual revolution, leading to more liberal attitudes towards various sexual practices, is just one example of this. Free citizens want to control their own medical and psychiatric treatment because it is up to them to decide which treatment is for their good, not only in a non-moral sense, but also in a moral sense. They claim the freedom to decide whether they want to have a child or not and whether abortion is morally justified. Finally, they want to decide themselves whether further suffering is an acceptable part of their dying process of whether they want to avoid further suffering through euthanasia or assisted suicide.

These criticisms on paternalism and moralism set the background for most of the current literature on law and morality, like the Hart-

---

[18] Cf. Kuitert, op. cit.: 64–71.

BIOETHICS AND LAW: A DEVELOPMENTAL PERSPECTIVE 97

Devlin debate, culminating in Feinberg's four-volume series on the moral limits of the criminal law.[19] There are, however, other elements of the moralist-paternalist model that, though they have attracted less direct attention from moral philosophers, are equally important reasons for abandoning the model. A third objection to the model is that it is too static and does not provide solutions to the problems that arise as a result of changes in society, technology and health care practice. Societal structures and processes are changing so rapidly that an appeal to the moral tradition and trust in a gradual adaptation of implicit morality to changing circumstances simply is no longer adequate. Professional morality would soon loose contact with social reality if it were not an explicit object of open, critical discussion, reflection and adaptation. (This phenomenon of losing touch with social reality can most clearly be seen in the deep cleft between the static official Roman Catholic moral doctrine on sexuality and the practice of most believers who simply ignore the official doctrine.) Technology poses many new problems to which traditional morality does not offer answers — issues like embryo research, organ transplants and the treatment of severely handicapped newborns that in the past simply would not have survived. Health care practice has changed from a practice in which the individual physician had a personal relationship with a patient to a situation in which teamwork and interdisciplinary co-operation are normal. Each of these three essential changes makes it necessary to make moral norms and values explicit so that they can be discussed, critically analysed and adapted to new circumstances or new opinions. They also make the need for law more clearly felt, to guide those developmental processes and to prevent excesses as a result of normative uncertainty. When traditional morality no longer provides adequate guidance, and a new morality is still developing, we can no longer put our trust completely in the medical judgement because the risk of erring is too great.

These latter remarks already point to a fourth criticism of the model. It knows no checks and balances, no external control mechanisms. Even if almost all medical professionals act in a decent or even highly laudable way, there will always be the need to correct the small minority of practitioners who do not. In a small-scale profession with strong mechanisms of social control, it may be largely

---

[19] Cf. Dworkin, R. (ed.) *The Philosophy of Law*, Oxford University Press, 1977. Feinberg, J., *The Moral Limits of the Criminal Law* New York: Oxford University Press, Vol. I *Harm to Others*, 1984, Vol. II *Offence to Others*, 1985, Vol. III *Harm to Self*, 1986, Vol. IV *Harmless Wrongdoing*, 1990, and Dworkin, G. (ed.) *Morality, Harm, and the Law*, Boulder: Westview Press, 1994.

98 WIBREN VAN DER BURG

adequate to trust informal and internal methods of correction and control, e.g. through disciplinary proceedings. But in a more anonymous large-scale medical practice this simply does not suffice. Moreover, it does not give the patients adequate protection against and compensation for medical malpractice. The Nazi experiments are often mentioned as the primary reason why the need for control became felt. But other situations also gave rise to the demand for legal control of medical practice, especially in the field of psychiatry. Everyone with power runs the risk of abusing it; the more power the medical profession is given by modern technology, the greater the need for control and checks and balances. In combination with the growing emancipation of patients, this has led to increasing direct legal intervention in medical practice.

These four critical objections to the moralistic-paternalistic model are the major factors that have led to its abandonment in favour of a new model, the liberal model. It is important to understand that the reasons for abandoning it are not only new normative opinions on paternalism and moralism, but that the changes are also responses to developments in Western society and in medical practice itself. The old model is simply no longer functional in various respects. This means that a reactionary return to this model — even if someone were to suggest this and defend it from a normative point of view — is likely to be counterproductive, simply because the social context in which it once worked no longer exists.

3 THE LIBERAL MODEL

Each of the four objections to the paternalistic-moralistic model suggests, by contrast, characteristics of an alternative model. Both the anti-paternalism and the anti-moralism criticisms suggest a model that explicitly recognises and protects patient autonomy and patient rights, and that is based on a more equal relationship between physicians and patients. Because autonomy and rights are so dominant in this new model (partly as a reaction against the old paternalism and moralism), I will call it the liberal model.[20]

The third objection I mentioned is that the old model is too static, because it is based on an implicit professional morality that can only

---

[20] Beauchamp and Childress op. cit,.: 78 consider the postulates of individual autonomy, rights against the state and neutrality towards conflicting values to be the central elements of liberalism. My conception of liberalism here is both broader and narrower. Neutrality is not essential, but the concept of rights applies also to other institutions than the state and to other individuals, like health care professionals.

very gradually adapt to new circumstances. This point suggests that the professional morality should be made more explicit and should be an object of ethical reflection, discussion and reformulation in the light of changing circumstances. Changes in society, technology and health care practice result in the need for bioethics as a discipline that supports this continuous process of reflection, discussion and reformulation. Changes in health care practice, moreover, require that medical ethics is broadened to bioethics or health care ethics, and that medical law is broadened to health care law, so that both include all health care professions (like nurses) and the organisation of the health care system as a whole. Changes in society require that bioethical discussions are not confined to health care professionals, but that health care consumers are involved as well, which means society as a whole. All these rapid and radical changes, but especially those in technology, clearly demand more than superficial ethical analyses, which means that we need specialists to make them; in other words, we need bioethics as an independent (philosophical or theological) discipline.

Finally, the fourth objection mentioned above is that the moralistic-paternalistic model does not provide adequate mechanisms of control and correction, let alone the protection of patients and third parties. The most obvious institution for control is the law. This means that new legislation and regulations are needed in a practice that, so far, has not been used to much external regulation. This almost automatically leads to the establishment of a new field of law with its own specialists in health law as a new professional discipline.

In the transformation process from the moralistic-paternalistic model to the liberal one, the new disciplines of bioethics and health law profit from a close co-operation.[21] They have many things in common: no firm theoretical ground to stand on, demanding tasks and, as is usual in a starting period, a very small number of competent ethicists and lawyers. Moreover, both disciplines often — though not always — have to struggle against the resistance of settled interest groups, especially physicians. But most importantly, they have a common mission: to elaborate the liberal programme in a theoretically satisfying way and to implement it in health care practice.

[21] Cf. Leenen, H.J.J. 'Vijfentwintig jaar gezondheidsrecht', in: J.H. Hubben and H.D.C. Roscam Abbing (eds.), *Gezondheidsrecht in Perspectief*, Utrecht: De Tijdstroom, 1993: 21; Clouser, K.D. and Kopelman, L.M. 1990, 'Philosophical Critique of Bioethics: Introduction to the Issue', *Journal of Medicine and Philosophy*, 15 1990, 2: 121–122.

In such a situation, it is only natural that both disciplines collaborate closely and find intellectual inspiration in each other's work. Why not try to construe a theory on informed consent in a common effort by lawyers and ethicists? Why should lawyers not try to build on ethical theories regarding the status of the human embryo when developing suggestions for legislation on abortion or on embryo research? Moreover, it is not only intellectually helpful, but also strategically important to join forces if one of your aims is to change health care practice and opposition is strong.

This sketch may explain why co-operation between both disciplines is stimulated, but this does not mean co-operation is possible. If lawyers are talking about patient rights while ethical analysis focuses on professional virtues and fundamental views of life, co-operation will not be easy. So a further condition for co-operation must be that both disciplines use the same framework for analysis and this is, indeed, characteristic of the liberal model.

Firstly, both health law and bioethics take what I shall call a 'product approach'. When studying law, one may focus on law as a product, which means that one regards law as a system of rules and principles or as a collection of statutes, customary rules and judicial decisions.[22] But one may also focus on the practice of law, on the legal process, on law as an interpretative and argumentative activity.[23] Similarly with ethics: one may focus on moral theory as the construction of principles for the basic structure of society or as the construction of rules and principles for action and, on the basis of this, of concrete moral judgements.[24] But one may also focus on morality as a practice, as an activity in which we are continually interpreting, reconstructing and trying to realise our central moral values.[25] The distinction between law and morality as a product and law and

---

[22] This approach seems dominant among positivists like Hans Kelsen, but is most obvious in the way many legal textbooks tend to present 'the law' on certain subjects: as a coherent doctrine of norms, based on a collection of legal materials like statutes and case-law.

[23] Lon L. Fuller, *The Morality of Law*, New Haven: Yale University Press, 1969 and Ronald Dworkin (though the latter is sometimes ambiguous in this respect) exemplify this approach. I should add that most philosophical authors try to combine both approaches, but the resulting theories are never fully adequate. The two approaches seem partly incommensurable. Therefore they can, in my view, never be combined in one coherent theory, just as we may regard an electron as particle or as wave, but not as both at the same time.

[24] Examples abound, which shows how dominant this way of thinking is (e.g., Rawls, Hare, Gert).

[25] MacIntyre, A. *After Virtue*, Notre Dame: University of Notre Dame Press, 1981 and philosophers of medicine in the hermeneutic tradition are the obvious examples here.

BIOETHICS AND LAW: A DEVELOPMENTAL PERSPECTIVE 101

morality as a practice or process has important implications. In a product view, it is usually easy to defend simple distinctions between law as it is and law as it ought to be, between law and morality, or between positive and critical morality.[26] The product is usually easily identifiable by some test of pedigree or by empirical research. But in a practice or a process view, these distinctions are not so simple; for instance because legal and moral argument cannot be separated, or because most positive moralities include mechanisms of self-criticism and self-improvement by reflection on critical morality.[27]

In the liberal model, both health law and bioethics put strong emphasis on the product rather than on the activity or practice. They try to develop new theories, principles, rules or concrete advice for the new problems that arise (or the old ones seen in a new light): the plight of psychiatric patients, the possibilities and risks of new technologies. Bioethicists try to construct new moral guidelines and suggest solutions for concrete problems and moral dilemmas; often they also try to argue for new legal rules. The product approach is best exemplified by the central role the 'four principles of biomedical ethics' play in the ethical literature.[28] Health lawyers also focus on products in the form of legislation, other types of regulation and judicial decisions. They continually try to construct law as a coherent system of rules and principles. Thus, both disciplines have a similar orientation towards law and morality as a product. This is different from the moralistic-paternalistic model, in which professional morality is that of good medical practice, whereas law mainly consists of a small number of rules and provisions in criminal law and thus takes a product approach.

Secondly, bioethics and health law both use the same conceptual categories. In both disciplines, principles, patient rights, concrete rules and procedures take pride of place. This allows (at least superficially) a translation of legal analysis into moral analysis and vice versa, an essential precondition for successful co-operation.[29]

---

[26] Cf. Hart, H.L.A. 'Positivism and the Separation of Law and Morals', in: R. Dworkin (ed.), *The Philosophy of Law*, Oxford University Press, 1977, pp. 17–65.

[27] Cf. Brom, F.W.A., J.M.G. Vorstenbosch and E. Schroten, 'Public Policy and transgenic animals: case-by-case assessment as a moral learning process', in: P. Wheale and R. von Schonberg (ed.), *The Social Management of Biotechnology: Workshop Proceedings*, Tilburg University, Faculty of Philosophy, 1996 p. 73–86.

[28] Cf. Beauchamp and Childress op. cit., and Gillon, R. (ed.) *Principles of Health Care Ethics*, Chichester: John Wiley and Sons, 1994. Even many critics of 'principlism' still take a product view, like in the theory of moral rules suggested by Clouser, K.D. and Gert, B. 1990, 'A Critique of Principlism,' *Journal of Medicine and Philosophy*, 15 1990, 2, p. 219–236.

[29] A simple illustration: Some years ago, I was invited to present an analysis of the ethical aspects of a controversial epidemiological research project of HIV

Ethicists can participate in legal discussions because they largely use the same framework (though the precise meanings and roles of the principles and rights are usually not identical in law and ethics, a fact which is too often neglected by lawyers and ethicists alike). Lawyers can make a useful contribution to ethical discussions because legal experience often provides valuable insights into the way in which a moral right like that of privacy could be elaborated.

Here again, there is a difference with the moralistic-paternalistic model, in which professional morality focuses on virtues and on categories like the good doctor, whereas criminal law emphasises strict rules of action. Of course, there is an overlap between the two with respect to material implications, but there is no easy translation from the moral category of the good doctor to the question of whether abortion should be legal.

Thirdly, both health law and bioethics concentrate on what is minimally necessary rather than on the ideal situation or the perfect doctor.[30] In a situation in which a quick transformation is deemed desirable or even necessary, it is wise to start with the minimum, for making practitioners comply with this minimum may already be a major achievement. If doctors are not used to give full information to their patients, the most urgent task is to make at least a decent minimum of information available; only in a later stage it may make sense to aim for more perfectionist standards of giving information. If the general idea of legalising abortion is still controversial, it may be wise to stress the woman's right to free choice and leave the more subtle moral questions — like the precise conditions under which an abortion is morally justified — out of the public debate. As long as the minimally decent has not been realised, it may not be very effective, even counterproductive, to aim for the excellent. Again, this guarantees good co-operation in the liberal model between health law and bioethics because law is not an adequate instrument for enforcing excellence. There is a standard saying which states that law is a minimum morality. I think this saying is not entirely correct, if only because it is not very useful to conceptualise law as a form of

---

infection. On this occasion I noticed that the analysis by the legal expert was almost identical to mine, with one major exception: his appeal to the authority of law. The basic principles from which we both started — respect for physical integrity and for privacy — are laid down in the Dutch Constitution as constitutional rights. When, on another occasion, I was invited to discuss both the ethical and the legal aspects, it was, therefore, no problem to integrate these into one coherent story.

[30] The trend to structure the physician-patient relationship in a contractual form is also a sign of this minimalism. Cf. May, W.F. 'Code and Covenant on Philosophy and Contract?', in: S. Gorowitz et al. (eds.), *Moral Problems in Medicine*, Englewood Cliffs (New Jersey): Prentice Hall, 1983; Schneider op. cit.: 18.

morality; yet there is an important core of truth in it. The higher we get on the continuum from the morality of duty to the morality of aspiration, the less effective law can be.[31]

Thus, health law and bioethics both take the product view; both use the same conceptual framework and both focus on the minimally decent rather than on the ideal. These three characteristics are largely formal characteristics. But the most important factor that guarantees successful co-operation is the fourth one (which is closely connected with the other three factors); they are both committed to the same substantive normative theory. Patient autonomy and patient rights — in other words liberalism — are central to the modern bioethical and legal discourse.[32] Because bioethics and health law share this commitment to liberal values, they not only speak the same language, but also take similar stances, at a more theoretical and at a more practical level. Moreover, a theory based on autonomy and patient rights offers simple solutions for most of the problems that were central in the early days of bioethics and health law. On abortion and on euthanasia, on the plight of psychiatric patients and on medical experiments, the paradigm of patient rights gives a clear and simple answer: the patient has to decide.[33] Against the traditional background of moralism and paternalism this is real progress. Moreover, autonomy means that individuals are entrusted with the responsibility for moral dilemmas rather than the law, or society as such. Thus, the more subtle and controversial moral issues are effectively removed from the public sphere. This makes it much easier, in modern pluralist societies, to reach an overlapping consensus on the moral issues that remain in the public sphere; who would oppose patient autonomy as such?

4 PROBLEMS OF THE LIBERAL MODEL

It may be good to stress at this point that this is only an ideal-typical sketch of a model. There is no country that has fully implemented the

---

[31] The distinction between the morality of duty and the morality of aspiration is at the core of Fuller op. cit. and also Selznick, P. *The Moral Commonwealth: Social Theory and the Promise of Community*, Berkeley: University of California Press, 1992. The implications for the health care professional have been elaborated in Van der Burg and Ippel et al., 1994, 'The care of a good caregiver. Legal and ethical reflections on the good health care professional', *Cambridge Quarterly of Health Care Ethics*, Vol. 3, nr. 1 Winter 1994, p. 38–48.

[32] Cf. Ippel, P. 'Gezondheidsrecht en gezondheidsethiek', in: W. van der Burg en P. Ippel (ed.), *De Siamese tweeling*, Assen: Van Gorcum, 1994; Schneider, op. cit.: 18.

[33] With respect to abortion, this conclusion only follows once it has been decided that the foetus is not a full person.

liberal model, if only because its shortcomings are too obvious. Many countries are still only starting its implementation; Sweden, perhaps, is an example. In strongly pluralist societies, like the US and the Netherlands, it seems to have been most effective for obvious reasons: the more a society is characterised by moral pluralism, the less a policy of legal moralism is possible. Even within one country or legal system there may be important differences. Thus, so far, most countries have been non-liberal on the subject of euthanasia and physician-assisted suicide, even those that have been very active with respect to patient rights in general.[34]

Yet, I think the conclusion is warranted that, in most Western countries, the liberal model currently is or is becoming the dominant approach to bioethics and health law. The basic ideas have now been successfully elaborated theoretically and have gained broad support. They have won legal recognition — patient rights have been laid down in statutes or even been included in constitutions and international human rights treaties.[35]

The success of the liberal model now also seems to be the reason for its decline: once the most important advantages of the model have been realised, the disadvantages become clearer and are beginning to weigh more heavily. Especially in the recent ethical literature, we can find a great deal of criticism that stresses the objections to the liberal model.

For, effective and attractive as this model may be, it does have major disadvantages as well. Each of the four characteristics that are responsible for the liberal success result in a certain one-sidedness. The focus on product may neglect practice, the way in which the rules and principles can effectively be interpreted and implemented. Ethical theory and legal doctrine may sometimes be satisfactorily elaborated at a certain reflective distance of the practice, if only because there may be good reasons for changing the practice. But in the end, it is the practice that counts, rather than the law in the books or the ethical

---

[34] In some cases, of course, the opposition against (partly) legalising euthanasia is liberal as well; consider, for instance, the argument that it will lead to situations in which the elderly will feel under pressure to ask for euthanasia and for that reason, in order to protect their autonomy, we should not legalise euthanasia. Most objections, however, are non-liberal, like reference to the sanctity of life or protecting the distinct medical ethos that doctors should never kill.

[35] Cf. the Patient Self-Determination Act in the US, or the new Constitutional clauses in the Netherlands on privacy and physical integrity. In Leenen et al., op. cit., a broad study of health law in most European countries, it is argued that there has been an 'emergence all over Europe of a social and cultural reassertion of the values of individual freedom and self-determination that sustain the concept of patients' rights' (at vii).

© Blackwell Publishers Ltd. 1997

BIOETHICS AND LAW: A DEVELOPMENTAL PERSPECTIVE

principles in the textbooks, and if the elaboration of ethical and legal doctrine overburdens practice, we should be careful. And, indeed, we can hear complaints from practitioners and ethicists alike implying that medical ethics has lost touch with reality, or that health law has become a threat to good medical practice.[36] Even though some of these complaints are based on caricatures and misperceptions or simply on practitioners' dislike of external interference, I think it is important to see the core of truth in it. And it is likely that the more the product is elaborated in ethical theories and positive law, the more strongly the tensions with the demands of practice will be felt.

The second characteristic of the liberal model, the emphasis on principles, rights, rules and procedures, has received so much criticism lately that I will not elaborate on it. Whatever the suggested alternative is, like virtue ethics or ethics of care, they show that ethical analysis only in terms of the liberal model neglects certain dimensions of moral experience.[37]

The third characteristic, minimalism, results in the neglect of perfectionist dimensions of morality and law. In my view, however, perfectionist standards and ideals are essential to bioethics and also to law, though in a different way. We cannot fully understand a profession, unless we realise that it is partly oriented towards some professional ideals.[38] If this is true, then the rise of liberalism led to a morally impoverished image of professional morality and needs to be complemented by richer analysis.

The fourth characteristic, the substantive orientation towards liberalism, may seem to be the most controversial to attack. Do criticisms of liberalism not automatically lead us back to an anti-liberal moralistic position? I do not think so. We should distinguish two shortcomings of the liberal emphasis on rights and autonomy. The first shortcoming is that it simply does not give an answer. It seems to me that this is the case with many issues that we have to confront once liberalism has been realised. Autonomy and rights are of little relevance to the problem of embryo experimentation. When

---

[36] Cf. Vandenbroucke, P. 1990, 'Medische ethiek en gezondheidsrecht: hinderpalen voor de verdere toename van kennis in de geneeskunde?', *Nederlands Tijdschrift voor Geneeskunde* 1990, 5–6.

[37] Cf. Shelp, E.E. (e.a.) *Virtue and Medicine: Explorations in the Character of Medicine*, Dordrecht: Reidel 1985, and the literature inspired by Gilligan, C. 1982, *In a Different Voice: Psychological Theory and Women's Development*, Cambridge, Mass: Harvard University Press, 1982.

[38] Cf. Campbell, A.W. 'Ideals, the Four Principles and Practical Ethics', in: R. Gillon, *Principles of Health Care Ethics*, Chichester: John Wiley and Sons 1994, 241 makes a related point: we cannot fully understand moral principles unless we see that they are connected to more fundamental ideals. Cf. Van der Burg and Ippel et al. op. cit.: 42.

discussing preconception sex selection of children, ethical analysis based on the autonomy of the parents only seems to give part of the story because we cannot neglect the wider context of discriminatory social attitudes. Once we accept that abortion should be a free choice for women, the real problem for them is still there: whether or not to have an abortion in their specific situations. We cannot understand the full ethical dimensions of prenatal diagnosis, unless we understand what it means for women to have a 'tentative' pregnancy,[39] and unless we see what having a handicapped child may mean in this specific woman's biography. The liberal framework does not offer adequate possibilities to analyse these richer dimensions; yet, as long as it is not made absolute it need not prevent us from adding other elements.

Thus, one type of shortcoming of liberalism is that it simply does not enable us to address certain dimensions of a situation. This could, in principle, be solved by supplementing liberalism with richer perspectives, as many authors are currently trying to do. A more problematic shortcoming is that, at times, liberalism presents us unacceptable solutions for a problem and effectively excludes other ways of conceptualising the problem.[40] If we take autonomy as the primary basis for moral and legal judgements, we may find that we have inadequate legal mandate to treat schizophrenic patients in the early stages of their illness, or to prohibit euthanasia or assisted suicide in cases where we do not think it morally justified. (An example could be a patient in a very early stage of cancer demanding euthanasia, even though there are still reasonable chances of curing it.) If we make liberalism too dominant in law, this may lead to a legal doctrine that does not allow enough space for professional autonomy in those cases where patient rights become counterproductive. The rise of preventive medicine may have to do with too much emphasis in law on the liberal model and its rights orientation.

Each of the four characteristics of the liberal model thus corresponds with a certain one-sidedness. A further central characteristic of the liberal model, as I have sketched it, is the close co-operation between health law and bioethics. The advantages of this co-operation were most important in the early years of these disciplines, but once they have become settled, the disadvantages begin to weigh heavier. To put it more simply, a too close co-operation may lead to a neglect of important differences between law and morality. Law is an institution with a distinct role and distinct functions in society. This leads to specific possibilities and limitations of what law can and cannot achieve. For instance, the use of force and

---

[39] Cf. Rothman, B. Katz *The Tentative Pregnancy*, New York: Viking, 1986.
[40] As suggested by Trappenburg op. cit.

sanctions, which is often associated with law, means that law usually has more effective instruments than morality, but it also means that legal regulation is often perceived as threatening by physicians.[41] Both effects should be assessed when discussing legislation, and often this type of evaluation means that we should not enforce moral duties through law. Similar illustrations can be made about the specific possibilities of morality, which may be neglected if ethics is too closely connected with law.[42] For instance, morality should also give guidance in situations where law leaves full discretion to autonomous decision making by patients or physicians; it can only do so if ethics is not too closely associated with law.

5 THE POSTLIBERAL MODEL

We may conclude that the more the liberal model is realised, the stronger its disadvantages become clear. This suggests that it will be succeeded by a different model. As that alternative model is still only in an emergent and implicit state, only a tentative sketch is possible. Just as it was possible to predict the outline of the liberal model partly from the defaults of its moralistic-paternalistic predecessor, it is possible to predict the outline of the postliberal model partly from the defaults of its liberal predecessor. The extrapolation of criticism must be strongly evaluative, because criticism can be met in various ways. Before going into details, however, some preliminary remarks should be made.

A first point I would like to stress is that, despite the criticisms, the advantages of the liberal model are substantial. We should not give up the idea of patient autonomy and go back to paternalism and moralism; anyway, this is not likely to be a feasible alternative. So the new model should include the liberal model, elaborate on it and perhaps in some minor ways correct it rather than replace it by a completely new model. Thus, the new model should be postliberal rather than anti-liberal.

Secondly, the disadvantages mentioned above need not have the same implications for law and for ethics. It is very likely even that the criticisms lead to different reactions for health law and for ethics. For instance, health law should, in my view, largely stick to liberal minimalism and, in some respects, become even more minimalist so as to leave more room for perfectionism in the exercise of professional

---

[41] Cf. Mason and McCall Smith op. cit.: 14–17; Schneider op. cit.: 21–22.

[42] For similar criticism, see Holm, S. 1994, 'American Bioethics at the Crossroads: A critical Appraisal', *European Philosophy of Medicine and Health Care*, 2:2, 1994, p. 6–31.

autonomy, whereas bioethics should incorporate perfectionist ideas more directly. The answer to the criticisms will differ, precisely because health law and bioethics are different, and one of the criticisms of the liberal model is that it does not adequately acknowledge these differences.

This suggests a third point. Law and ethics should become more independent and distinct. The reasons for co-operating so intensely have become less important and the disadvantages of the close connection are becoming more visible. This means that critical reflection on and empirical study of the distinct roles of law and morality have become more urgent and that only on the basis of this we may be able to make adequate judgements about the desirable relationships between law and morality. In the future model, the relationships will probably be more loose than they are in the liberal model. Therefore, I will discuss the implications for law and for morality separately.

During the liberal phase, health law undergoes quite radical changes and elaborations, culminating in some form of codification or, at least, the establishment of a generally recognised body of legal norms of precedent. It seems to be time for the stabilisation and refinement of, and critical reflection on, such a body of norms. A further development of law beyond the liberal model, based on various forms of theoretical study and reflection, should proceed along three lines.

1. One line of development should be based on reflection on the integrity of law as a whole. As a result of its strong connection with bioethics in the liberal model, health law runs the risk of becoming isolated from adjacent fields of law. This may imply that its doctrines become inconsistent with the legal system as a whole.

I will illustrate this with an example from Dutch law.[43] In Dutch health law, constitutional rights have been interpreted in a way that significantly differs from the role they have in constitutional or criminal law. Constitutional rights are usually regarded as a corrective mechanism against the abuse of power by government. In the health law doctrine, constitutional rights and underlying principles like the right to self-determination and the right to health care are seen as the basis for the legal doctrine. If, however, what is meant to be primarily a corrective mechanism on official action is misconstrued as the primary basis of all legal responsibilities, things

---

[43] This example has been elaborated in Van der Burg, W. and H. Oevermans 'Grondrechten in het gezondheidsrecht', in: W. van der Burg and P. Ippel (ed.), *De Siamese tweeling*, Assen: Van Gorcum, 1994: 187–203.

© Blackwell Publishers Ltd. 1997

BIOETHICS AND LAW: A DEVELOPMENTAL PERSPECTIVE 109

are turned upside down. Health law doctrine should start with the primary goal of medicine, i.e. the cure and care of the patient, and then construct constitutional rights as a protective countermechanism or as a symbolic point of orientation. If you make rights the basis of health law, as the liberal orientation on autonomy and patient rights has at least a tendency to do, then you loose contact with the primary goal of health care. Thus, the liberal rights orientation may, if taken too far, lead to results that are contrary to its primary aim: serving the patient's interest.[44] It seems to me that closer contact with traditions in adjacent fields of law and less intense contact with bioethics might have prevented this, and could have led to a better health law.

This example shows how the separation of health law as a distinct subfield of law — though in itself not objectionable — may lead too far, especially if health law is too strongly connected to bioethics. A stronger orientation of health law towards the legal system as a whole and to the integrity of law may lead to significant corrections in health law doctrine and especially to a more modest role of the law.

2. A second line of health law development should be based on a further reflection on the societal role, functions and limitations of law in general and of health law in particular.[45] As a result of its orientation towards bioethics, health law may become too ambitious and thus counterproductive in trying to change medical practice. But law is not always effective and it has often many side-effects that should be taken into account. This problem of effectiveness and side-effects is particularly important in the context of biomedical practice. Legal control is difficult, if only because medical confidentiality often shields the profession from external intervention. Thus, traditional models of enforcement are usually not effective unless the profession itself largely co-operates voluntarily — the problem of illegal euthanasia practices in many countries may be an example. Simple instrumentalist views of law often just do not work; in order to influence professional practice, the communicative function of law should be stressed.[46] Moreover, the side-effects of legal intervention may be far-reaching: relationships of trust could be damaged.[47]

Thus, both the directly intended effects of legislation and the

---

[44] This critical reappraisal of the rights orientation is what is now happening, indeed, in Dutch health law. Its 'founding father', H.J.J. Leenen, has gradually retreated from his earlier stance that these rights are the 'pillars' of health law; compare the first (1978) and third (1994) editions of his *Handboek Gezondheidsrecht*.
[45] Cf. Schneider op. cit.
[46] Cf. Legemaate, J. *Recht en realiteit: Juridische normering en het therapeutisch proces* (oratie Rotterdam), Houten: Bohn Stafleu Van Loghum, 1994: 23.
[47] Cf. Mason and McCall Smith op. cit.: 16–17.

© Blackwell Publishers Ltd. 1997

indirect effects or side-effects should be counted. For instance, if legal regulation both leads to the desirable goal of enforcing patient rights and to the unintended result of defensive medicine because doctors feel threatened by the law, we should balance these two effects before deciding in favour of legislation. We should also consider possible alternatives for state regulation, such as instituting (partly) independent regulatory bodies in which both the public and the profession are represented; forms of self-regulation and convenants between the state and the business sector (a common practice in environmental law in many countries) may also be a good alternative.

3. A third line of further health law development should be based on the development of normative theories regarding the limits of state and law. As I have mentioned earlier, most of the current theories only focus on the moral limits of criminal law. Normative theory on the proper limits of tort law or administrative law is still lacking. There are some strong political positions, obviously, but these are often highly ideologically coloured (especially by strong anti-state sentiments) or merely pragmatic. What we need is more nuanced theoretical work on what the state should or should not do and what the law should or should not regulate if we take ideals like the rule of law or democracy seriously, and especially how then this should be done. When is civil law and when is criminal law adequate? When should we leave issues to internal self-regulation? The case of surrogacy presents a good example. Presumably, criminal sanctions will not only be partly ineffective but, according to most authors, also unjustified.[48] How the law of contract or internal hospital regulations should deal with the issue is still open then.

For each of these three lines of health law development we need a certain reflection on and distance from biomedical practice: studies in political philosophy, in the sociology of law, and in general jurisprudence and the philosophy of law will be necessary. But in each of these fields there seems to be the same trend: in a postliberal model, health law should be more modest and should show self-restraint and acknowledge its inherent and normative limits.[49]

With respect to ethics, the general trend seems to be different. I will only give a very simple indication here, because I am primarily

---

[48] According to Mason and McCall Smith op. cit.: 70, in the Anglophone world, almost no legal system has criminalised the procedure as such — Queensland being the exception.

[49] Mason and McCall Smith op. cit.: 16 seem to suggest that in the English courts this self-restraint is now, indeed, being practiced, whereas they had expressed their fears as to the contrary in a previous edition.

interested in the relationship between law and ethics. For this purpose it suffices to see that, in whatever direction we may expect and hope the development in ethics to go, it will presumably always be a direction away from law.

The four general characteristics of the liberal model that I discussed earlier, and their concomitant shortcomings, have been strongly criticised in recent ethical literature; they should each be complemented to develop a richer, pluralist view of ethics. Some authors have argued for replacing (some of the characteristics of) the liberal model in ethics, but most critics have taken an intermediate position. They want to supplement the liberal model with elements that it has neglected rather than construing a completely new model. Many representatives of the liberal model have accepted the challenge and have tried to include elements of the criticisms or to emphasise non-liberal elements that so far have not received due attention. It seems that we are heading towards an enriched and pluralist view of ethics.[50] We should not only study the product in the form of theories, but also analyse good practice. Studies based on rights perspectives and principlism should be supplemented by studies based on, e.g. virtue ethics or ethics of care, simply because each of these alternative approaches has its own blind spot. The minimalism that was adequate in the early days of bioethics can now be enriched by going beyond the minimum and reflecting on the ideal of good medical practice. Finally, the strong orientation on individual rights and autonomy — which may still be quite acceptable in legal philosophy — should be nuanced and supplemented by views in which the full dimensions of the good life and of the good society at large are elaborated.[51]

An example may make clear what I mean. If we look at the relationship between patient and doctor, we need a plurality of approaches for an adequate ethical analysis. We should both look at minimum standards or duties that every doctor should always respect, and to maximum standards or professional ideals that he should aspire to. We should, as in the liberal model, analyse the actions of

---

[50] There is a growing recognition of the need for a plurality of methodological and normative-ethical approaches; see, e.g., Gustafson, J.M. 1990, 'Moral Discourse About Medicine: A Variety of Forms', *Journal of Medicine and Philosophy*, 15 1990 p. 125–142, and even Beauchamp and Childress op. cit.: 111. See also Van der Burg, Ippel, et al., op. cit.

[51] Even in legal philosophy, however, the liberal rights orientation will not always be adequate, as R. Dworkin's *Life's Dominion*, New York: Alfred A. Knopf, 1993, shows. The most ardent supporter of rights theories had to switch to value theories in order to present an adequate analysis of legal issues connected to bioethics.

112 WIBREN VAN DER BURG

the physician in terms of rules, principles and protocols as well as in terms of the rights of the patient — but this is only part of the story. We should also articulate what a virtuous doctor is and we need a perspective of an ethics of care to supplement the contractualist (and therefore minimalist) understanding of the relationship between patient and doctor. So, to understand all the relevant aspects of the norm of a good caregiver, we need indeed a plurality of ethical approaches. Focusing on only one or two approaches, as in the liberal model, leads to a reductionist and distorted picture of this highly complex phenomenon.[52]

As a result of these two trends in health law and bioethics, we may expect (and should support) a divergence between the legal and the moral point of view. If law, generally speaking, should be more modest and conscious of its inherent and normative restraints, whereas ethics should rather take a richer and more ambitious self-image, the two diverge.[53] If ethics is to go beyond liberalism, to address the ideal as well as the minimum and so on, whereas law sticks to the minimum and to liberalism, or even partly retreats from it in the light of a better understanding of its specific role, further divergence will become necessary. Loosening the bonds between law and bioethics is thus the result of developments in the postliberal phase. In a sense, it is also a condition for a further development of both health law and bioethics. For as long as both are so closely connected, it will also be difficult for each to go its own way. If the public moral debate on abortion is closely linked to the debate on the desirable legislation or judicial decisions, an open moral discussion on how this freedom should be exercised will be frustrated. Legal freedom does not imply a full moral license. The motives of a woman requesting abortion may be legally irrelevant, but the request is not morally neutral, let alone that it is emotionally easy. To help women (and men) handle these difficult decisions which they face, a public moral debate can be important, but this will only work if there is no suspicion of hidden agendas to change the law.[54]

The same goes for law. If health law tries no longer — often in vain or quite forcefully — to justify each and every single rule in moral terms, it may be easier to get a workable practice. The example of embryo legislation has been mentioned above. It seems to me that we will only make progress in the legislative debate once

---

[52] Cf. Van der Burg and Ippel et al. op. cit: 40.
[53] Schneider op. cit. makes a similar point.
[54] Schneider op. cit.: 21 gives a similar example: the question whether we have a moral obligation to donate blood tends to be restructured as the question whether there should be a legal obligation.

© Blackwell Publishers Ltd. 1997

we see that legal rules and legal lines, like a three-months or a fourteen-days line in rules on embryo experiments or abortions, need not be directly justifiable in moral terms — law knows many arbitrary lines.[55] The law as a whole should be as morally justifiable as possible, but this does not mean that we should be able to give a direct moral foundation to each individual statutory rule or judicial ruling seen in isolation.

6 CONCLUSIONS

In this paper I have sketched a developmental theory of the relationships between health law and bioethics. This theory can give us a good understanding of why, in many Western countries, health law and bioethics are so closely intertwined. Understanding the specific historical setting that facilitated this close connection may help us recognise the time for a new phase in which the bonds are loosened. Obviously, a sketch that is meant to outline some general trends in all Western countries must be either too vague or will not fit readily in some countries. Indeed, this is only an ideal-typical sketch of three models: no country fully embodies or once embodied either of the three models. Yet I would hold that central elements of the first two models can be found in the historical development of these countries that I know best: the Netherlands and the USA, and probably also in most of the Anglophone world and Germany. The third model is more tentative; it is an emergent model, and perhaps, in some respects, I have misinterpreted some of the current tendencies; perhaps I fell victim to wishful thinking.

Presently, most of the Western countries are still in the process of realising the liberal model. What does my analysis mean for those countries? Should they stop this development and try to skip the liberal phase, because of the criticisms? Some of the critics of the liberal model seem to suggest so: we should go back to Aristotle or back to traditional morality. In my view this would be the wrong reaction, and I think this development approach shows why.

There were good reasons to leave the pre-liberal phase. Going back to old times will not help us, because the old model is no longer functional in modern societies, and is no longer acceptable to the public at large in pluralist cultures. A regression to the pre-liberal phase is nevertheless possible, even though it will not be very effective. Just like Nonet and Selznick (1978) argued in their developmental model of law that there can be 'two ways law can

---

[55] C. Van der Burg, W. 1996, 'Legislation on Human Embryos: From Status Theories to Value Theories', *Archiv für Rechts– und Sozialphilosophie*, 82: 1 1996, 73.

© Blackwell Publishers Ltd. 1997

114 WIBREN VAN DER BURG

die', there may be two ways liberalism can die: regression to pre-liberalism and progression to post-liberalism.[56] I suggest that we take the second way, and incorporate the sound parts of the anti-liberal criticisms into the postliberal model, rather than simply abandon the liberal model.

In order to preserve the valuable core of liberalism, we should go beyond it.

Schoordijk Institute for Jurisprudence and Comparative Law
Tilburg University

---

[56] Cf. Nonet, P. and Selznick, P. *Law and Society in Transition: Toward Responsive Law*, New York: Harper and Row, 1978: 115.

© Blackwell Publishers Ltd. 1997

Part III
Bioethics and Religion

Religion and the Secularization of Bioethics
by Daniel Callahan

The occasion of this special supplement on religion and bioethics serves to remind me, once again, that the field of bioethics as we now know it is a creature of its time and history. It grew up during the 1960s and 1970s in an era of affluence and social utopianism, in a culture that was experimenting with an expansive array of newly found rights and unprecedented opportunities for personal freedom, and in the context of a national history that has long struggled to find the right place for religion in its public life. For medicine it was a time that combined magnificent theoretical and clinical achievements with uncommonly difficult moral problems, many of them bearing on the self-identity and goals of medicine. The story of contemporary bioethics turns on the way in which those problems intersected with, and whose understanding was shaped by, that larger temporal and social context.

The most striking change over the past two decades or so has been the secularization of bioethics. The field has moved from one dominated by religious and medical traditions to one now increasingly shaped by philosophical and legal concepts. The consequence has been a mode of public discourse that emphasizes secular themes: universal rights, individual self-direction, procedural justice, and a systematic denial of either a common good or a transcendent individual good.

Let me, if I may, use myself as an illustration of this trend, as well as an example of some considerable uneasiness left in its wake. When I first became interested in bioethics in the mid-1960s, the only resources were theological or those drawn from within the traditions of medicine, themselves heavily shaped by religion. In one way, that situation was congenial enough. I was through much of the 1960s a religious person and had no trouble bringing that perspective to bear on the newly emergent issues of bioethics. But that was not to be finally adequate for me. Two personal items were crucial. My religious belief was by then beginning to decline, and by the end of the decade had all but disappeared. My academic training, moreover, was that of analytic philosophy, and I wanted to bring that work to bear on bioethics. Was it not obvious, I thought, that moral philosophy, with its historical dedication to finding a rational foundation for ethics, was well suited to biomedical ethics, particularly in a pluralistic society? Just as I had found I did not need religion for my personal life, why should biomedicine need it for its collective moral life?

The answer to that last question has been less obvious than I originally thought. If my life has been, in a way, relieved by the absence of religion as a guiding force, I cannot say that it has been enriched or that I am a better person for that. Nor can it be said, I think, that biomedical ethics is demonstrably more robust and satisfying as a result of its abandonment of religion. To say that of course is not to make a case for the validity of religion, which must be made on its own merits, not on its potential contribution to bioethics. Some nineteenth century thinkers, we might recall, came to think that, although religion was false as a way of understanding the world, it was socially useful to sustain as a source of discipline and political stability. There was always something slightly cynical in that view, and doubly so because it was meant to strengthen the hand of those in authority. Nonetheless, it is not necessary to entertain such a position to recognize that, whatever the ultimate truth status of religious perspectives, they have provided a way of looking at the world and understanding one's own life that has a fecundity and uniqueness not matched by philosophy, law, or political theory. Those of us who have lost our religious faith may be glad that we have discovered what we take to be the reality of things, but we can still recognize that we have also lost something of great value as well: the faith, vision, insights, and experience of whole peoples and traditions who, no less than we unbelievers, struggled to make sense of things. That those goods are part of a garment we no longer want to wear does not make their loss anything other than still a loss; and it is not a negligible one.

But need that be the end of the story? Can those of us who share my lack of belief still make use of at least some of the insights and perspectives of religion, even as we reject its roots? Or are they meaningless without their connection to those roots? Are there some questions about our lives and destiny that philosophy, science, or other secular disciplines can't help us get hold of with any telling force, and that only religion has been able to accommodate? Is it wrong, or a form of illogical sentimentality, to continue feeding off of religious traditions and ways of life that one has, in fact, rejected at their core? Does intellectual honesty demand that we have the courage of our convictions (or lack thereof) and construct our view of the world out of the whole cloth of unbelief, not borrowing to suit our own purposes those valuable bits, pieces, and parts of a garment we have thrown off? And of course there is another question that might be entertained: if we agree that religion, even if wrongheaded, provides ways of understanding not otherwise attainable, should we then never allow ourselves to close the door on the possibility of a renewed belief? Even if we have not the faintest idea (as I do not) about where that renewal might come from?

Daniel Callahan is a philosopher and director of The Hastings Center.

Those are some questions I have put to myself over the years. I will not try to answer them directly here, and do not in any event think I have good answers. I will instead say something about the unfolding of contemporary bioethics, inviting others to see whether that history provides some answers to the questions I have raised.

A Short History of Bioethics

Joseph Fletcher's book *Medicine and Morals* (1954) has often, and correctly, been cited as the first truly fresh manifestation of a growing interest in medical ethics in the post-World War II era. That Fletcher was at the time an Episcopalian theologian might easily lead one to think of the book as a "theological" contribution. Its contents, however, suggest a very different interpretation. By his emphasis upon "choice" as the heart of morality, his rejection of moral theories (particularly Roman Catholic) that would look to nature for ethical guidance, and his celebration of the power of medicine to open new opportunities for moral freedom, Fletcher was in fact opening a direct assault upon some long-standing religious constraints on medicine. That Fletcher's moral theory was based on what he called "situation ethics"—emphasizing the uniqueness of each moral choice and therefore the irrelevance of binding moral rules and principles—signalled all the more the depth of his attack on some characteristic religious values. The possibility also of detecting, just below the surface, an additional powerful strain of utilitarianism in Fletcher's book underscored the depth of the break he was working to engender.

Medicine and Morals did not, in the 1950s, have a great impact in the medical world, even if Fletcher's situation ethics had a telling appeal among many physicians whose clinical experience resisted general moral rules. But that was not an era when the writings of outsiders, religious or not, were likely to be taken seriously. It was not until the middle of the 1960s, in the controversies that developed over human subject experimentation, that those outside voices began to make themselves heard. The quick appearance thereafter of increasingly public struggles over the definition of death and the care of the terminally ill, genetic counseling and prenatal diagnosis, and organ transplantation, brought the field of bioethics into being. The Protestant theologian Paul Ramsey, first with *The Patient as Person* (1970) and then with other books in the 1970s, carried out one of the first comprehensive bioethical examinations of the newly emergent issues. James M. Gustafson added still another powerful theological impetus (even if, in what his writings actually said, the specific contribution of theology was rendered systematically ambiguous). All the while, Jewish and Roman Catholic theologians were carrying on the long-standing work of responding to medical advances and quandaries in light of their own traditions, though now with a new intensity. The writings of Seymour Siegel or David Feldman, from the Jewish side, or Richard McCormick and Charles Curran, from the Roman Catholic, provided evidence of that intensity.

Yet in many respects this early theological role in the emergence of the field was soon to decline. Part of the reason may be that the theological seminaries and departments of religion were in the 1970s drawn more to issues of urban poverty and race, and to questions of world peace in a nuclear age, than to bioethics. After a short burst of interest, the number of younger scholars drawn to the field seemed to decline as the decade came to an end (and many of those who were attracted seemed more comfortable speaking the language of philosophy than religion). No less importantly perhaps, once the field became of public interest, commanding the attention of courts, legislatures, the media, and professional societies, there was great pressure (even if more latent than manifest) to frame the issues, and to speak, in a common secular mode.

Here the philosophers and the lawyers came to take the lead. Samuel Gorovitz organized a 1974 conference on bioethics for philosophers at Haverford College, drawing a number of newcomers to the field, many of whom went on to considerable prominence. The Karen Ann Quinlan case in 1975 had a similarly potent effect on the law, making evident that bioethics would provide a steady stream of legal cases and a considerable body of unique issues for legal scholars. As the field of medicine became itself more engaged in the issues, it sought a way of framing and discussing them that would bypass religious struggles. Lawyers and philosophers were by no means seen as congenial allies of doctors, but they were preferable to theologians (especially those who spoke out of sectarian traditions). For all the steady interest of some physicians in religion and medicine, the discipline of medicine itself is now as resolutely secular as any that can be found in our society. It is a true child of the Enlightenment.

All of these trends were nicely epitomized in the two federal commissions established during the 1970s, the National Commission for the Protection of Human Subjects in 1974, and the President's Commission in 1979. Both the professional staffs of the two groups and those called upon to give testimony before them were drawn mainly from medicine, philosophy, the health policy sciences, and the law. The approaches and concepts commonly employed in their reports, moreover, showed not the least visible trace of religious influence. An ethic of universal principles—especially autonomy, beneficence, and justice—was given a place of prestige in the 1978 *Belmont Report* issued by the National Commission.

I do not want to imply that there was any outright hostility toward religion (even though I could detect that now and then in some philosophers I knew). On the contrary, it was for the most part bypassed altogether. Whatever place it might have in the private lives of individuals, it simply did not count as one of the available common resources for setting public policy. There was (and still is) a lurking fear of religion, often seen as a source of deep and unresolvable moral conflict as well as single-minded political pressure when aroused. For that matter, ours is a society extraordinarily wary of provoking fundamental debates about basic worldviews and ethical premises. Such debates are seen as more likely to produce destructive battles than illuminating social insights, more anger and intransigence than peace and compromise. Religious differences have commonly been seen as the most likely source of such struggles, and thus to be kept at arm's length—or, even better, off the political playing field altogether.

The Discontents of Secularization

Some important consequences of this general attitude seem apparent. It encourages a form of moral philosophy for use in the marketplace that aspires simultaneously to a kind of detached neutrality (what Thomas Nagel has called the "view from nowhere"), and a culture-free rationalistic universalism (which is suspicious of the emotions and the particularities of actual human communities). It is hardly surprising that the only theoretical debate taken to be of any great moral interest is that between deontologists (who can help the right trump the good), and utilitarians (who can allow a calculus of pleasures, pains, or preferences to trump both the right and the good). No less banished are more speculative forms of philosophy, especially those that might look to nature or organism for moral direction. Its worst failing may be its enormous reluctance to question the conventional ends and goals of medicine, thereby running a constant risk of simply legitimating, by way of ethical tinkering and casuistical fussiness, the way things are.

Another consequence is that it has either intimidated religion from speaking in its own voice, or has driven many to think that voice can be expressed with integrity only within the confines of particular religious communities. Time and again I have been told by religious believers at a conference or symposium that they feared revealing their deepest convictions. They felt the price of acceptance was to talk the common language, and they were probably right. Religious convictions are thought "personal" in two senses: they bespeak a particular cultural and ethnic background, and they reveal someone's inner life. Those of us who spend our time in the leading scientific and intellectual salons, and who have come to know the rules of the game, take great pains to conceal those features of our lives. I am no more enthused about letting my Irish-Catholic, parochial school background show (even if now put behind me) than I am to have a spot of gravy on my Brooks Brothers striped tie. (In fact the latter is preferable to the former; we all dribble from time to time, but not everyone has had a parochial school education—a tie can be cleaned in a way a psyche cannot be).

The net result of this narrowing of philosophy and the disappearance or denaturing of religion in public discourse is a triple threat. It leaves us, first of all, too heavily dependent upon the law as the working source of morality. The language of the courts and legislatures becomes our only shared means of discourse. That leaves a great number fearful of the law (as seems the case with many physicians) or dependent upon the law to determine the rightness of actions, which it can rarely do since it tells us better what is forbidden or acceptable than what is commendable or right.

It leaves us, secondly, bereft of the accumulated wisdom and knowledge that are the fruit of long-established religious traditions. I do not have to be a Jew to find it profitable and illuminating to see how the great rabbinical teachers have tried to understand moral problems over the centuries. Nor will Jews find it utterly useless to explore what the popes, or the leading Protestant divines, have had to say about ethics. This seems an obvious kind of point to make; but few actually make it.

It leaves us, thirdly, forced to pretend that we are not creatures both of particular moral communities and the more sprawling, inchoate general community that we celebrate as an expression of our pluralism. Yet that pluralism becomes a form of oppression if, in its very name, we are told to shut up in public about our private lives and beliefs and talk a form of what Jeffrey Stout has called moral esperanto. The rules of that language are that it deny the concreteness and irregularities of real communities, that it eschew vision and speculation about goals and meaning, and that it enshrine the discourse of wary strangers (especially that of rights) as the preferred mode of daily relations.

With so many riches at our disposal, why have we ended in the name of social peace with a salt that has lost its savor?

Religion and Moral Meaning in Bioethics

by Courtney S. Campbell

Few experiences in life seem more pointless, more suggestive that our lives are subject to powers that are arbitrary, abusive, and destructive, than the suffering and death of children. What possible account could be given to explain, let alone give meaning to such an event? Several years ago, I developed a friendship with a young couple who were anxiously awaiting the birth of their first child. What transpired, quite unexpectedly, was every prospective parent's nightmare: their child was born with serious congenital abnormalities, evidenced visibly by facial disfigurement and substantial respiratory difficulties. Following a short

Courtney S. Campbell is associate for religious studies at The Hastings Center and editor of the Hastings Center Report.

stay in an NICU, the neonatologists indicated that though they could not be sure when death would occur, they were certain that the child's prognosis was terminal, and asked the parents for their preferences regarding continuing or stopping treatment.

How might we think about such a problem in contemporary bioethics? We might invoke a benefits versus burdens calculation or a best interests standard, or take procedural recourse to an ethics committee, perhaps recommending withdrawal of life support. Or, we might consider the cogency of arguments supporting active killing as a compassionate act to spare the child what would inevitably be a painful life, whatever its duration. But the parents did not ask those kinds of questions; they instead brought to that very difficult situation an understanding that our lives are subject to ultimate powers which are creative, nurturing, and redeeming, and a way of construing the world shaped decisively by a set of religious convictions about the purpose of life, the meaning of death, and ultimate human destiny. Within that moral vision, Angela was not seen by her parents as a tragedy to be prevented (by prenatal diagnosis and abortion) or an unwanted burden whose life could easily be shortened, but instead as a gift in need of care. With minimal medical support, my friends took Angela home to begin their family life bound together, and over the next few months gave devoted and unceasing care until she died.

I do not relate this story to say the parents' choice to care for their daughter at home rather than let her die in the hospital was ethically right or justifiable. I am still unsure about that choice, even though the subsequent care Angela received was to me an exemplary witness of how we should collectively treat the vulnerable and voiceless in our midst. Rather, my point is that a world view provided meaning in a situation that seemed pervaded by arbitrariness and cruelty, a meaning that could not be supplied or sustained by our conventional bioethics maxims about "best interests" or "substituted judgment." The tragedy seen by others, including myself, was transformed into a gift. "Suffer the little children...for of such is the kingdom of God."

Religion offers an interpretation or revelation of reality that responds to what Max Weber referred to as the "metaphysical needs of the human mind" to seek order, coherence, and meaning in our lives, to understand ultimate questions about our nature, purpose, and destiny. Yet, in our common endeavor to do bioethics within the limits of reason alone, the discourse necessary to sustain the traditions of moral insight and meaning embedded in the practices and values of religious communities may be characterized as "private" and so considered largely irrelevant to the overriding objectives of bioethics. Indeed, prominent scholars have given serious consideration to whether traditions of theological ethics may constructively contribute to bioethics and to the practices of health care, and the conclusion on several accounts may often be that such a moral resource is dispensable: "Bioethics, where it succeeds, shows where it does not need theology."[1]

The tensions between religious discourse and bioethics pose dual challenges of *accessibility* and *meaning*. Insofar as the incorporation of moral claims from a specific religious tradition or community is deemed to undermine the possibilities for a generally accessible bioethics discourse, the significance of religious perspectives may be very limited. Yet the criterion of accessibility may limit the moral richness of bioethics, for the costs of conformity to public discourse requirements may be the loss of meaning and content about ultimate concerns embedded in a particular tradition, whether religious (as illustrated by the story of Angela's parents) or professional (for example, medicine or nursing).

The Public Limits of Religious Discourse

If it was premature to pronounce "the death of God" in the 1960s, it seems equally mistaken to begin doing post-mortems on the demise of theological and religious perspectives in bioethics. There are nevertheless several problems posed for religious thinkers by the criterion of a generally accessible bioethics discourse, as succinctly identified by Leon Kass:

Perhaps for the sake of getting a broader hearing, perhaps not to profane sacred teachings or to preserve a separation between the things of God and the things of Caesar, most religious ethicists entering the public practice of ethics leave their special insights at the door and talk about "deontological vs. consequentialist," "autonomy vs. paternalism," "justice vs. utility," just like everybody else.[2]

A first limit on religious discourse in bioethics, then, has to do with constructing a moral language appropriate to an interdisciplinary and public audience. Religious thinkers no longer converse only with members of a particular religious community affirming a common set of assumptions. The audience of bioethics is instead comprised of a broad range of academics and professionals, who likely do not share the same moral, let alone theological, language and concepts. In this setting, the substantive but private insights of a particular tradition may need to be translated into concepts that have public significance.

The linguistic compromises required to gain a "broader hearing," however, risk substantive compromises, since the common discourse of bioethics may not be sufficiently rich to convey the full meaning of relevant religious language. For example, the biblical concept of the "image of God" expresses a transcendent and relational understanding of the self that may be diminished by proposed equivalents of "personhood" or "autonomy," while both the motivational and substantive elements of "covenant" seem only minimally conveyed by the language of "contract." Moreover, though the principle of "beneficence" may be in the bioethics lexicon, even at its most morally demanding it is a very diluted form of "neighbor-love."

The problem of translating religious discourse into a common bioethics language, without attenuating or transforming its meaning, has for some religious thinkers illustrated the potential for cooptation involved in addressing a secular world on its terms and in its concepts. Rather than "profane sacred teachings" as Kass puts it, the alternative to this perceived compromise may be to affirm an ethic of an exemplary community that witnesses to the integrity of its religious convictions primarily in practice rather than discourse. Stanley Hauerwas, for example, has maintained that appreciating "the integrity of Christian discourse—[entails] that Christian beliefs do not need translation but should be demonstrated through Christian practices...."[3]

There is, to be sure, an important vocational reason for retaining the integrity of religious discourse. Unlike moral philosophers, for example, theologians do have a particular audience or constituency to whom they are accountable, namely, their various religious communities, whose historical traditions of reflection may be inadequate for the new questions of practical ethics raised by contemporary biotechnology and medicine. Part of the theological concern with addressing a public audience on generally accessible grounds, then, is that it may compromise not only a vocational responsibility to speak *out of* a particular religious tradition, but also a responsibility to speak *to* the tradition embodied in an identifiable community of believers.

Yet a third consideration to which Kass alludes is the church-state controversy, or the societal interest in preserving a wall of separation between religious and public concerns. This limit may be particularly significant in those settings where a specific kind of public bioethics is required—the articulation of public or institutional policy by advisory commissions or committees. The institutionalization of bioethics can reinforce the necessity for a generally accessible language, not only to facilitate ethical discourse among members of such commissions, but also so that they can explain and defend their recommendations to the public on grounds accessible to all.

In the process of public policymaking on bioethics issues, for example, religious themes are typically acknowledged, either through the appointment of particular commission members as representatives of a certain tradition or in public hearings in which invited representatives from a tradition present position statements. These statements may at times articulate distinctive conclusions on the issues under consideration based on the moral reasoning of a religious tradition, as exemplified by the testimony opposing the use of human fetal tissue for purposes of transplantation by Roman Catholic and Jewish scholars presented to an NIH panel in 1988. In other instances, the arguments of religious traditions may be "essentially the same" as the conclusions supported by secular moral reasoning.[4]

Whatever the contributions of religious traditions to the policymaking process, given the particular constitutional configurations of our polity the outcomes and conclusions need to be articulated and defended publicly on nonreligious, generally accessible grounds. That is, the constitutional requirements of a secular purpose for legislation and the constitutional restrictions on appeals to religious grounds as authorization for legislation impose political limits on the scope of religious argumentation.[5]

The sense that the contributions of religious discourse to contemporary bioethics are limited by these interdisciplinary, theological, and political parameters assumes of course that religious traditions have something substantively distinctive to communicate to a public, secular audience. But where might we locate these distinctive or special insights? I want to suggest that the answers to the conventional bioethics questions of "who should decide?" or "what should we do?" often—if we felt free to allow them to do so—would push back to fundamental issues that require a substantive account of the purpose of human life and destiny. These are common questions of meaning that religious communities have devoted considerable attention to in their theologies, rituals, and practical ethics.

The Anomaly of Suffering

The nature of the accessibility-meaning dichotomy can initially be illustrated by attending to some very contested questions in contemporary bioethics. Two examples will suffice.

In an influential discussion of the moral status of animals, one philosopher explains his neglect of religious argumentation for the concept of the "sanctity of life" because such views do not provide "reasoned explanation." Moreover, even sanctity of life proponents typically appeal to nonreligious reasons, since "[religious] doctrines are no longer as widely accepted as they once were."[6] Another has observed that religious arguments prohibiting active killing in medical practice have limited scope in the secular domain; even if one "eschews euthanasia on religious grounds, there will be the challenge of establishing in general terms why a secular society compassing a plurality of moral viewpoints may forbid euthanasia."[7] The constraints on religious discourse are in part its sociological inadequacy (because in our secular age purely religious appeals will not be sufficient for *public* moral reasoning), and in part its logical inadequacy (because the arational nature of such appeals will be unsatisfactory as a foundation for *moral* reasoning). For the sake of general accessibility, then, we may be tempted to do bioethics without recourse to important sources and traditions of meaning in our culture.

Yet if we consider what is driving moral debate on both "animal rights" and euthanasia, we are likely to find what has historically been deemed a question of religious meaning right at the core, for it is difficult to discuss either of these issues without invoking the notion of "suffering." The central question in attributing moral status to animals, in Jeremy Bentham's classic formulation, is, "Can they suffer?," while arguments on euthanasia often turn on the availability of alternatives to "relieve suffering." Our moral disagreements in bioethics over whether animals should be used in research or over appropriate care of the dying may thus reflect not only (if at all) differences in moral norms, but also various understandings of the place and meaning of suffering in our lives.

Even prior to its significance for such controversial issues, the concept of suffering seems central for the most fundamental concerns of bioethics. Suffering is in part constituted by the experience of a profound assault upon or threat to our sense of self and identity that we are unable to control. It is the experience of the inexplicably arbitrary and typically destructive, of what Weber referred to as the "ethical irrationality of the world." It is perhaps such a perception of illness and disease that lies behind the Latin root (*pati*) of our "patient," meaning "the one who suffers."

Religious traditions do not have a monopoly on discourse about suffering, nor is there a univocal understanding of suffering common to all religions. It is nevertheless the case that the meaning of suffering has long been a central concern of much theological reflection and many religious communities. If such a concept is a central presupposition of both basic conceptual (what is a "patient"?) and controversial pragmatic problems in bioethics (the human treatment of animals), the traditions of religious discourse about suffering would seem to present a rich resource for substantive insights. Some conceptual comprehension of "necessary suffering" is needed, for example, to make sense of moral arguments, let alone current public referenda proposals in Oregon and Washington that would sanction active euthanasia in cases of "unnecessary" suffering.

A Journey of Meaning

Suffering is not of course an end of religious experience but a problem demanding interpretation. Religious traditions have historically tried to give meaning to suffering by placing the experience in a context of broader questions about ultimate purpose in life, and even human destiny beyond life. The "ethically irrational" is typically explained by the construction of a theodicy that reconciles the presence of evil and suffering within a concept of salvation. In Buddhism, for example, suffering may be descriptive of life within the cycle of karma. In some Western traditions, suffering has been construed as having punitive, pedagogical, or redemptive purposes in human experience, though the incompleteness of all such constructions is suggested by the paradigmatic biblical story of the suffering of Job and, in our time, by the experience of the Jews in the Holocaust. Whether suffering does have a "point" and what that point may be will vary among religious traditions. My claim, however, is that the moral intelligibility of suffering is dependent on some account, theological or philosophical, of human nature and ultimate human ends; any conception of bioethics, therefore, that purports to take suffering seriously will likewise have to consider such ultimate questions.

The substantive responses of religious traditions to questions about our origins, who we are, what the nature and purpose of life is, and what constitutes our ultimate ends, account in part of course for the practical and moral differences among traditions. While acknowledging this diversity and complexity, I want to illustrate, by drawing on one fairly common interpretation of life in religious traditions, how such ultimate perspectives can present important implications for our models of bioethics. For many traditions, a fundamental metaphor for life is that of a *journey* or *pilgrimage*. The meaning of the journey is derived in part from its *telos*, the promise of passage or deliverance, including deliverance from the ills and adversity encountered in life, and which also gives point and purpose to morality as the requirements of character and action necessary to transform the kind of people we are (human nature) into the kind of people we ought to be (human destiny).

The life given to us by powers that are ultimately creating, sustaining, and redeeming is not without its thickets and thorns, yet it is precisely through the encounter with human (evil and sin) and natural (disease) forms of opposition that progress in the journey is possible, for such experiences shape decisively the identity and character of the moral self. Thus participation in the journey is intrinsically valuable, a source of meaning through experience of oppression, adversity, and perhaps even suffering. That meaning is constructed and explained, clarified and communicated, in stories and narratives of creation, alienation, and reconciliation told to others and retold as part of an ongoing tradition. The journey is thus as well a communal experience that involves the making of covenants and promises, the mutual binding together of former strangers for common purposes and ends, through which moral responsibilities are mediated.

This teleological account of human experience can reveal several features to us about the character of contemporary bioethics. It is part of our set of cultural assumptions that meaning is created (or not) by the autonomous individual. Consider, for example, how we understand our pervasive concern with "dying with dignity" in bioethics. A conventional explanation is that this involves returning to the patient control over his or her dying. But, as Kass has observed, it is far from clear that "dignity will reign only when we can push back officious doctors, machinery, and hospital administrators."[8] Dignity must be informed by meaning, and it is perhaps the case that we will achieve dying with meaning only as we understand the place of death within a notion of a meaningful life.

Moreover, within the vision of life as a journey, the hard cases, quandaries, and dramatic scenarios of bioethics are disclosed as but a time-slice in the narrative of a person's moral quest. A devotion to problem-solving both reflects and reinforces a cultural tendency to excise an individual from the social and temporal ties, from community and history, that present sources of meaning in the moral life.

Accommodating questions of meaning in bioethics will require that we broaden its scope beyond our current fixation with problem-solving, for some problems cannot be solved but must still be faced. This broader vision involves directing attention not only to the means of medicine, such as procedures for obtaining informed consent or the regulation of research protocols, but also the purposes of medicine within the context of a life conceived as a journey. For on such an account, health will be valued not merely for its own sake, but for the ends it allows us to pursue, while sickness and illness may signify not only inconvenient interruptions, but also teachers whose meaning we share with others through stories.

The journey metaphor, because it presupposes a conception of human ends, directly confronts us with questions about the moral presuppositions of a medicine wedded to technology and conquest of the endless frontier of scientific research. Formulating what these questions are, let alone answering them, is a task made more complex by the very successes of technological medicine, which may render prior, long-standing moral or religious concepts inadequate or in need of reinterpretation. For example, the suffering for generations associated with the experience of infertility—often reinforced culturally by religious worldviews—may now, through various technological interventions, be transformed into an instance of unnecessary suffering.

Is suffering such an unmitigated evil, and its perduring presence such a concession to failure, that medicine ought, as many have argued, to aspire to its elimination? Or does suffering require the compassion of persons who embody the meaning of care? Such matters are particularly acute in debates over active euthanasia, where eliminating suffering involves eliminating the person who suffers. Yet a medicine that aspires to achieve such a purpose may conflict with specific religious perspectives that see suffering as less a problem to be solved than as an unavoidable part of one's journey, and which assumes meaning in the context of that journey. For example, Paul Ramsey once rhetorically inquired whether "the purpose of modern medicine is to relieve the human condition of the human condition," by which Ramsey had particularly in mind the illness, disease, and suffering all persons experience as their mortal lot. Such an objective not only commits medicine to an impossible task, but one that risks dehumanizing its practitioners and patients.

To the extent that medicine is not morally bounded, or transforms conceptual boundaries, it may summon a theological critique essentially concerned with the theme of idolatry, of making of health an absolute, the end of the human journey, rather than a value whose meaning is intelligible only within some broader account of human nature and destiny. Such a critique will thus be directed against the assertion of an unbounded dominion expressed in some definitions of health, which threaten to transform every human problem into one that is or eventually can be susceptible to medical resolution. It is directed as well against pretensions to unbridled authority and control, and unlimited knowledge in the medical context, and against the well-intentioned aspiration to alleviate the common problems of the human condition in a way that is dehumanizing. Such pretensions and aspirations frequently converge in contemporary medicine's ongoing battle with the enemy of death.

In a culture void of meaning, death must appear as the crowning surd. Its power in our culture is disclosed in the ways we seek to evade it. The vast majority of persons now die in alien environments, institutions such as hospitals and nursing homes, which shelter the living from personally confronting death and may isolate the dying from all that has comprised their journey, including, at times, their families. For the living, moreover, our culture increasingly holds out a promise of technological deliverance, through the medicine of resuscitation or organ transplantation, for example, together with empirical data on "the risk" factor—typically the probability of contracting a disease or developing a condition that has some statistically significant correlation with death—of almost every conceivable activity. We seek to evade this ultimate assault on the self and yet, as Camus's Dr. Rieux comments, it organizes our lives and medical activities. "The order of the world is shaped by death."[9]

The value of life conveyed in the journey metaphor likewise implies that religious traditions cannot (and do not) look upon death with indifference. Indeed, on some accounts, death may be perceived as the pervasive sign of the intruding presence of evil. Life is a fundamental, even if not an absolute, good; the tragedy that we ascribe particularly to premature or "untimely" death from illness or accident is in part attributable to a sense that a person's journey has been interrupted.

Yet for all the shadows cast by death, we may also respond to it not as intruder but as deliverer from a completed mortal journey. That response underlies the interpretation of death as a "blessing" found in some traditions of religious ethics, often reflected in support for practices of only caring for the dying rather than prolonging life through unceasing technological support. The issue is not so much whether we can be delivered from death, either through relying on technological sustenance or institutional isolation, but rather how we might be delivered from meaningless death. The latter requires contextualizing death in a broader vision of human life, or as passage to ultimate destiny beyond life, and through practices of ministering to the dying in a community of care. In this respect, the traditions of religious discourse witness to a conviction that death is not the overriding power that governs our lives, but is itself subject to powers that are ultimate and supreme.

The nature and purpose of life, and the place of health, medicine, suffering, and death within a vision of human nature and destiny, while integral to religious discourse, are common human questions of meaning that often seem peripheral in the quandary-centered concerns of bioethics. A central contribution of religious traditions may therefore be to broaden our moral vision by raising issues of existential interest that are not typically addressed in contemporary bioethics. Precisely because these are human questions, they require examination, lest our assumptions about pluralism and ethics consequently compartmentalize our moral lives.

Priests and Prophets

We value bioethics in a pluralistic moral culture in part because of its capacities for peaceably resolving moral conflict about difficult practical dilemmas and hard cases. The success of bioethics in problem-solving is displayed in its increasing institutionalization in health care through the establishment of hospital ethics committees, ethics consultation groups, institutional review boards, and advisory commissions at state and national levels. In these various forums, bioethics discourse is prominently shaped by an ethic of principles—autonomy, beneficence, and justice—that seems well-suited as a method of conflict resolution because such norms are deemed to command general acceptance.

In managing and regulating the moral issues that arise in the delivery of health care, bioethics provides an important service for patients, their families, and clinical practitioners. Yet, while this "priestly" role (as it might be viewed in a religious perspective) is a necessary dimension of bioethics, it is not sufficient, for bioethics should be not only a source of solutions but also a source of problems.

Part of the responsibility of bioethics is to be "prophetic," challenging to accountability the institutional and professional presuppositions of the health care system and the society of which it is a part. No ethics committee can resolve the scandal of 31.5 million medically indigent persons in this country who may not have access to any institution to begin with. The prophetic responsibility of bioethics necessarily entails probing beneath the visible manifestations of the crisis to identify the root causes of the problem *and* articulating an alternative vision of the health care system based on ideals of justice in community that may be only approximated in practice. Religious traditions can enhance recognition and implementation of this responsibility, for it is the indicting message of the biblical traditions of this culture that the poor are not to be excluded from the community of moral concern.

Moreover, religious traditions can, in several respects, be significant for reminding us of the limitations of an ethic of principles. The normative principles of bioethics are not, for example, self-applying or self-interpreting, but instead require a context of application and a content informed by moral traditions—professional, secular, and religious. In this dialogue among traditions, religious discourse can illuminate and acknowledge the validity of a moral principle, even while challenging its conceptual presuppositions.

For example, central convictions of theological anthropology in biblical traditions, such as that human beings are created in the image of God, support the notion of intrinsic human dignity and respect for personal choice conveyed in bioethics discourse by the principle of autonomy. Yet such a principle will always appear theologically limited to the extent that its conceptual assumptions reflect an isolated individual severed from community and history. The scope of autonomous choices may be limited by the relational and narrative nature of the self, whose moral identity and character are forged in process of a temporal journey rather than in discrete instances of dramatic decisionmaking.

It would, moreover, be theologically narrow to focus on the moral self as a "decisionmaker" or "chooser." Human beings are more than the aggregate of their choices; the "person" whom one respects is an embodied self and the correlative attitude of "respect" must be holistic, acknowledging the moral significance of the bodily organism as well as concerns about liberty of action and freely willed decisions. The self is more than one's capacities for rational, cognitive activity just as the body is more than personal property. In addition, it may be misleading to understand autonomy as a moral ideal for human beings, since freedom of choice may be seriously compromised not only by illness, but also by what biblical traditions have typically designated as "sin," a condition that even Kant believed was so common and radical as to compromise the very conditions for autonomous choice.

An assessment of beneficence and justice can evoke similar kinds of overlap and critique. Beneficence conveys a sense of moral obligation and responsibility for the welfare of others, but its content and scope may seem minimalistic placed alongside norms of love of neighbor. Moral philosophers have often maintained that, beyond the fundamental requirement not to harm others, positive actions on behalf of the welfare of other persons are frequently discretionary, as suggested by the language of "imperfect duties" or "supererogation," or mediated by professional roles, such as those assumed by health care practitioners. The substantive requirements of love of neighbor, however, will often demand exceeding minimal or role responsibilities. The themes of self-sacrifice, assuming personal inconvenience and risk, and active seeking of the welfare of others beyond one's conventional community of concern, as displayed paradigmatically in the Christian narrative of the Good Samaritan, may entail that the discretionary takes on the character of the obligatory.

The sense that health care is a special kind of good has been an important conceptual underpinning for egalitarian schemes of allocating health care resources. This approach can be supported by the anthropology of the image of God, but it also may be qualified by a historically informed conception of preferential justice towards the poor, the oppressed, and the stranger. Justice may thus require more than a self-interested egalitarianism, namely, a commitment to give special priority to the health care needs of people and groups who have historically experienced oppression and marginalization in our culture. The preferential qualification of egalitarian justice reflects an attempt to redress inequalities stemming from natural and social "givens" with particular attention to the most vulnerable and voiceless in our society.

While religious traditions can point to the questions that need to be asked about the meaning and application of a moral principle, they can also inform judgments about what an ethic of principles neglects. For example, such an ethic assumes a sociology of strangers who share little in the way of common values and ends, and there are instances in medicine where such a situation obtains. It would be a mistake, however, to encompass all human relations, and thereby all human choices, under such a model. A richer sense of special moral relationships, embodied in families, friendships, congregations, or in professional collegiality, can attest to the moral significance religious traditions have historically placed on themes of community and covenant.

Nor do the normative principles of bioethics, to the extent that they focus our moral vision on questions of what should be done in a situation, give sufficient attention to the issue of what kind of people moral agents should be, or what kinds of virtues are necessary to sustain us in our temporal journey beyond the moment of decisionmaking. The moral teachings of religious traditions speak to matters of meekness, mercy, and purity; knowledge, temperance, and patience; gratitude, courage, and kindness; faith, hope, and love; issues of moral character and identity beyond the scope of decision-oriented principles. A comprehensive bioethics may find in religious discourse about virtues and dispositions an important source of moral correction and balance, one that places our decisions about health care within the context of a fuller account of purpose and meaning in life.

Acknowledgments

I wish to thank several persons who gave me helpful criticism and needed encouragement, particularly my colleagues at The Hastings Center, Daniel Callahan, Kathleen Nolan, Susan Wolf, and Michael Zeik, all of whom read prior versions of this article; Rabbi Marc Gellman, Ronald Green, Stephen Lammers, Richard Neuhaus, Philip Turner, and Alan Weisbard, who participated in a project meeting on Religion and Bioethics where another version of this article was discussed; and James F. Childress at the University of Virginia.

References

[1] H. Tristram Engelhardt, Jr., "Looking for God and Finding the Abyss: Bioethics and Natural Theology," in *Theology and Bioethics: Exploring the Foundations and Frontiers*, Earl E. Shelp, ed. (Boston: D. Reidel Publishing Company, 1985), 88.

[2] Leon R. Kass, "Practicing Ethics: Where's the Action?," *Hastings Center Report* 20:1 (January/February 1990), 6-7.

[3] Stanley Hauerwas, "The Testament of Friends," *The Christian Century* 107:7 (February 28, 1990), 213.

[4] President's Commission for the Study of Ethical Problems in Medicine and Biomedical and Behavioral Research, *Splicing Life* (Washington, D.C.: U.S. Government Printing Office, 1982), 54.

[5] For a more detailed account of this issue, see Kent Greenawalt, *Religious Convictions and Political Choice* (New York: Oxford University Press, 1988).

[6] Peter Singer, *Animal Liberation: A New Ethics for Our Treatment of Animals* (New York: Random House, Inc., 1975), 21.

[7] H. Tristram Engelhardt, Jr., "Fashioning an Ethic for Life and Death in a Post-Modern Society," *Hastings Center Report* 19:1 (January/February 1989), Special Supplement, 8.

[8] Leon R. Kass, "Averting One's Eyes, or Facing the Music?-On Dignity in Death," *Hastings Center Studies* 2:2 (May 1974), 69.

[9] Albert Camus, *The Plague* (New York: Vintage Books, 1948), 121.

Can Theology Have a Role in "Public" Bioethical Discourse?

by Lisa Sowle Cahill

Religious groups indubitably have been active in pressing their bioethical concerns in the public arena in the United States. One thinks preeminently of the efforts of the Roman Catholic Church and its representatives, or of religiously motivated "pro-life" activists, who quite visibly aim to influence public perceptions and policies on reproductive issues such as abortion and infertility therapies, and on dilemmas of life-prolongation, such as withdrawal of artificial nutrition and direct euthanasia. Have these church-based efforts any legitimacy in public policy formulation and if so, on what grounds? Or are they attempts to foist particularistic religious convictions on a pluralistic and otherwise free society, in violation of our prized tradition of separation of church and state?

At the same time that religious involvement in policy formation may seem unduly aggressive to some, from the perspectives of bioethics literature and medical practice or research, it often appears that theology brings little to bioethics which is even identifiably religious. When one inspects the work of individual theologians rather than ecclesial bodies—and especially when one advances beyond the well-tread ground staked out around abortion

Lisa Sowle Cahill is professor of Christian Ethics, Boston College, Boston, MA.

to tangle with issues such as genetic research or national health insurance—it may seem that religious faith and theological reflection fail to offer any guidance that could not have been arrived at by other means. Although "theologians" and "Christian ethicists" frequently address bioethics issues both in clinical settings and in print, even major figures such as Paul Ramsey and Richard McCormick often limit or avoid directly religious appeals in the interest of expanding their audience and hence influence. One might thus ask whether the result has any specifically theological stamp to it.

If by "theological" is meant a specific and unique line of religious argument entailing conclusions that also manifest a religious imprint, then theology is scarce in bioethics. Even clearly theological foundations, premises, and commitments do not necessarily lead to substantive moral principles, to arguments, or much less to concrete conclusions of a directly religious character, even though they may be endorsed strongly by religious groups. At the same time, the presence in bioethics of persons with theological training or with religious affiliations continues to give theology influence, even though this may not manifest itself in the explicit justification of moral conclusions. But it is more appropriate to construe theological contributions as overlapping and coinciding with philosophical ones, than to see secular, philosophical bioethics and religious, theological bioethics as two distinct or even competing entities.

As I see it, public bioethical discourse (or public policy discourse) is actually a meeting ground of the diverse moral traditions that make up our society. Some of these moral traditions have religious inspiration, but that does not necessarily disqualify them as contributors to the broader discussion. Their contributions will be appropriate and effective to the extent that they can be articulated in terms with a broad if not universal appeal. In other words, faith language that offers a particular tradition's beliefs about God as the sole warrant for moral conclusions will convince only members of that tradition. But faith commitments can legitimately motivate participants in public discussion to seek a moral consensus consistent with their faith while at the same time be congenial to members of other moral traditions, the persuasion of whom may be the object of religious groups and theologians who argue and act for social change.

A Commitment to Dialogue and Openness

As James Gustafson has indicated, theology rarely yields precise and concrete directives for bioethical decisionmaking, or commends insights and actions inaccessible to nonreligious persons. But theology does have a critical function in "public" discourse, if the edge of religious commitment càn be sharpened so as to cut through cultural assumptions.[1] Theologians and religious groups can introduce the civil community to insights borne by their own traditions, *on the assumption that and provided that* these traditions are not sheerly insular nor the civil community a wholly foreign country in which values with originally religious sponsorship are entirely unintelligible.

One should not, moreover, approach the issue of the contribution of theology to bioethics on the assumption that there exists some independent realm of secular or philosophical discourse, privileged as more reasonable, neutral, or objective, and less tradition-bound, than religious discourse. If such a realm is posited, then theology is seen potentially as entering it to be talkative, or remaining outside it in silence. To speak of distinctly secular language and arguments also implies that to be intelligible, religious or theological language must undergo some sort of "translation" into the lingua franca—into some different vocabulary universally understood. But this is a distorted understanding both of religious traditions and their theologies, and of what happens in "public" discourse about bioethics.

Bioethical discussions (and other "public" or intertraditional discussions of ethics) begin in situations of common *practical* interest; a dilemma about the nature of a *practical* moral obligation gives a common starting-point. A real or envisioned situation of moral agency presents questions and stimulates participants to think theoretically. Discussion partners come to be so on the basis of such situations, and they enter them as persons from quite different, yet sometimes shared, or overlapping, moral and religious communities. Attempts to fashion a life together, a life that necessarily involves moral obligations and decisions, force us to arrive at some mutual understanding of what that would mean—especially in its practical results. Yet we do not participate in this process via an objective, traditionless, secular version of philosophical reasoning. The preeminent and supposedly neutral vocabulary of public policy debates in the U.S. today (liberty, autonomy, rights, privacy, due process) itself comes out of a rather complex but distinct set of political, legal, philosophical, moral, and even religious *traditions*. Though these are far from universal to humankind, they have over a three-hundred-year period come to be constitutive of a certain shared North American perspective. As Jeffrey Stout puts it, there is no privileged vantage point "above the fray."[2]

To follow Stout's evocative terminology,[3] there is also no universal and neutral language, no "Esperanto," into which theological language can be translated. Moreover, it is mistaken to expect theologians to adopt some sort of "pidgin," implying that, even if not philosophically fluent, theologians ought to try to master some dominant language, a language rising above all special commitments and points of view, the language in which those no longer hampered by an immigrant, ghetto mentality are already conversing. What ethicists do manage, as they speak beyond but always out of their native traditions, is what Stout (reinterpreting the term from Claude Levi-Strauss) calls "bricolage," a borrowing of what is not only handy but appropriate and communicative in jostling, negotiating, and persuading toward a common moral sense.

It is also useful to keep in mind that ethical discourse occurs on different levels and in different contexts, and that differentiated methods and goals may be appropriate to each. In a reminder to this effect, James Gustafson distinguishes four complementary modes of ethics: analytical ethics, public policy ethics, narrative ethics, and prophetic ethics.[4] The first, which Gustafson calls "ethical discourse," is aimed at finding moral justifications for specific actions and decisions, while the interrelated modes of narrative and prophetic discourse present larger questions about worldview, community identity, and basic values. Public policy discourse can be "ethical discourse" when it is more disciplined and distanced from the actual political process. But policy discourse can also be carried out by persons with institutional roles, who ask practical questions. In such a case, bioethics is not "purely" ethical because it deals with the "enabling and limiting conditions" of practical social options, rather than with a more philosophical delineation of the ideally good society, institution, or policy.[5]

Using Gustafson's categories, one will note that policy discussions occur precisely in the arena in which some common courses of action must be agreed upon, despite less agreement at the "metaethical" level. To construct a language of "principles" that will serve this purpose is a necessary achievement, however limited. We will also discover that even analyses at the highest theoretical levels take place within some "narrative" traditions, that is, within communities shaped by, to use Gustafson's language, "formative narratives."[6] Both ethical and institutional varieties of policy discussion also occur within narratives, or at least on the basis of narratives that may be partially transcended as common ground is sought. Consensus-shaping policy efforts search for and build on the existing ground shared by traditions; they seek to illumine the aspects of a narrative that can encompass more particular stories.

Like narrative ethics, prophetic ethics advances special agendas over against common views or practices, and does so both by "indictment," and by "utopian" visions that can raise human aspirations.[7] Prophetic ethics has as its agenda the introduction of particular values into the mainstream, to shift the geography of the ground occupied in common, that is to say, to reconfigure the governing narrative.

It follows that it is best to construe "public discourse" not as a separate *realm* into which we can and ought to enter tradition-free, but as embodying a *commitment* to civil exchanges among traditions, many of which have an overlapping membership, and which meet on the basis of common concerns. The language of "secular" and "publicly accessible" serves exactly to exhort persons from traditions to adopt a stance of dialogue and openness, of mutual critique, of commitment to consensus and to hammering out institutions and policies that will affect the common life for "the better," as defined on the broadest consensus we can achieve. It is a commitment to the dialogic and consensual mode of discourse, or perspective, or attitude, or stance, that is indicated by the expectation that religious and other traditions will make public rather than particularistic appeals in addressing civil society or the body politic.

Community with Others

In struggling toward a conclusion within the "public" realm of discourse, Christians, Jews, or other religious persons will of course be influenced by their religiously based values. They will look for ways to live in community with others—that is, in the many communities in which they participate—that are consistent with their religious way of being (say, as a covenant people, or as disciples), as well as with their theoretical or theological reflection on that way of life. Biblical, especially New Testament, models exist for this sort of approach. St. Paul, for instance, borrows freely from the surrounding culture (as in the "vice lists" of *1 Corinthians* 5:11, and 6:9-10) in his writings about morality. Paul seems to feel no necessity to carve out something that is uniquely Christian in morality, for its own sake. His primary concern is to discern what sort of activity is appropriate for persons with a special religious identity. Then, on concrete moral issues he accepts or rejects cultural practices in view of their relation to the communal vocation of discipleship. Although Christianity poses profound questions about "wordly" power, authority, and values, it does not necessarily demand that all moral expectations which are not specifically Christian be set aside or judged irrelevant to the Christian portrayal of the moral life. As Wayne Meeks has observed, the New Testament literature expresses a process of "resocialization" in the early church, in which new social relationships and identities were forged, even though Christians might simultaneously continue to live as members of other communities with their own values, sometimes overlapping with Christian values, and sometimes challenged by them.[8]

Meeks has also suggested that the importance of religious commitment for ethics lies in its function to form communities that then interact with the broader culture in provocative ways. Just as the biblical narratives were generated by a social environment in which the new religious identity of Christianity served a critical function, so Christian communities today mediate their religious commitment into society through a "hermeneutics of social embodiment" of the biblical witness.[9] The relevance of religion to bioethics does not lie primarily in any distinct or specific contribution to the process of moral argumentation, nor in lifting up "religious" behaviors defensible only on faith, revelation, or church authority. Rather it depends on the formation of socially radical communities that challenge dominant values and patterns of social relationship, not by withdrawing from the larger society, or by speaking to it from outside, but by participating in it in challenging and even subversive ways.

A Countercultural Edge

It is important that, in thinking bioethically, theologians hone the critical edge of religious or theological interest. To be more specific, a person from a Jewish or Christian religious tradition might have sensibilities and interests that would make her or him more attuned to certain biblically based themes, such as the well-being of creation, God's providence, human responsibility, and human finitude and sinfulness.[10] Other themes include love of neighbor and a "preferential option for the poor" and vulnerable, mercy to others as God is merciful to us, forgiveness of others as we expect to be forgiven by God, and repentance for our sins. In nonreligious terms these themes cash out as service, not only autonomy; solidarity and integration within community; the dignity of all human beings, and special advocacy for the most vulnerable; sensitivity to our own finitude and the limits that we confront in all the projects we undertake. Recognizing and retaining the countercultural edge of such commitments is the first task of the theologian, even as he or she acknowledges that it will have few direct payoffs in particular bioethical decisions and analyses.

For instance, invoking the narrative, prophetic mode, Protestant theologians Stanley Hauerwas and Allen Verhey criticize decisions to let severely abnormal newborns die. They draw on Christian themes without claiming either that these themes *require* particular decisions, or that *only* these themes would enjoin decisions to sustain life. Hauerwas claims, "The cross provides a pattern of interpretation which allows one to locate the pointlessness of suffering within a cosmic framework,"[11] while Verhey maintains that "the eschatological vision of Christianity—and the entire Jesus story—enlists us on the side of life and health in a world where death and evil still apparently reign." This vision also "calls us to identify with and to serve especially the sick and the poor, the powerless and the despised, and all those who do not measure up to conventional standards."[12] Although many Christians would no doubt see acceptance of death as an appropriate choice for some infants, they would agree nonetheless that the tradition would make such choices a rare exception within an ethos of nurturance and sacrifice.

Hauerwas and Verhey represent a somewhat more biblical and confessional strand within Christian theology; their audience is characteristically the Christian community itself. Hence they emphasize the specifically Christian "narrative" and themes, while "prophetically" exhorting the community to create patterns of moral action that correspond to its religious commitments. A contrasting approach is represented by Roman Catholicism. Catholic moral theology historically has manifested a greater interest in explicitly "public" discourse and has in its service developed a "natural law" moral language claiming to analyze with some precision shared human (not religious) values. While doctrines such as creation, humanity's status as "image of God," and the supernatural destiny of human beings lie in the background of the natural law approach, it still assumes that there are basic human characteristics and values which obtain cross-culturally, and which ought to provide a basis for moral thinking and social order. The nature and extent of these "basics," as well as their practical implications, provide the often controversial subject matter of ethics. As articulated by Joseph Fuchs, S.J., Catholic ethics is based in faith in the sense of a deep personal "giving and entrusting" to God, but "no concrete ethics" can be developed out of faith so understood. Thus, Catholic ethics "has generally presented itself as a philosophical ethics: its reflections, its principles, and its reasonings differ hardly at all, in a formal sense, from those of a philosopher."[13]

Yet even contemporary natural law thinkers are increasingly ready to recognize the "postmodern" emphasis on contextualism, particularity, and tradition, and hence also to recognize that Catholic natural law thinking, while aiming at the "universal," is worked out within a historically particular religious tradition: Christianity as Catholicism. Nonetheless, the tradition continues to represent a commitment to cross-traditional communication, aiming at the broadest community possible. In the modern papal encyclicals from John XXIII forward, the community addressed has even been global, for example, in regard to the "universal common good," on issues such as arms control and international development. In narrower political communities, such as the nation, local prelates may work to raise moral consciousness about issues whose practical importance they consider not to be limited to their own church. Their effectiveness in achieving this goal—and even their legitimacy in attempting to achieve it—depends on their success in framing the moral issues in terms that can in fact strike a responsive chord in a constituency formed from a plurality of communities within the larger political order.

If religiously motivated speakers from particular traditions are to contribute to the sort of public consensus that can support policy initiatives, they will need to do so on the basis of moral quandaries, moral sensibilities, moral images, and moral vocabulary shared among other religious and moral traditions (as an ethics without tradition does not exist.) Such morally formative factors are not sheerly "universal," nor need they be. Consensus in and about the public order is contingent not on genuine universality, but on intelligibility and persuasiveness within a community of communities broad enough to encompass the society to be ordered. (This is not to deny that at least at a very fundamental level, the whole human race might be considered a "community," sharing certain minimal moral insights in common. But even if so, such insights would *practically* demand to be worked into consistent moral expectations and social institutions within derivative communities shaped historically in more differentiated ways.)

In the United States, a Roman Catholic example of the explicitly intertraditional appeal is the writings and addresses of Joseph Cardinal Bernardin. During the 1984 presidential election, Bernardin shaped a moral vision ("the consistent ethic of life") based on the interconnection of "life issues," including but not limited to abortion, capital punishment, and nuclear war. Although obviously a religious leader wielding both religious and moral authority, Bernardin does not advance his position on specifically religious grounds. In a recent address focused on abortion (Georgetown University, March 20, 1990), Bernardin tried to persuade his audience that the moral issue of who decides should not overwhelm the issue of what it is that is decided. Specifically, how does a community grant or refuse the recognition of "humanity" in debatable cases? Appealing for a consensus that "at the very heart of public order is the protection of human life and basic human rights," Bernardin asks, "What happens to our moral imagination and social vision if the right to life is not protected for those who do not look fully human at the beginning or end of life?" Recognizing that a large percentage of Americans do not identify themselves either with pro-choice or pro-life positions, the Cardinal "invites" this constituency to agreement that the human fetus is a value to be protected, and thus to "join us in setting significant limits on abortion."[14] His intended audience may or may not come to concur that although early fetuses do not "look" human, they deserve the full protection due children and adults; nor may it be persuaded that the limits on abortion ought to be "significant." The point here is rather that Bernardin's identity as a religious leader does not disqualify his participation in the public debate, and his success in this forum will depend precisely on his ability to join issues in a way that can elicit or instigate broad agreement. No politician, philosopher, or "humanist" marches into the contest armed only with the sharp sword of reason, stripped naked of the costume of any moral culture—however invisible he or she might wish that clothing to be. Each will succeed on demonstrated ability to find and enlarge the common ground on which originally disparate forces can be joined around a mutual cause.

Jeffrey Stout's notion of a "creole" language is illuminating here: a language that begins as a simplified "bridge dialect" to enable communication among unconnected communities, but "eventually gets rich enough for use as a language of moral reflection (e.g., the language of human rights)."[15] Bernardin puts his case in the vocabulary of public order, human life, and basic human rights, hoping to be persuasive on grounds that are not narrowly "Catholic" or "religious." Where Bernardin and other Roman Catholic representatives might differ with historically more biblical communities and theologians such as Stanley Hauerwas and Allen Verhey is in the former's confidence that essential and recognizable human values (e.g., human life) ground any cultural specification; in their stronger belief that religion supports these human values; and in their optimism about the ability of discussion partners in good faith to come to agreement not only on what the basic values are, but on how they should be implemented practically. Hauerwas and Verhey would emphasize the critical or "witnessing" function of religion (its narrative and prophecy), while Fuchs and Bernardin would stress the motivation it gives to join in moral analysis and public efforts toward consensus on better social institutionalization of "human" values (the contributions it makes to ethical discourse and to policy). As Gustafson has argued, these contributions are not mutually exclusive but complementary.

Roles of Theology in Bioethics

The role of theology in bioethics is, first of all, to clarify for the religious community itself what the shape of its life should be in the relevant areas. Even within the community, however, theology will yield fewer specific norms than it will more fundamental affirmations of the values and commitments that should undergird the identity and challenge the decision-making of religious persons. Indeed, articulating moral norms will usually require the interaction of religious values and theological reflection with other sources, such as philosophy, the natural and social sciences, and careful analysis of implications and consequences. The second role of theology is to move the religious community toward active participation in the broader or overlapping communities with which its members are in some way affiliated, and in which specific norms and policies for those communities are hammered out. Beginning especially from questions of common practice, theology can influence policy through a prophetic function that challenges the civil community to consider more seriously values and alternatives which other traditions and established forms of life may have neglected. Theology also contributes at a more precise analytic level, in which a common language of moral analysis is forged by traditions that are on speaking terms, and which, more importantly, share a commitment to mutual criticism and to progress toward consensus.

References

1. James M. Gustafson, *The Contributions of Theology to Medical Ethics* (Milwaukee, WI: Marquette University Theology Department, 1975).
2. Jeffrey Stout, *Ethics After Babel: The Languages of Morals and Their Discontents* (Boston: Beacon Press, 1988), 282.
3. Stout, *Ethics After Babel*, 294.
4. James M. Gustafson, "Moral Discourse About Medicine: A Variety of Forms," *The Journal of Medicine and Philosophy* 15:2 (1990), 125-42.
5. Gustafson, "Moral Discourse," 140-41.
6. Gustafson, "Moral Discourse," 137.
7. Gustafson, "Moral Discourse," 130-31.
8. Wayne Meeks, *The Moral World of the First Christians* (Philadelphia: Westminster Press, 1955), 126.
9. Wayne Meeks, "A Hermeneutics of Social Embodiment," *Harvard Theological Review* 79:1-3 (1986), 176-86.
10. Gustafson, *Contributions of Theology*, 18-25.
11. Stanley Hauerwas, "Reflections on Suffering, Death, and Medicine," in *Suffering Presence: Theological Reflections on Medicine, the Mentally Handicapped, and the Church* (Notre Dame, IN: University of Notre Dame Press, 1986), 31.
12. Allen Verhey, "The Death of Infant Doe: Jesus and the Neonates," in *On Moral Medicine: Theological Perspectives in Medical Ethics*, Stephen E. Lammers and Allen Verhey, eds. (Grand Rapids, MI: Eerdmans, 1987), 492.
13. Joseph Fuchs, "'Catholic' Medical Moral Theology?," in *Catholic Perspectives on Medical Morals*, Edmund D. Pellegrino et al., eds. (Dordrecht: Kluwer, 1989), 85, 83.
14. As quoted by Thomas H. Stahel, "Cardinal Bernardin on the 'Forgotten Factor' and Other Gaps in the Abortion Debate," *America* 162:13 (1990), 354-56.
15. Stout, *Ethics After Babel*, 294.

Bioethics and the Contemporary Jewish Community

by David Novak

The enormous growth of interest in questions of normative ethics, which has come in direct response to the even greater growth of medical technologies during the past twenty-five years or so, has had a profound resonance in the contemporary Jewish community. Many prominent Jewish scholars have taken it upon themselves to address questions of bioethics, drawing upon the vast resources of the normative Jewish tradition. In these efforts they have received much encouragement from the wider Jewish community; indeed,

David Novak is the Edgar M. Bronfman Professor of Modern Judaic Studies at the University of Virginia, Charlottesville, VA.

a few scholars have gained considerable recognition both within the Jewish community and beyond it because of their ability to articulate their own expertise in this new area of intense public interest. And not only has bioethics raised the whole field of normative Jewish ethics to a level of public prestige it has not enjoyed since premodern times, it has also placed more traditionalist rather than more liberal scholars in a new position of authority as spokespersons for Judaism to the wider non-Jewish world. This quiet revolution in the Jewish community can be appreciated only against the backdrop of the rise of bioethics as an area of intellectual and political interest in our society.

Normative Authority and the Holocaust

For all the centuries when Jews had communal sovereignty, and the relative social and cultural isolation it presupposes, traditional Jewish law known as *halakhah* (what Christians have usually seen as "the Law") governed the communal and individual lives of Jews. There was no area of human activity with which it was not concerned and about which it did not have much to say. Even though Jewish intellectual pursuits were certainly not exclusively confined to questions of *halakhah* as normative ethics, *halakhah* always functioned minimally as the negative limit for Jewish discourse and action. Ultimately, nothing was allowed to contradict its norms.

This situation changed radically when the communal sovereignty of the Jewish community was eliminated by the emergence of the modern national state, which eventually accorded Jews the rights of full citizenship as individuals. The Enlightenment brought with it a secularism that most Jews welcomed as giving them, at long last, equal social space in European civilization and the opportunities to become fully contributing members. For most Jews, the Enlightenment was seen as the emancipation from the ghetto and all its restrictions. However, these cultural developments accorded nothing to the traditional Jewish community as the mediating social structure between individual Jews and the non-Jewish body politic. One immediate and profound result of this radical shift was that *halakhah* no longer served as the norm for all of Jewish life. The structure of all-encompassing authority it presupposed was simply no longer present.

Within the Jewish community, the most secularist elements saw this shift as the end of the authority of *halakhah* in toto. In this view, Jews were now entirely part of another world and would have to derive normative guidance for how to live from the moral resources of that world. Either explicitly or by strong implication, these Jews advocated abrupt, or more often gradual assimilation into the surrounding society.

Except for ultraorthodox East European Jews, especially the Hasidim, who rejected this new situation of modernity altogether and strove to retreat from its advance, even many Orthodox Jews were willing to formulate Jewish responses to the questions raised by the modern world in a decidedly nonhalakhic way. Thus, the leader of this more worldly orthodoxy in Germany, Samson Raphael Hirsch (1808-1888), characterized his approach as *Torah im Derekh Eretz*, roughly translated as, "The Torah together with worldliness." Whereas more specific internally Jewish questions pertaining to such areas as diet, family status, and worship were still discussed according to the ancient norms of *halakhah*, more general questions pertaining to such areas as politics and economics were now addressed according to the general principles of what was considered to be "universal ethics" (which almost always meant Kantian ethics).

Inasmuch as thinkers from the more liberal religious elements in the Jewish community, usually from the Reform movement, felt greater comfort with this new universal ethics, they typically articulated Jewish responses to these more general questions, such as the standards for a just society and proper role of Jews within it. Orthodox thinkers who attempted to deal with these new questions within the old halakhic framework rarely had much of an audience among acculturated Jews, and virtually none at all among non-Jews.

The rise of bioethics has, however, effected a profound change in discourse about ethics in the Jewish community. Bioethics shifted ethical concern toward the more specific normative questions that arise in the wake of new medical technologies and away from abstract discussion of general principles or the analysis of the logic of general ethical language (metaethics). Bioethics has brought "hard cases," which had usually been relegated to the suspect discipline of "casuistry," to the center stage of ethical discourse. This concern with specifics forced ethicists generally to look at traditions of religious ethics with a new interest and respect, since these traditions had dealt with specific issues of practical ethics over a long period of time, amassing a considerable body of precedent for contemporary research.

This shift in interest from the general to the specific, and thereby from the novel to the historical, has permitted traditionalist legal scholars, such as David Feldman, J. David Bleich, and this author, at long last to belie the charge made by Jewish and even non-Jewish liberals that *halakhah* is basically irrelevant, that it cannot deal with the questions of real concern in the modern world. It has granted both *halakhah* and those committed to its continuing authority an unaccustomed prominence. A new group of prospectors are suddenly interested in tapping the riches of religious traditions, and the Jewish tradition in particular. And these new prospectors are in need of reliable and knowledgeable guides to show them just where within the labyrinths of this gold mine the richest deposits lie. This new interest has made some traditionalist experts in normative Jewish ethics now feel like the rabbinical student who reputedly one day burst into the Talmudic academy proclaiming, "I have an answer, I have an answer—please ask me a question!" There is no greater stimulus to research and publication of one's results than to learn that there is indeed an audience for what is to be uncovered and applied.

Another stimulus for the particular Jewish interest in bioethics is the fact that Jews still very much live in the dark shadow of the Holocaust. When one speaks of bioethics, especially as it pertains to the activities of physicians and others who directly treat human bodies, Jews become acutely aware that concentration camp inmates, mostly Jews, were made the subjects of the most ghastly tortures, which were rationalized as experiments for the sake of medical progress. Thus Jews are intensely sensitive to what happens when medicine is conducted without ethical restraint and direction, without which it can and did degenerate into organized sadism.

For example, the shadow of the Holocaust effects the Jewish approach to such moral problems as abortion and euthanasia. Concerning abortion, one sees the generally restrictive approach of the halakhic tradition reinforced by an affirmation of a pronatal policy, at least in the Orthodox community. The fact that virtually no Jewish children survived Nazi captivity, and that abortions were regularly performed on Jewish women, certainly influences this pronatal stance. Regarding euthanasia, many Jews express an abhorrence for the general notion, prevalent today, that some persons are better off dead than alive. This abhorrence is decisively shaped by the Nazi policy of genocide, which was proceeded by a policy of mass euthanasia (*unwerteslebens Leben*).

Tradition and Society

These two elements, the renewed interest in specifically normative ethics and the perversion of medicine by Nazi physicians, have made bioethics an area of intense Jewish inquiry. That shows no sign of abating. The methodological question that is just beginning to be discussed, however, is exactly how the teachings of Jewish tradition can be included in the world of general moral discourse without being absorbed by it.

In dealing with the bioethical revolution in society at large, more traditionalist thinkers in the Jewish community, precisely because they are rooted in a normative base that, for them, has remained fundamentally intact, rushed to the fore to become the spokespersons for the community. Such a development seemed to be almost a fulfillment of the prophetic prediction that the gentiles would eventually come to Zion to be instructed out of the Torah of the Lord. Nevertheless, the problem faced by such thinkers was just how one speaks to a general, secular society out of a singular religious tradition. Christian ethicists face the same problem, albeit from a different angle. Whereas Jews must devise ways to speak to a world that has never been theirs, Christians must devise ways to speak to a world that once was theirs but is no longer.

Jewish approaches to bioethical questions (and other questions of social import as well) reflect two distinct models, although they are often not explicated in the course of dealing with the specific normative issues at hand. These ought to be identified, however, since their respective methodologies will frequently lead to quite different practical conclusions.

The first model has tended to be the *modus operandi* of most Orthodox Jewish thinkers in bioethics such as Immanuel Jakobovits, Moses Tendler, and Fred Rosner. It is a model that contains a hidden triumphalist premise: God has given a full and sufficient law to the Jews and a partial law to the gentiles. The law for the Jews, which is the Mosaic Torah along with its rabbinic interpretations and elaborations, contains numerous norms of great specificity, whereas the law for the gentiles contains a mere seven very general norms. This general, gentile law is known in Jewish tradition as the "noahide commandments" or "noahide law"—"Noahides" (the descendants of Noah) being a synonym for humankind. Since the revelation to the Jews is both necessary and sufficient for moral direction whereas the revelation to the gentiles is only necessary but quite insufficient because of its vague generality, it seems to follow that the traditional Jewish community assumes the role of guardian of pure revelation. As such, the community is clearly meant to function as the moral decisor for the rest of the world, from whom the true meaning of the law must be sought. In fact, what emerges from this model is that the Torah has both a direct application to the Jews themselves and an indirect application to the rest of the world. All of this is very similar to the concept and institution of *jus gentium* in Roman law. There a civil law (*jus civile*, literally "the city law") obtained for full Roman citizens, and the more general *jus gentium* bound non-Roman citizens who lived under Roman political jurisdiction. The important point of this analogy is that *jus gentium* was interpreted and enforced by Roman authorities.

In this model, then, there will be spokespersons eager and ready to present "the Jewish position" on any and every ethical question. However, once the triumphalist assumption is exposed, it is difficult to see how the conclusions based on it can be accepted by anyone not personally committed to the full hegemony of Jewish tradition. Can one accept Judaism as the final moral arbiter without, in good faith, becoming a Jew? Indeed, many have accused the Roman Catholic Church of relying on the same assumption, namely, asserting that natural law is something that obtains for all human beings in any society, while the final arbiter of what natural law is and is not turns out to be the magisterium of the Church. The same problem many non-Roman Catholics (and many Roman Catholics as well) have with this approach is one, *mutatis mutandis*, many non-Jews should have with the triumphalist Jewish approach, once its premises and conclusions are understood.

A second model present in Jewish approaches to bioethics is more closely akin to the concept of *jus naturale*. It asserts that certain basic moral norms can be held in common by all rational persons and can thus function as a foundation for a common life together. Hence, if the Jewish tradition has something to say to the world, it will not be conveyed in the authoritative sense described above. Rather, the tradition can present its insights as a body of rich information for rational deliberation in a common realm of discourse and action. This model has been used in the recent past more by liberal Jewish thinkers than by traditionalists, and it is likewise reflected in most statements on ethical questions issued by the major Jewish organizations in the U.S. The problem with this model is that in contemporary society the language of natural law has evolved into the language of minimalist natural rights. And unlike classical natural law theory, theories of natural rights proposed by thinkers like John Rawls and Ronald Dworkin have no place for religious claims at all.

Religious Pluralism and a Public Philosophy

In the Jewish community, therefore, one can adopt an authoritative, traditionalist, approach or a natural rights approach. The former model supposes acceptance of the moral authority of a singular religious community, something impossible for most outsiders short of actual conversion. The latter model, conversely, seems to eliminate religious claims altogether. Is there any third alternative—one that can avoid the pitfalls of these two other approaches?

It seems to me that before a religious community can address the wider public square it first must address other religious communities in a pluralistic democratic context. In my own case, involvement in Jewish-Christian dialogue over several years has very much influenced the way I deal with issues of public ethics—particularly bioethical issues—that concern the full range of humankind. For what Jews and Christians share in common is a *theonomous* ethics, that is, some basic norms whose ultimate context is the covenantal relationship with God lived by Judaism and Christianity in their respective ways. For example, I have identified four areas of commonality between Judaism and Christianity, all of which have immediate ethical significance. These include: (1) the primary purpose of human life is to be related to God; (2) the relationship with God is primarily practical rather than contemplative; (3) human sociality in relationship with God and other persons is covenantal; and (4) ultimate human fulfillment will come only through a redemptive act of God.[1]

It is not only that Jews and Christians each see their tradition as emerging out of the Hebrew Bible, which both communities revere as the word of God, but equally important that both communities have developed remarkably similar ways of treating human persons. This results in a common ethical stance on many issues of import, including issues of bioethics.

What Jews and Christians can do when addressing bioethical questions in concert is to demonstrate to the larger world that their common approach offers a more coherent means for dealing with specific ethical questions than secular methods. This approach may demonstrate, for example, that a more inclusive notion of humanness can be seen in the Judeo-Christian doctrine of the human person as *imago Dei* than from competing secularist ideas of either individual autonomy or collective heteronomy. This is surely important because abuses of medical treatment are most likely to occur when too many are relegated to nonhuman status.

The discussion of bioethical and other issues in our society today by Jews requires developing a public philosophy that can constitute a pluralism of religious traditions, and even have it extend to the value democratic secularists extol most—tolerance. This new religious pluralism can make room for secularists in public discourse more than secularism can make room for Jewish and Christian believers, for religious pluralism can constitute the integrity of the secular realm far better than secularism can constitute the integrity of the religious realm. Thus, for example, this new religious pluralism can fully accept the intellectual independence of science and the freedom of inquiry it requires, because this religious pluralism does not claim cultural sufficiency. Secularism, conversely, by claiming such cultural sufficiency, cannot accept the public presence of religious traditions and can only relegate them, at best, to an absolutely private realm. As such, this public philosophy can display a rhetoric where religious traditions *inform* ethical discourse without also insisting that theological premises be accepted in advance.

This is the lesson to be learned from Jewish-Christian dialogue at its best. Instead of demanding theological compliance as a pre-condition for deducing practical conclusions, the dialogue begins with practical problems—especially ethical problems—and attempts to construct a common approach based on overlapping theological principles. But it is always aware that, short of the final redemption of the world by God, this commonality can only be partial. Thus it can affirm a common Judeo-Christian *ethic* on a number of key points without denying that there is Jewish *theology* and Christian *theology*. Just as Jews, then, can cogently recognize the integrity of Christianity without becoming Christians, and Christians can recognize the integrity of Judaism without becoming Jews, this new public philosophy can show how Jews and Christians can recognize the integrity of the secular realm without thereby become secularists.

This, it seems to me, provides the most generous atmosphere possible for the discussion and common resolution of the ethical problems that have become so acute in the contemporary world, bioethical problems being among the most obvious examples. Jewish thinkers are quite well prepared to make their own contribution in this area if they have learned much from their tradition, from their experience in the modern world, and from their critical reason.

Reference

[1] David Novak, *Jewish-Christian Dialogue: A Jewish Justification* (New York: Oxford University Press 1989).

What Can Religion Offer Bioethics?

by James P. Wind

The fact that we have to ask what religion can offer bioethics points to an enigma present within bioethics and in American society as a whole. As specialized professionals and as a people we make room for individuals with religious perspectives at the same time that we conduct our daily affairs as if those perspectives made little difference. Religion permeates American lives, but its actual contributions to our common life remain in doubt.

In comparison with well-entrenched disciplines in the modern university, bioethics is a young field where people from many backgrounds—including religious ones—can carve out niches. No entrance requirements exist to screen out people who wish to draw upon religious or theological perspectives. Moreover, many of the field's early shapers were theologians or people open to discourse about theology.

Yet the discipline of bioethics came of age just as secularism crested as a social movement (the 1960s) and was formed by people—including some theologians—who often found secular institutions and causes more promising than religious ones. The ethos of bioethics is now pronouncedly secular. That is due in part to its subject matter and social location. Its issues arise within and between medical, scientific, legal, economic, and political worlds—contexts where technical, professional, and secular ways of thinking and speaking are most in vogue. This secular tone is also attributable to the socialization patterns of most of those drawn to bioethics. By and large they are products of graduate and professional schools that nurture and reward secular habits of thought. Further, those who address bioethics issues are acutely aware of modern pluralism and seek a public discourse that transcends worlds of particular beliefs and commitments. They feel the pressure of new life-or-death problems that demand immediate response and are wary of debates that can bog down in the minutiae of insiders' conversations. Thus, despite openness to religious perspectives and a historic indebtedness to a distinguished generation of theological ethicists, it remains unclear just what religion can offer the young and complex field of bioethics. Is it possible to identify some potential contributions that religion might make to our current bioethical discourse?

An Honest Appraisal

It is best to begin cautiously and honestly. Some will fear—for biographical and historical reasons—that religion's main contributions to bioethics will be chaos, confusion, and hostility. These critics will point to the package of problems we call "pluralism." Religion and theology bring to public discourse particular truth claims, private languages, and special warrants that do not convince people who do not share heritages and basic assumptions about the world. Thus to invite religious traditions to contribute to public bioethics discourse seems like an invitation to conflict and entanglement in unresolvable debates. The spectre of lethal religious conflict haunts both our newspapers and our history books. What contributions could possibly be so important that we would risk letting this menacing genie out of the two-hundred-year-old bottle fashioned by the Enlightenment?

Such a view overlooks the fact that pluralism has more than a contentious downside—much more. If we consider the 218 denominations, the more than 200 seminaries, the many religion departments in U.S. colleges and universities, and the more than 340,000 local congregations that various statisticians monitor,[1] the breadth and pervasiveness of American religiosity becomes apparent. To attempt to deal with life and death decisions, with matters of health and suffering—the special interests of bioethics—as if this teeming religiousness did not exist is therefore to engage in a self-deception of monumental proportions. Their secular "everydayishness" notwithstanding, the majority of Americans express themselves religiously. They come to their moments of medical decisionmaking (both personal and political) with particular beliefs and commitments.

Attending to religion requires us both to be honest about who we are as a people and to be more responsive to the full humanity with which we deal in bioethics. Religion's first contribution, then, is to furnish a more accurate view of the human beings whom we encounter in the secular worlds of the academy, health care, and public policy. If, as many argue, our secular ethical language of rights and duties screens out the religious interpretations and perspectives people carry into these settings, the result is human fragmentation and alienation. Patients, policymakers, and health care professionals do not park their beliefs at the bioethical door. Instead they smuggle them in—in plain wrappers—beneath the surface of much of our technical secular discourse. An honest encounter with religious pluralism can make us more responsive to human particularity, more compassionate, able to offer more complete care.

At their best, religious communities and their theologians can contribute

---

James P. Wind is program director, Religion Division, Lilly Endowment, Inc. He was formerly senior associate at the Park Ridge Center, and editor of Second Opinion.

to the emergence of fuller, more complete views of the human. Religious communities have views of humanity that are often higher and lower than our conventional wisdom. These traditions know limits and face them (an ability that is still quite underdeveloped in our culture.) Some remind us of finitude and fallenness at the same time that they draw upon deep reservoirs of hope. Many challenge false optimisms and undermine the many determinisms that are part of our collective consciousness. They reflect experience with surprise and tragedy, and foster self-criticism and openness to corrective vision from others.

In articulating their fundamental visions and purposes these communities and traditions can contribute to a more variegated or motley view of humanity, helping us see more of the full marvel present in each human being. Instead of a restrictive or reductionistic view they can suggest more expansive ones, ones that remind us of mystery and possibility.

It must be admitted that to welcome this contribution is to open the door to complexity. Bioethics will become more colorful and less tidy. But it will also deal more adequately with human intersubjectivity; it will move closer to human experience and to the agents' interpretations of that experience. It will also mean a stronger commitment to the hermeneutical, interpretive dimensions of the bioethical task—dimensions championed by philosophers like Daniel Callahan, sociologists like Renee Fox, physicians like Arthur Kleinman, and theologians like Don S. Browning.[2]

Communities of Moral Discourse

The statistical size of American religiousness suggests a second contribution. If we add up the congregations, seminaries, denominations, and religion departments—not to mention all the religious groupings that escape the church watchers' eyes—we will find the largest collection of communities of moral discourse in our society. Religious communities provide already existing places where people can talk about some of the most vexing issues that we encounter. In our court rooms, legislatures, and hospital rooms we regularly find people confronted by decisions for which they are unprepared. Our existing religious communities *could* be places of preparation, places where people are morally and ethically equipped for times of decisionmaking.

It is important to be candid about the health of these communities of discourse. While they bear traditions of moral discourse much older and much richer than the thin tradition that currently shapes our public conversation, they also find themselves partially estranged from the very traditions they seek to embody and represent. Many of our religious communities have so accommodated themselves to the American ethos of individualism that they no longer risk serious moral conversation. And some of them have fostered bigotry, closemindedness, and tunnel vision. So their contribution must be labelled as "potential," not automatic.[3]

Yet even if many religious communities seem morally anemic there are significant reasons for taking seriously their potential contribution. Such communities provide an alternative to a simplistic approach to American public life. Too often we mistakenly divide American life into two realms: public and private. We assume that there is one megapublic world where each speaks to all, and countless private worlds where each speaks to the like-minded. It is a commonplace to lump congregations and other religious communities into this private zone and to miss their public character. Many, if not all, American religious communities are publics in their own right. In a society accustomed to segmenting people along lines of class, race, profession, gender, etc., these institutions cross lines of age, ethnicity, educational background, profession, income and the other barriers that subtly ghettoize our moral discourse.

As theologians like Stanley Hauerwas have noted, religious communities, when they are true to their distinctive characters, can offer "contrast models" to a culture's habitual ways of perceiving and acting. Such traditions can provide ways first to face and then address the deepest of human questions, such as our response to suffering, questions of ultimate meanings that our current functional rationality steadfastly avoids.[4] And these traditions provide access to fundamental claims that, while taking various particular forms, may open out into universal concerns and commitments.

Alternative Imaginations

Embedded in religious communities and theological traditions are "alternative imaginations" that allow us to approach enduring human riddles like suffering, health, death, procreation, and the like from different vantage points. For example, most of the religious communities of our land bear traditions of love for the neighbor and concern for creation that can serve as healthy contrast models to the individualism and anthropocentrism that shape so much of our common life. In essence these communities and traditions can increase our imaginative repertoire, making it possible to envision new options and solutions.

Religious communities may also function to widen current bioethical horizons. An example of such widening is provided by a Carter Center conference in October, 1989 at which former President Jimmy Carter invited leaders of America's religious communities to consider "The Church's Challenge in Health Care." The conference participants devoted little if any time to the individual quandaries that take up so much space on conventional bioethics agendas. Rather they addressed major ethical issues like access to health care, or personal and societal responsibility for healthy behavior, as well as national policies that support exporting cigarettes to the third world or inadequately foster safety in home and workplace. Such topics seem remote from conventional bioethics discussions about termination of treatment or organ transplantation, but the challenge presented by this religious conversation is whether our bioethics agenda is too often oriented by quandaries.

Another potential contribution, although it is much less immediate than the ones proposed so far, is the possibility that religious communities might help us develop a more adequate ethical language. Here I allude to Jeffrey Stout's recommendation that religious ethicists be invited back into our moral discourse.[5] If that invitation were accepted, Stout believes, several things would occur. First, we would discover what Mary Midgely calls the "sad little joke" that almost no one speaks the universal moral language of the experts. If theologians and religious scholars re-enter the conversation Stout believes that our "first moral language" will be seen as a pidgin (a sparse dialect used only for communicating with strangers) or a creole (a mixture of fragments from other linguistic traditions) rather than a full blown linguistic tradition. That discovery would help those Stout calls "esperantists" (the designers of universal languages) to discover their own location within larger ethical traditions.

Such discoveries would have considerable implications for bioethics. The enterprise would become more comparative and historical; it would include a kind of "reflexive ethnography" that takes seriously the traditions and cultural contexts which stand behind all ethical constructs.

What Bioethics Can Offer Religion

Stephen Toulmin has written that the encounter with concrete cases and issues in medicine and biomedical research helped reorient philosophical ethics from a drift toward abstraction and irrelevance.[6] It is only fair, after suggesting potential contributions that might flow from religion to bioethics, to ask if someday a religious thinker might write a similar article about medicine's impact upon religion. I raise this prospect to signal a mutual enriching that might be hoped for between realms that have been increasingly estranged from each other. In interactions with each other, medicine and religion might come to fresh appreciations of the distinctive and *limited* contributions each has to offer humanity.

For religious communities, this means that encounters with the life and death quandaries of modern medicine present opportunities to dust off the enduring genius of a particular tradition and to reconnect to moorings that have been lost from view. It is a commonplace in modern discourse to talk about the pervasive identity confusion that exists within religious communities. In the face of a bewildering variety of religious and secular interpretations, it is difficult to speak with certainty about religious meanings and beliefs.

Yet the majority of our religious traditions came to life in equally confusing encounters with human suffering and dying. The religious figures who first articulated distinctive interpretations that later became "great traditions" (Moses, Jesus, Mohammed) arrived at their insights through dark nights of the soul, in times of great ethical and cultural confusion. When confronted with modern questions about the meaning of suffering or the possibility of a good death, the religious interpreter is offered an existential bridge into the heart or core of a tradition. Delving there can result in a fresh perception that allows religious communities to see that they are different from the surrounding culture and why their differences matter.

Such shocks of recognition can ripple across a tradition or religious community. Academic theological reflection, for example, might (just as Toulmin argued with respect to philosophy) reorient itself away from some of the fine points, abstractions, and specialized interests that keep religious journals and graduate schools humming tunes few in America's religious communities sing. A fresh confrontation with the primal reality of a tradition and with modern medical experience can turn religious institutions away from the many concerns of institutional self-preservation and toward human need. In a time when most American denominations are feeling the weight of rising costs and parallel diminishment of support from their constituency, life and death encounters can remind beleaguered leaders and followers of fundamental reasons for being.

Finally, religious traditions and communities, like individual patients and whole societies, can become ill. They can become so entangled in pathological situations that they too need healing. Almost all the religious traditions in our society have a fundamental commitment to love God and neighbor at their core. Even those communities that do not affirm the existence of a particular deity seek to awaken compassion and care in their members. Yet modern religious communities have found it ever more difficult to keep such commitments lively and central. They too have accepted the modern division of labor that delegates "caring" to certain professionals and "religion" to others.

The encounter with life and death worlds of members and strangers points out the unhealthy side affects of such ways of life. It sets inquirers out in search of other, healthier, patterns. And it can revive those who find themselves weary from life along modernity's dividing line. Such inquirers may even find that experiences of a shared mandate to care and heal that crosses the lines of faith traditions and religious communities makes possible new alliances on behalf of a public good for a land with a serious case of individualism and privatism.

References

[1] Constant H. Jacquet, Jr., *Yearbook of American and Canadian Churches 1990* (Nashville: Abingdon Press, 1990.)

[2] Daniel Callahan, *Setting Limits: Medical Goals in an Aging Society* (New York: Simon and Schuster, 1987); Renee C. Fox, *The Sociology of Medicine: A Participant Observer's View* (Englewood Cliffs, NJ: Prentice Hall, 1989); Arthur Kleinman, *The Illness Narratives: Suffering, Healing and the Human Condition* (New York: Basic Books, Inc., 1988); Don S. Browning, "Hospital Chaplaincy as Public Ministry," *Second Opinion* 1 (March 1986), 66-75.

[3] For the contribution to be realized, religious communities must revitalize their traditions and strengthen their abilities at moral discourse. How they might accomplish such revitalization is too complex a subject to be addressed here. Graduate schools, seminaries, denominations, and independent research institutes like the Park Ridge Center for the Study of Health, Faith, and Ethics are attempting to respond to these needs.

[4] Stanley Hauerwas, *Suffering Presence: Theological Reflections on Medicine, the Mentally Handicapped, and the Church* (Notre Dame, IN: University of Notre Dame Press, 1986).

[5] Jeffrey Stout, *Ethics After Babel: The Languages of Morals and Their Discontents* (Boston: Beacon Press, 1988).

[6] Stephen Toulmin, "How Medicine Saved the Life of Ethics," *Perspectives in Biology and Medicine* 25:4 (1982), 736-50.

Part IV
The Principle-Based Approach

[9]

Principles and Particularity: The Roles of Cases in Bioethics

JOHN D. ARRAS[*]

INTRODUCTION

Twenty-five years ago, when I was a graduate student in philosophy, the study of ethics had fallen on hard times. Some of the leading exponents of ethical theory had succeeded, for the time being, in showing either that all ethical judgments were reducible to emotive reactions—and hence irrational and indefensible[1]—or that the study of ethics, properly understood, had more to do with probing the nuances of the "language of morals"[2] than with reflecting on the normative moral experience of real people in their mundane or professional capacities. The study of ethics had become a rarefied, specialized, technical, and, above all, dry discipline. Given the sad state of the field, many had begun to wonder whether political philosophy was dead. To be sure, books and articles continued to be written, and courses continued to be taught, but for many of us at the time such behaviors might have resembled the residual motions of patients in a persistent vegetative state more than genuine signs of life. The real "action" in philosophy lay elsewhere, around the "linguistic turn"[3] or in continental theory, but certainly not in ethics.

Not coincidentally, during my undergraduate and graduate years I was never exposed to anything remotely resembling a "case study" in ethics. If ethics was ever to establish itself as an intellectual enterprise worthy of respect, students were told, it would have to ignore the grubby world of everyday moral concerns and concentrate instead on theory, abstraction, and the meaning of various moral terms.[4] In my work today, however, I am mired in cases, both at the hospital, where the exigencies of clinical problems preclude leisurely invocations of philosophical theory, and even in my university classes on bioethics and the philosophy of law. This Article inquires how this dramatic shift from theory-driven to case-driven ethics came about and

---

[*] Division of Bioethics, Montefiore Medical Center/Albert Einstein College of Medicine, Department of Philosophy, Barnard College. Ph.D., 1972, Northwestern University. The author thanks Jeffrey Blustein and Norman Care for helpful discussions, and Richard Miller and Susan Williams for stimulating commentary at this symposium.

1. *See, e.g.*, ALFRED J. AYER, LANGUAGE, TRUTH AND LOGIC (2d ed. 1946); C.L. STEVENSON, ETHICS AND LANGUAGE (1944).

2. R.M. HARE, THE LANGUAGE OF MORALS (1972 reprint).

3. THE LINGUISTIC TURN (Richard Rorty ed., 1967).

4. Felicitous exceptions in my own education were the courses of Professor Henry B. Veatch, which, while not "applied" in the contemporary sense, were rooted in the normative quest for goods and virtues.

attempts to chart some of its implications for the practice and teaching of ethics.

I. EXAMPLES IN THE SERVICE OF THEORY

Although neither classical nor contemporary moral philosophers dealt with what is now called a "case study," they frequently cited *examples* designed to substantiate their theoretical points. Thus, Mill deployed the example of someone inciting an angry mob poised on the corn dealer's doorstep in connection with his theory of the limits of free expression;[5] and Kant mentioned, less helpfully, examples of honest dealing, suicide, and failure to develop one's talents as illustrations of his "categorical imperative."[6] The partisans of "linguistic ethics" would also occasionally cite an example of moral behavior, though these tended to be uniformly unimaginative and trivial.[7]

There was, to be sure, an occasional philosophical example sketched with some detail and literary flair, such as Sartre's memorable reference to a young man tragically torn between the incompatible demands of caring for his mother and joining the Free French struggle against fascism.[8] Indeed, Sartre produced not merely a few apt examples, but also a remarkable literary corpus of novels and dramatic works, much of which was self-consciously devoted to the illustration of the philosopher's theories of freedom, identity, and responsibility.[9]

The common thread uniting these examples, both the trivial and the tragic, is their subservience to philosophical theory. The philosophers' examples and hypotheticals were designed to make theoretical points, not to shed light on various moral problems independently articulated by practical people enmeshed in the realities of everyday personal and professional life. Indeed, to the proponents of linguistic ethics, the true task of moral philosophy simply involved the clarification of moral language; while, to the philosophical emotivist, the yearning for a normative theory of responsibility or justice stemmed from a failure to acknowledge the non-cognitive status of all moral values. The ethical concerns of spouses, lovers, parents, legislators, workers, revolutionaries, doctors, nurses, lawyers, and social workers thus were condescendingly delegated to parties occupying lower rungs on the

---

5. JOHN S. MILL, ON LIBERTY 53 (David Stitz ed., 1975).
6. IMMANUEL KANT, KANT'S GROUNDWORK OF THE METAPHYSICS OF MORALS 89-90 (H.J. Paton trans., 1961).
7. Indeed, a review of the ethics literature produced in the 1950's and 1960's could easily give a present-day reader the impression that civilization had in those days been brought to its knees by hordes of ruthless pedestrians bent on violating posted warnings not to trespass on the grass.
8. JEAN-PAUL SARTRE, L'EXISTENTIALISME EST UN HUMANISME (1946). For another memorable example of a story in the service of philosophy, see SOREN KIERKEGAARD, FEAR AND TREMBLING (1843).
9. JEAN-PAUL SARTRE, WHAT IS LITERATURE? (1948). Typical examples of Sartre's philosophical fiction include the novel, LA NAUSÉE (1938), and such plays as LES MOUCHES (1941) and HUIS CLOS (1944).

academic/intellectual food chain, such as journalists, ministers, and politicians.[10] In view of this cleavage between the goals of moral philosophy and the practical world, it is not surprising that the practice and teaching of ethics did not refer to case studies.

II. THE RISE OF "APPLIED ETHICS"

The current revival of interest in "practical ethics"—that is, the use of the concepts and methods of ethical theory towards the resolution of concrete moral problems—is generally credited to the publication of John Rawls' monumental work, *A Theory of Justice*.[11] For serious intellectuals struggling with issues of race and the moral dilemmas occasioned by the Vietnam war, Rawls' book rekindled hope that reason—rather than emotion, custom, or sheer political force—might be fruitfully applied to clarify and resolve real ethical-political problems in public life. Although Rawls' book was exclusively concerned with the explanation and justification of a morally *ideal* blueprint for just social institutions, and even though it contained no actual case studies and few examples of how his theory might be applied,[12] *A Theory of Justice* nevertheless generated a heady optimism regarding the potential of moral theory to solve real world problems. In no time, it seemed, a fledgling "industry" had been launched, complete with its own journals and think-tanks. For those working in the field at that time, it seemed that the rational, definitive resolution of some of the most vexing social conflicts merely awaited the proper formulation and application of the best ethical theory that moral philosophy could provide.[13] The heyday of "applied ethics" had dawned.

Different styles of moral analysis eventually emerged under this rubric of applied ethics. By far the most theoretically confident, and the most problematic style might be described as a kind of moral deductivism.[14]

---

10. *See* STEVENSON, *supra* note 1, at 1:
The purpose of an analytic or methodological study, whether of science or of ethics, is always indirect. It hopes to send others to their tasks with clearer heads and less wasteful habits of investigation. This necessitates a continual scrutiny of what these others are doing, or else analysis of meanings and methods will proceed in a vacuum; but it does not require the analyst, as such, to participate in the inquiry that he analyzes. In ethics any direct participation of this sort might have its dangers. It might deprive the analysis of its detachment and distort a relatively neutral study into a plea for some special code of morals. So although normative questions constitute by far the most important branch of ethics, pervading all of common-sense life, and occupying most of the professional attention of legislators, editorialists, didactic novelists, clergymen, and moral philosophers, these questions must here be left unanswered.
The present volume has the limited task of sharpening the tools which others employ.
As we shall soon see, the above project is the exact opposite of contemporary casuistry in every detail.
11. JOHN RAWLS, A THEORY OF JUSTICE (1971).
12. Rawls' only deviation from the development of so-called "ideal theory" concerned the conditions for justifying the practice of civil disobedience. *Id.* at 333-91.
13. For example, see RONALD M. DWORKIN, TAKING RIGHTS SERIOUSLY 149 (1977).
14. Just as H.L.A. Hart discovered the difficulty of tracking down actual specimens of the legal realists' *bête noire*, the advocates of so-called "mechanical jurisprudence," so is it hard to pin down actual exemplars of so-called deductivistic bioethics. *See* H.L.A. Hart, *Positivism and the Separation of Law and Morals*, 71 HARV. L. REV. 593 (1958). A deductivistic approach is certainly implied in a

According to this approach, the task of the "applied philosopher" was to start with a philosophical theory—presumably, the best and most comprehensive account available—then to develop various mid-level normative principles, such as those bearing on truth-telling, paternalism, and confidentiality. With the theory and derivative principles firmly in place, the practical philosopher needed only to feed the relevant factual data into the moral equation to yield the appropriate moral conclusion.[15]

For reasons that shall be explained presently, this sort of deductivistic appeal to comprehensive moral theory found few adherents, especially among professionals seeking the advice of the applied ethicist. However, a far more theoretically modest approach, focusing on the development, application, and refinement of a small set of mid-level principles, was to prove spectacularly successful. This "principlist" approach (or "bioethical mantra")[16] posited the existence of objective, universal principles that ought to govern moral behavior, social policy, and legislation. Developed and popularized by philosophers Tom Beauchamp and James Childress,[17] this approach soon became the dominant paradigm for serious work in bioethics.

In contrast to the reductionistic tendencies of the more hard-core variety of applied ethicists, principlists neglected ultimate or foundational questions in favor of a more pluralistic and "intuitionistic" approach. The partisans of applied moral theory tended to reduce the sources of normative criticism to a single, overarching value (for example, Kantian respect for persons or the maximization of utility) that would then definitively settle all conflicts between values and principles. The principlists settled for a small cluster of disparate fundamental values (autonomy, beneficence, nonmalificence, and justice), no one of which was granted a priori primacy over the others.

The relationship between these mid-level principles and cases within the theory of principlism has been somewhat ambiguous and subject to historical fluctuation. The basic question is whether one ought to conceive this relationship in uni-directional or in dialectical terms. As a uni-directional relationship, one can hold either that judgments about cases are entirely determined by appeal to governing principles or that principles are merely derivative "summary formulations" of incremental judgments about cases. As a dialectical relationship, one can claim that principles both shape and are shaped by the responses to particular cases. According to this latter interpretation, principles would retain normative dominion over what ought to be done

---

much-quoted chart in TOM L. BEAUCHAMP & JAMES F. CHILDRESS, PRINCIPLES OF BIOMEDICAL ETHICS 32 (1st ed. 1979), that plots the path of ethical justification from cases to rules to principles to theory. Perhaps the philosophers whose works come closest to a highly theory-laden, deductivist approach are H. TRISTRAM ENGLEHARDT, JR., THE FOUNDATIONS OF BIOETHICS (1986), and PETER SINGER, PRACTICAL ETHICS (1979).

15. Implicit in this approach was a rather clear-cut division of labor: the applied philosopher was the expert with regard to moral theory and practical reasoning, while "the facts" would be furnished by others, such as physicians, social workers, or business executives.

16. I believe I might have actually coined this derogatory epithet at a lecture on "Methodology in Bioethics" at the University of Texas Medical Branch, Galveston, 1986.

17. BEAUCHAMP & CHILDRESS, supra note 14.

in specific circumstances, while the developing intuitive responses to cases would add content to principles and help formulate their proper boundaries.

During the early, heroic phase of applied ethics, the principlists were partisans of a decidedly "top down" orientation devoted to applying principles to the moral data of concrete cases.[18] Moral objectivity and justification were found, not in the messy details of the cases, but rather in "the principles of bioethics." Although many clinicians continued to complain that even this more modest version of applied ethics was too abstract to be well suited to clinical decision-making, many others viewed principlism as a source of objective moral knowledge and useful advice. These physicians tended to view the bioethicist as a kind of "moral expert," and as a purveyor of "principled" moral judgments.

During this early period in the development of bioethics as a field, the case study emerged as an object of serious consideration. At first, case studies were often employed in the traditional manner as illustrations of how a particular ethical theory might bear on moral problems. For example, a case involving the use of placebos in medical research would be used as a prism through which to view the salient features of Kantian or rule-utilitarian reasoning. Many, however, increasingly used case studies not just as illustrations, but as objects of interest in their own right. Case studies posed intellectual and moral problems that called for a solution. It was important to get the right (or at least an acceptable) answer, not simply in order to exhibit the properties of one's favorite theory, but to help determine the fates of living, breathing individuals, many of whom posed moral dilemmas of excruciating difficulty. The moral philosopher was fast becoming an "applied ethicist," and the ethicist was no longer an isolated theorist, but was now enmeshed in the problems, dilemmas, and crises of professional life. Indeed, the theorist was well on his or her way to becoming a consultant, moving from being a detached observer to a player in the professionals' drama.

The case studies that developed in the literature of this period shared two salient features. First, professionals tended to define them.[19] Second, the case studies were brief and "thin." Except for legal cases, the cases presented for consideration in the bioethics literature rarely exceeded a few paragraphs. Crucial medical facts (for example, the patient's diagnosis, options, and prognosis as affected by various treatment choices) would be presented, the shape of the ethical quandary would be sketched, and the care provider's position clarified. Such cases seldom painted a more fleshed out portrait of

---

18. *See supra* notes 16-17 and accompanying text.
19. Recall the established division of intellectual labor within the applied ethics movement. *See supra* note 15 and accompanying text. The philosopher/ethicists would be responsible for the application of theory and principles, while the factual "case material" would be provided by doctors, nurses, or social workers. The problems thus tended to be shaped according to the conceptual, axiologic, and linguistic frameworks of the caregivers. A good example of this phenomenon is the packaging of difficult issues in obstetrics under the heading of "maternal/fetal conflicts." Although I disagree with those who would deny or minimize the possibility for such conflicts, I think that this way of framing many of these issues obscures other conflicts (for example, maternal/professional) and often ignores or legitimates unjust or discriminatory background conditions of the conflicts.

the various actors and the implications of the choices before them. The audience of such case studies often had extremely limited information about, for example, the patients' perception of their disease and the meaning of treatment options as mediated by their social and family history, race, economic class, prior medical encounters, and psychological characteristics.

A typical example of this "bare bones" approach to case studies, drawn from the experience of my colleague Nancy Dubler, might have gone something like this:

> The medical housestaff at a public hospital in the Bronx confronts a difficult case involving a "problem patient." Mr. Jones is an IV drug user who also happens to be infected with HIV and tuberculosis. The TB has been diagnosed as being of the multi-drug resistant variety, and thus poses a serious threat of potentially lethal infection to anyone coming into casual contact with Mr. Jones. The problem is that the patient insists upon leaving his room so he can be free to wander the corridors and lobby of the hospital. The staff are extremely upset and worried that these expeditions outside of his room will lead to the infection of other patients, caregivers, or hospital visitors.

As presented, this case poses a conflict among the patient's individual rights, the public's legitimate interest in protection from harm, and the hospital's fiduciary obligations to its patients and employees. Where should the line be drawn between civil liberties and public health? Would it be ethically justifiable to lock the patient in his room against his will? I shall return to this case later in this Article.

III. THE DECLINE OF THEORY IN BIOETHICS

Notwithstanding the initial wave of enthusiasm that followed in the wake of Rawls' theory of justice, attempts to yoke moral theory into the service of practical ethics were destined to founder on philosophers' ambivalence and on the intrinsic limitations of ethical theory for practical purposes.

While some applied ethicists immediately embraced the role of practical consultant to professional colleagues,[20] many ethical theorists continued, even during the salad days of applied ethics, to view the application of moral theory primarily as a vehicle for enriching philosophical moral theory.[21] Thus, even when they were ostensibly addressing a medical audience, many philosophers appeared more concerned with how other philosophers and theorists of medicine would receive their views. Indeed, many philosophers working in ethics during this period were profoundly ambivalent towards applying their theories to practical affairs. While the revival of normative ethical theory in the 1970's was to a great extent fuelled by philosophers' expectations of "making a difference in the real world," many of these same

---

20. *See, e.g.*, Albert R. Jonsen, *Can an Ethicist Be a Consultant?*, in FRONTIERS IN MEDICAL ETHICS 157 (Virginia Abernethy ed., 1980).

21. Good examples of this ambivalently practical and heavily theory-laden work in ethics can be found in such journals as *Philosophy & Public Affairs* and *Journal of Medicine and Philosophy*.

theorists instinctively recoiled at the thought of becoming mere "moral valets" in the service of some other profession.[22] Their work was thus "theory driven" in yet another sense: in addition to being governed by the application of philosophical or theological theories, their work had been yoked primarily to the service of ethical theorizing as an activity in its own right. Needless to say, clinicians had very little use for this genre of applied ethics.

Although most philosophers working in this field would eventually overcome their residual discomfort with the practical domain, variants of applied ethics based primarily on the invocation of philosophical ethical theory were doomed to fail for reasons internal to such a project. Recall that the "theory driven" model assumes that the proper task for the applied ethicist is to assemble all the relevant ethical theories, with their corresponding principles and likely implications for a particular case, and deploy them for those seeking the ethicist's counsel. But what then? Two possibilities suggest themselves.

First, the ethicist could offer advice in the vein of a "Consumer Reports" service:[23] "Well, in this situation a Kantian would do 'X,' a utilitarian would promote 'Y,' and a natural rights theorist would advocate 'Z.'" Needless to say, such "advice" might not prove enormously helpful to those doctors, nurses, and social workers who haven't yet quite figured out where they stand in the ongoing debate between the partisans of Kant, Mill, and Locke.

Second, the ethicist could attempt to vindicate her favored theory and then apply it to the case at hand. The obvious problem with this gambit is the seemingly interminable nature of philosophical argument about the foundations of morals. To put the point bluntly, after more than two thousand years of ethical debate among philosophers with rival views, no clear winner has emerged, and clinicians cannot be blamed for doubting that one ever will. As eminently practical people, they cannot afford the luxury of awaiting the development of an ethical theory capable of routing this contentious field by force of argument alone.

Even if the theory-driven applied ethicist were miraculously to establish the philosophical supremacy of a single, comprehensive theory of morals, her project would have foundered on the emergence of disagreements among adherents to that very theory. Thus, a utilitarian would have to worry not merely about the challenges posed by rival theories, but also about profound intramural disagreements among adherents to the theory of utility. What shall count as the true meaning of "utility?" How will it be measured? Which form of utilitarianism (for example, act or rule) is correct? These seemingly intractable questions, along with many more, would continue to vex even the champions of the dominant ethical theory before they could begin to apply their doctrine to cases.

---

22. See Annette Baier's translation of Hegel's phrase, "Kammerdiener der Moralität." Annette Baier, *Doing Without Moral Theory?*, in POSTURES OF THE MIND 228, 236 (Annette Baier ed., 1985).
23. *See id.*

Suppose further that, per impossibile, philosophers could agree upon both the general outlines of the correct theory as well as on its precise formulation Even with the unlikely advent of this particular millennium, theorists would still be unable to provide clinicians and policy experts with unambiguous moral solutions derived from the theory. This is because many disputes in clinical bioethics and health policy turn, not on theoretical differences, but on such nettlesome issues as the value that should be accorded to different forms of human and animal life, the factual prediction of likely consequences, and the most rational attitude towards risk.

The problem of active euthanasia provides a good illustration of all three problems. Theorists who agree entirely on the moral theory level may yet part company on the crucial issue of how we should value biological human life.[24] Even theorists who agree on that difficult question may disagree on the likelihood of bad consequences ensuing from a shift towards a more permissive policy and on the question of who should bear the burden of proof.[25]

The more theory-driven approaches to applied ethics suffer a further liability embedded in widespread notions of what an ethical theory ought to look like. The common wisdom is that an ethical theory ought to be a large body of ethical propositions derivable from one or a few basic moral principles. When people speak of ethical theory in this way, they are usually thinking of some version of Kantian deontology,[26] utilitarianism,[27] or Lockean natural rights.[28] The theorists who support these different ethical theories are responding to the question, "What is *the* rational foundation of moral philosophy?" As philosophers such as Thomas Nagel, Bernard Williams, and Charles Taylor have convincingly argued, however, this enterprise is problematic.[29] It assumes that the chiaroscuro of our moral experience can be reduced to one or two overarching sources of moral value, such as maximization of happiness or respect for human freedom. While such an assumption is likely to please theorists bent upon achieving simplicity and efficiency, it will not do justice to the rich diversity inherent in the moral lives of individuals and societies. Consequently, even if the proponents of theory were to agree upon a moral theory so defined, and even if they could apply unambiguously the theory to concrete moral problems, the end result of

---

24. RONALD M. DWORKIN, LIFE'S DOMINION (1993).
25. See, for example, the contrasting views of Daniel Callahan, *When Self-Determination Runs Amok*, HASTINGS CENTER REP., Mar.-Apr. 1992, at 52; and Margaret P. Battin, *Voluntary Euthanasia and the Risks of Abuse: Can We Learn Anything from the Netherlands?*, L. MED. & HEALTH CARE, Spring-Summer 1992, at 133.
26. *See, e.g.*, IMMANUEL KANT, FOUNDATIONS OF METAPHYSICS OF MORALS (Oskar Priest ed. & Lewis W. Beck trans., 1959); RAWLS, *supra* note 11.
27. *See, e.g.*, JOHN S. MILL, UTILITARIANISM, LIBERTY, AND REPRESENTATIVE GOVERNMENT (1910); SINGER, *supra* note 14.
28. *See, e.g.*, ROBERT NOZICK, ANARCHY, STATE, AND UTOPIA (1974); ENGLEHARDT, *supra* note 14.
29. THOMAS NAGEL, MORTAL QUESTIONS 128 (1979); BERNARD WILLIAMS, ETHICS AND THE LIMITS OF PHILOSOPHY (1985); Charles Taylor, *The Diversity of Goods*, in UTILITARIANISM AND BEYOND 129 (Amartya Sen & Bernard Williams eds., 1982).

this reductivist enterprise would still leave us with an impoverished understanding of the problems, solutions, and sources of moral value.

IV. PRINCIPLISM UNDER SIEGE

As I have shown, the "principlist" version of applied ethics was able to virtually corner the methodological market in bioethics by abandoning the foundationalist pretensions of reductionist ethical theory while elaborating a network of principles that offered the hope, or at least the appearance, of ethical objectivity. Without having to bother with the Sisyphusian task of grounding their ethical judgments in ultimate theoretical norms, clinicians could pronounce them justified by appealing to such objective and universal principles as autonomy, beneficence, and justice. By the late 1980's, however, this approach to practical ethics was coming under fire from two diametrically opposed camps.

A. Principlism Not Theoretical Enough

From one flank, the partisans of a comprehensive philosophical theory attacked principlism for its relative insouciance regarding first principles,[30] that is, for not being theoretical enough. This group of critics found especially galling principlism's inability or unwillingness to provide a rationally defensible framework for settling conflicts between competing principles. Clearly, the critics had a point. Utilitarians or Rawlsians, unlike principlists, could settle, at least to their own satisfaction, the inevitable conflicts of the moral life through appealing to some overarching principle of "lexical ordering."[31] The principlists forthrightly admitted that the moral principles came with no pre-established theoretical weights and, consequently, that conflicts arising among these principles would have to be settled through a subtle process of weighing and balancing *in medias res*.[32] Although the partisans of theory find this approach to conflict resolution to be unacceptably subjective or "intuitionistic,"[33] there is wisdom in the principlists' modesty. Their critics have neither established the clear superiority of any monistic theory, such as utilitarianism, nor have they produced a convincing account of why within more pluralistic systems certain lexically favored values, such as utility or liberty, should *always* prevail over all other competing values in a myriad of convoluted real world situations.

---

30. K. Danner Clouser & Bernard Gert, *A Critique of Principlism*, 15 J. MED. & PHIL. 219 (1990); Ronald M. Green, *Method in Bioethics: A Troubled Assessment*, 15 J. MED. & PHIL. 179 (1990).
31. Utilitarians are supposed to resolve all such conflicts by bringing them under the common metric of "utility." Rawlsians give moral priority to liberty in conflicts with "welfare." *See* RAWLS, *supra* note 11.
32. TOM L. BEAUCHAMP & JAMES F. CHILDRESS, PRINCIPLES OF BIOMEDICAL ETHICS 51 (3d ed. 1989).
33. RAWLS, *supra* note 11, at 34-40.

B. Principlism Too Mechanistic

From the opposite flank, the partisans of a more case-driven approach to practical ethics began to attack principlism for being too formal, mechanistic, and deductive. Although the nuanced ethical analyses of its founding expositors were anything but simplistic or mechanistic, principlism's epigones, many of whom lacked even the equivalent of "basic training" in ethics, often did convey the impression that one merely had to slap one or more principles on a given set of facts to derive the morally correct result. More often than not, their "method" was to recite what each of the principles seemed to require, even if they conflicted with one another, then simply to *announce* a conclusion. Allusions to the "bioethical mantra" were in large measure a reaction to precisely this kind of bastardized principlism.

1. From Deductivism to Reflective Equilibrium

The broad-based dissatisfaction with the regnant paradigm harbored two more serious contentions about principlism and its way of configuring the relationship between principles and case judgments. First, the partisans of casuistry or case-based reasoning objected to the apparently uni-directional movement from principles to cases within principlism.[34] A careful analysis of Beauchamp and Childress' early editions of *Principles of Biomedical Ethics*[35] might suggest a more complicated relationship between principles and cases in the process of moral justification, but an oft-cited chart in that book gave the distinct impression that theory justified principles, that principles justified moral rules, and that rules justified moral judgments in particular cases.[36] According to the critics, this uni-directional picture distorted or totally ignored the pivotal role of intuitive, case-based judgments of right and wrong. To be sure, the judgments in question were not to be confused with just any responses to cases, no matter how prejudiced, ill-considered, or subject to coercion they might be. Rather, the critics had something in mind more akin to John Rawls' notion of "considered" moral judgments[37]—the judgments about whose genesis and moral rectitude we feel most confident, such as our sense that slavery is wrong. It is precisely these judgments, they claimed, that give concrete meaning, definition, and scope to moral principles and that provide critical leverage in refining their articulation.

The critics were claiming, in effect, that principles and cases have a dialectical or reciprocal relationship. The principles provide normative guidance, the cases provide considered judgments. The considered judgments, in turn, help shape the principles that then provide more precise guidance for

---

34. ALBERT R. JONSEN & STEPHEN TOULMIN, THE ABUSE OF CASUISTRY (1988).
35. TOM L. BEAUCHAMP & JAMES F. CHILDRESS, PRINCIPLES OF BIOMEDICAL ETHICS (2d ed. 1983).
36. *Id.* at 5.
37. *See* RAWLS, *supra* note 11, at 47-48.

more complex or difficult cases. Following Rawls' terminology, principles and cases exist together in creative tension or "reflective equilibrium."[38]

The principlists responded to this line of criticism by simply embracing it, over time, with increasing forthrightness and enthusiasm. Although they may have been slower than others to discern the formative and critical roles of case analysis with regard to principles and theories, Beauchamp and Childress now embrace reflective equilibrium as *the* methodology of principlism and emphatically denounce deductivism for precisely the same reasons given by their critics.[39] One can view principles as the primary substance of ethical analysis, they conclude, without being a deductivist.

2. Principlism, Indeterminacy, and Moral Justification

A large part of the initial appeal of principlism lay in its promise of providing *principled* solutions to moral problems, solutions that could claim to be more than the "merely subjective" biases of practitioners or consultants. As one physician-graduate of the Kennedy Institute's week-long bioethics seminar explained to me, "This [method] is what our student-doctors need. It's really objective, based on principles, just like a science." This promise of objectivity appeared to be based on the expectation that individual actions or social policies could be justified by applying the enumerated principles.

In some very simple moral situations consisting, for example, of a clear and uncontested moral rule and a fact pattern that contradicts it, this promise could be vindicated. Suppose, for example, that a physician decides to lie to her patient in order to improve his spirits and possibly facilitate his recovery. One could say that this doctor's act violates the principle of autonomy and the law of informed consent. Indeed, one could deploy reasoning in this case as a deductive syllogism: "It is wrong to lie to patients. Dr. Jones has told a lie. Therefore, Dr. Jones has done something wrong."

The problem, of course, is that even in a simple, straightforward case, this reasoning has suppressed a conflicting principle—the principle of beneficence. This is precisely the principle that Dr. Jones would appeal to should she try to defend her lie. ("I did it for his benefit. I was just following my Hippocratic impulses!") At first glance, this opposing principle may not be noticeable because the principle of autonomy has prevailed within the biomedical ethics community over the principle of beneficence in this type of case. One should remember, however, that the predominance of the autonomy principle was not always this clear, that the debate between autonomy and paternalistic medicine rages on in other countries,[40] and that the eventual victory of autonomy in

---

38. *Id.* at 48-51. Rawls' notion of reflective equilibrium, somewhat sketchily drawn in his book, is clarified and defended in Norman Daniels, *Wide Reflective Equilibrium and Theory Acceptance in Ethics*, 76 J. PHIL. 256 (1979).

39. *See* TOM L. BEAUCHAMP & JAMES F. CHILDRESS, PRINCIPLES OF BIOMEDICAL ETHICS (4th ed. 1994).

40. *See* Nicholas A. Christakis, *The Ethical Design of an AIDS Vaccine Trial in Africa*, HASTINGS CENTER REP., June-July 1988, at 31; Antonella Surbone, *Letter from Italy: Truth Telling to the Patient*,

the areas of truth-telling and informed consent, at least in theory, was won after a protracted ideological struggle.[41] As a result, the biomedical community now assigns much greater weight to respecting patients than to easing their psychological burdens.

Principlism may provide the kind of moral justification sought in the easy cases, but what about the complicated cases in which battles between competing principles continue to rage—the cases in which clinicians and policy-makers seek the advice of bioethicists? The "tough" cases will inevitably present not one clear-cut and uncontested principle, but rather two or more conflicting values that require some sort of reconciliation. Precisely what kind of moral justification can principlism offer in the face of serious moral ambiguity and conflict? To what extent does the "application of principles" actually *justify* the moral choices that we make, both individually and collectively?

Another way to formulate these questions is to ask about the capacity of principlism to generate *determinate* answers to moral quandaries. Doubts about the justificatory power of principlism's principles arise on several levels of moral reflection.

Interpreting the principles. The principles themselves require a great deal of interpretation and ordering before they can begin to shape the conclusion of a moral argument. The bioethical literature abounds with superficial claims to the effect that "the principle of autonomy (or of beneficence, or of the 'best interest' of the patient) *requires* that we do such and such." The problem with this common formulation is that it ignores the difficulty (or the vacuousness) of passing immediately from very abstract statements of principle to very concrete conclusions about what to do here and now. Quite apart from the vexing problem of rank-ordering *competing* principles in morally complex situations, a problem I shall treat separately, one first must determine exactly what these abstract formulations of principle actually mean.

What does it mean, for example, to invoke the "best interests" principle in the case of a severely impaired newborn? What content can one give to this expression? How are the interests of such a child to be assessed, and according to which conception of the good?[42] Some might argue that a vitalist's conception of the good should shape our understanding of the child's interests; others might advocate a hedonistic conception of the good that would restrict the notion of interests to the qualia of pleasure and pain; while still others might advance a conception of the good based on conceptions of

---

268 JAMA 1661 (1992). A recent television documentary provided a riveting portrayal of cultural differences regarding the practice of truth-telling. The physicians and nurses in a Japanese cancer ward were shown grappling with a cultural surd: a cancer patient who not only wanted to know the truth about her condition, but actually had the unbridled temerity to *talk to other patients* about their common plight. Their temporary solution: send the woman on lots of long walks in the hospital gardens! See *The Art of Healing* (David Grubin Productions, Inc. & Public Affairs Television, Inc.), *reproduced in Healing and the Mind: The Art of Healing* (Ambrose Video Publishing, Inc. 1993).

41. JAY KATZ, THE SILENT WORLD OF DOCTOR AND PATIENT (1984).

42. *See* EZEKIEL J. EMANUAL, THE ENDS OF HUMAN LIFE: MEDICAL ETHICS IN A LIBERAL POLITY (1991).

human flourishing and dignity, which might lead to nontreatment decisions even in the absence of pain and suffering.

Whatever the merit of these individual suggestions, the point is that unless one *interprets* "the principles of bioethics," they will merely play the role of empty "chapter headings,"[43] doing little if any actual work in moral analysis. Unless one furnishes principles with a definite shape and content, they will merely lend a patina of objectivity to bioethical debates while masking the need to make arguments and choices regarding the substance of those principles.[44]

It is important to recall that the meaning of principles is shaped, not simply by explicit and constructive ethical theorizing, but also by the largely implicit influences of culture.[45] The seemingly univocal "principle of autonomy" will mean different things and have different weights in different cultural settings. Compare, for example, the way in which the right of reproductive self-determination functions in the abortion debates of the United States and Germany. In this country, longstanding legal traditions of rugged individualism have yielded, albeit after many years of bloody and ongoing conflict, a right that has been aptly characterized as nearly absolute but entirely asocial.[46] So while a woman's claims to (nearly) absolute personal sovereignty have trumped the interests of husbands, parents, and the values of a large countervailing segment of the community, women remain largely isolated in their freedom, unsupported by the community's resources and concern. In Germany, by contrast, the principle of autonomy exercises considerable force, to be sure, but its meaning and scope have been mediated by a public philosophy, traceable back to Rousseau, that stresses the complimentary nature of individual freedom and social responsibility. Thus, Germans significantly curtail, by American standards, a woman's right to obtain an abortion, but German women who obtain abortions are given community services and abortion funding.[47] Such differences in the presentation of various principles in diverse cultural settings have prompted Mary Ann Glendon to speak, not of "rights talk" tout court, but rather of different "rights dialects."[48]

Interpreting conflicting principles. In hard cases, principles conflict. That is why they are hard. Can principlism provide a means to justify resolutions to moral conflict? What help can principlism provide, for example, when the principle of autonomy is at odds with the so-called "harm principle," as in cases involving maternal-fetal conflict or cases involving decisions to

---

43. *See* Clouser & Gert, *supra* note 30, at 221.
44. Precisely the same critical point can be made with regard to the other "principles of bioethics." "The" principle of justice is, if anything, a highly contested concept, not a univocal principle. In the words of Alasdair MacIntyre, one might well ask, "Whose Justice, Which Rationality?" *See generally* ALASDAIR C. MACINTYRE, WHOSE JUSTICE? WHICH RATIONALITY? (1988).
45. *See, e.g.*, Robert M. Cover, *Nomos and Narrative*, 97 HARV. L. REV. 4 (1983).
46. *See* MARY ANN GLENDON, RIGHTS TALK: THE IMPOVERISHMENT OF POLITICAL DISCOURSE 55-61 (1991).
47. *Id.* at 61-66.
48. *Id.*

reproduce in a context of genetic disease or AIDS? According to the principlists, the only available remedy for such conflicts of principle is to judiciously weigh and balance the competing moral claims as they arise in different circumstances.[49] If a woman is overwrought and her judgment skewed by excessive fear and faulty reasoning, and if her choice would impose severe and irreparable harm on her offspring, then a principlist might find the harm principle to outweigh the claims of self-determination.

This weighing and balancing, some critics contend, is inherently subjective and unpredictable.[50] Suppose two observers—for example, an ardent feminist and a staunch "pro-lifer"—happen to disagree about the above outcome? The latter approves, while the former sees it as a violation of the woman's integrity and as reducing her to the demeaning status of "fetal container." Can principlism help sort out, according to some canon of rational justification, the rival "intuitions" of the disputing parties?

According to Clouser and Gert, these kinds of intuitive conflicts will only be resolved on the higher plane of philosophical theory.[51] Until the principlists develop a more robust ethical theory, a theory that would ultimately assign determinate weights to such competing values, these critics contend that its resolutions of hard cases must remain ad hoc, fundamentally *unprincipled*, and therefore unjustified.[52]

Philosopher David DeGrazia has developed a more constructive critique of principlism.[53] While DeGrazia shares Clouser and Gert's worries about the ad hoc and unprincipled character of the weighing and balancing required by principlism, he adopts a strategy of amendment rather than abandonment.

Drawing on Henry Richardson's influential article on specification in moral reasoning,[54] DeGrazia contends that in many hard cases what is really going on is not the weighing and balancing of *conflicting* principles by unsupported intuition, but rather the progressive *specification* of more abstract norms. According to this view, initial abstract formulations of principles will become increasingly concrete, specified, and delimited as one approaches the level of the particular case. Thus, what begins as a straightforward, abstract, and seemingly absolute principle—that women (and men) have a right to make reproductive choices unfettered by government or medical professionals—might end as a complex and richly nuanced principle with built-in exceptions for factors such as compromised rationality and severe and irreversible harm, as in the above example. The advantage of thinking of moral reasoning in terms of specification rather than balancing is, according to DeGrazia and Richardson, that one's final practical judgments remain

---

49. *See, e.g.*, BEAUCHAMP & CHILDRESS, *supra* note 32, at 228-47.
50. *See* Clouser & Gert, *supra* note 30; *see also* David DeGrazia, *Moving Forward in Bioethical Theory: Theories, Cases, and Specified Principlism*, 17 J. MED. & PHIL. 511 (1992).
51. Clouser & Gert, *supra* note 30.
52. Given the importance of this theoretically justified balancing scale for the principlist project, one wonders why Clouser and Gert have not simply *loaned* one to Beauchamp and Childress.
53. DeGrazia, *supra* note 50.
54. Henry S. Richardson, *Specifying Norms as a Way to Resolve Concrete Ethical Problems*, 19 PHIL. & PUB. AFF. 279 (1990).

tethered to a single principle capable of bestowing rational justification upon them.[55]

Although DeGrazia's amendment to principlism is much richer than this short synopsis will allow, and although his theory of moral justification ultimately hinges on the sort of justification that reflective equilibrium affords,[56] this particular aspect of his amendment simply redescribes, rather than solves, the problem of indeterminacy. Indeed, the specter of indeterminacy that haunts the project of balancing within principlism threatens specification as well. If weighing and balancing competing principles in the above reproductive case falls short of rational justification for want of a hierarchy of values that is theoretically justified, then the specification of abstract principles through the process of reflective equilibrium will also fall short. Just as the competing principles of reproductive autonomy and "nonmaleficence" appear to require ad hoc, context specific, nuanced judgments unsupported by higher level, lexically ordered principles, so too will efforts to specify the principle of reproductive freedom down to the level of the particular case. Indeed, what motivates and guides the modification and specification of abstract principles, what compels one to lard them with qualifying clauses, if not precisely the sort of countervailing values and principles encountered by the principlist? Thus, whether one calls this balancing or specification, the respective weights of competing considerations must be sorted out. Unless DeGrazia has a rationally defensible, higher level, lexical ordering principle at his disposal, his "specifiers" are in the same boat as the principlists' "weighers and balancers." Neither, in short, can vindicate the claim to rational justification that gave to principlism much of its initial appeal.

Interpreting types of cases. Apart from the indeterminacies involved in balancing and specifying principles, the corresponding moral situation requires extensive, non-rule bound interpretation as well. In some contexts, this might mean developing an appropriate moral vocabulary to describe what is happening in certain kinds of situations. It seems that moral progress often depends as much on finding (or fashioning) the right words as on applying the right principles. This is especially the case in the areas of bioethical investigation defined by rapid technological change—such as genetic engineering, prenatal interventions on the fetus, and the withholding of life-sustaining treatments. For example, the tentative search for compelling descriptions has created much of the recent perplexity over the withholding of artificial food and fluids. One questions what is really going on in such cases. Is the withholding of artificial nutrition through a nasogastric tube an example of intentional "killing" or an example of a humble, merciful withdrawal of ineffective medical treatments?

Those who breezily claim that bioethics is the application of principles to "the facts" forget that, apart from the indices of bioethics periodicals, the

---

55. DeGrazia, *supra* note 50; Richardson, *supra* note 54.
56. That is, not on a straightforwardly foundationalist or deductivist approach.

facts do not come neatly labelled. Cases and issues must be described, individuated, and labelled well before any principles can be applied.

Interpreting the case. Even after developing a vocabulary to describe a particular moral situation, the application of moral principles must await the results of yet another layer of interpretation: the interpretation of actions, gestures, and relationships *within* the case. Even if one decides that a specific refusal of treatment does not necessarily amount to a form of suicide or intentional killing, one still must determine the meaning of that refusal in the context of its own setting and history. Indeed, some of the most illuminating writing in the field of bioethics has dealt precisely with this type of searching hermeneutic of the individual case.

Recall Robert Burt's brilliant and disturbing psychoanalytic interpretation of a burn patient's adamant refusal to be treated and articulate request to die.[57] While Burt acknowledged the validity of the principle of autonomy as well as the sincerity of the patient's request to die, he enlarged the understanding of this case by attempting to place the patient's treatment refusal in its emotional context. Perhaps, Burt suggested, the patient's refusal was less an unambiguous thrust of freedom than a plea for recognition, acceptance, and love from those surrounding him.[58] Instead of being a statement, perhaps the refusal was a question in disguise: "Do you still care for me? Would you banish me from your sight?"

Clearly, the relevance of the principle of autonomy for this case depends upon whether one interprets the patient's refusal as a statement or as a query. For example, if the patient is in fact testing the commitment of those around him, a mechanical application of the principle of autonomy to his expressed refusal could lead to a tragic result. Whether or not one agrees with Burt's controversial gloss on this case, his work shows that one can do creative and exciting work in bioethics while paying scant attention to the analysis or application of moral principles.

The search for moral justification through the application of principles thus proves to be a far more complicated matter than the followers of principlism appear to have initially discerned. While it still makes sense to talk about the "application" of principles to cases, this application is no simple matter of deduction but actually involves multiple layers of interpretation and substantive moral reflection. The crucial point, however, is that each of these interpretative layers—of the principles, of their relative weights, of case description, and of the meaning of individual gestures—is a locus of interpretive *conflict*. Bioethics requires one to articulate and attempt to resolve the conflicts at all of these levels. This is a difficult task. Reference to the "application" of principles to cases tends to mask these difficulties. It gives the impression that the task is "merely" one of intellectual procedure rather than substance.

---

57. ROBERT A. BURT, TAKING CARE OF STRANGERS: THE RULE OF LAW IN DOCTOR-PATIENT RELATIONS (1979).
58. *Id.* at 10-11.

Likewise, when people speak of this sort of "application" as *justifying* particular moral judgments, they appear to assume that, from among a welter of serious yet conflicting views at all levels, a justified choice must select the correct principles, their correct formulation, their correct weight, the correct typology of the situation, and the correct "reading" of the case details. This assumption places inordinate demands upon the notion of moral justification, especially since there are no clear and uncontested criteria for making precisely these kinds of judgments.

This picture of what moral justification entails, a picture that early confidence in principlism seems to have assumed, simply cannot bear the weight that has been put on it. Indeed, as the principlist partisans of reflective equilibrium now admit, the conception of moral justification as a *correspondence* between individual judgments and theoretically validated moral principles must be abandoned. In its place, a conception based upon the overall *coherence* of our case-based judgments, mid-level principles, and theoretical and cultural commitments would seem a more realistic goal. That is, instead of seeking ultimate justification in an appeal to some rock solid, freestanding principle, the quest should be for answers to how well an action or policy comports with the considered judgments, principles, and values already embedded in the web of our collective moral life.[59] Sometimes such an inquiry will yield a clear-cut answer, but most of the time it will create genuine controversy that will be played out over time. Some arguments will be more or less plausible, more or less rational than others.[60] They will never, however, be purely objective "just like a science."

V. THE PARTICULARIST PROJECT IN BIOETHICS

As the initial promise of principlism began to fade, a small cluster of alternative methodological approaches in bioethics emerged.[61] They pressed the critique of the dominant paradigm while attempting to articulate a more "particularist" moral vision. Much of this critique has already been adumbrated in the short history of principlism. Examples include: the attack on the reductionist and foundationalist aspirations of ethical theory, understood as

---

59. *See* MICHAEL WALZER, INTERPRETATION AND SOCIAL CRITICISM (1987); *see also* GEORGIA WARNKE, JUSTICE & INTERPRETATION (1993).

60. *See* RICHARD J. BERNSTEIN, BEYOND OBJECTIVISM AND RELATIVISM (1983).

61. In addition to casuistry and narrative ethics, the two alternative methodologies that I shall discuss, a complete account of challenges to principlism would have to include feminist theory as well. Feminist theories in bioethics have much in common with casuistry and narrative ethics: All three approaches are skeptical of standard ethical theories, attempt to root their moral analyses in the particularities of complex situations, and give greater weight to the role of emotions and relationships in moral life. While I would argue that feminist theory adds little, if anything, to the particularist critique of principlism, feminist theorists have convincingly argued that the reigning paradigm of bioethics has been insufficiently attentive to problems of power and domination. *See, e.g.*, FEMINIST PERSPECTIVES IN MEDICAL ETHICS (Helen B. Holmes & Laura M. Purdy eds., 1992); SUSAN SHERWIN, NO LONGER PATIENT: FEMINIST ETHICS AND HEALTH CARE (1992); FEMINISM AND BIOETHICS: BEYOND REPRODUCTION (S. Wolf ed., forthcoming 1994).

some version of Kantianism or utilitarianism;[62] the insistence upon the multiple layers of difficult interpretive work that are obscured by talk of "applying" principles; and the dialectical role of cases in generating, specifying, and reformulating ethical principles. My aim in this section is to give a brief but more positive account of these new directions in bioethics. Then, in conclusion, I will reflect on the implications of this methodological shift for the role of case studies in the practice and teaching of bioethics.

A. Casuistry

The renaissance of casuistry, or case-based reasoning, in practical ethics has stressed the pivotal role of cases while de-emphasizing the role of theory and routinized appeals to "the principles of bioethics."[63] According to its leading proponents, a casuistical method must begin with a typology or grouping of cases around a paradigm of a moral rule or principle. In the area of research ethics, for example, the atrocities of Nazi medicine still are an exemplar of unethical dealing with human subjects. From this signal case one then branches out by a method akin to "moral triangulation" to analogous cases of lesser or greater difficulty, such as research on children or the demented elderly. As one proceeds from case to case responding to the particular settings, treatments, and categories of research subjects, the principle becomes increasingly refined and complex.

Crucially, the casuists contend that whatever "weight" a principle has vis-a-vis competing principles, one must determine that weight, not in the abstract, but in response to the details of individual cases.[64] Suppose, for example, the medical director of a reputable nursing home wishes to study the causes and treatment of the refusal to eat by elderly patients with Alzheimer's disease. Suppose further that informed consent to participate in the study cannot be expected from this patient population. According to the dictates of our paradigm case—for example, the infamous hypothermia experiments of the Nazi doctors—the principle of respect for persons always requires the free and informed consent of the research subject. According to the casuists, to determine whether the principle of autonomy should prevail over the principle of beneficence in nursing home research requires a more nuanced investigation into the "who" (enslaved ethnic populations vs. patients with Alzheimer's disease), the "what" (lethal hypothermia experiments vs. studying and filming patients' eating behaviors), the "where" (death camps vs. a regulated nursing

---

62. *See, e.g.*, Barry Hoffmaster, *Can Ethnography Save the Life of Medical Ethics?*, 35 SOC. SCI. & MED. 1421-31 (1992); Barry Hoffmaster, *The Theory and Practice of Applied Ethics*, 30 DIALOGUE 213-34 (1991).
63. *See, e.g.*, BARUCH A. BRODY, LIFE AND DEATH DECISION MAKING (1988); JONSEN & TOULMIN, *supra* note 34; John D. Arras, *Getting Down to Cases: The Revival of Casuistry in Bioethics*, 16 J. MED. & PHIL. 29 (1991); *see also* A. Mackler, Cases and Judgments in Ethical Reasoning: An Appraisal of Contemporary Casuistry and Holistic Model for the Mutual Support of Norms and Case Judgments (1992) (unpublished Ph.D. dissertation, Georgetown University).
64. *See* Albert R. Jonsen, *Of Balloons and Bicycles; or The Relationship Between Ethical Theory and Practical Judgment*, HASTINGS CENTER REP., Sept.-Oct. 1991, at 14.

home with a competent research review board), and the "when" (after capture and before execution vs. after the loss of capacity, the consent of family, and approval and ongoing oversight of an ethics committee). Casuistry holds that rather than assigning a timeless relative weight to a certain principle, details should determine the weight. Thus, in this hypothetical, the facts and setting of the proposed study might be so far removed from our paradigm of unethical research that they justify moral approval even without the patient's consent.

Presented in this way, the casuistical method obviously has much in common with the method of the common law. Indeed, given the pivotal and ubiquitous role of legal cases in the recent history of bioethics—a history punctuated by such names as Karen Quinlan,[65] Claire Conroy,[66] Nancy Cruzan,[67] Helga Wanglie,[68] and Baby M[69]—it was entirely natural for bioethicists to begin seeing parallels between case-based reasoning in ethics and law. On both fronts, ethicists seem to reason from the "bottom up" (from cases to fleshed-out principles) rather than from the "top down" (as most versions of applied ethics imply). The principles themselves are consequently "open textured" and always subject to further revision and specification, and the final judgments usually turn on a fine-grained analysis of the particularities of the case.

To many working in the field, this account of reasoning in both ethics and law accurately describes how ethicists actually think, both in clinical situations and in the classroom. That is, they tend to think in terms of cases, which serve as exemplars—a kind of shorthand for moral analysis and assessment: "This is a Cruzan-type case, except here, instead of a feeding tube, the issue is antibiotics" (or minimal conscious awareness, or a family insisting that everything be done, etc.). How do these different facts alter one's perception of the case? Are they so different as to dictate an alternative result? Instead of ritualistically invoking the mantra, these ethicists propose that normative accounts of ethical reasoning should more closely conform to actual practices.

Just as the casuists insist that the weight of principles resides in the details, so they insist that moral certainty resides in our responses to paradigmatic cases, rather than in appeals to theory or principle. One is, in fact, much more confident in the knowledge that torturing and killing Jews to learn about hypothermia is wrong than in the assessment of which moral theory or principles best describes why. One is much more likely to switch allegiance to a different moral theory or conception of principles than to change his or her mind about what the Nazi doctors did. Indeed, if an alternative moral theory were to approve of the Nazis' experiments, most would reject the theory based on that approval.

---

65. *In re* Quinlan, 355 A.2d 647 (N.J. 1976).
66. *In re* Conroy, 486 A.2d 1209 (N.J. 1985).
67. Cruzan v. Director, Missouri Dep't of Health, 497 U.S. 261 (1990).
68. Wanglie v. Minnesota, 398 N.W.2d 54 (Minn. Ct. App. 1986).
69. *In re* Baby M, 537 A.2d 1227 (N.J. 1988).

This emphasis on the case as the locus of moral certainty reveals an important split within the casuistical camp. On the one hand, some "hard core" casuists have little, if any, use for either principles or higher level theory.[70] According to this view, the principles invoked in moral argument are nothing more than tidy summaries of moral thought as it grapples analogically with cases. Such principles might serve as useful shorthand, these critics concede, but they might also mislead by allowing one to impute normative significance to mere summaries of what one has already decided.

This hard-core version of casuistry has little in common with the great historical tradition of casuistry, and it presents a problematic account of moral reasoning. As Jonsen and Toulmin's historical chapters on the rise and fall of casuistry attest, the adherents of the casuistical method have always seen their task as one of fitting the abstract principles of moral doctrine's sources, such as the Bible, ancient philosophers, moral theology, or international law, to the circumstances of cases.[71]

Moreover, doing without moral principles that not only summarize past behavior but also guide future conduct may be the equivalent of throwing the baby out with the bathwater. This radically anti-principlist stance derives its plausibility from the fact that, according to the theory of reflective equilibrium, moral principles originate as summations of responses to experience of particular cases. If this is so, one might reason, then it is intuitive responses alone, not the principles, that do the real work in moral decision-making. Moral principles, on this view, are thus nothing more than factual summaries incapable of providing positive moral guidance.

This radically particularistic account of moral decision-making seems to assume that if principles initially grow out of individual responses to situations, then they will be incapable of transcending the domain of the purely factual. But this assumption may give too much credit to the supposed dichotomy between facts and values. The principles that gradually emerge from one's experience with cases might be more profitably viewed as repositories of congealed value judgments. They are expressions of what is valued and disvalued in the world of moral experience. Thus, the principle of confidentiality that prohibits health care providers from exposing the secrets of their patients (apart from certain compelling exceptional circumstances) can serve as a general, action-guiding norm: Unless you have a good reason, it is generally wrong to violate a patient's confidence. It makes perfect sense to say that such principles can and do guide deliberations in particular cases. Even though general moral principles must usually be supplemented by a fine-grained, particularistic assessment of a morally complex situation, they still

---

70. *See, e.g.*, Stephen Toulmin, *The Tyranny of Principles*, HASTINGS CENTER REP., Dec. 1981, at 31. Toulmin's position on principles is echoed by Richard Rorty who claims that the legacy of Hegel, Marx, and Dewey is the realization that "the search for principle is a primitive stage of moral development. What counts as moral sophistication is the ability to wield complex and sensitive moral vocabularies, and thereby to create moral relevance." Richard Rorty, *Method and Morality, in* SOCIAL SCIENCE AS MORAL INQUIRY 174 (Norma Haan et al. eds., 1983).

71. *See* JONSEN & TOULMIN, *supra* note 34, at 1-228.

provide a kind of general orientation or moral compass. They provide, that is, reasons for acting certain ways. In depriving ethicists of the grounds for this kind of reason-giving, the radical particularists fundamentally distort one of the most basic features of ordinary moral experience.

Another problem with this view is that it appears to embrace the dubious notion that one can grasp the moral essence of individual cases through a kind of "immaculate perception" unmediated by reference to general propositions. It assumes that agents can traverse the field of their moral experience, moving from case to case, unaided by appeals to principles, theory or other abstract notions. The problem, however, is how one might decide to align any particular case against a paradigm or series of precedent cases. In order to determine that a certain case belongs to this line of cases rather than that, the casuist will require norms, whether implicit or explicit, of moral relevance. Thus, the casuist's efforts to categorize cases are necessarily "theory laden," at least in the sense that they implicate some kind of more general moral appeal.[72] Thus, following MacIntyre, one might say that cases elucidate ethical "theory," while theory is a kind of story about how cases are to be described.[73]

More moderate versions of casuistry make room for principles, theories, and cultural norms, while still insisting on the priority of the particular. Instead of imposing a false choice between responses to cases and principles, these ethicists envision, in the words of Martha Nussbaum, a "process of loving conversation between rules and concrete responses, general conceptions and unique cases, in which the general articulates the particular and is in turn further articulated by it."[74] These more general propositions play a role, but rarely, if ever, as mere axioms from which moral conclusions might be deduced. Whatever validity or usefulness these general notions might have will depend upon the ethicist's insight, moral sensitivity, and casuistical skill in applying them to a case.

At this point in the history of principlism and the emerging paradigm of casuistry, it should be clear that these two approaches are not as antithetical as their respective partisans often suggest. On the contrary, reformed principlists who have abandoned deductivism and moderate casuists who admit a role for principles and general notions could endorse Martha Nussbaum's dictum with equal enthusiasm. Her dictum is, after all, just another way of calling for reflective equilibrium between principles and cases.

---

72. *See* Arras, *supra* note 63.
73. *See* MACINTYRE, *supra* note 44, at 7-11. For additional criticisms of "radical particularism," see Jeffrey Blustein, *Principlism and the Particularity Objection* (unpublished manuscript on file with author).
74. MARTHA C. NUSSBAUM, LOVE'S KNOWLEDGE: ESSAYS ON PHILOSOPHY AND LITERATURE 95 (1990).

B. The Ascendancy of Narrative

The casuists' emphasis upon the particularities of moral situations is also a recurring theme within the emerging literature of "narrative ethics."[75] Although this classification harbors an array of writers with widely divergent viewpoints on the relationship between ethics and stories, they would agree, in common opposition to a top-down "applied ethics" model, that the story or history is the most appropriate form of representing moral problems.

To support this claim, the partisans of narrative can point to the history of contemporary bioethics, which is in a sense a history of the "big cases." Whatever the so-called principles of bioethics might mean at this juncture, they have achieved their meaning through collective reflection upon a set of compelling stories. While the two dominant theoretical paradigms in ethics, Kantianism and utilitarianism, have been consistently indifferent or hostile to the role of narrative in ethical reasoning, the field of bioethics has moved the story or case study to center stage.

While some partisans of narrative ethics advance very strong and controversial claims,[76] I think all would agree that a complete story or history is a prerequisite to any responsible moral analysis. Before one can attempt to judge, one must understand, and the best way to understand is to tell a nuanced story.

Thus, to debate the issue of assisted suicide, for example, one should not rely on abstract, asocial, and timeless propositions, but rather begin within the context of a full-bodied case. Dr. Timothy Quill's well-known case study of Diane, a patient requesting assisted suicide, provides an excellent illustration of this narrative approach.[77] Instead of focusing on the derivation and specification of principles, Dr. Quill gives us a rich picture of the "players" and their characters. First, there was Diane, a courageous but fearful cancer patient seeking control of her dying process, a woman who had already overcome a previous cancer threat and her own debilitating alcoholism. Next, there was Dr. Quill himself, a competent and clearly compassionate physician torn between loyalties to his patient and professional ethics, a man courageous enough to "take small risks for people [he] really know[s] and care[s] about."[78] Then Dr. Quill explores the roles that the players occupy: a doctor trained to preserve life rather than end it; a patient who is also a wife, mother, and respected friend. He tells us about their prior and ongoing relationship: how he had witnessed and rejoiced when Diane triumphed over adversity, and

---

75. *See, e.g.*, HOWARD BRODY, STORIES OF SICKNESS (1987); ALASDAIR C. MACINTYRE, AFTER VIRTUE (1984); NUSSBAUM, *supra* note 74; Margaret U. Walker, *Keeping Moral Spaces Open: New Images of Ethics Consulting*, HASTINGS CENTER REP., Mar.-Apr. 1993, at 33; David Burrell and Stanley Hauerwas, *From System to Story: An Alternative Pattern for Rationality in Ethics*, in KNOWLEDGE, VALUE, AND BELIEF 111-52 (H.T. Englehardt, Jr. & Daniel Callahan eds., 1977).

76. Nussbaum, for example, argues that narrative is the *only* proper medium for some philosophical issues. *See* NUSSBAUM, *supra* note 74, at 3.

77. Timothy E. Quill, *Death and Dignity: A Case of Individualized Decision Making*, 324 NEW ENG. J. MED. 691 (1991).

78. *Id.* at 694.

how he anguished with her over the current threat. He describes his own doubts and hopes for Diane's future and the future of their relationship. He wonders whether prescribing a lethal dose might restore her spirits and give her more emotional comfort in her final struggle. He also alludes to the institutional and social context, albeit in my opinion not sufficiently,[79] with references to the current state of the law.

Although a reconstructed principlist might object at this point that all the above matters can and should be folded into a principlistic analysis as components of "the case," I think it remains true that the partisans of moral theory and principlism have not given many of these issues their due. This is especially true of Quill's concern to sketch the moral character of his players, the nature of their past and future relationships, and the fine details of their institutional and social context. As Bernard Williams has argued, most received moral theories operate with impoverished or empty conceptions of the individual.[80] To bring the moral individual into clearer focus, he claims, one must attend to his or her differential particularity, to the desires, needs, and "ground projects" that coalesce into the *character* of the person. But if one is concerned with the depiction, understanding, and assessment of character, one can do so only by telling and retelling stories.[81]

Finally, note that there is an important pedagogical value of narrative approaches to ethics. A common thread uniting these "new paradigms" in bioethics is their emphasis upon particularity—of persons, character, situations, and histories. Both the casuists and narrativists insist that if one is to "do ethics" well, one must be, in the words of Henry James echoed by Martha Nussbaum, "finely aware and richly responsible"[82] to precisely these particularities.

It may be that the study of ethical theories and a concern for properly defining and specifying principles will make one a better judge of moral problems and policies. But without an equal if not greater concern for the particularities and nuances of specific situations, the "applied ethicist" will be operating as if in the dark. One very important way for students of morality, both young and old, to acquire and refine this sensitivity is to encounter complex narratives of real or fictional characters, situations, and events. Whereas philosophers' examples and at least one philosopher's[83] fiction tend to present narratives clearly in the service of some doctrine or rule, stories cultivate, in Nussbaum's fine phrase, "our ability to see and care for

---

79. Indeed, in my opinion, Quill's major failing is to have inadequately considered the implications of introducing the *practice* of assisted suicide within the context of a society that fails to provide adequate health care, including pain relief and treatment for depression, to millions of potential candidates.
80. Bernard Williams, *Persons, Character and Morality, in* MORAL LUCK 1, 1-19 (1981).
81. For a more fully developed statement of the fit between narrative and the depiction of character, see TOBIN SIEBERS, MORALS AND STORIES 15 (1992).
82. NUSSBAUM, *supra* note 74, at 148.
83. *See generally* SARTRE, *supra* note 8.

particulars, not as representatives of a law, but as what they themselves are . . . ."[84]

VI. THE ROLE OF CASES RECONSIDERED

What are the implications of these challenges to the reigning paradigm for the understanding and use of case studies? As has been seen, the "applied ethics" movement, while continuing the long tradition of viewing cases as mere illustrations of more theoretical propositions, began to envision cases as problems in their own right that required the assistance of philosophical theory. The particularist critique of this "applied ethics" model suggests two additional roles for case studies within the practice and teaching of bioethics.

First, the critique of deductivism, endorsed now by reformed principlists and casuists alike, assigns an important role to cases in the dialectic of reflective equilibrium. Instead of viewing cases as entirely subordinate to theory and/or principles, there is now common agreement that cases provide the considered judgments from which principles eventually evolve. There is also widespread agreement that while principles may continue to exercise normative force over judgments in particular cases, those very judgments can serve to test, specify, and even disprove particular formulations of principle and theory.

The analysis and assessment of case studies thus assumes a much more integral role in the process of moral reflection and theorizing than either the standard applied ethics model or the philosophical tradition had envisioned. Indeed, in such a constructivist model the very notion of "applied ethics" is redundant, since all ethics is "applied" in the sense that it grows out of particularities and is constantly tethered to them in a process of perpetual readjustment.

A second new role for case studies within particularized bioethics is to serve as a laboratory for students and teachers alike to learn how to perceive, comprehend, and judge ethically. Whereas the more mechanistic variants of applied ethics simply assumed that all the ethical heavy lifting went into the formulation of theory and principles and that the process of "application" was only a matter of bringing factual particulars under the rule of normative principle, the emerging paradigms in bioethics draw attention to neglected aspects of moral reasoning and to skills that can be developed and nurtured through narratives and case analysis. Importantly, again in contrast to the nearly exclusive emphasis on principles and rule-governed behavior within applied ethics, most of these skills are not rule-governed and do not fit within a paradigm based upon a correspondence theory of ethical truth.

Consider, for example, what I have elsewhere called the skill of "moral diagnosis."[85] The very first step in moral analysis is the question: "What kind of case is this?" Confronted with a particular case, one must immediately

---

84. NUSSBAUM, *supra* note 74, at 184.
85. Alan R. Fleischman & John D. Arras, *Teaching Medical Ethics in Perinatology*, 14 CLINICS IN PERINATOLOGY 395 (1987).

start casting about for an appropriate general description. Since cases do not come pre-labelled, and since different observers can and do disagree about what certain cases are "really about," an essential part of one's "moral education" should involve the process of "diagnosing" morally problematic aspects of cases. Although some judgments are clearly better than others in this domain, the process is anything but rule-governed. Indeed, it requires a great deal of moral imagination and creativity to plot where the most important problems lie or to reframe the terms of a protracted debate in a way that both sides can accept and use as the platform for a fruitful compromise.[86]

The development of this sort of diagnostic skill or art is crucial in clinical and policy settings, especially in view of the temptation for consultant ethicists to simply accept at face value the presuppositions of professionals in their labelling of cases. Although I am not advocating a return to heavily theory-driven examples and cases, it is naive to think that moral problems exist independently of theory, broadly understood to encompass views of the good, principles, virtues, or professional ideology. Without careful attention to developing this skill of collaborative moral diagnosis, consultant ethicists will be reduced to playing the role of Jeeves to their respective employers.

In addition to the art of moral diagnostics, exposure to cases and narratives fosters other non-rule-governed skills crucial to ordinary moral reasoning. As Martha Nussbaum emphasizes, exposure to stories (especially the novels of Henry James) develops the ability to discern the particularities of morally charged situations, to be "finely aware and richly responsible."[87] Likewise, observing skilled clinical casuists at work can hone one's capacities for analogical reasoning—the engine that drives most practical reasoning—and for judiciously weighing and balancing competing values. Finally, exposure to case studies can acquaint students of ethics with various practical strategies for coping with risk and uncertainty,[88] and with exemplars of morally necessary (and unnecessary) compromise among equally well-informed and well-meaning participants.[89]

---

86. During the course of a heated case conference in our Intensive Care Unit ("ICU") at Montefiore Medical Center regarding a case involving a family's request to wind down aggressive treatments, my colleague Nancy Dubler made the suggestion that this case was "really" about how to offer a patient hospice care in the context of an ICU. Both sides of the argument, those who favored the gradual withdrawal of life-sustaining treatment and those who opposed it on the ground that the mission of the ICU is to provide precisely this kind of aggressive care, welcomed this "reframing" of the issue as a way out of their quagmire. There is nothing rule-governed about this skill; it grows out of experience, imagination, and good judgment.

87. NUSSBAUM, *supra* note 74, at 148.

88. Nancy K. Rhoden, *Treating Baby Doe: The Ethics of Uncertainty*, HASTINGS CENTER REP., Aug. 1986, at 34.

89. MARTIN BENJAMIN, SPLITTING THE DIFFERENCE: COMPROMISE AND INTEGRITY IN ETHICS AND POLITICS (1990).

VII. THE RECALCITRANT PATIENT RECONSIDERED

To bring the form of this Article into closer conformity with its point, I shall conclude with a case and commentary that illustrate the value of enhanced particularity for ethical analysis. The case concerns the same recalcitrant TB patient encountered earlier, presented this time with a semblance of the detail demanded by the "emerging paradigms" in bioethics:

> The patient AB is a 42 year old Hispanic male. He has known that he is HIV-positive since 1989. He has been and continues to be an intravenous drug user. He was found by the Emergency Medical Service team in early April 1992, wandering and disoriented with a tourniquet still attached to his arm. He was brought to the hospital to rule out TB and endocarditis because of an active cough and a temperature of 105 degrees.
>
> Upon admission to the hospital, the patient's previous admissions were not immediately discovered because his two prior chart histories in the record room were linked to two different names and sets of personal data. Because of his admitting condition, however, and an X-ray that showed severe upper lobe infiltrates, he was placed in a single room and initially begun on INH, RIF, PZA, and EMB.
>
> Once the patient's medical history was reconstructed from the previous admissions, he was shown to have had two admissions in the previous three months and to be HIV-positive. He had received three or four weeks of therapy during that time, although none of it was consecutive. TB had been first diagnosed in January, it was sensitive to all drugs. A drug-resistant strain was confirmed upon sputum culture in March during his second admission; the organism was identified as resistant to INH and PZA. Upon the third admission, as on the prior two admissions, AB was placed in a negative pressure isolation room and ordered not to leave this space. When his prior drug sensitivities became available, he was placed on a six-drug regimen that included parenteral amikacin.
>
> The patient refused to stay in his room. He had been promised that a television and a telephone would be connected. When neither happened, he went in search of both. He also complained that the room was very cold and uncomfortable. After he had been found in the elevators and in the lobby of the hospital, the nurses took away his clothes. He was again found wandering in the hall. At that point the resident on duty called the guard and had the patient handcuffed to the bed by his hands and feet. He was also "posied", confined by a bed jacket with straps that were tied to the bed.
>
> The room was in fact quite cold, as is often the case with negative pressure, highly ventilated rooms. In addition, blankets were in very short supply in the hospital. As some patients were being given a stack of sheets in lieu of blankets, the nurses did not feel that they could give this particular patient more blankets. Even if the supply had been adequate, staff might not have been forthcoming. Once he had been gowned, cuffed, and posied, AB was quite cold and miserable.
>
> The next morning after the patient had been released from restraints for breakfast and was again found in the lobby, the resident called for a guard and asked the Department of Health for a detention order; it was issued.
>
> During this time the staff caring for the patient had no special protections. No "microspore" masks were available. The rumor in the hospital was that some would be available soon. The most effective masks, however, would be available only for special technicians such as those

doing induced sputum cultures. Masks at the next level of effectiveness would be available to the general staff. At this point, none were available except for those "liberated" from a nearby hospital. The resident in charge of the patient was pregnant and very afraid of contracting TB; she had, therefore, not actually seen or spoken to him.

Once the detention order was issued, the hospital placed the patient under "one-to-one" surveillance with a guard beside the door at all times. The cost of such supervision is approximately $100,000 per year.

Once the guard had been posted, the patient began refusing medications selectively. Some of the refusals seemed random. Some, however, were comprehensible. For example, he refused to take amikacin. The administration of this medication can be either intramuscular or intravenous. Assuming that there were no available veins to administer the drug intravenously, the staff had begun the intramuscular administration that he regularly refused because of the pain and discomfort. They then discovered that it was, indeed, possible to administer the medication intravenously. He did not refuse the medication in this form.

Approximately one week after admission, AB was shifted to a different single room that was less cold. He was also provided with a television and a working telephone. After four weeks of treatment, his fever abated, and he felt much better. He began to talk about leaving the hospital. He also began pulling out the intravenous drips used to administer the amikacin. His last three smears were negative, but his X-ray continued to show a large upper lobe infiltrate.[90]

In the first encounter with Mr. AB, the issue was simple: Should the patient be permitted to roam the corridors and lobby of the hospital where he might infect others with a potentially lethal strain of TB, or should he be forcibly detained in his room or, if necessary, on his bed? While the above "thicker" description of the case poses the same question, it reveals particularities about the patient's life in the hospital and his relations with others that might fundamentally alter one's attitude towards the case and the patient.

The second version of the case tells the story of a patient who exists, and is expected to tolerate existing, in near total isolation from the outside world. He has no phone, no radio, and no TV. Because his virulent strain of TB might be easily communicated to the staff, Mr. AB's own physician, a pregnant resident, refuses to enter his room. In addition, his room is now described as exceedingly cold and uncomfortable. Blankets would help, but they are unavailable. This is, after all, a chronically underfunded and ill-equipped public hospital. Clothes would help too, but they have been taken away by nurses to prevent him from wandering.

The relationship between Mr. AB and the hospital nursing staff emerges as a distinct theme in the second version. It is a terrible relationship. Mr. AB is no doubt acting in an irresponsible and disrespectful manner towards the nurses, and the nurses regard him, an HIV-infected drug abuser, as the classic "hateful patient." The narrative implies that even if the nurses had the

---

90. NANCY DUBLER ET AL., A SPECIAL REPORT, THE TUBERCULOSIS REVIVAL: INDIVIDUAL RIGHTS AND SOCIETAL OBLIGATIONS IN A TIME OF AIDS app. C, at 33-34 (United Hospital Fund of New York, 1992).

requisite blankets, they may not have given him some, just to punish him for his ongoing bad behavior.

The second narrative better details the handling of this difficult patient. It spells out in graphic detail exactly what it means for public health concerns to prevail over individual liberty on the floors of this particular hospital. In order to neutralize Mr. AB as a threat to the health of others, he is stripped of his clothing, placed in four point "restraints" (or handcuffs), and posied to the bed. The second account also shows that the patient may not be the irrational maniac suggested by the first description. After he finally gets a new room and some conveniences to occupy his time, he begins to cooperate with his treatment regimen, and some of his aversions are found to have a rational basis: they hurt and other modalities are available.

The thicker account of the case prompts reflection on additional ethical issues. The first issue concerns the meaning of this patient's "noncompliance." The first version does not explain his behavior; the second, expanded version allows one to comprehend and to "deconstruct" the notion of noncompliance. Mr. AB belongs to a class of patients who combine drug use with HIV-infection and TB. Many are homeless and impoverished; most who are noncompliant tend to manifest definite psychiatric disturbances. In the stressed and chaotic setting of the urban, public hospital, the needs of such patients often go unmet. With the lack of adequate social and medical supports, it is not surprising that people like Mr. AB have trouble cleaving to an extraordinarily strenuous and demanding medical regimen.

Who is to blame for Mr. AB's situation—Mr. AB or the social system that makes it nearly impossible for him to succeed? Seen through the "thick" account, the patient's "noncompliance" reveals an unnoticed social dimension of utmost importance both for individual patient care and social policy.

The second set of issues flagged by the thicker description concerns the relationships between Mr. AB and his health care providers. Although nurses, at least in my limited experience, generally tend to be more caring and compassionate with patients than physicians, the nurses in this case may have crossed the line between understandable exasperation with a difficult case and patient abuse. It is one thing to resent the hostile, noncompliant, and dangerous behavior of a patient, but it is something else again to strip him of his clothes in a frigid room, strap him down, and force toxic antibiotics into his body. This episode prompts one to reflect upon how powerful emotional responses can cloud judgment and interfere with professional behavior.

A related issue posed by this version of the case concerns the limits of one's professional obligation to treat difficult or dangerous patients. For the medical team, Mr. AB presents a triple threat: he is a potentially violent drug abuser, is HIV-infected, and is the host of a drug-resistant strain of TB. While the first two threats do not prevent most health care providers from attending to such patients, the third posed a serious problem for Mr. AB's pregnant resident physician.

What are the limits of professional obligation, especially for pregnant professionals, when confronted by serious health risks? In considering this, also recall the additional element of this case: This hospital failed to provide its physicians and nurses with the kinds of masks needed to protect themselves against the deadly strain of TB. Can the hospital expect its physicians and nurses to fulfill their ethical obligations to patients when it has not provided them with adequate protection? Again, a thicker description reveals the distinct social dimensions of the problem.

Finally, this more robust account of Mr. AB demonstrates the danger for ethical analysis of relying exclusively on certain actors' pictures of "the case." For example, relying on the housestaff and nurses probably would have produced a picture resembling the first sketch. With this limited picture, one sees the patient's vexing and dangerous behavior, but misses the additional issues the second sketch reveals. Thus, the testimony of social workers familiar with society's shocking neglect of such patients is welcome and necessary. To be sure, the perspectives of physicians and nurses involved in a case are indispensable in the construction of an adequate story, but they only provide a part of the story. To develop a larger psychological, social, and ethical context, the ethicist-consultant must actively participate in the development of "the case," rather than play the role of a passive recipient of professionals' stories.

Conclusion

What is the role of cases and case studies within the discipline of bioethics? This survey of the emergence of "applied ethics" and of the challenge of "new paradigms" reveals different answers to this question that reflect different conceptions of moral inquiry.

The philosophical tradition, with few exceptions, makes use of "examples" designed to illustrate theory, but has no use for case studies as we know them. The "applied ethics" movement in its early, "heroic" phase embraced case studies not merely as another vehicle for exemplifying theory, but as real-life problems to be solved with the aid of philosophical theory and moral principles.

The critiques of "applied ethics" and principlism by the partisans of casuistry and narrative ethics have further expanded the importance and role of case studies. For the casuists, cases provide the considered judgments and paradigms from which moral principles ultimately are derived and to which they must remain faithful within the creative tension of reflective equilibrium. Cases also put flesh on abstract moral principles, giving them concrete meaning, weight, and specificity. For the partisans of narrative, cases or stories provide the best window into the phenomenon of moral character while sharpening our ability to see particulars, "not as representatives of a law, but as what they themselves are . . . ."[91] For both casuists and narrativists, cases provide a laboratory for the development and nurturing of many important non-rule-governed aspects of moral reflection, such as the ability to reframe

---

91. NUSSBAUM, *supra* note 74, at 184.

and diagnose moral problems, to reason by analogy, and to engage in the judicious weighing and balancing of competing principles and values in concrete circumstances.

This shift towards the particular as the focus of moral inquiry has been accompanied by a parallel movement towards a different conception of moral justification. The applied ethics movement began in a powerful burst of enthusiasm for theory as the ultimate warrant for the rectitude of moral judgments. With the waning of this theory-driven, top-down, deductivist model of moral reasoning, justification was sought in moral principles derived through a process of reflective equilibrium. Instead of viewing moral justification as a question of correspondence between case judgments and the correct moral principle, justification is now sought in the overall coherence among case judgments, principles, cultural values, and ideals.

Implicit in this shift from correspondence to coherence is a parallel shift in emphasis from the individual to the social group as the focus of moral justification. Instead of searching for moral justification in a connection between an individual's judgment and some objective, universal, moral principle or theory, the particularist paradigms point, either implicitly or explicitly, to the social group as the ultimate "ground" or "foundation" of moral truth. Just as Thomas Kuhn has argued that the authority of scientific judgments resides in the consensus of its practitioners—that there is no transcendent warrant for different pictures of the world or scientific paradigms[92]—recent developments in bioethics also point to consensus within the community of inquirers, which includes the professions and the general public, as the ultimate but provisional warrant for actions and policies.[93]

As good Kuhnian paradigms, these particularist movements generate new problems as they challenge old methods. Perhaps foremost among these are the problems of critique and intercultural conflict. Just a few words about each may be in order before closing.

The great virtue of deductivism and of principlism in its early days of methodological slumber was their ability to criticize paternalistic assumptions and practices deeply embedded in the medical community. Of course, the norms on which this critique was based—such as respect for persons, for truth-telling, and justice—did not come from some detached realm of moral truth. Even if they were not embedded in medical practice, they belonged to the moral vocabulary of the larger society, where all the patients lived. What is one's response, however, when skeptics challenge the received wisdom and moral consensus of this larger society? What is the response when, for example, a long line of cases, developed casuistically and analogically, seems headed in the wrong direction? What should be done, in other words, about the problem of "bad coherence"?[94]

---

92. Gary Gutting, *Paradigms and Hermeneutics: A Dialogue on Kuhn, Rorty, and the Social Sciences*, 21 AM. PHIL. Q. 1, 4 (1984).

93. JONATHAN MORENO, THE SENSE OF THE HOUSE: BIOETHICS AND MORAL CONSENSUS (forthcoming 1995).

94. Margaret J. Radin, *The Pragmatist and the Feminist*, 63 S. CAL. L. REV. 1699, 1710 (1990).

This old question continues to haunt the partisans of particularism, including pragmatists and communitarians. One response, explored by Michael Walzer, is to emphasize the richness and diversity of most developed cultures, which usually harbor within themselves sufficient resources for vigorous critiques of existing assumptions and arrangements.[95] Another suggestion, offered by Tom Beauchamp at this Symposium, is that this task of correcting misguided casuistical analysis naturally falls to moral principles.[96] Indeed, Beauchamp argued that a continuing emphasis upon principles is necessary in order to steer casuistical analysis in the right direction.[97] In any case, the partisans of particularity need to grapple more carefully with this problem.

A related issue facing these new paradigms in bioethics is the problem of identifying the "we" that is the subject of moral consensus and devising ways of mediating conflicts between competing communities of inquiry and meaning. In the early years of the "applied ethics" movement, it was basically assumed that the so-called principles of bioethics were objective, timeless, and universal. Given the intellectual indebtedness of this movement to utilitarianism and Kantianism—two theories that fancied themselves as being objective in this sense—this was a thoroughly predictable assumption. The more one probes the particularities of different communities and cultures, however, the more likely one will discern differences in the meaning and weight of various moral principles, values, and ideals—differences that tend to preclude the kind of consensus sought.

Who, then, shall count as a member of the "community of inquiry"? A seventeen-year-old Latina, infected with HIV, who wishes to have a child in spite of the thirty percent risk of infecting her offspring with a lethal disease? Is her behavior "rational" or "responsible" according to her community? Is it rational according to "ours"? In case of a disagreement, how should one proceed?

Although a precarious consensus has emerged on a surprising number of bioethical issues, one must be alert to the fact that a heightened sensitivity to social and cultural particularity will often subvert consensus rather than foster

---

95. WALZER, *supra* note 59, at 39, 50.
96. Tom L. Beauchamp, *Principles and Other Emerging Paradigms in Bioethics*, 69 IND. L.J. 955, 962-66 (1994).
97. *Id.* Although I agree with Tom Beauchamp that principles may serve as a beacon for casuistical analysis—along with notions of the good life, virtues, cultural commitments, etc.—I am skeptical of his claim that principles will be especially useful in keeping casuistical reasoning on the straight and narrow. In the first place, as I have discussed, the way of ethical truth, mediated as it is by community and consensus, is neither particularly straight nor narrow. In many instances in bioethics, the ultimate question seems to be: "What kind of life are we forging together?", rather than: "Is this particular approach, for example, to reproductive technologies, morally correct?". Second, since our principles in large measure stem from our considered judgments about particular cases, they are likely to be "infected" by the same misguided casuistry they are supposed to correct. (The fault will often lie in our considered judgments. The Greeks, for example, found slavery to be perfectly natural.) And third, there is no reason to think that the existence and invocation of moral principles will necessarily serve as reliable correctives regarding moral truth. Casuists have no natural advantage over principlists in their ability to generate bad lines of case judgments. Having moral principles at your disposal does not guarantee that you will "apply" them well. Until principles are joined to the particularities of cases, they will remain abstract "chapter headings" capable of "justifying" contradictory case interpretations.

it. Partisans of the new paradigms of bioethics must prepare to meet this new challenge.

DAVID DEGRAZIA

MOVING FORWARD IN BIOETHICAL THEORY: THEORIES, CASES, AND SPECIFIED PRINCIPLISM*

ABSTRACT. The field of bioethics has deployed different models of justification for particular moral judgments. The best known models are those of deductivism, casuistry, and principlism (under one, rather limited interpretation). Each of these models, however, has significant difficulties that are explored in this essay. An alternative model, suggested by the work of Henry Richardson, is presented. It is argued that specified principlism is the most promising model of justification in bioethics.

Key Words: casuistry, deductivism, ethical theories, intuition principlism, specified principlism, specification

I. INTRODUCTION

These are troubled times for ethical theory. Many philosophers, and perhaps more nonphilosophers working in bioethics, have lost their hope of discovering an adequate ethical theory in the traditional sense – which would serve as the ultimate court of appeal in the justification of particular moral judgments (see, e.g., Williams, 1985; MacIntyre, 1984; Baier, 1985, chs. 11–12). An ethical theory in the traditional sense is a unified, comprehensive ethical system comprising one or more principles or rules related to each other in explicit ways; I will call such theories 'deductivist' and the general approach of working from them 'deductivism'. Just as troubling as the perceived failure of deductivism is the fact that no alternative model has earned greater theoretical confidence. Clearly, this problem concerns ethical theory as a whole. But attempts to develop detailed theoretical frameworks in bioethics (e.g., for justice in health care microallocation), and to use theory in clinical teaching and practice, have played a major role in revealing the current difficulties. For that reason, and because of the intrinsic interest of some recent developments in bioethics, this paper will focus on approaches developed by scholars

---

David DeGrazia, Ph.D., Departments of Philosophy and Health Care Sciences, George Washington University, Washington, D.C. 20052, U.S.A.

working in that field – i.e., on contributions in *'bioethical* theory'.[1]

While deductivism has been the dominant model among moral philosophers throughout the century,[2] it has been viewed somewhat less favorably in bioethics. One of the most commonly cited alternative models, which has most influenced the way bioethics is spoken about and taught, has recently been called 'principlism'. Principlism, the approach taken in Tom Beauchamp's and James Childress's *Principles of Biomedical Ethics* (Beauchamp and Childress, 1989), has lately come under severe attack.[3] One of the sharpest challenges has come in an article by Dan Clouser and Bernard Gert, who argue that principlism cannot provide genuine action-guides and that an adequate ethical theory is needed (Clouser and Gert, 1990). Another attack – on both deductivism and principlism (though these are not clearly distinguished) – has been made by Albert Jonsen and Stephen Toulmin, who call for a revival of casuistry, an inductive model with roots in Aristotle that was greatly developed by the Jesuits (Jonsen and Toulmin, 1988).

Bioethical theory does not seem to be advancing much today. Some have suggested that this sluggishness is due to the quality, or to the dearth, of scholarship in relevant theoretical areas (see, e.g., Brody, 1990; Green, 1990). I suggest that the difficulties lie with the leading models themselves, or perhaps with the way they are understood. This paper will examine and summarily criticize deductivism, casuistry, and principlism (which I take to be the leading models). Henry Richardson's idea of specification will then be introduced as a crucial contribution to our understanding of the relationship between general ethical norms and concrete cases. I will then argue that a 'specified principlism' is the most promising model – though it requires development.

II. DEDUCTIVISM

What makes an ethical theory deductivist is its having a theoretical structure sufficiently well defined that all justified moral judgments (or all within some specified domain) – given knowledge of relevant facts – purport to be derivable from the structure, in principle. So, once the correct structure or theory has been identified, there is no need to appeal to intuitions in arriving at correct moral judgments – either in balancing conflicting principles or in making particular judgments. (By 'intuitions' I mean judgments made simply because they seem correct, and not because they are believed to be justified by further considerations.)

The reasons for favoring deductivism are very powerful, so its dominance is not surprising. To be credible, moral judgments must be made for reasons. Claims that certain appeals count as good reasons in support of particular judgments (e.g., that an act's being a case of gratuitous torture makes it wrong) must also, up to a point, be made for reasons (e.g., that gratuitous torture is a case of unnecessary and significantly harming). It would seem, then, that ultimately there must be one or more general norms that serve as the final justification for all more specific moral judgments. And, if there is more than one such ultimate norm, how to adjudicate among them must be made explicit; otherwise, choosing among competing moral judgments, each of which is justified by *one* of the ultimate norms, could not be a rational procedure. While oversimplified, this argument explains why a deductivist theory that is rationally necessary (to the exclusion of all competing theories) would be the theoretically most adequate approach: Such a theory would, in principle, provide a method for justifying all correct moral judgments.[4]

Unfortunately, deductivism seems to be a failure. While this bald statement deserves a thorough defense, here I only highlight a few supporting arguments. First, unless almost all moral philosophers are mistaken, no deductivist theory has been shown to be rationally necessary; nor has any won the allegiance of most of this group.[5] Since no such theory appears to be rationally necessary, it is fair to judge theories partly by the intuitive plausibility of their implications. (Only the rational necessity of a theory would make intuitive plausibility entirely irrelevant.[6]) On this test, too, I suggest (here without argument), most, if not all, deductivist theories are inadequate, having too many highly counterintuitive implications.

Deductivist theories have also struck many theorists and clinicians as of limited use in bioethics. One problem is that, contrary to their pretensions, deductivist theories (including those limited to some specified domain) are *indeterminate*. That is, even with knowledge of relevant facts, deductivist theories cannot determine an answer for each moral problem; in fact, they generally do not come close (a point developed by modern-day casuists – see below).[7] Consider, for example, questions of justice in the microallocation of health care resources. Take any principle or set of explicitly-related principles constituting an ethical theory or theory of justice. Ask whether this principle or set of principles can determine (1) criteria for eligibility for a scarce resource when there is not enough to go around, or (2) criteria for final selection. Ask whether it can answer certain more specific questions without the help of other moral considerations. For example, if a patient awaiting admission to a full I.C.U. better fulfills admission criteria than someone already admitted, is it ever right to admit the first patient when doing so would entail a real loss to the second? If I am right, answers to these questions cannot be derived from the theory alone.

For many people working in bioethics, another weakness of deductivist theories is their remoteness from the actual cases on which they are supposed to bear (see, e.g., Baier, 1985). Moral philosophers who have taught medical ethics in clinical settings are often surprised to learn how infrequently it seems necessary to refer to theories, as opposed to principles or rules supportable by various theories. Indeed, for such teachers, tracing these norms back to theories often seems irresponsible, for risking unnecessary complication of the issues, or for dogmatic adherence to a theory when pluralism seems more appropriate. And actual ethical decision-making in medicine suggests the remoteness of ethical theories. While the relevance of such experiences to the *truth or correctness* of deductivism is disputable,[8] I here only flag a type of consideration that has made some scholars and teachers sceptical of that approach.

A final difficulty of many deductivist theories is their misplacement of moral certainty (a point taken up by the casuists).[9] In these theories specific moral judgments, rules, and 'mid-level' principles are all to be justified by appeal to the theory's supreme principle or set of explicitly-related principles. This terminus is supposedly more clearly justified, if not rationally necessary. Yet it is quite implausible to hold that *any* ethical theory has greater moral certainty than certain more specific norms – e.g., 'It is wrong to torture for fun', or better, 'It is prima facie wrong to torture'.

III. CASUISTRY

An alternative to deductivism that has received increasing attention is casuistry, a method of moral reasoning reawakened from three centuries' slumber with the recent publication of Albert Jonsen's and Stephen Toulmin's *The Abuse of Casuistry* (Jonsen and Toulmin, 1988). Following Aristotle and numerous other moral philosophers and theologians throughout the ages, Jonsen and Toulmin contend that deductivism completely fails to express the nature of moral reasoning. (In truth, they never clearly distinguish deductivism from principlism and their critique appears to be aimed at both.[10] For brevity I refer only to deductivism.)

First, no deductivist theory captures all our leading moral ideas (Jonsen and Toulmin, 1988, p. 297; cf. Brody, 1988, pp. 9–11). Second, the model of logical entailment embodied in deductivism – with moral principle as major premise, factual premise stating that the case at hand falls under the principle's scope as minor premise, and moral judgment as conclusion – cannot work in the rough terrain of moral living. Deductive arguments work only where the *relevance* of particular considerations and the *applicability* of principles are not in doubt, as in geometry (Jonsen and Toulmin, p. 327). It requires *practical wisdom* to determine which ethical norm applies in a complicated or ambiguous case. Not surprisingly, then, major ethical theories proved of limited use as modern bioethics began to emerge: "...disputations between 'consequentialists' and 'deontologists', or between Kantians and Rawlsians, were not of much help in settling vexed practical issues, such as the question, 'How much responsibility should physicians allow gravely ill patients (and their closest relatives) in deciding what treatments they shall undergo?'" (Jonsen and Toulmin, 1988, p. 305).

Most importantly, deductivist theories miss the fact that moral certainty, when it exists, is about particular cases, not abstract norms. This lesson was learned by the National Commission for the Protection of Human Subjects of Biomedical and Behavioral Research:

The *locus of certitude* in the commissioners' discussions did not lie in an agreed set of intrinsically convincing *general* rules or principles, as they shared no commitment to any such body of agreed principles. Rather, it lay in a shared perception of what was *specifically* at stake in particular kinds of human situations. Their practical certitude about specific types of cases lent to the commission's collective recommendations a kind of conviction that could never have been derived from the supposed theoretical certainty of the principles to which individual commissioners appealed in their personal accounts (Jonsen and Toulmin, 1988, p. 18).

This brings us to the heart of casuistry. Casuistry begins with clear 'paradigm' cases in which some norm is clearly relevant and indicates the right judgment or action. For example, if we see a man thrashing his child violently and without special cause, we know he is acting wrongly. From that (and similar) cases we can generalize, 'Violence against the innocent is wrong,' which guides our judgments in the absence of any excuse or extenuation (Jonsen and Toulmin, 1988, p. 323). Such paradigm cases serve to illuminate other cases using argument by analogy. 'Presumptions' are refined as new cases are encountered in which the norms apply *ambiguously* (say, if the child stole something, so that his innocence is debatable), or *in conflict* (say, if the child, who is very large, has begun to attack a smaller child who needs protection). Or, to think of it slightly differently, the norms acknowledged through paradigms may remain the same, while the understanding of exceptions may develop in considering further cases.

Thus in a particular case we must first determine which paradigms are relevant. Difficulties arise, then, if (1) paradigms fit only ambiguously or (2) two or more paradigms apply in conflicting ways. Jonsen and Toulmin see the cultural history of moral practice as revealing a progressive clarification of the applicability of paradigms and of admitted exceptions. Moral reasoning about cases, then, does not and cannot proceed de novo:

In ethics as in medicine, this "practical experience" is as much collective as personal. The priorities that have important roles in moral reflection and practice are, in part, outcomes of the lives and experiences of different individuals; but in part, they are also the products of each individual's professional, social background. One sadly neglected field of historical research is the history of ethics – ... an understanding of the ways in which moral practice, with its social, cultural, and intellectual contexts, has evolved over the centuries (1988, p. 314).

Thus casuistry is rooted in traditions and practices, not in pure reason or a special faculty of moral intuition.

How adequate is casuistry as a model of bioethical theory? Its advantages include avoiding the weaknesses that we have seen to plague deductivism, while (unlike some intuitionist theories) providing an account of the source of our intuitive understanding of particular cases, namely, traditions and practices. Casuistry also seems to be a realistic account of how we acquire moral understanding.

But note that the latter apparent advantage is of debatable value. Ethical theories are not necessarily models of how actual moral reasoning takes place. Actual moral reasoning might, in the main, be highly flawed; more likely, it is often incomplete. A successful ethical theory, however, must provide a valid justification procedure that extends to the highest possible level of generality while retaining plausibility. Thus it would explain how justification *could* go (soundly), whether or not it typically *does* go that way. The weaknesses of casuistry, I think, concern its failure to meet this standard adequately.

First, casuistry relies excessively on intuitive judgments in cases of conflict.[11] If it is replied that appeal to tradition or prevailing practices can guide one through difficult conflict cases, two responses are in order. First, such appeal may prove impotent if the case is sufficiently novel, for it might transcend tradition and practices. Second and more decisively, when such appeal does seem to settle the issue, it is vulnerable to the charge of begging questions, bringing us to the next problem.

Casuistry seems too accepting of prevalent beliefs and practices. We noted that one criticism of deductivism that motivates contemporary casuistry is the fact that no deductivist theory captures the full gamut of our moral concerns. But why assume that the latter are self-validating? Maybe some common moral concerns – e.g., partiality towards members of one's own social group, religion, or nation – are groundless. And why take at face value the ethical convictions woven into our broad cultural traditions and professional practices? John Arras argues that because of the casuists' view of ethical norms as

mere summaries of our intuitive responses to paradigmatic cases, their method might suffer from ideological distortions and lack of a critical edge. Moreover, relying so heavily on the perceptions and agenda of health care professionals, casuists might tend to ignore the existence of important issues that could be revealed by other theoretical perspectives, such as feminism (Arras, 1991, p. 49).

For example, professional practices – even when 'corrected' on the basis of values embedded in the practices – may embody a vision of the physician-nurse relationship that appears elitist and male-centered, when subjected to criticisms developed in feminist thinking. As another example, neither broad cultural traditions nor the professional practice of researchers may have sufficient critical edge to confront squarely the question of whether the interests of animals should be given equal consideration to the like interests of humans.

The last point takes us to a final criticism. By focussing on cases, casuistry risks missing global ethical issues the resolution of which may be entirely relevant to specific cases. Issues tied to the moral status of animals is one example. A second is the broad issue of distributive justice. Which theory, or set of theories, in the range from libertarianism to radical egalitarianism should a nation like ours embrace (implictly) in deciding, for example, whether to create a national health plan? Consider also a related concern expressed by Arras. A casuist, he argues, is likely to reason as follows about the problem of whether to fund heart transplants. Our society is already committed to paying for renal dialysis and transplantation, open-heart surgery, and many other, comparably expensive 'high-tech' therapies. So long as heart transplants qualify medically as a proven therapy, there is no reason why Medicare and Medicaid should not fund them. But should these other therapies be funded in the first place? Arras concludes that "such contested practices raise troubling questions that tend not to be asked, let alone illuminated, by casuistical reasoning by analogy" (1991, p. 46). I think, then, that unless supplemented with tools allowing for criticism on various levels, casuistry cannot be considered an adequate model.

IV. PRINCIPLISM

'Principlism' is a recently coined term for theories whose structure at the most general level (clarified by the theory) consists in a plurality of nonabsolute principles of obligation. Although he used the language of 'prima facie duties' rather than 'principles', W.D. Ross (1930) was a principlist; William Frankena (1973) was as well, his theory asserting prima facie principles of beneficence and justice. Principlism has been especially important in bioethics due to the influence of Beauchamp's and Childress' *Principles of Biomedical Ethics* and the *Belmont Report* (National Commission, 1979). These documents have given rise to the 'mantra' of bioethics: 'autonomy, beneficence, nonmaleficence, and justice'.[12]

Since principlism as it relates to bioethics is best expressed in *Principles of Biomedical Ethics*, I focus on this book.

Early in *Principles* the authors express an ambivalent attitude about ethical theories. On the one hand, they suggest that ethical theories have an important role in justifying principles: "To be justified, one's principle's must themselves be defensible" (1989, p. 6). They then present a commonly cited diagram showing particular judgments and actions being justified by rules, which are justified by principles, which are in turn justified by ethical theories.[13] On the other hand, they concede that they do not think any available theory is quite adequate:

For one author of this volume, a form of rule utilitarianism is more defensible than any available deontological theory; for the other, a form of rule deontology is more acceptable than any version of utilitarianism. ... Still, for both of us the most satisfactory theory is only slightly preferable, and no theory fully satisfies the tests explicated [earlier] (1989, p. 44).

They go on to develop an account of prima facie principles, which they refer to as their 'theory'. So why are the 'higher' theories necessary? They appear to play no significant justificatory role in their system, yet invite seemingly pointless disputes between rule-utilitarians and -deontologists. What is important is the convergence of the two theories, and the convergence occurs at the level of principles and at 'lower' levels. Let us turn, then, to their principlism.

The first thing to note is that the metaethical theory is not rationalist, and the normative structure not deductivist – though many critics (e.g., Clouser and Gert, 1990) assume one or both of these falsehoods.[14] What establishes a justified theory is a dialectical approach, not a knock-down rationalist argument establishing indubitable first principles. (An argument is rationalist if it purports to establish that its conclusion is rationally necessary; a theory is rationalist if it purports to be rationally necessary.) The authors say this:

We develop theories to illuminate experience and to determine what we ought to do, but we also use experience to test, corroborate, and revise theories. If a theory yields conclusions at odds with our ordinary judgments – for example, if it allows human subjects to be used merely as means to the ends of scientific research – we have reason to be suspicious of the theory and to modify it or seek an alternative theory (1989, p. 16).

Thus it is wrong "to say that ethical theory is not *drawn from* cases but only *applied to* cases," (ibid). It is astonishing how often critics of this book fail to observe this point.

The authors are on more solid ground when they emphasize the principles that represent the most general agreed-upon level of justification:

> The four core principles are intended to provide a framework of moral theory for the identification, analysis, and resolution of moral problems in biomedicine. Deliberation and justification occur in applying the framework to cases. ... We can also say, without undue paradox, that the different tiers of justification – judgments, rules, principles – can be used to test one another (ibid).

Here it becomes evident that Beauchamp and Childress endorse reflective equilibrium. My reading is that reflective equilibrium establishes the *framework* of principles and more specific rules, which is then applied to cases (although principles and rules are subject to further revision in the light of reflection on the cases).

But there is still a problem of interpretation. Given the role of cases and the structure of reflective equilibrium, is their framework simply a form of inductive intuitionism, in which theories are formed entirely on the basis of specific intuitive judgments (see, e.g., Brody, 1988)?

The answer turns on the matter of whether the principles have a source other than, or in addition to, cases. And I think the answer is yes. A quiet statement in a footnote suggests that principles are partly grounded in tradition:

> By proposing the need for an *external* basis for justification in ethics, we do not embrace foundationalism in moral justification, in the sense of holding that moral theories are rooted in some ahistorical domain rather than in history and tradition. To the contrary, we would support (if we could develop the argument here) a robust historicism in preference to foundationalism (1989, p. 24).

But we may still ask whether tradition simply feeds into judgments about cases, which ground the principles, or whether tradition feeds (also or exclusively) into the principles, distinguishing this approach from inductivism (either casuistry or intuitionism). I assume the latter interpretation because of the author's emphasis on reflective equilibrium and the lack of textual evidence supporting the inductivist interpretation.

What the authors arrive at, of course, is a plurality of prima facie principles:

> We [treat] principles and rules as prima facie binding. The theory we defend may be called a composite theory. ... A composite theory permits each basic principle to have weight without assigning a priority weighting or ranking. Which principle overrides in a case of conflict will depend on the particular context, which always has unique features (1989, p. 51).[15]

But how is one to know which principle to favor when two or more of autonomy, beneficence, nonmaleficence, and justice conflict? The authors claim that "agents are not left with only intuition as a guide" (1989, p. 62). What is the guide, then?

The next sentence states that they have "proposed a process of reasoning that is consistent with both a rule-utilitarian and a rule-deontological theory" (ibid), a process that will become evident when they explore the content of the principles in the chapters that follow. I am not sure the process ever does become evident. First, the discussions that follow never seem to draw explicitly from utilitarianism (whose justification procedure may be inconsistent with reflective equilibrium, anyway). Second, while these discussions certainly *involve* rules and are therefore *consistent* with rule-deontology, this claim is rather empty. Because we are never told what deontological consideration is supposed to unite the rules (as utility unites rules in rule-utilitarianism), how except intuitively, are we supposed to know what rules are right? The discussions seem in no explicit way to be *guided by* 'rule-deontology'.

Another way of reading their remark is to take the 'process of reasoning' to be, or include, a list of requirements they provide for infringements of prima facie principles or rules – e.g., that such an infringement "be necessary in the circumtances, in the sense that there are no morally preferable alternative actions that could be substituted ..." (1989, p. 53). But, like the other requirements, this is so breathtakingly obvious (imagine someone disagreeing with it!) that it can hardly be thought to get the agent significantly away from intuition. The authors never make explicit the way in which their theory provides agents with a significant advance over intuitive balancing or 'judging' in cases of conflict. (However, I take up another interpretation of their 'procedure' below.)

How strong an alternative to deductivism and inductivism is

principlism, as expounded by Beauchamp and Childress? Under one common interpretation, the theory as a whole seems to suffer from this serious difficulty: Either it is radically indeterminate, failing on a large scale to generate solutions to concrete problems, or, if it does yield answers, they lack discursive justification. This can be seen by asking how we are to apply the framework of principles to cases which involve a conflict among principles (a problem discussed above). When a competent patient refuses to consent to life-sustaining treatment that seems to be in her interests, creating a conflict between autonomy and beneficence, how should we decide? Clearly we cannot just apply the principles, since they conflict; we need a rule. The tentative rule they propose opposes strong paternalism (which infringes someone's autonomous wishes) in almost all instances (1989, pp. 219–20). How was this rule arrived at? Certainly, mere consideration of autonomy and beneficence does not yield this result. If the balancing or judgment is said to be intuitive, this forfeits any claim to discursive justification. This is the basic problem under a common interpretation of principles, which is that the framework of principles is supposed to imply certain rules that can guide us in particular cases – call this *the 'free-floating principles' interpretation*.

But perhaps the anti-paternalistic rule is itself the product of reflective equilibrium, which includes consideration of intuitive judgments about particular cases. If so – and I favor this interpretation – critics regularly miss this point. For example, Clouser and Gert (who, strangely, cite the 2nd edition of the book, though the 3rd was available), write the following: "Since there is no moral theory that ties the 'principles' together, there is no unified guide to action which generates clear, coherent, comprehensive, and specific rules for action nor any justification of those rules," (1990, p. 227). It is true that there is no unified theory from which rules follow. So to the extent that the authors claim that their framework of principles can be *applied* to generate rules and judgments in cases of conflict – and in places they do suggest this – they seem to be mistaken. Under this understanding of their model, it is, again, either indeterminate or lacking in discursive justification.

However, this might not matter if reflective equilibrium can do what the authors sometimes (and their critics usually) suggest the principles should be doing. But there remains the general problem of resolving conflicts between rules. Is this too to be taken care of by reflective equilibrium, this time between cases and rules? If so, their diagram on justification is very misleading. In either case, one would like to know more about the relationships among principles, rules, and specific judgements than simply that they involve (1) application or (2) reflective equilibrium.

Another problem concerns ultimate foundations. We are told that a 'robust historicism' is to provide external justification for the ethical theory. Why assume that the values embedded in our traditions are worthy of acceptance? I will say little about this issue here, since it was discussed with respect to casuistry. Let me simply assert that, if there is any way of identifying tools of ethical criticism that are valid for all human contexts, they are to be preferred to historically grounded values (even if the former cannot vindicate a deductivist theory).

V. SPECIFIED PRINCIPLISM

A. Introduction: Thesis and Assessment of Principlism

We have now examined two important alternatives to classical deductivist theories. Developed with an eye toward the resolution of bioethical issues, both, it seems fair to say, have proven more fruitful in bioethics than has deductivism. Yet, we have found that they have significant shortcomings. Neither is likely to be a very inspiring model for students of ethical theory and bioethics, or for theoretically interested clinicians. Is there any way forward?

My thesis is that principlism, self-consciously developed along the lines of what Richardson calls 'specification', is the most promising model for bioethical theory. 'Specified principlism', as I call this model, has the following features: (1) It has one or more (probably more) general principles 'at the top'; (2) It employs casuistry but is by no means reducible to it; (3) It allows the drawing and explication of relationships between norms of different levels, relationships usually irreducible to 'derivation' or 'entailment'; and (4) It allows for discursive justification throughout the system.

In order to explain this program, it will be best to begin with principlism, stating its strengths and reviewing where it needs modification or supplementation. In a nutshell, principlism has the following relevant virtues: (1) It acknowledges the lack of a rationalist foundation for morality, thereby vindicating the use of intuition at some level; (2) It acknowledges the lack of a supreme moral principle or set of explicitly-related principles from which all correct moral judgments can be *derived*; and (3) It acknowledges the need for a justification procedure that can (at least generally) distinguish correct intuitive judgments from incorrect ones, so that the whole theory is not reducible to intuitionism.

At the same time, principlism, as presented by Beauchamp and Childress, has the following weaknesses: (1) It mistakenly suggests, in places, that ethical theories (more general than the principles) have a significant role in justification; (2) To the extent (which is unclear) that any general norms are to be cited in order to generate more specific norms or judgments, no clear method affording discursive justification has been presented for dealing with conflicts; (3) To the extent that reflective equilibrium (which does allow for discursive justification) is to be used, it is not clear in what ways and at what levels; (4) Assuming that the principles are at least partly grounded in tradition, no defense of that foundation – or explanation of what it amounts to – has been offered.

These criticisms are largely calls for clarification and development. I disagree with those critics who believe the problems of principlism amount to its death sentence as a theory; I think such a conclusion is warranted only on the 'free-floating principles' interpretation. Surely, if principlism attempted to mimic deductivism, applying its principles in such a way as to *derive* rules and judgments, it would fail. Free-floating principles are not explicitly related and therefore cannot entail anything when they conflict. But the 'free-floating principles' interpretation is, again, incorrect.

B. Specification

Let us turn now to the basic ideas of specification, to see how they can advance principlism. Specification is the subject of an article by Henry Richardson that, to my mind, may be the most significant contribution to our understanding of bioethical theory in some time (Richardson, 1990). The essay's first sentences indicate that specification is intended as a way of advancing once we have seen the dead-ends of deductivism and intuitive balancing:

Starting from an initial set of ethical norms, how can we resolve concrete ethical problems? We may try to *apply* the norms to the case, and if they conflict we may attempt to *balance* them intuitively. The aim of this paper is to show that a third, more effective alternative is to *specify* the norms (1990, p, 279).

Turn now to a case Richardson uses to illustrate his thesis.

Consider this seemingly reasonable initial norm and the dubious conclusion to which it leads: (1) It is wrong for lawyers not to pursue their clients' interests by all means that are lawful; (2) In this case of defending an accused rapist, it would lawfully promote the clients's interest to cross-examine the victim about her sex life in such a way as to make sexist jurors think that she consented; therefore (3) It would be wrong not to cross-examine the victim in this way. A different, equally plausible norm leads to a conflicting conclusion: (4) It is wrong to defame someone's character by knowingly distorting her public reputation; (5) To cross-examine the victim about her sex life in such a way as to make sexist jurors think that she consented would be to defame her character by knowingly distorting her public reputation; therefore (6) It would be wrong to cross-examine the victim in this way (1990, pp. 281–2). How can the dilemma be resolved, since application is contradictory and balancing would lack discursive justification?

Richardson's answer is to tailor one of the norms to make it more specific. For example, (1) might be replaced with (1'): It is wrong for lawyers not to pursue their clients' interests by all means that are *both* lawful *and ethical*. This amendment by itself does not settle the conflict, but it motivates a reexamination of the scope of (4). While attacking a witness' character is common practice among lawyers, perhaps a rape victim needs special protections for her allegations. So we might replace (4) with (4'): It is always wrong to defame *a rape victim's* character by knowingly distorting her public reputation. With the specifications expressed in (1') and (4') the conflict seems to be settled (1990, p. 283). (Below I take up the question of how we are to know which possible specifications are justified.)

At this point the question arises as to whether the norms that result from specification (e.g., (1') and (4')) are absolute. Richardson's answer is reminiscent of Aristotle and the modern-day casuists:

Fortunately, there is no need to settle individual cases deductively in order to settle them on rationally defensible grounds. ... [O]nce our norms are adequately specified for a given context, it will be sufficiently obvious what ought to be done. ... A conclusion supported by considerations that hold only "for the most part" is, of course, rebuttable by further deliberation; but that is the way our moral reasoning goes. The ability to bring norms to bear on cases even while leaving them nonabsolute is a distinctive feature of the model of specification (1990, p. 294).

Specified norms need not be absolute; they may be qualified by 'generally' or 'for the most part'. Even those specified norms, like (1') and (4'), that are not so qualified, could be. For in this model, norms are always subject to future revision: "the complexity of the moral phenomena always outruns our ability to capture them in general norms" (1990, p. 295). (The "always" of this claim may seem exaggerated. Consider 'It is always wrong to torture babies just for fun'. While Richardson is not concerned to argue that there are no such absolute norms, he thinks that the norms of greatest interest in moral theory are nonabsolute (Richardson, 1991b)).) So fairly specific norms can often be stated in absolute form, even if they are admittedly subject to revision; 'It is always wrong to defame ...', is an example. At the same time, it does not seem helpful to state norms of great generality (e.g., a principle of beneficence) in absolute form, unless it is noted that they hold only 'for the most part'.

This last point might be taken simply to mean that we must regard our most general norms as prima facie, as they are regarded in *Principles*. There are several possible reasons for abandoning this qualifier.[16] First, it is closely associated with Ross' theory, which has the agent settle conflicts between prima facie duties with nothing more than an intuitive judgment, apparently precluding discursive justification. Second, 'prima facie' is generally understood to suggest that, absent conflict, a norm can be directly applied — that is, a correct moral judgment can be derived from it. This is no doubt true in some cases. But, as the casuists have shown, this deductive image is appropriate only when the applicability and relevance of norms to particular cases is beyond dispute (and there is no conflict) — and this sort of neat application is uncommon. Third, 'prima facie principle' might suggest a static norm, whereas in the model of specification, all that is interesting occurs as norms get tailored.

Thus Richardson suggests that, instead of saying, e.g., 'It is prima facie wrong to lie', we say 'It is generally wrong to lie' and move on from there. However, if we wish to emphasize that *sometimes*, absent conflict, deduction of moral judgments is straightforward, we could say this: 'It is generally wrong to lie, and always wrong to lie unless there is a competing obligation requiring us to do so – in which case go by the best specification', (Richardson, 1991b). But the difference between these two formulations is, I think, mostly a matter of style.

But by now the reader might be puzzled. In the block quote above it was asserted that that cases did not have to be settled deductively in order to be settled rationally. And Richardson has severely criticized the model of intuitive balancing or judging, as I have, on that grounds that it forfeits any claim to discursive justification. Then how does specification do any better? What determines whether a given specification is rationally justified? Other specifications were possible in the above case about the rape victim. If all we can say is that we made the intuitively most attractive specification, it is unclear how this is any better than – or even different from – intuitive balancing of conflicting norms.

Richardson's short answer is that "all such questions are to be answered in terms of the overall coherence and mutual support of the whole set of norms" (1990, p. 299). Specification depends on the possibility of reasoned criticism afforded by a coherence theory of ethical justification. Such an approach is enjoying increasingly wide support, as noted in a recent article by Brock:

The current conventional philosophical view of justification in ethics acknowledges that ethical judgments do express attitudes ... but also that they have substantial cognitive content and are backed by reasons that make them capable of support and admitting of reasoned argument. In this view, justification is usually developed along coherentist lines with one or another version of John Rawls' "reflective equilibrium" (1971, sec. 9) at the heart of the view (1991, p. 34).

Richardson states that the coherence standard to be used for specification "in effect carries the Rawlsian idea of "wide reflective equilibrium" down to the level of concrete cases" (1990, p. 300).

But what does this amount to? Richardson stresses that coherence involves not only logical consistency, but also argumentative support, so that some norms explain other norms (which is the idea of providing reasons mentioned by Brock) (Brock, 1991, p. 34). Moreover, a later summary comment indicates that coherence is not the only index for rational justification: "A specification is rationally defensible, then, so long as it enhances the mutual support among the set of norms *found acceptable on reflection*," (1990, p. 302, my emphasis). Thus, intuitive plausibility plays a role, but is not the way to determine the correctness of a particular specification. A specification can be *proposed* on any basis (e.g., intuitive plausibility, trial and error), but its correctness is testable by how well it coheres with the overall set of norms found to be intuitively plausible on reflection.[17] As a concluding remark, Richardson summarily notes that specification "benefits from a considerable degree of casuistical flexibility without sacrificing a potentially intimate tie to guiding theories; and it is able to proceed from norms looser and hence more acceptable than the completely universal ones required by the deductivist to reach a conclusion through a Peripatetic syllogism" (1990, p. 308).

C. *The Structure Clarified*

The idea is to think of principlism and specification united. That would mean, roughly, that a small number of principles – perhaps Beauchamp's and Childress' four – would, through specification, branch into more and more specific norms, reaching down to judgments about specific cases. Now let us revisit the problems of Beauchamp's and Childress' version of principlism, to see whether specification can help.

The easiest problem to solve is (1), though specification is not needed to do it. (1) is the misleading suggestion that ethical theories (more unified than the principles themselves) play an important role. The authors plausibly maintain that two distinct theories (rule-utilitarianism and rule-deontology) are equally adequate. This pluralistic claim suggests that neither theory itself plays an essential role. And if I have been right that no unified deductivist theory is adequate, then we should simply drop these theories from the picture.[18] *The entire network of principles and their specifications becomes the theory.*[19] If this sounds odd, that is only because of the continuing influence of the deductivist picture, which we have rejected.

More importantly, we now have the solution to (2), the problem that attempts to apply general norms in cases of conflict seemed to leave no possibility of discursive justification. Rather than intuitively balancing or judging, one revises one of the conflicting norms into a more specific norm that resolves the conflict – in such a way that maintains or increases the coherence of the total set of norms found reflectively acceptable. So, for example, a proposed specification that contradicted other norms in the system would be rejected (unless the whole package could be made more coherent and plausible by changing the ones it contradicted). Now avoiding contradiction is an aspect of coherence that is easy to understand. Less easy is *mutual support*, which I now illustrate.

Suppose someone claimed that we should understand the scope of moral concern to extend beyond humanity, but only to turtles. There is no contradiction in saying that the interests of humans and turtles alone count morally. Still, it is incoherent, for any attempt to provide reasons for this judgment will ultimately fail to fit well with many other judgments that seem reflectively plausible. Attempts to cite characteristics that humans and turtles share will either (1) bring other species into the moral domain, on pain of contradiction (as with sentience), or (2) seem incredibly ad hoc, defeating any claim of *argumentative support* (as with some bizarre disjunction of genotypes). Moreover, the judgment would fail to cohere with many reflective intuitions about the wrongness of certain kinds of treatment of other animals.

Specification also takes care of (3), the problem that it was unclear in what ways and at what levels reflective equilibrium has a role. It is not that reflective equilibrium will establish the principles, which will then be applied to cases (as, I think, the authors sometimes suggest).[20] First, that is too static a picture. Second, and more importantly, principles cannot really be applied because they hold only 'generally'. They can be specified all the way down to cases, and then no further application is necessary. Reflective equilibrium is to be sought throughout the system, on an ongoing basis, as norms are specified and revised. So the famous diagram of justification in *Principles* should probably be omitted or significantly revised. Arrows going in one direction wrongly suggest a model of application, as noted above. Moreover, the hierarchy of four levels may unnecessarily oversimplify the relationships among norms; there are any number of levels.

A bit more must be said about reflective equilibrium, however. Several critics of this method have claimed that it is, at bottom, warmed-over intuitionism, simply systematizing particular intuitions that have no claim to epistemological priority (see, e.g.,

Singer, 1974; Hare, 1975; and Brandt, 1979, ch. 1). Daniels has plausibly argued that this charge might be true of *narrow* reflective equilibrium (NRE) but not *wide* reflective equilibrium (WRE) (Daniels, 1979). Very roughly, NRE involves a person's identifying a set of considered judgments, formulating principles that largely account for or synthesize them, and revising principles or judgments until a stable equilibrium is reached.[21] So NRE is a form of inductive intuitionism and therefore suffers from excessive dependence on the people's considered judgments. Now consider WRE. While descriptions vary somewhat, in rough terms WRE requires one to compare the principles that would be obtained in NRE to principles supported by background philosophical theories believed to be true – and then revise the considered judgments, principles, and background theories as necessary, until reaching equilibrium. By employing background theories that are independent of the original considered judgments, WRE, proponents argue, gains a measure of theoretical independence from specific moral intuitions that greatly enhances its credibility[22]

Reflective equilibrium in the present model is closer to WRE, as commonly described, than NRE. It involves much more than revisions and systematization of an initial set of considered judgments. And, as we will see, it is importantly linked to background theories (viz., a theory of the nature and point of morality, and a theory of fundamental interests or value[23]). These background theories, as well as certain ethical theoretical considerations (e.g., the rejection of deductivism and inductive intuitionism) motivate a starting point that distinguishes this approach from inductive theories, including NRE: a plurality of principles. (These theories and other considerations, incidentally, explain why specification and principlism not only *can* be united, but *should* be.)

Yet specified principlism adds to common conceptions of WRE in describing a web of mutual support, without implying clearly discrete levels of principles and considered judgments (as common conceptions tend to imply).[24] Also, an apt metaphor for specified principlism, but probably not WRE as commonly conceived, is one of *growth* – as norms get further specified. Since relatively general norms are understood to hold only generally, they are usually not *revised*, as in common conceptions of WRE, but made more specific.[25]

Returning to the difficulties of principlism cited above, specification does not take care of (4), the problem that no defense or explanation of the foundation of tradition has been given. Nor is such a foundation essential to principlism. I would recommend that efforts be made to maximize critical tools that do not depend on tradition – so that we can do justice to the fact that some aspects of even well-developed traditions are criticizable.

To start, while I do not believe that universalizability (in combination with certain features of moral language) can provide us a complete ethical theory, as Hare does (1981), I think it can do significant work. Universalizability demands the citing of relevant differences to justify differences in treatment. Not every factual difference can count as morally relevant, a point well brought out by the observation that coherence involves argumentative support. Invoking universalizability and demanding relevant differences can, by the requirements of coherence, defeat racism, sexism, and some other forms of differential treatment (possibly including the giving of unequal consideration to the like interests of humans and animals). I am claiming that the availability of these argumentative tools, and possibly others, in an important sense transcends traditions – they are valid no matter what tradition one is in (and regardless of whether their validity is recognized). Some will argue that *what is to count as a relevant difference* will be determined by values embedded in a given tradition. But such relativity, if well-founded at all, can only go so far; for example, it was always wrong to treat blacks as less than equals. However, I will have to save further pursuit of these ideas for another occasion.

From the preceeding it should be clear that casuistry operates within specified principlism. Careful examination of real and hypothetical cases allows us to specify norms, by settling conflicts, determining the boundaries of rights, specifying conditions under which certain forms of harm are justified, and so forth. However, since general principles and critical tools are established independently of case analysis, the content of norms is not determined by examination of cases alone.

This brings us to the question of where the principles come from in the first place. What justifies the most general principles? I have expressed doubts about relying exclusively on tradition, and, in discussing casuistry, even less confidence in relying on practices (e.g., that of American medicine). I have also criticized the tendency of inductivism to base norms of every level of generality ultimately on specific judgments about cases. Add my rejection of rationalist foundations for morality, and it may look as if nothing is left.

I do not think matters are so bleak, although what I say here is more of a suggestion than a carefully developed proposal. Consideration of the nature and point of morality provides a rough starting point of the sort we seek. Anything we consider a moral system in some way requires an agent to respect the *interests, well-being, or points of view of other individuals*; the point of morality is to uphold or protect the interests or well-being of individuals, to allow life to go well (or better) for them.[26] And, as emphasized by many scholars, intrinsic to the idea of morality is the notion of impartiality (see, e.g., Gert, 1988, pp. 77–95). Thus morality in some way involves the overcoming of partiality; the 'others' whose interests one is to uphold are not simply friends, family, and so on, but some universal group (e.g., moral agents, human beings, sentient creatures).[27] Well, what are the most fundamental ways in which an individual's interests or well-being can be affected?

One plausible answer is this: by having one's autonomy respected or disrespected (if one is capable of autonomous action), by being benefitted or not, harmed or not, and treated justly or unjustly.[28] Any adequate moral system will in some way cover at least these fundamental moral concerns. This need not be worked out in terms of four principles. Respect for autonomy, for example, might be viewed as among the most important forms of benefit and as subsumable under beneficence and nonmaleficence – or under a single principle of utility.[29] (The latter possibility would not entail the deductivist theory of utilitarianism, because specifications would be guided by the coherence and plausibility of the whole set of norms, not by deduction from the original principle.) The ideas covered in the principle(s) of justice might be expressible in rights language applied to other principles or their specifications.[30]

Several points should be noted about this proposal. First, the precise content of the principles is not as crucial as it would be in a deductivist theory. This is because the principles are only starting points; their precise content is determined by specification, which, as we have seen, is not governed by logical entailments from the principles. That means that different sets of principles might yield similar, or identical, specifications. But, second, it is crucial to have some such plausible starting point to prevent us (with the help of other critical tools) from being either radically dependent on specific current intuitions and practices, or at a loss when such intuitions differ greatly from person to person. In considering what duties, if any, we have to those in the third world, we may find that while our tradition and common intuitions suggest little or no obligation to contribute, a more impartial consideration of fundamental interests yields a different conclusion. Third, the vindication of the principles need not amount to a rationalist demonstration to be compelling. This starting point is, again, justified by the combined force of arguments about the nature and point of morality, certain background theories (e.g., any plausible value theory), and ethical theoretical considerations such as the refutation of other models. These together form a suggestive argument, not a rationalist demonstration.

Before closing, I wish to emphasize that the model I have begun to sketch is not very new. It is largely found in Richardson's proposals. But, interestingly, Richardson writes this in his article: "My purpose in working out this model is to reform the way many of those working on these issues understand what they are doing and to articulate more explictly what has already been done by others," (1990, p. 280). He believes that some of the best work in bioethics employs specification implicitly – and I concur. What I have tried to do is unite principlism and specification explicitly and defend their union. But, to my mind, in spite of an unhappy effort to explain what they were doing, Beauchamp and Childress were already using the methods of specification throughout their text. That explains how they could move from general principles (so often considered 'free-floating') to more specific norms and particular judgments, without deducing the latter from the former.

Let me close with a very simple stated agenda for the future. First, the foundations of specified principlism have to be worked out more fully and explicitly. Second, details of the model must be filled in (1) at the more general levels, including the basic principles and norms closely related to them,[31] and (2) in particular areas that interest us. Due to the nature of the model, which is grounded in the nature of morality, we will never have a complete model of specified principlism – and whatever we have will be tentative. That is why I suggest no more than the two goals above.

At the same time – due also to the nature of the model – we will never have an ethical theory whose content can be articulated fully, the way most of us hoped (and some of us believed) could be done with the principle of utility, the categorical imperative, Rawls' principles of justice, or some other easily stated formula. At the same time, I believe that we now have a theoretical model whose overall plausibility moves us a healthy step forward.

NOTES

* A draft of this paper was presented at the Kennedy Institute of Ethics, Georgetown University on May 21, 1991. I thank the scholars who attended, especially Tom Beauchamp and Henry Richardson, for their helpful comments; I also benefitted from follow-up discussions with Richardson. A second draft was presented to members of the Program in Bioethics at George Washington University on August, 5, 1991. I am grateful to them for their thoughtful criticisms and suggestions. Finally, I thank an insightful reviewer from *The Journal of Medicine and Philosophy*.

[1] Strictly speaking, the only difference between ethical theory and what I call 'bioethical theory' is that, while the former is usually quite general, the latter extends all the way down to concrete cases in what we know as bioethics. The conclusions of this paper, however, may add to the growing doubt about the usefulness of distinguishing ethical theory from applied ethics, including bioethics. On this topic, see Beauchamp, 1984.

[2] A reviewer from *The Journal of Medicine and Philosophy* challenged this claim, suggesting that coherence theories, often employing Rawls' idea of reflective equilibrium (to be discussed below), have been dominant in the last two decades. I disagree. While coherence theory and reflective equilibrium have had an important impact on American ethical theory – and perhaps more on American social and political philosophy – I submit that a majority of the most significant contributions to ethical theory in the last twenty years have been deductivist. Consider, e.g., Nozick's *Anarchy, State, and Utopia* (1974), Donagan's *The Theory of Morality* (1977), Gewirth's *Reason and Morality* (1978), Brandt's *A Theory of the Good and the Right* (1979), Hare's *Moral Thinking* (1981), Parfit's *Reasons and Persons* (1984), Gauthier's *Morals by Agreement* (1986), and Griffin's *Well-Being* (1986).

[3] Even among those who think quite highly of the book, it is commonly criticized from the perspective of ethical theory. For example, after acknowledging that "[t]hroughout, the quality of discussion is very high," Ronald Green comments that "[f]rom an ethicist's perspective, what is most striking about this volume ... is its almost deliberate avoidance of deep engagement with basic theoretical issues in ethical theory," (1990, p. 188).

[4] The case for deductivism is elegantly and powerfully made by Henry Sidgwick in *Methods of Ethics* (Sidgwick, 1907). For a painstakingly careful examination of

Sidgwick's argumentation (though not just for deductivism), see Richardson, 1991a.

[5] This second point is only suggestive (while the first is, of course, tentative). Admittedly, it is conceivable that moral philosophers have failed to appreciate an argument, already proffered, that demonstrates the rational necessity of some deductivist theory; less implausibly, there may be such an argument that remains undiscovered.

[6] In *Interests, Intuition, and Moral Status* (DeGrazia, 1989), ch. 3, I argue that, unless an ethical theory is alleged to be rationally necessary, intuitions must be appealed to at some level in the process of justifying the theory. Intuitions, again, are judgments that are asserted because they seem correct and not for any further reason. The only way a theory could be formed without intuition, then, would be if *all* of the moral judgments it implied were believed to be justified by some reason other than their seeming correct – up to some terminus (the theory itself) that is believed to be justified by being rationally necessary.

[7] Utilitarians would insist that specific versions of their theory are exceptions to this indeterminacy thesis. Perhaps that is true. But when applied to a wide range of concrete problems in health policy, for example, utilitarianism quickly reveals ambivalence about what should count as good consequences, what as evil ones, about the role of intermediate rules, and even about what beings (e.g., fetuses) fall within the scope of moral concern. Versions of the theory specific enough to address these concerns are still dogged by the difficulties of predicting consequences with sufficient assurance to justify particular policy recommendations.

[8] Hare argues that everyday moral decision-making need not make any reference to an ultimate ethical theory, yet the norms that should guide such everyday thinking are derivable from an ethical theory that can be reflected upon in moments of leisure (1981).

[9] This criticism does not affect those deductivist theories whose most general principles are justified, wholly or in part, by appeal to more specific judgments or norms. Thus theories established by considerations of coherence or reflective equilibrium are immune to the present charge.

[10] This odd conflation is consistently displayed in an article by Jonsen, who treats prima facie duties – proposed by Ross as an *alternative* to absolute principles – as if they were themselves absolute principles: "Autonomy, beneficence, non-maleficence and justice became the bioethicists' distant echoes of the Calvinist's Decalogue. These principles were law-like statements ..." (Jonsen, 1990, p. 127).

[11] This is also a major difficulty of Brody's pluralistic, inductive intuitionism, an alternative to deductivism that I have not discussed for reasons of space. This theory uses intuitions about particular actions, social arrangements, and the like to generate a list of irreducible moral considerations – viz., rights, consequences, respect for persons, virtues, and cost-effectiveness and justice. These considerations are to guide us in moral decision-making, but when they conflict, the agent has no specific procedure or rule for deciding: "This final process ... is a process of judgment," (Brody, 1988, p. 77). This idea of 'judgment' is like the Rossian idea

of individual decisions' resting with 'perception' (Ross, 1930), i.e., intuition.

While this criticism concerns the use of intuition *at the moment of judging*, another problem is the use of intuition in *forming the tools to be used* in judging. The ultimate source of *all* levels of the theory is particular intuitive judgments. Such excessive reliance on intuitions may rightly be regarded as question-begging (a point developed with respect to casuistry).

[12] Actually, the *Belmont Report* subsumes nonmaleficence under beneficence (National Commission, 1978).

The 'mantra' label has been used to express some people's feeling that these terms are incessantly parroted without real understanding of their meanings – and with the uncritical assumption that the essential normative ideas of bioethics must be articulated in this form. However, the label 'mantra' has become as parroted as the mantra, so I will avoid this term.

[13] This diagram is just as commonly misunderstood. Critics frequently interpret it as indicating that the authors advocate a theory whose principles are arrived at independently of reflection on specific cases. What they miss, as we will see, is that theories, or at least the basic principles, are justified by reflective equilibrium.

[14] John Arras includes *Principles* as among those works that "begin from 'on high' with the working out of a moral theory and culminate in the deductivist application of norms to particular factual situations," (1991, p. 30).

[15] The last phrase is unfortunate. Taken literally, it is trivially true that the contexts of different cases always have unique features – they are numerically distinct. On the other hand, taking it to mean that each different context has unique *morally relevant* features is false, unless situationalism, which they reject, is true. They are wise to reject situationalism, since the latter fails to acknowledge the rules that can be generated by appeal to universalizability.

[16] In this paragraph I go somewhat beyond Richardson's article, though I attempt to capture its spirit. I am influenced here by Richardson (1991b).

[17] Thus this approach is rather Quinean. (See. e.g., Quine's classic, 'Two dogmas of empiricism' [Quine, 1951].) No norm or judgment is deemed immune from doubt (and possible revision) on account of its own intuitive plausibility. Still, the cost of revising some norms or judgments, in terms of other revisions that would be required to maintain coherence, might be so high that we could not seriously imagine revising them (see Daniels, 1979, p. 267). Contrast a foundationalist intuitive theory that treats certain judgments as immune from doubt and as forming a foundation for the rest of the theory.

[18] Here I assume that rule-deontology (if it meets the authors' claims) is a unified, deductivist theory. Although, as mentioned above, the book never explains what deontological consideration unites the four principles, the claim that these principles are justified by theories (one of which is rule-deontology) logically requires a deontological theory that can unite the principles (just as rule-utilitarianism does).

My conviction, of course, is that the principles do not need to be justified by a more general theory – which is suggested by *some* of the authors' remarks (see sec. IV) – so that the absence of a unified rule-deontology is no loss.

[19] I leave open the possibility that this network of norms might eventually be found to have a single principle or set of principles 'at the top', uniting various principles like those of Beauchamp and Childress. But since the relationship of such a 'theory' to other norms would not be that of logical entailment, given our rejection of deductivism, it would still be best to take our theory to be the whole set of norms. Also, since no supreme principle or explicitly-related set has been identified, yet specification flourishes anyway, it is hard to see how any such principle or set can be considered essential.

[20] See, e.g., where they speak of applying the framework of principles (Beauchamp and Childress, 1989, p. 16). But, clearly, in other places the authors suggest a picture more like the one I am developing, if less explicitly. (See extended discussions of quotes from p. 16 in sec. IV.)

[21] Thus NRE is in some important ways analogous to descriptive syntactic theory in linguistics (Daniels, 1980a).

[22] See Daniels, 1979. For a subtle argument that NRE and WRE are complementary – not competing – approaches, but that we have some reason to prefer NRE methodologically, see Holmgren, 1989.

[23] I speak now of *my* development of this model. These particular background theories are not essential to specified principlism.

[24] This attribution must not be overstated, however. Although Rawls originally (Rawls, 1951) restricted considered judgments to judgments about particular cases (so that principles and considered judgments constituted clearly discrete levels), he later allowed considered judgments to have any level of generality (Daniels, 1979, p. 258).

[25] There are many more important questions about reflective equilibrium than I can tackle here. In addition to the works already cited, see Daniels, 1980b and DePaul, 1986 for deeper exploration of this method.

[26] A much more complete defense of these claims is provided in DeGrazia, 1989, ch. 1; see also Warnock, 1971, ch. 2.

[27] Explaining what morality essentially involves does not explain why anyone should be moral. But that is another question.

[28] This is all very crude, as stated. Its full vindication and a specification of its content would require the support of a plausible value theory (as well as a theory of autonomy) – except for justice, which concerns the *distribution* of valuable things. A principle of justice, therefore, is independent of and presupposes a value theory.

[29] Griffin, for example, treats autonomy as intrinsically valuable in a consequentialist theory (1986).

[30] The possibility of expressing ideas of justice in terms of rights, without appeal to a separate principle or rule of justice, is demonstrated by Gewirth, whose entire normative theory is captured in rights to freedom and well-being (1978).

[31] But, again, there may be several equally plausible ways of articulating the

most general norms (or norm).

REFERENCES

Arras, J.D.: 1991, 'Getting down to cases: The revival of casuistry in bioethics', *Journal of Medicine and Philosophy* 16, 29–51.
Baier, A.: 1985, *Postures of the Mind*, University of Minnesota Press, Minneapolis, Minnesota.
Beauchamp, T.L.: 1984, 'On eliminating the distinction between applied ethics and ethical theory', *Monist* 67, 515–31.
Beauchamp, T.L. and Childress, J.F.: 1989, *Principles of Biomedical Ethics*, 3rd ed., Oxford University Press, New York.
Brandt, R.B.: 1979, *A Theory of the Good and the Right*, Clarendon Press, Oxford, England.
Brock, D.W.: 1991, 'The ideal of shared decision making between physicians and patients', *Kennedy Institute of Ethics Journal* 1, 28–47.
Brody, B.A.: 1988, *Life and Death Decision-Making*, Oxford University Press, New York.
Brody, B.A.: 1990, 'Quality of scholarship in bioethics', *Journal of Medicine and Philosophy* 15, 161–78.
Clouser, K.D. and Gert, B.: 1990, 'A critique of principlism', *The Journal of Medicine and Philosophy* 15, 219–236.
Daniels, N.: 1979, 'Wide reflective equilibrium and theory acceptance in ethics', *Journal of Philosophy* 76, 256–82.
Daniels, N.: 1980a, 'On some methods of ethics and linguistics', *Philosophical Studies* 37, 21–36.
Daniels, N.: 1980b, 'Reflective equilibrium and archimedean points', *Canadian Journal of Philosophy* 10, 83–103.
DeGrazia, D.: 1989, *Interests, Intuition, and Moral Status* (a Georgetown University dissertation).
DePaul, M.R.: 1986, 'Reflective equilibrium and foundationalism', *American Philosophical Quarterly* 23, 59–69.
Donagan, A.: 1977, *The Theory of Morality*, University of Chicago Press, Chicago.
Frankena, W.K.: 1973, *Ethics*, 2nd ed., Prentice-Hall, Englewood Cliffs, New Jersey.
Gauthier, D.: 1986, *Morals by Agreement*, Clarendon Press, Oxford, England.
Gert, B.: 1988, *Morality: A New Justification of the Moral Rules*, Oxford University Press, New York.
Gewirth, A.: 1978, *Reason and Morality*, University of Chicago Press, Chicago.
Green, R.M.: 1990, 'Method in bioethics: A troubled assessment', *Journal of Medicine and Philosophy* 15, 179–97.
Griffin, J.: 1986, *Well-Being: Its Meaning, Measurement and Moral Importance*, Clarendon Press, Oxford, England.
Hare, R.M.: 1975, 'Rawls' theory of justice', in Daniels, N. (ed.), *Reading Rawls*,

Basic Books, New York.

Hare, R.M.: 1981, *Moral Thinking: Its Levels, Method, and Point*, Clarendon Press, Oxford, England.

Holmgren, M.: 1989, 'The wide and narrow of reflective equilibrium', *Canadian Journal of Philosophy* 19, 43–60.

Jonsen, A.R.: 1990, 'American moralism', *Journal of Medicine and Philosophy* 16, 113–130.

Jonsen, A.R. and Toulmin, S., 1988: *The Abuse of Casuistry: A History of Moral Reasoning*, University of California Press, Berkeley, California.

MacIntyre, A.: 1984, *After Virtue*, 2nd ed., University of Notre Dame Press, Notre Dame, Indiana.

National Commision for the Protection of Human Subjects of Biomedical and Behavioral Research: 1978, *The Belmont Report: Ethical Principles and Guidelines for Research Involving Human Subjects*, Government Printing Office, Washington, D.C.

Nozick, R.: 1974, *Anarchy, State, and Utopia*, Basic Books, New York.

Parfit, D.: 1984, *Reasons and Persons*, Clarendon Press, Oxford, England.

Quine, W.V.: 1951, 'Two dogmas of empiricism', *The Philosophical Review* 60, 20–43.

Rawls, J.: 1951, 'Outline for a decision procedure for ethics', *Philosophical Review* 60, 177–97.

Rawls, J.: 1971, *A Theory of Justice*, The Belknap Press of Harvard University Press, Cambridge, Massachusetts.

Richardson, H.S.: 1990, 'Specifying norms as a way to resolve concrete ethical problems', *Philosophy and Public Affairs* 19, 279–310.

Richardson, H.S.: 1991a, 'Commensurability as a prerequisite of rational choice: an examination of Sidgwick's position', History of Philosophy Quarterly 8, 181–97.

Richardson, H.S.: 1991b, (personal correspondence, June 3, 1991).

Ross, W.D.: 1930, *The Right and the Good*, Oxford University Press, Oxford, England.

Sidgwick, H.: 1907, *The Methods of Ethics*, 7th ed., Hackett, Indianapolis, Indiana (reprint).

Singer, P.: 1974, 'Sidgwick and reflective equilibrium', *Monist* 58, 490–517.

Warnock, G.J.: 1971, *The Object of Ethics*, 7th ed., Hackett, Indianapolis, Indiana (reprint).

Williams, B.: 1985, *Ethics and the Limits of Philosophy*, Harvard University Press, Cambridge, Massachusetts.

HENRY S. RICHARDSON

Specifying Norms as a Way to Resolve Concrete Ethical Problems

> We want to walk: so we need *friction*. Back to the rough ground!
> Ludwig Wittgenstein

I. INTRODUCTORY

Starting from an initial set of ethical norms, how can we resolve concrete ethical problems? We may try to *apply* the norms to the case, and if they conflict we may attempt to *balance* them intuitively. The aim of this paper is to show that a third, more effective alternative is to *specify* the norms. The problems that I am concerned with are of a sort typically ranged under the rubric of "applied ethics"—that is, relatively particular questions about what should be done in individual cases (e.g., Baby Doe's) or concretely described types of cases (e.g., Baby Doe cases). Although some who have worked most fruitfully on concrete ethical problems have begun to chafe at the "application" label,[1] no alternative metaphor has taken hold.[2] I aim to develop an alternative metaphor—that of

---

This paper specifies ideas first inchoately presented to an audience at the Hastings Center in June 1985. Since then, other versions have been presented at the Kennedy Institute of Ethics at Georgetown University and the Program in Ethics and the Professions at Harvard University. Those present at each of these occasions were most helpful. In addition, I am especially indebted to Tom L. Beauchamp, Sissela Bok, Wayne Davis, Ezekiel Emanuel, Linda Emanuel, Andreas Føllesdal, Alfonso Gomez-Lobo, Steven Kuhn, Aaron Mackler, Dennis Thompson, Kenneth Winston, and the Editors of *Philosophy & Public Affairs* for their detailed criticisms and suggestions. I am grateful to Georgetown University and to the Program in Ethics and the Professions for their generous financial support.

1. See, e.g., Albert Jonsen and Stephen Toulmin, *The Abuse of Casuistry* (Berkeley: University of California Press, 1988); Michael D. Bayles, "Moral Theory and Application," *Social Theory and Practice* 10 (1984): 97–120; and Tom L. Beauchamp, "On Eliminating the Distinction Between Applied Ethics and Ethical Theory," *Monist* 67 (1984): 515–31.

2. In lieu of "applied ethics," some now employ "practical ethics." The latter, however, does not suggest any particular methodological understanding, except insofar as it implies a contrast, which I would reject, with "theoretical ethics." I would instead follow Aristotle in thinking of ethics as a whole as a practical subject. Within that subject, concrete problems about what should be done are but a subclass of the important questions—as is emphasized by, for example, Edmund Pincoffs, "Quandary Ethics," *Mind* 80 (1971): 552–71.

specification—into a model that will promote a better methodological understanding than the currently prevailing models, those invoking only the operations of application and intuitive balancing. My purpose in working out this model is to reform the way many of those working on these issues understand what they are doing and to articulate more explicitly what has already been done by others.[3] While much of the best work that has been done undoubtedly already accords with the model of specification to some degree, making this alternative approach explicit should bolster these efforts. By stemming the skeptical doubts fostered by the failure of pure application while avoiding the excuses for inarticulateness that an excessive reliance on intuition affords, the model of specification should encourage a more fruitful approach to the difficult problems of concrete ethics.

By a "model of how to resolve concrete ethical problems" I mean a schema of what it would be to bring norms to bear on a case so as to indicate clearly what ought to be done. The deductive application of rules to cases and the intuitive weighing of considerations are the two cognitive operations usually thought central to this task. I seek to add specification as a third, even more important operation. A *pure* model would see only one of these operations as involved in settling concrete cases. Most models actually defended are, in fact, to some degree hybrids, giving some role to application and some to intuitive balancing. I will criticize these hybrids, arguing that instead of a hybrid view built upon these two commonly understood operations, what is needed is a model built around specification: a true third way, rather than just a mixture. To be sure, once the operation of specification has been adequately understood, it may then be admitted that it should be supplemented by application and balancing in a more complex hybrid model. For convenience, I will refer to this eventual hybrid centered on the idea of specification as "the model of specification." The main task of this paper, however, is simply to make out the nature and the promise of specification as a third way.

In concentrating on the form of reasoning involved in bringing norms to bear on cases, I largely set aside the heuristics of ethical discussion and deliberation. It is of course true that discerning morally relevant features of a case, marshaling facts, analyzing arguments and ideas, citing

---

3. My aim is not, for instance, to capture the a priori structure of concrete ethical reasoning or the logic of "practical inference."

Specifying Norms as a Way to Resolve Concrete Ethical Problems

examples, and comparing the case at hand with a range of related cases ("the case method") are generally indispensable means to productive discussion and deliberation about concrete ethical issues. Each of the models I will consider recognizes this.[4]

Let me begin by describing the pure operations from which the common hybrids are built, namely, application and intuitive balancing. I will hijack the term *application* to name a quite pure deductivist approach to ethical problems. It is appropriate to start by considering a deductivist model, for the problems with which we are concerned all pertain to individual cases—sometimes as sui generis but more likely as occurring regularly under some description. Either way, the crucial question is how ethical norms reach down to individual cases. The answer given by the pure model of application, as I am defining it, is: by deductive inference that subsumes the case under a rule.[5]

This said, it becomes obvious that a natural train of thought leads many to shift from the pure model of application to a hybrid including intuitive balancing, as follows. When working with a strictly individual case, the pure model of application must work along the lines of a "Peripatetic syllogism" of the following form:

(i) For all actions x, if Ax then x is (is not) permitted (obligatory).

(ii) Aa.

Therefore,

(iii) Action a is (is not) permitted (obligatory).

In these formulas, A stands for a description of an action that might be complex, and might include information about the circumstances or occasion of the action, the agent, or the persons affected, in addition to the type of action to be performed or avoided. For example:

(1) It is wrong for lawyers not to pursue their clients' interests by all means that are lawful.

(2) In this case of defending an accused rapist, it would lawfully promote the client's interest to cross-examine the victim about her

---

4. Thus I agree with many of the positive suggestions about ethical heuristics put forward by Jonsen and Toulmin, Bayles, and Beauchamp.

5. This subsumption, of course, need not be seen as a mechanical process, but instead may (as Kant emphasized) call upon the faculty of judgment: see Onora O'Neill, "The Power of Example," *Philosophy* 61 (1986): 5–29.

sex life in such a way as to make sexist jurors think that she consented.

Therefore,

(3) It would be wrong not to cross-examine the victim in this way.

Yet in addition to the norm stated in (1) there is another that is relevant and is no less true, that may even be subscribed to by the lawyer in question, and that leads to an opposite conclusion:

(4) It is wrong to defame someone's character by knowingly distorting their public reputation.
(5) To cross-examine the victim about her sex life in such a way as to make sexist jurors think that she consented would be to defame her character by knowingly distorting her public reputation.

Therefore,

(6) It would be wrong to cross-examine the victim in this way.

Here we have at least an apparent moral dilemma, potentially generated even out of the moral convictions of one central actor and certainly out of principles common in our culture (with its adversarial legal system), that is not easily brushed aside. Even apart from whether this dilemma amounts to an intolerable logical contradiction, it frustrates the purpose of a model for resolving concrete ethical problems, for the very least we can say is that (3) and (6) give conflicting advice.[6] In the face of such a quandary, one natural response is to try to "balance" the ethical considerations represented by (1) and (4)—no longer seen as peremptory or absolute—by assessing how much weight they are to be assigned in these circumstances. In this way, the pervasiveness of ethical conflicts—together with their centrality to our notion of an ethical "problem"—leads many from the pure model of application to a hybrid model including balancing. The question for balancers, in turn, will be how their weightings are to be explained or justified. To anticipate my arguments in a later section, we will see that to the extent that the balancing is

---

6. Logical contradiction might be avoided by, for instance, severing the connection between "wrong" and that moral sense of "ought" that invokes the principle that "'ought' implies 'can'." On these issues see the useful collection *Moral Dilemmas*, ed. Christopher Gowans (New York and Oxford: Oxford University Press, 1987).

283   *Specifying Norms
as a Way to Resolve
Concrete Ethical Problems*

genuinely distinct from application it affords no claim to rationality, for to that extent its weightings are purely intuitive, and therefore lack discursively expressible justification.

The third model I shall develop and defend here, that of specification, aims to be more flexible, realistic, fruitful, and attainable than that of application without sacrificing its claim to discursive rationality. While the model of specification will be more precisely defined in Section III, its leading ideas are simple enough and may be briefly described at once. The model of specification concurs with the balancing approaches in seeing a need to qualify our commitments, but insists that this be done not by a quantitative weighting or discounting but instead by qualitatively tailoring our norms to cases. Thus, one is urged not merely to reflect and change one's mind in a way that resolves a conflict in an acceptable way, but to revise one's normative commitments so as to make at least one of them more specific. For instance, in our example of cross-examining the rape victim, one might get a narrowed version of (1):

(1′) It is wrong for lawyers not to pursue their clients' interests by all means that are *both* lawful *and ethical.*

By itself, of course, this amendment does not settle the issue; but it does focus attention on the strength of the role-excuse provided by the lawyer's place in the adversary system. In particular, it forces one to reconsider the breadth of (4). On the one hand, publicly undercutting a witness's character is a stock in trade of cross-examiners, and to that extent may appear to be an ethical tactic; but on the other, there are reasons to think that a rape victim requires special social protection for her allegations, just as the accused is due the adversarial protections of the presumption of innocence.[7] Accordingly, we might reaffirm a narrowed version of (4):

(4′) It is always wrong to defame *a rape victim's* character by knowingly distorting her public reputation.

And it looks as if (1′) and (4′) settle the conflict in favor of restraint.

As I shall show, there are at least four reasons to build an alternative model around the idea of making a norm more specific. The first, and

---

7. I am here abbreviating the sophisticated casuistical discussion of this case in David Luban, *Lawyers and Justice: An Ethical Study* (Princeton: Princeton University Press, 1988), pp. 150–52.

most obvious, is that it helps us imagine how our ethical precepts, many of which are very general and abstract, can reach concrete cases without generating unacceptable implications. A second important reason for this requirement of greater specificity is that it helps ensure (without merely stipulating) that the reasonable motivation behind the initial, unqualified norm is still captured by what one ends up with. As we shall see, a third is that the notion of specification, conceived thus as a relation between two norms, allows us to understand in a precise way how a "mid-level" norm can serve as a bridge between a general precept and a concrete case.[8] Fourth, this same notion can also explain how a moral theory can remain the subject of a more or less stable attachment despite the sort of revision that moral conflicts engender. It is only concurrence on such a relatively stable moral theory that can assure that different people will reach the same conclusions in employing the model of specification; the same, of course, is true of the model of application.

It will require some work to show that the model of specification is truly distinct from the other two, for there is always a strong tendency to redescribe the unfamiliar (specification) in terms of the familiar (application and balancing). Accordingly, in the next section I set out the models of application and balancing and explain their principal defects. Specification is then defined, in Section III, in a way that makes clear how it is a genuine alternative to the model of application. The fourth section undertakes to show that there are rational constraints on specification that preserve its claim to discursive justification and hence distinguish it from an intuitive balancing model; and Section V gives some examples that exhibit this possibility concretely. The final section of the paper will compare the three models, arguing in general terms for the superiority of the model of specification.

II. Deficiencies of the Traditional Models

The two dominant pictures of how to bring ethical norms to bear on concrete questions of practice—application and intuitive balancing—can seem to exhaust the possibilities.[9] One abstract explanation for this false appearance is the following. Recall that in characterizing what the dif-

---

8. The notion of "mid-level bridging principles" is given prominence in Bayles, "Moral Theory and Application," but the bridging relation receives little analysis in his treatment.

9. See, for example, F. H. Bradley, "My Station and Its Duties," in his *Ethical Studies*, 2d ed. (Oxford: Clarendon Press, 1927), pp. 193–99.

285   *Specifying Norms
                       as a Way to Resolve
                       Concrete Ethical Problems*

ferent models are models *of*, I said that we may suppose that the deliberators or discussants start with a set of ethical norms to which they are in some important way initially committed. For our purposes, it does not matter where these norms come from, whether they change over time, or how they are grounded, if at all. Suppose that someone tries to apply them to concrete issues using deductive means to produce answers or decisions—not expecting a complete decision procedure, but hoping to avoid inconsistency. There seem to be two possibilities: either the norms are orderly enough to allow deductive application to avoid dilemmas or they are not. If, say, the norms can be lexically ordered according to higher-order priority rules, then the model of application may succeed. If, by contrast, there is no way to order the norms so as to preclude apparent dilemmas, then one seems forced to fall back on an intuitive balancing of the clashing norms—for by hypothesis there are no higher-order rules that could settle the conflicts in a nonintuitive way.

The idea of balancing, *sans phrase*, could arise under each of these possibilities, depending upon whether or not the "weights" are taken to reflect criteria that exist antecedently to and independently of the act of weighing. Antecedent weighting principles might exist, for example, if the "weight" of a norm were a homogeneous and objectively measurable feature of it, or else if the weights derived from a set of implicit priority rules that ranked the norms in question. Under either of these suppositions, balancing could be assimilated to the pure model of application. In the former case, the single highest-order principle would be to choose the option with the greatest net weight of reasons in its favor.[10] In the latter case, the implicit priority rules could be made explicit, if not in the context of deliberation, then at least for the purposes of justifying some choice after the fact. For example, one might grade students' philosophy papers rather intuitively or impressionistically, yet be able to reconstruct one's implicit reasons afterward by noting that one ranks making arguments above expounding texts. Or again, one might justify breaking a promise to a friend in order to save a drowning person on the grounds that saving a life is more important than keeping a promised social engagement.[11] In each case, one has invoked a priority rule, however vague. This then returns one to the question of the orderliness of these

---

10. For grounds for doubting that the use of comparison cases is a good way of bringing out antecedent, implicit weights, see Shelley Kagan, "The Additive Fallacy," *Ethics* 90 (1988): 5–31.

11. I am here indebted to the comments of an anonymous reviewer for this journal.

priority rules: if the implicit rules are consistent and sufficiently complete, then they could be deductively applied. If not, the need for a more intuitive sort of balancing may arise.

If the balancing of norms is thought not to be getting at antecedent weighting principles, but to be creating or supplying them, or merely to be providing particular judgments that might inductively support some weighting principle, then it is what I am calling "intuitive balancing." In intuitive balancing, any weighting principle—and therefore the notion of weight as a homogeneous property, as discussed in the last paragraph—is consequent upon the weighing.[12] An analogy would be the case of Von Neumann–Morgenstern utility functions, which are consequent upon (induced by) a consistent set of preferences. In teleological versions of intuitive balancing, values are balanced.[13] In nonconsequentialist versions—I will get to Ross in a moment—principles are balanced.[14] There are various labels for the faculty exercised in intuitive balancing: intuition, judgment, perception. The balancing might occur within a theory that had reduced all moral considerations to two heads, assessing only, for instance, the relative weight of autonomy and beneficence in a given case; or the balancing might be more open-ended, declaring the "balance of reasons" tentatively to favor one option over another.

It is widely if not universally recognized that the two pure models involving only application or balancing are each seriously deficient. The pure model of application depends upon an ideal achievement of moral theory that is beyond our grasp. The claims of certain versions of natural law theory notwithstanding, we are unable to systematize our commonsense norms sufficiently to preclude widespread and serious conflicts

---

12. One can therefore understand Alan Donagan's complaint in *The Theory of Morality* (Chicago: University of Chicago Press, 1979), p. 23, that to call this intuitive assessment "weighing" or "balancing" is "fraudulent"; but this metaphorical use of these terms is well entrenched in Western culture—embodied, as it is, in the figure of blind Justice—and is a convenient one for the comparative intuitive assessment of competing considerations.

13. Although there are elements of teleological balancing in G. E. Moore and Hastings Rashdall, the implications of this for concrete ethics are obscured by their overall utilitarianism. A less ambiguous statement of this sort of view is found in Thomas Nagel, "The Fragmentation of Value," in his *Mortal Questions* (Cambridge: Cambridge University Press, 1979).

14. One nonconsequentialist balancing view that is purer than Ross's is that of Bradley in "My Station and Its Duties." See also Robert M. Veatch, *A Theory of Medical Ethics* (New York: Basic Books, 1981), pp. 303–4, and Baruch Brody, *Life and Death Decision Making* (New York and Oxford: Oxford University Press, 1988), esp. pp. 77–79.

287   *Specifying Norms
                       as a Way to Resolve
                       Concrete Ethical Problems*

among them. Utilitarianism would introduce system, but at too high a price, requiring too great a departure from norms to which we are firmly committed. This is no contingent limitation of our current ethical knowledge or sophistication. The inherent particularity and variability of the subjects with which ethics has to deal will prevent us from ever being able to present a system of rules that takes account of all the needed qualifications and distinctions.[15] Since it is inherent to the nature of the subject, this limitation is not merely contingent upon the present stage of progress in ethical theory. Consider the parallel issue in the law. All operating legal systems have accepted severe limitations on treating law as a deductive system, and have instead developed case-oriented and precedent-bound approaches that make room for equity, as described by Aristotle (in the *Nicomachean Ethics*, bk. V) and as familiar in English common law, namely, scope for the judge to modify the rules to fit the case at hand.[16] Given the role of law in the public legitimation of the state and in grounding stable expectations for commerce and society, there is every reason to strive for a rule-bound, deductive approach to adjudication. Since even the law is forced to give up on the pure deductive ideal, it is hardly likely that ethics, where the motivations for deductive transparency are much weaker, could succeed in living up to it. The pure model of application is doomed to be hamstrung by dilemmas and strained by the effort to accommodate the diversity of moral experience.

Intuitive balancing, by contrast, is all too easy. As preference utilitarians are fond of reminding us, we do it all the time. The problem with intuitive balancing is not its unattainability but its arbitrariness and lack of rational grounding. By whatever name the balancing faculty is graced, its operations seem intrinsically beyond the pale of justification. There is no faculty of ethical intuition (or perception or judgment) whose discursively unjustifiable deliverances carry their warrant with them. Since intuitive balancing does not proceed by measuring any objective feature of the world or of our system of reasons, what it does do remains mysterious

---

15. This Aristotelian theme is nicely developed by a series of writings by Martha Nussbaum, including *Aristotle's De Motu Animalium* (Princeton: Princeton University Press, 1978), essay 4; *The Fragility of Goodness: Luck and Ethics in Greek Tragedy and Philosophy* (Cambridge: Cambridge University Press, 1986), esp. chap. 10; and "The Discernment of Perception," in *Proceedings of the Boston Area Colloquium in Ancient Philosophy*, vol. 1, ed. J. Cleary (Lanham, Md.: University Press of America, 1986).

16. If this is right, then it betrays a misconception of the law to speak of the model of application as "ethical legalism."

or, at best, subjective. The balance we strike can be taken as a primitive, as a *datum*; but that is again just to admit that we cannot give it a rational grounding.[17]

As I have noted, most influential models of concrete ethics are hybrids that combine elements of application with elements of balancing. What these hybrid approaches have in common is the thought that although moral conflicts frustrate a purely deductive model, there is nonetheless considerable room for deductive application. A common metaphor for a hybrid approach is that of core and penumbra. Ethical principles are taken as having a core zone in which deductive application may proceed confidently, and a penumbral zone in which there can be no secure application—whether or not there are conflicts with other norms. In this picture, intuitive judgment is called in more to settle the uncertain meaning of a single norm than to adjudicate a conflict between norms.[18] But since norms will conflict, we should consider hybrid models that account for this possibility. The most influential and interesting of these is W. D. Ross's account of prima facie duties. A prima facie duty is a norm that does serve as an adequate basis for deducing actual duty in a given situation so long as it does not come into conflict with any other norm.[19] When prima facie duties do conflict, however, none of them is any longer allowed to serve as a basis for deducing actual duty.[20] In cases of conflict,

---

17. For a frank casting of preference formation as primitive in this way, see James Griffin, *Well Being: Its Meaning, Measurement and Moral Importance* (Oxford: Clarendon Press, 1986), pp. 36, 103.

18. The distinction between core and penumbra is recently familiar from H.L.A. Hart's jurisprudence: see "Positivism and the Separation of Law and Morals," in Hart's *Essays in Jurisprudence and Philosophy* (Oxford: Clarendon Press, 1982), pp. 63–64. A development of the metaphor of core and penumbra for moral purposes is found in classical Catholic casuistry, as expounded by Jonsen and Toulmin in *The Abuse of Casuistry*, chap. 16. Central to this conception of casuistry is the idea of a paradigm case and progressive departures from it until things become muddy, when "discernment" is needed.

19. W. D. Ross, *The Right and the Good* (Oxford: Clarendon Press, 1930; repr. Indianapolis: Hackett, 1988), p. 19. On pp. 30–34 Ross develops the claim that every possible act is the subject of conflicting moral considerations. In describing Ross's view as a hybrid model in the text, I have been supposing that this is not necessarily the case. If it is, then Ross's view obviously collapses back into the pure model of balancing.

20. My reading of Ross's notion of "prima facie duty" focuses on the contrast with "actual duty," thus coming close to John Searle's helpfully critical interpretation, in "*Prima Facie* Obligation," in *Practical Reasoning*, ed. Joseph Raz (Oxford: Oxford University Press, 1978), pp. 81–90, of what he calls Ross's "official view." Because he focuses solely on conflict situations, Searle gives insufficient weight to Ross's insistence that a prima facie duty is one that will be an actual duty so long as no other duties conflict with it.

289   *Specifying Norms*
               as a Way to Resolve
               Concrete Ethical Problems

Ross says, quoting Aristotle, "the decision rests with perception."[21] Accordingly, on Ross's view, the model of application prevails so long as there are no conflicts; and where there are, we turn to intuitive balancing.[22]

These hybrid views fare no better than their purer counterparts. In conceding that the ideal of pure application is beyond our grasp, and therefore relying considerably on intuitive balancing, they undercut the former model without explicating the latter. Perception's decision of conflicts between prima facie duties, like judgment within the penumbra, remains mysterious. It undercuts the idea of application by the admission that it is not the only model of practical reasoning and by declaring certain norms not to "apply" in the penumbral or conflicted cases. The universal norms appealed to by a pure model of application get much of their support from their claim to introduce a deductively consistent and complete hierarchical order into our moral thinking. Since the hybrid models largely give up on this ambition, they tend to weaken the rationale of the norms with which they start without providing an alternative picture of systematization to replace that of deductive hierarchy. In this respect, these hybrid models appear as application manqué, as deductivism thrown back on intuitionist resources by the harsh realities of moral conflicts.

Given these difficulties both with the pure models of application and balancing and with hybrids that mix them, it is not surprising that philosophers have been casting about for alternative ways of relating ethical norms to concrete issues of practice. A common tack is to accept Ross's basic framework while looking for a supplement that would provide for a more discursive resolution of conflicts among the prima facie duties.[23] A

21. Ross, *The Right and the Good*, p. 42, quoting Aristotle, *Nicomachean Ethics* 1109b23; cf. 1126b5.

22. Instead of using the Peripatetic syllogism to represent the deductive aspect of a Rossian hybrid view, it might be more accurate to follow G. H. von Wright's suggestion of thinking of obligatoriness, permittedness, and so on *both* as predicates of individual actions *and* as operators on propositions applied to types of action ("On the Logic of Norms and Actions" in *New Studies in Deontic Logic: Norms, Actions, and the Foundations of Ethics*, ed. Risto Hilpinen [Dordrecht: Reidel, 1981], pp. 3–35). It would still be the case, however, that *every* act that fell under a forbidden (or permitted) category of action and no other morally relevant category would be forbidden (or permitted).

23. The view that Ross's position is all right as far as it goes but needs a significant supplement has been embraced by moral philosophers of as diverse positions as Albert Jonsen, one of the coauthors of *The Abuse of Casuistry*, for whom the supplement is an

surprising number of these attempts follow Ross in recalling Aristotle's protean account of practical wisdom (*phronêsis*) without doing the philosophical work necessary to explain how discursive reasoning figures in this account. One thoughtful critic who has emphasized how the Aristotelian ideal of practical wisdom can both help us understand how we may rationally cope with moral conflicts and serve as a prop to obscurity finishes by saying that although judgment is essential, no theory of practical judgment is possible.[24] Despite this warning, I will use the notion of specification to begin to develop one that replaces Ross's framework rather than merely supplementing it.

III. Specification as an Alternative to the Dominant Models

The reason that the models of application and balancing do not exhaust the field is that they each suppose that the set of norms invoked in ethical discussion and deliberation is held fixed. As has been emphasized especially strongly by Deweyan ethical pragmatism, however, and as is also implied by the Rawlsian idea of wide reflective equilibrium, our norms are subject to revision. The model of specification starts from this recognition of revisability, but reestablishes a kind of constancy or stability not implied either by the general pragmatist approach or by the idea of reflective equilibrium. This stability is essential to the claim that the initial norms are in some way *brought to bear* on concrete cases by means of more specific norms.

It will be useful to see how the model of specification both incorporates aspects of the pragmatist approach—which is currently enjoying something of a revival[25]—and adds to it a crucial missing element. In the face

---

ordered appeal to paradigm cases (personal communication); and R. M. Hare, for whom the supplement is "critical level" thinking, which is allegedly utilitarian. See Hare's "Comments" in *Hare and Critics: Levels of Moral Thinking*, ed. Douglas Seanor and N. Fotion (Oxford: Clarendon Press, 1988), p. 223.

24. Charles E. Larmore, *Patterns of Moral Complexity* (Cambridge: Cambridge University Press, 1987), pp. 18–20.

25. See, e.g., Andrew Altman, "Pragmatism and Applied Ethics," *American Philosophical Quarterly* 20 (1983): 227–35; and James D. Wallace, *Moral Relevance and Moral Conflict* (Ithaca: Cornell University Press, 1988). An uncritical and antitheoretical version of the pragmatist approach—one hardly hospitable to the ideal of wide reflective equilibrium—is criticized in Bayles, "Moral Theory and Application." In the present article, I abstract from the consequentialism that Altman takes to be central to the pragmatist account of justification. My approach is particularly close to Wallace's, and I would endorse many of the

291   *Specifying Norms*
                       as a Way to Resolve
                       Concrete Ethical Problems

of conflicts, Dewey wrote, deliberation will be reasonable if it can devise a *"way* to act," or light upon a conception of the object of action, "in which all [competing tendencies] are fulfilled, not indeed in their original form, but in a 'sublimated fashion,' that is, in a way which modifies the original direction of each by reducing it to a component along with others in an action of transformed quality."[26] Since an explanation of the way in which the action reflects the "original" norms would be facilitated if the principle of the action were explicitly stated rather than simply left to the observer to infer from the action's features, we might think the following reformulation of Dewey's idea by James Wallace to be an advance: "[When moral considerations conflict,] the aim [of deliberation] must be to modify one or more considerations so that it applies, so that its original point is to some degree preserved, and so that one can live with the way [of proceeding] so modified."[27] In fact, without necessarily buying into broader pragmatist assumptions about the nature of truth, the model of specification will take this general description of practical reasoning as its point of departure. The key unanswered question, however, for both Dewey's and Wallace's versions of this pragmatist account is, What licenses us to call a modification or sublimation of an original norm still in some significant sense the *same* norm that we started out with? Why is it not a self-contradiction to speak of modifying a consideration so that *it* applies? Is not what "applies," in the end, just a different norm or consideration?[28] If so, then so far as *concrete* ethics is concerned, it would look as if the pragmatic approach posed no alternative to the hybrids we have already discussed: changes in norms are arrived at intuitively, and once the change has occurred, the new norms can be deductively applied.

The idea of specification aims to complement this general pragmatic approach by laying down conditions on the relation between the initial norm or norms and their modifications that explain how the original norms *are* being respected (in a "sublimated fashion"). Answering this question of stability serves two purposes. First, in this way, the idea of

---

points made in his stimulating book. It is the idea of specification that is lacking from his account, and that is needed to fill out the general pragmatist approach that he sets out.

26. John Dewey, *Human Nature and Conduct* (New York: Henry Holt, 1922), p. 194.
27. Wallace, *Moral Relevance and Moral Conflict*, p. 86.
28. I am indebted to Nathan Salmon for having pressed me for an answer to this question.

specification converts the general pragmatist approach into a truly distinct model for concrete ethics. Second, we want some such notion of constrained change both to allow the development of a stable moral theory and to give us some assurance that the commitment that underlay the initial norm is being appropriately honored. Yet there are three reasons not to simply stipulate that an acceptable specification is one that captures this initial commitment and leave it at that: (1) We may not be aware just what the contours of this initial commitment are. The model of specification lets these emerge on reflection. (2) If the underlying rationale of a norm being specified can be laid out, then this just means that we have looked through it to some other norms, which are then what should be in play. (3) To honor the initial "point" or source of commitment is easier said than done. For all these reasons, in defining the notion of specification I will seek to delineate a notion that will not merely posit stability but will explain it.

For this sort of stability in the course of revision to be possible, it must be the case that the norms being specified are not "absolute" in logical form the way (i) is, that is, are not strictly universal with respect to the domain of possible acts. Instead of being, in this sense, prefaced by an "always," they must be seen as implicitly beginning with a "generally speaking." To see why the latter form is necessary to stability, note that there are two possibilities: either the more specific norm that results from deliberation replaces the initial norm it specifies or else it stands alongside it. If it stands alongside, it would mark an expansion of the set of norms. If it replaces, that would be a true revision of the set of norms.[29] If the initial norm were strictly universal, then a specification that stood alongside it would be otiose, since it would already be implied in the initial norm, and could be omitted as an unnecessary step in a deductive argument to a practical conclusion. For example, if we began with "it is always wrong to lie," then "it is wrong to lie to someone who has a right to the truth" would be redundant. As Kant held, the right to the truth would be irrelevant to the permissibility of lying. If the more specific norm replaced the one it specifies, however, the result would be an implied exception that would be logically incompatible with the initial norm's universal command, making it difficult to see any stability. Accordingly, to conceive of a kind of stability over the course of a path of

---

29. For the terminology of revision and expansion, see Peter Gärdenfors, *Knowledge in Flux: Modeling the Dynamics of Epistemic States* (Cambridge, Mass.: MIT Press, 1988), sec. 3.1.

293   *Specifying Norms
as a Way to Resolve
Concrete Ethical Problems*

specification that does useful work, one must suppose that the norms being specified are not absolute in the fashion of (i).

This supposition poses no difficulty, for the norms to which we are commonly committed are not plausibly viewed as formally absolute in this way. Rather, they are typically qualified, at least implicitly, by variants of "generally" or "for the most part." This sort of looseness is a common feature of our norms as we find them, whether they be prohibitions, positive duties, or ends. As T. M. Scanlon has written, "common-sense moral principles ... are not simple self-contained rules.... Qualifications having to do with intent, justifications, excuses, and so on, while not always explicit in any formulation of the principle, are part of the idea referred to (though their exact boundaries are never clear)."[30] That blanket prohibitions on lying and killing are not universally applicable is widely recognized. The kind of looseness our norms allow is often thought of as making implicit room for exceptions. Another way of regarding it is to use Kant's notion of "latitude." This idea is different insofar as it suggests that the exact extent and nature of the duty may require further specification. Thus, in presenting the positive duty of beneficence, Kant presents it as not specifying when, exactly, one must help others, what one must do to help them, or to what degree one must sacrifice one's own welfare in doing so. Nonetheless, there is an "imperfect" duty to do *something* for the sake of helping others.[31] I believe that our common beliefs about beneficence are similarly latitudinarian; and our ends and values are even more obviously qualified in this way. To be sure, many philosophical debates begin by supposing they are not: we may think, for instance, that a political regime must do everything it can to promote liberty *and* everything it can to promote equality, and end up having to cope with the resulting conflict.[32] Yet most ends, including these political ideals, fall short of requiring that we do everything possi-

---

30. T. M. Scanlon, "Levels of Moral Thinking," in *Hare and Critics: Levels of Moral Thinking*, ed. Seanor and Fotion, p. 134. Despite this talk of reference to an idea, Scanlon states clearly that he does "not mean to suggest that there is a fixed set of moral ideas" to be simply discovered (p. 137). Hare, responding to Scanlon in ibid., p. 263, poses the challenge that I am now addressing of how a norm can be seen as "the same" before and after revision.

31. Immanuel Kant, *The Metaphysics of Morals*, pt. 2 (*Tugendlehre*), Introduction, secs. 7–8.

32. For a sketch of the importance of the idea of specification for liberal political theory, see sec. 8 of my essay "The Problem of Liberalism and the Good," in *Liberalism and the Good*, ed. Gerald M. Mara, R. Bruce Douglass, and Henry S. Richardson (New York: Routledge, 1990).

ble that can be done in their service. For instance, a serious commitment to the end of liberty does not imply that one must shield pornographers or reduce government regulation to an absolute minimum.

While the model of specification begins with norms that allow for latitude, it also ends with them; and this feature is crucial to its status as a distinct model. It is not realistic to view the goal of concrete ethical discussion or deliberation as coming up with adequately limited ("midlevel") though still strictly universal norms. To be sure, if we never arrive at norms of this form, then since deductive application along the lines of the Peripatetic syllogism must begin from a norm of the form of (i), it will prove impossible. That it is impossible was argued in the previous section, precisely on the grounds that the complexity of the moral phenomena always outruns our ability to capture them in general norms. Fortunately, there is no need to settle individual cases deductively in order to settle them on rationally defensible grounds. The central assertion of the model of specification is that specifying our norms is the most important aspect of resolving concrete ethical problems, so that once our norms are adequately specified for a given context, it will be sufficiently obvious what ought to be done. That is, without further deliberative work, simple inspection of the specified norms will often indicate which option should be chosen.[33] A conclusion supported by considerations that hold only "for the most part" is, of course, rebuttable by further deliberation; but that is the way our moral reasoning goes. The ability to bring norms to bear on cases even while leaving them nonabsolute is a distinctive feature of the model of specification.

Having thus sketched the model of specification, I am now in a position to define the specification relation more precisely. Doing so will require some preliminary definitions of component notions. Although the model of specification supposes that the norms to which we are actually committed are typically not absolute, it will be convenient to define the relation of specification by reference to artificially tightened versions of these norms that, unlike a norm that begins with "generally" or "for most actions," can have well-defined and presumably bivalent conditions of

---

33. As Aristotle would put it, once the norm (end) is sufficiently specific, there is no need for further deliberation, and it is "perception" that must supply the "premise" that a currently possible action satisfies the norm. See, e.g., *De Motu Animalium*, chap. 7, and the discussion thereof by David Charles, *Aristotle's Philosophy of Action* (Ithaca: Cornell University Press, 1984), p. 96.

295 Specifying Norms
as a Way to Resolve
Concrete Ethical Problems

satisfaction. Without undue violence, then, the typical looseness of ordinary norms could be represented as taking the following form:

(i*) For *most* actions x, if Ax then x is (is not) permitted (obligatory).

The *absolute counterpart* of a norm of the form of (i*) is one that restores it to the form of (i) by replacing the hedging "for *most* actions" with the absolute "for *all* actions."[34] The detailed way in which the satisfaction of a norm is to be understood will presumably depend upon the *type* of norm involved, that is, upon whether it is an end, permission, requirement, or prohibition. In general, we can say that an *instance* of an absolute norm is an alternative that satisfies it. An instance of an end is an example of what amounts to its achievement or actualization; an instance of a permission is an example of what is permitted; and an instance of a prohibition is an example of avoiding what is prohibited. Given the generality of my account, it would be wrong to try for too much precision in the notion of satisfaction that underlies this extended usage of the term *instance*.[35]

On the basis of these other definitions, I now define *specification*, considered as a relation between two norms, as follows:

Norm p is a *specification* of norm q (or: p specifies q) if and only if

(a) norms p and q are of the same normative type;[36]
(b) every possible instance of the absolute counterpart of p would count as an instance of the absolute counterpart of q (in other words, any act that satisfies p's absolute counterpart also satisfies q's absolute counterpart);
(c) p qualifies q by substantive means (and not just by converting universal quantifiers to existential ones) by adding clauses indicating what, where, when, why, how, by what means, by whom, or to whom[37] the action is to be, is not to be, or may be done or

---

34. If a norm is already absolute, then its absolute counterpart is itself. I remind the reader that the absoluteness I have in mind is a matter of logical form, not epistemic basis.

35. See the instructive worrying of this notion of satisfaction in Ludwig Wittgenstein, *Philosophical Investigations*, 3d ed. (New York: Macmillan, 1958), pt. 1, secs. 437–39.

36. Ideally, this restriction on cross-type specification should be overcome; but I have thought it better to avoid the complications that would come with the attempt.

37. This clause uses the traditional list of "circumstances" developed by the casuists: see Jonsen and Toulmin, *The Abuse of Casuistry*, p. 253. The list goes back to Aristotle's theory of the "predicables" in the *Categories*.

the action is to be described, or the end is to be pursued or conceived; and

(d) none of these added clauses in p is irrelevant to q.

Several comments are in order. First, by referring to the absolute counterpart of the specified norm, clause (b) enables specification to be defined in terms of the ordinary notion of containment without requiring that specification proceed from absolute norms.[38] It can therefore rule out making an exception by disjunction. That is, if the original norm says "when you have received great benefits from someone that were not simply your due, you should generally express your gratitude to him or her," this cannot be specified to read "when you have received great benefits from someone that were not simply your due, you should generally *either* express your gratitude to him or her *or surreptitiously aid his or her child*."[39] An act that satisfied the second norm by aiding the child could fail to satisfy the first norm's absolute counterpart. Second, clause (c) implies that the sense in which a specification is more "specific" than what it specifies goes beyond the "subset" requirement of clause (b), ruling, for instance, that a move from "torture is always wrong" to "torture is sometimes wrong" is not a specification. Specification proceeds by setting out substantive qualifications that add information about the scope of applicability of the norm or the nature of the act or end enjoined or proscribed. Sometimes it will do both. For instance, "euthanasia is generally wrong" might be specified by "it is generally wrong to shut off the respirator of a patient in a potentially reversible coma." Third, while clause (b) rules out specification by disjunction, clause (d) rules out some forms of specification by conjunction. For instance, it blocks taking "to promote the health of my patients and to write a great opera" as a specification of the end of promoting the health of one's patients. The

---

38. Specification might begin from an absolute norm—and for this reason some instances of deductive application are also instances of superfluous specification—but it need not.

39. This restriction on the logical means available in specification is rather narrowly drawn. One might achieve much the same effect by putting the "exception" into the circumstances: "When you have received great benefits from someone that were not simply your due, and when you do not have an opportunity to aid their child surreptitiously, you should express your gratitude." This norm, however, is of narrower scope than that in which the exception is by disjunction; in particular, the former does not say what one's duty is in those circumstances in which one does have this opportunity, whereas the latter explicitly leaves the agent two options in those cases.

Specifying Norms as a Way to Resolve Concrete Ethical Problems

element referring to opera is (presumably!) irrelevant to the patients' health.[40]

Finally, note that in the definition of specification as a relation between two norms, there is no mention of any temporal or justificatory priority between the two. To be sure, my thesis is that in the attempt to resolve a concrete issue, the most important thing will be to make our norms more specific; but it is also important that we sometimes *revise* an end or principle, for what we consider to be good reasons, in a way that will not count as a specification of it. Sometimes we move to a *less* specific formulation of a norm, for instance. Even here, however, the notion of specification can be useful, depending upon the nature of the grounds for claiming that this change is a rational one. In many of these cases, our appeal in changing a norm is to a deeper or more general norm that underlay it, which we now claim to understand better, and for which we provide a new specification. An example of this kind will be given in Section V.

In light of my definition of specification, I can now elaborate on some of the advantages of the model of specification briefly mentioned in the first section. The first is that it allows for a strong reply to the objection that a pragmatist view underestimates the seriousness of our commitments to our initial norms. Although we recognize that they cannot be regarded as absolute, if we suppose that they need to be and are specified further we can nonetheless genuinely claim to be appealing to *them*. This is because the definition of specification assures as nearly as is possible without stipulating it that the commitments expressed in the initial norm would be honored in the satisfaction of the specified norm. While the basic notion of extensional narrowing in clause (b) is important to this result, clauses (c) and (d) reinforce this tendency. Although this will not guarantee the preservation of commitment, it does rule out many of the likely threats to it.[41]

Second, by giving us a way to articulate how a specific norm is meaningfully related back to a more abstract one, the model of specification helps secure a role for a stable ethical theory that seems as elusive on

---

40. There is no pretense, here, that any account of relevance can be innocent of substantive ethical presuppositions.

41. My thinking on these issues, and on the model of specification in general, is much influenced by David Wiggins, "Deliberation and Practical Reason," *Proceedings of the Aristotelian Society* 76 (1975–76): 29–51; repr. in *Practical Reasoning*, ed. Raz.

the general conception of a change in view as it is unattainable conceived as a deductive hierarchy. System is more attainable by specification because the norms need not be taken as fixed or as formally absolute, and so will conflict less readily and adjust more easily than the sort of norms postulated by a pure model of application. Nonetheless, the connection back to an initial norm afforded by the notion of an instance of a general norm's absolute counterpart enables one to set out clearly what has remained the same in the course of specification. By making clear what remains constant despite modifications that are occurring, the model of specification allows one to distinguish the progressive refinement of a theory that remains the same in essentials from the mere shifting from one holistic equilibrium to another.

Third, and by the same token, the notion of specification provides a clear sense to the notion of a "mid-level bridging principle" which might otherwise be lacking. There is no trouble with "mid-level," understood loosely in terms of a rough sense of degrees of generality: the difficulty is in explaining the "bridging" relation. A mid-level norm that specifies a general one and thereby helps mediate the latter to a concrete case serves as a bridge in a quite definite sense—one across which, as I have just claimed, the discussant's or deliberator's commitment will likely travel. A series of progressively more specific norms would provide a bridge with multiple spans.

In addition, the model of specification can explain how it is that contingently conflicting norms "hang around" even after a conflict of norms has been resolved, sometimes giving rise to what Ross called "compunction" and to a duty to make reparations.[42] As John Searle has argued, Ross's own explanation of this phenomenon conflicts with his "official" view that in cases in which prima facie obligations conflict, they do not state actual duties.[43] On the model of specification, however, the general but nonabsolute norm, understood as stating an actual obligation, can stand alongside the specified version that averts the particular conflict at issue.[44] Take the example of a clash between a requirement to respect

---

42. Ross, *The Right and the Good*, p. 28. Regarding this paragraph, I have benefited from the friendly skepticism of Arthur Applbaum and Amy Gutmann, in addition to that of others named above.

43. Searle, "*Prima Facie* Obligation," p. 83. See also Bernard Williams, *Ethics and the Limits of Philosophy* (Cambridge, Mass.: Harvard University Press, 1985), pp. 176–77.

44. The sense in which nonuniversal norms can conflict will be explicitly explored in the next section.

299   Specifying Norms
                       as a Way to Resolve
                       Concrete Ethical Problems

one's promises and a prohibition on hurting others, in which you have promised to a person now dead to use their estate to build a research center on a certain plot of land you own, and only later find out that doing so would seriously disrupt the town water supply. Suppose that the initial conflict is averted by specifying the prohibition on breaking promises in a way limited in scope: "When the promisee is dead, respect for one's promises requires fulfilling the spirit of the promise but need not bind one to its precise terms." As the scope limitation allows, suppose further that the original norm has not been thoroughly rejected. Thus, if you subsequently find out that the town has switched to a new reservoir (and you have not yet spent the money), then there will be strong reason both to follow the letter of the promise and to add a further clause limiting the original qualification: ". . . need not bind one to its precise terms *when following them would be seriously disadvantageous to the public*." Here, the initial specification is rebutted (in practical effect) by a further specification that derives its force partly from the importance of the initial, general prohibition on promise-breaking, which has been retained.

A similar argument could explain how the persistence of this initial prohibition—which is still seen as stating an actual duty—is relevant to accounting for the appropriateness of reparations. Thus, if no alternative water supply turns up, the appropriate secondary specification, instead of referring to public disadvantage, might require paying deference to the deceased's wishes in some more symbolic fashion. To be sure, when a more general norm is denied application to a particular case by a specification (via a scope restriction, for example), whether the specification replaces or stands alongside what it specifies, and in the latter case, whether it gives rise to a duty of reparations are questions that must be addressed on a case-by-case basis. As I shall argue in the next section, all such questions are to be answered in terms of the overall coherence and mutual support of the whole set of norms. If the initial general prohibition remains among them, then coherence grounds may support setting a threshold for its violation, requiring that the "least restrictive alternative" be chosen, or requiring reparations.

So far, then, we have seen that the model of specification is genuinely distinct from the model of application, since a specification will in general not follow deductively from what it specifies. This alternative model escapes the apparently exhaustive choice between deductively applying absolute norms and qualifying norms solely by "weights" by denying that the norms with which one starts are always, or even usually, absolute. Nonetheless, the notion of specification has enough structure to represent a significant improvement over the bare pragmatist idea of a change in view, and offers a number of other advantages besides. To show that the model of specification is also a genuine alternative to intuitive balancing, however, I must go further, and explain how specification can be rational—and in particular, how it can be discursively justified.

IV. Rational Specification

Are there rational constraints on specification? Unless there were, and unless the superiority of one specification over another could thereby be defended, it would be hard to see how specification could be anything but a special employment of intuition. I will propose a coherence standard for the rationality of specification. This standard in effect carries the Rawlsian idea of "wide reflective equilibrium" down to the level of concrete cases.[45] The power and interest of this coherence standard is underestimated if it is seen simply as requiring an absence of logical contradictions. In the last section, we saw how the relation of specification allowed for a stable development of theory despite revisions; now I suggest that developing a theory—even if only one quite limited in scope—is crucial to the rational defense of any specification. A (successful) theory importantly makes intelligible logical connections among the norms to which one is committed that do not merely demonstrate that they are logically compatible with each other, but also explain some of them in terms of others. It is this kind of argumentative support, and not mere lack of incoherence, that can justify.[46] Note that although there is no meaningful measure of the strength of argumentative support, it remains—unlike the grounds invoked by the intuitionist—fully subject to discursive statement and criticism.

There are two reasons why building explanatory or intelligible argumentative connection is vital to the rationality of the model of specifica-

---

45. The notion of wide reflective equilibrium was introduced, although without the label, in John Rawls, *A Theory of Justice* (Cambridge, Mass.: Harvard University Press, 1971), p. 49. The label is applied in Rawls's Presidential Address, "The Independence of Moral Theory," *Proceedings and Addresses of the American Philosophical Association* 47 (1974–75): 8.

46. On the importance of mutual support to justification, see Rawls, *A Theory of Justice*, pp. 21, 579.

301   *Specifying Norms as a Way to Resolve Concrete Ethical Problems*

tion. The first, as Gilbert Harman has emphasized, is just that it is important to the rationality of any "change in view."[47] The second is that developing a theory is an important means of avoiding contingent practical conflicts. These matter because the enterprise of deciding what ought to be done in a concrete situation (if not all of ethics) is a practical enterprise. This fact puts it in the same camp as intending or willing: if we believe it impossible—even contingently impossible—to do both x and y, then we have reason to revise the set of norms leading to the conclusion that we ought to do both. (This contrasts with wishing and desiring, for which jointly incompatible objects are perfectly normal and apparently acceptable.)

When a conflict of norms is the result of some contingent fact about the world, it is of course an important question whether we should not try to avert the conflict by changing the world rather than by changing our norms.[48] Often, there will be good reason to do both. For example, suppose that contingent limitations of technology now prevent us from being able to protect hospital populations from the spread of a potentially fatal disease except by severely limiting the work of surgeons discovered to be carriers of this disease. We cannot well serve both the epidemiological interests of the hospital population, the professional interests of the infected surgeons, and the interests of the patients potentially benefited by their surgical talents. In such a situation, we surely have reason *both* to seek improved technologies to block the spread of the disease *and* to attempt to resolve this contingent clash between the ends involved in a way that takes for granted the limitations of current technology. In doing so, it will be important to arrive at a finer-grained specification of the aims that guide us in this situation. For instance, the "interests of the surgeons" might be factored into financial security and the liberty to pursue their calling. The former interest might be satisfied by a special indemnity for those found to be carriers, while the latter might be further specified in a way that makes plain that it cannot be consistently achieved in a way that involves inflicting harm on patients, even unwittingly, by spreading disease. The fact that some such specification of the

47. Gilbert Harman, *Change in View: Principles of Reasoning* (Cambridge, Mass.: MIT Press, 1986), pp. 32–33 and chap. 7.
48. See Ruth Barcan Marcus, "Moral Dilemmas and Consistency," *Journal of Philosophy* 77 (1980): 121–36, repr. in *Moral Dilemmas*, ed. Gowans; and the criticism of Marcus in Alan Donagan, "Consistency in Rationalist Moral Systems," *Journal of Philosophy* 81 (1984): 291–309, repr. in *Moral Dilemmas*, ed. Gowans, p. 281.

ends involved could avoid the contingent conflict between the surgeons' interests (unspecified) and those of the patients provides one reason for specifying in this way.

Ross and F. H. Bradley were right, then, that such practical conflict among our norms is ubiquitous, but wrong in thinking that this fact left us with no alternative but intuitive and ad hoc balancing.[49] The owl of Minerva can do better than that. Because of the pervasiveness of potential conflicts, however, the only way to have any grounds to hope that a specification does not simply avert one local conflict at the cost of giving rise to worse ones elsewhere is to begin to develop a relatively stable moral theory.

These extensions of the idea of consistency of norms in the direction of practical or contingent consistency and mutual argumentative support explain the possibility of a conflict between norms that are not strictly universal. Even if such norms cannot be logically inconsistent with one another, they can be practically inconsistent insofar as they guide choice in opposite directions and disturb our attempts at theoretical systematization. Thus, consider the difficulties on both counts that have been posed by the clash between the views that it is generally wrong to lie and that it is important to prevent others from coming to harm.

A specification is rationally defensible, then, so long as it enhances the mutual support among the set of norms found acceptable on reflection. Typically, the removal of a conflict will enhance mutual support, but not always. In such matters, it is vain to strive after an ephemeral ideal of the total absence of conflict—especially since sometimes, on reflection, we see no acceptable way to rationalize away a given practical conflict. Still, there will be clear cases in which a shift in specification yields a more coherent overall view by acceptably removing a given conflict.

V. Examples of Specification

To reinforce my claim that specification can be discursively pursued and justified, I will present two schematic examples of it. One is set in a medical context in which the ruling model is that of a hybrid deontology

---

49. For Bradley's claim that conflicting considerations are pervasive, see "My Station and Its Duties," pp. 196–97 (footnote). For Ross's, see *The Right and the Good*, pp. 30–34. For Bradley's Hegelian view that philosophy cannot guide, but can only understand, see "My Station and Its Duties," p. 193.

303   *Specifying Norms*
                         as a Way to Resolve
                         Concrete Ethical Problems

along the lines of Ross, and the other is a case that would be treated as ethical only by certain value-maximizing or value-balancing ethical views.

First, then, let us consider a hypothetical and simplified course of deliberation about whether to withhold nutrition and hydration from a severely malformed newborn so as to let it die. I ask the reader to suspend any dissent from the particular norms mentioned, and to concentrate upon the relations among them. Our hypothetical agent will be imagined to hold certain views, not only about the case in question (which I will not describe exactly) but also about a range of related cases with respect to which—seeking rationality in specification—she aims to work out a consistent view. In the debate over the Baby Doe cases, it appears that at least three main principles are in contention, each of which our deliberator begins by accepting in nonabsolute form: (1) a prohibition on directly killing innocent persons (here, the newborn), (2) a duty to respect the reasonable choices of parents regarding their children (suppose that in this case the mother and father want to let their baby die), and (3) a duty to benefit the persons over whom one has responsibility (here, from the point of view of the medical personnel, the patients—i.e., the infant and the mother).[50] Assuming that the prohibition on directly killing innocent persons is not to be evaded, in the case in question, either on double-effect grounds (i.e., on the grounds that the killing is not "direct") or on act-omission grounds (i.e., on the grounds that withdrawing nutrition and hydration is merely "letting die" and not killing), there is a conflict between the first principle and the other two. An analysis of the concept of personhood will not help much here, for our deliberator quails at the implications *either* of classing these newborns as persons and sticking by the prohibition on killing *or* of classing them as nonpersons and thereby treating that prohibition as irrelevant. She finds the first option terrible from the point of view of benefit—cui bono? The second option she deems unacceptable partly on its own account and partly because of its implications by analogy for the treatment, say, of the elderly and the mentally retarded. The suggestion of the model of specification, by contrast, is that we must not assume that the principles mentioned are all fixed in their content, leaving us only to understand the terms of

50. Cf. the principles invoked by Laurence B. McCullough and Catherine Myser, "Recent Developments in Perinatal and Neonatal Medical Ethics: A US Perspective," *Seminars in Perinatology* 11 (1987): 216–23.

the principles precisely and to describe the case accurately so as to determine correctly which principle applies. I want to illustrate the idea of specification at work in two ways in a possible course of deliberation: first, in helping understand a revision of a norm that is not itself a case of specification, and second, in a specification proper.

Suppose, as a first step, that our deliberator is led by this practical conflict to examine her reasons for accepting the general prohibition on killing, and suppose that these revolve around the notion of respect for persons. What is it about persons, she wonders, that demands respect? These difficult cases involving severely defective infants force this question upon her. Suppose that she decides, on reflection, that the prohibition on killing is, in effect, a specification of a more general principle requiring respect for self-conscious life, and that she is led to revise the prohibition, replacing it with one that specifies the underlying norm differently. Suppose, also, that the present practical conflict leads her to qualify the revised prohibition on killing further by reference to the principle of benefit. As a result of these deliberations, she specifies the prohibition on directly killing innocent persons to read "it is generally wrong directly to kill innocent human beings who have attained self-consciousness, and generally wrong directly to kill human beings with the (genetic?) potential to develop self-consciousness who would not be better off dead, but it is not generally wrong directly to kill human beings who meet neither of these criteria." Although its explicit exception prevents this norm from being a specification of the original prohibition (1), it can still claim some support as a specification of the underlying norm of respect for life. It can also be defended more particularly by reference to the fact that it resolves many conflicts among the norms governing the treatment of defective newborns. As always, of course, if resolving these conflicts provokes other ones, this defense of the specification may be rebutted. To reflect this, and taking to heart the maxim that "hard cases make bad law," the deliberator may wish to preface her specifications with a scope limitation, such as "in all cases involving defective newborns. . . ."

Let us suppose, however, that the particular case facing our agent is one in which it does not appear that the infant in question would be better off dead. Of course, one might at this stage seek a resolution by specifying further the tremendously vague notion of "benefit" as it appears in the principle she arrived at in the preceding paragraph; but let us suppose, instead, that she first works with the principle of respect for

305   *Specifying Norms*
                           as a Way to Resolve
                           Concrete Ethical Problems

parental choice, since there remains a clash between the revised prohibition and the wishes of the parents. In this case, there is a specification readily available in the ethical tradition which will lessen the practical conflict she is facing by restricting the range of the principle of respect for parental choices to choices that themselves express respect for their children. (Compare Kant's version of respect for autonomy.) Accordingly, she may specify this principle as requiring "that one respect the reasonable choices of parents regarding their children so long as they respect the children's rights." She might, further, decide that this narrowed version of respect for parental choice ought to be taken to *replace* the initial, unqualified version, thereby freeing herself from a requirement to respect the wishes of the parent if they would go against the infant's right to life.

While the course of this hypothetical path of deliberation has been highly controversial and considerably oversimplified, let me highlight the two features that give rise to its claim to be a rational process. First, the specifications and respecifications offered do manage to avert a practical conflict among principles—a conflict that in itself seems rationally unacceptable. Since they therefore enhance the fit among our principles, at least within this limited domain, these specifications mark an improvement in coherence that might be counted as being, in itself, strong (though hardly conclusive) grounds for the rationality of this change. Second, although each of these specifications is controversial, their grounds are not some kind of private and nondiscursive perception or intuition. Rather, they rest on grounds open to rational public debate and assessment, such as those arguments resting on the underlying theory of respect for persons. For instance, the specification of the prohibition on killing offered above could be rationally rejected on the basis of an argument to the effect that the grounds of the prohibition are quite independent of its specifying the ideal of respect for persons.

For a second example, I will shift from the tragic to the merely distasteful, and discuss a choice that is the personal counterpart of what is now a major policy question.[51] It is a choice faced by a committed environmentalist—one convinced that he should, within reason, live his life

---

51. In this essay I have generally tried to avoid getting into the complications that arise when the decision to be made is, in an important way, joint, public, or interpersonal. While one might claim that an advantage of, say, some forms of preference utilitarianism is that they leave controversial questions of value specification to individuals, I believe that this is a misleading dodge.

so as to minimize his adverse impact on the ecosystem. And now the momentous question is: Should he use disposable diapers for his baby or cloth ones? He is enough of an environmentalist that we may ignore questions of convenience and the baby's well-being (allergies, dryness, and so on), and focus solely on the relevant environmental values.[52]

Here is one approach our environmentalist might take: he might make a list of all of the kinds of environmental damage relevant to this choice. In using disposables there is tree loss, topsoil lost and species disturbed at the logging site, air pollution from logging vehicles, water pollution from the pulp plant, oil consumed and air polluted during plastics manufacture, energy consumed in disposable diaper production, the bulk of disposable diapers as a strain on available landfill space, and the biological hazards posed by disposing of soiled diapers. In using cloth diapers there are pesticides used in farming cotton, air pollution from the farming vehicles, energy consumption in manufacturing cotton diapers, energy consumption in transporting and washing cotton diapers, the incremental strain on the sewage system of emptying the cloth diapers into the public sewers, and water pollution from the detergent and bleach used in cleaning the cloth diapers. Being compulsive enough to develop such a list, our deliberator is certainly not going to rest content with an intuitive balancing of this complex set of pros and cons. In order to be more systematic, he instead may try to develop an "environmental impact index" that (1) develops a measure of each of these different types of effect and (2) assigns that measure a weight. But how is such a weighting to be rationally defended? The task seems hopeless, and its value merely heuristic. If this factoring into pros and cons is just a more complicated version of intuitive balancing, it might be easier just to go by his gut reaction to the overall choice.

This abortive effort at weighting these different types of environmental harm, however, will not be in vain if it leads our deliberator to reflect on the way he would specify his guiding norm. We started by supposing that his single overriding relevant principle was to protect and preserve the

---

52. Since the following paragraphs were written, Arthur D. Little Inc., a respected consulting company, published a "life cycle analysis" of the two types of diaper, much along the lines suggested in the text. It concludes that neither type of diaper is clearly better for the environment. Although the study was funded by one of the makers of disposables, the spokesman for one national environmental organization complained only that the study ignored the pesticides used in growing the cotton for cloth diapers. See John Holusha, "Diaper Debate: Cloth or Disposable?" *New York Times*, 14 July 1990, late edition, p. 46.

307 *Specifying Norms as a Way to Resolve Concrete Ethical Problems*

environment: but what shall he mean by this? Preserve it in what state, from what dangers? Reflection on the various pros and cons can be of heuristic value in helping him further specify his central principle. Thus, while many of the harms on either side seem to cancel out, in a rough way, there remains a salient difference between the two options—one which might be captured by the notions of material flow versus energy expenditure. Disposable diapers come from the forests and the oil reserves and end up in landfills. Cloth diapers stick around, but require a lot of pollution-generating energy consumption to do so. This overall contrast suggests that it will be important, for the purposes of making this choice, whether our environmentalist specifies his leading norm in one of two broadly familiar ways. First, there is the more old-fashioned conception of the conservationist: the supporter of wilderness areas, hiker (or perhaps NRA member), and reader of John Muir, whose notion of preserving the environment centers on the idea of keeping those parts of nature not yet touched by man from becoming disrupted. Second, there is the newer, more urban-oriented and liberal environmentalist who focuses on those parts of the earth where man's influence is already noticeable, is concerned largely with human health, and seeks to minimize the pollution of populated areas. The first specification would lend differential support to the use of cloth diapers, the second to the use of disposables (at least if the biohazard can be contained). How will our deliberator decide which specification of his guiding norm to adopt (supposing he is initially unsure)? Here is where his effort at ranking the particular harms involved, though incomplete and insufficiently precise to yield a single-valued index, will nonetheless help, for it is likely that his pattern of ranking reflects one of these specifications more than the other. This differential could draw his attention to the way he would specify his guiding norm. Once he focuses on this question, it is likely that this more finely specified version of his environmental end will fit with and will help make sense of a broad range of his policy positions. This fit would justify or explain his adopting that specification. If he can specify his guiding norm more finely in one of these two ways, then which diaper option he should choose will become relatively obvious.

To be sure, once he has settled upon one of these specifications—or perhaps upon a more complex one that crafts a compromise—this would provide a better basis for constructing an index. Obviously, however, the resulting weighting would not be one that was antecedent to the choice.

Furthermore, since other choices might call for a still finer grained specification, or one that qualified along a different axis, it would be unwise to place too much confidence in the weighting that seems implied by this particular choice.

In this second example, as in the first, the claim to rationality for the specification stems from the possibility of setting out discursively the reasons for holding that it yields a better fit than its rival. Here, there is no conflict averted; but where it had seemed that the choice would have to be made purely intuitively, we have instead an argument that is open to assessment. The claim, in this example as in the prior one, is that one can see how the specifications involved count as courses of reasoning—not that one can see that rationality dictates a unique answer.

VI. Conclusion

I have argued that the model of specification is not only distinct from the pure models of application and balancing and their hybrids, but also superior to each of them. It deals constructively with moral conflicts rather than being stymied by them, as is the pure model of application; and it has a claim to proceeding by discursive rationality that intuitive balancing cannot share. It benefits from a considerable degree of casuistical flexibility without sacrificing a potentially intimate tie to guiding theories; and it is able to proceed from norms looser and hence more acceptable than the completely universal ones required by the deductivist to reach a conclusion through a Peripatetic syllogism. By showing, without relying upon universal norms, how a theory might remain stable in the face of conflicts, the model of specification also undercuts the argument for ethical skepticism that departs from the fact that norms will conflict.

The decisive advantage of the model of specification lies in its attitude to conflicts of norms. Whereas the pure model of application is bedeviled by conflicts and the pure model of intuitive balancing sails through them untouched, the model of specification learns from the conflicts it faces, exploiting their friction to push off toward a more concrete and definite understanding of the relevant norms. If we assume that our norms cannot be absolute, then they will naturally be qualified in the course of resolving concrete ethical problems. The model of specification searches out qualifications that are specific to the content of the norm being specified (recall the relevance requirement), tailored to the situation being addressed, and articulate as to their rationale.

309 *Specifying Norms
as a Way to Resolve
Concrete Ethical Problems*

While the superiority of the model of specification's attitude to conflicts over those of the pure models of application and balancing is perhaps obvious, its superiority in this respect in comparison to a hybrid such as Ross's, which combines these two operations, needs more elaboration. I have already commented upon the superior ability of the model of specification to account for the phenomenon of general norms "hanging around" even though they are not followed in a given case. Beyond this, however, is a deeper difference in attitude. This hybrid model has served the very important and constructive function of convincing many that we need not cast aside a nonconsequentialist attachment to moral principles simply on account of counterexamples to each principle taken absolutely—for these can all too readily be generated from our considered judgments about hypothetical and real examples. Shifting from an "absolute" to a "prima facie" interpretation of moral principles allows the nonconsequentialist to survive in the face of such objections. But in the field of medical ethics, at least, it would seem that this hybrid model has won this battle. It turns out, however, that the prima facie principles that have been put forward in this field settle few questions by themselves: rather, one gets a sense of a pervasive conflict between, say, autonomy and beneficence. Because of the nature of the hybrid model's framework, there is little theoretical incentive to refine these prima facie principles in a way that expands the constructive role of discursive reasoning. This lassitude derives from the very feature that gave Rossian intuitionism such appeal in the first place, namely, its ability to brush aside counterexamples. A Rossian intuitionist need not worry about presenting a very vague and overly inclusive interpretation of "autonomy" as "self-determination," for instance, because when a concrete case arises in which the demands of autonomy so interpreted seem unacceptable, it is highly likely that this unacceptability can be explained in terms of a clash with another prima facie principle, therefore depriving any principle of straightforward application. Combine this universal stopgap with the claim that "the decision rests with perception" when the various prima facie principles conflict, and you can see that this hybrid approach offers no logical requirement to go any further than listing a few prima facie principles, the exact contours of which one need not worry much about. If one does start to worry about these—wondering, for instance, why autonomy in the control of one's body is more important than autonomy in the control over the use of one's surgical capacities (say, when there is a conflict over whether the surgeon should amputate a patient's leg), then one has started down the road of specification.[53] Many of the most thoughtful writers on concrete ethics do just this. They should then recognize that Ross's hybrid model no longer adequately describes what they are doing.

In contrast to its alternatives, as I have stressed, the model of specification typically uses practical conflicts, in which unacceptable implications of norms arise, as occasions that give one *pro tanto* grounds for more finely specifying these norms. This feature of the model of specification was apparent in the hypothetical deliberation concerning malformed newborns, in which a more fine-grained interpretation of autonomy was generated in response to the case at hand. It is this sort of further specification that is now needed, I suggest, in relatively well developed areas of concrete ethics such as medical ethics. Unless we can learn from our ethical conflicts in this way, our prospects for a reasonable and rational treatment of the problems of concrete ethics are dim indeed.

53. I doubt that this differential between the body and the use of professional capacities may be deduced from the concept of autonomy. It seems, rather, to reflect an independent set of norms, of the sort that are embodied in the law of torts.

[12]

The Tyranny of Principles
by STEPHEN TOULMIN

If this were a sermon (and perhaps it is), its text would be the quotation attributed to H. L. Mencken that hangs in the staff lounge at The Hastings Center:

> For every human problem, there is a solution that is simple, neat, and wrong.[1]

Oversimplification is a temptation to which moral philosophers are not immune, despite all their admirable intellectual care and seriousness; and the abstract generalizations of theoretical ethics are, I shall argue, no substitute for a sound tradition in practical ethics.

These days, public debates about ethical issues oscillate between, on the one hand, a narrow dogmatism that confines itself to unqualified general assertions dressed up as "matters of principle" and, on the other, a shallow relativism that evades all firm stands by suggesting that we choose our "value systems" as freely as we choose our clothes. Both approaches suffer from the same excess of generality. The rise of anthropology and the other human sciences in the early twentieth century encouraged a healthy sense of social and cultural differences; but this was uncritically taken as implying an end to all objectivity in practical ethics. The subsequent reassertion of ethical objectivity has led, in turn, to an insistence on the absoluteness of moral principles that is not balanced by a feeling for the complex problems of discrimination that arise when such principles are applied to particular real-life cases. So, the relativists have tended to overinterpret the need for discrimination in ethics, discretion in public administration, and equity in law, as a license for general personal subjectivity. The absolutists have responded by denying all real scope for personal judgment in ethics, insisting instead on strict construction in the law, on unfeeling consistency in public administration, and—above all—on the "inerrancy" of moral principles.

I propose to concentrate my attention on this last phenomenon—the revival of a tyrannical absolutism in recent discussions about social and personal ethics. I find it reflected in attitudes toward politics, public affairs, and the administration of justice, as much as toward questions of "ethics"

STEPHEN TOULMIN *is professor, Committee on Social Thought and department of philosophy, University of Chicago. This article is adapted from a presentation at The Hastings Center's General Meeting held on June 19, 1981. It was also presented, in a somewhat different version, at Osgoode Hall Law School and will be published in that version in the Osgoode Hall Law Journal.*

in a narrower and more personal sense. My main purpose will be to ask: What is it about our present situation that inclines us to move in that direction? By way of reply, I shall argue that, in all large industrialized societies and cultures—regardless of their economic and political systems—ethics, law, and public administration have recently undergone similar historical transformations, so that all three fields are exposed to the same kinds of pressures, face common difficulties, and share in the same resulting public distrust. And I shall try to show what we can learn about those shared problems, and about the responses that they call for, by studying the common origins of our basic ethical, legal, and political ideas. All my central examples will be concerned with the same general topic: the nature, scope, and force of "rules" and "principles" in ethics and in law. Three personal experiences helped to bring these problems into focus for me.

Three Personal Experiences

Human Subjects Research. For several years in the mid-1970s, I worked as a staff member with the National Commission for the Protection of Human Subjects of Biomedical and Behavioral Research, which was established by the U.S. Congress, with the task of reporting and making recommendations about the ethics of using human subjects in medical and psychological research. Eleven commissioners—five of them scientists, the remaining six lawyers, theologians, and other nonscientists—were instructed to make recommendations about publicly financed human experimentation: in particular, to determine under what conditions subjects belonging to certain vulnerable groups (such as young children and prisoners) could participate in such research without moral objection.[2]

Before the Commission began work, many onlookers assumed that its discussions would degenerate into a Babel of rival opinions. One worldly commentator remarked in the *New England Journal of Medicine*, "Now (I suppose) we shall see matters of eternal principle decided by a six to five vote."[3] But things did not work out that way. In practice, the commissioners were never split along the line between scientists and nonscientists. In almost every case they came close to agreement even about quite detailed recommendations—at least for so long as their discussions proceeded taxonomically, taking one difficult class of cases at a time and comparing it in detail with other clearer and easier classes of cases.

Even when the Commission's recommendations were not unanimous, the discussions in no way resembled Babel: the commissioners were never in any doubt what it was that they were *not quite unanimous about.* Babel set in only afterwards. When the eleven individual commissioners asked themselves what "principles" underlay and supposedly justified their adhesion to the consensus, each of them answered in his or her own way: the Catholics appealed to Catholic principles, the humanists to humanist principles, and so on. They could agree; they could agree what they were agreeing about; but, apparently, they could not agree why they agreed about it.

This experience prompted me to wonder what this final "appeal to principles" really achieved. Certainly it did not add any weight or certitude to the commissioners' specific ethical recommendations, for example, about the kind of consent procedures required in biomedical research using five-year-old children. They were, quite evidently, surer about these shared, particular judgments than they were about the discordant general principles on which, in theory, their practical judgments were based. If anything, the appeal to principles undermined the recommendations by suggesting to onlookers that there was more disharmony than ever showed up in the commissioners' actual discussions. So, by the end of my tenure with the Commission I had begun to suspect that the point of "appealing to principles" was something quite else: not to give particular ethical judgments a more solid foundation, but rather to square the collective ethical conclusions of the Commission as a whole with each individual commissioner's other *non*ethical commitments. So (it seemed to me) the principles of Catholic ethics tell us more about Catholicism than they do about ethics, the principles of Jewish or humanist ethics more about Judaism or humanism than about ethics. Such principles serve less as foundations, adding intellectual strength or force to particular moral opinions, than they do as corridors or curtain walls linking the moral perceptions of all reflective human beings, with other, more general positions—theological, philosophical, ideological, or *Weltanschaulich.*

Abortion. The years of the National Commission's work were also years during which the morality of abortion became a matter of public controversy. In fact, the U.S. Congress established the Commission in the backwash of the Supreme Court's ruling on the legality of abortion, following a public dispute about research on the human fetus. And before long the public debate about abortion acquired some of the same puzzling features as the proceedings of the Commission itself. On the one hand, there were those who could discuss the morality of abortion temperately and with discrimination, acknowledging that here, as in other agonizing human situations, conflicting considerations are involved and that a just, if sometimes painful, balance has to be struck between different rights and claims, interests and responsibilities.[4] That temperate approach underlay traditional common law doctrines about abortion before the first statutory restrictions were enacted in the years around 1825. It was also the approach adopted by the U.S. Supreme Court in the classic case, *Roe* v. *Wade*; and, most important, it was the approach clearly spelled out by Thomas Aquinas, whose position was close to that of the common law and the Supreme Court. (He acknowledged that the balance of moral considerations necessarily tilts in different directions at different stages in a woman's pregnancy, with crucial changes beginning around the time of "quickening."[5]) On the other hand, much of the public rhetoric increasingly came to turn on "matters of principle." As a result, the abortion debate became less temperate, less discriminating, and above all less resolvable. Too often, in subsequent years, the issue has boiled down to pure head-butting: an embryo's unqualified "right to life" being pitted against a woman's equally unqualified "right to choose." Those who have insisted on dealing with the issue at the level of high theory thus guarantee that the only possible practical outcome is deadlock.

Social Welfare Benefits. My perplexities about the force and value of "rules" and "principles" were further sharpened as the result of a television news magazine program about a handicapped young woman who had difficulties with the local Social Security office. Her Social Security payments were not sufficient to cover her rent and food, so she started an answering service, which she operated through the telephone at her bedside. The income from this service—though itself less than a living wage—made all the difference to her. When the local Social Security office heard about this extra income, however, they reduced her benefits accordingly; in addition, they ordered her to repay some of the money she had been receiving. (Apparently, they regarded her as a case of "welfare fraud.") The television reporter added two final statements. Since the report had been filmed, he told us, the young woman, in despair, had taken her own life. To this he added his personal comment that "there should be a *rule* to prevent this kind of thing from happening."

Notice that the reporter did not say, "The local office should be given discretion to waive, or at least bend, the existing rules in hard cases." What he said was, "There should be an *additional* rule to prevent such inequities in the future." Justice, he evidently believed, can be ensured only by establishing an adequate system of rules, and injustice can be prevented only by adding more rules.

Hence, the questions that arise from these experiences: What force and function do rules or principles truly possess, either in law or in ethics? What social and historical circumstances make it most natural and appropriate to discuss legal and ethical issues in the language of "rules" and "principles"? Why are our own contemporary legal and ethical discussions so preoccupied with rules and principles? And to what extent would we do better to look for justice and morality in other directions?

Rules in Roman Law

Far from playing an indispensable part in either law or ethics, "rules" have only a limited and conditional role. The current vogue for rules and principles is the outcome of certain powerful factors in recent social history; but these factors have always been balanced against counterweights. Justice has always required both law and equity, while morality has always demanded both fairness and discrimination. When this essential duality is ignored, reliance on unchallengeable principles can generate, or become the instrument of, its own subtle kind of tyranny.

My reading soon led me back to Peter Stein's *Regulae Juris*, which traces the development of the concept of a "rule" in Roman law from its beginnings to the modern era.[6] His account of the earliest phases of Roman law was for me the most striking part. For the first three hundred years of Roman history, the legal system made no explicit use of the concept of rules. The College of Pontiffs acted as the city's judges, and individual pontiffs gave their adjudications on the cases submitted to them. But they were not required to cite any general rules as justifications for their decisions. Indeed, they were not required to give reasons at all. Their task was not to argue, but rather to pontificate.

How was this possible? How can any system of law operate in the absence of rules, reasons, and all the associated apparatus of binding force and precedent? Indeed, in such a situation can we say a true system of law exists at all? Those questions require us to consider the historical and anthropological circumstances of early Rome. Initially Rome was a small and relatively homogeneous community, whose members shared a correspondingly homogeneous tradition of ideas about justice and fairness, property and propriety, a tradition having more in common with Sir Henry Maine's ideas about traditional "customary law" than with the "positive law" of John Austin's *Province of Jurisprudence Determined*.[7] In any such community the functions of adjudication tend to be more arbitral than regulatory. Like labor arbitrators today, the judges will not be as sharply bound by precedent as contemporary high court judges. So the disputes that the pontiffs adjudicated were typically ones about which the traditional consensus was ambiguous; the balance of rights and obligations between the parties required the judgment call of a trusted and disinterested arbitrator. In these marginal cases all that the arbitrator may be able to say is, "Having taken all the circumstances into account, I find that on this particular occasion it would, all in all, be more reasonable to tilt the scale to A rather than to B." This ruling will rest, not on the application of general legal rules, but rather on the exercise of judicial discrimination in assessing the balance of particulars. Initially, "pontificating" did not mean laying down the law in a dogmatic manner. Rather, it meant resolving marginal disputes by an equitable arbitration, and the pontiffs had the trust of their fellow citizens in doing so.

This state of affairs did not last. Long before the first Imperial codification, Roman law began to develop the full apparatus of "rules" with which we ourselves are familiar. Stein suggests that five sets of factors contributed to this new reliance on *regulae*.[8] First, as the city grew, the case load increased beyond what the pontiffs themselves could manage. Junior judges, who did not possess the same implicit trust as the pontiffs, were brought in to resolve disputes; so the consistency of their rulings had to be "regularized." Second, with the rise of lawyering as a profession, law schools were set up and *regulae* were articulated for the purpose of teaching the law. Discretion, which had rested earlier on the personal characters of the pontiffs themselves and which is not so easy to teach, began to be displaced by formal rules and more teachable argumentative skills. Third, Rome acquired an empire, and foreign peoples came under the city's authority. Their systems of customary law had to be put into harmony with the Roman system, and this could be done only by establishing a concordance between the "rules" of different systems. Fourth, the empire itself developed a bureaucracy, which could not operate except on the basis of rules. Finally, the intellectual discussion of law was pursued in the context of Greek philosophy. Although Cicero, for example, was a practicing attorney, he was also a philosophical scholar with a professional interest in the Stoic doctrine of the *logos*, or "universal reason."

What followed the resulting proliferation of rules and laws is common knowledge. First, a functional differentiation grew up between two kinds of issues. On the one hand, there were issues that could be decided by applying *general* rules or laws, on the basis of the maxim that like cases should be treated alike. On the other hand, there were issues that called for discretion, with an eye to the *particular* features of each case, in accordance with the maxim that significantly different cases should be treated differently. This functional differentiation became the ancestor of our own distinction between legal and equitable jurisdiction. Second, the Emperor Constantine decided as a matter of imperial policy to bring equitable jurisdiction under his personal control by reserving the equitable function to his own personal court and chancellor. Out in the public arena, judges were given the menial task of applying general rules with only the minimum of discretion. Once legal proceedings were exhausted, the aggrieved citizen could appeal to the Emperor as *parens patriae* ("father of the fatherland") for the benevolent exercise of clemency or equity. Politically, this division of labor certainly did the Emperor no harm; but it also sowed the first seeds of public suspicion that the Law is one thing, Justice another.[9]

Carried over into the modern English-speaking world, the resulting division between courts of law and courts of equity is familiar to readers of Charles Dickens. And although during the twentieth century most Anglo-American jurisdictions have merged legal and equitable functions in the same courts,[10] it is still widely the case that equitable remedies can be sought only in cases where legal remedies are unavailable or unworkable—so that in this respect the dead hand of Constantine still rules us from the grave.

The Ethics of Strangers

Life in late-twentieth-century industrial societies clearly has more in common with life in Imperial Rome than it has with the Rome of Horatius at the Bridge or with Mrs. Gaskell's *Cranford*. Our cities are vast, our populations are mixed and fragmented, our public administration is bureaucratic, our jurisdictions (both domestic and foreign) are many and varied. As a result, the moral consensus and civic trust on which the pontificate of early Rome depended for its general respect and efficacy often appear to be no more than a beguiling dream. The way we live now, people have come to value uniformity above responsiveness, to focus on law at the expense of equity, and to confuse "the rule of law" with a law of rules. Yet the balance between law and equity still needs to be struck, even if new ways need to be found that answer our new needs. From this point on, I shall work my way toward the question: how, in our actual situation, can that balance best be redressed?

In law, in ethics, and in public administration alike, there is nowadays a similar preoccupation with general principles and a similar distrust of individual discretion. In the administration of social services, the demand for equality of treatment makes us unwilling to permit administrators to "temper the wind to the shorn lamb"—that strikes us as unfair, and therefore unjust.[11] (The equation of justice with fairness is thus a two-edged sword.) In the professions, a widespread fear that professionals are taking unfair advantage of their fiduciary positions has contributed to the recent wave of malpractice suits. In the courts, judges are given less and less room to exercise discretion, and many lawyers view juries as no more trustworthy than judges; the more they are both kept in line by clear rules, or so it seems, the better.[12] As for public discussions of ethics, the recognition of genuine moral complexities, conflicts, and tragedies, that can be dealt with only on a case-by-case basis, is simply unfashionable. Victory in public argument goes, rather, to the person with the more imposing principle. Above all, many people involved in the current debate seem to have forgotten what the term "equity" actually means. They assume that it is just a literary synonym for "equality."[13] So, a demand for the uniform application of public policies leads to a submerging of the discretionary by the rigorous, the equitable by the equal. Faced with judicial injustices, we react like the television reporter, declaring, "There ought to be a law against it," even where it would be more appropriate to say, "In this particular case, the law is making an ass of itself." The same applies to the operation of our bureaucracies, and to the emphasis on principles in moral judgments.

In all three fields, we need to be reminded that equity requires not the imposition of uniformity or equality on all relevant cases, but rather reasonableness or responsiveness (*epieikeia*) in applying general rules to individual cases.[14] Equity means doing justice with discretion around, in the interstices of, and in areas of conflict between our laws, rules, principles, and other general formulas. It means being responsive to the limits of all such formulas, to the special circumstances in which one can properly make exceptions, and to the trade-offs required where different formulas conflict. The degree to which such marginal judgments can be regularized or routinized remains limited today, just as it was in early Rome. Faced with the task of balancing the equities of different parties, a judge today may well be guided by previous precedents; but these precedents only illuminate broad maxims, they do not invoke formal rules.[15] Likewise, professional practice may be described in cut-and-dried terms as a matter of "routine and accepted" procedures only in the artificial context of a malpractice suit. In the actual exercise of his profession, a surgeon, say, may sometimes simply have to use his or her own best judgment in deciding how to proceed conscientiously. Finally, in ethics, moral wisdom is exercised not by those who stick by a single principle come what may, absolutely and without exception, but rather by those who understand that, in the long run, no principle—however absolute—can avoid running up against another equally absolute principle; and by those who have the experience and discrimination needed to balance conflicting considerations in the most humane way.[16]

By looking at the effects of changing social conditions and modes of life on our ethical perceptions, I believe we can best hit on the clues that will permit us to unravel this whole tangle of problems. A century ago in *Anna Karenina* Leo Tolstoy expressed a view which, though in my opinion exaggerated, is none the less illuminating. During his lifetime Tolstoy lived to see the abolition of serfdom, the introduction of railways, the movement of population away from the country to the cities, and the consequent emergence of modern city life; and he continued to have deep reservations about the possibility of living a truly moral life in a modern city. As he saw matters, genuinely "moral" relations can exist only between people who live, work, and associate together: inside a family, between intimates and associates, within a neighborhood. The natural limit to any person's moral universe, for Tolstoy, is the distance he or she can walk, or at most ride. By taking the train, a moral agent leaves the sphere of truly moral actions for a world of strangers, toward whom he or she has few real obligations and with whom dealings can be only casual or commercial. Whenever the moral pressures and demands become too strong to bear, Tolstoy has Anna go down to the railway station and take a train somewhere, anywhere. The final irony of Tolstoy's own painful life was that he finally broke away from his home and family, only to die in the local stationmaster's office.[17] Matters of state policy and the like, in Tolstoy's eyes, lay quite outside the realm of ethics. Through the figure of Constantin Levin, he made clear his skepticism about all attempts either to turn ethics into a matter of theory or to make political reform an instrument of virtue.[18]

What Tolstoy rightly emphasized is the sharp difference that exists between our moral relations with our families, intimates, and immediate neighbors or associates, and our moral relations with complete strangers. In dealing with our children, friends, and immediate colleagues, we both expect to—and are expected to—make allowances for their individual personalities and tastes, and we do our best to time our actions according to our perception of their current moods and plans. In dealing with the bus driver, the sales clerk in a department store, the hotel barber, and other such casual contacts, there may be no basis for making these allowances, and so no chance of doing so. In these transient encounters, our moral obligations are limited and chiefly negative—for example, to avoid acting offensively or violently. So, in the ethics of strangers, respect for rules is all, and the opportunities for discretion are few. In the ethics of intimacy, discretion is all, and the relevance of strict rules is minimal.[19] For Tolstoy, of course, only the ethics of intimacy was properly called "ethics" at all—that is why I described his view as exaggerated. But in this respect the ethics of John Rawls is equally exaggerated, though in the opposite direction. In our relations with casual acquaintances and unidentified fellow citizens, absolute impartiality may be a prime moral demand; but among intimates a certain discreet partiality is, surely, only equitable, and certainly not unethical. So a system of ethics that rests its principles on "the veil of ignorance" may well be "fair," but it will also be—essentially—an ethics for relations between strangers.[20]

The Stresses of Lawsuits

Seeing how Tolstoy felt about his own time, what would he have thought about the life we lead today? The effects of the railways, in blurring the boundary between the moral world of the immediate community and the neutral world beyond, have been only multiplied by the private car, which breaks that boundary down almost completely. Living in a high-rise apartment building, taking the car from its underground garage to the supermarket and back, the modern city dweller may sometimes wonder whether he has any neighbors at all. For many of us, the sphere of intimacy has shrunk to the nuclear family, and this has placed an immense strain on family relations. Living in a world of comparative strangers, we find ourselves short on civic trust and increasingly estranged from our professional advisors. We are less inclined to give judges and bureaucrats room to use their discretion, and more determined to obtain equal (if not always equitable) treatment. In a world of complete strangers, indeed, equality would be about the only virtue left.

Do not misunderstand my position. I am not taking a nostalgia trip back to the Good Old Days. The world of neighborliness and forced intimacy, of both geographical and social immobility, had its vices as well as its virtues. Jane Austen's caricature of Lady Catherine de Burgh in *Pride and Prejudice* reminds us that purchasing equity by submitting to gross condescension can make its price too dear:

> God bless the Squire and his relations,
> and keep us in our proper stations.

Any biography of Tolstoy reminds us that his world, too, had a darker side. Those who are seduced by his admiration for the moral wisdom of the newly emancipated peasantry will find an antidote in Frederick Douglass's memoirs of slave life on the Maryland shore. Nor am I deploring apartment buildings and private cars. People usually have reasons for living as they do, and attacking modernity in the name of the morality of an earlier time is an act of desperation, like building the Berlin Wall. No, my question is only: If we accept the modern world as it is—apartment buildings, private cars, and all—how can we strike the central balance between the ethics of intimates and the ethics of strangers, between uniformity of treatment and administrative discretion, and between equity and law, in ways that answer our contemporary needs?

To begin with the law: current public stereotypes focus on the shortcomings of the adversary process, but what first needs to be explained is just where the adversary system has gone astray, and in what fields of law we should be most concerned to replace it. That should not be hard to do. Given that we handle our moral relations with intimates and associates differently from our moral relations with strangers, is not some similar differentiation appropriate between our legal relations with strangers, on the one hand, and with intimates, associates, and close family members on the other?

Even in the United States, the homeland of the adversary system, at least two types of disputes—labor-management conflicts and the renegotiation of commercial contracts—are dealt with by using arbitration or conciliation rather than confrontation.[21] That is no accident. In a criminal prosecution or a routine civil damage suit arising out of a car collision, the parties are normally complete strangers before the proceedings and have no stake in one another's future, so no harm is done if they walk out of the court vowing never to set eyes on each other again. By contrast, the parties to a labor grievance will normally wish to continue working together after the adjudication, while the disputants in a commercial arbitration may well retain or resume business dealings with one another despite the present disagreement. In cases of these kinds, the psychological stresses of the adversary system can be quite destructive: by the time an enthusiastic litigating attorney has done his bit, further labor relations or commercial dealings may be psychologically impossible. So in appraising different kinds of court proceedings, we need to consider how particular types of judicial episodes fit into the larger life histories of the individuals who are parties to them, and what impact the form of proceedings can have on those life histories.

A lawsuit that pits the full power of the state against a criminal defendant is one thing: in that context, Monroe Freedman may be right to underline the merits of the adversary mode, and the positive obligations of zealous defense advocacy.[22] A civil suit that pits colleagues, next-door neighbors, or family members against each other is another thing: in that context resort to adversary proceedings may only make a bad situation worse. So, reasonably enough, the main locus of dissatisfaction with the adversary system is those areas of human life in which the psychological outcomes are most damaging: family law, for example. By the time that the father, mother, and children involved in a custody dispute have all been zealously represented in court, the bad feelings from which the suit originally sprang may well have become irremediable. It is just such areas as family law that other nations (such as West Germany) have chosen to handle by arbitration rather than litigation, in chambers rather than in open court, so providing much more room for discretion.

I am suggesting, then, that a system of law consisting wholly of rules would treat all the parties coming before it in the ways appropriate to strangers. By contrast, in legal issues that arise between parties who wish to continue as close associates on an intimate or familiar level, the demands of equality and rule conformity lose their central place. There, above all, the differences between the desires, personalities, hopes, capacities, and ambitions of the parties most need to be taken into account; and only an adjudicator with authority to interpret existing rules, precedents, and maxims in the light of, and in response to, those differences will be in a position to respect the equities of all the parties involved.

Reviving the Friendly Society

In public administration, especially in the field of social services, the crucial historical changes were more recent, yet they appear much harder to reverse. Two centuries ago most of what we now call the social services—then known, collectively, as "charity"—were still dispensed through the churches. Local ministers of religion were generally trusted to perform this duty equitably and conscientiously; and in deciding to give more to (say) Mrs. Smith than Mrs. Jones, they were not strictly answerable to any supervisor, still less bound by a book of rules. (As with the Squirearchy, of course, this arrangement had its own abuses: the Rev. Mr. Collins could be as overbearing in his own way as Lady Catherine de Burgh.) Even a hundred years ago many such charitable functions were still carried on by private organizations, like those in Britain which were charmingly known as "friendly societies." But by this time things were beginning to change. A friendly clergyman is one thing, but a friendly *society* is more of an anomaly: in due course irregularities in the administration of those organizations—like those in some trade union pension funds today—provoked government supervision, and a Registrar of Friendly Societies was appointed to keep an eye on them.

From that point on, the delivery of social services has become ever more routinized, centralized, and subject to bureaucratic routine. It should not take horror stories, like that of the handicapped young woman's answering service, to make us think again about the whole project of delivering human services through a bureaucracy: one only has to read Max Weber. The imperatives of bureaucratic administration require determinate procedures and full accountability; while a helping hand, whether known by the name of "charity" or "social services," can be truly equitable only if it is exercised with discretion, on the basis of substantive and informed judgments about need rather than formal rules of entitlement.

What might be done, then, to counter the rigors of bureaucracy in this field? Or should late-twentieth-century societies look for other ways of lending a collective hand to those in need? In an exemplary apologia for bureaucracy, Herbert Kaufman of the Brookings Institution has put his finger on many of the key points.[23] If we find public administration today complex, unresponsive, and procedure-bound, he argues that this is almost entirely our own fault. These defects are direct consequences of the demands that we ourselves have placed on our public servants in a situation increasingly marked by diversity, democracy, and distrust. Since we are unwilling to grant discretion to civil servants for fear that it will be abused, we leave ourselves with no measure for judging administrators' performance other than *equality*. As Kaufman remarks, "If people in one region discover that they are treated differently from people in other regions under the same program, they are apt to be resentful and uncooperative."[24]

Hence there arises a "general concern for uniform application of policy," which can be guaranteed only by making the rulebook even more inflexible. Yet is our demand for equality and uniformity really so unqualified that we are determined to purchase it at any price? If we were certain that our own insistence on absolute fairness made the social services dehumanizing and dehumanized, might we not consider opting for other, more *equitable* procedures even though their outcomes might be less *equal?*

Alternatively, perhaps we should reconsider the wholesale nationalization of charity that began in the early twentieth century. Plenty of uncorrupt private pension funds still operate alongside governmental retirement and old-age pension schemes, and a few communally based systems of welfare and charity remain trusted just because their accountability is to a particular community. Among the Ismailis, for instance, the world-wide branch of Islam of which the Aga Khan is the head, tithing is still the rule, and no promising high school graduate misses the chance of going to college merely because he comes from a poor family. Despite governmental programs, that is no longer true of the United States. So perhaps we have let ourselves become too skeptical too soon about the friendliness of "friendly societies," and we should take more seriously the possibility of reviving social instruments with local roots, which do not need to insist on rigidly rule-governed procedures. That is of course a large "perhaps." The social changes that led to the nationalization of charity are powerful and longstanding, and thus far they have shown little sign of weakening. Given a choice, people may prefer to continue putting up with bureaucratic forms and procedures that they can grumble at with impunity if in this way they can avoid putting themselves at the mercy of social or communal relationships that they may find onerous.

Frail Hopes and Slender Foundations

In the field of ethics, all these difficulties are magnified. There I have one firm intellectual conviction, and one somewhat frailer hope on the social level.
'In a 1932 poem Robert Frost wrote:
Don't join too many gangs. Join few if any.
Join the United States, and join the family.
But not much in between, unless a college.[25]

Frost, in his curmudgeonly way, captures that hostility toward communal ties and restraints which, since Tolstoy's day, has continued to undermine our "intermediate institutions" or "mediating structures." Toward the nuclear family and the nation, people do indeed still feel some natural loyalty; "but not much in between, unless a college." During the last thirty years, even the nation-state has lost much of its mystique, leaving the family exposed to stresses that it can hardly support. It is my frail social hope that we may find some new ways of shaping other intermediate institutions toward which we can develop a fuller loyalty and commitment: associations larger than the nuclear family, but not so large that they defeat in advance the initial presumption that our fellow members are trustworthy. For it is only in that context, I suspect, that the ethics of discretion and intimacy can regain the ground it has lost to the ethics of rules and strangers.

Where might we look for the beginnings of such associations? Traditionally their loci were determined by religious and ethnic ties, and these are still sometimes used constructively to extend the range of people's moral sympathies beyond the immediate household. But we scarcely need to look as far as Ulster or Lebanon to see the other side of that particular coin. Membership in schools and colleges has some of the same power, as Frost grudgingly admits, though it is a power that tends to operate exclusively rather than generously. The great ethical hope of the Marxists was that "working-class solidarity" would, in effect, create a vast and cohesive extended family within which the dispossessed would find release from psychological as well as from political and economic oppression. But by now, alas, the evidence of history seems to show that awareness of shared injuries sets different groups against one another quite as often as it unites them. For some of us, the bonds of professional association are as powerful as any. The physicians of Tarrytown or the attorneys of Hyde Park probably have a close understanding of, feeling for, and even trust in one another; and despite all other reservations about my fellow academics, I do still have a certain implicit trust in their professional responsibility and integrity. So each year, without any serious anxiety, I vote for colleagues whom I have never even met to serve on the boards that manage my pension funds. If it were proved that those elected representatives had been milking the premiums and salting them away in a Swiss bank, that revelation would shake up my moral universe more radically than any dishonesty among public figures on the national level.

True, these are frail hopes and provide only slender foundations to build on. Yet, in the realm of ethics, frail hopes and slender foundations may be what we should learn to live with as much better than nothing. And that brings me to the intellectual point about which I am much more confident. If the cult of absolute principles is so attractive today, that is a sign that we still find it impossible to break with the "quest for certainty" that John Dewey tried so hard to discredit.[26] Not that we needed Dewey to point out the shortcomings of absolutism. Aristotle himself had insisted that there are no "essences" in the realm of ethics, and so no basis for any rigorous "theory" of ethics. Practical reasoning in ethics, as elsewhere, is a matter of judgment, of weighing different considerations against one another, never a matter of formal theoretical deduction from strict or self-evident axioms. It is a task less for the clever arguer than for the *anthropos megalopsychos*, the "large-spirited human being."[27]

It was not for nothing, then, that the members of the National Commission for the Protection of Human Subjects were able to agree about the ethical issues for just so long as they discussed those issues taxonomically. In doing so they were reviving the older, Aristotelian procedures of the casuists and rabbinical scholars, who understood all along that in ethics, as in law, the best we can achieve in practice is for good-hearted, clear-headed people to triangulate their way across the complex terrain of moral life and problems. So, starting from the paradigmatic cases that we do understand—what in the simplest situations harm is, and fairness, and cruelty, and generosity—we must simply work our way, one step at a time, to the more complex and perplexing cases in which extremely delicate balances may have to be struck. For example, we must decide on just what conditions, if any, it would be acceptable to inject a sample group of five-year-old children with an experimental vaccine from which countless other children should benefit even though the risks fall on those few individuals alone. Ethical argumentation thus makes most effective progress if we think of the "common morality" in the same way as we think about the common law:[28] if, for instance, we develop our perception of moral issues by the same kind of progressive triangulation that has extended common law doctrines of tort into the areas, first of negligence and later of strict liability.[29]

Meanwhile, we must remain on guard against the moral enthusiasts. In their determination to nail their principles to the mast, they succeed only in blinding themselves to the equities embodied in real-life situations and problems. Their willingness to legislate morality threatens to transform the most painful and intimate moral quandaries into adversarial confrontations between strangers. To take one example, by reintroducing uncompromising legal restraints to enjoin all procedures of abortion whatever, they are pitting a woman against her own newly implanted zygote in some ghastly parody of a landlord-tenant dispute. This harsh inflexibility sets the present day moral enthusiasts in sharp contrast to Aristotle's *anthropoi megalopsychoi*, and recalls Tolstoy's portrait of Alexei Karenin's associate, the Countess Ivanovna, who in theory was a supporter of all fashionable good causes but in practice was ready to act harshly and unforgivingly.

When Pascal attacked the Jesuit casuists for being too ready to make allowances in favor of penitents who were rich or highborn, he no doubt had a point.[30] But when he used this point as a reason for completely rejecting the case method in ethics, he set the bad example that is so often followed today: assuming that we must withdraw discretion entirely when it is abused and impose rigid rules in its place, instead of inquiring how we could adjust matters so that necessary discretion would continue to be exercised in an equitable and discriminating manner. I vote without hesitation against Pascal and for the Jesuits and the Talmudic scholars. We do not need to go as far as Tolstoy and claim that an ethics modeled on law rather than on equity is no ethics at all. But we do need to recognize that a morality based entirely on general rules and principles is tyrannical and disproportioned, and that only those who make equitable allowances for subtle individual differences have a proper feeling for the deeper demands of ethics. In practice the casuists may occasionally have been lax; but they grasped the essential, Aristotelian point about applied ethics: it cannot get along on a diet of general principles alone. It requires a detailed taxonomy of particular, detailed types of cases and situations. So, even in practice, the faults of the casuists—such as they were—were faults on the right side.

REFERENCES

[1]President Jimmy Carter used this quotation in a speech and attributed it to H. L. Mencken. However, the Humanities Section of the Enoch Pratt Library in Baltimore has been unable to locate it in Mencken's works.
[2]The work of the U.S. National Commission for the Protection of Human Subjects of Biomedical and Behavioral Research will be discussed more fully in a paper to be published in a forthcoming Hastings Center volume on the "closure" of technical and scientific discussions.
[3]So, at any rate, current legend reports. On the other hand, having worked through the files of the *Journal* for 1974-75 without finding any article or editorial on the subject, I am inclined to suspect that this may have been a casual remark by the late Dr. Franz Ingelfinger, the distinguished editor of the periodical.
[4]Daniel Callahan, *Abortion: Law, Choice and Morality* (New York: Macmillan, 1970); John T. Noonan, Jr., ed., *The Morality of Abortion: Legal and Historical Perspectives* (Cambridge, Mass.: Harvard University Press, 1970).
[5]Thomas Aquinas, *Commentarium Libro Tertio Sententiarum*, D.3. Q.5, A.2, Solutio.
[6]Peter Stein, *Regulae Juris* (Edinburgh: Edinburgh University Press, 1966), pp. 4-10.
[7]Lloyd A. Fallers, *Law without Precedent* (Chicago: University of Chicago Press, 1969): see also the classical discussion by Sir Henry Maine in *Lectures on the Early History of Institutions* (1914).
[8]Stein, pp. 26ff, 80-82, 124-27.
[9]For the subsequent influence of this division on the Anglo-American legal tradition, see (e.g.) John H. Baker, *An Introduction to English Legal History* (Toronto and London: Butterworths, 1979).
[10]Politically speaking, of course, the decline of monarchical sovereignty made the formal division of law from equity less functional; so it is no surprise that the nineteenth century saw its abolition both in the constitutional monarchy of England and also in the republican United States.
[11]John Rawls, *A Theory of Justice* (Cambridge, Mass.: Harvard University Press, 1971) is only the most recent systematic exposition of this position, which has become something of a philosophical commonplace, at any rate since Kant raised the issue of "universalizability" in the late eighteenth century.
[12]See, e.g., Kenneth C. Davis, *Discretionary Justice* (Urbana, Ill., Univ. of Illinois Press, 1969); Ralph A. Newman, *Equity and Law* (Dobbs Ferry, NY: Oceana, 1961); and particularly Ralph A. Newman, ed., *Equity in the World's Legal Systems* (Brussels: Bruylant, 1973).
[13]This seems to be true even of so perceptive an author as Herbert Kaufman, in his ingenious tract, *Red Tape: its Origins, Uses and Abuses* (Washington, D.C.: Brookings Institution, 1977), pp. 76-77: "Quite apart from protective attitudes toward specific programs, general concern for uniform application of policy militates against wholesale devolution. Not that uniformity automatically assures equity or equality of treatment. . . ."
[14]The *locus classicus* for the discussion of the notion of *epieikeia* (or "equity") is Aristotle's *Nicomachean Ethics*, esp. 1136b30-1137b32. See also Max Hamburger's useful discussion in *Morals and Law: the Growth of Aristotle's Legal Theory* (New Haven: Yale University Press, 1951).
[15]Henry L. McClintock, *Handbook of the Principles of Equity*, 2nd ed. (St. Paul, Minn.: West, 1948) pp. 52-54; John N. Pomeroy, *A Treatise on Equity Jurisprudence* (San Francisco: Bancroft Whitney, 1918-19), secs 360-63.
[16]Hence Aristotle's emphasis on the need for a person of sound ethical judgment to be an *anthropos megalopsychos*.
[17]This image of the steam locomotive had a powerful hold on Tolstoy's imagination: it recurs, for example, in *War and Peace*, where he compares the ineluctable processes of history to the movements of the pistons and cranks of a railway engine, as a way of discrediting the assumption that "world historical figures" like Napoleon can exercise any effective freedom of action in the political realm.
[18]This is the central theme of the closing book of *Anna*, in which Tolstoy documents his own disillusion with social and political ethics through the character of Constantin Levin.
[19]Notice how Aristotle treats the notion of *philia* as complementary to that of "equity." As he sees, the nature of the moral claims that arise within any situation depend on how closely the parties are related: indeed, it might be better to translate *philia* by some such term as "relationship" instead of the customary translation, "friendship," since his argument is intended to be analytical rather than edifying.

[20] Rawls, *Theory of Justice*.
[21] In United States labor law practice, arbitrators are guided by the published decisions of previous arbitrations, but not bound by them, since their own decisions normally turn on an estimate of the exact personal and group relations between the workers and managers involved in the particular dispute. Indeed, in Switzerland—here, as elsewhere, an extreme case—the results of labor arbitrations are not even published, on the ground that they are a "purely private matter" as between the immediate parties.
[22] Monroe Freedman, *Lawyers' Ethics in an Adversary System* (Indianapolis: Bobbs Merrill, 1975). In this connection, current Chinese attempts to turn criminal proceedings into a species of chummy conciliation between the defendant and his fellow citizens can too easily serve to conceal tyranny behind a mask of paternalistic goodwill.
[23] Kaufman, *Red Tape*.
[24] *Ibid.*, p. 77.
[25] Robert Frost, "Build Soil—a Political Pastoral," in *Complete Poems of Robert Frost* (New York: Holt, Rinehart & Winston, 1949), pp. 421-32, at p. 430.
[26] John Dewey, *The Quest for Certainty* (New York: Putnam, 1929).
[27] Aristotle's "large spirited person"—commonly but wrongly translated as "great souled man," ignoring the care with which the Greeks differentiated between *anthropoi* (human beings) and *andres* (men)—is the final hero of the *Nicomachean Ethics*: the key feature of such a person was, for him, the ability to act on behalf of a friend from an understanding of that friend's own needs, wishes, and interests.
[28] We are indebted to Alan Donagan for reintroducing the idea of the "common morality" into philosophical ethics, in his book, *The Theory of Morality* (Chicago: University of Chicago Press, 1977).
[29] Edward H. Levi, *Introduction to Legal Reasoning* (Chicago: University of Chicago Press, 1948).
[30] Pascal's *Lettres Provinciales* were originally published in 1656-57, during the trial of his friend Antoine Arnauld, whose Jansenist associations made him a target for the Jesuits. Pascal's journalistic success with these letters did a great deal, by itself, to bring the tradition of "case reasoning" in ethics into discredit: so much so that the art of casuistics has subsequently been known by the name of "casuistry"—a word which the *Oxford English Dictionary* first records as having been used by Alexander Pope in 1725, and whose very form, as the dictionary makes clear, is dyslogistic. (It belongs to the same family of English words as "popery," "wizardry" and "sophistry," all of which refer to the *disreputable* employment of the arts in question.)

K. DANNER CLOUSER AND BERNARD GERT

A CRITIQUE OF PRINCIPLISM

ABSTRACT. The authors use the term "principlism" to refer to the practice of using "principles" to replace both moral theory and particular moral rules and ideals in dealing with the moral problems that arise in medical practice. The authors argue that these "principles" do not function as claimed, and that their use is misleading both practically and theoretically. The "principles" are in fact not guides to action, but rather they are merely names for a collection of sometimes superficially related matters for consideration when dealing with a moral problem. The "principles" lack any systematic relationship to each other, and they often conflict with each other. These conflicts are unresolvable, since there is no unified moral theory from which they are all derived. For comparison the authors sketch the advantages of using a unified moral theory.

Key Words: bioethical principles, medical ethics, moral theory, principlism

I. INTRODUCTION AND OVERVIEW

Throughout the land, arising from the throngs of converts to bioethics awareness, there can be heard a mantra "...beneficence...autonomy...justice..." It is this ritual incantation in the face of biomedical dilemmas that beckons our inquiry.

In the last twenty years the field of biomedical ethics has expanded in an unprecedented way. The numbers of persons involved, its acceptance as an important field, the myriad university courses, the ubiquitous workshops and conferences, and the plethora of articles, books, and journals have exceeded all expectations. In response to this enormous demand for training in ethics, there have appeared countless books, workshops, and courses that package the theories and methods of ethics, making them readily available to more people in a shorter time.

K. Danner Clouser, Ph.D., *Professor of Humanities (Philosophy), The Pennsylvania State University College of Medicine, The Milton S. Hershey Medical Center, Hershey, Pennsylvania 17033, U.S.A.*
Bernard Gert, Ph.D., *Stone Professor of Intellectual and Moral Philosophy, Dartmouth College, Hanover, New Hampshire 03755, U.S.A.*

The major strategy in the most influential of these responses is the deployment of "principles" of biomedical ethics. Conceptually, as diagrammed for example by Beauchamp and Childress (1983), the principles are located just below theories and just above rules. The general notion is that principles follow from moral theories and, in turn, generate particular rules that are then used to make moral judgments. Brandishing these several principles, adherents to the "principle approach" go forth to confront the quandaries of biomedical ethics.

We believe that the "principles of biomedical ethics" approach (hereinafter referred to as "principlism") is mistaken and misleading. Principlism is mistaken about the nature of morality and is misleading as to the foundations of ethics. It misconceives both theory and practice. By no means do we wish to impugn the many significant moral insights of the proponents of principlism. Our quarrel is not so much with the content of the various "principles" as it is with the use of "principles" at all. We consider this to be crucial and not just a matter of philosophical style. Our focus is on philosophical point: the conceptual or systematic status of "principles" as used in principlism.

Our bottom line, starkly put, is that "principle", as conceived by the proponents of principlism, is a misnomer and that "principles" so conceived cannot function as they are in fact claimed to be functioning by those who purport to employ them. At best, "principles" operate primarily as checklists naming issues worth remembering when considering a biomedical moral issue. At worst "principles" obscure and confuse moral reasoning by their failure to be guidelines and by their eclectic and unsystematic use of moral theory.

It is important that the nature of this article be understood at the outset. We are criticizing a highly influential trend in biomedical ethics, and our focus is on that trend and not on its perpetrators. That is, though we illustrate our points by citing several authors, our mission is not to refute this or that author but rather to show why a certain way of thinking about morality is wrong-headed. Citing chapter and verse of individual authors on individual points, and then defending our interpretations, would detract significantly from the thrust of our major points about a trend which is not author specific, but which is exemplified in various aspects and parts by many authors and editors.

II. THE USELESSNESS OF "PRINCIPLES"

Though principlism is widely prevalent, we will cite only two particular texts to illustrate our points. One is William Frankena's *Ethics* (1973), and the other is Beauchamp and Childress's *Principles of Biomedical Ethics* (1983). Though he does not specifically deal with biomedical ethics, we chose Frankena because he seems to be the progenitor of this approach. And we chose Beauchamp and Childress, because theirs is by far the most influential book exemplifying principlism.

A. Our General Claim

Our general contention is that the so-called "principles" function neither as adequate surrogates for moral theories nor as directives or guides for determining the morally correct action. Rather they are primarily chapter headings for a discussion of some concepts which are often only superficially related to each other. When, for example, we are told that a particular case calls for the application of the principle of beneficence, this can mean that the case involves either (1) the utilitarian ideal of promoting some good, or (2) the moral ideal of preventing some harm or removing some harm, or (3) some duty which is morally required. This use of "principles" bears no similarity to principles that "summarize" theories, e.g., as used by Rawls and Mill. Rawls' principle of justice and Mill's principle of utility or principle of liberty are directives toward a moral resolution of particular cases. The principles of Rawls and Mill are effective summaries of their theories; they are shorthand for the theories that generated them. However, this is not the case with principlism, because principlism often has two, three, or even four competing "principles" involved in a given case, for example, principles of autonomy, justice, beneficence, and nonmaleficence. This is tantamount to using two, three, or four conflicting moral theories to decide a case. Indeed some of the "principles" – for example, the "principle" of justice – contain within themselves several competing theories.

Classically, a principle embodies the moral theory (or part thereof) that spawned it; it is used by itself to enunciate a meaningful directive for action. "Do that act which creates the greatest good for the greatest number", "Maximize the greatest amount of liberty compatible with a like liberty for all". The thrust of the directive is clear; its goal and intent are unambiguous. Of course, there are often ambiguities and differing interpretations with respect to how the principle applies to a particular situation. But the principle itself is never used with other principles that are in conflict with it. Furthermore, if a genuine theory has more than one general principle, the relationship between them is clearly stated, as in the case of Rawls' two principles of justice. Unlike principlism, we are not given a number of conflicting principles and then told to pick whatever combination we like.

By contrast, for proponents of principlism "principles" seem primarily to name important aspects of morality, and, as such, a principle functions mainly as a check list of considerations. When we read their chapters discussing a principle, we get a description of several ways in which the authors think beneficence or autonomy or justice is a relevant moral consideration; we do not get a specific directive for action. Partly, that is because each "principle" includes quite disparate moral matters, unrelated by systematic considerations.

Why do we make so much of the fact that in principlism the "principles" provide no systematic guidance? After all, the proponents of principlism would simply say, "Principles are complicated directives. When we say 'apply the principle of beneficence', we mean consider those points that we discuss in our chapter on the principle of beneficence". In other words, they would say that "the principle of beneficence" is shorthand for their discussion of beneficence. But in that case there is really nothing to be "applied". In effect the agent is being told "think about beneficence and here's thirty pages of distinctions and deliberations to get you started", and that is very different from being told, e.g., "Do that act which will create the greatest good for the greatest number". At best the agent may be reflecting on the relevance of beneficence to the current problem, but he is only deceiving himself if he believes that he has some useful guideline to apply.

There are two problems with an agent's being deceived about whether or not he has a principle that can be applied. One is that the principles are assumed to be firmly established and justified. A person feels secure in applying or in presuming to apply them. The other problem is that an agent will not be aware of the real grounds for his moral decision. If the principle is not a clear, direct imperative at all, but simply a collection of suggestions and observations, occasionally conflicting, then he will not know what is really guiding his action nor what facts to regard as relevant nor how to justify his action. The language of principlism suggests that he has applied a principle which is morally well-established and hence *prima facie* correct. But a closer look at the situation shows that in fact he has looked at and weighed many diverse moral considerations, which are superficially interrelated and herded under a chapter heading named for the "principle" in question.

The agent meanwhile may have "applied" other competing "principles" as well, e.g., autonomy and justice, to the same case. This actually amounts simply to thinking about the case from diverse and conflicting points of view. By "applying" the "principles" of autonomy, beneficence, and justice, the agent is unwittingly using several diverse and conflicting accounts rather than simply applying a well-developed unified theory. It is risky to be doing the former while believing one is doing the latter. A unified moral theory reflects the unity and universality of morality. While it does not eliminate all moral disagreement, it does show what is responsible for that disagreement, e.g., that it is a disagreement about the facts, or about the ranking of different goods and evils, or whatever.

Using principles in effect as surrogates for theories seems to us to be an unwitting effort to cling to four main types of ethical theory: beneficence incorporates Mill; autonomy, Kant; justice, Rawls; and nonmaleficence, Gert. Presenting the matter as so many principles suggests that the principles have been integrated into one unified theory, whereas the exact opposite is true. The four main theories are reduced to four principles from which agents are told to pick and choose as they see fit, as if one could sometimes be a Kantian and sometimes a Utilitarian and sometimes something else, without worrying whether the theory one is using is adequate or not.

B. Our Thesis Illustrated with Frankena

It is necessary to see some real examples of principlism. But we wish to reiterate our earlier caveat that we use aspects of individual authors only illustratively. An early and influential example can be seen in William Frankena's *Ethics* (1973). Frankena gives great prominence to the principle of beneficence. He finds it to be presupposed by the principle of utility (which principle he ultimately rejects) and ranks it, along with the principle of justice, as one of the two basic principles of all morality.

But precisely what are his principles of beneficence and of justice? What directive is the moral agent following when he "applies" one of these principles? In reality what we have are two basic types of ethical theory – utilitarian and deontological – presented as if they were simply two principles of a single moral theory. Yet there is no attempt to work out that single theory so it would actually incorporate both types of consideration into a coherent whole. We do not deny that both consequences (utilitarianism) and rules (deontology) are essential features of morality. Rather our point is that it is not sufficient simply to say they are essential, but one must also *show how* they are related to each other.

Frankena gives several descriptions of the principle of beneficence, treating them as if they were identical, thus committing what we call "the fallacy of assumed equivalence". When he first mentions that the principle of utility presupposes another more basic principle (namely, beneficence), he characterizes it as "that we ought to do good and to prevent or avoid doing harm" (p. 45). Later, on the same page, he describes it as "that of producing good as such and preventing evil". In still another place he says that the principle "tells us to do good and to eschew evil and eliminate evil" (p. 53). He further complicates the "principle" (p. 47) by saying that, even if it is not required, it is a "desirable" and "important" part of morality!

In his most systematic attempt to spell out the principle of beneficence Frankena cites four directives: (1) one ought not inflict evil, (2) one ought to prevent evil, (3) one ought to remove evil, (4) one ought to promote good (p. 47). He expresses uncertainty as to whom and for whom they are binding. And he suggests that very likely they are arranged in descending order of priority, such that directive #4 may not even be a duty. Though he does not define duty, he clearly does not use it in the ordinary sense, where it is restricted to duties imposed by roles, professions, circumstances, etc. Furthermore he entertains the possibility that there should be a fifth directive which would settle conflicts among the other four. It would read "do what will bring about the greatest balance of good over evil". Overall it should be clear that in presenting the principle of beneficence he is really presenting a substitute for a moral theory rather than putting forth either a well worked out theory or a useful action-guide.

How can Frankena's principle be "applied"? "Not inflicting evil" is very different from "preventing evil", and "promoting good" is significantly different from them both. Several persons being told to apply the principle of beneficence to a situation could each end up doing very different things. There are two significant observations concerning this state of the "principle". One is that the "principle" itself is not capable of determining what action should be taken. There must be other factors (intuitions, rules, theories, or whatever) that are surreptitiously and otherwise influencing the agent's decision making. The other observation is that the four or five different "directives" of the principle need justification which is not provided. They are not tied together systematically by an underlying theory whose supporting arguments could then be explicitly assessed and from which moral rules could be derived to apply to real cases.

Frankena's principle of justice (the other one of the twosome on which he bases all of morality) exemplifies the same difficulties we have seen with beneficence (pp. 51–54). Again it fails to be a straightforward action-guide. He holds what he calls the "equalitarian" view of distributive justice. This commits us to the *prima facie* obligation of treating people equally. But of course it is impossible to treat everyone equally. Thus, he presents various modifications. Treat them equally according to morally relevant similarities and dissimilarities – that is, as he says, "the ones that bear on the goodness or badness of people's lives", such as abilities, interests, and needs (p. 51). It is still an impossible principle to follow. Given that there are billions of people, could we really treat every person equally with respect to their abilities, interests, and needs – to name only three of the presumably large reservoir of matters "that bear on the goodness or badness of people's lives"? And we are not helped on this score by the additional modification: we have to make only the same *relative* contribution to the goodness of each of their lives. Relative to what? Ability? Interest? Need? Merit? And this is further modified by his saying that this proportional distribution of goodness takes place "once a certain minimum has been achieved by all" (p. 51). There is no explanation of where that modification came from, what justifies it, or how we can know when it obtains.

According to Frankena, the principle of justice may on occasion be overridden by the principle of beneficence (which itself has internal conflicts) but there is no formula for determining those occasions (p. 51). We suspect that he fails to recognize that he has no theory, and so does not recognize that a theory needs to specify how it is to be applied. As with his principle of beneficence, his principle of justice is also of no practical use in determining action. If a person claimed to have decided on a line of action simply by virtue of applying either of these principles or some combination of them, we would know that he was mistaken and that he had unwittingly employed other beliefs, intuitions, rules or whatever in order to make that decision. It is generally acknowledged that any adequate moral theory must incorporate considerations about consequences, about rules, about impartiality, etc. But it is not an adequate moral theory simply to say that all of these kinds of considerations must be included. That is all that principlism does. Rather, an adequate theory must show how all of these considerations should be integrated.

C. Our Thesis Illustrated with Beauchamp and Childress

The same type of conceptual confusions can be found in what is surely the most popular of all biomedical ethics textbooks, Beauchamp and Childress's *Principles of Biomedical Ethics* (1983).[1] The authors enunciate four basic principles, each of which illustrates the problems that we have been delineating. Consider their principle of beneficence. For Beauchamp and Childress beneficence is a duty "to help others further their important and legitimate interests" (1983, p. 149); it is morally required (p. 148). The "principle" explicitly prescribes at least two very different kinds of action: (1) to prevent and remove harm, and (2) to confer benefits. These are both included in the general duty of beneficence. Additionally, there seem to be other subprinciples buried in the general "principle". Some are genuine duties to help, which accrue by virtue of special relationships and roles, whereas others are triggered by needs and one's ability to meet those needs, though without clear limitations on the scope of such obligations. All these are included in "*the* principle of beneficence". Clearly, this "principle" is simply a chapter heading under which many superficially related topics are discussed; it is primarily a label for a general concern with consequences. But by being called a principle, it avoids the kind of fundamental questioning that a theory would undergo.

Beauchamp and Childress are obviously sensitive to and articulate about many nuances of morality. But our focus here is on the lack of a systematic account of the "principles" themselves and of the relationships between the "principles". At best, the "principles" function as hooks on which to hang elaborate discussions of various topics that are sometimes only superficially related. When they refer to a principle, in effect they are saying, "go read the chapter on beneficence, justice, autonomy, or nonmaleficence and take all those diverse considerations into account when thinking about the situation". To regard all of those diverse considerations as "a principle", and to treat them as such is, as we have described, to be misled both practically and theoretically.

The Beauchamp and Childress "principle of justice" manifests our point even more than their other "principles". There is not even a glimmer of a usable guide to action. There is a discussion of the concept of justice and about various well-known and conflicting accounts of justice, yet there is no specific action-guide stated. Nevertheless, they refer to a principle of justice as though it is something we ought to apply to moral situations. It is clearly not a guide to action, but rather a checklist of considerations that should be kept in mind when reflecting on moral problems. Not being the kind of classical principle that summarizes a theory and yields specific action-guides, it is deceptive in purporting to have conceptual status and systematic validity. Their "principle" is neither derived from a theory nor does it provide a usable guide to action.

III. PRINCIPLISM: SYSTEMATIC CONSIDERATIONS[2]

A. Lack of Systematic Unity and Some Consequences

The points we want to raise are rarely if ever addressed in the literature. Therefore it is important that we make clear what our focus is. It is that principlism lacks systematic unity, and thus creates both practical and theoretical problems. Since there is no moral theory that ties the "principles" together, there is no unified guide to action which generates clear, coherent, comprehensive, and specific rules for action nor any justification of those rules.

For example, Beauchamp and Childress (1983) list five conditions necessary in order for a general duty of beneficence to become a specific duty of beneficence to another person (p. 153). But whence these conditions? Are they integrated into a moral theory? And what precisely is the relation between the general duty of beneficence and the specific duty of benevolence? On what is the general duty of beneficence founded? The authors suggest some possibilities, but not really in an argued, systematic way. They recommend reciprocity as a good possibility, but they toss in Rawls' "duty of fair play" for good measure (pp. 155–6).

In principlism each discussion of a "principle" is really an eclectic discussion that emphasizes a different type of ethical theory, so that a single unified theory is not only not presented, but the need for such a theory is completely obscured. Rather we are given a number of insights, considerations, and theories, along with instructions to use whichever one or combination of them seems appropriate to the user. But what is needed is that which tells us what actually is appropriate in a consistent and universal fashion. Certainly the "principles" themselves, as portrayed by principlism do not do so. Rather, it is a moral theory that is needed to unify all the "considerations" raised by the "principles" and thus to help us determine what is appropriate.

When an author does not put forward a theory explicitly, he does not subject himself to the same standards of rigor as one who does. Neglecting to do serious ethical theory in favor of making general observations about various principles can lead to some unfortunate arguments. Principlism, in failing to operate within an overall unified moral theory, defaults to eclectic, *ad hoc* "theories" which ultimately obfuscate moral foundations and moral reasoning.

Given space limitations, one example will have to suffice. Consider the argument for and some of the consequences of making beneficence a moral requirement, that is, a duty. (Autonomy would be an even better example, but its problems are so extensive as to deserve a separate article.) How could benefiting others ever become a moral duty required of everyone? After all, systematic considerations would convince us that impartiality is an essential feature of moral requirements. But the "duty" of beneficence cannot be impartially followed. That is, it is impossible for us to do good toward everyone, impartially, all the time.

Nevertheless, Beauchamp and Childress, for example, argue

that beneficence is a requirement, duty, or obligation, and not an ideal or supererogatory moral act. Their reason seems to be: "if there is a competing duty of confidentiality, beneficence may outweigh it" (p. 155). But that suggests what must surely be false, namely, that only a duty can outweigh another duty, and that a supererogatory act or moral ideal cannot outweigh a duty. Ergo, beneficence must be a duty, and not merely supererogatory. However, consider some heroic act in which one puts himself at considerable risk and which everyone regards as supererogatory. If the harm that one is preventing is a significant harm for many people, then one would be right to do it even if it involved causing some minor harm to others. In harming others one is violating a moral rule (or, as Beauchamp and Childress would say, the principle of nonmaleficence), yet, as in this example, that violation is outweighed by the moral ideal or supererogatory act. Our point is that a comprehensive and unified theory which gave an account of the support for moral ideals and their relation to the morally required would have avoided this line of reasoning.

Another unfortunate consequence of the conceptual mistake of making beneficence a requirement is that it obscures the role that real duties play. Real duties must be distinguished from what is morally required of all those subject to morality. Making beneficence morally required and calling it a duty distorts the essence of moral requirements (i.e., impartiality) and misleads as to the nature of real duties, which are created by special relationships and roles. Beauchamp and Childress do extensively address specific relationships and roles in connection with duties, but they are not able to give an adequate account of these in terms of principles. That is, for example, there is no systematic moral explanation of the relationship between the "general duty of beneficence" and customs, standards of practice, and codes such that we could morally evaluate the various duties established by virtue of these relationships and roles.

Taking what is properly the moral *ideal* of helping others (and hence not morally required), and lumping it under a "principle" of beneficence along with genuine duties (which *are* required), e.g., the duty of health care professionals to help their patients, leads to confusion and misunderstanding. The confusion basically results from treating beneficence as if it were morally required just as noninterference with the freedom of others is morally required. But only in the context of a comprehensive and unified theory would the significant difference in their moral status become clear. We believe that this conceptual mistake is the result of having no comprehensive moral theory, whose absence is barely noticed because of the flurry of attention and deference given instead to "principles".

A universal moral theory can systematically accommodate and account for the significance of particular circumstances. For example, if we understood the philosophical foundation for "Do Your Duty" as a universal moral rule, we would then understand how duties would be more precisely and appropriately fashioned for particular roles, times, and places. An adequate moral theory would set limits on what health professionals are allowed to do; however, it would also acknowledge that their duties cannot be completely determined *a priori*, but instead must be based on the relevant customs and practice of a particular culture. Just as morality sets limits on when one is morally required to obey the law, so morality sets limits on when health care professionals are morally required to follow the standard custom and practice in treating patients. And just as, within these limits, the law often determines what one is morally required to do, so within the limits of morality, custom and practice often determine how a health care professional is morally required to act. Thus, there is no incompatibility at all between a single unified moral theory and the acceptance of a difference in the duties of health care professionals based upon different customs and practices. Indeed, it is the theory that is necessary to indicate what is relevant and to set limits; it guides one through the endless variations in customs and circumstances.

B. Relativism: The Anthology Syndrome

Beauchamp and Childress accompany their account of moral reasoning with a diagram:

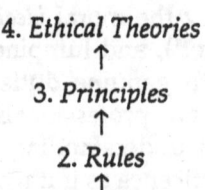

4. *Ethical Theories*
↑
3. *Principles*
↑
2. *Rules*
↑
1. *Particular Judgments and Actions*

A Critique of Principlism

"According to this diagram, judgments about what ought to be done in particular situations are justified by moral rules, which in turn are justified by principles, which ultimately are justified by ethical theories" (p. 5). Admitting that their diagram "may be oversimplified", they nevertheless claim that "its design indicates that in moral reasoning we appeal to different reasons of varying degrees of abstraction and systematization" (p. 5).

The authors give no argument for this account of moral reasoning. We suspect that they give no argument because none exists to support the role of principles in the hierarchy they propose. We believe that giving principles a significant role in moral reasoning is not only mistaken, but it also has unfortunate practical and theoretical consequences.

We had earlier seen a kind of relativism embodied by their "principles". Each principle seemed to have a life and logic of its own, as well as a number of internal conflicts. This relativism seems to be endorsed by their diagram having *theories* at the top of the hierarchy rather than a single unified ethical theory. This same kind of ethical relativism is endorsed by almost all anthologies in medical ethics, as well as in all other areas of applied and professional ethics. These anthologies (as well as most courses) almost invariably start by providing brief summaries of some standard ethical theories, e.g., utilitarianism, Kantianism, and contractualism. Next, the inadequacies of each of these theories are pointed out. There is no attempt to repair or remedy these defects, nor to present readers with a theory that they can actually use in solving the problems that are presented in the main body of the book (or course). Rather, the theories are either completely ignored and each problem is dealt with on an *ad hoc* basis, or the student is told to apply whatever inadequate theory he thinks is most useful in dealing with the problem at hand. Often he is told to apply several different, inadequate theories to a given problem, using whatever part of each theory seems most appropriate. This is an extraordinary way to proceed. It is difficult to imagine any respectable discipline proceeding in a similar fashion. Having acknowledged that all of the standard theories are inadequate, one is then told to apply them anyway, and even to apply competing theories, without any attempt to show how the theories can be reconciled.

In effect, the "anthology" approach is that of principlism. The proponents of principlism claim to derive principles from several different theories, none of which they judge to be adequate, and then they urge the student or health care professional to apply one or more of these competing principles to a given case. There is no attempt to show how or even whether these different principles can be reconciled. There is no attempt to show that the different theories, from which the principles are presumably derived, can be reconciled, or that any one of the theories can be revised so as to remove its defects and inadequacies. In the case of Beauchamp and Childress, this strongly suggests that there are several competing but equally good sources of final justification. And since "ethical theories" are at the very top of their hierarchy of justification, there would seem to be no way to adjudicate between them. This relativism is supported by their inadequate account of what an ethical theory is: "*theories* are bodies of principles and rules, more or less systematically related. They include second-order principles and rules about what to do when there are conflicts" (p. 5).

C. Morality vs. Moral Principles

An adequate ethical theory should not be just some more or less systematically related set of principles and rules. Rather it should provide an explanation of our moral agreement and disagreement; it should organize our moral thinking; it should tell us what is relevant to a moral judgment. In formulating theory we start with particular moral judgments about which we are certain, and we abstract and formulate the relevant features of those cases to help us in turn to decide the unclear cases. Simply to use the phrase "ethical theory" to refer to some historical examples of theories, e.g., those of Kant and Mill, which everyone recognizes to be inadequate, makes ethical theory irrelevant to practical moral reasoning. Thus in principlism, although "ethical theories" are at the top of the hierarchy of justification, it is no surprise that they play no role whatsoever in practical moral reasoning. Instead, as we have seen, moral "principles" are *de facto* the final court of appeal.

The appeal of principlism is that it makes use of those features of each ethical theory that seems to have the most support. Thus, in proposing the principle of beneficence, it acknowledges that Mill was right in being concerned with consequences. In proposing the principle of justice, it acknowledges that Rawls was right in being concerned with the distribution of goods. In proposing the principle of autonomy, it acknowledges that Kant was right in emphasizing the importance of the individual person. In proposing the principle of nonmaleficence, it acknowledges that Gert was right in emphasizing the importance of avoiding harming others. But there is no attempt to see how these different concerns can be blended together as integrated parts of a single adequate theory, rather than disparate concerns derived from several competing theories.

An adequate moral theory is one that will encompass all the major thrusts of each "principle", showing how they are related to each other. It will explain both our moral agreement and disagreement, and show which disagreements can be settled and which cannot, and why. This theory will resemble in part various historical ethical theories, because it will incorporate those aspects of each theory which made that theory seem so plausible. Thus, an adequate theory will include as essential to morality (1) a concern with consequences, (2) a concern with how these consequences are distributed, (3) acknowledgment of the importance of the individual, and (4) the centrality of prohibitions against harming individuals. But more than this, it will show how these features are related to each other, integrating them into a clear, coherent, and comprehensive system that can actually be used to solve real moral problems that arise in medicine and other fields.

Insofar as an adequate moral theory has any unacceptable conclusions, it will, like scientific theories, be revised. For an ethical theory, properly understood, is not an historical relic, created at a given time and frozen in that form for eternity. It is an ongoing attempt to explain and justify our common moral intuitions. An adequate moral theory should provide a description of morality, i.e., of the moral system that is actually used by thoughtful people in making judgments about what to do in particular cases. Such a theory will be complicated, but, after all, morality is a very complex phenomenon, and we can hardly expect a theory that explains it to be statable in one sentence slogans.

The value of using a single unified moral theory to deal with the ethical issues that arise in medicine and all other fields, is that it provides a single clear, coherent, and comprehensive decision procedure for arriving at answers. All of those dealing with the problem can communicate easily with one another; they will agree on what the relevant features of the case are, and how changes in those features can change the decisions that should be made. This does not require that they always arrive at the same decision, for they may rank the different values involved somewhat differently. But even then, they will know precisely where they disagree and why. And even if the theory provides an unacceptable answer, one can go back to the theory and attempt to revise it. Contrariwise, with principlism, disagreements are often not only unresolvable, but one often does not even know what the basis of the disagreement is or what change in facts would produce agreement. Furthermore, an unacceptable answer is of no value to principlism, since there is no theory to revise accordingly.

An adequate account of morality would see morality as a public system that applies to all rational persons. By "a public system" we simply mean a system that is understandable and acceptable to all those to whom it applies, e.g., as the rules of a game form a public system which is understandable and acceptable to all those who play the game. Since morality applies to all rational persons, it must be understandable and acceptable to all rational persons. The moral theory, in turn, would justify the moral system (which tells us how to make moral judgments) by showing why morality would be supported by all impartial rational persons. It would provide an explicit description of the various parts of the moral system: (1) the moral rules, e.g., "Don't kill", "Don't deceive", "Keep your promise", and "Do your duty", for which punishment for unjustified violations is appropriate, (2) moral ideals, such as relieving pain and preventing death, for which punishment for failure to follow is inappropriate, unless such a failure is also a violation of a duty, (3) the procedure for determining when a violation of a moral rule is justified, which would include an explicit statement of what counts as morally relevant features, several of which would be the harms caused, avoided, and prevented by violation. And, finally, (4) a moral theory would explain the disagreement about the scope of morality, i.e., whether the moral rules protect only actual moral agents or whether it has a wider scope, including, e.g., some or all potential moral agents, namely infants and fetuses, and some or all sentient beings such as nonhuman mammals.

This account of a moral theory is obviously more complex than that presented by many historical ethical theories. But in one respect it is simpler than the account offered by Beauchamp and Childress: there is neither room nor need for principles between the theory and the rules or ideals which are applied to particular cases. Rather, one applies the relevant rules and ideals and then, after taking into account all of the morally relevant features, one decides whether or not it is justified to violate a particular moral rule. The decisive question in determining whether or not to violate the rule is whether or not one would advocate that this kind of violation be publicly allowed, i.e., whether one would allow this kind of violation to be part of the public moral system. Although this resembles Kant's Categorical Imperative, it is significantly different. It captures the impartiality that is an essential part of morality without leading to the absurdities that Kant's theory does. And, just as important, in determining the *kind* of action, it takes into consideration the action's foreseeable consequences, thus capturing the concern with consequences that is the strongest feature of Utilitarianism – but without leading to the absurdities of Utilitarianism. We believe that this kind of theory does accurately describe the kind of moral reasoning that thoughtful people go through when they make moral judgments in particular cases. An excellent example of such a unified theory is Bernard Gert's *Morality: A New Justification of the Moral Rules* (1988).

D. And Finally

We believe, in the sense given to "principle" by Frankena and by Beauchamp and Childress, that for all practical and theoretical purposes there are no moral principles. Rather, for the former it is merely a way of combining some aspects of utilitarian and deontological theories without actually working out how they can be combined. For the latter, moral principles seem primarily to be chapter headings, which pen together superficially related topics. Although we find their discussions of these individual topics often to be extremely well done, we think that grouping them together under the heading of their "principles" gives a misleading account of moral reasoning.

Invocations of these principles leads to *neglect* of (1) the theories from which the principles supposedly are derived, (2) the individual rules and ideals that apply to the particular case, (3) the procedure that should be used in applying the rule to the particular case, and (4) the statement of the particular duties of a profession. And, most importantly, by invoking several "principles" they implicitly deny the unity of morality. As John Stuart Mill says in the first chapter of *Utilitarianism*,

...there ought either to be some one fundamental principle or law at the root of all morality, or if there be several, there ought to be a determinate order of precedence among them; and the one principle, or the rule for deciding between the various principles when they conflict, ought to be self evident (paragraph #3).

We do not concur with Mill's implication that there has to be agreement about the answer to all moral questions, but we do accept that everyone must agree on the procedure to be used in deciding moral questions.

NOTES

[1] A third edition of *Principles of Biomedical Ethics* was published in mid-1989. Nevertheless we have continued to cite the second edition for two reasons. At this time it is more likely that readers will have copies of and be familiar with the second edition thus making reference checking more convenient. And secondly, not pursuing the third edition underlines our emphasis on not criticizing individual authors but rather on criticizing a conceptual "gestalt" which we see manifested in various forms and places, and the second edition is sufficient for that.

[2] Two other authors in this issue make charges similar to ours. Both Baruch Brody and Ronald Green note the insufficiency of principles: conflicts among, and unclarity within them, and of lack of a unifying theory. Brody emphasizes the difficulty in application with respect to scope, conditions for applying, etc. and the lack of a more fundamental theory (pp. 165–169). Whereas he concludes that we need to improve the principles, we argue that they have no role whatsoever within a unified moral theory whose derived rules are the proper and sufficient guides to action. Green not only notes that a fundamental moral theory is missing in the approach of Beauchamp and Childress but also claims that biomedical ethics in general has avoided serious attention to basic theoretical issues in ethics (pp. 187–190).

REFERENCES

Beauchamp, T.L., and Childress, J.F.: 1983, *Principles of Biomedical Ethics*, second edition, Oxford University Press, New York.
Brody, B.A.: 1990, 'Quality of scholarship in bioethics', this issue, pp. 161–178.
Frankena, W.: 1973, *Ethics*, second edition, Prentice-Hall, Englewood Cliffs, New Jersey.
Gert, B.: 1988, *Morality: A New Justification of the Moral Rules*, Oxford University Press, New York.
Green, R.M.: 1990, 'Method in bioethics: a troubled assessment', this issue, pp. 179–197.

Part V
The Absolute Rule Approach

[14]

Medalist's Address: Action, Intention and 'Double Effect'

by G. E. M. Anscombe

It is customary in the dominant English and related schools of philosophy to restrict the terms "action" or "agency." That is, when the topic is 'philosophy of action'. This is often done by an appeal to intuition about a few examples. If I fall over, you wouldn't usually call that an *action* on my part; it's not something that I *do*, it is rather something that happens to me. Donald Davidson has made a more serious attempt than this at explaining a restriction on the term "action," or what he means by "agency." "Intentional action" is an insufficient designation for him: it determines no class of events, because an action which is intentional under one description may not be intentional under another. And anyway there are unintentional actions, which he doesn't want to say are not actions in the restricted sense in which he wants to apply the term. So he suggests that we have an action (in the restricted sense) if what is done (no restriction on the ordinary sense here) is intentional under *some* description. This allows pouring out coffee when I meant to pour out tea to be an action, being intentional under the description "pouring out liquid from this pot." I fear, however, that it may allow tripping over the edge of the carpet to be an action too, if every part of an intentional progress across the room is intentional under that description. But Davidson doesn't want to count tripping as an action. If this is right, then his account is wrong because it lets in what he wants to exclude. Furthermore, I don't think it comprises omissions, which are often actions.

I am inclined to think that the attempt, brave as it was, was misconceived anyway. There is a goal in view when people want to introduce a restricted sense of "action," but I don't think it can be attained by trying to find a characterisation of a sub-class of events.

All the same, the point about there being many descriptions of any action, as indeed of any event or any object, is true. It has an importance which we shall see later.

What is being aimed at, I think, is the category called "human action" by some scholastics: They made a contrast between 'human action'—*actus humanus*—and 'act of a human being'—*actus hominis*. Again, this is usually explained by examples. Idly stroking one's beard, or idly scratching one's head, may be an 'act of a human being' without being a 'human act.'[1] And I expect falling over or tripping up is so too; at any rate I lay it down that I will use the term 'act of a human being' in such a way that those things come under that heading. Also, that 'act of a human being' is a wider notion, which includes 'human action'.

The contrast is that human actions *are under the command of reason*: This does not mean just that reason *can* intervene to forbid—for that holds of idle actions too. What it does mean beyond that will, I hope, emerge

We might say that human action = voluntary action. But that raises a question of meaning, like what we have just glanced at in the last paragraph. We are speaking of voluntary action *not* in a merely physiological sense; not in the sense in which idly stroking your beard *is* a voluntary action. Notice, too, that what is voluntary under one description may be non-voluntary or counter-voluntary under another. We are not, like Davidson, attempting a classification which will divide all events into members and non-members of a class.

Nor are we using "voluntary" as Aristotle uses ἐκούσιον, generally translated "voluntary." For Aristotle says that beasts and babies have the voluntary, but we would not say so in the sense of "voluntary" that we are trying to introduce.

Aristotle too introduces a restricted sense of "action"—praxis, which beasts and babies don't have. But it is a bit too limited for us. It wouldn't include omissions unless calculated, or sudden impulsive actions.

Voluntariness does not require that there be any act of will, any formation of intention, any choice of what is voluntary; or even any positive voluntary act. What you were able to do and it was needful you should do, if you omit it in forgetfulness or sloth, falling asleep perhaps and sleeping through the time when you should have been doing it—your omission of it is voluntary. Unless indeed you fell asleep because you were drugged without the slightest consent on your part. Consent may reside in not taking care when you could have, and in the nature of the case as available to your understanding, you needed to.

I will now put forward a thesis, which I will later give reason for:

All human action is moral action. It is all either good or bad. (It may be both.)

This needs a lot of clarification. First, let me point to an implication. It means that "moral" does not stand for an extra ingredient which some human actions have and some do not. The idea of the moral as an aspect that is to be seen in some human actions, or felt by the agent, and which may be lacking, perhaps is lacking if it is not felt by the agent—this idea is rejected by the equation "Human action = moral action." Or at least "Human action = moral action of a human being." For I am not concerned with angels, demons, fairies or Martians. I shall hope to shew that this equation is not a mere 'extensional equivalence'—two descriptions which happen to be true of the same things. The descriptions are equivalent in content.

All the same, not all human-action descriptions are moral action-descriptions. E.g. "walking," if a human being other than an infant is said to walk, is normally a human-action description, but it is not a moral action-description. (I say it is *normally* a human-action description to allow exclusion of sleep-walking (say), which would be the act of a human being, but not a human action.) "Chucking a pebble into the sea" is another such description, or "Picking a flower." Like "walking," these are *indifferent* human-action descriptions.

This fact, that there are indifferent human-action descriptions, might lead someone to think that there are indifferent human actions. But that does not follow at all. It is the *particular* action that is always good or bad.

Note also that not all action-descriptions which can, and in the particular case often do, describe human actions, are such that whatever acts fall under them are good or bad human actions. For example the description, even when it does describe the action of a human being, still may *not* be describing a human action. As an instance, take "Killing someone." Suppose I am a parcel—I mean I've been made up into a parcel—and by sheer accident I get set rolling down a hill in such circumstances that I kill someone by knocking him over into the path of a rapid vehicle—that's not a human action on my part. It *is*, if I kill someone by an accident in driving my car—I reverse it by mistake, say, and kill a small child standing behind it.

As I said: "Walking," though if it is applied to a non-infant human being it is normally a human-action description, is nevertheless not a moral action-description. By a moral action-description I mean one at least *suggesting* some *specific* goodness or badness about an act that falls under it. "Walking," even when it is used to report a particular human action, does not suggest anything specific.

It is not even true that every *moral* action-description, as a description of a particular human action, entails that that particular action was good, or again, that it was bad. It may only entail that the action was, say, good, unless some aspect makes it bad. Or was bad, unless some excuse or justification either lets it have a certain goodness inasmuch as it is an action which is not wicked, or actually renders it specifically good.

This working of excuse may astonish. Someone has killed someone, let us say. We ask: Was it his *fault*? It turns out that it was not; although the action which as it turned out resulted in death *was* a human action. So: he has an excuse, he is perhaps exonerated; he is not *guilty of homicide*. But does that mean his action was *good*? If all actual human action that occurs is either good or bad, it seems as if his *excuse* renders his action *good*! But isn't that too paradoxical? Don't we want something between good and bad in actual particular occurrences of action?

Assume his action is not good *qua* killing, *qua* resulting in death. And we can suppose it was no particular species of good action; not the act of any specific virtue. But, just as anything that has positive being is good *qua* being (even if it is something that for some reason ought not to exist) so action is good as being action, i.e., *qua* belonging to the genus 'action'. (And it would be so, even if there were no specific goodness about it.) Suppose, then, that all the things about it which make one want to say it was bad turn out to be not his fault: suppose they were just accidents for which he had no responsibility, except in the sense of (involuntarily) contributing some of the causation of a bad result. Then, there is not the *quicunque defectus* to make his action a bad human action.

Here I am invoking the principle "Bonum ex integra causa, malum ex quocunque defectu." This might be rendered: "Something is good by reason of being good in every respect, bad from being bad in any." Here respects of good and bad have to belong to the thing under the description under which it is described as good or bad. Thus there might be a good human action—good *tout court*, not just good in this respect or that—which was by sheer accident an intervenient cause of some evil. Here some might say that that *act of a human being* had something bad about it, and so wasn't good *tout court*. That is, *if* I am right in the extensive application I give to the expression "act of a human being." But the human act has not got something wrong with it *qua* human act from being an involuntary cause of some evil. That respect of badness does not belong to it as a human act. For being the involuntary cause of something does not belong to it as a human act.

On the other hand, there might be nothing good about it *qua* human action, *except* that it was human action. I am still thinking of the same case, where the evil result is pure accident, not voluntarily caused by the agent. But he is presumably engaged in something or other in his being there or at least in his motion, if that is voluntary; and what he is up to may itself have been for a bad end, and hence bad on its own account.

Or it may have been subordinated to a bad end. But here I get into deep water. Is a wicked man, who keeps himself in good trim by physical exercise so as to pursue his life's purposes, acting badly or well in taking that exercise? I cannot answer this question, and to investigate it now would take too long.

It will be apparent why I said that an action—a human action—may be both good and bad. It may be good only in a certain respect, and bad in others; then it is not good *tout court*, but bad. And the respect *may* be: generically. In *this* respect all human actions are good, though many are bad *tout court*.

So far we've been speaking in a uniform way about the case of the bad upshot, whether there is excuse *or* exoneration. Alternatively, we may want to distinguish between these. With exoneration, an agent is in the clear; but if there is less than exoneration, we may say his action was bad as needing excuse and *therefore* pardon. In such a case we may say it was mixed. In *that* way, it was bad—if he had taken more care, he would have avoided the result; and yet the result was not one that, as we say, 'was to be expected in the nature of the case'. And in this way it was mixed; it had the goodness of being a human action and perhaps of being whatever sort of action he was engaged in intentionally; it lacks the defect of being a specifically wicked action, since it does not get this from the bad accidental result; and yet it has something of badness, that makes it seem to need pardon. For if we do distinguish between exoneration and excuse in this sort of case, this is where the distinction must be made. If it merits complete exoneration, then it has no badness from the bad upshot—e.g. the unfortunate result is 'utterly accidental, he couldn't have avoided it, it was sheer bad luck'.

From considering good and bad, we see that the extension of "human action" is wider than that of "intentional human action." That is to say: something may be a human action under a description under which it is not an intentional action. Acts of carelessness, negligence and omission may be of this character. For though they can be intentional, they may not be so, but their not being intentional does not take the character of human action away from them. But a human action does not have something wrong with it qua human act—i.e., so as to be to that extent a bad human action—from being an involuntary cause of some evil. The involuntariness does mean that the badness is not in a respect belonging to it as a human action. By parity of consideration, voluntariness would mean that it was bad in such a respect.

To repeat: when I speak of moral action-descriptions, I mean ones which suggest, at least suggest, good or bad—unlike neutral or indifferent action-descriptions, which suggest nothing either way. However, one might object that *if* just being an action is good, then neutral action-descriptions must after all mention something good. (Even if in the particular case it also fails in goodness because of something bad about it then and there.) So how can I say that there are neutral action-descriptions? The answer is that the good or bad suggested by moral action-descriptions is *specific* goodness or badness. That in the particular case each human action is good or bad is a different point from the generic goodness of any action as being an action: it means that each human action is specifically good or specifically bad. It will be good, if good, for more than just being an action. Firstly, the particular thing that is done may itself be more than generically good. But also there are circumstances and ends to consider. For suppose the particular thing that is done is sufficiently specified by a neutral action-description, so that it—the particular thing that is done—might be called "no more than generically good": then, if the agent's purpose or purposes in doing it are specifically good and circumstances import nothing bad about doing that thing for those purposes, the action will be specifically good. A neutral action-description reporting a human act may give 'the particular thing that was done' sufficiently for us to say: "That was all right, unless the purpose or circumstances put a different complexion on it." Or, it may be an inadequate description of the particular thing that was done: he didn't 'merely write his name on a bit of paper', he was signing such-and-such a contract.

To say that "human action" and "moral action (*sc.* of a human being)" are equivalent is to say that all human action *in concreto* is either good or bad simpliciter. There is no need to insert "morally" and say "morally good or bad." The term "moral" adds no sense to the phrase, because we are talking about human actions, and the 'moral' goodness of an action is nothing but its goodness as a human action. I mean: the goodness with which it is a good action. 'Moral' goodness is: goodness of actions, passions, and habits of action and feeling. The term is however a distinguishing one, restricted to specific goodness, goodness simpliciter, or to what comes closer to that than the generic good of being a human action or passion or disposition.

The idea that a human action could be called a "pre-moral evil," or evil in a pre-moral sense, is extremely confused. Examples which are offered to prove it are killing and amputation.

Death is an evil, and a killing (of a human by a human) may not be a wicked action. For it may be blamelessly accidental and so, it is suggested, a 'pre-moral evil'. The amount of truth there is in this conclusion consists in this: the description "killing someone" may be the description of an *act of a human being* (actus hominis) without describing a *human act* (actus humanus)—as when I was a parcel rolling down the hill. Note that when it *is* the description of an act of a human being, even though not of a human act, it is still a moral action-description. At least this is so if I am right in my application of these terms. For we ask whether it was the person's fault, was there excuse, and so on. If, as in the parcel case, it turns out that the act of knocking the victim over to his death wasn't a human act, that is sufficient to answer those questions: it wasn't his fault, it was in no way voluntary on his part. Only in the sense in which "responsibility" means "causality" was he responsible.

The fact that "killing," even when applied to the interaction of two human beings, has this somewhat generic character, does not prove that a particular *human action* of killing someone is not established with a definite character of moral evil once it is clear that it was intentional and also was private—i.e., was not an action belonging to the exercise of civil authority. I would prefer to say "a definite character of evil" because of my opinion that the term "moral" there is strictly redundant; but I have to put it in as I am commenting on a conception of 'pre-moral evil' according to which an action of killing someone, fully deliberate, fully intentional, may only be evil in a 'pre-moral' sense. That is, as so far described or proposed it may be so.

Now this, if true, would not be true in the way in which the evil was pre-moral in the parcel case: namely, because, while death is an evil, it was not brought about by a human action. It would, rather, be true because of what is excluded by my word "private." Intentional killing in warfare, or by police in fighting violent criminals, or by execution of a death sentence—all these *can* be murderous, but they are not necessarily so, and that means that "intentional killing of one human being by another" is a moral action-description whose applicability does not *eo ipso* prove the wickedness of the deed. The description is more determinate than is the bare word "killing"; yet it is still somewhat indeterminate. But this indeterminateness of description does not signify an indeterminateness in the quality of the human act, given the sanity of the killer and the circumstances which make it 'private'.

If anyone thinks otherwise, he must have been misled by bad teaching. Or simply by a bad philosophic tradition, according to which the intentionalness of an action (a) can't be known to anyone but the agent and (b) is a matter of what the agent did it *for*—intention being often taken to mean purpose, or intention of the end. Now as to (a), "intention can't be known, because it is something private," that is in general absurd. It is often, nay *usually* quite apparent that someone is doing such-and-such on purpose. It is no objection to this that error on the point is possible. Nor yet, that it is more difficult to know someone's further intentions, or the intentions with which he was doing what he was obviously doing on purpose, or what he was doing it all for.

Murder is a complex concept with many disparate elements in it. But you don't have to know what some private person killed his uncle for in order to know he committed murder, so long as he was awake, *compos mentis* and was doing the killing on purpose. (I say "some private person" to exclude the cases of capital punishment, cops and robbers, and warfare all in a lump).

This means that although the mental element of *mens rea* is important in identifying a killing as a murder, the question whether someone has committed a murder can usually be answered as soon as the relevant facts are in, and having the facts in doesn't mean that all we have ascertained is the occurrence of a 'pre-moral evil'.

Amputation—of a limb, say—is a more pressing example for our immediate enquiry. This is because what someone is doing an amputation for is all-important. If it is needed for the life or health of the victim because of the physical condition or situation of his body, then it is all right as far as purpose goes, otherwise not. And this seems to lend real substance to the idea of a 'pre-moral evil' which is deliberately encompassed by a human action for the sake of a greater good. Someone cut off someone's hand, let us say. That sounds awful—could it be an indeterminate description of an action justified by circumstances: by who he was, and who his victim was? Suppose he was the public executioner and his victim a thief being punished according to law? If that would make it all right, then amputation as a moral problem would be rather like killing. But we don't have amputations as punishment 'in civilised countries'. I don't wish to raise the question whether such punishment is admissible at all: but the fact that we don't have it puts amputation into a special position: an evil inflicted, not as a punishment, but for the sake of a greater good in some other way. The evil is all in the particular thing that is purposely done, but the evil of it and the intentionalness do not determine the quality of the act. That is principally determined by what it was done for. So you have a pre-moral evil, and the goodness or badness of the action of *doing* it is principally a matter of the intention of the end. This gives us a pattern which, it might be said of, we can surely apply elsewhere: "If deliberately cutting off a hand is so far forth only pre-moral evil, then can't the same be said of killing your uncle, or aborting your baby or . . . ? What will give it its *moral* character (and maybe a lovely one) is what you do it for."

"Cutting off a limb" is a moral action-description by my criteria. It is also indeterminate, suggesting evil, raising the question of excuse or justification. Who did it to whom, in what circumstances, and what for? When we know the answer to these questions we should be able to tell the quality of the act. The thing that makes it of importance for our discussion is the dominant role of the question "What for?" If this role is described by reference to 'a greater good', then the road is thrown open to a generalisation which threatens to destroy many absolute prohibitions of kinds of act.

The important thing about a justified amputation—as we 'in civilised countries' understand it—is that it is for the life, health or capacity-to-function of the individual human being who suffers it. The lesser evil for that human being's physical condition or integrity is chosen for the sake of the greater good of that human being's life or condition or capacity. So there really is here a case in which *an* intrinsic evil is inflicted for the sake of a more valuable good. But the evil and the good concern the bodily condition of the single human individual. He occupies a pre-eminent position in questions about good and bad action.

Once this is clear, it should also be clear that in this case too we have an indeterminate description whose kind of indeterminateness is exploited to argue for a characterisation of many bad actions as so far 'pre-moral evils'. Because in *this* case the principal determinant is the 'what for', it is suggested that this is quite generally so. Old authorities are invoked, who wrote of all the factors that go to determine the specific goodness or badness of actions. These factors certainly include intention. Against the background of certain modern traditions in philosophy—especially the Cartesian—it is hardly noticed that intention may relate to the intentionalness of the particular act that is done, as well as to the purpose for which it is done. Now there are several kinds of action which, if they are done intentionally, are evidently evil actions, no matter what they are done for. The good end only sanctifies such means as either are good considered in themselves, or would naturally fall merely under a neutral action-description.

My phrase "if they are done intentionally" signifies a sufficient condition, not a necessary one. This will become clear if we return to our earlier topic of murder.

For here there can be borderline cases arising because murder is not committed only where there was an intention to kill. The arsonist who burns down a house, not caring that there are people there, is as much a murderer if they are burned to death by his action, as if he had aimed to kill them. This action falls squarely within a penumbra surrounding the hard-core part of the concept of murder, which contains only intentional killing. The penumbra is fuzzy at the outer edges—that is, there are borderline cases. But that fact does not mean that an absolute prohibition on murder makes no sense.

And similarly for other intrinsically evil deeds. The descriptions might be simple and easy to apply, like "sodomy," or have cases in which the application was somewhat obscure or disputable, like "lying"; but none of that creates a conceptual difficulty about the notion of absolute wrongness—whether great wrongness, or small as in many instances of lying.

The fact that there is murder where death foreseeably results from one's action, without the actual intention of killing, naturally leads to a problem. One cannot say that *no* action may be done which foreseeably or probably leads to some death, or that all such actions are murderous. Why, the very begetting of a child would be murder at that rate—for the child will surely die. Or if that seems too zany an example: you can't build roads and fast vehicles, you can't have various sports and races, you can't have ships voyaging over the seas, without its being predictable that there will be deaths resulting. And much that is done in medicine and surgery is done knowing it involves the risk of death—pain-killing drugs which may kill the patient before his disease does, and high-risk surgery.

Therefore some distinction needs to be made, or some distinctions.

This is a problem for those who hold that deliberately killing is absolutely out in the sort of case we may have to consider. If you don't hold that, it seems you don't get into a bind. For the whole thing begins by saying

(a) You must not kill either as an end or as a means to some end.
(b) Not all action that leads to someone's, or people's death, though this is not intended, is murderous and so forbidden.
(c) Often such action *is* murderous, and so is forbidden.

It is here that we have the famous 'doctrine of double effect'. "Double effect" is an unfortunate Latinism. What we are talking about is death as a side-effect which is brought about as well as the effect being aimed at.

I will call it the "principle of side-effects" that the prohibition on murder does not cover *all* bringing about of deaths which are not intended. Not that such deaths aren't often murder. But the quite clear and certain prohibition on intentional killing (with the relevant 'public' exceptions) does not catch you when your action brings about an unintended death.

So much seems clear. But notice that the principle is modest: it says "where you must not aim at someone's death causing it does not *necessarily* incur guilt."

The principle is unexceptionably illustrated by some examples of dangerous surgery, by some closings of doors to contain fire or water; or by having ships and airlines. In these we are helped by thinking of the deaths as either remote or uncertain. But an unintended death which is a foreseeable consequence of one's action may be neither. *Then* we are confronted with cases where it strikes people that there is little difference between direct and indirect killing. Imagine a pot-holer[2] stuck with people behind him and water rising to drown them. And imagine two cases: in one, he can be blown up; in the other, a rock *can* be moved to open another escape route, but it will crush his head. He will be killed by it.

Someone who will equally choose either course clearly prefers saving these lives to the avoidance of any intentional killing. Such cases are discussed with a note of absolute necessity about savings lives—a presupposition that is paramount.

The example of the stuck pot-holer was invented (without the choice of ways of escape) to illustrate the iniquity of abortion: you wouldn't say you could kill the pot-holer to get out—it was argued. But people did say just that—at least if the posture of the pot-holer was so described that he was going to get drowned too!

Yet situations must often have occurred where people were in a tight corner, could have saved themselves by killing one of their number, and that has not occurred to them as an option at all.

If that were the attitude of the people in the cave, they wouldn't do either thing.

Indeed someone might say of moving the rock and crushing his head: "Isn't that direct killing too?" The point of not calling it direct was that it isn't his being crushed that gives the escape route—and so his being crushed can be something you don't *intend*.

"Direct" and "indirect" are dodgy terms; sometimes they relate to offshoots, as it were, from a given sequence of causes, and sometimes to immediacy or remoteness, and sometimes to what is intended or not. I note with curiosity that McCormick uses the concepts of direct and indirect intention, saying that they are centuries old tools of moral theology. If that is so, I'd like to know the sources. I myself know of "direct" and "indirect" intention only as terms introduced by Jeremy Bentham. He called it "indirectly intended" if you took a shot at something and hit something else, if you knew that was a possibility. Fr. McCormick's sense seems to be the same. "Indirectly intended" thus means "Unintended, but the possibility was foreseen." While I am speaking of Fr. McCormick, I will also remark on his curious use of "intention in a psychological sense."[3] With respect, there is no other relevant sense.

Returning to the pot-holer, I note that the 'doctrine of double effect' is supposed to say that the people could move the rock, though they must *not*, not on any account, blow up the pot-holer. And this is what is found intolerably artificial and unnatural. But we may ask: Is that because of what is allowed, or what is forbidden? What I've called "the principle of side effects" is related to an absolute prohibition on seeking someone's death, either as end or as means. I've spoken of that. Now, if the objection is to what is here *allowed*, note that the principle of side effects does not state or imply that they can move the rock. It does not say *when* you may foreseeably cause death.

And why should we have a package deal here, as in what is called the "doctrine of double effect"?

Now—perhaps because of this teaching—there might be people among those in the cave who, even seeing the undesired consequence, would move the rock, though they would refuse to blow the man up because that would mean choosing his death as means of escape. This is not a meaningless stance. They'd be shewing themselves as people who will reject any policy making the death of innocent people a means or an end.

But, to repeat: you cannot deduce the permissibility of moving the rock from the principle of side-effects. It determines nothing about that, except perhaps that it is not excluded on the score of being intentional killing. We have to say "perhaps" because of the possible closeness of the result. As I have described the case, we are only given that moving the rock will crush the pot-holer's head. This might be a result so immediate that the action could not be called "taking the risk that that would happen." If so, then it is at best a dubious business to say "We don't intend that result." At most, it is no part of the aim, in securing the opening, that the man's head should be crushed.

At this point the Doctrine of Double Effect helps itself to an absurd device, of choosing a description under which the action is intentional, and giving the action under that description as *the* intentional act. "I am moving what blocks that egress," or "I am removing a rock which is in the way." The suggestion is that that is *all* I am doing as a means to my end. This is as if one could say "I am merely moving a knife through such-and-such a region of space" regardless of the fact that that space is manifestly occupied by a human neck, or by a rope supporting a climber. "Nonsense," we want to say, "doing that is doing this, and so closely that you can't pretend only the first gives you a description under which the act is intentional." For an act does not merely have many descriptions, under some of which it is indeed not intentional: it has several under which it is intentional. So you cannot choose just one of these, and claim to have excluded others by that. Nor can you simply bring it about that you intend *this* and not *that* by an inner act of 'directing your intention'. Circumstances, and the immediate facts about the means you are choosing to your ends, dictate what descriptions of your intention you must admit. *Nota bene* that here "intention" relates to the intentionalness of the action you are performing as means.

Suppose for example that you want to train people in habits of supporting the Church with money. If you exact money from them as a condition of baptism you cannot say you are not making them pay for it.

All this is relevant to our pot-holer only where the crushing of his head is an immediate effect of moving the rock. Here a ground for saying you can intend to move the rock and not intend to crush the head is that you might not know that in moving the rock you would crush his head. That is true, we may suppose; which does differentiate this case from the simoniacal one. But if you *do* know, then where the crushing is immediate you cannot pretend not to intend it if you are willing to move the rock.

Let us now consider the case where the result is not so immediate—the rock you are moving has to take a path after your immediate moving of it, and in the path that it will take it will crush his head. Here there is indeed room for saying that you did not intend that result, even though you could foresee it. And that is the sort of case we have to consider. The Doctrine of Double Effect is supposed to allow you to move the rock, if the balance of good over bad results is favourable. The Principle of Side Effects says no more than that moving the rock is not excluded by the prohibition on intentional killing. For, as I have explained it, that principle is not a package deal and it does not say what circumstances or needs excuse unintended causing of death.

Some principle or principles are needed, and if we adopt that one principle, of the balance of good over evil in the expected upshot, then it becomes obscure why we could not do this where the causation of death was perfectly intentional. And that seems to be the principal ground on which some thinkers throw the whole package out of the window, and talk about a deliberate killing, for example, as *so far* a 'pre-moral evil'. They may help themselves by the confused considerations I discussed earlier, but the nerve of the rejection of former doctrine is here.

I formerly understood the doctrine of double effect, *not* as a package deal, but rather as what I have called the "principle of side-effects," and I thought I was only doing a work of clarification in formulating it and remarking that it does not tell us what to allow and what to forbid when we have left the area of intentional killing.[4] I have come to realise that the Doctrine of Double Effect comprises several things, merely *including* this 'principle of side effects', and that we should split it up.

Having accepted the principle of side effects, we need some further principle or principles on which to judge the unintended causing of death. There is one which both seems obvious and covers a good many cases. The intrinsic certainty of the death of the victim, or its great likelihood from the nature of the case, would exclude moving the rock. Here is a reasonable principle. Surgery would be thought murderous, even though it was not done in order to kill, but, say, to get an organ for someone else, if the death of the subject were expected as a near consequence, pretty certain from the nature of the operation.

It will be apparent that this principle tells you rather what you can't do than what you can. Also, it is particularly devised for the causing of death; causing of other harm is not covered by it. I think that these are not faults.

I will end by protesting at the ascription of the Doctrine of Double Effect to Aquinas: The phrase "duplex effectus" occurs in his discussion of killing in self-defence. (*Summa Theologica* IIa IIae, Q.64 art. 7) "Ex acu ergo alicuius se defendentis duplex effectus sequi potest: unus quidem, conservatio propriae vitae; alius autem, occisio invadentis." His doctrine is severe: he holds that one may not aim at the death of one's assailant, but one is guiltless if it occurs unintended as a result of one's use of means proportionate to the end of repelling him. One must moderate the force one uses, to suit the end; if one uses more than is required (si utatur maiori violentia quam opporteat) one's act is rendered illicit. Those who wished to see in this text the package Doctrine of Double Effect claimed that in speaking of proportionate means St. Thomas was introducing their doctrine of a proportion of good over evil in the upshot. I am not concerned to discuss St. Thomas' view on self-defence, only to note the false interpretation.

If we want to know St. Thomas' general opinion on responsibility for evil consequences of actions, this is not the place to look, but rather at what he says about the relation of an *eventus sequens* to the goodness or badness of an action (Ia IIae, Q.20 art. 5):

> Si est praecogitatus, manifestum est quod addit ad bonitatem vel malitiam. Cum enim aliquis cogitans quod ex opere suo multa mala possunt sequi nec propter hoc dimittit: ex hoc apparet voluntas eius esse magis inordinata.
>
> Si autem eventus sequens non sit praecogitatus, tunc distinguendum est. Quia si per se sequitur ex tali actu, et ut in pluribus, secundum hoc eventus sequens addit ad bonitatem vel malitiam actus: manifestum est enim meliorem actum esse ex suo genere, ex quo possunt plura bona sequi; et peiorem ex quo nata sunt plura mala sequi. Si vero per accidens, et ut in paucioribus, tunc eventus sequens non addit ad bontiatem vel ad malitiam actus: non enim datur de re aliqua secundum illud quod est per accidens, sed solum secundum quod est per se.[5]

New Hall, Cambridge University
  Cambridge, England

NOTES

1. I use the words "act" and "action" interchangeably without intending any difference of sense.
2. A cave explorer.
3. My references are to his *Ambiguity in Moral Choice*.
4. See Chapter III, section of *Euthanasia and Clinical Practice, The Report of a Working Party*, published by The Linacre Centre, London, 1982.
5. *Translation:* If it (the consequent event) is pre-conceived, it manifestly adds to the goodness or badness of the action. For when someone considers that much that is bad can follow from what he does, and does not give it up on that account, this shows that his will is the more inordinate. But if the consequent event is not pre-conceived, then it is necessary to distinguish. For if it follows from that kind of action *per se* and in most cases, then the consequent event does accordingly add to the goodness or badness of the action; for it is clear that that action is better in kind, from which more goods can follow, and worse, from which more evils are liable to follow. But if it is *per accidens*, and in rather few cases, then the consequent event does not add to the goodness or to the badness of an action: for there isn't judgment on any matter according to what is *per accidens*, but only what is *per se*.

JOSEPH BOYLE

WHO IS ENTITLED TO DOUBLE EFFECT?

ABSTRACT. The doctrine of double effect continues to be an important tool in bioethical casuistry. Its role within the Catholic moral tradition continues, and there is considerable interest in it by contemporary moral philosophers. But problems of justification and correct application remain. I argue that if the traditional Catholic conviction that there are exceptionless norms prohibiting inflicting some kinds of harms on people is correct, then double effect is justified and necessary. The objection that double effect is superfluous is a rejection of that normative conviction, not a refutation of double effect itself. This justification suggests the correct way of applying double effect to controversial cases. But versions of double effect which dispense with the absolutism of the Catholic tradition lack justification and fall to the objection that double effect is an unnecessary complication.

Key Words: double effect, intention, side effect

The doctrine of double effect (hereafter DDE) emerged within Roman Catholic moral theology as a procedure for guiding some decisions which arise in a class of morally ambiguous situations – namely, those in which a straightforward application of an exceptionless moral norm appears to exclude an action for which there are good, and even morally compelling, reasons. DDE rests on a distinction between what a person intends in acting and what a person brings about as a side effect of an intentional action. According to DDE this distinction has moral significance: it is sometimes permissible to bring about as a side effect of one's intentional action what it would be wrong to bring about intentionally.

Within the Catholic tradition DDE has been formulated in various, more or less complicated ways (Mangan, 1949; Boyle, 1980, pp. 528–530). The common core of these formulations is the idea that there are conditions for the permissibility of bringing

---

Joseph Boyle, Professor of Philosophy, St. Michael's College, Centre for Bioethics, University of Toronto, Toronto, Ontario, M5S 1J4, Canada

about certain kinds of harms to people. The harms in question are taken by the tradition to be of various sorts (bodily harms such as death or injury to the agent or to another, and moral harms such as helping someone commit sin or putting oneself in an occasion of sin) but they have in common that they are all harms which it would be absolutely impermissible to bring about intentionally. The double effect doctrine states that such harms may be brought about if two conditions are met: (1) the harms are not intended but brought about as side effects; and (2) there are sufficiently serious moral reasons for doing what brings about such harms.[1]

Plainly, DDE has important applications within bioethical casuistry. Indeed, with the possible exception of its application in the casuistry of self-defense and warfare, the best known use of DDE by Catholic moralists is its use in the context of abortion; indirect abortions are those which can be justified by DDE. But other bioethical applications abound: to distinguish intentional sterilization from actions which sterilize as a side effect, to distinguish from prohibited killing acts of providing analgesics which may shorten life, to distinguish cooperation in evil action which might be morally justifiable from that which, because it takes on the intentions of the one helped, cannot be, and to distinguish morally justifiable decisions to forgo life-extending treatments from decisions to let die which constitute immoral "passive euthanasia".[2]

Casuistical reasoning and debate about these and related issues is an abiding part of the ongoing dialogue of bioethics. For this reason the applications of DDE will likely continue to be a source of philosophical concern. Those influenced by or committed to the Catholic moral tradition will continue to be part of this dialogue, and this tradition itself, as one of developed sources of casuistical reasoning, will likely be explored and mined for the assistance it can provide. This is especially true in the present context because a number of non-consequentialist moral philosophers are showing a new found appreciation for DDE, even as they reject many of the characteristic themes of traditional Catholic morality.

In this dialectical context, it is not satisfactory simply to develop the casuistry which depends on DDE in the way the Catholic moral tradition has done for several centuries. DDE itself must be subjected to analytical scrutiny. For the casuistry which makes use of DDE cannot itself determine how its underlying distinctions are to be understood, and there is considerable disagreement, particularly concerning the exact meaning of the distinction between intentionally harming someone and harming someone as a side effect. This disagreement can be decisively settled only by considering the normative justification of DDE. For only thus will we be able to judge which of the various ways of drawing this distinction is compatible with justified applications of DDE. A consideration of the justification of DDE is also necessary for evaluating the force of the objection that DDE is superfluous and dispensable. This objection can be addressed to the traditional Catholic versions of DDE and to the contemporary, philosophical versions which dispense with many of the assumptions of the tradition.

In this paper I will deal with the justification of DDE. I will argue that in its traditional absolutist version DDE is justified and needed, and that those who reject it as superfluous have no specific objection to DDE but a normative disagreement with the absolutism of the Catholic tradition. This justification settles some of the disputes about how the distinction between intentionally harming and harming as a side effect is to be applied. I will also argue that contemporary, non-absolutist versions of DDE are left without justification, and cannot answer the objection that DDE is superfluous. Outside the absolutist context of the Catholic tradition, DDE is not needed; and those who reject this context are not entitled to use it.

THE REQUIREMENT OF PROPORTIONATE REASON

There is considerable unclarity in the tradition about how the second condition of DDE – that there must be a sufficiently serious moral reason for bringing about the harmful side effect – is to be understood and applied. It is clear, however, that it directs us to consider a highly variable and circumstantial set of factors quite unlike those which might be relevant in determining the morality of intentionally bringing about the harms in question. Surely, also, this condition directs us to consider anything about the act having harmful side effects which might provide grounds for foregoing the act, for example, that it would be unfair to someone to perform an act having these side effects, or that one has some special duty to prevent these side effects, and so on (Grisez and Boyle, 1978, pp. 388–390; Finnis et al., 1987, p. 292). Since the discussion of this condition has not been at the center of disputes about the defensibility of DDE and its applications, I will not discuss its details (Quinn, 1989, p. 334).

However, the simple fact that, in addition to the condition concerning intention, there is another necessary condition for the permissibility of bringing about harms of the kind in question is important for forestalling certain objections to DDE. For it is commonly believed that, according to DDE, acts which bring about harms as side effects only are so far permissible. This false belief leads some to suppose that DDE is committed to holding that people are responsible only for what they bring about intentionally, and that there is no responsibility for side effects (Donagan, 1977, pp. 122, 164). But if there is no responsibility for side effects, then it would hardly be relevant to state a moral condition for the permissibility of bringing them about. As Anscombe has noted, the first condition of DDE, which she calls "the principle of the side effect", says nothing about the permissibility of bringing about harmful side effects beyond the fact that they are not excluded by the absolute prohibitions which exclude intentionally bringing about the kind of harm in question: "But notice that the principle is modest: it says, 'where you must not aim at someone's death [the only harm she is considering] causing it does not *necessarily* cause guilt'" (1982, p. 21). Thus, Baruch Brody's worry that attributing to intention the role it has in DDE might lead to the consequence that we can only kill someone when we intentionally cause his or her death (1988, p. 25) is not substantial. As Anscombe's statement suggests, there is nothing about DDE which implies that such things as negligent or wanton killings are permissible or even less bad or not worse than intentional killings.

INTENTIONALLY HARMING AND HARMING AS A SIDE EFFECT

The first condition of DDE has been the focus in recent discussions and disputes about the doctrine and its applications. The distinction between what is brought about intentionally and what is brought about as a side effect, and the claim that in the case of actions which cause certain harms this distinction marks an important moral difference – the difference between what is always impermissible and what might be morally permissible – raise difficult and controversial issues.

Twenty years ago there was substantial skepticism among philosophers about whether the distinction between what an agent intends and what the agent brings about as a side effect could be drawn (Chisholm, 1970, pp. 636–637). There was also skepticism about whether the distinction, even if it could be drawn in a rough, intuitive way, was clear enough to be applied rigorously to the kind of cases requiring careful casuistical analysis. This latter scepticism arose from H.L.A. Hart's argument that certain actions which were not thought to be allowed by traditional applications of DDE were analytically indistinguishable from actions which were allowed by traditional applications (Hart, 1968, p. 123). This scepticism increased as a result of Philippa Foot's development of Hart's argument into a general suggestion that the DDE provides no "criterion of closeness" to distinguish cases in which a result is intended from cases in which it is a side effect (Foot, 1978, p. 23).

These concerns about the distinction which underlies DDE and its application to cases are not now regarded by philosophers as seriously damaging or fatal to DDE (Foot, 1985, pp. 25–26; Nagel, 1986, p. 179). An argument for this judgment can be stated as follows: The notion of intention used in traditional discussions of DDE is, fundamentally, a philosophical construction which has come to affect the ordinary English usage of "intention" but which is neither based on that usage nor identical with it (Boyle and Sullivan, 1977). On this conception, one intends one's ends, the states of affairs one aims to achieve in action, and one also intends one's means, that is, the precise steps one takes to achieve one's ends. Features of one's voluntary actions which are not one's ends or means are side effects. Side effects are consequences or other aspects of one's actions which are neither the goals one seeks in acting nor the precise states of affairs one is committed to realizing for the sake of these goals. They are properly regarded as outside one's intention in acting because their occurrence does not contribute to one's purposes; they are not part of what one wants to occur or of what, strictly, serves one's purposes. But they are voluntarily brought about if they are foreseen or should be foreseen. For one brings them about knowingly and has some control over whether they will occur, even if one is indifferent to their occurrence, and even if one acts in spite of the expectation of their occurrence. Thus, the tradition maintains that one "permits" side effects, and one might better say that one "accepts" them. So, there is a basis for making the distinction upon which DDE depends (Boyle, 1980, pp. 533–536).

Furthermore, although there are likely to be borderline cases in which it will be difficult, or perhaps even impossible, to determine whether some state of affairs a person voluntarily brings about is a side effect or part of what the person intends, not all applications of DDE concern such difficult applications, and the underlying concepts are not so vague as to prevent serious argumentation about whether or not certain applications are correct.

Thus, for example, the death of the one who is killed by the craniotomy in Hart's famous example is not intended in the sense of intention clarified two paragraphs above: that individual's death does not contribute to saving the mother's life; what contributes to it is the removal of the individual from the birth canal; this is achieved by crushing the individual's skull, and that surely causes death, but it is the removing and the crushing, not the death or the causing of death which are intended (Boyle, 1977; Quinn, 1989, p. 341). What settles cases like this is an analysis of the intentional structure of actions, not appeal to a general criterion of closeness.

This way of dealing with the craniotomy example has been found unacceptable on several grounds: it appears counterintuitive to many, and it seems to destroy the natural applications of DDE. To avoid these difficulties a different basis for the DDE has been suggested (Quinn, 1989, pp. 335–344). Furthermore, even granted that the death in this example is a side effect, some have maintained that, since this fact is not sufficient to morally justify the craniotomy, it remains reasonable to regard side effects as close to intentional actions as this one as if they were for purposes of moral evaluation part of what the agent intends (Anscombe, 1982, pp. 21–22; Linacre Centre, 1982, p. 35).

But none of these worries and alternatives provides a suggestion that the underlying distinction of DDE cannot be formulated in a way that is sufficiently intelligible and determinate to allow for rational application of DDE to cases.

JUSTIFICATION OF NON-ABSOLUTIST VERSIONS OF DDE

The moral relevance of the distinction between side effects and what is intended is more difficult to establish, and has become the object of considerable discussion among moral philosophers. Recent philosophical writing on DDE has emphasized that it captures pre-philosophical intuitions which are shared by many people and which constitute an important part of the non-consequentialist morality of common sense (Foot, 1985, pp. 25–26; Nagel, 1986, pp. 179–185). Thus, many non-consequentialist moral philosophers appear to think that the distinction between intentionally harming someone and harming as a side effect is morally significant, and that this significance is similar to that attributed to the distinction within the Catholic tradition.

The main difference between the contemporary, philosophical view of DDE and the traditional Catholic understanding is that the former separates DDE and its underlying distinctions from the moral absolutism which provides the context for DDE within the Catholic tradition. Thus, Warren Quinn formulates DDE in a way that does not presuppose a moral view which includes absolute prohibitions of inflicting kinds of harms, but instead provides a basis for discriminating in favor of certain actions and against others: "It discriminates against agency in which there is some kind of intending of an objectionable outcome as conducive to the agent's end, and it discriminates in favor of agency that involves only foreseeing but not that kind of intending, of an objectionable outcome" (1989, p. 335).

This non-absolutist formulation of DDE is appealing insofar as it avoids controversial claims about exceptionless prohibitions against inflicting certain kinds of harms. Moreover, it seems to capture what is intuitively appealing about DDE and to highlight just those features of it which make it so compelling as an irreducible and non-consequentialist part of everyday, common sense morality.

However, DDE is hard to defend in this form. For if there is no justification of this form of DDE, it remains plausible to think either that the distinction to which it attributes considerable moral weight in fact lacks moral significance, however deeply it might be embedded in ordinary moral thought, or that some other moral considerations in fact bear the moral weight mistakenly attributed to DDE. And this condition, as far as I can determine, is met. Justifications of this form of DDE do no more than elaborate the intuitive appeal which striking examples illustrate. Therefore, the dilemma posed above is a serious one.

Nagel, for example, holds that DDE, for all its difficulties of application, "provides a rough guide to the extension and character of deontological constraints [on the pursuit of agent neutral goals]" (1986, p. 179). He goes on to provide a phenomenology of the action of doing what is evil for the sake of a good purpose, and then asks how DDE is justified. He replies that there is no decisive answer (p. 183). By this he seems to mean that there is no general way to say whether the agent relative perspective of DDE or the agent neutral perspective of promoting good outcomes should be normatively dominant. But this assumes that from the agent relative perspective DDE is justified. And he provides no argument for that assumption, beyond the phenomenology which elaborates common intuitions about the difference between harms one intends and harms one brings about as side effects. So Nagel faces the dilemma: perhaps there is nothing of normative significance in the phenomena he details, and the force of the agent's subjective perspective is normatively illusory, or perhaps something else more adequately captures the agent relative intuitions on which he focuses.

Alan Donagan's argument that DDE is superfluous (1977, pp. 163–164) exemplifies the difficulty involved in the second horn of the dilemma. Donagan maintains that within common morality, which within Donagan's Kantian framework is systematically agent relative, there is a structural principle for ordering moral obligations, which he names "the Pauline Principle" after St. Paul's saying that one may not do evil that good might come of it (*Romans* 3:8). This principle relies on an interpretation of Kant's distinction between perfect and imperfect duties, and requires that one not violate perfect duties in fulfillment of imperfect duties. This requirement follows from the first moral principle as understood by Kant, since the goals to which imperfect duties direct us are not mandatory in every situation but are rightly pursued only by actions which do not violate the perfect duties which follow from the principle of respect for persons (pp. 154–155).

Donagan understands DDE as a replacement for the Pauline Principle (p. 156). He argues that this replacement is not needed *unless* the perfect duties in question are understood as absolute prohibitions against certain kinds of harming as such (pp. 159, 163). For if the perfect duties are not exceptionless, but proscribe only harming *at will*, as Donagan thinks they do, then the plausible exceptions, such as killing in self-defense or the sorts of abortions which the Catholic tradition regarded as 'indirect' will not be ruled out by the perfect duty.

Whether or not Donagan is correct in thinking that DDE is a replacement for the Pauline Principle, and whether or not he has precisely stated the condition necessary to warrant such a replacement, his argument is effective against a position like Nagel's. For it makes clear that agent centered constraints on the pursuit of good need not be grounded on DDE and its underlying distinction, unless those agent centered constraints are more generally stated than Nagel gives us reason for thinking them to be, and surely more generally stated than those who wish to defend DDE on non-absolutist grounds are willing to allow.

Warren Quinn develops a justification for a revised version of DDE which seems to avoid the force of Donagan's argument, and which is plainly more than an elaboration of common sense intuitions. His revisions, in effect, provide a position which avoids the horns of the dilemma to which other non-absolutist defenses of DDE are subject. His revisions, however, are such that what he defends is not DDE, at least as understood within the Catholic tradition, but another doctrine which does not have the range of application of DDE (Quinn, 1989, p. 343) nor, if I am correct about the craniotomy case, the same results in cases to which both seem to apply (1989, p. 343).

In addition to his rejection of the absolutism of the Catholic version of DDE, Quinn's revision includes two essential elements. One has already been noted: in order to exclude the possibility that the death in the craniotomy case will be in the relevant sense outside the agent's intention, he does not base the DDE on the distinction between what is intended and side effects. His basis for the DDE is the fact that some who are harmed by our actions are what he calls "intentional objects" whereas others are not. In the former case but not the latter, the agent deliberately involves those harmed in something "in order to further his purpose precisely by way of their being so involved" (1989, p. 343). Thus, "The doctor in CC [the craniotomy example] strictly intends to produce an effect on the fetus so that the mother can be saved by that effect" (p. 342).

The second element in Quinn's revision is that DDE is taken to apply only to harms which the agent brings upon other people, and indeed applies only when there is a conflict between the moral claims of different people (p. 342).[3]

The justification Quinn offers for his version of DDE is worth considering: Whenever a person harms another by his or her agency, the person does what is bad and perhaps prima facie wrong. But when a person harms another who could volunteer or refuse to volunteer to be harmed but is not asked to volunteer then the agent does a further wrong to the one harmed. For in such cases one subordinates the other person to one's own goals, and literally uses the person. When one intentionally harms another, one uses him or her in this way; when one brings harm on another as a side effect one does not. So there is an additional wrong-making factor in cases of intentionally harming a person, and so a basis for discriminating against agency which involves such harming.

Intentionally harming a person makes the person play a role within one's strategic thinking. That person's being harmed serves one's purposes. Thus it is something one might ask the person to do, and which they might conceivably consent to do. But in cases where harm is brought about as a side effect, volunteering would be irrelevant; any harm which might come to a person harmed as a side effect does not serve one's purposes; they make no contribution to the agent's plans (Quinn, 1980, pp. 348–349).

Quinn's claim that there is a duty not to use people which goes beyond the duty not to harm them is plausible enough, and the contours of this duty closely track some intuitions about DDE, at least for some cases in which harms are inflicted on others. But it is not clear that Quinn's argument provides a general basis for discriminating against intentionally harmful agency.

As Quinn notes, it is surely possible to wrong people by harming them as a side effect (p. 348). This would be failing to respect them, though it would not be using them. However, he does not consider the possibility that bringing about harms as side effects is in some cases as wrongful as, or even worse than, bringing about those harms intentionally. One who wantonly disregards the interests of those harmed by his or her actions surely need show no lesser disrespect for those people than if he or she had intentionally harmed them in the same way, and so used them. Thus, even if intentionally harming always adds a wrong-making feature to an act which harms others, it is by no means clear that this justifies generally discriminating against intentionally harmful agency.

Another, deeper difficulty in Quinn's account arises from the fact that it attributes moral significance to the distinction between what an agent intends and side effects only in cases in which the intended harm is not voluntarily accepted by the victim and only in cases in which the harm is to another. This limitation has a troubling implication concerning the beliefs of those who hold that the distinction between intentionally harming and harming as a side effect has the same moral significance in cases in which Quinn thinks it not justified as it does in the cases he thinks it justified. On Quinn's account such people are simply guilty of a mistake. Yet such people seem to be guilty only of having normative convictions slightly different than Quinn's own – convictions which are quite natural within common sense morality and which do not presuppose the absolutism of the Catholic tradition.

For if one assumes that it is possible to wrong oneself by harming oneself, then it seems that whether one harms oneself intentionally or as a side effect should make a difference similar to the difference it makes when applied to harms inflicted on others. Similarly, if one supposes that there are harms one can inflict on others which wrong them even if they voluntarily consent to them, then it seems that whether one harms the person intentionally or as a side effect should make a difference similar to the difference Quinn sees between intentionally harmful actions without the consent of the victim and actions which harm as a side effect. Thus, those who believe that killing oneself is wrong are likely to think there is a morally significant difference between intentionally ending one's life and ending it as a side effect of other actions. Similarly, those who think it is wrong to kill another even if the other consents to being killed are likely to think that the difference between intentional killing and killing as a side effect is morally relevant to evaluate the agent's act.

In other words, Quinn seems to have constructed a defense for a version of DDE which grounds its moral force in considerations which, while they have their own intuitive power, do not mesh well with the intuitions of many who have thought DDE to be true. For both in Catholic moral thinking and common sense morality, there are normative convictions which appear to bring DDE into play where Quinn's account implies that it has no application.

In short, it seems that contemporary philosophical discussions of DDE do not provide an account which justifies the moral significance which many think attaches to the distinction between intentionally harming and harming as a side effect. Absent such a justification, current claims that the DDE captures an important part of people's pre-philosophical and non-consequentialist moral intuitions are not compelling, and no grounds are provided for a non-consequentialist casuistry.

AN ABSOLUTIST JUSTIFICATION OF DDE

As far as I am aware, there is no systematic attempt within the Catholic moral tradition to provide a justification for DDE. Much like contemporary philosophers who accept some version of DDE, Catholic moralists since Aquinas have assumed that the distinction between intentionally harming and harming as a side effect bears considerable moral weight, no doubt for similar, intuitively grounded reasons.[4]

There is, however, a justification of DDE which emerges within the framework of the moral absolutism which characterizes the Catholic tradition. This absolutism is not, of course, specific to the Catholic tradition but would be a feature of any moral theory according to which there were exceptionless moral norms prohibiting inflicting certain kinds of harms on people. Furthermore, as will become clear shortly, the justification of DDE within such a moral framework does not establish the truth of its absolute prohibitions, but assumes there are some.

The justification is as follows: if it is absolutely impermissible to inflict some kinds of harms on people, there is a natural and, indeed, unavoidable, question about the extension of the norms prohibiting such harms. This question arises because of the possibility that there are situations in which, whatever one chooses to do, one will inflict the prohibited harm on someone. If there are cases of this kind, moral norms which absolutely exclude inflicting such harms cannot be so general as to prohibit inflicting them in these cases. For a moral norm which literally cannot be followed cannot perform its function of guiding choice. There are, plainly, cases of this kind – cases in which, whatever one does, someone will be the victim of a harm it is presumably wrong to inflict. Thus, whatever the precise extension of the prohibition, it must be limited so as not to cover such cases. In other words, absolute prohibitions against inflicting harms on people cannot sensibly be formulated as prohibitions against *inflicting* or even *knowingly inflicting* the harms in question, although, of course, absolute prohibitions of some kinds of actions could be sensible if they were not based on considerations about the harms they inflict.

Who is entitled to double effect?

The distinction between actions in which one intentionally harms someone and those in which someone is harmed as a side effect provides the needed limit on the extension of norms absolutely prohibiting inflicting certain kinds of harms. For it is always possible (although sometimes extremely difficult and costly) for a moral agent to follow a norm which absolutely prohibits intentionally harming someone. For this reason, acts of intentionally harming someone appear to be paradigm cases of what norms which absolutely exclude inflicting harms would prohibit. By way of contrast, it would not be always possible (indeed is frequently impossible) to follow an absolute prohibition against inflicting harms if that were taken to apply to harms brought about as side effects. For there are many circumstances, hard to specify in any very general way, in which, whatever one does, one will cause harm as a side effect.

Thus, it is not incompatible with the idea of a moral norm to think that there are moral norms which direct that actions which intentionally harm someone should never be done, but it is incompatible with this idea to think that these norms should be extended so as to prohibit absolutely harms caused as a side effect (Finnis et al., 1987, p. 292).

Thus, as Anscombe has emphasized, the primary point of the distinction between intentionally harming someone and harming someone as a side effect is to limit the extension of the relevant absolute prohibitions (1982, p. 21). But my justification of DDE along these lines has implications which Anscombe may not want to accept. For she seems to suggest that in cases in which it is hard to see the difference between intentionally harming and harming as a side effect, the latter should be morally evaluated in the same way as the former. Thus, referring to actions having death as a side effect, she maintains that when the death is intrinsically certain or very likely in the nature of the case, then it is wrong to do the action which brings it about (1982, p. 24). But in the cases she discusses, death is also a side effect, and a fairly certain one at that, of the decision to forgo the actions she wishes prohibited. The immediacy or certainty of a side effect's occurring is surely relevant to the moral evaluation of the act which brings it about, but anything approaching an absolute prohibition of actions having harmful side effects appears to run afoul of the limitations which my argument sets for absolute prohibitions against inflicting harms.

The character of this justification of DDE can be made more precise and its force put into perspective by considering its bearing on Donagan's argument that DDE is superfluous. Contrary to what Donagan supposes (1977, pp. 159, 164), DDE does not arise because there is an established and determinate prohibition against certain kinds of harming as such, and therefore a need to limit responsibility to harms intentionally inflicted in order to avoid the impossibilities to which such a prohibition would lead. It arises instead because there is a prohibition against (at least) intentionally inflicting certain kinds of harms, and therefore a question whether this prohibition can be extended to cover inflicting harmful side effects. DDE gives a negative answer to this question.

Thus, it seems clear that DDE is not a replacement for the Pauline Principle, and is in no conflict with it, but rather provides a ground for clarification of the precise extent of some of the perfect duties to which it gives priority. Donagan is correct, of course, in thinking that this sort of precision about the extent of perfect duties would be otiose if the duties themselves were not absolute. But Donagan's disagreement with the Catholic tradition about this matter is a normative disagreement about the character of norms which prohibit inflicting harms. If the Catholic tradition is correct in its conviction that there are absolute norms prohibiting intentionally inflicting harms – a conviction which must be justified independently of considerations about DDE – then his objection to DDE is not substantiated.[5]

In short, if my justification of DDE is correct, the objection that DDE is superfluous is sound when directed against non-absolutist versions, but when directed at absolutist versions, it challenges not DDE itself but the absolutist framework it assumes. Both implications are important. For the first means that many who would like to make use of DDE, for example, contemporary theologians who reject the Catholic tradition's moral absolutes and anti-consequentialist philosophers, are not entitled to help themselves to its use. And the second means that those who object to the implications of the application of DDE within the traditional Catholic context have no specific objection to DDE and so should direct their criticisms at the absolute norms on whose extension DDE provides a control.

DIFFICULTIES

It might be objected that my justification of DDE is at least as far away from accounting for all its plausible uses as is Quinn's. For my justification applies only when there is a situation of what might be called 'moral impossibility', that is, a situation in which one lacks the capacity to prevent the harmful side effect from occurring. And this situation may seem to obtain in only a few of the situations to which DDE plausibly applies.

I consider first the cases in which there clearly is moral impossibility – deflection cases in which the situation is defined in such a way that it is not within one's power to prevent a harm from falling on some who are caught up in the situation, but in which one does have a choice about which of these people are to be the victim. Here one causes the harm to fall on some to save another or others; the harm to the victim is a side effect. Plainly, the choice to bring it upon some person rather than others is subject to moral evaluation, but this evaluation plainly cannot be based on an absolute prohibition against inflicting the harm.

Many classical cases used to illustrate DDE are structurally similar – the indirect abortion cases, for example. In these cases, and in the craniotomy case if my analysis of it is correct, the established situation determines that at least one of the parties will die. The choice to do or refrain from doing the medical procedure determines which will die as a side effect: the indirect abortion causes the death of the fetus as a side effect, the refusal of the procedure results in the mother's death as a side effect.

A similar analysis applies to decisions to allocate scarce medical resources. These decisions provide scarce resources to some who need them, and deny them to others who as a result will die or live on miserably. These are not structurally identical to deflection cases. For, unlike deflection cases, they involve saving some at the price of *letting* harm fall on others. The fact that the harm is allowed to fall on some rather than being inflicted by the agent's initiative raises familiar difficulties about agency, causality and omissions. But these complications do not alter the situation of moral impossibility, and do not show that the harm permitted is not a side effect. For the harm would not have fallen on its specific victim except for the agent's decision, and the harm in the cases described is not intended: as in deflection cases, the harm to those left untreated to save scarce resources for others are not what serve the purposes of those who decided to save others' lives. But these harms to certain individuals are within the agent's power to prevent. So, they are side effects, and not reasonably evaluated by absolute prohibitions against inflicting harms.

Still, it seems odd to many to consider as harmful side effects of one's choices things which one does not actually cause, and this sense of oddity increases when one considers the reverse side of this idea, namely, that an agent can intentionally harm someone without causing the harm, merely by wanting the harm to occur and choosing not to prevent it. Baruch Brody thinks that this possibility unnecessarily complicates the ethics of decision making about the termination of life saving treatment. For this possibility implies that "either a great deal of killing is morally permissible or that we are required to treat a very large number of terminally ill patients so as to avoid killing them" (Brody, 1988, p. 25). He prefers a strictly causal theory of killing, which avoids these complications.

But Brody's disjunction is incomplete. Defenders of DDE will hold that there is another possibility besides keeping people alive so as to avoid killing them and killing them intentionally by omission. The traditional understanding of the doctrine of ordinary and extraordinary treatments provides that possibility. According to this view, one can choose to omit life preserving treatments not only for the sake of ending the patient's life but for the sake of avoiding various burdens of the treatment. Thus, if it were true that the only way to avoid intentionally killing people would be to continue to treat them, then we would be obligated by a norm absolutely prohibiting intentional killing by causing death or by omission to treat an implausibly great number of patients, but treating people is not the only alternative to intentionally killing them.

This approach to the ethics of terminating treatment is more complicated than Brody's strictly causal approach, but it is not clear that the causal approach is therefore preferable. If one supposes, as Brody appears to suppose, that there is no absolute prohibition against intentional killing by omission, then the intentional approach of DDE and the ordinary and extraordinary treatments doctrine is bound to give the wrong results, and indeed is not needed or justified. But rejecting this normative belief of the Catholic tradition does little to justify Brody's alternative. For, as he admits, one who intentionally kills by omission does contribute to the death. It follows that the agent bears responsibility for the death of a kind similar to the responsibility one would have for causing it. Given this, it is a mystery why the relevant norms, however they are precisely formulated, should prohibit only the causing of death (in Brody's sense of "cause"), and not also the contribution to death which comes about in intentional omissions.

In short, the application of the distinction between intentionally harming and harming as a side effect to cases where the agent deliberately refrains from doing something seems justified, and, since situations of moral impossibility arise in cases where one of the alternatives is not to do something, the limitation of absolute prohibitions applies here as well as in cases in which the harmful side effects are caused.

Still, many cases usually thought to be covered by DDE do not have even the similarity to deflection cases of those in which one has a choice between letting a harm fall on one as a side effect or causing it to fall on another as a side effect. For in many cases, the harms which come about as a side effect of whatever one chooses to do will fall upon the same person. But the identity of the victim of the harmful side effects of either choice does not remove the situation of moral impossibility. For example, one who faces a choice between death from a disease and very risky surgery to deal with the disease must accept the likelihood of death as a side effect of either choice.

Another important class of cases usually covered by DDE is quite different from deflection cases in that the harms which are the side effects of choosing one alternative are different in kind from those which would occur if one chose another alternative. But again this difference does not remove the situation of moral impossibility. Consider the case of building highways, or the standard example of giving a person analgesics which are required to control pain but will probably shorten the patient's life. In both cases the side effects of taking the action will include the probability of death, but the side effects of the alternatives are also bad, and indeed include some which it is plausible to think would be absolutely impermissible to inflict intentionally. So there remains here a situation in which, whatever one does, harms will occur which it would be absolutely wrong to bring about intentionally, and so a pair of norms each of which excluded absolutely bringing about the side effects of each alternative would be impossible to follow.

In short, the objection that my justification of DDE as determining the limits of the extension of absolute prohibitions against harming people does not cover the range of application of DDE is not sound. Any action which has as a side effect the sort of harming of someone which it is plausible to think absolutely prohibited if brought about intentionally is covered by DDE, and this class of actions is very extensive indeed, certainly extensive enough to cover the cases to which DDE is thought to apply.

NOTES

[1] This formulation implies that traditional Catholic formulations in terms of three or four conditions are, strictly speaking, superfluous. See Boyle, 1980, p. 532 for an explanation of why, given their concern about casuistical application, traditional moralists found it useful to formulate DDE in theoretically superfluous ways.

[2] See Ashley and O'Rourke, 1981, pp. 227–238, 276–284, 375–387 for a contemporary Catholic statement of many of these issues. See also Grisez and Boyle, 1979, Chapter 12, for a systematic account of those among them which relate to the ethics of killing.

[3] A curiosity of Quinn's approach is worth noting. He is convinced that it would destroy the natural application of DDE if one were to allow that the craniotomy does not violate the first, intentional condition of DDE. Yet he is not troubled by the fact that his revision of DDE excludes other natural applications which are used as standard examples, such as the difference between using analgesics which shorten life for the sake of easing pain and the use of the same or other analgesics with the intention of shortening life. The grounds for regarding one application as essential and others as dispensable are not clear.

[4] In his famous discussion of killing in self-defense, which is widely regarded as the first statement of DDE, Thomas Aquinas provides only one sentence by way of justification of the distinction between intentionally harming and harming as a side effect – the cryptic remark that "moral acts receive their species according to what is intended" (*Summa Theologiae*, 2-2, q. 64, a. 7, trans. author). Neither he nor the tradition elaborates this idea. But there is a hint within the more recent tradition which points in the direction of the argument I begin here. This part of the tradition does not sharply distinguish between justification and excuse, and tends to express DDE in terms that suggest it to be a principle of excuse. That, of course is a mistake (Boyle, 1980, pp. 529–530). But it suggests what is true and important for the justification of DDE, namely, that the character of one's responsibility for side effects is different from that for what one intends. It is also worth noting that there is a deep, theological precedent for the distinction: part

of the Catholic solution to the problem of evil is that God does not intentionally bring it about but only accepts it as a side effect.

[5] The absolute prohibitions against intentionally harming persons which characterize the Catholic moral tradition have been defended, and not simply on the basis of a divine command theory (Finnis et al., 1987, pp. 281–294). The defense of these moral absolutes by Catholics does not presuppose moral principles very different than those Donagan endorses (Donagan, 1977, pp. 57–66). For one natural interpretation of the Kantian principle of respect for rational creatures implies that they never be intentionally harmed in certain ways. Donagan's non-absolutist interpretation is not obviously better, and requires an enormously complex and intuitive procedure for determining when the norms prohibiting harming people at will are applicable (pp. 66–74).

[6] I thank John Finnis, John Hartley and Elmar Kremer, who read an earlier draft of this paper, and both corrected a number of mistakes and suggested improvements. The main ideas of this paper are the result of countless discussions with Germain Grisez; the justification of the DDE presented here emerged in one of these discussions, and was first stated in Finnis et al. (1987, p. 292).

REFERENCES

Anscombe, E.: 1982, 'Action, intention and "double effect"', *Proceedings of the American Catholic Philosophical Association* 54, 12–25.

Aquinas, T.: 1942, *Summa Theologiae*, Second Part of the Second Part, Volume Three, Institute of Medieval Studies, Ottawa.

Ashley, B., and O'Rourke, K.: 1981, *Health Care Ethics: A Theological Analysis*, 2nd Edition, The Catholic Health Care Association of the United States, St. Louis.

Boyle, J.: 1977, 'Double effect and a certain type of embryotomy', *The Irish Theological Quarterly* 44, 303–318.

Boyle, J.: 1980, 'Toward understanding the principle of double effect', *Ethics* 90, 527–538.

Boyle, J., and Sullivan, T.: 1977, 'The diffusiveness of intention principle: A counter-example', *Philosophical Studies* 31, 357–360.

Brody, B.: 1988, *Life and Death Decision Making*, Oxford University Press, New York, Oxford.

Chisholm, R.: 1970, 'The structure of intention', *The Journal of Philosophy* 67, 633–647.

Donagan, A.: 1977, *The Theory of Morality*, University of Chicago Press, Chicago.

Finnis, J., Boyle, J., and Grisez, G.: 1987, *Nuclear Deterrence, Morality and Realism*, Oxford University Press, Oxford and New York.

Foot, P.: 1978, 'The problem of abortion and the doctrine of double effect', in *Virtues and Vices*, University of California Press, Berkeley, pp. 19–32. Originally published in 1967, *Oxford Review* 5.

Foot, P.: 1985, 'Morality, outcome and action', in T. Honderich (ed.), *Morality and Objectivity: A Tribute to J. L. Mackie*, Routledge & Kegan Paul, London, pp. 23–38.

Grisez, G., and Boyle, J.: 1979, *Life and Death with Liberty and Justice: A Contribution to the Euthanasia Debate*, University of Notre Dame Press, Notre Dame.

Hart, H. L. A.: 1968, 'Intention and punishment', in *Punishment and Responsibility: Essays in the Philosophy of Law*, Oxford University Press, New York, pp. 113–135.

The Linacre Centre: 1982, *Euthanasia and Clinical Practice; Trends, Principles and Alternatives: The Report of A Working Party*, The Linacre Centre, London.

Mangan, J.: 1949, 'An historical analysis of the principle of double effect', *Theological Studies* 10, 41–61.

Nagel, T.: 1986, *The View from Nowhere*, Oxford University Press, New York.

Quinn, W.: 1989, 'Actions, intentions, and consequences: The doctrine of double effect', *Philosophy and Public Affairs* 18, 334–351.

ALAN DONAGAN

MORAL ABSOLUTISM AND THE DOUBLE-EFFECT EXCEPTION: REFLECTIONS ON JOSEPH BOYLE'S *WHO IS ENTITLED TO DOUBLE EFFECT?*

ABSTRACT. Joseph Boyle raises important questions about the place of the double-effect exception in absolutist moral theories. His own absolutist theory (held by many, but not all, Catholic moralists), which derives from the principles that fundamental human goods may not be intentionally violated, cannot dispense with such exceptions, although he rightly rejects some widely held views about what they are. By contrast, Kantian absolutist theory, which derives from the principle that lawful freedom must not be violated, has a corollary – that it is a duty, where possible, to coerce those who try to violate lawful freedom – which makes superfluous many of the double-effect exceptions Boyle allows. Other implications of the two theories are contrasted. *Inter alia*, it is argued that, in Boyle's theory, that a violation of a fundamental human good can be viewed as a cost proportionate to a benefit obtained, cannot yield a double-effect exception to the prohibition of intentionally violating that good, because paying a cost cannot be unintentional.

Key Words: cost-benefit analysis, double effect, intention, side effect

Most Catholic moralists, especially those who have to do with the practice of medicine, have long accepted that some moral prohibitions are not absolute, but admit exceptions when what is putatively prohibited because of a bad effect has a counterbalancing good effect. In recent years their doctrine has attracted much interest and some favor among secular non-Catholics. Moralists influenced by Kant, however, tend to resist 'double-effect' exceptions as superfluous. The issues are confusing, because not only are theories of the double-effect exception various, but so also are theories according to which it is superfluous. Joseph Boyle's illuminating exploration of some of the theories in the field, both Catholic and non-Catholic, and his exposition and persuasive

---

Alan Donagan, late Doris and Henry Dreyfuss Professor of Philosophy, California Institute of Technology, Pasadena, California 91125, U.S.A.

defence of a particular Catholic theory of it, disentangle some of my own perplexities (Boyle, 1991); and in what follows, I shall try to disentangle some others.

I pass over the double-effect exception in nonabsolutist moral theories, like those of Philippa Foot (1978) and Warren Quinn (1989), and confine myself to its place in absolutist ones, that is, to ones in which "there are exceptionless moral norms prohibiting inflicting certain kinds of harms on people" (Boyle, 1991, p. 486).

1. ACTIONS, INTENDED AND UNINTENDED: THE CASE OF CRANIOTOMY

Boyle would agree, I believe, that the human actions that are subject to moral judgement are changes or persistences in an agent's bodily or mental state brought about by his will, or 'voluntarily', in the technical sense of that word. Hence refusing to bring about such a change is as much an action as bringing one about.[1] An agent *voluntarily* causes an effect of such a voluntary change or persistence if and only if he believes that it can have that effect, not necessarily that it must. And he *intentionally* causes an effect he voluntarily causes if that effect is either the end for which he causes it, or among "the precise steps [he] takes to achieve" that end (Boyle, 1991, p. 479).

What you intend is therefore what you *plan* to do, whether as your end or as among the means by which you plan to accomplish it. You do not intend something you will to do if you will it neither as your purpose nor as contributing to your purpose, even if you foresee that carrying out your plan will cause it. A good test of whether or not you intend a particular foreseen effect of an action is to suppose that, by some fluke or miracle, the action does not have the effect you foresee, and to ask whether you then consider your plan carried out and your purpose accomplished. Boyle contends that, if intended effects are conceived as planned, the distinction between them and unintended side-effects is clear in principle, although there will be borderline cases.[2] Confusion arises when unintended effects are conceived, not as planned, but as causally more remote from the change or persistence in the agent's body that causes them than are intended effects.

Some Catholic moralists resist Boyle's analysis on the ground that no effect of an action can be a side-effect if any step the agent takes to bring about his end is a sufficient condition for it. For example, Stephen Theron argues as follows that killing a foetus, while an unintended side-effect of a hysterectomy performed to prevent its mother from being killed by her uterine cancer, is an intended effect of a craniotomy performed to prevent its mother from being killed by the blockage of her birth canal.

> If I could remove the cancerous womb without causing death I would. But I can't credibly say, if I could do the craniotomy ... without causing death I would. For the *point* of th[is] act is to cause death, and that is why it is killing, whereas the point of removing the cancerous womb and foetus is to save life, and that is why it is not killing, even though it causes death. The craniotomy may also have the point of saving life, but that is through its aim of killing. The hysterectomy has the point of saving life through its aim of removing a womb (Theron, 1984, p. 76).[3]

Presumably Theron's reason for asserting that the "aim" of craniotomy is killing is that the "precise step" in it by which the foetus is made removable from the birth canal is the crushing of its skull, which is a sufficient condition of its death. By contrast, none of the precise steps by which a cancerous womb is removed kills the foetus: it is killed by the removal itself.

Boyle implicitly rejects reasoning like Theron's for two reasons. First of all, an action, whether it is a voluntary change of the agent's state or a voluntary persistence in the same state, is inescapably the causing of *all* the effects of that change or persistence. Since, in the normal course of nature, hysterectomy and craniotomy both cause the death of the foetus concerned, a hysterectomy is as much a killing as a craniotomy, even though the foetus is not killed by any "precise step" in carrying it out. And secondly, since the point of crushing the foetus's skull in craniotomy is not to kill it, but to make it removable from the birth canal, its death is no more the point of the operation than is the death of a foetus the point of hysterectomy. Despite his bold tone, Theron has no credible answer to the question Boyle would presumably ask: "Why can a surgeon performing a craniotomy not 'credibly say' that, if he could crush the foetus's skull in a way that would neither kill nor irreparably injure it, he would?"

2. HOW THE EFFECTS OF AN ACTION AND THE SCOPE OF INTENTION ARE LIMITED BY INTERVENING ACTIONS

The moral implications of the above conception of human action vary according to the conception of cause and effect with which it is associated. Both Catholic and Kantian moral absolutists, and in general, all moralists who accept the freedom of the will in a non-compatibilist sense, limit an action's effects, and *a fortiori* what its agent intends to bring about in doing it, to those that follow from it in the course of nature and the ordinary operation of social institutions, and not from the free reactions of others to it. (Thus actions in the ordinary course of business, for example, those of postal officers in delivering a letter that has been mailed, are not counted as free reactions.) The principle on which they do so is that a free reaction to an action is a 'new action' ('*novus actus*'), the effects of which are their effects, and not those of the action to which they are reactions. It follows that a *novus actus interveniens* terminates not only the effects of the original action, but also what its agent intentionally brings about in doing it. And it also follows that what an agent plans or intends can extend beyond what he plans or intends to bring about. He may intend that others react in a certain way to what he does; but he cannot intend to bring it about that they do, because bringing that about is not in his power.

These distinctions are the foundation of both Catholic and Kantian views of the treatment of action in face of threats, whether by radically unjust legal authority or by private criminals. History offers numerous and horrible examples of somebody powerful and evil commanding somebody else to do something morally abominable (e.g., to choose patients for lethal or radically injurious medical experiments) under the threat that otherwise he will have something even more abominable done. Sophie's predicament in William Styron's novel *Sophie's Choice*, is an example: she is told that if she does not choose one of her two children to be sent to the gas chamber, both will be sent. Although the case is fictional, the records of the concentration camp crimes of the Nazis contain numerous similar ones, many of them even more vile. Yet, as most Jewish writers on the Nazi genocide have concluded, such cases, although agonizing for the victims, are not morally problematic. Given that it is absolutely morally prohibited to collaborate in certain irreparable wrongs, as it will be in any absolutist moral system, that others will react to your refusal to collaborate by doing some graver wrong cannot be a morally relevant reason for your not refusing. By not refusing you will collaborate in a wrong for which there are no amends. Yet you cannot plead that if you refuse, you will cause that graver wrong; for you will not cause it. Nor can you plead that, in failing to refuse, you intended only to prevent the graver wrong, and that your collaboration was the unintended side-effect of trying to prevent it; for even if the threatener refrained from doing what he threatened, you did not prevent him from doing it: that is, you neither caused nor could have caused his not doing it. Your belief that you intended to is at best self-deception.[4]

3. BOYLE'S REVISIONARY THEORY OF THE DOUBLE-EFFECT EXCEPTION

Having got rid of the irrelevancy of harms caused by new intervening actions, we may now turn to Boyle's revisionary theory of double effect exceptions. It is as follows.

Catholic moral absolutism absolutely prohibits intentional invasions of the human goods that are fundamental; and, as a rule but not absolutely, it also prohibits even unintentional invasions of these goods. Since Catholic morality accepts the Pauline principle that it is absolutely prohibited to do evil that good may come of it, it makes no end obligatory that can only be brought about by absolutely prohibited means. Hence none of its absolute moral prohibitions are such that they can be observed only by violating some other. However, situations may occur in which whatever one does will have unintended side-effects that it would be absolutely prohibited to bring about intentionally. For example, a surgeon may be confronted with a situation in which he must either refrain from saving a mother's life or kill her child by craniotomy. In both cases he will cause the death of what, on the face of it, is a materially innocent life: something he is absolutely prohibited from doing intentionally. If he operates with the end of saving the mother's life, he must unintentionally take her child's; and if he refuses to operate with the end of avoiding killing the child, he will refrain from saving its mother's. Yet he is not absolutely prohibited from doing either of these things unintentionally. That is the ground of the 'double-effect exception'. Unintentionally invading a fundamental human good is not prohibited when its end is to avoid some other proportionate invasion of such a good (see Boyle, 1991, pp. 486f.).

For a reason that I shall examine below (in Section 5), Boyle's reasoning holds only if the conflicting plans between which the agent must choose are independent. A physician morally considering whether a craniotomy should be performed is not making a cost-benefit choice between the mother's life and the foetus's: his purpose is to save the mother's life, if he can, by all morally permissible means; and he has concluded that, to accomplish it, he must extract the foetus from her birth canal, which he can do only by crushing its head, which in turn will kill it. In maintaining that such a plan is morally permissible, Boyle assumes that the foetus's death is unplanned and unintended, and not a cost deliberately paid. A physician whose purpose is to save the foetus's life could likewise plan to save its life, with the mother's death as an unintended side-effect. Since under either plan the intended good and unintended harm are the same – saving a human life and causing a human death – it would, according to Boyle's analysis, be morally permissible to carry out either.

4. KANTIAN MORAL ABSOLUTISM, AND ITS REASON FOR DISPENSING WITH THE DOUBLE-EFFECT EXCEPTION

Consider now a Kantian moral absolutism[5] founded on the fundamental principle that, in every voluntary action, every rational being must always be treated as an end, and never as a means only.[6] Two sorts of absolute prohibition follow from this principle: prohibitions of voluntarily doing anything that fails to treat any rational being (including yourself) as an end[7]; and prohibitions of voluntarily omitting to form and act on rational plans of life to perfect yourself and to promote the happiness of others as far as you permissibly and reasonably can. What you can permissibly do is determined by the prohibitions of the first sort; and, given your capacities, what you can reasonably do to perfect yourself is limited and by what you can reasonably do to promote the happiness of others, and *vice versa*. Since absolute prohibitions of the latter sort prohibit only failing to form and act on some plan of self-perfection and beneficence, and not failing to do the specific actions required by any particular plan, the prohibitions of specific actions they entail are 'imperfect', that is, conditional upon the plan adopted.

Since Kantian moral absolutists deny that absolute prohibitions of voluntary actions derived from their fundamental principle can come into conflict, they are predisposed to dismiss double-effect exceptions as superfluous. Obviously, prohibitions entailed by reasonable plans of self-perfection and beneficence cannot conflict with prohibitions of the first sort, because they are conditional upon their observance; nor can they conflict with one another, because plans generating such conflicts are defective and must be revised. But can prohibitions of the first sort themselves come into conflict? That they are all derived from a single substantive principle does not show that they cannot, because that principle may itself be inconsistent; and since it is not logically formalizable, it cannot rigorously be proved consistent. However, Kantians contend that it has never been shown that treating a rational being as an end in some given way can either fail to treat that being as an end in some other way, or fail to treat any other rational being as an end.

Here Boyle would presumably object, "But how does an absolutist Kantian morality treat cases in which a choice must be made between killing a baby by performing a craniotomy, or its mother by not performing one? Both are voluntary actions, and presumably both are absolutely prohibited: one as voluntarily killing an innocent, and one as voluntarily and unnecessarily allowing an innocent to die. Unless it is revised to allow double-effect exceptions, is not Kantian morality, if interpreted as absolutist, inconsistent?" Although he was never to my knowledge confronted with this objection, Kant would have met it by invoking what he called "the universal principle of *Recht*". That principle, that "Every action is *recht* that in itself or in its maxim is such that the freedom of the will of each can coexist together with the freedom of everyone in accordance with a universal law" (Kant, 1797, p. 230)[8], he considered to follow immediately from his fundamental principle of morality; and he inferred from it that "if a certain use of freedom is itself a hindrance to freedom according to universal laws (that is, is *unrecht*), then the use of coercion to counteract it ... is consistent with freedom according to universal laws; in other words ... is *recht*", or, in other words, that "*Recht* is united with the authorization to use coercion against anyone who violates *Recht*" (Kant, 1797, p. 231). Hence, in all situations in which an innocent's lawful freedom is threatened or obstructed by another, even non-voluntarily, if that threat or obstruction can be removed only by invading that other's fundamental good, it is not only permissible to invade it, but impermissible not to.

In requiring this invasion, Kantian morality claims to be no less absolutist than Catholic morality, as Boyle presents it. However, what is absolutely prohibited, according to it, is not intentionally causing or allowing certain fundamental harms, but voluntarily causing or allowing invasions of lawful freedom. Because of this difference, it does not need double-effect exceptions in order to permit invasions of the fundamental good of those who, voluntarily or not, threaten or obstruct somebody's lawful freedom. Catholic morality does, because, as presented by Boyle, it lacks a counterpart of Kant's subordinate principle that "*Recht* is united with the authorization to use coercion against anyone who violates *Recht*". That is why situations that to Kantian moralists demand that a violator of *Recht*, perhaps a non-voluntary one, be coerced, confront Boyle's Catholic moralists with inescapable choices between unintentional causings of fundamental harms, which they legitimate by recognizing double-effect exceptions. However, except when the unintentional harms between which choices must be made are not proportionate, as killing and (say) knocking unconscious are not, the doctrine of double effect cannot guide choice. Hence in treating cases in which there is a violator of *Recht*, even a non-voluntary one, Kantian theory seems to me superior, especially as in many of them Catholic moralists will in fact recommend what it requires.

Although it is seldom discussed, and Boyle passes over it, Kantian moralists recognize a second large class of cases in which choices must be made between unavoidable fundamental harms: those in which an agent's violation of morality creates a situation in which whatever he does causes such a harm: for example, a surgeon has negligently promised to perform urgent operations at two different places at the same time, and when he finds out, it is too late to find another to do either. In such cases, both Catholics and Kantians agree that the least harm possible be chosen (*minima de malis eligenda*), but there is no double-effect exception. If your own wrongdoing has put you in a situation in which you cannot avoid voluntarily doing evil, you are doubly guilty, both for putting yourself in that situation and for the evil you do in it. That evil is not absolutely unavoidable, as it must be in genuine double-effect cases: it is conditional upon your having done what you could and should have refrained from doing.

5. HOW EXTENSIVE IS THE CLASS OF UNAVOIDABLE FUNDAMENTAL HARMS?

Kantian moralists freely acknowledge that there are two kinds of situation in which causing fundamental harms cannot be avoided: those in which only so can somebody's lawful freedom be safeguarded; and certain of those brought about by the agent's own wrongdoing. In situations of the former kind, they deny the need for double-effect exceptions, on the ground that what is absolutely prohibited is not intentionally invading fundamental goods, but failing to safeguard lawful freedom; and in situations of the latter, they deny their validity, on the ground that the agent could have avoided being in them. If fundamental harms are unavoidable only in situations of one of these kinds, then the Kantian doctrine that double-effect exceptions are superfluous seems to me to merit serious consideration by Catholic absolutists, at least if they agree with Boyle about the nature of human action.

Boyle, however, intimates that the class of unavoidable fundamental harms is much more extensive than that.

Any action which has as a side effect the sort of harming of someone which it is plausible to think absolutely prohibited if brought about intentionally is covered by the Doctrine of Double Effect, and this class of actions is very extensive indeed... (Boyle, 1991, p. 492).

Is it? The answer turns on how extensive is the class of unavoidably harmful side-effects. Boyle argues that it is very extensive, because plans of at least three common kinds involve such side-effects, namely: (i) plans to deflect harms from some to others; (ii) plans for allocating scarce resources; and (iii) plans to reduce harmful processes occurring in patients when the treatment of one such process involves neglecting or even exacerbating the other. If he were right about plans of these three kinds, Boyle would have made out his case; but Kantians contend that he is not. They dismiss (i) as bogus; and although they accept (ii) and (iii) as genuine plans, concerning (ii) they deny that a harm is caused by so allocating resources that it cannot be prevented, given that no other allocation would be more effective; and concerning (iii) they deny that a harm that is a chosen cost is a side-effect, because what is chosen is intended.

The most familiar examples of kind (i), plans to deflect harms from some to others, are invented "trolley cases", in which different individuals or groups have been tied, like the legendary Pauline, to different forks in a railroad down which an unstoppable trolley is approaching. Who among them will be killed depends on which fork it takes; that depends on whether the points at the fork remain as they are or are switched to the other fork; and that, finally, depends on some unfortunate who has one and only one choice: to switch the points (to deflect) or to leave them as they are (not to deflect).

Because *prima facie* their principle forbids deflecting harms from one set of innocents to another as reducing the latter to mere means to the good of the former, Kantians were apt to be discomposed by being mocked as upholding A.H. Clough's satirical commandment:

> Thou shalt not kill; but need'st not strive,
> Officiously, to keep alive.

Needlessly, however. They did not deny that to allow somebody to bleed to death by not applying a tourniquet to an accidentally severed artery is just as wrong as to cut his throat; and they should not have been ashamed to assert that it is wrong for a physician to endanger other innocents by recklessly speeding with help to a patient with a severed artery, even though, by refusing to endanger them, he might allow his patient to bleed to death before he brought help. There is nothing objectionable in the variant of Clough's commandment:

> Thou shalt not kill; but must not strive,
> By wrongful means, to keep alive.

Hence they should have declined to rush to judge imaginary trolley cases. If there has ever been an actual one, I am ignorant of it. A pilot or a truck-driver steering his crashing vehicle to cause the least possible harm does not choose between definite innocents he will harm: he tries to harm none at all. Nor is it hard to see why the literature on the subject avoids real cases. Trolleys crossing points are all too easily derailed, for example by setting the points in mid-position between the two forks; and, unless time is very short, those tied to the tracks (why on both forks?) can be released – helpers will multiply with each release. If it is stipulated that time is very short, how can any reliable judgement be made of what the situation is? And if such a judgement cannot be made, would not switching a railroad's points be culpably reckless? Kantian moralists are entitled to dismiss as bogus any imaginary deflection case that is not presented as comprehensively as a real one would be in any report of it that was credible.

The more comprehensively such cases are described, the more morally relevant information is apt to emerge; and judgements made in the absence of morally relevant information are worthless.

As Boyle points out, plans of his kind (ii), those for allocating scarce resources, structurally differ from those of kind (i) in that they are plans to save some at the price of *letting* others suffer. But that does not go far enough. On a Kantian analysis, all such cases fall under the 'imperfect duty' of benevolence. We each have an absolute duty to do what good we reasonably can, with whatever resources are at our command; but none of us are morally obliged to do more than we reasonably can. Although sometimes several allocations of resources will be equally reasonable, choosing and sticking to one rather than another until a better becomes available does not deny to *anybody* help that can reasonably be given: *all* are helped who reasonably can be. It would be as silly as it would be monstrous to describe a fireman who intentionally follows a reasonable procedure by which he rescues as many people trapped in a burning building as he can rescue, as *causing* the deaths of those he does not, because he could have chosen another reasonable procedure by which some of those rescued would have been different. In intentionally acting on any plan that is as good as possible, he cannot not save some whom he can save on another equally good; but that is not a good reason for not acting on it.

Here I believe I am generalizing Boyle's own objection to Baruch Brody's doctrine that intentionally letting some people die is intentionally killing them: namely, that the intention from which it follows that some people are not given life-saving treatment may not be that they die, but that scarce medical resources may be put to the best use (Boyle, 1991, p. 490). My only complaint is that he does not pursue its implications. The important questions scarce resources raise in medical ethics are about what allocations are reasonable, given that the end is to do as much good as possible, while treating all concerned as ends in themselves. If different allocations are equally reasonable, it is reasonable to choose one of them and stick to it until it is found how to improve upon it. Yet any reasonable plan for allocating scarce resources will set a limit to what can morally be done. A physician who chooses such a plan and sticks to it neither fails to help those he would have helped on the plans he rejects, nor causes the harms they suffer. They are caused by the scarcity of resources, not by how they were allocated; for they could not have been allocated better.

Plans of Boyle's kind (iii) are those in which different kinds of harm to one and the same person are allegedly side-effects of different courses of action between which a choice must be made: for example, between relieving a terminally ill patient's severe pain by analgesics that will probably shorten his life, and refraining from probably shortening his life by leaving his pain untreated.

> In both cases the side effects of taking the action will include the probability of death, but the side effects of the alternatives are also bad, and include some which it is plausible to think [it] would be absolutely impermissible to inflict intentionally (Boyle, 1991, p. 491).

In other words: when it is morally prohibited either intentionally to fail to relieve the patient, or intentionally to make it more probable that his life would be shortened, it is legitimate for a physician either to plan to relieve his pain, with the unintended side-effect of probably shortening his life, or to avoid probably shortening his life, with the unintended side-effect of not relieving his pain. Whichever harm is thus unintentionally caused, is excused by a double-effect exception.

Physicians mindful of the common law doctrine of informed consent, which Catholics as well as Kantians approve, will object that such choices are not theirs, but their patients', and that rational patients will each make them by deciding whether or not the benefit of relief of their pain is greater than the cost of a probable shortening of their lives. That is, they will each make cost-benefit calculations; and, in planning arising from such calculations, each will be confronted with a future in which he must endure one or another of two proportionately harmful processes, and must choose *either* that one be treated at the cost of accelerating the other, *or* that one not be accelerated at the cost of the other's not being treated. Such choices will be intentions that one harmful process be treated or not accelerated at the cost of accelerating or not treating the other. And just as you do not unintentionally part with your busfare in spending it on a glass of beer, so when you deliberately pay the cost of incurring or increasing one harm to yourself in order to obtain the benefit of avoiding or reducing another, you do not pay it unintentionally. In both cases, since paying the cost is as much part of the plan as gaining the benefit, it cannot be excused as an unintended side-effect.

Two conclusions follow. First, no moral system that prohibits *both* not procuring a benefit *and* paying its cost can be rescued from inconsistency by the doctrine of double effect, because costs cannot be paid voluntarily but unintentionally. Nor does Catholic morality, as Boyle presents it, need such rescue; for, since it regards as untreatable any condition of which the effective treatment is morally prohibited, its prohibition of not intentionally treating certain conditions *if they are treatable* cannot require intentional resort to any morally prohibited treatment. Secondly, any moral absolutism that mistakenly regards an individual's planning to obtain benefits as independent of the costs by which he plans to obtain them, and allows payments of costs to be excused as unintended side-effects, can be transformed into a form of good-maximizing consequentialism. Boyle will disarm his theory against such a transformation, unless he repudiates treating costs as unintended side-effects.

6. SUMMING UP

Although he has established that the doctrine of double effect is indispensable in any absolutist theory of morality, like his Catholic one, in which intentionally invading certain fundamental human goods is absolutely prohibited, Boyle seems to me to have exaggerated its importance even in such moralities; for it applies only to cases in which plans to observe one prohibition are made independently of plans to observe another. Kantian moralists must concede not only that Boyle's theory is impressive, but that the practical code that he fallibly derives from it is in the main sound. However, they believe that Boyle himself has succumbed to a danger in the doctrine: that of invoking it in cases in which, on his own theory, it is superfluous or misplaced. Thus it is superfluous in cases in which evils that cannot reasonably be avoided are mistakenly treated as effects of reasonable plans for using scarce resources; and it is misplaced in cases of an individual's choosing to obtain a benefit at the cost of incurring a harm, where incurring the harm cannot be an unintended side-effect.

NOTES

[1] A fuller exposition and defence of my views about the nature of human action may be found in Donagan, 1987. Although Boyle's approach, in which he largely follows Grisez, differs from mine, they seem to me to coincide with respect to causation and intention.

[2] This analysis of action is largely the work of Germain Grisez. It has been adopted by his collaborators John Finnis and Boyle himself. It coincides in many respects with contemporary analytic theories, especially that of Donald Davidson. How it may be put to work in moral theory may be studied at length in the admirable and inevitably controversial treatment of the (now) apparently successful U.S. policy of nuclear deterrence in Finnis, Grisez, and Boyle, 1987.

[3] Theron 1984, p. 76. Theron is criticizing my endorsement (Donagan, 1977, p. 159) of an analysis by Germain Grisez anticipating Boyle's, but he does not refer to Grisez directly.

[4] Theron's bewilderment at my refusal to call martyred Christians suicides betrays either ignorance that actions do not cause voluntary reactions to them, or oblivion that the martyring of Christian confessors is a voluntary reaction by others to their confessions of faith (Theron, 1984, p. 75).

[5] Boyle expressly recognizes that an absolutist interpretation of Kant is possible (Boyle, 1991, p. 493), although he mistakenly concludes that mine is not for a reason examined in note 7 below.

[6] Although my understanding of Kant's absolutism is not that of all Kantians, as Boyle's of Catholic absolutism is not that of all Catholics, it is revisionary only in taking the second of Kant's three formulas of the categorical imperative, the formula of the end in itself, to be fundamental, and not equivalent, as he himself believed, to the first, the formula of the universal law of nature. The reasons I have given for this in Donagan, 1977, still seem to me sound.

[7] Boyle interprets my version of Kantian morality (in Donagan, 1977) as absolutist only in name, on the mistaken ground that it absolutely prohibits only the causing of certain harms *at will* while permitting it in an indefinite set of conditions, arrived at by an "enormously complex and intuitive" procedure (Boyle, 1991, p. 493). Of course, I think my procedure neither intuitive in any sense in which Boyle's for arriving at his list of fundamental harms is not, nor more complex than that of any other moral theory that seriously claims to be complete in outline, including his. But, however that may be, he is flatly mistaken about what I tried to do. I began by determining the kinds of action it is impermissible to do at will only as the first step to specifying the kinds it is impermissible to do under any circumstances. E.g., observing that falsehood at will is absolutely prohibited was my first step towards specifying what lying is (viz., falsehood in free communication, when it is not expected under some convention, e.g., of courtesy); and I concluded that lying is absolutely prohibited.

[8] I have departed from Ladd's translation only in leaving the noun '*Recht*' and cognate expressions untranslated.

When juxtaposed with their absence from absolutist moral theories like Kant's, the paucity of the cases in which the doctrine of double effect is indispensable in theories like Boyle's suggests another possibility. Perhaps the doctrine of double effect, which notoriously did not become explicit until very late, is an intruder in the Catholic moral tradition; and perhaps Kant was not mistaken in failing to discern any fundamental difference between Catholic and Lutheran views of common human morality, and in imagining that his theory captured the essence of both.

REFERENCES

Boyle, J.: 1991, 'Who is entitled to double effect?', *Journal of Medicine and Philosophy* 16, 475–494.
Donagan, A.: 1977, *The Theory of Morality*, Chicago University Press, Chicago.
Donagan, A.: 1987, *Choice: The Essential Element in Human Action*, Routledge and Kegan Paul, New York.
Finnis, J., Grisez, G., and Boyle, J.: 1987, *Nuclear Deterrence, Morality and Realism*, Clarendon Press, Oxford.
Foot, P.: 1978, *Virtues and Vices*, University of California Press, Berkeley, pp. 19–32.
Kant, I.: 1797, *Metaphysik der Sitten*, J. Nicolovius, Koenigsberg, 2 vols. Page references are to Vol. 6 of the Pussian Academy's edition of Kant's works. The translation used is by J. Ladd: 1965, *Kant: The Metaphysical Elements of Justice*, Bobbs-Merrill, Indianapolis.
Quinn, W.: 1989, 'Actions, intentions and consequences: The doctrine of double effect', *Philosophy and Public Affairs* 18, 334–351.
Theron, S.: 1984, 'Two criticisms of double effect', *The New Scholasticism* 58, 67–83.

Part VI
Utilitarianism and Bioethics

CONSEQUENTIALISM, REASONS, VALUE AND JUSTICE[1]

JULIAN SAVULESCU

ABSTRACT

Over the past 10 years, John Harris has made important contributions to thinking about distributive justice in health care. In his latest work,[2] Harris controversially argues that clinicians should stop prioritising patients according to prognosis. He argues that the good or benefit of health care is providing each individual with an opportunity to live the best and longest life possible for him or her. I call this thesis, opportunism. For the purpose of distribution of resources in health care, Harris rejects welfarism (the thesis that the good of health care is well-being) and argues that utilitarianism in general may lead to de facto discrimination against groups of people needing health care. I argue that well-being is a superior theory of the good of health care to Harris' opportunism. Harris' concerns about utilitarianism can be better addressed by: (i) relating justice more closely to reasons for action; (ii) by conceptualising the relationship between reasons for action and the value of the consequences of those actions as a plateau rather than scalar relationship. Justice can be understood as satisfying as many equally rational claims on resources as possible. The rationality of a person's claim on health resources turns on the strength of that person's reasons to promote certain health-related states of affairs. I argue that the strength of that reason does not track the expected value of that state of affairs in a fully scalar fashion. Rather a person can have most reason to promote some state of affairs, even though he or she could promote other more valuable states of affairs. Thus there can be equal reason for a distributor of public resources to save either of two people, even though one will have a better and more valuable life. This approach, while addressing many of Harris' concerns about utilitarianism, does not imply that doctors should give up prioritising patients according to prognosis altogether, but it does allow that patients with lower but reasonable prognosis should have a share of public resources.

---

[1] I would like to thank David McCarthy, Derek Parfit, Tony Hope and especially Klemens Kappel for helpful comments on earlier drafts.
[2] J. Harris, 'What Is the Good of Health Care?' *Bioethics* 10 (1996), pp. 269–291. All page references in parentheses refer to this work.

In Sheffield, England, publicly funded in vitro fertilisation (IVF) is a scarce resource and is available only to women most likely to successfully bear a live child. Roughly, a 30 year old infertile woman has a 15% chance of bearing a child with IVF, but the chance drops by 2/3 by the time she gets to 40, that is, to roughly 5%. On the basis of this observation, older women are effectively not offered IVF. While the primary motive of this distributive procedure is to achieve as good an outcome as possible (maximisation of outcome), the result is that older women are not treated. The prioritisation of individuals according to outcome goes far beyond the allocation of IVF treatment in England. It is probably the most widely used method of prioritising patients.

Such a system is unfair in one sense. Dora, a 40 year old infertile woman, could claim,

> 'I admit that my chance of becoming pregnant is only 5%, but IVF might be successful. That is my only chance. I have paid taxes for 20 years and now when I need the health service, I am denied a chance of effective treatment. Why has a 30 year old woman like Jean who happens to have 3 times my chance of becoming pregnant a greater claim on the services that I contributed to, perhaps even more than she has?'

Indeed, Dora could argue that her need for a child is the same as Jean's. Since their needs are the same, why are they being treated differently?

The theory of distributive justice which motivates much medical decision-making such as that of gynaecologists in Sheffield is utilitarianism. Utilitarianism has three components.[3] The first is an account of what is good. According to welfarism, the predominant account of the good used in health care, the value of a state of affairs is given entirely by the welfare (well-being) of individuals in that state.[4] The second component of utilitarianism is the thesis that actions are to be chosen on the basis of their consequences. This is called consequentialism. Utilitarianism is a version of welfarist consequentialism which requires simply adding up individual's well-being to evaluate consequences. This is the third component and has been called 'sum-ranking'.[5] Both because this terminology is not descriptive for non-specialists and because Harris does not himself use it, I will refer to sum-ranking versions of consequentialism as maximising versions, and all other versions as submaximising versions. Submaximising versions

---

[3] A. Sen, 'Utilitarianism and Welfarism' *Journal of Philosophy* 76 (1979), pp. 463–89.

[4] A. Sen, *Choice, Welfare, Measurement*, (Basil Blackwell, Oxford, 1982), pp. 28, 227.

[5] A. Sen and B. Williams, 'Introduction' in A. Sen and B. Williams, *Utilitarianism and Beyond*. (Cambridge University Press, Cambridge, 1982), p. 4.

of consequentialism include satisficing theories (according to which some states of affairs are good enough to justify promoting them, even though more valuable states could be promoted[6] and versions which give weight to the fairness of distribution of welfare. Utilitarianism is, in my terminology, welfarist maximising consequentialism. When consequences are not certain, utilitarianism requires that we should choose that course of action which maximises expected value, and it is on this basis that utilitarians would treat Jean in preference to Dora.

In what follows, I will argue that Harris advances a new conception of the good. I aim to show that this is implausible, and that the problems with utilitarianism are better understood as being based on an inaccurate relationship between reasons for action and the value of the expected consequences of action.

HARRIS' WORRIES ABOUT UTILITARIANISM

All three elements of utilitarianism – welfarism, consequentialism and maximisation – have attracted scholarly criticism.[7] One widely discussed problem with utilitarianism is that, in the pursuit of maximising welfare, it gives insufficient weight to desert, rights or fairness. It does not matter how welfare is distributed across individuals, as long distribution produces maximum welfare.[8] In this vein, Harris objects that utilitarianism fails to treat people as equals. It results in the systematic neglect of certain groups of individuals in need.[9] His arguments have been directed against the use of Quality Adjusted Life Years (QALYs) as a measure of the good of health care, but they apply equally to all forms of welfarist maximising consequentialism. Consider two of Harris' examples.

In the **life-boat example**, a naval disaster has occurred. Two ships are sinking, one with 13 crew (the big boat) and the other with 6 (the little boat). Utilitarians would save the 13. However, Harris also argues we should save the 13 (281–2).

In the **medical example**, a surgeon has 26 patients on her waiting list who will all die in a couple of weeks if not operated on. She only has time to operate on 13. If she operates on the first 13, A–M, they will all survive; if she operates on the second 13, N–Z, only about half will

---

[6] See below and J. Broome, *Weighing Goods*, (Basil Blackwell, Cambridge, Ma, 1991), p. 7.
[7] Sen and Williams, 'Introduction', pp. 4–5.
[8] J. Rawls, *A Theory of Justice*, (Oxford University Press, Oxford, 1972), p. 26.
[9] See for example, his: 'QALYfying the Value of Life', *Journal of Medical Ethics*, Sept 1987, pp. 117–123; 'More and Better Justice' in ed. J.M. Bell and S.M. Mendus *Philosophy and Medical Welfare*, (Cambridge University Press, Cambridge, 1988); *The Value of Life*, (Routledge, London, 1985).

© Blackwell Publishers Ltd. 1998

survive. Let's say that A–M have appendicitis and N–Z have brain tumours. The surgeon is faced with the choice of saving 13 or 6 lives. A utilitarian would save A–M, those with appendicitis, since this would save the most lives and so produce the most welfare.[10]

According to utilitarianism, we should provide aid so as to maximise human welfare. One consequence of this utilitarian decision procedure is what Harris calls *de facto discrimination*.[11] The utilitarian decision procedure rules those with brain tumours out of eligibility, even though they have similar needs. Indeed, arguably, they are already worst off and suffer a double injustice. In other cases, utilitarianism can be, Harris has claimed, 'economist' (it discriminates against those whose disease is more expensive to treat), racist (it discriminates against racial groups with a poorer prognosis[12]), ageist (discriminating against the old) and sexist.[13] In the case of IVF treatment, it has been observed that lower socio-economic groups have a worse prognosis.[14] Utilitarians would seek out patients from the upper socio-economic classes. Such a system would be classist.[15]

One terminological point. Harris is right to draw attention to the implications of a utilitarian decision procedure. *De facto* discrimination is morally objectionable in one sense. Recently, the age limit for post-doctoral scholarships was increased in the England because it was recognised that the previous limit discriminated against women who take time out to have children. But there was no intention in the original policy to disadvantage women, nor was there any presumption behind this policy that women are in any way less

---

[10] Consequentialism can be stated in a negative form: to act so as to prevent the most harm. In the life-boat case, the choice is between preventing 13 people dying and preventing 6 people dying. Negative consequentialism requires that we prevent the 13 dying. In the medical example, the choice is between 20 people dying and 13 people dying. Negative utilitarians would prevent the 20 people dying.

[11] There are other problems with consequentialism as a theory of distributive justice. See for example, Rawls, *A Theory of Justice.*, Sen and Williams, 'Introduction'. and W. Kymlicka, *Contemporary Political Philosophy*, (Oxford University Press, Oxford, 1990), Chapter 2.

[12] M. Lowe, I.H. Kerridge, K.R. Mitchell, ' "These sorts of people don't do very well": race and allocation of health care resources' *Journal of Medical Ethics* 2 (1995), pp. 356–60.

[13] 'QALYfying the Value of Life'

[14] Ian Cooke, personal communication. Michael Lockwood envisaged this general possibility in 'Quality of Life and Resource Allocation' in Bell and Mendus, *Philosophy and Medical Welfare*, p. 44.

[15] Full-blooded egalitarians could argue that Harris' own intuition that we should save the 13 in the life-boat example is another instance of *de facto* discrimination: 'little boatism' in which people are denied rescue because they happen to be in a little boat rather than a big boat, through no fault of their own.

© Blackwell Publishers Ltd. 1998

worthy of scholarships. Racism is discrimination *based on* race. Terms like ageism, sexism and racism imply a high degree of blame. They are not justified in evaluating utilitarian attempts to secure a just distribution since the intention here is to promote all people's well-being. We should stick to the term '*de facto* discrimination.'[16]

Harris concludes that utilitarian providers and funders of health care will choose those who are easiest to treat, those with the least expensive diseases to treat and those with the best prognosis, skimming the cream of those who are ill. In the limit, those who need health care the most are most likely to be denied it.

OPPORTUNISM

Where does utilitarianism go wrong? Harris' solution is to reject welfarism. He plausibly claims that each rational person wants at least 3 things from health care: (i) the maximum possible life-expectancy *for him or her*; (ii) the best quality of life *for him or her*; (iii) the best opportunity or chance *for him or her* of getting both (i) and (ii) (270). According to his rival theory of the good which I call opportunism,

> the good of health care is a state of affairs which provides people with the best chance or opportunity to achieve what is for them the best life (iii).[17]

As Harris puts it,

> 'The fact that each person *counts* – matters morally, is recognised when their moral claims are respected, and this happens when their chances of continued life are given equal weight with the, necessarily different, chances of anyone else. (282)'

Harris retains a commitment to maximisation (281–2). He writes, 'So the maximising requirement of consequentialism is met when the claims to chances of continued life, of equal numbers of people, are given equal respect (282).'[18] While this is true, it does not capture the scope of maximisation. According to what can be called **opportunist maximising consequentialism**,

> the right course of action is that course of action which **maximises** the number of persons who will receive the opportunity to realise

---

[16] Thanks to Derek Parfit for this example and observation.

[17] While strictly speaking, it is these states which provide opportunity which are good, for brevity I will write as if opportunity itself were the good of health care.

[18] This passage illustrates that Harris assumes that all versions of consequentialism are maximising. On my taxonomy, this is not the case.

what is **the best life for them** (given their situation and all possible courses of action).

In the medical example, an opportunist maximising consequentialist is faced with a dilemma: giving 13 people (A–M) their chance of the best life or giving a different 13 (N–Z) their chance. Harris argues that the surgeon should not prefer those with appendicitis, simply based on prognosis. He raises the possibility of treatment on a 'first come, first served basis' (274,282). In the lifeboat example, an opportunist maximiser should save the 13 (281–2), since this gives the greater number of people their opportunity to live. This example establishes Harris as a maximiser.

In my experience, Harris' intuitions about these two examples are shared by many people. Opportunist consequentialism is consistent with these intuitions. However, I will presently examine these intuitions in detail and offer a more plausible alternative.

Opportunist maximising consequentialism, like utilitarianism, has some counterintuitive implications. For example, it requires giving those with brain tumours the same chance of treatment even if they only have a one in a million chance of cure or if a cure would only result in them living for a few more days. That is absurd.

It is also hard to square Harris' opportunism with his rejection of economism. Imagine that, in the medical example, performing an appendicectomy costs $1000 whereas removing a brain tumour costs $2000. If there were 13 people with each disease but only $13,000 in public resources, saving those who happen to have appendicitis is like saving those who happen to be on the big life boat in the life boat example: given the constraints of our situation, we can give more people their opportunity to live if we go for those with appendicitis. Harris' rejection of economism prevents him from giving preference to those with appendicitis if that disease is cheaper to treat, but I can see no morally significant difference in these examples between the cost of one's disease (which allows distributors of public resources to put that person in one of two groups in which either more or less people are saved) and whether one happens to find oneself be in a big or little boat, with more or less people.

Both welfarist and opportunist maximising consequentialism have counterintuitive implications. However, there are more principled reasons to reject Harris' opportunism.

IS THE GOOD OF HEALTH CARE OPPORTUNITY?

How should we interpret Harris' claim that the good of health care is opportunity? One obvious interpretation is that giving people an opportunity is a constraint on distributive schemes aimed at maximising welfare. That constraint is necessary to promote a just and fair society. It is good *that* people have opportunity. Harris in the past has certainly said this kind of thing. He wrote,

> 'Equality requires both that we treat as many people as we can [the maximising element] and that we ensure so far as possible that certain sorts of people be not systematically ignored.'[19]

> '[W]e have two equally plausible moral principles here [maximising welfare and equality] and that pull in opposite directions. When this is true some means of doing justice to each must be found and it is not enough merely to opt for one.'[20]

This, however, is not very new and many critics of utilitarianism have given variants of this argument. Moreover, Harris himself seems to be saying something new, and not merely restating his old arguments. If he is saying something new and interesting, I think we should understand him literally as saying that the good of health care *is* opportunity, not welfare, and that opportunities are to be distributed among people, as utilitarians distributed welfare. This squares with his talk of the 'benefit' of health care, 'conceptions of the good', and his apparent sympathy for some maximising version of consequentialism, albeit a different one to that employed by clinicians and health economists. Thus Harris concludes, 'While it is true that funders and providers might legitimately wish to take into account the amount of benefit that their money and/or efforts will provide, discounted by the probability of that benefit being achieved. I have argued that there is another perspective to consider and another interpretation of what 'benefit' legitimately means.' (290; see also 274, 281–2)

There are three ways in which Harris' claim that opportunity is literally a good can be interpreted. He might mean that opportunity is good in itself (that is, an intrinsic good) or is a means to other states of affairs which are good in themselves (that is, opportunity is an instrumental good), or both. An example of an intrinsically good state is being happy; an example of an instrumentally good state is having money. Some good states like having knowledge may be both intrinsically good and a means to other intrinsically good states like being happy. In this section I will argue that on any of these

---

[19] 'More and Better Justice', p. 95.

[20] *Ibid.*, pp. 94–5. This is in response to a similar challenge from Michael Lockwood ('Quality of Life and Resource Allocation', p. 54). This is like John Broome's suggestion that we should trade some good for fairness ('Good, Fairness and QALYs' in Bell and Mendus, *Philosophical Medical Welfare*.)

interpretations, Harris' intuitions about these cases cannot be justified.

The claim that opportunity has instrumental value is most easily dealt with and clearly will not justify Harris' intuitions. On this reading, we should interpret the claim that opportunity is good to mean that it has value as a means to prolonging a good life. But if it has only this instrumental value, then what is ultimately good is a good life. Let's give every person's good life the value of 1, with death being 0. Operating on those with brain tumours realises 6 units of value while operating on those with appendicitis realises 13 units. We should operate on those with appendicitis.

However, Harris is best understood as suggesting that opportunity is of value in itself, of intrinsic value.[21] If opportunity is an intrinsic good, then this would distinguish the life-boat from the medical example. When we attempt rescue or medical treatment, we provide opportunity, regardless of outcome. If providing a person with an opportunity counts as value 1, and not providing opportunity is 0, then if we rescue the 13 people in the naval disaster, we provide 13 units of value; if we rescue 6 people, we provide 6 units. If we are to choose that option with the best consequences, we should rescue the 13. If we operate on the 13 patients with brain tumours, we provide 13 units of value; if we operate on the 13 patients with appendicitis, we provide 13 units of value. There is no reason to prefer those with appendicitis over those with brain tumours.

But can opportunity be an intrinsic good? Entering a lottery is a means to our ultimate ends, such experiencing pleasure, achieving worthwhile things with the money and so on. Losers of lotteries often console themselves by pointing out that money did not make the winner any happier. Watching the lottery wheel spin may be fun, but the value of this experience lies in the pleasure it provides, and not in the mere participation in a lottery itself. Chance or opportunity is not of objective intrinsic value.

Some would deny this and claim that there is value in just having a chance. However, Harris himself rejects the concept that chance or opportunity has an objective intrinsic value, as his commitment to the Argument against Potentiality implies. This argument is deployed in the abortion and other debates, and goes something like this:

Premise 1. Potential persons have the same rights as persons.
Premise 2. The fetus is a potential person.

---

[21] Utilitarians can attribute intrinsic value to both the outcomes of an act and the act itself (S. Scheffler, *The Rejection of Consequentialism* (Oxford University Press, Oxford, 1982), pp. 1–2; Broome, *Weighing Goods*, p. 4).

© Blackwell Publishers Ltd. 1998

So, the fetus has the same rights as a person (including a right to life).[22]

Harris has rejected the first premise. '[T]he bare fact that something will become X ... is not a good reason for treating it now as if it were in fact X. We will all inevitably die, but that is ... an inadequate reason for treating us now as if we were dead.'[23] Not only does Harris believe that potential persons do not have the same rights as persons, he also believes that they do not have the same value as persons and on this grounds it is not wrong to kill fetuses.[24] In this context, potential is just another word for chance or opportunity. Harris could not make the claims he does regarding the value of the fetus' life if potential or chance or opportunity to realise something valuable had substantial value in itself.

There is one further way in which opportunity may have intrinsic value. Rather than having an objective intrinsic value, it may have subjective intrinsic value.

VALUING OPPORTUNITY

Harris asserts that a person's life matters 'not because it is a life, but because it is *someone's* life, because her life is an enterprise in which she has, and takes, an interest (282).'[25] The suggestion here is that life *per se* is not of value, but of value to the extent that a person values it.[26] As we have seen, this strategy will not justify Harris' intuitions in the medical example because, even if every patient's life has value of 1, we must discount the value of operating on patients with a brain tumour by the probability that the operation will not achieve that valued outcome.

However, the implication of these claims is that each person *values having the operation to the same degree.* On this view, opportunity is good to the extent that it is valued. Thus, if Tom, who has a brain tumour,

---

[22] *The Value of Life*, p. 11. Strictly, this example is not relevant. It demonstrates that the fact that something will lose value does not justify treating it as if it has already lost that value. However, we are interested in the claim that because something will have a certain value it should be treated now as if it has that value.

[23] *Ibid.*

[24] *Ibid.*, p. 159.

[25] This is similar to Kamm's suggestion that 'we count equally each individual's preference, understood not as the *object* of his preference but as the fact *that he prefers it*' and that the fact that he prefers some state of affairs should make a difference in the process of deciding whether to bring that state of affairs about (F.M. Kamm, 'Equal Treatment and Equal Chances', *Philosophy and Public Affairs*, 14 (1985), pp. 177-194, esp. p. 181).

[26] *The Value of Life*, Ch. 1 and 2.

wants the opportunity to live just as much as Alex, who has appendicitis, this grounds an equal moral claim, regardless of how great their chances are. The relevant difference between the life-boat example and the medical example is that in the former, the choice is between respecting the values of 13 people or 6 people, while in the latter the choice is between respecting the values of 13 people or a different 13 people.

There are several problems with this account of the goodness of opportunity.

(i) It is not the way we value opportunity.

To value opportunity or treatment itself as an end and not as a means would be quite unusual. According to this view, we might value holding a ticket in a lottery not because of the money we might win, but simply for the chance to participate in the lottery. An extreme example of this pattern of concern would be a person who valued entering lotteries, but did not care about the result at all. Seeing that he has won, he walks off, not interested in collecting the prize money. Such a person, perhaps suffering from a psychological disorder, might be said to have missed the point of entering a lottery.

I myself have difficulty understanding how opportunity could have intrinsic value or how one could intelligibly value it for its own sake. Nonetheless, people do value some pretty bizarre things and part of the value of participating in risky sports may be taking risk.[27] And doctors sometimes justify the disastrous result of some medical adventure by saying, 'At least he was given a chance.'

(ii) Present Preferences

On Harris' view, the goodness of a state of affairs is a function of people's desires for that state of affairs. But which desires? Desires we now have or desires we will have? According to a principle of temporal neutrality,[28] if the value of a state of affairs is determined by our desires for that state, we should appeal not only to what people now desire, but also what they will desire. And if we consider future preference satisfaction, we must discount the value of that satisfaction

---

[27] Though more plausibly the contrast with death enhances the value of life. The psychological heuristic of contrast is described in D. Kahneman and C. Varey, 'Notes on the psychology of utility,' in ed. J. Elster and J.E. Roemer, *Interpersonal Comparisons of Well-Being*, (Cambridge University Press, Cambridge, 1991), pp. 127–63.

[28] H. Sidgwick, *The Methods of Ethics*. (Macmillan, London, 1963), p. 111; T. Nagel, *The Possibility of Altruism*. (Clarendon Press, Oxford, 1970), pp. 60, 72.

by the probability of it not occurring. Thus, the value of operating on patients with brain tumours must be reduced by 50% in Harris' medical example.

Harris must reject this kind of temporal neutrality. On his view, what is good is not preference satisfaction *per se*, but present preference satisfaction. Thus Harris' consequentialism is different from preference utilitarianism which counts all preferences, across all times. I note in passing that this theory shares many formal features with the Instrumental and Deliberative Versions of Derek Parfit's Present-aim Theory of reasons for action. According to the Instrumental version, what each of us has most reason to do is whatever would best fulfil our present desires.. Parfit himself goes on to reject this view, as I will suggest we should, in favour of an objective theory, the Critical Present-aim Theory, which I will describe presently.

(iii) Other Present Preferences

But let us assume for argument's sake that the only relevant preferences are present preferences. Even if opportunity has intrinsic value to the extent that it is valued, life itself, if of a certain quality or kind, is also surely valued. So, on a subjective account of value, life is also of value. If life is also presently valued, the moral imperatives derived from the need to save life would direct us, as I have argued, to save those most likely to live.

To illustrate, imagine that we accord equal weight to valued opportunity and valued life. If we treat 10 people with brain tumours, we expect to realise 10 units of opportunity value and 5 units of life value. If we treat 10 people with appendicitis, we realise 10 units of opportunity value and 10 units of life value. We should give priority to those with appendicitis.

(iv) Subjectivism

One significant problem with Harris' view that an outcome is valuable to the extent that individuals value it is that it is a subjectivist account of value. On this view, if an individual does not want to live, her life has no value, and it might not be wrong to kill her. While this may be true if there is some objective reason for her not wanting to live, such as she is racked with incurable pain from imminently terminal cancer, in the absence of such an objective justification, it is absurd to suggest that because someone happens to want to die her life is not of value. Subjectivists have responses to this argument, and I will only signal that I do not believe that a subjectivist account of value is plausible and that objectivist alternatives are practicable.[30] Moreover, there are possible responses to my preceding arguments against the claim that opportunity has value because it is valued. Some of these turn on what it means to treat an individual as an end in himself or herself.[31] For present purposes, the preceding objections are sufficient to call into question the concept of the good of health care as opportunity.

BEYOND OPPORTUNISM

If we do reject the concept of the good as opportunity, there are at least two moves open. One is to give up commitment to maximisation and go for some submaximising form of consequentialism, such as Harris has described in the past, or perhaps even nonconsequentialism. Another strategy would be to further revise the conception of the good. Harris could claim that both welfare and fairness are good. On this approach, a plausible form of consequentialism involves weighing both these goods.[32]

There is much more to be said for these alternatives than I can say here, and there are many ways understanding what it is to treat a person as an equal.[33] But let me signal that I have some doubt that giving weight to fairness as Harris has conceived of it will square with Harris' intuitions about the life-boat and medical examples. Harris elsewhere claims that 'the equality principle demands that each person be given an equal chance of benefiting from health care.'[34] If Harris is to be taken literally, giving significant weight to fairness and equality requires that we give everyone an equal chance of being saved. Fairness, on this view of equality, requires that in choosing whether to save those in the big boat or the small boat, rescuers should toss a coin.[35]

---

[29] D. Parfit, *Reasons and Persons*, (Clarendon Press, Oxford, 1984), p. 117.

[30] J. Savulescu, 'Rational Non-Interventional Paternalism: Why Doctors Ought to Make Judgements of What Is Best for Their Patients', *Journal of Medical Ethics* 21, 6 (Dec 1995), pp. 327-31 J. Savulescu, 'Liberal Rationalism and Medical Decision-Making', *Bioethics*, 11 (1997), pp. 115–129.

[31] F.M. Kamm, *Morality, Mortality*, Part I (Oxford University Press, New York, 1993).

[32] Broome, J. *Weighing Goods*, Chapter 1.

[33] See for example the works by Kamm previously cited.

[34] 'More and Better Justice,' p. 86. This view is shared by Dan Brock ('Ethical Issues in Recipient Selection for Organ Transplantation' in ed. D. Mathieu, *Organ Substitution Technology: Ethical, Legal, and Public Policy Issues*, (Westview Press, Boulder, Colorado, 1988).

[35] J.M. Taurek, 'Should the Numbers Count?' *Philosophy and Public Affairs*, 6 (1977), pp. 293-316. Kamm's response to this paper in both the works cited outlines

I will leave both these possibilities open. I will not address the non-consequentialist literature around equality as respect for persons.[36] Rather, I will offer a version of maximising consequentialism which I believe is closer to what Harris has in mind, and which squares with Harris' intuitions about these cases. But first we need to discuss the relationship between reasons for action and value, and between reasons for action and distributive justice.

REASONS AND JUSTICE

A reason for acting is a fact or circumstance forming a sufficient motive to lead a person to act. Knowing a person's reasons allows us to understand why a person acted as he did. These are explanatory or motivating reasons. For example, a person's reason for buying a lottery ticket might be the fact that he believes that this is his lucky week and he wants to win a large sum of money. Reasons for acting can be good or bad. For example, 'His reason for removing the pollution control device on his car was to reduce petrol consumption, but that wasn't a good reason to do that.' A reason for action is good if it meets a standard, that is, if it conforms to a set of norms governing that behaviour. Good reasons for action are called normative or justifying reasons for action. In what follows, I will only consider normative and not motivating reasons for action.

What is the relationship between a person's normative reasons and her entitlement to health resources? To have a *prima facie* entitlement to health resources, the state which there is reason to promote must be some relevant health-related state, like regaining sight or being free of pain. But it requires more than this.

Justice is concerned with providing what there is good reason to provide for people. Let's say that a person has a rational claim to have some state of affairs, p, promoted if there is good reason to promote p.

---

several other non-consequentialist procedures such as various gambles and majority rule, which claim to treat people as equals without necessarily according everyone an equal chance of being saved.

[36] In particular, her principle of majority rule (*Morality, Mortality* pp. 116ff and 'Equal Treatment and Equal Chances') would justify Harris' intuitions about the life-boat and medical case, if the interests of all those involved in receiving treatment or being saved were the same. However, I have questioned whether the interest in treatment of a patient with a brain tumour (who has a 50% chance of surviving with treatment) is the same as the interest of a person with appendicitis (who has a 100% chance of surviving). I will argue that their reasons for action are the same strength, though the expected value of those actions is different. Kamm herself gives some weight to outcome (at least length of life – 257–260) in the distribution of scarce medical resources. She does not directly address prognosis or chance of good outcome.

According to one version of consequentialism,

C1. the good of health care is satisfying a rational claim for some health-related state.

C2. the right distribution is that distribution which maximises the number of people whose equally rational health-related claims are fully satisfied.

Call this view reasons-based maximising consequentialism, or reasons-based consequentialism for short.[37] According to reasons-based consequentialism, the following claims are true:

C3. If a person (including a distributor of public resources) has equal reason to promote p, q or r, and that person can promote either p and q, or r, then he or she should promote p and q.[38]

C4. If a person, A, has the same strength reason to promote p as another person, B, has to promote q, there is as much reason to promote p as q. Thus, if A has the same strength reason to promote p as B has to promote q, then a distributor of public resources, X, has as much reason to promote p as to promote q.

C3 applied to the life-boat example implies that we should save the 13 rather than the 6, assuming there is equal reason to save each person's life.[39] C3 seems obviously true.

C4 is less obviously true, though I believe it is true. An example of the principle properly specified is that if A (who is a professional footballer) has as much reason to have a knee reconstruction as B (who is a professional tennis player) has to have an elbow reconstruction, then there is as much reason for the distributor of public resources to provide A with resources for a knee reconstruction as there is to provide B with those needed for an elbow reconstruction. The idea is that reasons have a force which is determined by the particular set of circumstances and apply to anyone in a relevantly similar situation. The return of normal function of a joint which is crucial for performing properly in a professional capacity provides a

---

[37] If duties provide reasons, this becomes a very broad reading of consequentialism which encompasses much of deontology. For a similarly broad interpretation, see D. Sosa, 'Consequences of Consequentialism', *Mind*, 102 (1993), pp. 101–22.

[38] Provided, of course, that there are no negative interactive effects between p and q. Both C3 and C4 concern only the agent-neutral component of reasons, as we shall see.

[39] Our intuitions about this example would change if the 13 were patients with terminal cancer expected to die in the next week and the 6 were healthy.

© Blackwell Publishers Ltd. 1998

reason, and that same reason is what should determine allocation of resources to A and B.

C4 is easily misinterpreted and its scope over-extended. Taurek, for example, in an often-cited work, argues that if it is morally permissible to save oneself rather than 5 strangers, then it is morally permissible for another person to save one stranger rather than 5 strangers. Taurek might be interpreted (erroneously) as appealing to something like C4: if (1) there is at least as much reason for A to save A as there is for A to save B-F, then (2) there is at least as much reason for a distributor of public resources, X, to save A as there is to save B-F. Claim (2), however, does not follow claim (1)

Taurek's version of consequentialism involves evaluations of outcomes relative to individuals' own interests (it is permissible for A to save herself rather than 5 strangers), combined with an agent-neutral conception of reasons. An agent-neutral reason applies to any agent in relevantly similar circumstances. Agent-neutral reasons can be specified without making essential reference to the agent.[40] An agent-relative reason applies to some agents in virtue of their relationship with the state to be promoted and make essential reference to the agent. For example, I may have a reason to save X rather than Y and Z because X is my child. However, you may have reason to save Y and Z because they are all strangers to you. Your reason is agent-neutral whereas mine is agent-relative.[41]

Parfit objects that Taurek is really discussing agent-relative reasons when he claims to describing about agent-neutral reasons.[42] The only conclusion one can draw from the claim that A can have as much reason to save himself as 5 strangers is that anyone can have as much reason to save himself as 5 strangers. Thus, at most, all that follows from Taurek's claim (1) that there is as much reason for A to save A as for A to save B-F is (2*) that there is as much for

---

[40] T. Nagel, *The View from Nowhere*, (Oxford University Press, New York, 1986), p. 153.
[41] M. Smith, *The Moral Problem*, (Blackwell, Oxford, 1994), p. 169.
[42] D. Parfit, 'Innumerate Ethics', *Philosophy and Public Affairs*, 7 (1978), pp. 285-301 at p. 287. Parfit uses the term agent-neutral in a later work (*Reasons and Persons*).

This distinction is in some ways unhelpful. All reasons are relative, in that they are relative to the relevant features of the circumstances including relevant features of the agent and his or her relationships. However, all reasons are agent-neutral in that they apply to any agents (irrespective of identity) in those circumstances. Thus if I have reason to save my child rather than two strangers, any father (in relevantly similar circumstances) has reason to save his child rather than two strangers. If you have a reason to save two strangers rather than one stranger, any person has a reason to save two strangers rather than one stranger. These reasons are both agent-relative and neutral.

a distributor of public resources to save himself as there is for him to save B-F.[43]

My claim, C4, refers to the agent-neutral component of a person's reasons. In the example of joint the reconstructions, what I am claiming is that if there is a reason of strength R to provide A with a knee reconstruction and there is a reason of strength R to provide B with an elbow replacement, then there is equal reason for a distributor of public resources to provide A with a knee reconstruction as there is to provide B with an elbow reconstruction. These reasons apply in virtue of the suffering or disability each experiences.[44]

C4 applied to the medical example would support Harris' intuition that we should not prefer those with appendicitis over those with brain tumours if there is as much (agent neutral) reason to treat a person with appendicitis as there is to treat a person with a brain tumour. Is there as much reason to treat patients with brain tumours as there is to treat patients with appendicitis? How are reasons for action related to the expected value of the consequences of that action?

REASON AND VALUE

Harris' move to opportunism was motivated, in part, by (widely-held) intuitions about cases like the medical example. However, I have argued that this thesis has counterintuitive implications and is an implausible account of value. Harris was close, but not spot-on in his diagnosis. A better solution is based on a new understanding of the relationship between reasons and value.

The relationship between reasons and value which is assumed by most discussions of reasons for action is a scalar one: increases in the expected value of action result in roughly linear increases in the strength of our reasons to perform those actions. That is, the more good an action would achieve, the more reason (the stronger) there is to perform the action.[45] On this account, those with brain tumours have less reason to seek out operation than those with appendicitis because they have half the chance of achieving the good outcome (prolonging a good life).

---

[43] Other things being equal, which they would not typically be because distributors of public resources have special duties to B-F which other individuals would not have.

[44] There may of course be other agent-relative reasons but I am not referring to these.

[45] I am not distinguishing in this paper between the strength of reason, the rationality of a reason and the amount of reason.

However, reasons and value may be related in a different, non-scalar way. The relationship may be of a plateau kind such that the strength of reason to act increases as the value promoted by that action increases, until some plateau is reached where strength of reason no longer increases despite increments in value. Thus a person may have most reason to perform some act, even though other actions would promote more value, if the consequences of the chosen act are good enough.

I have argued elsewhere[46] that the relationship between reasons and value is a plateau type on Derek Parfit's Critical Present-aim Theory (CP). The central features of this theory are:

1. each of us has most reason to satisfy his set of rational present desires.
2. a set of rational present desires includes those desires we would have if we knew the relevant facts and were thinking clearly.
3. all intrinsically irrational desires are excluded from this set. An intrinsically irrational desire is a desire which is in no sense worth achieving.[47]
4. all rationally required desires are included in this set. A rationally required desire is a desire which each of us has reason to cause to be fulfilled, whether or not we actually have this desire.[48]
5. the set of desires is itself not irrational (e.g., no inconsistent or intransitive preferences).[49]

Elsewhere,[50] I have argued that according to the Critical Present-aim Theory:

- for a choice or act to be rational, the state of affairs promoted by that choice or act must be worth promoting. That is, it must promote some objectively valuable state such as well-being, achievement, knowledge, justice, and so on.
- the state of affairs promoted must have an expected value which is good enough relative to other available alternatives.
- we are not rationally required to give up a concern for one objectively valuable state which is good enough for a relevantly

---

[46] J. Savulescu, 'The Present-aim Theory: A Submaximizing Theory of Reasons?', *Australasian Journal of Philosophy*, forthcoming.
[47] Parfit, *Reasons and Persons*, p. 122.
[48] *Ibid.*, p. 131.
[49] *Ibid.*, p. 119. Framing CP in terms of desires and aims is potentially misleading. CP is an objective theory of reasons for action. What generates a reason is the objective value of the object of that aim.
[50] Savulescu, 'The Present-aim Theory: A Submaximizing Theory of Reasons?'

different state which is more valuable. Some present rational concerns are good enough.

Thus, I said that CP is a 'submaximising' theory of reasons for action, that is, a theory which allows that a person can have most reason to act in some way even though other actions would realise more value. Submaximisation has been proposed by some philosophers as being rational and morally acceptable,[51] but, as Harris notes, it is generally argued to be irrational.[52] I have here described the relationship between reasons and value as plateau rather than submaximising to avoid confusion with a submaximising theory of justice. These are different, and one can be (as I am) a submaximiser about individual reason for action but a maximiser about justice.

The Present-aim Theory, when interpreted this way, gives some weight *to what agents now actually care about*.[53] Can an individual have most reason to promote a states of affairs which has less value than other states of affairs which she could promote?

I have given arguments elsewhere[54] that she can. Here is a one example. Imagine that Peter's wife, Andrea, becomes an alcoholic. If Peter stayed with her, he could help her, and their relationship would be good in some ways. However, it would be a difficult life, and they would probably not be able to bring up children together. If he left her, he could love an old friend, Mary. They would have a rich and happy relationship, and be able to have and care properly for children. Loving Mary would likely produce more value for him and overall. If Peter chose to stay with Andrea, his justification would be, in part, that Andrea happens to be the woman he now actually cares about.

Let's assume that, if Peter left Andrea for Mary, Peter's pattern of concern would change and he would care most for Mary. If Peter is rationally justified in staying with Andrea, there is at least as much reason for Peter to love Andrea as there is for him to love Mary. My claim is that Peter is rationally justified in staying with Andrea, if she is the person he most cares about.

---

[51] M. Slote, 'Satisficing Consequentialism', *Proceedings of the Aristotelian Society*, Suppl. 58 (1984) pp. 139-63. M. Slote, *Common-Sense Morality and Consequentialism*, (Routledge and Kegan Paul, London, 1985). M. Stocker, *Plural and Conflicting Values*, (Clarendon Press, Oxford, 1990), Part IV.

[52] P. Pettit, 'Satisficing Consequentialism', *Proceedings of the Aristotelian Society*, Suppl. 58 (1984), pp. 164-76.

[53] For a number of examples, see Savulescu, 'The Present-aim Theory: A Submaximizing Theory of Reasons?'

[54] *Ibid.*

230   JULIAN SAVULESCU

FROM REASON AND VALUE TO JUSTICE

If the relationship between reasons and value is a plateau one, this has important implications for distributive justice. Imagine that only the following conditions obtain:

1. there is a distributor of public resources who can promote either p or q, but not both.
2. A has at least as much reason to promote p (because that is what she now cares about) as she would have to promote q (if that were what she cared about).
3. A could change her pattern of concern to care about q (A*).
4. q is more valuable than p.

If A can have most reason to promote p if that is what she most cares about, then according to C4, the distributor of public resources can have most reason to provide A with the resources so that p rather than q is promoted, if that is what A wants, and this does not conflict with other people's rational claims.

Here is a medical example. Imagine that A must have an operation on his spine. If the operation is performed one way, there will be no damage to the nerves to his legs but A will certainly be impotent. If another operation is performed, A will not be impotent but there will be a small chance that he will be left paralysed. A is 48 years old and values his potency. He chooses to have the operation which will preserve his potency. Now it may be that it is better to be impotent than paralysed by a long way (let's assume that it is), and that this choice does not maximise expected value. Nonetheless, it may be the choice A has most reason to make. If that is so, distributors of public resources should not require him to have the operation which will avoid paralysis with certainty.

Distributors of public resources should not require that agents change what matters most to them, provided that the object of that pattern of concern is worth achieving and good enough relative to other alternatives. But, *a fortiori*, agents should not be required to give up altogether what matters most to them (unless it is not worth achieving) for the sake of what matters to *others* in order to maximise value.

Imagine now that the following conditions obtain:

1. there is a distributor of public resources who can promote either p or q, but not both.
2. A has most reason to promote p and B has most reason to promote q.
3. q is more valuable than p.

If the preceding argument is correct, the distributor can have as much reason to provide A with the resources so that p is promoted as she can to provide resources to B to promote q. To use the preceding example, if A and B both have the same disorder, and A prefers to have the potency-preserving operation, and B prefers to have the paralysis-avoiding operation, distributors should not prefer B to A, even if the expected value of B's choice is greater.

C4 implies:

> A distributor of public resources can have the same strength reason to promote A in p (if that is what A most cares about) as to promote B in q (if that is what B most cares about), even if q is more valuable than p.

There are limits to this principle. When the expected value of one option greatly outweighs the expected value of another option, we are rationally required to choose the former. Thus while it may be up to A to choose between the potency-preserving operation and the paralysis-avoiding operation, distributors of public resources are not required to provide resources for A to have a herbal therapy of no benefit, even if A strongly desires this. Thus, the difference between the expected value of treating A and the expected value of treating B must be below some threshold or limiting amount, or else there is more reason to treat B.

If C4 and its implications are true, these together would justify Harris' intuitions about the medical example. Can we find other support for it? Consider a related but slightly different example. Two 70 year old men have cancer and will die without treatment. Each loves his family dearly. In each case, the man's family is grown up, but they are poor. Each old man is trying to decide whether to use all his remaining assets to pay for a new experimental treatment. If he spends his remaining assets, his family will be worse off, and this weighs heavily with him. With treatment:

> Man A has a 1/50 chance of survival.
> Man B has a 1/100 chance of survival.

Each asks, in a state of genuine uncertainty, 'What should I do?' Let's assume that each decides to take a chance on life.

Now my intuition about this case is that there is as much reason for each man to choose a chance on life rather than his family's welfare. Each has the same reason to bequeath money to his family. So, the reason giving force of a chance of continued life is the same for each, even though the chances are different.[55]

---

[55] An alternative explanation of these intuitions is that in each case the chance of life is so much greater in value than providing for one's family that setting aside

If you do not share the intuition that each is equally rational in choosing a chance of life, change the relevant probabilities to 1/50 and 1/51. At some point, the probabilities are so close that any difference is not relevant to the old man's reasons in this situation. There is a range of probabilities which are so close to 1/50, say, that the difference is not relevant to rational deliberation. For example, it may be down to 1/55, or 1/60, or 1/100, or 1/200. The point is that reasons are not so fine grained as to be sensitive to small changes in expected value.

Compare these men to Man C. He has the same disease, the same assets and the same concern for his family. However, he has a 1/1 000 000 chance of survival. Man C is relevantly different to Men A and B. If Man C cares greatly about his family's welfare, he should not spend his money on the experimental treatment. The expected value of the operation is so small that the strength of his reason to have the operation is weaker.

Importantly, whether the expected value of a course of action is good enough to justify performing that action depends on the expected value of the alternatives. If Man C did not have a family, he would have most reason to spend his money on the treatment. But not, I am suggesting, as much reason as A and B. In deciding whether to distribute resources to Man A, B or C, I am claiming that there is as much reason to provide resources to Man A as there is to Man B, but less reason to treat C.

To return to Harris' medical example, whether there is equal reason to treat those with appendicitis as those with brain tumours turns on whether individuals with appendicitis have as much reason to seek treatment as individuals with brain tumours. Here, Harris' intuitions may be justified. It seems plausible to suggest that if operation for brain tumour had a 50% chance of success then those with brain tumours have as much reason to seek treatment as those with appendicitis. They could plausibly say that it is their only chance at their own life, and 50% success is enough.

What are the limits to this principle? When is one option of lesser value good enough compared to other options? Kamm suggests that '[o]nly equal or approximately equal individual interests or rights should be matched against each other in deciding who or what may

---

one's family tells us nothing of the relative reason-giving force of the chosen alternative. But this does not seem to me to be a case of this kind. In each case, the alternative of bequeathing the money to the family is roughly of similar reason-giving force to taking a chance on prolonging one's own life. That is why it is a dilemma for each man.

be a contestant for a good'.[56] She notes that 'the fact that someone values his own cut-off toenail as much as someone's life is not thought ... to make it morally acceptable for him not to give up the toenail to save a life.'[57] Kamm describes this as an objective constraint on the subjective weight we give to our own interests.

Taurek, for example, suggested that it would be permissible to prevent one person losing her arm rather than prevent one person dying.[58] Parfit, in what has been taken to be an endorsement of maximisation (289), denies this claim.[59] He and probably Harris (289) believe that there is more reason to save lives than limbs. Some people, however, choose to die rather than lose a limb. Is a person who chooses an operation for some serious spinal condition with a 10% chance of death in preference to another operation with a 10% chance of loss of limb irrational? It is hard to see that he is.

Kamm draws the line differently to Parfit and Harris. She claims that it would be rational for a person to give more weight to his own legs than another person's life, though (citing an observation of Parfit's) that same person would be rational if he chose to give up his legs to save another's life. My claim is that saving legs and preserving life both provide an equal reason for action, and are good enough relative to each other to ground an equal claim to health care resources. While Kamm believes that the loss a person's legs can be compared with the loss of a life, she believes that the loss of an arm cannot be compared with the loss of a life.[60] There is more work to be done in determining which options are good enough compared to available alternatives.

There are, of course, many situations arising in real life which are outside the scope of C2 and reasons-based consequentialism. What

[56] Kamm, *Morality, Mortality*, p. 148.
[57] *Ibid.*, p. 153.
[58] Taurek, 'Should the Numbers Count?'
[59] Parfit, 'Innumerate Ethics'.
[60] Kamm, *Morality, Mortality*, p. 154. She states that 'an arm and a life do differ too radically.'

While Kamm's approach is non-consequentialist, mine is consequentialist. Our views may differ in other ways. On Kamm's preferred analysis of interests, subjectivism, for the losses of A and B to be comparable, what A would lose must be as important to A as what B would lose would be to B (and these losses are roughly objectively comparable, *Ibid.*, p. 154). On Kamm's view, if A happens to care less about the loss of his legs than B (say, he is more stoic), though A still most wants to keep his legs, there is a reason for a distributor of public resources to give preference to B because B's loss is more important to him. On my view, the loss of one's legs in relevantly similar circumstances provides an equal reason for action (provided that a person cares more about that loss than other alternatives). Our views differ on the life-boat case, with Kamm's preferred analysis of interests, subjectivism, requiring that everyone be given equal chances or proportional chances (*Ibid.*, p. 156).

© Blackwell Publishers Ltd. 1998

should be done when there are insufficient resources and we have a group of people who have equally rational claims which can be either partially or fully satisfied? For example, we could save A for 10 years, or B for 10 years, or A and B each for 6 years. When outcomes are comparable, like being saved for 6 or 10 years, we should defer to individual autonomy: would A (and B) prefer a 50% chance of surviving 10 years or a certainty of 6 years? The question here is whether a 50% chance of 10 years provides the same reason for action as a certainty of 6 years, and this is, I believe, a matter of individual judgement, which should be accommodated as far as possible.

Secondly, what should be done when not all individual claims on resources are equally strong? For example, we could save A for 10 years or B–Z for 6 months. Here there are at least two alternatives:

1. the priority view: we should satisfy those first whom individually there is most reason to save.[61]
2. the additive view: would be to give some but less weight to less rational claims and these claims can be summed together.

I am attracted to the priority view but I will not argue for this here.

OPPORTUNIST OR REASONS-BASED CONSEQUENTIALISM?

Reasons-based consequentialism avoids one absurd implication of Harris' argument: that any chance of good life, no matter how small, justifies a claim on resources. Thus, in the medical example, if those with brain tumours had only a 0.1% chance of survival, it would be appropriate to give preference to patients with appendicitis. That chance is too small compared to the certainty of saving patients with appendicitis.

It is worth noting that reasons-based consequentialism will not avoid one of Harris' criticisms of utilitarianism: the charge that it is economist. But nor, as I previously noted, will Harris' preferred solution: opportunist consequentialism. Economism cannot be avoided if we aim to maximise the satisfaction of the legitimate claims which people have on public resources. The cost of treatment may put a person in a group, in the same way as happening to find himself in a

---

[61] Is this still a version of consequentialism? I am not sure. It may be that the satisfaction of rational claims of differing strength are non-comparable goods and that consequentialism can accommodate a lexical priority to goods. That is, if A and B are non-comparable goods, and A has lexical priority to B, we should maximise A before we maximise B.

small life-boat puts a person in a group, a group in which, because of the circumstances, there is less reason for distributors of public resources to save than other groups.

FINAL REMARKS

Harris argues that utilitarianism unfairly neglects the claims of some people in its quest to maximise welfare. In his most recent contribution, Harris suggests that doctors should give up prioritising patients according to prognosis. Harris argues that the good of health care is opportunity. However, I have argued that this approach is problematic on several grounds. I have offered a different alternative: reasons-based maximising consequentialism. Justice, I have argued, involves giving weight to individual's reasons, and what is expected to be good them. On the conception of justice which I favour, distributors of public resources should seek to maximise the satisfaction of equally rational health-related claims which people make on those resources. However, reasons themselves are not tied to the expected value of actions in a scalar (maximising) way, but rather there is a plateau (submaximising) threshold relationship. There can be equal reason to save each of two people, even though the expected value of saving each is different. This approach requires that we give preference to the best prognosis patient in preference to someone with a *much worse* prognosis, but that when prognoses are comparable, we are not rationally required to provide treatment to the patient with the best prognosis.

Centre for Human Bioethics
Monash University

JUSTICE AND EQUAL OPPORTUNITIES IN HEALTH CARE

JOHN HARRIS*

ABSTRACT

The principle that each individual is entitled to an equal opportunity to benefit from any public health care system, and that this entitlement is proportionate neither to the size of their chance of benefitting, nor to the quality of the benefit, nor to the length of lifetime remaining in which that benefit may be enjoyed, runs counter to most current thinking about the allocation of resources for health care. It is my contention that any system of prioritisation of the resources available for healthcare or of rationing such resources must be governed by this principle.

This can have apparently paradoxical conclusions in that it can seem wasteful to give someone with a very slim chance of a lifesaving treatment the same priority as someone with a much better chance. In an important and thoughtful recent paper, Julian Savulescu has concentrated on this apparent weakness and has argued for a particular conception of the good or benefit to be achieved by a healthcare system which purports to demonstrate the inadequacies of an equal opportunities approach to prioritisation and to replace it with an altogether better account. This paper will show that a rational 'reasons based consequentialism' is more in line with the equal opportunities approach, which I defended some time ago in these pages, than with that of Savulescu. I shall then examine more closely the conception of equal opportunities in health care and show that if we give weight to an individual's reasons, and what is expected to be good for them, we will opt for exactly the equality based account of distributive justice that I have recommended.

The principle that each individual is entitled to an equal opportunity to benefit from any public health care system, and that this entitlement is proportionate neither to the size of their

* Thanks are due to two anonymous referees for *Bioethics*.

chance of benefitting, nor to the quality of the benefit, nor to the length of lifetime remaining in which that benefit may be enjoyed, runs counter to most current thinking about the allocation of resources for health care. It is my contention that any system of prioritisation of the resources available for healthcare or for rationing such resources must be governed by this principle.

This principle can lead to apparently paradoxical conclusions in that, for example, it can seem wasteful to give someone with a very slim chance of a lifesaving treatment the same priority as someone with a much better chance. I set out the above ideas in this journal some time ago,[1] and in an important and thoughtful recent paper,[2] Julian Savulescu has concentrated on this apparent weakness and has argued for a particular conception of the good or benefit to be achieved by a healthcare system which purports to demonstrate the inadequacies of my approach and to replace it with an altogether better account.

Savulescu identifies my theory of the good of healthcare as providing each individual with an opportunity to live the best and longest life possible for him or her, and dubs this theory 'opportunism'. Savulescu notes that for the purposes of distribution of resources, I reject welfarism (the thesis that the good of health care is well-being) and that I have argued that utilitarianism in general may lead to *de facto* discrimination against groups of people needing health care. It is true that I do reject the thesis that the good of healthcare is well-being, but if welfare is defined in terms of *preference satisfaction* as it very often is, then what I have to say about equal opportunities in health may well be compatible with welfarism thus conceived.[3]

Savulescu argues that well-being is a superior theory of the good of health care to mine and that the weaknesses of utilitarian approaches that I have identified can be better addressed in two ways, by: (1) relating justice more closely to reasons for action and (2) by conceptualising the relationship between reasons for action and the value of the consequences of those actions as a

---

[1] John Harris 'What Is the Good of Health Care?' *Bioethics* 10:4 1996 269–291. Justine Burley and Søren Holm have made helpful comments on an earlier draft of this paper. The author thanks the *European Commission* (DG XII) for a project grant, which made this work possible.
[2] Julian Savulescu, 'Consequentialism, Reasons, Value and Justice' *Bioethics* 12:3. 1998. 212–235.
[3] See for example Amartya Sen, 'Well-Being, Agency and Freedom', *Journal of Philosophy* 82, 1985. 187ff. See also G.A. Cohen 'On the Currency of Egalitarian Justice', *Ethics* 99. 1989 pp. 906–909.

394 JUSTICE AND EQUAL OPPORTUNITIES

plateau rather than as a scalar relationship. Justice, Savulescu suggests, can be understood as satisfying as many equally rational claims on resources as possible and that the rationality of a person's claim on health resources turns on the strength of that person's reasons to promote certain health-related states of affairs.

Savulescu's point is that 'the strength of that reason does not track the expected value of that state of affairs in a fully scalar fashion. Rather a person can have most reason to promote some state of affairs, even though he or she could promote other more valuable states of affairs. Thus there can be equal reason for a distributor of public resources to save either of two people, even though one will have a better and more valuable life.' Savulescu's claim is that this 'approach, while addressing many of Harris's concerns about utilitarianism, does not imply that doctors should give up prioritising patients according to prognosis altogether, but it does imply that patients with lower, but reasonable prognosis should share in public resources'.

The concentration on a reasons based solution to problems of allocation has many attractions and is worth pursuing. I shall first show that a rational 'reasons based consequentialism' is more in line with my 'equal opportunities for health' than with Savalescu's position. I shall then examine more closely the conception of equal opportunities in health care that is at issue between us and show that if we give weight to an individual's reasons, and to what is expected to be good for them,[4] we will opt for exactly the equality based account of distributive justice that I have recommended.

REASONS BASED CONSEQUENTIALISM

What does a rational person have good reasons to promote?

If we ask what state of affairs I (or anyone) has most reason to promote, an obvious answer would be our own survival.[5] It surely must always be *rational* for someone who wants to live to choose a chance of continued survival over earlier death, even where the survival period will be relatively short or where the chances of survival are slim, so long as the life to be continued will likely be of acceptable quality. The *strength* of the agent's reason will be relative to the desire to live or to the fear of death, not to the

---

[4] Savulescu 1998 p. 235.
[5] We'll ignore cases in which our survival is incompatible with that of someone we care deeply about.

chances of survival. If the chances of my survival are slim, I may be irrational to believe that I *will in fact* survive, but I surely am not irrational to take any chance of survival that offers, unless other costs to me (or to things I ought to value more, or would be irrational not to value more,) are greater. And here, of course, the strength of the desire to take a chance on life need not be proportional to the chances of that desire being realised.

We should note that while pursuing goals with scant chance of success is often an irrational activity, it is *so because there are better* (more rational) *uses of one's time*. So it would be irrational for a person to pursue a course of professional training if there were very little prospect of gaining anything useful from it. But if it is irrational, it is so because there are better (more likely successful) uses of that person's time, the course is literally time wasted. But where what is pursued is continued existence, which is the *sine qua non* of the pursuit of almost all other goals, it can hardly be irrational or unreasonable to pursue life however slim the chance. There are no more rational uses of that person's time for that person is pursuing time itself,[6] nor are there more rational goals he might pursue, for what he is pursuing is the condition of almost all other objectives he may have. A slim chance of something[7] is always better (more objectively rational) than a certainty of nothingness.

Reasons and Justice

Savulescu sets out a plausible account of reasons-based justice and applies it to health related claims. Savulescu outlines his position as follows, and I will quote in sufficient detail to make the subtlety of his argument clear:

> Justice is concerned with providing what there is good reason to provide for people. Let's say that a person has a rational claim to have some state of affairs, p, promoted if there is good reason to promote p. According to one version of consequentialism,
>
>> C1. The good of health care is satisfying a rational claim for some health-related state.
>> C2. The right distribution is that distribution which maximises the number of people whose equally rational health-related claims are fully satisfied.

[6] With apologies to St. Augustine!
[7] If desired.

396 JUSTICE AND EQUAL OPPORTUNITIES

Call this view reasons-based maximising consequentialism for short. According to reasons based consequentialism the following claims are true:

> C3. If a person (including a distributor of public resources) has equal reason to promote p, q or r, and that person can promote either p and q, or r, then he or she should promote p and q.

> C4. If a person, A, has the same strength reason to promote p as another person, B, has to promote q, there is as much reason to promote p as q. Thus, the distributor can have as much reason to provide A with the resources so that p is promoted as she can to provide resources to B to promote q. To use the preceding example...

> A distributor of public resources can have the same strength reason to promote A in p (if that is what A most cares about) as to promote B in q (if that is what B most cares about), even if q is more valuable than p.

There are limits to this principle. When the expected value of one option greatly outweighs the expected value of another option, we are rationally required to choose the former... Consider... a related but slightly different example. Two 70 year old men have cancer and will die without treatment.

[Each loves his family dearly, the treatment is expensive and will leave each with little to bequeath]

Man A has a 1/50 chance of survival.
Man B has a 1/100 chance of survival.

> [M]y intuition about this case is that there is as much reason for each man to choose a chance on life rather than his family's welfare...[8]

Compare these men to Man C. He has the same disease, the same assets and the same concern for his family. However, he has a 1/1000000 chance of survival. If Man C cares greatly about his family's welfare, he should not spend his money on the experimental treatment. The expected value of the operation is so small that the strength of his reason to have the operation is weaker...[9]

---

[8] This is an astonishing claim for someone sporting utilitarian credentials because *any* gain in utility is a gain in utility!

[9] Ibid. p. 232.

Savulescu says of man C who has only 1/1000000 chance of survival: 'The expected value of the operation is so small that the strength of his reason to have the operation is weaker'. But this is neither true nor plausible unless stipulated so to be. The value of the operation is as great as it could conceivably be, it is a life saving operation, it is C's only chance of continued life, just as for A and B who have a 1/50 and 1/100 chance respectively. On the view of what each stands to gain the value is equal, it is the value of a chance of survival versus the value of no chance of survival. True, C will not be rational if he believes that he has a *good chance* of survival, but then neither will A or B. True, also, C has a much worse chance of survival than A or B. I have suggested that in cases like this the value of the operation to A, B or C is the value of a chance of survival. The moral reason to afford any of them that chance is simply that equality demands it. The requirement that each person is shown the same concern, respect and protection as is shown to any, requires that the life of each person be equally respected. In this sort of case, I have suggested, this means giving to each his or her chance,[10] whatever that chance may be.[11]

Perhaps Savulescu has a false analogy in mind here. If I am faced with a choice between rival therapies for the same condition, and one has a much greater chance of success than the other, I have a stronger reason to prefer the therapy that offers the best chance. But this case tells us nothing about 'stronger reasons' when we are comparing not a slim chance with a fat chance, but a slim chance with no chance at all; or when the slim and the fat chances fall to different people.

Savulescu, like many before him, is playing fast and loose with the meaning of the crucial phrase 'expected value'. He started by using the term 'expected value' to refer to the *magnitude or importance* of the benefit to be achieved by treatment, not to the *likelihood* of the benefit being realised. I agree with Savulescu when 'expected value' refers to magnitude and importance of the benefit. I have always maintained, as Savulescu concedes, that for example, life saving procedures are usually to be preferred to life enhancing procedures, precisely because of the magnitude of

---

[10] If that chance is wanted or claimed.

[11] Remember, although it may be hard to calculate, each claimant on health resources has, in fact, a different chance of benefit so any requirement to give all an equal chance cannot coherently refer to size of benefit or to the magnitude of the chance of obtaining that benefit unless equal just means 'proportional to size of benefit'.

398 JUSTICE AND EQUAL OPPORTUNITIES

the benefit.[12] And I also agree with him that except where differences in magnitude are clear and sizeable it is better to respect a person's own preferences. Thus a distributor of public resources can have the same strength reason to promote what A most cares about as to promote what B most cares about, even if one is more valuable than the other.

I have argued that the value of someone's life either cannot, or should not, be proportional to their life expectancy, nor to their chances of achieving that expectancy.[13] There are many reasons for this and here I will mention two. Genome analysis will soon be able to reveal, at conception or birth, many reliable differences between individuals with respect to their life expectancy and their chances of continued existence when genetically predicted illnesses take hold. It would surely be invidious to distinguish between individuals on this basis, not least because it would amount to renunciation of the equality principle. If equality of consideration varies with life expectancy or chances of successful treatment and these are for everyone unique, then the value of each life is different, not equal.

Savulescu partly accepts this but believes that really slim chances change the game, a 1/1000000 compared with a 1/100 chance for example. There is some plausibility to this, but there are a number of problems too. First, I doubt there would be any consensus about how small a chance carries with it loss of equality of status.[14] Many would think 1/100 chance is far too small. What rational person would play 'Russian Roulette' where the chance is 1/6? The answer of course is it depends what is at stake. No rational person would play for a 1/6 chance of death, but when it is the only chance of life why not take even a 1/1000000 chance? It can't be irrational to take such a chance, although it may be selfish when costs to others are included in the calculation. In

---

[12] Savulescu, like several of my other critics, seems unable to distinguish between situations where life is at stake and situations where a person will survive with better or worse quality of life. In the former case it is always rational to take a very small chance on life, in the latter it may be rational to discount the value of the various outcomes with the probability of achieving them.

[13] See for example my 'More & Better Justice' in Sue Mendus and Martin Bell Eds. *Philosophy And Medical Welfare*, Cambridge, University Press, 1988. 75-97. 'QALYfying the value of life' in *The Journal of Medical Ethics* Vol.13 No 3. September 1987. p. 118. 'Could we hold people responsible for their own adverse health?' in *The Journal of Contemporary Health Law and Policy* Vol. 1 1996. 100–106. 'What the principal objective of the NHS should *really* be' in *The British Medical Journal* 314. 1st March 1997. And my *The Value of Life* Routledge & Kegan Paul 1985.

[14] For that's what it amounts to.

such a case, the argument must be about enforcing 'altruism' or about the objectivity of the size of the benefits, that is about the superiority of a maximising consequentialism.

But reasons based maximising consequentialism, of the sort espoused by Savulescu, cannot help here because it implies that the rationality of reasons for doing x is proportionate to the likelihood of achieving x; but this depends on what is at stake and what the alternatives are. When life is at stake and one alternative offers a chance of life (and there are no other alternatives which offer any chance of continued existence for the agent) then, arguably, any chance is worth having and therefore rational. This will be true unless the reasons the agent has to give others a chance of rescue are for some reason stronger than those she has to save her own life.

II. EQUAL OPPORTUNITIES AND DISTRIBUTIVE JUSTICE

Savulescu suggests that if I am saying 'something new and interesting, I think we should understand [Harris] literally as saying that the good of health care *is* opportunity not welfare, and that opportunities are to be distributed among people, as utilitarians distributed welfare'.[15] He then identifies three ways in which opportunity as a good might be interpreted and finds fault with all of them. These are, crudely, that opportunity might be an intrinsic good, an instrumental good or what he calls a subjective intrinsic good. He points out, rightly, that each of the first two alternatives is flawed if strictly and exclusively interpreted. However, I am not claiming that equal opportunities for health care are either intrinsic or instrumental goods, they are *both and more*, like other accounts of the moral requirement for equal opportunities.

A denial of equal opportunities is a slap in the face; it is an existential rejection disproportionate to the value of the good or welfare that the opportunity might have afforded. So it is not the case that the opportunity is valuable only for what it is an opportunity to do or to be, nor is it merely valuable in itself. Equal opportunities recognise the existential or intrinsic value of people, they are neither simply intrinsic goods nor are they simply instrumental. Rather it is the case that the keeping open of opportunities is expressive of, and recognises that the person's objectives (whatever they are — however trivial or important) matter. When people champion equal opportunities in

---

[15] Savulescu 1998, pp. 217–218.

400 JUSTICE AND EQUAL OPPORTUNITIES

education, or to use public utilities (buses, for example, or lavatories) the liberty is not valuable in proportion to the importance of the particular object of the liberty (to make a journey by bus or wash your face). They are important because the denial of them is a rejection of equality and therefore an affront to human dignity.

Counting and discounting

Savulescu[16] attributes to me the suggestion that 'life *per se* is not of value, but of value to the extent that a person values it.' I stand by this remark so far as it goes. Savulescu goes on to claim that 'this strategy will not justify Harris' intuitions in the medical example because, even if every patient's life has value of 1, we must discount the value of operating on patients... by the probability that the operation will not achieve the valued outcome'.[17] Savulescu believes that the 'implication of these claims is that each person *values having the operation to the same degree*. On this view, opportunity is good to the extent that it is valued. Thus, if Tom, who has a brain tumour, wants the opportunity to live just as Alex, who has appendicitis, this grounds an equal moral claim, regardless of how great their chances are.' And Savulescu interprets this position as amounting to 'holding a ticket in a lottery not because of the money we might win, but simply for the chance to participate in the lottery'. But this is surely wrong. Tom has more than a chance of *participating*, and he wants more; he has and wants a chance of *winning*, winning the thing that matters most to him, his continued existence.

Of course, the opportunity of the operation is valued because it is seen as a means to continued existence. Tom and Alex each want *the same thing*, a chance of continued existence; although for each the chance is different and for each continued existence will be different (different length, different quality etc.). This no more shows that what each wants must be discounted for its peculiar value than does the fact that each human being is different show that the value of life is different for each and hence that there can be no such thing as a principle of equality.

To assert 'even if every patient's life has a value of 1, we must discount the value of operating on patients by the probability that the operation will not achieve the valued outcome' involves a

[16] Ibid. p. 219.
[17] Ibid. p. 220.

fundamental fallacy. If every opportunity had to be discounted by the probability that it will achieve its objective there could be absolutely no claim to the equality of public provision of anything. Education is effective in proportion to the intelligence, ability to concentrate, application, capacity for hard work etc. of each and every student and these are different for each and every student. Access to education must be finely graded accordingly. The value of the provision of public lavatories is, on this view, proportionate to the strength of the bladder of individual users, in that the utility of the operation in question, how long before another, similar operation is required, is one obvious measure of the utility of restroom provision.

The fallacy of the principle of temporal neutrality

Savulescu also appeals to this principle of discounting when discussing the so called 'principle of temporal neutrality'. According to this principle if 'the value of a state of affairs is determined by our desires for that state, we should appeal not only to what people now desire, but also to what they will desire. And if we consider future preference satisfaction, we must discount the value of that satisfaction by the probability of it not occurring'.[18] Imagine a nation state 'Temporal Neutralitovia' (TN) that has two potential and very powerful enemies. One declares all out war reducing the chances of survival of all TN's inhabitants by 50%. The second enemy can now reason, correctly according to Savulescu, that if it also declares war the wrong it will do in waging war and probably killing many of TN's inhabitants is only half what it was previously, because the value of the lives of all the inhabitants of TN must be reduced by 50%, must, in short, be discounted by the probability of their survival.

To move from the cataclysm of war to more mundane and realistic policy choices: we can imagine two towns of exactly the same size in the European Union, one in the north of England, 'Ancient', and the other in the south of Italy, 'Vecchio'. Both towns are claimants for Community resources available to care for the elderly. As is well known, life expectancy is greater in southern Italy than in northern Europe, perhaps due to the famous 'Mediterranean diet' of olive oil and cooked tomatoes. The citizens of both towns want the security of better health provision in old age. They want it now and will still want it when they are old. However, although both towns have equal size

---

[18] Ibid. p. 221.

populations, since life expectancy in Vecchio is much superior to that in Ancient, we must discount the value of devoting resources to the elderly the probability that the allocation will not achieve the valued outcome. That is, fewer elderly will benefit in Ancient than in Vecchio. Is it clear that the citizens of Vecchio have the better claim, and that the European Commission, for example, should allocate resources accordingly? Should Italy and Greece always win out over the United Kingdom and Denmark when such resources are available? I doubt this would (or should) strike the European Parliament, for example, as an equitable allocation of resources between member states.

The fallacy of the principle of temporal neutrality lies in attempting to extrapolate from decisions within particular lives to comparisons between lives where life itself is at stake. If the claim that 'if we consider future preference satisfaction, we must discount the value of that satisfaction by the probability of it not occurring' has any validity this derives from its application within a particular life. I would be irrational to plan for future preferences I am unlikely to be able to satisfy. But this is entirely different, as the above examples show, to the false claim defended by Savulescu, that we must discount the existential value of a life by the probability of its not continuing.

In any event Savulescu has already conceded enough of the point. He allows that it is invidious to prefer a 1/50 chance of life to a 1/100 chance so it is clearly not true that in his view we *must* discount for probability of occurrence. However, if, as I have argued, the value lies in giving the person an equal chance of continued existence, and that doing so recognises their equal standing in the community, then *that* is the value of the opportunity. And we have already seen that the explanation of this exception cannot be simply a matter of the externally assessed rationality or of the strength of the agent's reasons for the choice.

Thresholds and plateaux

Savulescu's claim is not that it is simply a matter of the strength of the agent's reasons for choice, but of that strength *once a certain threshold or plateau is reached.* His suggestion is that 'the strength of reason to act increases as the value promoted by the action increases, until some plateau is reached where strength of reason no longer increases despite increments in value. Thus a person may have most reason to perform some act, even though other actions would promote more value, if the consequences of the chosen act are good enough'.[19] Savulescu makes clear that 'Distributors of public resources should not require that agent's change what matters most to them, provided that the object of that pattern of concern is worth achieving and good enough relative to other alternatives'.[20] The crucial point is that Savulescu believes that a slim chance of life is not a reason on the plateau, not something either worth achieving or good enough relative to other values.

I have argued that a chance of continued existence that is desired is always worth taking and that it is only other values of the same agent that can eclipse that chance. The object of the chance of life is not, as Savulescu sometimes implies, the particular percentage chance, but the opportunity of life when the alternative is death. Thus the measure of the good to be achieved does not reside in the percentage chance of achieving it, but in the nature of what is to be achieved. Continued existence as opposed to immediate death is desired because it is everything as opposed to nothing. There could not be a more valuable objective or a more rational one. This must be on Savulescu's plateau if anything is.

What Savulescu must surely do is provide a principled account of when precisely differences in degree make for differences in quality, or in his terminology when scalarity breaks down. Without a principle for recognising the point of scalar shift, we have been given no account of anything, but merely a re-description of Savulescu's intuitions.

The value of life

The plateau or threshold is I concede attractive. Savulescu is certainly right to suggest that most people's intuitions suggest that really small chances of survival are not worth providing (as opposed to taking) when the same resources could be used to give better chances to others and hence save more lives. The same seems to be true where even good chances of continued life are available, but where the continuance will be only for very short periods, days or weeks for example. It may be that this is an objective matter in that a vast majority would see small chances or short periods of remission as obviously worthless or worth less. However, this paper has suggested that such plateaux are not supported by reasons based consequentialism, relying as it does

---

[19] Ibid. p. 228.
[20] Ibid. p. 230.

404 JUSTICE AND EQUAL OPPORTUNITIES

on measures of the objective strength of reasons particular people have. There are various other ways such a rejection of small chances of life or small amounts of remaining life-span, might be supported. Such a plateau might, for example, be supported by some overarching theory of distributive justice. Such a theory might of course run into equally counter-intuitive conclusions in other areas, as I have suggested is the case with Savulescu's version of reasons based consequentialism.

For these reasons I believe the paradoxical consequences of according equal concern and respect to claims to small chances of life, or small periods of continued existence, is more apparent than real. A reasons based consequentialism which is not burdened by the absurdities of the principle of temporal neutrality and is sensitive to the strength of reasons that particular individuals have to take their own chances on life, would probably be fully compatible with the position that I have defended. We must remember, however, that the crucial issue is that of distributive justice, of how public resources may be allocated to do justice to the equal claims of individual citizens. What matters therefore, is what a distributor of the public resources available for healthcare should do.

There is, I believe, no way to formalise at the level of public policy the information necessary to be fully sensitive to, and respectful of, individual reasons and circumstances. A distributor of public resources cannot (and perhaps should not) know or enquire into the detailed reasons why even a small chance of life or a short period of remission is wanted and needed. Such a distributor should be 'blind' to these individual differences, for to evaluate them violates the equality principle. This is why a distributor of public resources must afford equal opportunities for healthcare and not formalise principles that may accord different value to the lives of equals.

The Institute of Medicine, Law and Bioethics
The University of Manchester

Part VII
Virtue Ethics

VARIETIES OF VIRTUE ETHICS

Justin Oakley

Abstract
The revival of virtue ethics over the last thirty-five years has produced a bewildering diversity of theories, which on the face of it seem united only by their opposition to various features of more familiar Kantian and Utilitarian ethical theories. In this paper I present a systematic account of the main *positive* features of virtue ethics, by articulating the common ground shared by its different varieties. I do so not to offer a fresh defence of virtue ethics, but rather to provide a conceptual map that locates its main claims and arguments in relation to those of rival theories, and identifies its distinctive contribution to contemporary ethics. I set out *six* specific claims which are made by all forms of virtue ethics, and I explain how these claims distinguish the theory from recent character-based forms of Kantian ethics and Utilitarianism. I then use this framework to briefly survey two main strands of virtue ethics which have been developed in the literature.[1]

The current renewal of philosophical interest in the virtues is one of the most noteworthy developments in contemporary ethical theory. The first signs of this revival appeared in 1958, when Elizabeth Anscombe called for the restoration of Aristotelian notions of goodness, character, and virtue as central concerns of moral philosophy.[2] While initial reactions to Anscombe's call were modest, interest in the virtues gathered momentum during the 1980s, largely due to the work of philosophers such as Philippa Foot, Bernard Williams, and Alasdair MacIntyre. There is now a bewildering variety of claims made by philosophers in the name of virtue ethics.[3] Many of those claims are put in negative form, and are expressed in terms of an opposition to an 'ethics of principles', or to an 'impartialist ethics', or to 'abstract ethical theory', or simply to an 'ethics of action'. Unfortunately, this negative

---

[1] I would like to thank Brad Hooker, John Campbell, John Cottingham, Per Sandberg and Christine Swanton, for their very helpful comments on earlier versions of this paper. I am especially grateful to Dean Cocking for many insightful discussions of the topics in this paper and for his contribution to our work together on virtue ethics.

[2] G. E. M. Anscombe, 'Modern Moral Philosophy', *Philosophy* 33 (1958).

[3] For a comprehensive bibliography, see Robert B. Krushchwitz & Robert C. Roberts, *The Virtues: Contemporary Essays on Moral Character* (Belmont: Wadsworth, 1987). See also Peter A. French, Theodore E. Uehling, and Howard K. Wettstein (eds.), *Midwest Studies in Philosophy, Volume 13; Ethical Theory: Character and Virtue* (Notre Dame: Notre Dame University Press, 1988); Gregory E. Pence, 'Recent Work on the Virtues', *American Philosophical Quarterly* 21 (1984), pp. 281–97; and Gregory Trianosky, 'What is Virtue Ethics all About?' *American Philosophical Quarterly* 27 (1990).

emphasis has resulted in virtue ethics becoming better known to many by what it is *against*, rather than by what it is *for*. Of course, given that the revival of virtue ethics has been sparked by dissatisfaction with standard Kantian and Utilitarian ethical theories, it is not surprising that those negative claims have gained prominence. However, to focus only on those claims in an outline of virtue ethics and its variants would be inadequate, for this would not sufficiently distinguish it from other approaches – such as an ethics of care, and various forms of feminist ethics – which are also often advanced in terms of a rejection of similar features of orthodox ethical theories. While virtue ethics does share certain common targets with these and other ethical theories, it can be more clearly distinguished from them by its positive features.

When virtue ethicists *do* enunciate their positive claims, however, there is often a lack of clarity and specificity which does not help in fixing the theory's distinctive content. For instance, when virtue ethicists suggest how the theory can overcome many of the perceived vices of Kantianism and Utilitarianism, there is often a failure to articulate virtue theory in ways which make clear how or why its features cannot simply be appropriated by more sophisticated or ecumenical forms of these more familiar ethical theories. This is complicated by the fact that these latter theories do, in fact, seem to have incorporated certain characteristics of a virtue ethics approach, as I shall explain. Thus, in order to show how virtue ethics resists assimilation to a form of Kantianism or Utilitarianism, one needs to bring out which features of virtue ethics could not be consistently endorsed by someone who holds one of those theories. In setting out the main positive claims made by virtue ethics then, I will explain *which* of these claims distinguish the approach from both traditional and contemporary versions of Kantianism and Utilitarianism, and also from standard forms of Consequentialism.

The essential features of virtue ethics

I shall outline *six* claims which appear to be essential features of *any* virtue ethics view. The first and perhaps best-known claim, which is central to any form of virtue ethics, is the following:

(a) An action is right if and only if it is what an agent with a virtuous character would do in the circumstances.

This is a claim about the primacy of *character* in the justification of right action. A right action is one that is in accordance with what a virtuous person would do in the circumstances, and what *makes* the action right is that it is what a person with a virtuous character would do here.[4] Thus, Philippa Foot argues that it is right to save another's life, where life is still a good to that person, because this is what someone with the virtue of benevolence would do. A person with the virtue of benevolence would act in this way because benevolence is a virtue which is directed at the good of others, and to have the virtue of benevolence, according to Foot, is to be disposed to help others in situations where we are likely to be called upon to do so.[5] Similarly, Rosalind Hursthouse argues that it is right in certain circumstances to reveal an important truth to another, even though this may be hurtful to them, because a person with the virtue of honesty would tell the truth here. For example, if my brother asks me whether his wife is being unfaithful, and I happen to know what she is, I ought to answer him truthfully because this is what a person with the virtue of honesty would do here.[6] Likewise, in regard to justice, Foot argues that I ought to repay you the money I have borrowed, even if you plan to waste it, because repaying the money is what a person with the virtue of justice would do.[7]

Now, the primacy given to character in (a) might also seem to be endorsed by recent influential forms of Kantianism, Utilitarianism, and Consequentlialism, which invoke one of these theories to give content to the notion of a 'virtuous person'. For example, Barbara Herman has argued that the Kantian Categorical Imperative, which provides the standard of rightness for actions, is best understood as a normative disposition in the character of a good agent to rule out certain courses of conduct as impermissible.[8]

---

[4] For an explicit statement of this claim, see eg. Rosalind Hursthouse, 'Virtue Theory and Abortion', *Philosophy and Public Affairs* 20 (1991), p. 225. See Aristotle, *Nicomachean Ethics*, II, 6, 1107a1–2.

[5] See Philippa Foot, 'Euthanasia', p. 54; and 'Virtues and Vices', p. 4, both in her *Virtues and Vices* (Berkeley: University of California Press, 1978). Foot sometimes calls this virtue 'benevolence', while at other time she refers to it as 'charity'.

[6] See Hursthouse, 'Virtue Theory and Abortion', pp. 229, 231.

[7] See Foot, 'Euthanasia', pp. 44–5, and 'Virtues and Vices'. See also William Frankena, *Ethics*, 2nd ed. (Englewood Cliffs: Prentice-Hall, 1973), pp. 63–71. The impact of virtue ethics' emphasis on the importance of character is beginning to be felt in areas beyond ethical theory. See eg. William Galston, *Liberal Purposes: Goods, Virtues, and Duties in the Liberal State* (New York: Cambridge University Press, 1991); Will Kymlicka & Wayne Norman, 'Return of the Citizen: A Survey of Recent Work on Citizenship Theory', *Ethics* 104 (1994), pp. 352–81; and Stephen Macedo, *Liberal Virtues: Citizenship, Virtue, and Community in Liberal Constitutionalism* (Oxford: Clarendon Press, 1990).

[8] See Barbara Herman, 'The Practice of Moral Judgment', and other essays in her *The Practice of Moral Judgment* (Cambridge MA: Harvard University Press, 1993).

Similarly, Peter Railton has argued that the Consequentialist requirement to maximise agent-neutral value can be understood as a normative disposition in the character of the good agent, and R. M. Hare suggests that the Utilitarian requirement to maximise utility can be thought of in the same way.[9] How can (a) help distinguish virtue ethics from these other theories?

Virtue ethicists give primacy to character in the sense that they believe reference to character is *essential* in a correct account of right and wrong action. This distinguishes virtue ethics from *act*-consequentialist theories such as those of Hare and Railton, since both of these latter theories allow us to say what acts are right without referring to character at all. For example, act-consequentialists hold simply that an act is right if and only if it would result in the best consequences. They typically add that the best humanly possible character is the one with the best consequences. But the best humanly possible character *may* be one that will *not* allow the agent in every possible situation to do the act with the best consequences. Thus, act-consequentialists admit that a person with a virtuous character may not always do the act with the best consequences – ie., may not always do what is right according to act-consequentialism.

However, some forms of Utilitarianism, Consequentialism, and Kantianism do give character an essential role in the justification of right action, for they hold that right actions must be guided by a certain sort of character, and that such actions are justified because they flow from agents having the requisite kind of character. For example, Richard Brandt proposes a form of rule-utilitarianism which

> orders the acceptable level of a version to various act-types in accordance with the damage ... that would likely be done if everyone felt free to indulge in the kind of behaviour in question ... The worse the effect if everyone felt free, the higher the acceptable level of aversion.[10]

On this view, we cannot say what rightness is without referring to the aversions in the character of the agent. Indeed, some have taken the idea of a character-based Utilitarian or Kantian ethics to

---

[9] Peter Railton, 'Alienation, Consequentialism, and the Demands of Morality', in Samuel Scheffler (ed), *Consequentialism and its Critics* (Oxford: Oxford University Press, 1988), pp. 93–133; R. M. Hare, *Moral Thinking* (Oxford: Oxford University Press, 1981).

[10] Richard B. Brandt, 'Morality and its Critics', *American Philosophical Quarterly* 26 (1989), p. 95. See also Brad Hooker, 'Rule-Consequentialism', *Mind* 99 (1990), pp. 67–77.

© Blackwell Publishers Ltd. 1996

suggest that these theories can actually be recast as derivative forms of virtue ethics. For example, Philippa Foot has suggested that we could consider Utilitarianism a form of virtue ethics, insofar as it tells us that we ought to act as a person with a good Utilitarian character would. The character of such a person, as Foot sees it, would be governed by just *one* disposition – the virtue of universal benevolence – and the rightness of their actions would be judged according to whether they conformed with what such a disposition would have them do.[11] Likewise, Barbara Herman suggests that Kant (especially in his later work) tells us to act as a good Kantian agent would, and that such an agent would have and act out of certain emotional and partial dispositions, which are regulated by a commitment to not acting impermissibly.[12] These forms of Utilitarianism and Kantianism indicate that it will clearly not do to talk about virtue ethics as distinctive simply by the primacy it gives to *character* in the determination of right action.[13] One needs to point to additional features in order to show what is distinctive about virtue ethics as a form of character-based ethics.

One important way of distinguishing virtue ethics from Kantian and Utilitarian forms of character-based ethics is by bringing out the differences in how each theory grounds the relevant normative conception which would govern the character of a good agent. Kantians claim that the goodness of an agent's character is determined by how well they have internalised the capacity to test the universalisability of their maxims, while Utilitarians claim that a person with a good character is one who is disposed to maximise

---

[11] Philippa Foot, 'Utilitarianism and the Virtues', in Scheffler (ed)., *Consequentialism and its Critics*, pp. 224–42.

[12] See Barbara Herman, 'Agency, Attachment, and Difference', and other essays in her *The Practice of Moral Judgment*. See also Kurt Baier, 'Radical Virtue Ethics', in French *et al.* (eds.), *Midwest Studies in Philosophy, vol. 13*; Robert Louden, 'Kant's Virtue Ethics', *Philosophy* 61 (1986), esp. pp. 478–9, 484–9; Robert Louden, 'Can we be too Moral?' *Ethics* 98 (1988); Onora O'Neill, 'Consistency in Action', in N. Potter & M. Timmons (eds.), *Morality and Universality* (Dordrecht: Reidel, 1985); and Nancy Sherman, 'The Place of Emotions in Kantian Morality', in Owen Flanagan & Amelie O. Rorty (eds.), *Identity, Character, and Morality: Essays in Moral Psychology* (Cambridge MA: MIT Press, 1990). A criticism analogous to that which Foot makes of a Utilitarian virtue ethics may also be made of a Kantian virtue ethics, which took conscientiousness (as the disposition to act according to duty) as the only virtue. See N. J. H. Dent, *The Moral Psychology of the Virtues* (Cambridge: Cambridge University Press, 1984), pp. 27–31; and James D. Wallace, *Virtues and Vices* (Ithaca: Cornell University Press), p. 130.

[13] See Frankena, *Ethics*, pp. 63ff; Pence, 'Recent Work on the Virtues'; and Gregory E. Pence, 'Virtue theory' in Peter Singer (ed.), *A Companion to Ethics* (Oxford: Blackwell, 1991); and Gary Watson, 'On the Primacy of Character', in Flanagan & Rorty (eds.), *Identity, Character, and Morality*.

© Blackwell Publishers Ltd. 1996

utility. Virtue ethicists, however, reject both Kantian universalisability and the maximisation of utility as the appropriate grounds of good character, and instead draw on other factors in substantiating the appropriate normative conceptions of a good agent.

There are broadly speaking two main kinds of approach taken by virtue ethicists in grounding the character of the good agent. The more prominent of these approaches draws on the Aristotelian view that the content of virtuous character is determined by what we need, or what we are, qua *human* beings. Many virtue ethicists develop one particular version of this approach, taking the eudaimonistic view that the virtues are character-traits which we need to live humanly flourising lives. On this view, character-traits such as benevolence, honesty, and justice are virtues because they feature importantly among an interlocking web of intrinsic goods – which includes courage, integrity, friendship, and knowledge – without which we cannot have eudaimonia, or a flourishing life for a human being. Moreover, these traits and activities, when co-ordinated by the governing virtue of phronesis (or practical wisdom), are regarded as together partly *constitutive* of eudaimonia – that is, the virtues are intrinsically good components of a good human life.[14] Aristotle thought that humans flourish by living virtuous lives because it is only in doing so that our rational capacity to guide our lives is expressed in an excellent way. Human good is a function of our rational capacity because what counts as good in a species is determined by its characteristic activity, and the exercising of our rational capacity is the characteristic activity of human beings.[15] On this view, the good is not a passive external consequence of acting virtuously, and so it would be incorrect to say (as Utilitarians might) that acting virtuously typically results in our living a good human life; rather, the good is active, and acting virtuously is a constituent part of what a good human life consists in.

Some virtue ethicists develop this general approach by grounding the virtues not so much in the idea of a good human being, but rather in what is good *for* human beings. The best-known exponent of this view is Philippa Foot, who in her early work argued that a feature of the virtues is that they are beneficial to their possesor.

---

[14] See Aristotle, *The Nicomachean Ethics*. See also John M. Cooper, *Reason and Human Good in Aristotle* (Indianapolis: Hackett, 1975), pp. 79–88; and J. L. Ackrill, 'Aristotle on Eudaimonia', in Amelie O. Rorty (ed.), *Essays on Aristotle's Ethics* (Berkeley: University of California Press, 1980).

[15] This is Aristotle's well-known *ergon* argument, found in *Nicomachean Ethics*, I, 7.

Foot thought this helped explain why courage and temperance count as virtues. However, she later found this rationale unpromising with such common-sense virtues as justice and benevolence; so she broadened her account to derive virtues from what is beneficial to humans either individually or as a community.[16] This brought her closer in some respects to Alasdair MacIntyre, who argues that such qualities as truthfulness, courage, and justice are virtues because they enable us to achieve the goods internal to the characteristically human practices which strengthen traditions and the communities which sustain them.[17]

An alternative version of a broadly Aristotelian approach is put forward by perfectionists, who reject both the eudaimonistic idea that virtuous living is necessary for happiness, and the idea that such a life must be overall beneficial to the person living it. Perfectionism derives the virtues from those characteristics which most fully develop our essential properties as human beings. For example, love of knowledge, friendship, and accomplishment count as virtues because these states most fully realise our essential capacities for theoretical and practical rationality. And further, loving these goods would count as virtuous even when a person would lead a happier life, and would benefit more, by not loving them – say, because his accomplishment can be gained only at the cost of enormous personal hardship.[18] Nevertheless, despite the differences between this and the eudaimonistic development of the Aristotelian approach, both views agree that to live a life without the virtues would in some sense be to go against our basic nature.

A different kind of approach to grounding virtuous character also rejects the eudaimonistic idea that the virtues are given by what humans need in order to flourish, and instead derives the virtues from our commonsense views about what character-traits we typically find admirable. According to this non-Aristotelian approach, developed principally by Michael Slote, there is a

---

[16] See Foot, 'Virtues and Vices', and 'Moral Beliefs', both in her *Virtues and Vices*.

[17] See Alasdair MacIntyre, *After Virtue*, 2nd ed. (Notre Dame: University of Notre Dame Press, 1984), esp. ch. 14.

[18] See Thomas Hurka, 'Virtue as Loving the Good', in Ellen F. Paul, Fred D. Miller & Jeffrey Paul (eds.), *The Good Life and the Human Good* (Cambridge: Cambridge University Press, 1992), esp. pp. 153–5; Thomas Hurka, *Perfectionism* (New York: Oxford University Press, 1993); and L. W. Sumner, 'Two Theories of the Good', in Paul *et al.* (eds.) *The Good Life and the Human Good*, esp. pp. 4–5. See also John McDowell, 'The Role of *Eudaimonia* in Aristotle's Ethics', in Rorty, *Essays on Aristotle's Ethics*, esp. pp. 370–1, and Christine Korsgaard, 'Aristotle on Function and Virtue', *History of Philosophy Quarterly* 3 (1986), pp. 277–8.

© Blackwell Publishers Ltd. 1996

plurality of traits which we commonly find admirable in human beings in certain circumstances, and one way we can determine what these are is by examining our responses to the lives led by various admirable exemplars. Further, when we look at such exemplars, we see that some are quite different from those which would be held up by Kantians and Utilitarians. For example, while people like Mother Theresa are undoubtedly thought admirable on account of the benefits they have bestowed on humanity, Slote claims that we may well regard people like Albert Einstein or Samuel Johnson as just as admirable as Mother Theresa, even though Einstein and Johnson were not exactly *benefactors* of mankind.[19] On this view then, benevolence, honesty, and justice are virtues because, even if they are not necessary for human flourishing, they are nevertheless character-traits which we ordinarily find deeply admirable in human beings.

The differences between these forms of virtue ethics, on the one hand, and character-based forms of Kantianism and Utilitarianism, on the other hand, would become apparent in practice in their different ways of handling cases where certain values conflict. Thus, consider a case where the requirements of duty or utility conflict with what a good or admirable friend would do. For example, suppose I console a close friend of mine who is grieving over the irretrievable breakdown of his marriage, and that in consoling him, I stay with him longer than would be required by my duty to him as a friend. A virtue ethicist might regard my staying longer to console him as right, even if my doing so meant cancelling an appointment with a business associate I'd promised to meet for lunch, and also meant that I thereby failed to maximise overall utility. What makes it right to console the friend here is that this is the sort of thing which someone with an appropriate conception of friendship will be disposed to do, rather than because this brings about the best overall consequences, or because this is our duty as a friend.

But this does not fully explain how (a) is meant to operate as a standard for determining the rightness of actions. For example, is (a) meant to provide a purely 'external' criterion of right action, which a person may meet no matter what kinds of motives, dispositions, or character they act from in performing the action the criterion directs them to do? On this interpretation, acting rightly

---

[19] See Michael Slote, *From Morality to Virtue* (New York: Oxford University Press, 1992); and Michael Slote, *Goods and Virtues* (Oxford: Clarendon Press, 1983).

would not require modelling oneself on a virtuous person or a particular aspect of their character, but would involve merely having a good idea of what kinds of acts such a person would perform in various circumstances. In that case, (a) would be analogous to the role in certain ethical theories of an Ideal Observer, whose deliverances may guide one even though one lacks the qualities of such an observer onself (and indeed, even if there were no Ideal Observers at all).[20] Or, does the criterion of right action in (a) carry certain 'internal' requirements, such that we can act rightly only if we have and act out of the kinds of motives, dispositions, or character-traits that a virtuous agent would have and act out of in the circumstances?

The examples of benevolence and honesty given above suggest that (a) is to be understood according to the first interpretation, as setting only an external criterion of right action, since they indicate what would be the benevolent or honest thing to do, with no explicit requirement to act out of certain motives or dispositions. However, a closer look at what virtue ethicists say shows that they mean (a) to be understood in the second way – that is, 'doing what a virtuous person would do' is to be understood as requiring not merely the performance of certain acts, but also acting out of certain dispositions and (in many cases) motives. So, acting rightly requires our acting out of the appropriate dispositions and motives. Or better, we cannot meet the criterion of right action in (a) in a particular case unless we ourselves have and act out of the virtuous disposition appropriate to the circumstances.[21] For example, to act as a person with the virtue of justice would do, I must not only repay my debt, but I must do so out of an appropriate sense of justice. To be sure, while virtue ethics holds that acting out of the appropriate motives and dispositions is *necessary* for right action, it does not claim that acting out of such motives and dispositions is *sufficient* for right action. As we see below, virtue ethics recognises that there is a variety of reasons why good dispositions and motives may lead one to act wrongly.

Generally speaking then, having a particular virtuous disposition

---

[20] See Roderick Firth, 'Ethical Absolutism and the Ideal Observer', *Philosophy and Phenomenological Research* 12 (1952), pp. 317–45. I thank John Campbell for pointing out this similarity between Virtue Ethics and an Ideal Observer theory.

[21] Compare Aristotle: 'It is not merely the state in accordance with the right rule, but the state that implies the *presence* of the right rule, that is virtue' (*Nicomachean Ethics* VI, 13, 1144b26–9; see also II, 4 1105a26–33). See Cooper, *Reason and Human Good in Aristotle*, p. 78; and Korsgaard, 'Aristotle on Function and Virtue', pp. 266–8.

requires internalising a certain normative standard of excellence, in such a way that one is able to adjust one's motivation and conduct so that it conforms – or at least does not conflict – with that standard. Thus, to have the virtue of *friendship*, one must have an appropriate normative conception of what kind of relationship friendship is, and of what sorts of motives and conduct would be appropriate to such a relationship. And in order to do this, one must have developed one's motivation and perception to a certain level. For in exemplifying the virtue of friendship, one does not act for the sake of *friendship* per se, nor even for the sake of *this* friendship, but rather for the sake of this *person*, who is one's friend. And one can properly be said to be acting for the sake of this person only if one has shaped one's perception in certain ways – ie., one must have developed some kind of understanding of what this person's well-being consists in, and of which ways of acting would promote it. Thus, a virtuous agent will have certain standing commitments or normative dispositions, which need not always be consciously formulated or applied, but which will govern and shape their motivations and actions. We can call such commitments 'regulative ideals'.[22]

A common criticism of virtue ethics is that in deriving right action from virtuous character, it seems to make the actions of a virtuous person 'self-justifying'.[23] There are two different objections which critics may have in mind here. One is that, while acting from good character might be sufficient for right action, virtue ethics' requirement in (a) is circular – that is, right action is given by what a virtuous person would do, but we are to determine who counts as a virtuous person by looking at the rightness of their actions. This objection is overcome by explaining how virtuous character-traits are derived independently of some prior notion of right action – ie. from their admirability or their involvement in flourishing, as explained earlier.

The other objection critics may have in mind is that virtue ethics seems to make acting from good character itself sufficient for right action, which seems implausible. Robert Veatch expresses the worry by saying:

> I am concerned about well-intentioned, bungling do-gooders. They seem to exist with unusual frequency in health care, law,

[22] See Dean Cocking and Justin Oakley, 'Indirect Consequentialism, Friendship, and the Problem of Alienation', *Ethics* 106 (1995).

[23] See Robert B. Louden, 'On Some Vices of Virtue Ethics', *American Philosophical Quarterly* 21 (1984).

© Blackwell Publishers Ltd. 1996

and other professions with a strong history of stressing the virtue of benevolence with an elitist slant.[24]

However, conceiving of virtues as regulative ideals helps virtue ethics meet this criticism, because it allows for the possibility that an action done out of good motives or good intentions may fail to reach the appropriate standard of excellence which one is normatively disposed to uphold. For example, in seeking to help a friend who is despairing at finding a suitable job, I might bring to his attention a certain weakness which I think may be impeding his chances. However, I might later come to realise that it was a mistake to do so at the time, because I failed to sufficiently appreciate the nature and depths of my friend's despair, and that such comments were contrary to what can reasonably be expected of a good friend in such circumstances. There is a variety of reasons – such as false beliefs, insufficient attention, care, energy, or simply bad luck – why a virtuous person may on a particular occasion fail to act as his regulative ideals would dictate, but the regulative ideals of virtue ethics nevertheless provide a standard for act evaluation which allows us to see that acting out of good motives or good intentions, while it may be necessary for right action,[25] is not sufficient for the rightness of one's action. So virtue ethics can recognise, as R. M. Hare reminds us, that 'it is possible for very virtuous people to do terrible things'.[26]

A second claim made by all varieties of virtue ethics is:

(b) Goodness is prior to rightness.

That is, the notion of goodness is primary, while the notion of rightness can be defined only in relation to goodness: no account can be given of what makes an action right until we have established what is valuable or good. In particular, virtue ethics claims that we need an account of *human* good (or of what are commonly regarded as admirable human traits), before we can determine what it is right for us to do in any given situation. In terms of a familiar taxonomy of normative theories, claim (b)

---

[24] Robert M. Veatch, 'The Danger of Virtue', *Journal of Medicine and Philosophy* 13 (1988), p. 445.

[25] Acting out of good motives is required for motive-dependent virtues, such as friendship and courage, but certain virtues may not have such a motive requirement: while acting justly requires that one acts from a just *disposition*, it may not require that one acts out of certain motives.

[26] R. M. Hare, 'Methods of bioethics: some defective proposals', *Monash Bioethics Review* 13 (1994), p. 41.

© Blackwell Publishers Ltd. 1996

makes virtue ethics a *teleological* rather than a *deontological* ethical theory, and so would seem to place virtue ethics in the same family as Utilitarianism and standard forms of Consequentialism.[27] However, as I explain shortly, there are important differences between virtue ethics' account of the good and those given by most versions of Utilitarianism and Consequentialism, and in light of this, it is misleading to group virtue ethics as a theory of the same type as Utilitarianism and Consequentialism. Indeed, we will see that virtue ethics has important similarities with nonconsequentialist and deontological ethical theories.

Claim (b) is actually implicit in (a) above, but making the claim explicit brings out an important difference between virtue ethics and any form of character-based ethics derived from traditional forms of Kantianism and deontology. For according to these latter theories, the notions of goodness and the good agent are derived from prior deontic notions of rightness and right action – a good agent is one who is disposed to act in accordance with certain moral rules or requirements (which themselves are derived from, eg. the nature of practical rationality). By contrast, virtue ethics derives its account of rightness and right action from prior aretaic notions of goodness and good character, which (in Aristotelian virtue ethics) are themselves grounded in an independent account of human flourishing that values our emotional as well as our rational capacities, and recognises that our goodness can be affected for the better or worse by empirical contingencies.

A third claim made by virtue ethics is:

(c) The virtues are irreducibly plural intrinsic goods.

The substantive account of the good which forms the foundation for virtue ethics' justification of right action specifies a range of valuable traits and activities as essential for a humanly flourishing life, or as central to our views of admirable human beings. These different virtues embody irreducibly *plural* values – ie. each of them

---

[27] This way of classifying normative theories is increasingly coming under attack as inadequately sensitive to the issues which divide contemporary consequentialists and nonconsequentialists. See Herman, *The Practice of Moral Judgment*, esp. ch. 10 'Leaving Deontology Behind'; and Watson, op. cit., p. 450. John Rawls, in *A Theory of Justice* (Oxford: Oxford University Press, 1972), p. 24, assumes that all teleological theories must be consequentialist, and indeed, John Broome, in *Weighing Goods* (Oxford: Blackwell, 1991), ch. 1, argues that *all* ethical theories can be regarded as forms of consequentialism. On the other hand, Watson sees the possibility of teleological theories which are not consequentialist. For a good discussion of these issues, see James Dreier, 'Structures of Normative Theories', *The Monist* 76 (1993).

is valuable in a way which is not reducible to a single overarching value.[28] The virtues themselves are here taken to be valuable *intrinsically* rather than *instrumentally* – ie. they are valuable for their own sake, rather than as a means to promoting or realising some other value. For example, Aristotle argued that friendship is 'choiceworthy in itself', apart from any advantages it may bestow upon us.[29] The plurality of the virtues distinguishes virtue ethics from older, monistic forms of Utilitarianism, which reduce all goods to a single value such as pleasure.[30] Claim (c) would also distinguish virtue ethics from a simple 'Utilitarianism of the Virtues', which would regard the virtues as good, but only *instrumentally* – ie. insofar as they produce pleasure.[31]

However, the evaluative pluralism of the virtues in (c) does not distinguish virtue ethics from contemporary preference-utilitarianism, which seems able to consistently recognise a plurality of things which are, at least in one sense, intrinsically valuable. For preference-utilitarianism attributes value to the plural things desired, and can allow that certain things – such as knowledge, autonomy, and accomplishment – have intrinsic value, at least in the sense that we desire to have these things for themselves, rather than for any consequences which having them may bring.[32] On this kind of view, the concept of 'utility' is not a substantive value, but is given a formal analysis in terms of the fulfilment of informed preferences. Thus, as James Griffin puts it,

> Since utility is not a substantive value at all, we have to give up the idea that our various particular ends are valuable only

---

[28] On the evaluative pluralism of virtue ethics, see Aristotle's criticisms of Plato, in *Nicomachean Ethics*, Book I, chapter 6; Wallace, *Virtues and Vices*, eg. pp. 27–32; Hursthouse, 'Virtue Theory and Abortion'; and Lawrence Becker, *Reciprocity* (London: Routledge & Kegan Paul, 1986), eg. ch. 4. Note that the Aristotelian notion of *eudaimonia* is not itself to be construed in an evaluative monist way. See the discussions of 'inclusivist' versus 'dominant' conceptions of *eudaimonia* in W. F. R. Hardie, 'The Final Good in Aristotle's Ethics', *Philosophy* 40 (1965), pp. 277–95; J. L. Ackrill, 'Aristotle on *Eudaimonia*'; and Cooper, *Reason and Human Good in Aristotle*, pp. 96–9.

[29] See John M. Cooper, 'Aristotle on Friendship', in Rorty, *Essays on Aristotle's Ethics*, eg. p. 338n18.

[30] See for example, Bentham's hedonistic Utilitarianism. But as Michael Stocker points out, in *Plural and Conflicting Values* (Oxford: Clarendon Press, 1990), pp. 184–93, hedonistic Utilitarians need not have been evaluative monists; for pleasure, when properly understood, can itself be plausibly thought of as plural.

[31] See e.g. Henry Sidgwick, *The Methods of Ethics*, 7th ed. (London: Macmillan, 1907) pp. 391–7, 423–57.

[32] See James Griffin, *Well-Being* (Oxford: Clarendon Press, 1986), p. 31; and R. M. Hare, 'Comments', in D. Seanor & N. Fotion (eds.), *Hare and Critics* (Oxford: Clarendon Press, 1988), pp. 239, 251.

© Blackwell Publishers Ltd. 1996

because they cause, produce, bring about, are sources of, utility. On the contrary, they [our various particular ends] are the values, utility is not.³³

Such a view might therefore allow that the virtues are plural, intrinsic values, in the sense that agents attach value to having them for their own sake.

Nevertheless, there is a further claim made by virtue ethics, which helps to distinguish it from any preference-utilitarian approach to the virtues, viz:

(d) The virtues are objectively good.

Virtue ethics regards the virtues as objectively good in the sense that they are good independent of any connections which they may have with desire.³⁴ What the objective goodness of the virtues means in positive terms depends on the particular rationale given for them. As we saw earlier, one approach bases the goodness of the virtues on the connections they have with essential human characteristics, such as theoretical and practical rationality; another approach derives the goodness of the virtues from admirable character-traits. But neither approach makes the value of any candidate virtue depend on whether the agent desires it (either actually or hypothetically). For example, courageousness would still count as a virtuous trait, even in a person who had no desire to be courageous.³⁵ Further, the virtues can confer value on *a life*, even if the person living it does not (actually or hypothetically) desire to have them.³⁶ So, while preference utilitarians might allow that certain character-traits have intrinsic value in the sense that

---

³³ *Well-Being*, p. 32n24. See also p. 89.

³⁴ For this use of 'objective good', see Hurka, *Perfectionism*, p. 5. See also Sumner, 'Two Theories of the Good'.

³⁵ Could Philippa Foot allow this, given her well-known claim that we cannot have a reason to pursue something unless it is linked appropriately to some desire of ours (see 'Morality as a System of Hypothetical Imperatives', in *Virtues and Vices*)? It would seem so, for in several places Foot suggests that a virtuous person is a good example of a human being. Foot's view then would be that while a person cannot have a reason to be virtuous unless this serves some desire of theirs, the *goodness* of their being virtuous does not depend on their desires. See 'A Reply to Professor Frankena', in *Virtues and Vices*, p. 178: "propositions of the 'good F' 'good G' form do not, in general, have a direct connexion with reasons for choice". See also 'Goodness and Choice', in *Virtues and Vices*, esp. pp. 145–7.

³⁶ This is not to say that the virtues increase one's *well-being*. There is disagreement amongst virtue ethicists about whether the virtues are good *for me*, or make me 'better off'. Foot claims that virtues generally (ie. except justice and benevolence) make their possessor better off; however Michael Slote rejects any such general claim: see *From Morality to Virtue*, p. 209. Some would question whether a person who achieves certain characteristic human

© Blackwell Publishers Ltd. 1996

we may desire to have them for themselves, preference-utilitarians would not allow that the value of the virtues can be independent of desire in these ways.

But while (c) and (d) distinguish virtue ethics from various forms of Utilitarianism, they leave open whether virtue ethics is different to those forms of Consequentialism which accept the idea of irreducibly plural *intrinsic* and *objective* values. For example, some Consequentialists believe that there are at least two irreducibly plural intrinsic and objective values – such as universal benevolence and fairness – while others believe that there is a whole range of such values – such as happiness, knowledge, purposeful activity, autonomy, solidarity, respect, and beauty.[37] What, if anything, is there to distinguish virtue ethics from these forms of Consequentialism?

Two further claims are essential to any form of virtue ethics, and these help distinguish virtue ethics from most forms of Consequentialism.

(e) Some intrinsic goods are agent-relative.

Among the variety of goods which virtue ethics regards as constituting a humanly flourishing life, some, such as friendship and integrity, are held to be ineliminably agent-relative, while others, such as justice, are thought more properly characterised as agent-neutral. To describe a certain good as agent-relative is to say that its being a good of *mine* gives it additional moral importance (*to me*), in contrast to agent-neutral goods, which derive no such additional moral importance from their being goods of mine.[38] For

---

excellences could be living a good life if they do not *desire* (either actually or hypothetically) to have those excellences. For it might be claimed that living a good life has an ineliminable *subjective* element. See Gregory W. Trianosky, 'Rightly Ordered Appetites: How to Live Morally and Live Well', *American Philosophical Quarterly* 25 (1988), pp. 1–12.

[37] See eg. T. M. Scanlon, 'Rights, Goals and Fairness', in Scheffler, *Consequentialism and its Critics*, pp. 74–92; Railton, 'Alienation, Consequentialism, and the Demands of Morality', pp. 108–10; Hurka, 'Virtue as Loving the Good'; Hurka, *Perfectionism*; Thomas Hurka, 'Consequentialism and Content', *American Philosophical Quarterly* 29 (1992), pp. 71–8; and the 'Ideal Utilitarianism' of G. E. Moore, in *Principia Ethica* (Cambridge: Cambridge University Press, 1903), ch. 6; and Hastings Rashdall, in *The Theory of Good and Evil*, vol. 1 (Oxford: Oxford University Press, 1907), chs. 7 & 8. David McNaughton and Piers Rawling, in 'Agent-relativity and the Doing-happening Distinction', *Philosophical Studies* 63 (1991), pp. 168–9, explain well how a Consequentialist might be able to allow for plural intrinsic values. See also Derek Parfit, *Reasons and Persons* (Oxford: Clarendon Press, 1984), p. 26; and David Sosa, 'Consequences of Consequentialism', *Mind* 101 (1993), pp. 101–22.

[38] I do not mean to suggest that agent-relative value must be understood as *aggregative*. In describing the value of a certain trait or activity as 'agent-relative', one may be making a claim about its *qualitative* character.

example, friendship could be regarded as either an agent-neutral or an agent-relative good. In the former case, it would be friendship *per se* which is intrinsically valuable, and a pluralistic Consequentialist who believed that friendship is an agent-neutral value would tell us to maximise (or at least promote) friendships themselves – say, by setting up a social club. On the agent-relative account of the value of friendship, however, the fact that a certain relationship is *my* friendship would give it more moral relevance to my acts than would be had by, say, the competing claims of your friendships. Virtue ethics sees friendship (and certain other virtues) as valuable in the latter sense – were performing a friendly act towards a friend of mine to conflict with promoting friendships between others (eg. by throwing a party for new colleagues), I would nevertheless be justified in acting for my friend.[39]

Claim (e) distinguishes virtue ethics from most forms of Consequentialism, whether monistic or pluralistic, since most Consequentialists regard all values as agent-neutral.[40] But there seems to be no in principle reason why a Consequentialist could not allow that some values are properly characterised as agent-relative. Indeed, some Consequentialists do seem to accept that certain values (such as friendship and integrity) are irreducibly agent-relative.[41] However, most of those consequentialists would stop short of endorsing the following claim made by virtue ethics.

(f) Acting rightly does not require that we maximise the good.

The core thesis of most versions of Consequentialism is the idea that rightness requires us to maximise the good, whether goodness is monistic or pluralistic, subjective or objective, agent-neutral across the board or agent-relative in some instances. Virtue ethics, by contrast, rejects maximisation as a theory of rightness. Thus, in a case where I can favour *my* friendships over promoting others' friendships, I am not required by virtue ethics to *maximise* my friendships. Neither am I required to have the best friendship(s) which it is possible for me to have.[42] Rather, I ought to have

---

[39] See Stocker, *Plural and Conflicting Values*, pp. 313–14; and Dreier, 'Structures of Normative Theories'.

[40] Samuel Scheffler (in his introduction to *Consequentialism and its Critics*) and Shelly Kagan, in *The Limits of Morality* (Oxford: Clarendon Press, 1989) regard a belief in the agent-neutrality of all value as a *sine qua non* of a Consequentialist theory.

[41] See eg. Railton, 'Alienation, Consequentialism, and the Demands of Morality'; and Sosa, 'Consequences of Consequentialism'.

[42] On Aristotle as a non-maximiser, see Stocker, *Plural and Conflicting Values*, pp. 338–42; and Cooper, *Reason and Human Good in Aristotle*, pp. 87–8, and ch. 2.

excellent friendships, relative to the norms which properly govern such relationships, and an excellent friendship may not be the very best friendship which I am capable of having. Virtue ethicists hold that in acting towards my friends I ought to be guided by an appropriate normative conception of what friendship involves (such as the account of character-friendship given by Aristotle in *Nicomachean Ethics* IX, 9).

Claims (a) to (f) are made by all forms of virtue ethics, and the different varieties of the theory can be distinguished according to which of these claims they emphasise, and their reasons for making these claims. Some philosophers who do not (or at least, not explicitly) call themselves virtue ethicists nevertheless endorse one or more of these claims as part of their criticisms of Kantian, Utilitarian, or Consequentialist theories.[43] However, taken as a whole, these claims help show how virtue ethics forms a distinct alternative to familiar forms of Kantianism, Utilitarianism, and Consequentialism. With this framework in mind, I will now describe and compare the most important and influential versions of the basic virtue ethics position.

Varieties of Virtue Ethics

The main forms of virtue ethics can be broadly divided into Consequentialist and Nonconsequentialist versions. In describing a theory as 'Consequentialist', I mean that it treats rightness as ultimately a function of the value(s) an agent *promotes* (or the values an agent's rules would promote, when followed by people generally), whereas in calling a theory 'Nonconsequentialist', I mean that it regards rightness as ultimately a function of the value(s) an agent *honors* or *exemplifies*.[44] This means that Consequen-

---

[43] See eg. Samuel Scheffler, *The Rejection of Consequentialism* (Oxford: Oxford University Press, 1982); Samuel Scheffler, *Human Morality* (New York: Oxford University Press, 1992); Michael Stocker, *Plural and Conflicting Values*; and Bernard Williams, 'Persons, Character, and Morality', in his *Moral Luck* (Cambridge: Cambridge University Press, 1981).

[44] See Phillip Pettit, 'Consequentialism', in Singer (ed.), *A Companion to Ethics*, pp. 230–41, for this way of characterising the distinction between Consequentialism and Nonconsequentialism. For application of this distinction to virtue ethics, see Christine Swanton, 'Satisficing and Virtue', *Journal of Philosophy* 90 (1993), pp. 33–48. There is debate over how best to distinguish between these two broad types of theories. Some writers (eg. Scheffler, Kagan) draw this distinction by contrasting agent-neutral theories with theories which allow for agent-relative values. However, as Sosa and Dreier argue, this seems to conflate two different distinctions. I base my discussion on the distinction between promoting vs. honoring values because these notions seem to me to best capture a broad contrast between two different strands of virtue ethics.

© Blackwell Publishers Ltd. 1996

tialist and Nonconsequentialist virtue theories would tell us to respond in different ways to the values inherent in the virtues. For example, where the value of integrity is at stake, a Consequentialist virtue theory would say that the virtuous agent referred to in claim (a) would promote (primarily their) integrity, whereas a Nonconsequentialist virtue theory would say that the virtuous agent would exemplify their commitment to being a person of integrity, quite apart from whether this also promotes integrity in themselves or others. I will begin by outlining nonconsequentialist forms of virtue ethics.

Nonconsequentialist virtue ethics

Since its revival in 1958, the dominant forms of virtue ethics have been of a nonconsequentialist kind. These forms of virtue ethics emphasise the importance of an agent's personal projects which help constitute their integrity, acting out of motives which express an agent's commitments to particular-directed relationships, and the requirement to acknowledge certain constraints in promoting the impersonal good. The main proponent of a nonconsequentialist type of virtue ethics is Philippa Foot, whose writings have had a significant influence on contemporary forms of virtue ethics. Inspired by Anscombe's criticisms of Consequentialism,[45] Foot emphasises the plurality and agent-relativity of the virtues – ie. claims (c) and (e) above – and the importance of observing certain rights, rules, and prohibitions, as well as being guided by certain ends. For example, Foot tells us that

> The virtue of justice ... is primarily concerned with the following of certain rules of fairness and honest dealing and with respecting prohibitions on interference with others rather than with attachment to any end.[46]

Foot also discusses the importance of truth-telling, promise-keeping, and helping others in need, and their correlative virtues (ie. honesty, fidelity, and charity).

Foot drives a wedge between virtue ethics and Consequentialism by rejecting the Consequentialist notion of best states of affairs *per*

---

[45] See eg. Anscombe, 'Modern Moral Philosophy', esp. pp. 183–8.

[46] Foot, 'Utilitarianism and the Virtues', p. 236. See also 'Euthanasia'. For other examples of Nonconsequentialist virtue ethics, see Rosalind Hurtshouse, *Beginning Lives* (Oxford: Blackwell, 1987), eg. pp. 239, 278–91; Hursthouse, 'Virtue Theory and Abortion'; Edmund Pincoffs, *Quandaries and Virtues* (Lawrence: University Press of Kansas, 1986), esp. pp. 101–114; Watson, 'On the Primacy of Character'; and Swanton, 'Satisficing and Virtue'.

© Blackwell Publishers Ltd. 1996

se as lacking any clear reference, and she criticises the impoverishment of classical Utilitarianism's evaluative monism. Foot does concede that we may be morally required to impartially benefit others in certain circumstances – and that the notion of better or worse states of affairs may be clear *within* this circumscribed context; indeed, she regards this as part of the virtue of benevolence. However, Foot questions the idea that, as classical Utilitarians would assume, benevolence could be the only virtue, and argues that there are other virtues – such as friendship and justice – with which benevolence may conflict.[47] Foot also argues that a person who possesses certain virtues will be disposed to observe certain agent-centred restrictions, as embodied in the Doctrine of Double Effect and (what might be called) the Doctrine of Doing and Allowing.[48] Indeed, Foot appeals to the virtues and human good to provide an underlying moral rationale for these constraints, by arguing that an agent's life goes better if they observe these constraints.[49]

Consequentialist virtue ethics
In contrast to Foot's approach, Consequentialist virtue ethicists would reject the idea that the appropriate way to respond to the values inherent in such virtues as integrity and friendship is to honor them. One reason for rejecting this is that it may be thought to recommend irrational courses of action. Thus, suppose we are in a position where we could produce either more or less integrity, but to honor our own integrity would entail that we would produce less integrity overall than we could otherwise do. For example, consider a variation on Bernard Williams' familiar case of George and the research job in the chemical and biological weapons laboratory.[50] As

---

[47] See Foot, 'Utilitarianism and the Virtues', p. 236: 'We find in our ordinary moral code many requirements and prohibitions inconsistent with the idea that benevolence is the whole of morality'. This kind of argument against Utilitarianism is also put forward by N. J. H. Dent, in *The Moral Psychology of the Virtues*, pp. 27–9.

[48] See Philippa Foot, 'Morality, Action and Outcome', in T. Honderich (ed.), *Morality and Objectivity: A Tribute to J. L. Mackie* (London: Routledge & Kegan Paul, 1985), pp. 23–38.

[49] This grounding of agent-centred restrictions in an account of the virtues and human good distinguishes Foot's approach from standard deontological and Kantian approaches. For criticism of a virtues-based rationale for agent-centred restrictions, see Samuel Scheffler, 'Agent-Centred Restrictions, Rationality, and the Virtues', in Scheffler (ed.), *Consequentialism and its Critics*, esp. pp. 255–6.

[50] From Bernard Williams, 'A Critique of Utilitarianism', in J. J. C. Smart & Bernard Williams, *Utilitarianism: For and Against* (Cambridge: Cambridge University Press, 1973), pp. 97–8.

we know, if George were to accept the position, he would have to set aside his strong opposition to chemical and biological warfare, and that would constitute a violation of his integrity. But suppose George knows that were he not to take the job, it will be divided in two and offered to two less talented chemists who, like George, are morally opposed to such research, but are currently unemployed and are having great difficulty supporting their families. Now, assume that the nature of these two chemists' opposition to such research is such that *their* integrity would be violated if *they* were to take the jobs. Now, since integrity is the very thing which is of value here, it would seem irrational to act so as to produce less of it than more. This kind of argument has been used to suggest that the appropriate way to respond to intrinsic values is to promote rather than to honor them.[51]

Thus, some forms of virtue ethics, while agreeing with the rejection of the maximisation requirement of standard consequentialism in (f), have nevertheless wanted to retain the basic idea of consequentialism that rightness is ultimately determined by what one *promotes* (or by what one's dispositions would promote, when internalised by people generally.)[52] Consequentialist theories of the virtues seem to take one of the following three forms, and the third position shares enough of virtue ethics' central tenets to be properly regarded as itself a form of the theory.

(i) Character-utilitarianism

Some philosophers have suggested that utilitarianism be applied to evaluations of motives and character, as well as to evaluations of actions. An agent would have a virtuous character, on this kind of view, when the nature and structure of their dispositions is such as

---

[51] For a similar argument, see Pettit, 'Consequentialism', esp. p. 238.

[52] See further Julia Driver, 'The Virtues and Human Nature', in Roger Crisp (ed.), *How Should One Live?* (Oxford: Oxford University Press, 1996); Hurka, 'Virtue as Loving the Good'; and Trianosky, 'What is Virtue Ethics All About?', p. 339. See also G. H. von Wright, *The Varieties of Goodness* (London: Routledge & Kegan Paul, 1963), ch. 7, eg. p. 140; and Joel Kupperman's discussion of his consequentialist 'ethics of character', in *Character* (New York: Oxford University Press, 1991), eg. p. 156n1. Alasdair MacIntyre also puts forward what seems to be a consequentialist form of virtue ethics, despite his criticisms of consequentialist virtue theories held by Benjamin Franklin and others: see *After Virtue*, ch. 14, especially MacIntyre's definition of a virtue on p. 191. John Stuart Mill evidently regarded Aristotle himself as advocating a consequentialist form of virtue ethics: see Mill's reference to Aristotle's ethics as a 'judicious utilitarianism', in 'On Liberty', in *Utilitarianism and other Writings*, ed. Mary Warnock (Glasgow: Fontana, 1962), ch. 2, p. 150.

to maximise utility.⁵³ Such a view could allow that virtues are irreducibly plural intrinsic values, at least insofar as agents valued having a virtue for its own sake. However, character-utilitarians would not regard the virtues as *objectively* valuable, since they take the value of the virtues as dependent on desire, and they would also see all goods as agent-neutral – that is, each person's virtue would count for one, and none for more than one. Thus, character-utilitarianism would reject claims (d), (e) and (f) above, and would therefore seem to have insufficient common ground with other kinds of virtue ethics to be properly classified as a form of the theory.

(ii) Aristotelian Perfectionism
Other philosophers proposing theories of the virtues have rejected the idea, implicit in a preference-utilitarian account of the virtues, that the value of the virtues is desire-dependent, and have thereby embraced the objective value of the virtues in claim (d). But they have retained a commitment to maximisation, and to the idea that all goods are agent-neutral, and so have rejected (e) and (f) above. For example, Thomas Hurka defends the claim that 'there are certain intrinsically valuable states of human beings, and . . . each of us should maximise the achievement of these states both in herself and in others'.⁵⁴ In regarding all goods as agent-neutral, this view holds that my becoming virtuous should be of no more importance to me than is your becoming virtuous, for 'we should all try to promote the living of virtuous lives in general'.⁵⁵ This view would hold, in our amended George example, that (other things being equal) George should take the job, since his doing so would maximise the integrity of those affected. This view has a stronger claim to be regarded as a form of virtue ethics than do the character-utilitarian theories in (i), since it recognises the objective value of the virtues. However, in maintaining a commitment to maximisation and to the agent-neutrality of all value, this view is

---

[53] See Robert M. Adams, 'Motive Utilitarianism', *Journal of Philosophy* 73 (1976); Roger Crisp, 'Utilitarianism and the Life of Virtue', *Philosophical Quarterly* 42 (1992), pp. 139–60; and Michael Slote, 'Utilitarian Virtue', in French *et al.* (eds.), *Midwest Studies in Philosophy*, vol. 13. See also Peter Railton, 'How Thinking about Character and Utilitarianism might lead to Rethinking the Character of Utilitarianism', in French *et al.* (eds.), *Midwest Studies in Philosophy*, vol. 13; and Watson, 'On the Primacy of Character', pp. 456–9.

[54] Thomas Hurka, 'The Well-Rounded Life', *Journal of Philosophy* 84 (1987), p. 727. Hurka calls this view 'Aristotelian Perfectionism'.

[55] Dreier, 'Structures of Normative Theories', p. 36.

sufficiently removed from the essentials of virtue ethics to be regarded as a different kind of theory.[56]

(iii) Satisficing Perfectionism

One might, however, retain the basic perfectionist idea that we ought to develop or promote the virtues, but deny both the claim that rightness requires us to *maximise* realisation of the virtues, and the claim that all goods are *agent-neutral*. For one might instead claim that we can, for instance, be 'satisficers' about virtue, and that certain virtues have agent-relative value.[57] This kind of view would hold that one ought to promote virtue to a level which is good enough, rather than necessarily to the highest degree, and that one is permitted to give special priority to promoting one's own virtue, over the virtue-claims of others. Thus, in our George example, this view would permit George to refuse the job, even though his doing so would most likely result in the other chemists' integrity being violated, because it would be morally permissible for George to give primary importance here to his *own* integrity, over the effects of his doing so on others' integrity. Of the three types of consequentialism mentioned here, satisficing perfectionism is the closest to a form of virtue ethics, since it accepts all of the claims made in (a)–(f).

Some of Michael Slote's early work on the virtues suggests the possibility of a form of virtue ethics which resembles the position in (iii). For example, in his defence of the rationality of satisficing over maximising forms of Consequentialism, Slote speaks of the satisficer as having the virtue of moderation in regard to their personal good, which involves being content to accept what is good enough, rather than always seeking to maximise the personal good one can gain from a situation.[58] Slote also discusses how the virtue of benevolence may not require us to maximise the goods of others, but may permit us to satisfice instead: 'Nothing in the idea of

---

[56] See Watson, 'On the Primacy of Character'; and Dreier, 'Structures of Normative Theories', pp. 35–6, who also argue that perfectionism, because it regards virtues as valuable only in agent-neutral terms, cannot be a form of virtue ethics. Despite its name, 'Aristotelian Perfectionism' does not capture all the important features of Aristotle's ethical theory. For there is good evidence to suggest that Aristotle himself was not a maximiser, and regarded some values (such as friendship) as properly agent-relative. (See notes 39 and 42.)

[57] For a satisficing approach to the virtues, albeit one founded in *nonconsequentialist* theory, see Swanton, 'Satisficing and Virtue'. Hurka, *Perfectionism*, pp. 56–7, considers and rejects satisficing forms of perfectionism.

[58] See Michael Slote, 'Moderation, Rationality, and Virtue', in Sterling P. McMurrin (ed.), *The Tanner Lectures on Human Values VII* (Salt Lake City: University of Utah Press, 1986), pp. 55–99.

© Blackwell Publishers Ltd. 1996

impartial, rational, benevolence or of universal sympathy entails a desire for the *greatest possible* human happiness'.[59] Further, while endorsing Scheffler's attack on the kinds of deontological agent-centred *restrictions* which Foot and others accept, Slote nevertheless thinks that the intuitive plausibility of agent-relative *permissions* (such as those illustrated in Williams' integrity objection to Utilitarianism) can be supported both by satisficing and by a virtue ethics based on notions of admirability and excellence.[60] This is consistent with the idea that certain virtues are agent-relative, as in (e) above. Nevertheless, Slote argues that I ought still to be concerned with promoting others' virtue: 'it is part of a common-sense virtue ethics to assume that people should be concerned with the happiness and virtue ... *both of others and of themselves*',[61] although Slote thinks this should take the form of a *balance* of concern between oneself and others *as a class*, rather than the agent-neutrality of Utilitarianism.

However, Slote's recent writings move away from any suggestion of a consequentialist form of virtue ethics, and indeed, he clearly distances his theory from perfectionism and pluralistic consequentialism.[62] Instead, as we saw earlier, Slote bases his virtue ethics on common-sense views about admirable and deplorable character-traits, although this theory says 'nothing explicitly about what sorts of considerations make for admirability and how they combine into overall judgements of admirability'.[63] Some have criticised Slote's virtue ethics as leaving too much to intuition; however, the merits

---

[59] Michael Slote, 'Satisficing Consequentialism', *Proceedings of the Aristotelian Society, Supp.* vol. 58 (1984), p. 162 (my emphasis); cf. p. 142. See also Michael Slote, *Beyond Optimizing: A Study of Rational Choice* (Cambridge MA: Harvard University Press, 1989), p. 26. Slote also considers broadening the application of satisficing from the virtues of moderation and benevolence, to motives and character in general (see 'Satisficing Consequentialism', p. 159).

[60] Scheffler's attack on agent-centred restrictions is found in *The Rejection of Consequentialism*. For Slote's criticisms of agent-centred restrictions, see *From Morality to Virtue*, eg. pp. 37–9; and 'Morality and Self-Other Asymmetry', *Journal of Philosophy* 81 (1984). On satisficing as a rationale for agent-relative permissions, see Slote, 'Satisficing Consequentialism', p. 158. On the compatibility between virtue ethics and agent-relative permissions, see Slote, *From Morality to Virtue* pp. 96–7; John Cottingham, 'Ethics and Impartiality', *Philosophical Studies* 43 (1983); and John Cottingham, 'The Ethics of Self-Concern', *Ethics* 101 (1991).

[61] *From Morality to Virtue*, p. 111. See also p. 230: 'The overarching standard or credo of virtue-ethical thinking ... recommend[s] that we improve others and ourselves with regard to admirability or the possession of various virtues'.

[62] See *From Morality to Virtue*, pp. 245–7.

[63] *From Morality to Virtue*, p. 230.

© Blackwell Publishers Ltd. 1996

of this kind of approach remain unclear until the proper grounds of admirability are brought out.[64]

I cannot here adjudicate between Consequentialist and Nonconsequentialist varieties of virtue ethics; indeed, both forms of the theory seem to have their strengths and weaknesses. For example, Nonconsequentialist virtue ethicists seem to have difficulties in providing a plausible rationale for agent-relative restrictions, while doubts persist over whether a Consequentialist virtue ethics is capable of giving adequate recognition to goods such as integrity and friendship.

Conclusion

In recent years, the virtue ethics movement has made significant progress towards establishing itself as a distinctive and plausible alternative to Kantian and Utilitarian ethical theories. In doing so, virtue ethics has highlighted some serious shortcomings in these traditional approaches, and has offered fresh insights in related areas such as moral psychology, political philosophy, and applied ethics.[65] However, the central features of virtue ethics had always been left rather inexplicit, and this had made the merits of the theory difficult to assess. In order to better understand and judge what virtue ethics has to offer, I have identified six key claims on which the many forms of the theory converge. The resulting basic position demonstrates how virtue ethics differs in important ways from Kantianism and Utilitarianism, and so explains why virtue ethics cannot simply be assimilated to a character-based form of those latter theories, as some philosophers have thought. In outlining the essential features of virtue ethics and their development by different theorists, I also hope to have given some idea of

---

[64] For critiques of Slote's virtue ethics, see the critical notice by Julia Driver in *Nous* 28 (1994), pp. 505–14; and the symposium on Slote, with comments by Michael Stocker, Stephen Darwall, and Henry Richardson (along with Slote's responses), in *Philosophy and Phenomenological Research* 54 (1994).

[65] In moral psychology, see especially John McDowell, 'Virtue and Reason', *The Monist* 62 (1979). In bioethics, see S. R. L. Clark, *The Moral Status of Animals* (Oxford: Oxford University Press, 1977); Rosalind Hursthouse, *Beginning Lives*; Edmund D. Pellegrino & David C. Thomasma, *The Virtues in Medical Practice* (New York: Oxford University Press, 1993); Gregory Pence, *Ethical Options in Medicine* (Oradell: Medical Economics Company, 1980). In business ethics, see Robert Solomon, *Ethics and Excellence: Cooperation and Integrity* (New York: Oxford University Press, 1992). In political philosophy, see the references in note 7.

© Blackwell Publishers Ltd. 1996

the distinctive contribution which the virtue ethics movement has made to contemporary ethics. Whether or not the recently revitalised virtue ethics will survive as an enduring feature of the ethical landscape remains to be seen. In any case, I hope this discussion helps to clarify its prospects.

Centre for Human Bioethics
Monash University
Clayton, Victoria, 3168
Australia

© Blackwell Publishers Ltd. 1996

PHILIPPA FOOT

Euthanasia

The widely used *Shorter Oxford English Dictionary* gives three meanings for the word "euthanasia": the first, "a quiet and easy death"; the second, "the means of procuring this"; and the third, "the action of inducing a quiet and easy death." It is a curious fact that no one of the three gives an adequate definition of the word as it is usually understood. For "euthanasia" means much more than a quiet and easy death, or the means of procuring it, or the action of inducing it. The definition specifies only the manner of the death, and if this were all that was implied a murderer, careful to drug his victim, could claim that his act was an act of euthanasia. We find this ridiculous because we take it for granted that in euthanasia it is death itself, not just the manner of death, that must be kind to the one who dies.

To see how important it is that "euthanasia" should not be used as the dictionary definition allows it to be used, merely to signify that a death was quiet and easy, one has only to remember that Hitler's "euthanasia" program traded on this ambiguity. Under this program, planned before the War but brought into full operation by a decree of 1 September 1939, some 275,000 people were gassed in centers which were to be a model for those in which Jews were later exterminated. Anyone in a state institution could be sent to the gas chambers if it was considered that he could not be "rehabilitated" for useful work. As Dr. Leo Alexander reports, relying on the testimony of a

© 1977 by Philippa Foot
I would like to thank Derek Parfit and the editors of *Philosophy & Public Affairs* for their very helpful comments.

neuropathologist who received 500 brains from one of the killing centers,

> In Germany the exterminations included the mentally defective, psychotics (particularly schizophrenics), epileptics and patients suffering from infirmities of old age and from various organic neurological disorders such as infantile paralysis, Parkinsonism, multiple sclerosis and brain tumors.... In truth, all those unable to work and considered nonrehabilitable were killed.[1]

These people were killed because they were "useless" and "a burden on society"; only the manner of their deaths could be thought of as relatively easy and quiet.

Let us insist, then, that when we talk about euthanasia we are talking about a death understood as a good or happy event for the one who dies. This stipulation follows etymology, but is itself not exactly in line with current usage, which would be captured by the condition that the death should *not* be an evil rather than that it *should* be a good. That this is how people talk is shown by the fact that the case of Karen Ann Quinlan and others in a state of permanent coma is often discussed under the heading of "euthanasia." Perhaps it is not too late to object to the use of the word "euthanasia" in this sense. Apart from the break with the Greek origins of the word there are other unfortunate aspects of this extension of the term. For if we say that the death must be supposed to be a good to the subject we can also specify that it shall be for his sake that an act of euthanasia is performed. If we say merely that death shall not be an evil to him, we cannot stipulate that benefiting him shall be the motive where euthanasia is in question. Given the importance of the question, For whose sake are we acting? it is good to have a definition of euthanasia which brings under this heading only cases of opting for death for the sake of the one who dies. Perhaps what is most important is to say either that euthanasia is to be for the good of the subject or at least that death is to be no evil to him, thus refusing to talk Hitler's language. However, in this paper it is the first condition that will be understood, with the additional proviso that by an act of euthanasia we mean one

---

1. Leo Alexander, "Medical Science under Dictatorship," *New England Journal of Medicine*, 14 July 1949, p. 40.

of inducing or otherwise opting for death for the sake of the one who is to die.

A few lesser points need to be cleared up. In the first place it must be said that the word "act" is not to be taken to exclude omission: we shall speak of an act of euthanasia when someone is deliberately allowed to die, for his own good, and not only when positive measures are taken to see that he does. The very general idea we want is that of a choice of action or inaction directed at another man's death and causally effective in the sense that, in conjunction with actual circumstances, it is a sufficient condition of death. Of complications such as overdetermination, it will not be necessary to speak.

A second, and definitely minor, point about the definition of an act of euthanasia concerns the question of fact versus belief. It has already been implied that one who performs an act of euthanasia thinks that death will be merciful for the subject since we have said that it is on account of this thought that the act is done. But is it enough that he acts with this thought, or must things actually be as he thinks them to be? If one man kills another, or allows him to die, thinking that he is in the last stages of a terrible disease, though in fact he could have been cured, is this an act of euthanasia or not? Nothing much seems to hang on our decision about this. The same condition has got to enter into the definition whether as an element in reality or only as an element in the agent's belief. And however we define an act of euthanasia culpability or justifiability will be the same: if a man acts through ignorance his ignorance may be culpable or it may not.[2]

These are relatively easy problems to solve, but one that is dauntingly difficult has been passed over in this discussion of the definition, and must now be faced. It is easy to say, as if this raised no problems, that an act of euthanasia is by definition one aiming at the *good* of the one whose death is in question, and that it is *for his sake* that his death is desired. But how is this to be explained? Presumably we are thinking of some evil already with him or to come on him if he continues to live, and death is thought of as a release from this evil. But this

---

2. For a discussion of culpable and nonculpable ignorance see Thomas Aquinas, *Summa Theologica*, First Part of the Second Part, Question 6, article 8, and Question 19, articles 5 and 6.

cannot be enough. Most people's lives contain evils such as grief or pain, but we do not therefore think that death would be a blessing to them. On the contrary life is generally supposed to be a good even for someone who is unusually unhappy or frustrated. How is it that one can ever wish for death for the sake of the one who is to die? This difficult question is central to the discussion of euthanasia, and we shall literally not know what we are talking about if we ask whether acts of euthanasia defined as we have defined them are ever morally permissible without first understanding better the reason for saying that life is a good, and the possibility that it is not always so.

If a man should save my life he would be my benefactor. In normal circumstances this is plainly true; but does one always benefit another in saving his life? It seems certain that he does not. Suppose, for instance, that a man were being tortured to death and was given a drug that lengthened his sufferings; this would not be a benefit but the reverse. Or suppose that in a ghetto in Nazi Germany a doctor saved the life of someone threatened by disease, but that the man once cured was transported to an extermination camp; the doctor might wish for the sake of the patient that he had died of the disease. Nor would a longer stretch of life always be a benefit to the person who was given it. Comparing Hitler's camps with those of Stalin, Dmitri Panin observes that in the latter the method of extermination was made worse by agonies that could stretch out over months.

> Death from a bullet would have been bliss compared with what many millions had to endure while dying of hunger. The kind of death to which they were condemned has nothing to equal it in treachery and sadism.[3]

These examples show that to save or prolong a man's life is not always to do him a service: it may be better for him if he dies earlier rather than later. It must therefore be agreed that while life is normally a benefit to the one who has it, this is not always so.

The judgment is often fairly easy to make—that life is or is not a good to someone—but the basis for it is very hard to find. When life is said to be a benefit or a good, on what grounds is the assertion made?

The difficulty is underestimated if it is supposed that the problem

---

3. Dmitri Panin, *The Notebooks of Sologdin* (London, 1976), pp. 66–67.

arises from the fact that one who is dead has nothing, so that the good someone gets from being alive cannot be compared with the amount he would otherwise have had. For why should this particular comparison be necessary? Surely it would be enough if one could say whether or not someone whose life was prolonged had more good than evil in the extra stretch of time. Such estimates are not always possible, but frequently they are: we say, for example, "He was very happy in those last years," or, "He had little but unhappiness then." If the balance of good and evil determined whether life was a good to someone we would expect to find a correlation in the judgments. In fact, of course, we find nothing of the kind. First, a man who has no doubt that existence is a good to him may have no idea about the balance of happiness and unhappiness in his life, or of any other positive and negative factors that may be suggested. So the supposed criteria are not always operating where the judgment is made. And secondly the application of the criteria gives an answer that is often wrong. Many people have more evil than good in their lives; we do not, however, conclude that we would do these people no service by rescuing them from death.

To get around this last difficulty Thomas Nagel has suggested that experience itself is a good which must be brought in to balance accounts.

> . . . life is worth living even when the bad elements of experience are plentiful, and the good ones too meager to outweigh the bad ones on their own. The additional positive weight is supplied by experience itself, rather than by any of its contents.[4]

This seems implausible because if experience itself is a good it must be so even when what we experience is wholly bad, as in being tortured to death. How should one decide how much to count for this experiencing; and why count anything at all?

Others have tried to solve the problem by arguing that it is a man's desire for life that makes us call life a good: if he wants to live then anyone who prolongs his life does him a benefit. Yet someone may cling to life where we would say confidently that it would be better

---

4. Thomas Nagel, "Death," in James Rachels, ed., *Moral Problems* (New York, 1971), p. 362.

for him if he died, and he may admit it too. Speaking of those same conditions in which, as he said, a bullet would have been merciful, Panin writes,

> I should like to pass on my observations concerning the absence of suicides under the extremely severe conditions of our concentration camps. The more that life became desperate, the more a prisoner seemed determined to hold onto it.[5]

One might try to explain this by saying that hope was the ground of this wish to survive for further days and months in the camp. But there is nothing unintelligible in the idea that a man might cling to life though he knew those facts about his future which would make any charitable man wish that he might die.

The problem remains, and it is hard to know where to look for a solution. Is there a conceptual connection between *life* and *good*? Because life is not always a good we are apt to reject this idea, and to think that it must be a contingent fact that life is usually a good, as it is a contingent matter that legacies are usually a benefit, if they are. Yet it seems not to be a contingent matter that to save someone's life is ordinarily to benefit him. The problem is to find where the conceptual connection lies.

It may be good tactics to forget for a time that it is euthanasia we are discussing and to see how *life* and *good* are connected in the case of living beings other than men. Even plants have things done to them that are harmful or beneficial, and what does them good must be related in some way to their living and dying. Let us therefore consider plants and animals, and then come back to human beings. At least we shall get away from the temptation to think that the connection between life and benefit must everywhere be a matter of happiness and unhappiness or of pleasure and pain; the idea being absurd in the case of animals and impossible even to formulate for plants.

In case anyone thinks that the concept of the beneficial applies only in a secondary or analogical way to plants, he should be reminded that we speak quite straightforwardly in saying, for instance, that a certain amount of sunlight is beneficial to most plants. What is in

---

5. Panin, *Sologdin*, p. 85.

91   *Euthanasia*

question here is the habitat in which plants of particular species flourish, but we can also talk, in a slightly different way, of what does them good, where there is some suggestion of improvement or remedy. What has the beneficial to do with sustaining life? It is tempting to answer, "everything," thinking that a healthy condition just is the one apt to secure survival. In fact, however, what is beneficial to a plant may have to do with reproduction rather than the survival of the individual member of the species. Nevertheless there is a plain connection between the beneficial and the life-sustaining even for the individual plant; if something makes it better able to survive in conditions normal for that species it is ipso facto good for it. We need go no further, and could go no further, in explaining why a certain environment or treatment is good for a plant than to show how it helps this plant to survive.[6]

This connection between the life-sustaining and the beneficial is reasonably unproblematic, and there is nothing fanciful or zoomorphic in speaking of benefiting or doing good to plants. A connection with its survival can make something beneficial to a plant. But this is not, of course, to say that we count life as a good to a plant. We may save its life by giving it what is beneficial; we do not benefit it by saving its life.

A more ramified concept of benefit is used in speaking of animal life. New things can be said, such as that an animal is better or worse off for something that happened, or that it was a good or bad thing for it that it did happen. And new things count as benefit. In the first place, there is comfort, which often is, but need not be, related to health. When loosening a collar which is too tight for a dog we can say, "That will be better for it." So we see that the words "better for it" have two different meanings which we mark when necessary by a difference of emphasis, saying "better *for* it" when health is involved. And secondly an animal can be benefited by having its life saved. "Could you do anything for it?" can be answered by, "Yes, I managed to save its life." Sometimes we may understand this, just as we would

---

6. Yet some detail needs to be filled in to explain why we should not say that a scarecrow is beneficial to the plants it protects. Perhaps what is beneficial must either be a feature of the plant itself, such as protective prickles, or else must work on the plant directly, such as a line of trees which give it shade.

for a plant, to mean that we had checked some disease. But we can also do something for an animal by scaring away its predator. If we do this, it is a good thing for the animal that we did, unless of course it immediately meets a more unpleasant end by some other means. Similarly, on the bad side, an animal may be worse off for our intervention, and this not because it pines or suffers but simply because it gets killed.

The problem that vexes us when we think about euthanasia comes on the scene at this point. For if we can do something for an animal—can benefit it—by relieving its suffering but also by saving its life, where does the greater benefit come when only death will end pain? It seemed that life was a good in its own right; yet pain seemed to be an evil with equal status and could therefore make life not a good after all. Is it only life without pain that is a good when animals are concerned? This does not seem a crazy suggestion when we are thinking of animals, since unlike human beings they do not have suffering as part of their normal life. But it is perhaps the idea of ordinary life that matters here. We would not say that we had done anything for an animal if we had merely kept it alive, either in an unconscious state or in a condition where, though conscious, it was unable to operate in an ordinary way; and the fact is that animals in severe and continuous pain simply do not operate normally. So we do not, on the whole, have the option of doing the animal good by saving its life though the life would be a life of pain. No doubt there are borderline cases, but that is no problem. We are not trying to make new judgments possible, but rather to find the principle of the ones we do make.

When we reach human life the problems seem even more troublesome. For now we must take quite new things into account, such as the subject's own view of his life. It is arguable that this places extra constraints on the solution: might it not be counted as a necessary condition of life's being a good to a man that he should see it as such? Is there not some difficulty about the idea that a benefit might be done to him by the saving or prolonging of his life even though he himself wished for death? Of course he might have a quite mistaken view of his own prospects, but let us ignore this and think only of cases where it is life as he knows it that is in question. Can we think that the prolonging of this life would be a benefit to him even though he would rather have it end than continue? It seems that this cannot be ruled out. That there is no simple incompatibility between life as a good and the wish for death is shown by the possibility that a man should wish himself dead, not for his own sake, but for the sake of someone else. And if we try to amend the thesis to say that life cannot be a good to one who wishes *for his own sake* that he should die, we find the crucial concept slipping through our fingers. As Bishop Butler pointed out long ago not all ends are either benevolent or self-interested. Does a man wish for death for his own sake in the relevant sense if, for instance, he wishes to revenge himself on another by his death. Or what if he is proud and refuses to stomach dependence or incapacity even though there are many good things left in life for him? The truth seems to be that the wish for death is sometimes compatible with life's being a good and sometimes not, which is possible because the description "wishing for death" is one covering diverse states of mind from that of the determined suicide, pathologically depressed, to that of one who is surprised to find that the thought of a fatal accident is viewed with relief. On the one hand, a man may see his life as a burden but go about his business in a more or less ordinary way; on the other hand, the wish for death may take the form of a rejection of everything that is in life, as it does in severe depression. It seems reasonable to say that life is not a good to one permanently in the latter state, and we must return to this topic later on.

When are we to say that life is a good or a benefit to a man? The dilemma that faces us is this. If we say that life as such is a good we find ourselves refuted by the examples given at the beginning of this discussion. We therefore incline to think that it is as bringing good things that life is a good, where it is a good. But if life is a good only because it is the condition of good things why is it not equally an evil when it brings bad things? And how can it be a good even when it brings more evil than good?

It should be noted that the problem has here been formulated in terms of the balance of good and evil, not that of happiness and unhappiness, and that it is not to be solved by the denial (which may be reasonable enough) that unhappiness is the only evil or happiness the only good. In this paper no view has been expressed about the nature of goods other than life itself. The point is that on any view of the goods and evils that life can contain, it seems that a life with more evil than good could still itself be a good.

It may be useful to review the judgments with which our theory must square. Do we think that life can be a good to one who suffers a lot of pain? Clearly we do. What about severely handicapped people; can life be a good to them? Clearly it can be, for even if someone is almost completely paralyzed, perhaps living in an iron lung, perhaps able to move things only by means of a tube held between his lips, we do not rule him out of order if he says that some benefactor saved his life. Nor is it different with mental handicap. There are many fairly severely handicapped people—such as those with Down's Syndrome (Mongolism)—for whom a simple affectionate life is possible. What about senility? Does this break the normal connection between life and good? Here we must surely distinguish between forms of senility. Some forms leave a life which we count someone as better off having than not having, so that a doctor who prolonged it would benefit the person concerned. With some kinds of senility this is however no longer true. There are some in geriatric wards who are barely conscious, though they can move a little and swallow food put into their mouths. To prolong such a state, whether in the old or in the very severely mentally handicapped is not to do them a service or confer a benefit. But of course it need not be the reverse: only if there is suffering would one wish for the sake of the patient that he should die.

It seems, therefore, that merely being alive even without suffering is not a good, and that we must make a distinction similar to that which we made when animals were our topic. But how is the line to be drawn in the case of men? What is to count as ordinary human life in the relevant sense? If it were only the very senile or very ill who were to be said not to have this life it might seem right to describe it in terms of *operation*. But it will be hard to find the sense in which the men described by Panin were not operating, given that they dragged themselves out to the forest to work. What is it about the life that the prisoners were living that makes us put it on the other side of the dividing line from that of some severely ill or suffering patients, and from most of the physicaly or mentaly handicapped?

It is not that they were in captivity, for life in captivity can certainly be a good. Nor is it merely the unusual nature of their life. In some ways the prisoners were living more as other men do than the patient in an iron lung.

The suggested solution to the problem is, then, that there is a certain conceptual connection between *life* and *good* in the case of human beings as in that of animals and even plants. Here, as there, however, it is not the mere state of being alive that can determine, or itself count as, a good, but rather life coming up to some standard of normality. It was argued that it is as part of ordinary life that the elements of good that a man may have are relevant to the question of whether saving his life counts as benefiting him. Ordinary human lives, even very hard lives, contain a minimum of basic goods, but when these are absent the idea of life is no longer linked to that of good. And since it is in this way that the elements of good contained in a man's life are relevant to the question of whether he is benefited if his life is preserved, there is no reason why it should be the balance of good and evil that counts.

It should be added that evils are relevant in one way when, as in the examples discussed above, they destroy the possibility of ordinary goods, but in a different way when they invade a life from which the goods are already absent for a different reason. So, for instance, the connection between *life* and *good* may be broken because consciousness has sunk to a very low level, as in extreme senility or severe brain damage. In itself this kind of life seems to be neither good nor evil, but if suffering sets in one would hope for a speedy end.

The idea we need seems to be that of life which is ordinary human life in the following respect—that it contains a minimum of basic human goods. What is ordinary in human life—even in very hard lives —is that a man is not driven to work far beyond his capacity; that he has the support of a family or community; that he can more or less satisfy his hunger; that he has hopes for the future; that he can lie down to rest at night. Such things were denied to the men in the Vyatlag camps described by Panin; not even rest at night was allowed them when they were tormented by bed-bugs, by noise and stench, and by routines such as body-searches and bath-parades—arranged for the night time so that work norms would not be reduced. Disease too can so take over a man's life that the normal human goods disappear. When a patient is so overwhelmed by pain or nausea that he cannot eat with pleasure, if he can eat at all, and is out of the reach of even the most loving voice, he no longer has ordinary human life in the sense in which the words are used here. And we may now pick up a thread from an earlier part of the discussion by remarking that crippling depression can destroy the enjoyment of ordinary goods as effectively as external circumstances can remove them.

This, admittedly inadequate, discussion of the sense in which life is normally a good, and of the reasons why it may not be so in some particular case, completes the account of what euthanasia is here taken to be. An act of euthanasia, whether literally act or rather omission, is attributed to an agent who opts for the death of another because in his case life seems to be an evil rather than a good. The question now to be asked is whether acts of euthanasia are ever justifiable. But there are two topics here rather than one. For it is one thing to say that some acts of euthanasia considered only in themselves and their results are morally unobjectionable, and another to say that it would be all right to legalize them. Perhaps the practice of euthanasia would allow too many abuses, and perhaps there would be too many mistakes. Moreover the practice might have very important and highly undesirable side effects, because it is unlikely that we could change our principles about the treatment of the old and the ill without changing fundamental emotional attitudes and social relations. The topics must, therefore, be treated separately. In the next part of the discussion, nothing will be said about the social consequences and possible abuses of the practice of euthanasia, but only about acts of euthanasia considered in themselves.

What we want to know is whether acts of euthanasia, defined as we have defined them, are ever morally permissible. To be more accurate, we want to know whether it is ever sufficient justification of the choice of death for another that death can be counted a benefit rather than harm, and that this is why the choice is made.

It will be impossible to get a clear view of the area to which this topic belongs without first marking the distinct grounds on which objection may lie when one man opts for the death of another. There are two different virtues whose requirements are, in general, contrary

97 Euthanasia

to such actions. An unjustified act of killing, or allowing to die, is contrary to justice or to charity, or to both virtues, and the moral failings are distinct. Justice has to do with what men *owe* each other in the way of noninterference and positive service. When used in this wide sense, which has its history in the doctrine of the cardinal virtues, justice is not especially connected with, for instance, law courts but with the whole area of rights, and duties corresponding to rights. Thus murder is one form of injustice, dishonesty another, and wrongful failure to keep contracts a third; chicanery in a law court or defrauding someone of his inheritance are simply other cases of injustice. Justice as such is not directly linked to the good of another, and may require that something be rendered to him even where it will do him harm, as Hume pointed out when he remarked that a debt must be paid even to a profligate debauchee who "would rather receive harm than benefit from large possessions."[7] Charity, on the other hand, is the virtue which attaches us to the good of others. An act of charity is in question only where something is not demanded by justice, but a lack of charity and of justice can be shown where a man is denied something which he both needs and has a right to; both charity and justice demand that widows and orphans are not defrauded, and the man who cheats them is neither charitable nor just.

It is easy to see that the two grounds of objection to inducing death are distinct. A murder is an act of injustice. A culpable failure to come to the aid of someone whose life is threatened is normally contrary, not to justice, but to charity. But where one man is under contract, explicit or implicit, to come to the aid of another injustice too will be shown. Thus injustice may be involved either in an act or an omission, and the same is true of a lack of charity; charity may demand that someone be aided, but also that an unkind word not be spoken.

The distinction between charity and justice will turn out to be of the first importance when voluntary and nonvoluntary euthanasia are distinguished later on. This is because of the connection between justice and rights, and something should now be said about this. I believe it is true to say that wherever a man acts unjustly he has infringed a right, since justice has to do with whatever a man is owed, and whatever he is owed is his as a matter of right. Something should

---

7. David Hume, *Treatise*, Book III, Part II, Section 1.

therefore be said about the different kinds of rights. The distinction commonly made is between having a right in the sense of having a liberty, and having a "claim-right" or "right of recipience."[8] The best way to understand such a distinction seems to be as follows. To say that a man has a right in the sense of a liberty is to say that no one can demand that he do not do the thing which he has a right to do. The fact that he has a right to do it consists in the fact that a certain kind of objection does not lie against his doing it. Thus a man has a right in this sense to walk down a public street or park his car in a public parking space. It does not follow that no one else may prevent him from doing so. If for some reason I want a certain man not to park in a certain place I may lawfully park there myself or get my friends to do so, thus preventing him from doing what he has a right (in the sense of a liberty) to do. It is different, however, with a claim-right. This is the kind of right which I have in addition to a liberty when, for example, I have a private parking space; now others have duties in the way of noninterference, as in this case, or of service, as in the case where my claim-right is to goods or services promised to me. Sometimes one of these rights gives other people the duty of securing to me that to which I have a right, but at other times their duty is merely to refrain from interference. If a fall of snow blocks my private parking space there is normally no obligation for anyone else to clear it away. Claim rights generate duties; sometimes these duties are duties of noninterference; sometimes they are duties of service. If your right gives me the duty not to interfere with you I have "no right" to do it; similarly, if your right gives me the duty to provide something for you I have "no right" to refuse to do it. What I lack is the right which is a liberty; I am not "at liberty" to interfere with you or to refuse the service.

Where in this picture does the right to life belong? No doubt people have the right to live in the sense of a liberty, but what is important is the cluster of claim-rights brought together under the title of the

---

8. See, for example D.D. Raphael, "Human Rights Old and New," in D.D. Raphael, ed., *Political Theory and the Rights of Man* (London, 1967), and Joel Feinberg, "The Nature and Value of Rights," *The Journal of Value Inquiry* 4, no. 4 (Winter 1970): 243–257. Reprinted in Samuel Gorovitz, ed., *Moral Problems in Medicine* (Englewood Cliffs, New Jersey, 1976).

right to life. The chief of these is, of course, the right to be free from interferences that threaten life. If other people aim their guns at us or try to pour poison into our drink we can, to put it mildly, demand that they desist. And then there are the services we can claim from doctors, health officers, bodyguards, and firemen; the rights that depend on contract or public arrangement. Perhaps there is no particular point in saying that the duties these people owe us belong to the right to life; we might as well say that all the services owed to anyone by tailors, dressmakers, and couturiers belong to a right called the right to be elegant. But contracts such as those understood in the patient-doctor relationship come in an important way when we are discussing the rights and wrongs of euthanasia, and are therefore mentioned here.

Do people have the right to what they need in order to survive, apart from the right conferred by special contracts into which other people have entered for the supplying of these necessities? Do people in the underdeveloped countries in which starvation is rife have the right to the food they so evidently lack? Joel Feinberg, discussing this question, suggests that they should be said to have "a claim," distinguishing this from a "valid claim," which gives a claim-right.

> The manifesto writers on the other side who seem to identify needs, or at least basic needs, with what they call "human rights," are more properly described, I think, as urging upon the world community the moral principle that *all* basic human needs ought to be recognized as *claims* (in the customary *prima facie* sense) worthy of sympathy and serious consideration right now, even though, in many cases, they cannot yet plausibly be treated as *valid* claims, that is, as grounds of any other people's duties. This way of talking avoids the anomaly of ascribing to all human beings now, even those in pre-industrial societies, such "economic and social rights" as "periodic holidays with pay."⁹

This seems reasonable, though we notice that there are some actual rights to service which are not based on anything like a contract, as for instance the right that children have to support from their parents and parents to support from their children in old age, though both

---

9. Feinberg, "Human Rights," *Moral Problems in Medicine*, p. 465.

sets of rights are to some extent dependent on existing social arrangements.

Let us now ask how the right to life affects the morality of acts of euthanasia. Are such acts sometimes or always ruled out by the right to life? This is certainly a possibility; for although an act of euthanasia is, by our definition, a matter of opting for death for the good of the one who is to die, there is, as we noted earlier, no direct connection between that to which a man has a right and that which is for his good. It is true that men have the right only to the kind of thing that is, in general, a good: we do not think that people have the right to garbage or polluted air. Nevertheless, a man may have the right to something which he himself would be better off without; where rights exist it is a man's will that counts not his or anyone else's estimate of benefit or harm. So the duties complementary to the right to life—the general duty of noninterference and the duty of service incurred by certain persons—are not affected by the quality of a man's life or by his prospects. Even if it is true that he would be, as we say, "better off dead," so long as he wants to live this does not justify us in killing him and may not justify us in deliberately allowing him to die. All of us have the duty of noninterference, and some of us may have the duty to sustain his life. Suppose, for example, that a retreating army has to leave behind wounded or exhausted soldiers in the wastes of an arid or snowbound land where the only prospect is death by starvation or at the hands of an enemy notoriously cruel. It has often been the practice to accord a merciful bullet to men in such desperate straits. But suppose that one of them demands that he should be left alive? It seems clear that his comrades have no right to kill him, though it is a quite different question as to whether they should give him a life-prolonging drug. The right to life can sometimes give a duty of positive service, but does not do so here. What it does give is the right to be left alone.

Interestingly enough we have arrived by way of a consideration of the right to life at the distinction normally labeled "active" versus "passive" euthanasia, and often thought to be irrelevant to the moral issue.[10] Once it is seen that the right to life is a distinct ground of

---

10. See, for example, James Rachels, "Active and Passive Euthanasia," *New England Journal of Medicine* 292, no. 2 (9 Jan. 1975): 78–80.

objection to certain acts of euthanasia, and that this right creates a duty of noninterference more widespread than the duties of care there can be no doubt about the relevance of the distinction between passive and active euthanasia. Where everyone may have the duty to leave someone alone, it may be that no one has the duty to maintain his life, or that only some people do.

Where then do the boundaries of the "active" and "passive" lie? In some ways the words are themselves misleading, because they suggest the difference between act and omission which is not quite what we want. Certainly the act of shooting someone is the kind of thing we were talking about under the heading of "interference," and omitting to give him a drug a case of refusing care. But the act of turning off a respirator should surely be thought of as no different from the decision not to start it; if doctors had decided that a patient should be allowed to die, either course of action might follow, and both should be counted as passive rather than active euthanasia if euthanasia were in question. The point seems to be that interference in a course of treatment is not the same as other interference in a man's life, and particularly if the same body of people are responsible for the treatment and for its discontinuance. In such a case we could speak of the disconnecting of the apparatus as killing the man, or of the hospital as allowing him to die. By and large, it is the act of killing that is ruled out under the heading of noninterference, but not in every case.

Doctors commonly recognize this distinction, and the grounds on which some philosophers have denied it seem untenable. James Rachels, for instance, believes that if the difference between active and passive is relevant anywhere, it should be relevant everywhere, and he has pointed to an example in which it seems to make no difference which is done. If someone saw a child drowning in a bath it would seem just as bad to let it drown as to push its head under water.[11] If "it makes no difference" means that one act would be as iniquitous as the other this is true. It is not that killing is *worse* than allowing to die, but that the two are contrary to distinct virtues, which gives the possibility that in some circumstances one is impermissible and the other permissible. In the circumstances invented by Rachels, both are

11. Ibid.

wicked: it is contrary to justice to push the child's head under the water—something one has no right to do. To leave it to drown is not contrary to justice, but it is a particularly glaring example of lack of charity. Here it makes no practical difference because the requirements of justice and charity coincide; but in the case of the retreating army they did not: charity would have required that the wounded soldier be killed had not justice required that he be left alive.[12] In such a case it makes all the difference whether a man opts for the death of another in a positive action, or whether he allows him to die. An analogy with the right to property will make the point clear. If a man owns something he has the right to it even when its possession does him harm, and we have no right to take it from him. But if one day it should blow away, maybe nothing requires us to get it back for him; we could not deprive him of it, but we may allow it to go. This is not to deny that it will often be an unfriendly act or one based on an arrogant judgment when we refuse to do what he wants. Nevertheless, we would be within our rights, and it might be that no moral objection of any kind would lie against our refusal.

It is important to emphasize that a man's rights may stand between us and the action we would dearly like to take for his sake. They may, of course, also prevent action which we would like to take for the sake of others, as when it might be tempting to kill one man to save several. But it is interesting that the limits of allowable interference, however uncertain, seem stricter in the first case than the second. Perhaps there are no cases in which it would be all right to kill a man against his will *for his own sake* unless they could equally well be described as cases of allowing him to die, as in the example of turning off the respirator. However, there are circumstances, even if these are very rare, in which one man's life would justifiably be sacrificed to save others, and "killing" would be the only description of what was being done. For instance, a vehicle which had gone out of control might be steered from a path on which it would kill more than one man to a path on which it would kill one.[13] But it would not be permissible to

---

12. It is not, however, that justice and charity conflict. A man does not lack charity because he refrains from an act of injustice which would have been for someone's good.

13. For a discussion of such questions, see my article "The Problem of Abortion and the Doctrine of Double Effect," *Oxford Review*, no. 5 (1967); reprinted in Rachels, *Moral Problems*, and Gorovitz, *Moral Problems in Medicine*.

103   Euthanasia

steer a vehicle towards someone in order to kill him, against his will, for his own good. An analogy with property rights illustrates the point. One may not destroy a man's property against his will on the grounds that he would be better off without it; there are however circumstances in which it could be destroyed for the sake of others. If his house is liable to fall and kill him that is his affair; it might, however, without injustice be destroyed to stop the spread of a fire.

We see then that the distinction between active and passive, important as it is elsewhere, has a special importance in the area of euthanasia. It should also be clear why James Rachels' other argument, that it is often "more humane" to kill than to allow to die, does not show that the distinction between active and passive euthanasia is morally irrelevant. It might be "more humane" in this sense to deprive a man of the property that brings evils on him, or to refuse to pay what is owed to Hume's profligate debauchee; but if we say this we must admit that an act which is "more humane" than its alternative may be morally objectionable because it infringes rights.

So far we have said very little about the right to service as opposed to the right to noninterference, though it was agreed that both might be brought under the heading of "the right to life." What about the duty to preserve life that may belong to special classes of persons such as bodyguards, firemen, or doctors? Unlike the general public they are not within their rights if they merely refrain from interfering and do not try to sustain life. The subject's claim-rights are two-fold as far as they are concerned and passive as well as active euthanasia may be ruled out here if it is against his will. This is not to say that he has the right to any and every service needed to save or prolong his life; the rights of other people set limits to what may be demanded, both because they have the right not to be interfered with and because they may have a competing right to services. Furthermore one must enquire just what the contract or implicit agreement amounts to in each case. Firemen and bodyguards presumably have a duty which is simply to preserve life, within the limits of justice to others and of reasonableness to themselves. With doctors it may however be different, since their duty relates not only to preserving life but also to the relief of suffering. It is not clear what a doctor's duties are to his patient if life can be prolonged only at the cost of suffering or suffering relieved only by measures that shorten life. George Fletcher has argued that what the doctor is under contract to do depends on what is generally done, because this is what a patient will reasonably expect.[14] This seems right. If procedures are part of normal medical practice then it seems that the patient can demand them however much it may be against his interest to do do. Once again it is not a matter of what is "most humane."

That the patient's right to life may set limits to permissible acts of euthanasia seems undeniable. If he does not want to die no one has the right to practice active euthanasia on him, and passive euthanasia may also be ruled out where he has a right to the services of doctors or others.

Perhaps few will deny what has so far been said about the impermissibility of acts of euthanasia simply because we have so far spoken about the case of one who positively wants to live, and about his rights, whereas those who advocate euthanasia are usually thinking either about those who wish to die or about those whose wishes cannot be ascertained either because they cannot properly be said to have wishes or because, for one reason or another, we are unable to form a reliable estimate of what they are. The question that must now be asked is whether the latter type of case, where euthanasia though not involuntary would again be nonvoluntary, is different from the one discussed so far. Would we have the right to kill someone for his own good so long as we had no idea that he positively wished to live? And what about the life-prolonging duties of doctors in the same circumstances? This is a very difficult problem. On the one hand, it seems ridiculous to suppose that a man's right to life is something which generates duties only where he has signaled that he wants to live; as a borrower does indeed have a duty to return something lent on indefinite loan only if the lender indicates that he wants it back. On the other hand, it might be argued that there is something illogical about the idea that a right has been infringed if someone incapable of saying whether he wants it or not is deprived of something that is doing him harm rather than good. Yet on the analogy of property we would say that a right has been infringed. Only if someone had earlier

---

14. *George Fletcher* "Legal Aspects of the Decision not to Prolong Life," *Journal of the American Medical Association* 203, no. 1 (1 Jan. 1968): 119–122. Reprinted in Gorovitz.

told us that in such circumstances he would not want to keep the thing could we think that his right had been waived. Perhaps if we could make confident judgments about what anyone in such circumstances would wish, or what he would have wished beforehand had he considered the matter, we could agree to consider the right to life as "dormant," needing to be asserted if the normal duties were to remain. But as things are we cannot make any such assumption; we simply do not know what most people would want, or would have wanted, us to do unless they tell us. This is certainly the case so far as active measures to end life are concerned. Possibly it is different, or will become different, in the matter of being kept alive, so general is the feeling against using sophisticated procedures on moribund patients, and so much is this dreaded by people who are old or terminally ill. Once again the distinction between active and passive authanasia has come on the scene, but this time because most people's attitudes to the two are so different. It is just possible that we might presume, in the absence of specific evidence, that someone would not wish, beyond a certain point, to be kept alive; it is certainly not possible to assume that he would wish to be killed.

In the last paragraph we have begun to broach the topic of voluntary euthanasia, and this we must now discuss. What is to be said about the case in which there is no doubt about someone's wish to die: either he has told us beforehand that he would wish it in circumstances such as he is now in, and has shown no sign of a change of mind, or else he tells us now, being in possession of his faculties and of a steady mind. We should surely say that the objections previously urged against acts of euthanasia, which it must be remembered were all on the ground of rights, had disappeared. It does not seem that one would infringe someone's right to life in killing him with his permission and in fact at his request. Why should someone not be able to waive his right to life, or rather, as would be more likely to happen, to cancel some of the duties of noninterference that this right entails? (He is more likely to say that he should be killed by this man at this time in this manner, than to say that anyone may kill him at any time and in any way.) Similarly someone may give permission for the destruction of his property, and request it. The important thing is that he gives a critical permission, and it seems that this is enough to cancel the duty normally associated with the right. If someone gives you permission to destroy his property it can no longer be said that you have no right to do so, and I do not see why it should not be the case with taking a man's life. An objection might be made on the ground that only God has the right to take life, but in this paper religious as opposed to moral arguments are being left aside. Religion apart, there seems to be no case to be made out for an infringement of rights if a man who wishes to die is allowed to die or even killed. But of course it does not follow that there is no moral objection to it. Even with property, which is after all a relatively small matter, one might be wrong to destroy what one had the right to destroy. For, apart from its value to other people, it might be valuable to the man who wanted it destroyed, and charity might require us to hold our hand where justice did not.

Let us review the conclusion of this part of the argument, which has been about euthanasia and the right to life. It has been argued that from this side come stringent restrictions on the acts of euthanasia that could be morally permissible. Active nonvoluntary euthanasia is ruled out by that part of the right to life which creates the duty of noninterference though passive nonvoluntary euthanasia is not ruled out, except where the right to life-preserving action has been created by some special condition such as a contract between a man and his doctor, and it is not always certain just what such a contract involves. Voluntary euthanasia is another matter: as the preceding paragraph suggested, no right is infringed if a man is allowed to die or even killed at his own request.

Turning now to the other objection that normally holds against inducing the death of another, that it is against charity, or benevolence, we must tell a very different story. Charity is the virtue that gives attachment to the good of others, and because life is normally a good, charity normally demands that it should be saved or prolonged. But as we so defined an act of euthanasia that it seeks a man's death for his own sake—for his good—charity will normally speak in favor of it. This is not, of course, to say that charity can require an act of euthanasia which justice forbids, but if an act of euthanasia is not contrary to justice—that is, it does not infringe rights—charity will rather be in its favor than against.

107 Euthanasia

Once more the distinction between nonvoluntary and voluntary euthanasia must be considered. Could it ever be compatible with charity to seek a man's death although he wanted to live, or at least had not let us know that he wanted to die? It has been argued that in such circumstances active euthanasia would infringe his right to life, but passive euthanasia would not do so, unless he had some special right to life-preserving service from the one who allowed him to die. What would charity dictate? Obviously when a man wants to live there is a presumption that he will be benefited if his life is prolonged, and if it is so the question of euthanasia does not arise. But it is, on the other hand, possible that he wants to live where it would be better for him to die: perhaps he does not realize the desperate situation he is in, or perhaps he is afraid of dying. So, in spite of a very proper resistance to refusing to go along with a man's own wishes in the matter of life and death, someone might justifiably refuse to prolong the life even of someone who asked him to prolong it, as in the case of refusing to give the wounded soldier a drug that would keep him alive to meet a terrible end. And it is even more obvious that charity does not always dictate that life should be prolonged where a man's own wishes, hypothetical or actual, are not known.

So much for the relation of charity to nonvoluntary passive euthanasia, which was not, like nonvoluntary active euthanasia, ruled out by the right to life. Let us now ask what charity has to say about voluntary euthanasia both active and passive. It was suggested in the discussion of justice that if of sound mind and steady desire a man might give others the *right* to allow him to die or even to kill him, where otherwise this would be ruled out. But it was pointed out that this would not settle the question of whether the act was morally permissible, and it is this that we must now consider. Could not charity speak against what justice allowed? Indeed it might do so. For while the fact that a man wants to die suggests that his life is wretched, and while his rejection of life may itself tend to take the good out of the things he might have enjoyed, nevertheless his wish to die might here be opposed for his own sake just as it might be if suicide were in question. Perhaps there is hope that his mental condition will improve. Perhaps he is mistaken in thinking his disease incurable. Perhaps he wants to die for the sake of someone else on whom he feels he is a burden, and we are not ready to accept this sacrifice whether for ourselves or others. In such cases, and there will surely be many of them, it could not be for his own sake that we kill him or allow him to die, and therefore euthanasia as defined in this paper would not be in question. But this is not to deny that there could be acts of voluntary euthanasia both passive and active against which neither justice nor charity would speak.

We have now considered the morality of euthanasia both voluntary and nonvoluntary, and active and passive. The conclusion has been that nonvoluntary active euthanasia (roughly, killing a man against his will or without his consent) is never justified; that is to say, that a man's being killed for his own good never justifies the act unless he himself has consented to it. A man's rights are infringed by such an action, and it is therefore contrary to justice. However, all the other combinations, nonvoluntary passive euthanasia, voluntary active euthanasia, and voluntary passive euthanasia are sometimes compatible with both justice and charity. But the strong condition carried in the definition of euthanasia adopted in this paper must not be forgotten; an act of euthanasia as here understood is one whose purpose is to benefit the one who dies.

In the light of this discussion let us look at our present practices. Are they good or are they bad? And what changes might be made, thinking now not only of the morality of particular acts of euthanasia but also of the indirect effects of instituting different practices, of the abuses to which they might be subject and of the changes that might come about if euthanasia became a recognized part of the social scene.

The first thing to notice is that it is wrong to ask whether we snould introduce the practice of euthanasia as if it were not something we already had. In fact we do have it. For instance it is common, where the medical prognosis is very bad, for doctors to recommend against measures to prolong life, and particularly where a process of degeneration producing one medical emergency after another has already set in. If these doctors are not certainly within their legal rights this is something that is apt to come as a surprise to them as to the general public. It is also obvious that euthanasia is often practiced where old people are concerned. If someone very old and soon to die is attacked by a disease that makes his life wretched, doctors do not always come in with life-prolonging drugs. Perhaps poor patients are more fortunate in this respect than rich patients, being more often left to die in peace; but it is in any case a well recognized piece of medical practice, which is a form of euthanasia.

No doubt the case of infants with mental or physical defects will be suggested as another example of the practice of euthanasia as we already have it, since such infants are sometimes deliberately allowed to die. That they are deliberately allowed to die is certain; children with severe spina bifida malformations are not always operated on even where it is thought that without the operation they will die; and even in the case of children with Down's Syndrome who have intestinal obstructions the relatively simple operation that would make it possible to feed them is sometimes not performed.[15] Whether this is euthanasia in our sense or only as the Nazis understood it is another matter. We must ask the crucial question, "Is it for the sake of the child himself that the doctors and parents choose his death?" In some cases the answer may really be yes, and what is more important it may really be true that the kind of life which is a good is not possible or likely for this child, and that there is little but suffering and frustration in store for him.[16] But this must presuppose that the medical prognosis is wretchedly bad, as it may be for some spina bifida children. With children who are born with Down's Syndrome it is, however, quite different. Most of these are able to live on for quite a time in a reasonably contented way, remaining like children all their lives but capable of affectionate relationships and able to play games and perform simple tasks. The fact is, of course, that the doctors who recommend against life-saving procedures for handicapped infants are usually thinking not of them but rather of their parents and of other children in the family or of the "burden on society" if the chil-

---

15. I have been told this by a pediatrician in a well-known medical center in the United States. It is confirmed by Anthony M. Shaw and Iris A. Shaw, "Dilemma of Informed Consent in Children," *The New England Journal of Medicine* 289, no. 17 (25 Oct. 1973): 885–890. Reprinted in Gorovitz.

16. It must be remembered, however, that many of the social miseries of spina bifida children could be avoided. Professor R.B. Zachary is surely right to insist on this. See, for example, "Ethical and Social Aspects of Spina Bifida," *The Lancet*, 3 Aug. 1968, pp. 274–276. Reprinted in Gorovitz.

dren survive. So it is not for their sake but to avoid trouble to others that they are allowed to die. When brought out into the open this seems unacceptable: at least we do not easily accept the principle that adults who need special care should be counted too burdensome to be kept alive. It must in any case be insisted that if children with Down's Syndrome are deliberately allowed to die this is not a matter of euthanasia except in Hitler's sense. And for our children, since we scruple to gas them, not even the manner of their death is "quiet and easy"; when not treated for an intestinal obstruction a baby simply starves to death. Perhaps some will take this as an argument for allowing active euthanasia, in which case they will be in the company of an S.S. man stationed in the Warthgenau who sent Eichmann a memorandum telling him that "Jews in the coming winter could no longer be fed" and submitting for his consideration a proposal as to whether "it would not be the most humane solution to kill those Jews who were incapable of work through some quicker means."[17] If we say we are *unable* to look after children with handicaps we are no more telling the truth than was the S.S. man who said that the Jews could not be fed.

Nevertheless if it is ever right to allow deformed children to die because life will be a misery to them, or not to take measures to prolong for a little the life of a newborn baby whose life cannot extend beyond a few months of intense medical intervention, there is a genuine problem about active as opposed to passive euthanasia. There are well-known cases in which the medical staff has looked on wretchedly while an infant died slowly from starvation and dehydration because they did not feel able to give a lethal injection. According to the principles discussed in the earlier part of this paper they would indeed have had no right to give it, since an infant cannot ask that it should be done. The only possible solution—supposing that voluntary active euthanasia were to be legalized—would be to appoint guardians to act on the infant's behalf. In a different climate of opinion this might not be dangerous, but at present, when people so readily assume that the life of a handicapped baby is of no value, one would be loath to support it.

Finally, on the subject of handicapped children, another word

17. Quoted by Hannah Arendt, *Eichmann in Jerusalem* (London 1963), p. 90.

III   *Euthanasia*

should be said about those with severe mental defects. For them too it might sometimes be right to say that one would wish for death for their sake. But not even severe mental handicap automatically brings a child within the scope even of a possible act of euthanasia. If the level of consciousness is low enough it could not be said that life is a good to them, any more than in the case of those suffering from extreme senility. Nevertheless if they do not suffer it will not be an act of euthanasia by which someone opts for their death. Perhaps charity does not demand that strenuous measures are taken to keep people in this state alive, but euthanasia does not come into the matter, any more than it does when someone is, like Karen Ann Quinlan, in a state of permanent coma. Much could be said about this last case. It might even be suggested that in the case of unconsciousness this "life" is not the life to which "the right to life" refers. But that is not our topic here.

What we must consider, even if only briefly, is the possibility that euthanasia, genuine euthanasia, and not contrary to the requirements of justice or charity, should be legalized over a wider area. Here we are up against the really serious problem of abuse. Many people want, and want very badly, to be rid of their elderly relatives and even of their ailing husbands or wives. Would any safeguards ever be able to stop them describing as euthanasia what was really for their own benefit? And would it be possible to prevent the occurrence of acts which were genuinely acts of euthanasia but morally impermissible because infringing the rights of a patient who wished to live?

Perhaps the furthest we should go is to encourage patients to make their own contracts with a doctor by making it known whether they wish him to prolong their life in case of painful terminal illness or of incapacity. A document such as the Living Will seems eminently sensible, and should surely be allowed to give a doctor following the previously expressed wishes of the patient immunity from legal proceedings by relatives.[18] Legalizing active euthanasia is, however, another matter. Apart from the special repugnance doctors feel

18. Details of this document are to be found in J.A. Behnke and Sissela Bok, eds., *The Dilemmas of Euthanasia* (New York, 1975), and in A.B. Downing, ed., *Euthanasia and the Right to Life: The Case for Voluntary Euthanasia* (London, 1969).

towards the idea of a lethal injection, it may be of the very greatest importance to keep a psychological barrier up against killing. Moreover it is active euthanasia which is the most liable to abuse. Hitler would not have been able to kill 275,000 people in his "euthanasia" program if he had had to wait for them to need life-saving treatment. But there are other objections to active euthanasia, even voluntary active euthanasia. In the first place it would be hard to devise procedures that would protect people from being persuaded into giving their consent. And secondly the possibility of active voluntary euthanasia might change the social scene in ways that would be very bad. As things are, people do, by and large, expect to be looked after if they are old or ill. This is one of the good things that we have, but we might lose it, and be much worse off without it. It might come to be expected that someone likely to need a lot of looking after should call for the doctor and demand his own death. Something comparable could be good in an extremely poverty-stricken community where the children genuinely suffered from lack of food; but in rich societies such as ours it would surely be a spiritual disaster. Such possibilities should make us very wary of supporting large measures of euthanasia, even where moral principle applied to the individual act does not rule it out.

ROSALIND HURSTHOUSE   Virtue Theory and Abortion

The sort of ethical theory derived from Aristotle, variously described as virtue ethics, virtue-based ethics, or neo-Aristotelianism, is becoming better known, and is now quite widely recognized as at least a possible rival to deontological and utilitarian theories. With recognition has come criticism, of varying quality. In this article I shall discuss nine separate criticisms that I have frequently encountered, most of which seem to me to betray an inadequate grasp either of the structure of virtue theory or of what would be involved in thinking about a real moral issue in its terms. In the first half I aim particularly to secure an understanding that will reveal that many of these criticisms are simply misplaced, and to articulate what I take to be the major criticism of virtue theory. I reject this criticism, but do not claim that it is necessarily misplaced. In the second half I aim to deepen that understanding and highlight the issues raised by the criticisms by illustrating what the theory looks like when it is applied to a particular issue, in this case, abortion.

VIRTUE THEORY

Virtue theory can be laid out in a framework that reveals clearly some of the essential similarities and differences between it and some versions of deontological and utilitarian theories. I begin with a rough sketch of fa-

Versions of this article have been read to philosophy societies at University College, London, Rutgers University, and the Universities of Dundee, Edinburgh, Oxford, Swansea, and California–San Diego; at a conference of the Polish and British Academies in Cracow in 1988 on "Life, Death and the Law," and as a symposium paper at the Pacific Division of the American Philosophical Association in 1989. I am grateful to the many people who contributed to the discussions of it on these occasions, and particularly to Philippa Foot and Anne Jaap Jacobson for private discussion.

miliar versions of the latter two sorts of theory, not, of course, with the intention of suggesting that they exhaust the field, but on the assumption that their very familiarity will provide a helpful contrast with virtue theory. Suppose a deontological theory has basically the following framework. We begin with a premise providing a specification of right action:

P.1. An action is right iff it is in accordance with a moral rule or principle.

This is a purely formal specification, forging a link between the concepts of *right action* and *moral rule*, and gives one no guidance until one knows what a moral rule is. So the next thing the theory needs is a premise about that:

P.2. A moral rule is one that . . .

Historically, an acceptable completion of P.2 would have been

(i) is laid on us by God

or

(ii) is required by natural law.

In secular versions (not, of course, unconnected to God's being pure reason, and the universality of natural law) we get such completions as

(iii) is laid on us by reason

or

(iv) is required by rationality

or

(v) would command universal rational acceptance

or

(vi) would be the object of choice of all rational beings

and so on. Such a specification forges a second conceptual link, between the concepts of *moral rule* and *rationality*.

We have here the skeleton of a familiar version of a deontological theory, a skeleton that reveals that what is essential to any such version is the links between *right action*, *moral rule*, and *rationality*. That these form the basic structure can be seen particularly vividly if we lay out the familiar act-utilitarianism in such a way as to bring out the contrasts.

Act-utilitarianism begins with a premise that provides a specification of right action:

P.1. An action is right iff it promotes the best consequences.

It thereby forges the link between the concepts of *right action* and *consequences*. It goes on to specify what the best consequences are in its second premise:

P.2. The best consequences are those in which happiness is maximized.

It thereby forges the link between *consequences* and *happiness*.

Now let us consider what a skeletal virtue theory looks like. It begins with a specification of right action:

P.1. An action is right iff it is what a virtuous agent would do in the circumstances.[1]

This, like the first premises of the other two sorts of theory, is a purely formal principle, giving one no guidance as to what to do, that forges the conceptual link between *right action* and *virtuous agent*. Like the other theories, it must, of course, go on to specify what the latter is. The first step toward this may appear quite trivial, but is needed to correct a prevailing tendency among many critics to define the virtuous agent as one who is disposed to act in accordance with a deontologist's moral rules.

P.1a. A virtuous agent is one who acts virtuously, that is, one who has and exercises the virtues.

This subsidiary premise lays bare the fact that virtue theory aims to provide a nontrivial specification of the virtuous agent *via* a nontrivial specification of the virtues, which is given in its second premise:

---

1. It should be noted that this premise intentionally allows for the possibility that two virtuous agents, faced with the same choice in the same circumstances, may act differently. For example, one might opt for taking her father off the life-support machine and the other for leaving her father on it. The theory requires that neither agent thinks that what the other does is wrong (see note 4 below), but it explicitly allows that no action is uniquely right in such a case—both are right. It also intentionally allows for the possibility that in some circumstances—those into which no virtuous agent could have got herself— no action is right. I explore this premise at greater length in "Applying Virtue Ethics," forthcoming in a *festschrift* for Philippa Foot.

P.2. A virtue is a character trait a human being needs to flourish or live well.

This premise forges a conceptual link between *virtue* and *flourishing* (or *living well* or *eudaimonia*). And, just as deontology, in theory, then goes on to argue that each favored rule meets its specification, so virtue ethics, in theory, goes on to argue that each favored character trait meets its.

These are the bare bones of virtue theory. Following are five brief comments directed to some misconceived criticisms that should be cleared out of the way.

First, the theory does not have a peculiar weakness or problem in virtue of the fact that it involves the concept of *eudaimonia* (a standard criticism being that this concept is hopelessly obscure). Now no virtue theorist will pretend that the concept of human flourishing is an easy one to grasp. I will not even claim here (though I would elsewhere) that it is no more obscure than the concepts of *rationality* and *happiness*, since, if our vocabulary were more limited, we might, *faute de mieux*, call it (human) *rational happiness*, and thereby reveal that it has at least some of the difficulties of both. But virtue theory has never, so far as I know, been dismissed on the grounds of the *comparative* obscurity of this central concept; rather, the popular view is that it has a problem with this which deontology and utilitarianism in no way share. This, I think, is clearly false. Both *rationality* and *happiness*, as they figure in their respective theories, are rich and difficult concepts—hence all the disputes about the various tests for a rule's being an object of rational choice, and the disputes, dating back to Mill's introduction of the higher and lower pleasures, about what constitutes happiness.

Second, the theory is not trivially circular; it does not specify right action in terms of the virtuous agent and then immediately specify the virtuous agent in terms of right action. Rather, it specifies her in terms of the virtues, and then specifies these, not merely as dispositions to right action, but as the character traits (which are dispositions to feel and react as well as act in certain ways) required for *eudaimonia*.[2]

[2] There is, of course, the further question of whether the theory eventually describes a larger circle and winds up relying on the concept of right action in its interpretation of *eudaimonia*. In denying that the theory is trivially circular, I do not pretend to answer this intricate question. It is certainly true that virtue theory does not claim that the correct conception of *eudaimonia* can be got from "an independent 'value-free' investigation of

Virtue Theory and Abortion

Third, it does answer the question "What should I do?" as well as the question "What sort of person should I be?" (That is, it is not, as one of the catchphrases has it, concerned only with Being and not with Doing.)

Fourth, the theory does, to a certain extent, answer this question by coming up with rules or principles (contrary to the common claim that it does not come up with any rules or principles). Every virtue generates a positive instruction (act justly, kindly, courageously, honestly, etc.) and every vice a prohibition (do not act unjustly, cruelly, like a coward, dishonestly, etc.). So trying to decide what to do within the framework of virtue theory is not, as some people seem to imagine, necessarily a matter of taking one's favored candidate for a virtuous person and asking oneself, "What would they do in these circumstances?" (as if the raped fifteen-year-old girl might be supposed to say to herself, "Now would Socrates have an abortion if he were in my circumstances?" and as if someone who had never known or heard of anyone very virtuous were going to be left, according to the theory, with no way to decide what to do at all). The agent may instead ask herself, "If I were to do such and such now, would I be acting justly or unjustly (or neither), kindly or unkindly [and so on]?" I shall consider below the problem created by cases in which such a question apparently does not yield an answer to "What should I do?" (because, say, the alternatives are being unkind or being unjust); here my claim is only that it sometimes does—the agent may employ her concepts of the virtues and vices directly, rather than imagining what some hypothetical exemplar would do.

Fifth (a point that is implicit but should be made explicit), virtue theory is not committed to any sort of reductionism involving defining all of our moral concepts in terms of the virtuous agent. On the contrary, it relies on a lot of very significant moral concepts. Charity or benevolence, for instance, is the virtue whose concern is the *good* of others; that concept of *good* is related to the concept of *evil* or *harm*, and they are both related to the concepts of the *worthwhile*, the *advantageous*, and the *pleasant*. If I have the wrong conception of what is worthwhile and ad-

---

human nature" (John McDowell, "The Role of *Eudaimonia* in Aristotle's Ethics," in *Essays on Aristotle's Ethics*, ed. Amelie Rorty [Berkeley and Los Angeles: University of California Press, 1980]). The sort of training that is required for acquiring the correct conception no doubt involves being taught from early on such things as "Decent people do this sort of thing, not that" and "To do such and such is the mark of a depraved character" (cf. *Nicomachean Ethics* 1110a22). But whether this counts as relying on the concept of right (or wrong) action seems to me very unclear and requiring much discussion.

vantageous and pleasant, then I shall have the wrong conception of what is good for, and harmful to, myself and others, and, even with the best will in the world, will lack the virtue of charity, which involves getting all this right. (This point will be illustrated at some length in the second half of this article; I mention it here only in support of the fact that no virtue theorist who takes her inspiration from Aristotle would even contemplate aiming at reductionism.)[3]

Let me now, with equal brevity, run through two more standard criticisms of virtue theory (the sixth and seventh of my nine) to show that, though not entirely misplaced, they do not highlight problems peculiar to that theory but, rather, problems that are shared by familiar versions of deontology.

One common criticism is that we do not know which character traits are the virtues, or that this is open to much dispute, or particularly subject to the threat of moral skepticism or "pluralism"[4] or cultural relativism. But the parallel roles played by the second premises of both deontological and virtue theories reveal the way in which both sorts of theory share this problem. It is at the stage at which one tries to get the right conclusions to drop out of the bottom of one's theory that, *theoretically*, all the work has to be done. Rule deontologists know that they want to get "don't kill," "keep promises," "cherish your children," and so on as the rules that meet their specification, whatever it may be. They also know that any of these can be disputed, that some philosopher may claim, of any one of them, that it is reasonable to reject it, and that at least people claim that there has been, for each rule, some culture that

---

3. Cf. Bernard Williams' point in *Ethics and the Limits of Philosophy* (London: William Collins, 1985) that we need an enriched ethical vocabulary, not a cut-down one.

4. I put *pluralism* in scare quotes to serve as a warning that virtue theory is not incompatible with all forms of it. It allows for "competing conceptions" of *eudaimonia* and the worthwhile, for instance, in the sense that it allows for a plurality of flourishing lives—the theory need not follow Aristotle in specifying the life of contemplation as the only one that truly constitutes *eudaimonia* (if he does). But the conceptions "compete" only in the sense that, within a single flourishing life, not everything worthwhile can be fitted in; the theory does not allow that two people with a correct conception of *eudaimonia* can disagree over whether the way the other is living constitutes flourishing. Moreover, the theory is committed to the strong thesis that the same set of character traits is needed for *any* flourishing life; it will not allow that, for instance, soldiers need courage but wives and mothers do not, or that judges need justice but can live well despite lacking kindness. (This obviously is related to the point made in note 1 above.) For an interesting discussion of pluralism (different interpretations thereof) and virtue theory, see Douglas B. Rasmussen, "Liberalism and Natural End Ethics," *American Philosophical Quarterly* 27 (1990): 153–61.

rejected it. Similarly, the virtue theorists know that they want to get justice, charity, fidelity, courage, and so on as the character traits needed for *eudaimonia*; and they also know that any of these can be disputed, that some philosopher will say of any one of them that it is reasonable to reject it as a virtue, and that there is said to be, for each character trait, some culture that has thus rejected it.

This is a problem for both theories, and the virtue theorist certainly does not find it any harder to argue against moral skepticism, "pluralism," or cultural relativism than the deontologist. Each theory has to stick out its neck and say, in some cases, "This person/these people/other cultures are (or would be) in error," and find some grounds for saying this.

Another criticism (the seventh) often made is that virtue ethics has unresolvable conflict built into it. "It is common knowledge," it is said, "that the requirements of the virtues can conflict; charity may prompt me to end the frightful suffering of the person in my care by killing him, but justice bids me to stay my hand. To tell my brother that his wife is being unfaithful to him would be honest and loyal, but it would be kinder to keep quiet about it. So which should I do? In such cases, virtue ethics has nothing helpful to say." (This is one version of the problem, mentioned above, that considering whether a proposed action falls under a virtue or vice term does not always yield an answer to "What should I do?")

The obvious reply to this criticism is that rule deontology notoriously suffers from the same problem, arising not only from the fact that its rules can apparently conflict, but also from the fact that, at first blush, it appears that one and the same rule (e.g., preserve life) can yield contrary instructions in a particular case.[5] As before, I agree that this is a problem for virtue theory, but deny that it is a problem peculiar to it.

Finally, I want to articulate, and reject, what I take to be the major criticism of virtue theory. Perhaps because it is *the* major criticism, the reflection of a very general sort of disquiet about the theory, it is hard to state clearly—especially for someone who does not accept it—but it goes something like this.[6] My interlocutor says:

---

5. E.g., in Williams' Jim and Pedro case in J.J.C. Smart and Bernard Williams, *Utilitarianism: For and Against* (London: Cambridge University Press, 1973).

6. Intimations of this criticism constantly come up in discussion; the clearest statement of it I have found is by Onora O'Neill, in her review of Stephen Clark's *The Moral Status*

Virtue theory can't *get* us anywhere in real moral issues because it's bound to be all assertion and no argument. You admit that the best it can come up with in the way of action-guiding rules are the ones that rely on the virtue and vice concepts, such as "act charitably," "don't act cruelly," and so on; and, as if that weren't bad enough, you admit that these virtue concepts, such as charity, presuppose concepts such as the *good*, and the *worthwhile*, and so on. But that means that any virtue theorist who writes about real moral issues must rely on her audience's agreeing with her application of all these concepts, and hence accepting all the premises in which those applications are enshrined. But some other virtue theorist might take different premises about these matters, and come up with very different conclusions, and, within the terms of the theory, there is no way to distinguish between the two. While there is agreement, virtue theory can repeat conventional wisdom, preserve the status quo, but it can't get us anywhere in the way that a normative ethical theory is supposed to, namely, by providing rational grounds for acceptance of its practical conclusions.

My strategy will be to split this criticism into two: one (the eighth) addressed to the virtue theorist's employment of the virtue and vice concepts enshrined in her rules—act charitably, honestly, and so on—and the other (the ninth) addressed to her employment of concepts such as that of the *worthwhile*. Each objection, I shall maintain, implicitly appeals to a certain *condition of adequacy* on a normative moral theory, and in each case, I shall claim, the condition of adequacy, once made explicit, is utterly implausible.

It is true that when she discusses real moral issues, the virtue theorist has to assert that certain actions are honest, dishonest, or neither; charitable, uncharitable, or neither. And it is true that this is often a very difficult matter to decide; her rules are not always easy to apply. But this counts as a criticism of the theory only if we assume, as a condition of adequacy, that any adequate action-guiding theory must make the difficult business of knowing what to do if one is to act well easy, that it must provide clear guidance about what ought and ought not to be done which

---

of Animals, in *Journal of Philosophy* 77 (1980): 440–46. For a response I am much in sympathy with, see Cora Diamond, "Anything But Argument?" *Philosophical Investigations* 5 (1982): 23–41.

any reasonably clever adolescent could follow if she chose. But such a condition of adequacy is implausible. Acting rightly *is* difficult, and *does* call for much moral wisdom, and the relevant condition of adequacy, which virtue theory meets, is that it should have built into it an explanation of a truth expressed by Aristotle,[7] namely, that moral knowledge—unlike mathematical knowledge—cannot be acquired merely by attending lectures and is not characteristically to be found in people too young to have had much experience of life. There are youthful mathematical geniuses, but rarely, if ever, youthful moral geniuses, and this tells us something significant about the sort of knowledge that moral knowledge is. Virtue ethics builds this in straight off precisely by couching its rules in terms whose application may indeed call for the most delicate and sensitive judgment.

Here we may discern a slightly different version of the problem that there are cases in which applying the virtue and vice terms does not yield an answer to "What should I do?" Suppose someone "youthful in character," as Aristotle puts it, having applied the relevant terms, finds herself landed with what is, unbeknownst to her, a case not of real but of apparent conflict, arising from a misapplication of those terms. Then she will not be able to decide what to do unless she knows of a virtuous agent to look to for guidance. But her quandary is (*ex hypothesi*) the result of her lack of wisdom, and just what virtue theory expects. Someone hesitating over whether to reveal a hurtful truth, for example, thinking it would be kind but dishonest or unjust to lie, may need to realize, with respect to these particular circumstances, not that kindness is more (or less) important than honesty or justice, and not that honesty or justice sometimes requires one to act unkindly or cruelly, but that one does people no kindness by concealing this sort of truth from them, hurtful as it may be. This is the *type* of thing (I use it only as an example) that people with moral wisdom know about, involving the correct application of *kind*, and that people without such wisdom find difficult.

What about the virtue theorist's reliance on concepts such as that of the *worthwhile*? If such reliance is to count as a fault in the theory, what condition of adequacy is implicitly in play? It must be that any good normative theory should provide answers to questions about real moral issues whose truth is in no way determined by truths about what is worth-

---

7. Aristotle, *Nicomachean Ethics* 1142a12–16.

while, or what really matters in human life. Now although people are initially inclined to reject out of hand the claim that the practical conclusions of a normative moral theory have to be based on premises about what is truly worthwhile, the alternative, once it is made explicit, may look even more unacceptable. Consider what the condition of adequacy entails. If truths about what is worthwhile (or truly good, or serious, or about what matters in human life) do *not* have to be appealed to in order to answer questions about real moral issues, then I might sensibly seek guidance about what I ought to do from someone who had declared in advance that she knew nothing about such matters, or from someone who said that, although she had opinions about them, these were quite likely to be wrong but that this did not matter, because they would play no determining role in the advice she gave me.

I should emphasize that we are talking about real moral issues and real guidance; I want to know whether I should have an abortion, take my mother off the life-support machine, leave academic life and become a doctor in the Third World, give up my job with the firm that is using animals in its experiments, tell my father he has cancer. Would I go to someone who says she has *no* views about what is worthwhile in life? Or to someone who says that, as a matter of fact, she tends to think that the only thing that matters is having a good time, but has a normative theory that is consistent both with this view and with my own rather more puritanical one, which will yield the guidance I need?

I take it as a premise that this is absurd. The relevant condition of adequacy should be that the practical conclusions of a good normative theory *must* be in part determined by premises about what is worthwhile, important, and so on. Thus I reject this "major criticism" of virtue theory, that it cannot get us anywhere in the way that a normative moral theory is supposed to. According to my response, a normative theory that any clever adolescent can apply, or that reaches practical conclusions that are in no way determined by premises about what is truly worthwhile, serious, and so on, is guaranteed to be an inadequate theory.

Although I reject this criticism, I have not argued that it is misplaced and that it necessarily manifests a failure to understand what virtue theory is. My rejection is based on premises about what an adequate normative theory must be like—what sorts of concepts it must contain, and what sort of account it must give of moral knowledge—and thereby claims, implicitly, that the "major criticism" manifests a failure to understand what an *adequate normative theory* is. But, as a matter of fact, I think the criticism is often made by people who have no idea of what virtue theory looks like when applied to a real moral issue; they drastically underestimate the variety of ways in which the virtue and vice concepts, and the others, such as that of the *worthwhile*, figure in such discussion.

As promised, I now turn to an illustration of such discussion, applying virtue theory to abortion. Before I embark on this tendentious business, I should remind the reader of the aim of this discussion. I am not, in this article, trying to solve the problem of abortion; I am illustrating how virtue theory directs one to think about it. It might indeed be said that thinking about the problem in this way "solves" it by *dis*solving it, insofar as it leads one to the conclusion that there is no single right answer, but a variety of particular answers, and in what follows I am certainly trying to make that conclusion seem plausible. But, that granted, it should still be said that I am not trying to "solve the problems" in the practical sense of telling people that they should, or should not, do this or that if they are pregnant and contemplating abortion in these or those particular circumstances.

I do not assume, or expect, that all of my readers will agree with everything I am about to say. On the contrary, given the plausible assumption that some are morally wiser than I am, and some less so, the theory has built into it that we are bound to disagree on some points. For instance, we may well disagree about the particular application of some of the virtue and vice terms; and we may disagree about what is worthwhile or serious, worthless or trivial. But my aim is to make clear how these concepts figure in a discussion conducted in terms of virtue theory. What is at issue is whether these concepts are indeed the ones that should come in, that is, whether virtue theory should be criticized for employing them. The problem of abortion highlights this issue dramatically since virtue theory quite transforms the discussion of it.

ABORTION

As everyone knows, the morality of abortion is commonly discussed in relation to just two considerations: first, and predominantly, the status of the fetus and whether or not it is the sort of thing that may or may not be innocuously or justifiably killed; and second, and less predominantly (when, that is, the discussion concerns the *morality* of abortion rather than the question of permissible legislation in a just society), women's rights. If one thinks within this familiar framework, one may well be puzzled about what virtue theory, as such, could contribute. Some people assume the discussion will be conducted solely in terms of what the virtuous agent would or would not do (cf. the third, fourth, and fifth criticisms above). Others assume that only justice, or at most justice and charity,[8] will be applied to the issue, generating a discussion very similar to Judith Jarvis Thomson's.[9]

Now if this is the way the virtue theorist's discussion of abortion is imagined to be, no wonder people think little of it. It seems obvious in advance that in any such discussion there must be either a great deal of extremely tendentious application of the virtue terms *just*, *charitable*, and so on or a lot of rhetorical appeal to "this is what only the virtuous agent knows." But these are caricatures; they fail to appreciate the way in which virtue theory quite transforms the discussion of abortion by dismissing the two familiar dominating considerations as, in a way, fundamentally irrelevant. In what way or ways, I hope to make both clear and plausible.

Let us first consider women's rights. Let me emphasize again that we are discussing the *morality* of abortion, not the rights and wrongs of laws prohibiting or permitting it. If we suppose that women do have a moral right to do as they choose with their own bodies, or, more particularly, to terminate their pregnancies, then it may well follow that a *law* forbidding abortion would be unjust. Indeed, even if they have no such right, such a law might be, as things stand at the moment, unjust, or impractical, or inhumane: on this issue I have nothing to say in this article. But, putting all questions about the justice or injustice of laws to one side, and sup-

---

8. It seems likely that some people have been misled by Foot's discussion of euthanasia (through no fault of hers) into thinking that a virtue theorist's discussion of terminating human life will be conducted exclusively in terms of justice and charity (and the corresponding vice terms) (Philippa Foot, "Euthanasia," *Philosophy & Public Affairs* 6, no. 2 [Winter 1977]: 85–112). But the act-category *euthanasia* is a very special one, at least as defined in her article, since such an act must be done "for the sake of the one who is to die." Building a virtuous motivation into the specification of the act in this way immediately rules out the application of many other vice terms.

9. Judith Jarvis Thomson, "A Defense of Abortion," *Philosophy & Public Affairs* 1, no. 1 (Fall 1971): 47–66. One could indeed regard this article as proto–virtue theory (no doubt to the surprise of the author) if the concepts of callousness and kindness were allowed more weight.

posing only that women have such a moral right, *nothing* follows from this supposition about the morality of abortion, according to virtue theory, once it is noted (quite generally, not with particular reference to abortion) that in exercising a moral right I can do something cruel, or callous, or selfish, light-minded, self-righteous, stupid, inconsiderate, disloyal, dishonest—that is, act viciously.[10] Love and friendship do not survive their parties' constantly insisting on their rights, nor do people live well when they think that getting what they have a right to is of preeminent importance; they harm others, and they harm themselves. So whether women have a moral right to terminate their pregnancies is irrelevant within virtue theory, for it is irrelevant to the question "In having an abortion in these circumstances, would the agent be acting virtuously or viciously or neither?"

What about the consideration of the status of the fetus—what can virtue theory say about that? One might say that this issue is not in the province of *any* moral theory; it is a metaphysical question, and an extremely difficult one at that. Must virtue theory then wait upon metaphysics to come up with the answer?

At first sight it might seem so. For virtue is said to involve knowledge, and part of this knowledge consists in having the *right* attitude to things. "Right" here does not just mean "morally right" or "proper" or "nice" in the modern sense; it means "accurate, true." One cannot have the right or correct attitude to something if the attitude is based on or involves false beliefs. And this suggests that if the status of the fetus is relevant to the rightness or wrongness of abortion, its status must be known, as a truth, to the fully wise and virtuous person.

But the sort of wisdom that the fully virtuous person has is not supposed to be recondite; it does not call for fancy philosophical sophistication, and it does not depend upon, let alone wait upon, the discoveries of academic philosophers.[11] And this entails the following, rather startling,

---

10. One possible qualification: if one ties the concept of justice very closely to rights, then if women do have a moral right to terminate their pregnancies it *may* follow that in doing so they do not act unjustly. (Cf. Thomson, "A Defense of Abortion.") But it is debatable whether even that much follows.

11. This is an assumption of virtue theory, and I do not attempt to defend it here. An adequate discussion of it would require a separate article, since, although most moral philosophers would be chary of claiming that intellectual sophistication is a necessary condition of moral wisdom or virtue, most of us, from Plato onward, tend to write as if this were so. Sorting out which claims about moral knowledge are committed to this kind of elitism

conclusion: that the status of the fetus—that issue over which so much ink has been spilt—is, according to virtue theory, simply not relevant to the rightness or wrongness of abortion (within, that is, a secular morality).

Or rather, since that is clearly too radical a conclusion, it is in a sense relevant, but only in the sense that the familiar biological facts are relevant. By "the familiar biological facts" I mean the facts that most human societies are and have been familiar with—that, standardly (but not invariably), pregnancy occurs as the result of sexual intercourse, that it lasts about nine months, during which time the fetus grows and develops, that standardly it terminates in the birth of a living baby, and that this is how we all come to be.

It might be thought that this distinction—between the familiar biological facts and the status of the fetus—is a distinction without a difference. But this is not so. To attach relevance to the status of the fetus, in the sense in which virtue theory claims it is not relevant, is to be gripped by the conviction that we must go beyond the familiar biological facts, deriving some sort of conclusion from them, such as that the fetus has rights, or is not a person, or something similar. It is also to believe that this exhausts the relevance of the familiar biological facts, that all they are relevant to is the status of the fetus and whether or not it is the sort of thing that may or may not be killed.

These convictions, I suspect, are rooted in the desire to solve the problem of abortion by getting it to fall under some general rule such as "You ought not to kill anything with the right to life but may kill anything else." But they have resulted in what should surely strike any nonphilosopher as a most bizarre aspect of nearly all the current philosophical literature on abortion, namely, that, far from treating abortion as a unique moral problem, markedly unlike any other, nearly everything written on the status of the fetus and its bearing on the abortion issue would be consistent with the human reproductive facts' (to say nothing of family life) being totally different from what they are. Imagine that you are an alien extraterrestrial anthropologist who does not know that the human race is roughly 50 percent female and 50 percent male, or that our only (natural) form of reproduction involves heterosexual intercourse, vivipa-

---

and which can, albeit with difficulty, be reconciled with the idea that moral knowledge can be acquired by anyone who really wants it would be a major task.

rous birth, and the female's (and only the female's) being pregnant for nine months, or that females are capable of childbearing from late childhood to late middle age, or that childbearing is painful, dangerous, and emotionally charged—do you think you would pick up these facts from the hundreds of articles written on the status of the fetus? I am quite sure you would not. And that, I think, shows that the current philosophical literature on abortion has got badly out of touch with reality.

Now if we are using virtue theory, our first question is not "What do the familiar biological facts show—what can be derived from them about the status of the fetus?" but "How do these facts figure in the practical reasoning, actions and passions, thoughts and reactions, of the virtuous and the nonvirtuous? What is the mark of having the right attitude to these facts and what manifests having the wrong attitude to them?" This immediately makes essentially relevant not only all the facts about human reproduction I mentioned above, but a whole range of facts about our emotions in relation to them as well. I mean such facts as that human parents, both male and female, tend to care passionately about their offspring, and that family relationships are among the deepest and strongest in our lives—and, significantly, among the longest-lasting.

These facts make it obvious that pregnancy is not just one among many other physical conditions; and hence that anyone who genuinely believes that an abortion is comparable to a haircut or an appendectomy is mistaken.[12] The fact that the premature termination of a pregnancy is, in some sense, the cutting off of a new human life, and thereby, like the procreation of a new human life, connects with all our thoughts about human life and death, parenthood, and family relationships, must make it a serious matter. To disregard this fact about it, to think of abortion as

12. Mary Anne Warren, in "On the Moral and Legal Status of Abortion," *Monist* 57 (1973), sec. 1, says of the opponents of restrictive laws governing abortion that "their conviction (for the most part) is that abortion is not a *morally* serious and extremely unfortunate, even though sometimes justified, act, comparable to killing in self-defense or to letting the violinist die, but rather is closer to being a *morally neutral* act, like cutting one's hair" (italics mine). I would like to think that no one *genuinely* believes this. But certainly in discussion, particularly when arguing against restrictive laws or the suggestion that remorse over abortion might be appropriate, I have found that some people *say* they believe it (and often cite Warren's article, albeit inaccurately, despite its age). Those who allow that it is morally serious, and far from morally neutral, have to argue against restrictive laws, or the appropriateness of remorse, on a very different ground from that laid down by the premise "The fetus is just part of the woman's body (and she has a right to determine what happens to her body and should not feel guilt about anything she does to it)."

nothing but the killing of something that does not matter, or as nothing but the exercise of some right or rights one has, or as the incidental means to some desirable state of affairs, is to do something callous and light-minded, the sort of thing that no virtuous and wise person would do. It is to have the wrong attitude not only to fetuses, but more generally to human life and death, parenthood, and family relationships.

Although I say that the facts make this obvious, I know that this is one of my tendentious points. In partial support of it I note that even the most dedicated proponents of the view that deliberate abortion is just like an appendectomy or haircut rarely hold the same view of spontaneous abortion, that is, miscarriage. It is not so tendentious of me to claim that to react to people's grief over miscarriage by saying, or even thinking, "What a fuss about nothing!" would be callous and light-minded, whereas to try to laugh someone out of grief over an appendectomy scar or a botched haircut would not be. It is hard to give this point due prominence within act-centered theories, for the inconsistency is an inconsistency in attitude about the seriousness of loss of life, not in beliefs about which acts are right or wrong. Moreover, an act-centered theorist may say, "Well, there is nothing wrong with *thinking* 'What a fuss about nothing!' as long as you do not say it and hurt the person who is grieving. And besides, we cannot be held responsible for our thoughts, only for the intentional actions they give rise to." But the character traits that virtue theory emphasizes are not simply dispositions to intentional actions, but a seamless disposition to certain actions and passions, thoughts and reactions.

To say that the cutting off of a human life is always a matter of some seriousness, at any stage, is not to deny the relevance of gradual fetal development. Notwithstanding the well-worn point that clear boundary lines cannot be drawn, our emotions and attitudes regarding the fetus do change as it develops, and again when it is born, and indeed further as the baby grows. Abortion for shallow reasons in the later stages is much more shocking than abortion for the same reasons in the early stages in a way that matches the fact that deep grief over miscarriage in the later stages is more appropriate than it is over miscarriage in the earlier stages (when, that is, the grief is solely about the loss of *this* child, not about, as might be the case, the loss of one's only hope of having a child or of having one's husband's child). Imagine (or recall) a woman who already has children; she had not intended to have more, but finds herself unexpectedly pregnant. Though contrary to her plans, the pregnancy, once established as a fact, is welcomed—and then she loses the embryo almost immediately. If this were bemoaned as a tragedy, it would, I think, be a misapplication of the concept of what is tragic. But it may still properly be mourned as a loss. The grief is expressed in such terms as "I shall always wonder how she or he would have turned out" or "When I look at the others, I shall think, 'How different their lives would have been if this other one had been part of them.'" It would, I take it, be callous and light-minded to say, or think, "Well, she has already *got* four children; what's the problem?"; it would be neither, nor arrogantly intrusive in the case of a close friend, to try to correct prolonged mourning by saying, "I know it's sad, but it's not a tragedy; rejoice in the ones you have." The application of *tragic* becomes more appropriate as the fetus grows, for the mere fact that one has lived with it for longer, conscious of its existence, makes a difference. To shrug off an early abortion is understandable just because it is very hard to be fully conscious of the fetus's existence in the early stages and hence hard to appreciate that an early abortion is the destruction of life. It is particularly hard for the young and inexperienced to appreciate this, because appreciation of it usually comes only with experience.

I do not mean "with the experience of having an abortion" (though that may be part of it) but, quite generally, "with the experience of life." Many women who have borne children contrast their later pregnancies with their first successful one, saying that in the later ones they were conscious of a new life growing in them from very early on. And, more generally, as one reaches the age at which the next generation is coming up close behind one, the counterfactuals "If I, or she, had had an abortion, Alice, or Bob, would not have been born" acquire a significant application, which casts a new light on the conditionals "If I or Alice have an abortion then some Caroline or Bill will not be born."

The fact that pregnancy is not just one among many physical conditions does not mean that one can never regard it in that light without manifesting a vice. When women are in very poor physical health, or worn out from childbearing, or forced to do very physically demanding jobs, then they cannot be described as self-indulgent, callous, irresponsible, or light-minded if they seek abortions mainly with a view to avoiding pregnancy as the physical condition that it is. To go through with a pregnancy when one is utterly exhausted, or when one's job consists of crawling along tunnels hauling coal, as many women in the nineteenth century were obliged to do, is perhaps heroic, but people who do not achieve heroism are not necessarily vicious. That they can view the pregnancy only as eight months of misery, followed by hours if not days of agony and exhaustion, and abortion only as the blessed escape from this prospect, is entirely understandable and does not manifest any lack of serious respect for human life or a shallow attitude to motherhood. What it does show is that something is terribly amiss in the conditions of their lives, which make it so hard to recognize pregnancy and childbearing as the good that they can be.

In relation to this last point I should draw attention to the way in which virtue theory has a sort of built-in indexicality. Philosophers arguing against anything remotely resembling a belief in the sanctity of life (which the above claims clearly embody) frequently appeal to the existence of other communities in which abortion and infanticide are practiced. We should not automatically assume that it is impossible that some other communities could be morally inferior to our own; maybe some are, or have been, precisely insofar as their members are, typically, callous or light-minded or unjust. But in communities in which life is a great deal tougher for everyone than it is in ours, having the right attitude to human life and death, parenthood, and family relationships might well manifest itself in ways that are unlike ours. When it is essential to survival that most members of the community fend for themselves at a very young age or work during most of their waking hours, selective abortion or infanticide might be practiced either as a form of genuine euthanasia or for the sake of the community and not, I think, be thought callous or light-minded. But this does not make everything all right; as before, it shows that there is something amiss with the conditions of their lives, which are making it impossible for them to live really well.[13]

The foregoing discussion, insofar as it emphasizes the right attitude to human life and death, parallels to a certain extent those standard discussions of abortion that concentrate on it solely as an issue of killing. But it does not, as those discussions do, gloss over the fact, emphasized by those who discuss the morality of abortion in terms of women's rights, that abortion, wildly unlike any other form of killing, is the termination

---

13. For another example of the way in which "tough conditions" can make a difference to what is involved in having the right attitude to human life and death and family relationships, see the concluding sentences of Foot's "Euthanasia."

of a pregnancy, which is a condition of a woman's body and results in *her* having a child if it is not aborted. This fact is given due recognition not by appeal to women's rights but by emphasizing the relevance of the familiar biological and psychological facts and their connection with having the right attitude to parenthood and family relationships. But it may well be thought that failing to bring in women's rights still leaves some important aspects of the problem of abortion untouched.

Speaking in terms of women's rights, people sometimes say things like, "Well, it's her life you're talking about too, you know; she's got a right to her own life, her own happiness." And the discussion stops there. But in the context of virtue theory, given that we are particularly concerned with what constitutes a good human life, with what true happiness or *eudaimonia* is, this is no place to stop. We go on to ask, "And is this life of hers a good one? Is she living well?"

If we are to go on to talk about good human lives, in the context of abortion, we have to bring in our thoughts about the value of love and family life, and our proper emotional development through a natural life cycle. The familiar facts support the view that parenthood in general, and motherhood and childbearing in particular, are intrinsically worthwhile, are among the things that can be correctly thought to be partially constitutive of a flourishing human life.[14] If this is right, then a woman who opts for not being a mother (at all, or again, or now) by opting for abortion may thereby be manifesting a flawed grasp of what her life should be, and be about—a grasp that is childish, or grossly materialistic, or shortsighted, or shallow.

I said "*may* thereby": this *need* not be so. Consider, for instance, a woman who has already had several children and fears that to have another will seriously affect her capacity to be a good mother to the ones she has—she does not show a lack of appreciation of the intrinsic value of being a parent by opting for abortion. Nor does a woman who has been a good mother and is approaching the age at which she may be looking forward to being a good grandmother. Nor does a woman who discovers that her pregnancy may well kill her, and opts for abortion and adoption. Nor, necessarily, does a woman who has decided to lead a life centered

---

14. I take this as a premise here, but argue for it in some detail in my *Beginning Lives* (Oxford: Basil Blackwell, 1987). In this connection I also discuss adoption and the sense in which it may be regarded as "second best," and the difficult question of whether the good of parenthood may properly be sought, or indeed bought, by surrogacy.

around some other worthwhile activity or activities with which motherhood would compete.

People who are childless by choice are sometimes described as "irresponsible," or "selfish," or "refusing to grow up," or "not knowing what life is about." But one can hold that having children is intrinsically worthwhile without endorsing this, for we are, after all, in the happy position of there being more worthwhile things to do than can be fitted into one lifetime. Parenthood, and motherhood in particular, even if granted to be intrinsically worthwhile, undoubtedly take up a lot of one's adult life, leaving no room for some other worthwhile pursuits. But some women who choose abortion rather than have their first child, and some men who encourage their partners to choose abortion, are not avoiding parenthood for the sake of other worthwhile pursuits, but for the worthless one of "having a good time," or for the pursuit of some false vision of the ideals of freedom or self-realization. And some others who say "I am not ready for parenthood yet" are making some sort of mistake about the extent to which one can manipulate the circumstances of one's life so as to make it fulfill some dream that one has. Perhaps one's dream is to have two perfect children, a girl and a boy, within a perfect marriage, in financially secure circumstances, with an interesting job of one's own. But to care too much about that dream, to demand of life that it give it to one and act accordingly, may be both greedy and foolish, and is to run the risk of missing out on happiness entirely. Not only may fate make the dream impossible, or destroy it, but one's own attachment to it may make it impossible. Good marriages, and the most promising children, can be destroyed by just one adult's excessive demand for perfection.

Once again, this is not to deny that girls may quite properly say "I am not ready for motherhood yet," especially in our society, and, far from manifesting irresponsibility or light-mindedness, show an appropriate modesty or humility, or a fearfulness that does not amount to cowardice. However, even when the decision to have an abortion is the right decision—one that does not itself fall under a vice-related term and thereby one that the perfectly virtuous could recommend—it does not follow that there is no sense in which having the abortion is wrong, or guilt inappropriate. For, by virtue of the fact that a human life has been cut short, some evil has probably been brought about,[15] and that circumstances

---

15. I say "some evil has probably been brought about" on the ground that (human) life

make the decision to bring about some evil the right decision will be a ground for guilt if getting into those circumstances in the first place itself manifested a flaw in character.

What "gets one into those circumstances" in the case of abortion is, except in the case of rape, one's sexual activity and one's choices, or the lack of them, about one's sexual partner and about contraception. The virtuous woman (which here of course does not mean simply "chaste woman" but "woman with the virtues") has such character traits as strength, independence, resoluteness, decisiveness, self-confidence, responsibility, serious-mindedness, and self-determination—and no one, I think, could deny that many women become pregnant in circumstances in which they cannot welcome or cannot face the thought of having *this* child precisely because they lack one or some of these character traits. So even in the cases where the decision to have an abortion is the right one, it can still be the reflection of a moral failing—not because the decision itself is weak or cowardly or irresolute or irresponsible or light-minded, but because lack of the requisite opposite of these failings landed one in the circumstances in the first place. Hence the common universalized claim that guilt and remorse are never appropriate emotions about an abortion is denied. They may be appropriate, and appropriately inculcated, even when the decision was the right one.

Another motivation for bringing women's rights into the discussion may be to attempt to correct the implication, carried by the killing-centered approach, that insofar as abortion is wrong, it is a wrong that only women do, or at least (given the preponderance of male doctors) that only women instigate. I do not myself believe that we can thus escape the fact that nature bears harder on women than it does on men,[16] but virtue theory can certainly correct many of the injustices that the emphasis on women's rights is rightly concerned about. With very little amendment, everything that has been said above applies to boys and men too. Although the abortion decision is, in a natural sense, the woman's decision, proper to her, boys and men are often party to it, for well

---

is (usually) a good and hence (human) death usually an evil. The exceptions would be (*a*) where death is actually a good or a benefit, because the baby that would come to be if the life were not cut short would be better off dead than alive, and (*b*) where death, though not a good, is not an evil either, because the life that would be led (e.g., in a state of permanent coma) would not be a good. (See Foot, "Euthanasia.")

16. I discuss this point at greater length in *Beginning Lives*.

or ill, and even when they are not, they are bound to have been party to the circumstances that brought it up. No less than girls and women, boys and men can, in their actions, manifest self-centeredness, callousness, and light-mindedness about life and parenthood in relation to abortion. They can be self-centered or courageous about the possibility of disability in their offspring; they need to reflect on their sexual activity and their choices, or the lack of them, about their sexual partner and contraception; they need to grow up and take responsibility for their own actions and life in relation to fatherhood. If it is true, as I maintain, that insofar as motherhood is intrinsically worthwhile, being a mother is an important purpose in women's lives, being a father (rather than a mere generator) is an important purpose in men's lives as well, and it is adolescent of men to turn a blind eye to this and pretend that they have many more important things to do.

CONCLUSION

Much more might be said, but I shall end the actual discussion of the problem of abortion here, and conclude by highlighting what I take to be its significant features. These hark back to many of the criticisms of virtue theory discussed earlier.

The discussion does not proceed simply by our trying to answer the question "Would a perfectly virtuous agent ever have an abortion and, if so, when?"; virtue theory is not limited to considering "Would Socrates have had an abortion if he were a raped, pregnant fifteen-year-old?" nor automatically stumped when we are considering circumstances into which no virtuous agent would have got herself. Instead, much of the discussion proceeds in the virtue- and vice-related terms whose application, in several cases, yields practical conclusions (cf. the third and fourth criticisms above). These terms are difficult to apply correctly, and anyone might challenge my application of any one of them. So, for example, I have claimed that some abortions, done for certain reasons, would be callous or light-minded; that others might indicate an appropriate modesty or humility; that others would reflect a greedy and foolish attitude to what one could expect out of life. Any of these examples may be disputed, but what is at issue is, should these difficult terms be there, or should the discussion be couched in terms that all clever adolescents can apply correctly? (Cf. the first half of the "major objection" above.)

245 Virtue Theory and Abortion

Proceeding as it does in the virtue- and vice-related terms, the discussion thereby, inevitably, also contains claims about what is worthwhile, serious and important, good and evil, in our lives. So, for example, I claimed that parenthood is intrinsically worthwhile, and that having a good time was a worthless end (in life, not on individual occasions); that losing a fetus is always a serious matter (albeit not a tragedy in itself in the first trimester) whereas acquiring an appendectomy scar is a trivial one; that (human) death is an evil. Once again, these are difficult matters, and anyone might challenge any one of my claims. But what is at issue is, as before, should those difficult claims be there or can one reach practical conclusions about real moral issues that are in no way determined by premises about such matters? (Cf. the fifth criticism, and the second half of the "major criticism.")

The discussion also thereby, inevitably, contains claims about what life is like (e.g., my claim that love and friendship do not survive their parties' constantly insisting on their rights; or the claim that to demand perfection of life is to run the risk of missing out on happiness entirely). What is at issue is, should those disputable claims be there, or is our knowledge (or are our false opinions) about what life is like irrelevant to our understanding of real moral issues? (Cf. both halves of the "major criticism.")

Naturally, my own view is that all these concepts should be there in any discussion of real moral issues and that virtue theory, which uses all of them, is the right theory to apply to them. I do not pretend to have shown this. I realize that proponents of rival theories may say that, now that they have understood how virtue theory uses the range of concepts it draws on, they are more convinced than ever that such concepts should not figure in an adequate normative theory, because they are sectarian, or vague, or too particular, or improperly anthropocentric, and reinstate what I called the "major criticism." Or, finding many of the details of the discussion appropriate, they may agree that many, perhaps even all, of the concepts should figure, but argue that virtue theory gives an inaccurate account of the way the concepts fit together (and indeed of the concepts themselves) and that another theory provides a better account; that would be interesting to see. Moreover, I admitted that there were at least two problems for virtue theory: that it has to argue against moral skepticism, "pluralism," and cultural relativism, and that it has to find something to say about conflicting requirements of different virtues.

Proponents of rival theories might argue that their favored theory provides better solutions to these problems than virtue theory can. Indeed, they might criticize virtue theory for finding problems here at all. Anyone who argued for at least one of moral skepticism, "pluralism," or cultural relativism could presumably do so (provided their favored theory does not find a similar problem); and a utilitarian might say that benevolence is the only virtue and hence that virtue theory errs when it discusses even apparent conflicts between the requirements of benevolence and some other character trait such as honesty.

Defending virtue theory against all possible, or even likely, criticisms of it would be a lifelong task. As I said at the outset, in this article I aimed to defend the theory against some criticisms which I thought arose from an inadequate understanding of it, and to improve that understanding. If I have succeeded, we may hope for more comprehending criticisms of virtue theory than have appeared hitherto.

Methods of bioethics: Some defective proposals

R.M.HARE

1. In these days of intense academic competition, which is supposed to keep us all on our toes, one has to publish or be damned; and for advancing one's career it is more important that what one publishes should be new, than that it should be true. Often it is not as new as one thinks it is; sometimes, if one looks back to the great philosophers of the past, one finds that one's bright new ideas have been anticipated by them. This has happened often enough to me.

As to being true, that is not so difficult. Most philosophical truths are fairly obvious, though people obscure them by their inability or unwillingness to express themselves clearly. The difficult thing is to grasp the whole truth. If one takes a number of supposedly divergent theories on almost any philosophical question, one will find in each of them some points which are right, and some which are wrong. Those who criticize these theories often rightly attack the points that are wrong, but do not see that not everything in a theory is wrong; it also, usually, has hold of important truths. So, in putting forward their own opposing theories, these philosophers discard the good with the bad, denying truths that their victims had grasped. So they too land themselves in a mixture of truth and error.

The difficult thing, as I said, is to grasp the whole truth. This entails carefully disentangling the truths from the errors in *all* the theories one studies. It is the mark of the good philosopher to be able to do this. All philosophers can profit from the advice that I regularly give to my students: pinch your opponents' clothes. That is, find out what is right about what they are saying, and say it yourself. You will then be less exposed to their counter-attacks. You will end up, as I have ended up, as an eclectic - not the sort of eclectic that borrows thoughts from all and sundry without seeking to make them consistent with one another, but the sort that sees that these thoughts are true, *and* that they can all be consistently held simultaneously. It is very difficult to be this kind of eclectic. It requires, above all, great clarity of thought and precision of expression.

I have called this paper 'Methods of Bioethics'. I could have called it, following Sidgwick, simply 'Methods of Ethics', because the appropriate methods for bioethics are not, so far as I can see, going to differ from those appropriate for ethics or moral philosophy in general. But in attending to a branch of applied ethics like bioethics, we have brought home to us a requirement of which those who propound ethical theories seem often to be unaware: the requirement to say something that will help us answer important practical moral questions, on our answers to which lives may depend. I shall be showing later that many of the theories that have recently won fame for their inventors are not of much use for this purpose.

In order to explain the scope of this paper, I need to distinguish between different kinds of thing that have been called ethical or moral theories. In order to keep within my time limit, I shall leave one of these kinds on one side, although it contains the more serious and useful sorts of ethical theory. I can do this, because I have written extensively about such theories in other places (H 1987, 1995). I mean theories about the

© Copyright 1994 RM Hare

nature and logical properties of the moral concepts, or the meanings of the moral words. This, I am convinced, has to be what we start with in any serious study of moral reasoning. But the advocates of the views I shall be discussing say little about ethical theory in this narrow sense. Perhaps if they did study these issues they would do more good. Ethical theories in the narrow sense, those that I shall be leaving aside, are such as naturalism, intuitionism, subjectivism, emotivism and my own prescriptivist theory. These theories are grappling with serious problems about the logic of moral reasoning - problems which we have to solve if we are to make any progress in it. But, as I said, the theories I shall be discussing do not move in that world.

2. Enough, then, for these very general remarks. I will now give some examples, from moral philosophy, of how people can be led into error by denying truths which they only deny because the truths are tangled up, in the writings of those who have grasped them, with errors, and it is hard to disentangle the truths from the errors.

I will start with an example which I can deal with briefly, because it is a fairly familiar one and I have discussed it before, though many people seem not to have taken in what I said (H 1981: 36, 39). This is the theory commonly known as situation ethics. Admirers of the existentialists often say the same sort of thing. The situation ethicists have hold of an important truth, that one has to judge each situation on its merits. Situations differ one from another, and the differences may be morally relevant. One cannot assume that they are not. But the situation ethicists go on from asserting this truth to asserting a dangerous falsehood. They say that in morals one cannot appeal to what they call 'general principles' or 'general rules'.

In order to see what is wrong with this, one has to make a distinction of which, even now, many of our philosophical colleagues seem to be unaware. This is the distinction between universality and generality. Many people think that 'universal' and 'general' mean the same. Most philosophers do indeed use them as if they meant the same. Aristotle was, I think, the first offender, because he used his expression *kath' holou*, usually translated, indiscriminately, 'general' and 'universal', without making clear that the term can have two entirely different meanings (see H 1972). In his *Ethics*, for example, he sometimes uses it in a quite different way from his use in his logical works (contrast, e.g., *EN* 1076b 13 with *An. Post.* 74a 25 ff.)

Consider the two statements, that one ought never to tell lies, and that one ought never to tell lies to one's business partners. Both these statements are <u>universal</u>. They start with a universal quantifier ('never') and contain no individual references. They apply, the first of them to <u>anyone</u> who says anything, and the second of them to anyone who says anything to a business partner of his. But the second is less <u>general</u> than the first. It is more specific, though no less universal.

We can now see the first thing that is wrong with what the situation ethicists say. 'Considering each situation on its merits' does entail not judging it by the simple application of very <u>general</u> rules or principles. The situation ethicists have a point there. But it does not entail refusing to judge it on highly specific but still <u>universal</u> principles. Suppose one goes into the utmost detail about the specifics of a situation, carefully noticing all the features of it which might be morally relevant. Suppose, even, if that were possible, that one <u>describes</u> the situation at enormous length, leaving out nothing that could possibly be relevant to a moral decision about it. Suppose, for example, that it is a situation in a short story - or even a very long story in several volumes. And suppose that one comes to a decision as to what one of the characters ought to have done at some point in the narrative. The moral statement that one then makes is still universal, logically speaking. It can begin with a universal quantifier, and not contain individual constants or references to individuals. It can say that anyone of a certain kind, in a situation of a certain kind (the kinds being as minutely specified as you like) ought to do a certain thing.

It is true that the character is represented in the story as an individual. But in order to represent him (or her) the novelist has to describe him. And the descriptions have all to be in universal terms, because there are no other terms available for the purpose. We cannot identify the person by pointing at him. What we have in the novel is a description, in universal terms, of a person of a very minutely specified kind, in a situation of a very minutely specified kind. Any moral statement that we make about him (or her) has to be of the form, that a person of that kind in that kind of situation ought to act in such and such a way.

The confusion between universality and generality, which I have been exposing, leads people to think that if one makes a universal judgement about a situation, one must be making a very general judgement about it. This is not so. The judgement can be specific enough to take in any details of the situation that anybody thinks relevant. Only a victim of the confusion I have been exposing will think that a statement cannot at the same time be universal and highly specific.

There is a lot more to be said on this topic, and many more mistakes that need to be pointed out. But since I have done this in other places (H 1972, 1981: 41), I can skip it now. I shall be explaining later how it is that, though we have to consider each situation on its merits, rather simple and general principles do, all the same, have a use in our moral thinking (H 1981: 35 ff., 43 ff.). I shall not have time to explain why it is important to have regard to universal but highly specific principles, although in the actual world no two situations are ever exactly alike (H 1981: 42). And I shall omit here any discussion of the familiar confusion between singular prescriptions like 'He ought to keep his promise to her' and universal relational prescriptions like 'One ought to keep one's own particular promises to the individual to whom one has made them'. The second, like 'One ought to be faithful to one's own wife', is a universal prescription, even though in most countries one can have only one wife (see H 1992).

3. I come now to my next example of a theory that has hold of part of the truth, but combines it with serious errors through denying other parts of the truth. This is the theory known as 'virtue ethics'. Its adherents often appeal to the authority of Aristotle, and repudiate that of Kant; but I very much doubt, after reading those great philosophers, whether the virtue ethicists have hold of the whole truth even about what they actually said.

An ethics of virtue is often contrasted with an ethics of duty, or with an ethics of principle. Let us consider first the alleged contrast between virtues and principles. The contrast is supposed to be between having good states of character (which is what virtues are) and following good or right principles. But suppose we ask some proponent of virtue ethics to tell us what one would have to do, or what states or dispositions of mind or of feeling one would have to cultivate, in order to acquire virtue. To answer this question, he will have to describe the states or dispositions, or the actions to which they lead. But now we have to ask, what is the difference between such a description, and a statement of the principles for living a good life. I cannot see any. It looks as if any ethics of virtue would have to borrow extensively from an ethics of principle in order even to tell us what virtue consists in.

To put it another way: suppose we have a <u>description</u> of one way of being virtuous (there are no doubt many ways). By a very simple grammatical manoeuvre, one can change the mood of this descriptive statement and put it into the imperative. It will then be a <u>prescription</u>. Or one could change it instead into an 'ought'-statement; it will then be another kind of prescription. Both these prescriptions will be different kinds of <u>principles</u>. They will be principles prescribing how one should behave, and how one should be feeling, in certain kinds of situation. Behaving and feeling like that is one way of displaying virtue. Neither an ethics of virtue nor an ethics of principle has to assume, though many do assume, that there is only one way of leading a good life. Both virtues and principles could be like recipes in a cookbook; one does not have to cook them all at the same time. It is another question whether the good life <u>is</u> like that (that is, whether there are alternative possible kinds of good life); but that is a question which affects both an ethics of virtue and an ethics of principle, so I do not need to discuss it now.

It is not surprising, in the light of what I have said, that Aristotle has a lot to say about principles, and Kant a lot to say about virtues (he devoted, after all, half of his *Metaphysic of Morals* to his *Tugendlehre* (*Doctrine of Virtue, Tgl.*). These great philosophers were not so one-sided as their modern self-styled disciples. To illustrate Aristotle's belief in principles, we have only to notice that the first premisses of his practical syllogisms were universal prescriptions, that is, principles - though not all of them were <u>moral</u> principles (e.g. 1147a 31). For Aristotle the better sort of people are those who 'desire and act in accordance with a rational principle'. They are contrasted with those immature people who 'live and pursue things in accordance with feeling' (1095a 8-10). And in the most famous passage of all he says, rightly, that virtue itself is 'a disposition governing our choices, lying in a mean, which is determined by a rational principle' (1107b 36). The word I have translated 'rational principle' is *'logos'* - the same word he uses for describing the universal prescriptions that form the first premisses of his practical syllogisms (see, e.g. <u>EN</u> 1147b 1 ff. They are the verbal expressions of the dispositions or traits of character that make us act as we do. But feelings are not left out of Aristotle's account. The mean is exhibited in feelings <u>and</u> in actions (1104b 13, 1106b 24, 1109b 30). Nor does Kant leave feelings out. His view is simply that the mere feeling without corresponding action is not enough, as he makes clear in his contrast between what he calls (unfortunately to modern ears) 'pathological' and 'practical' love (<u>Gr</u>. BA13 = 399; <u>Tgl</u>. A118 f. = 449 f.). 'Pathological' means, of course, consisting in having pathê, or feelings. Kant never denies that feeling is supportive of action, nor that it is important to have the right feelings. He says that one can do the right thing, fulfilling one's duty, even if one does not have them; but of course he could agree that this is much more difficult.

If virtue is contrasted with duty, the same happens. 'Duty' is thought nowadays, though it was not in either Kant's or Aristotle's days, to be a somewhat pompous expression. But Nelson was not being pompous when he said that England expected every man to do his duty. Come to that, 'virtue' is a pretty pompous expression too, if one uses it that way. When Aristotle says that both with virtuous action and with virtuous habits of mind it is a question of 'when one ought, and under what conditions, and towards whom and for what purpose and in what manner' (1106b 22), he was speaking of duty, or of what one ought to do or feel. One has a duty to cultivate the right feelings and to do the right actions. I can see no essential difference from Kant here. To delineate virtue is to say what feelings one ought to cultivate, and what actions one ought to do. This is a delineation of our duties, and requires statements of moral principles. The virtue ethicists, it appears, have, perhaps in the interests of novelty, been making a distinction without a difference. At the most they are emphasizing the importance of character for the moral life; but did Kant deny this?

4. Feelings are also stressed, to the exclusion of much else that is important, by the advocates of what we may call 'caring ethics'. I include in this class such writers as Gilligan (1982, and see refs. in Blum 1988) and Noddings (1984), as well as more professional philosophers like Lawrence Blum, who has written a good book in a somewhat similar vein (1980). He has also published recently an article explicitly supporting Gilligan (1988). Though I shall not have room to discuss Blum's arguments in detail, I must say that I think his choice of antagonists was a pity. Neither Gilligan nor Kohlberg is a very clear thinker, important as their ideas are. I do not know Gilligan, but I knew Kohlberg quite well and learnt a lot from him. However, he lacked the analytical skills to give a clear account of his higher stages of development. In particular, I think he failed to make clear the crucial distinction between universality and generality that I explained earlier. As a result he gets accused by Gilligan, not unfairly, of putting in his highest stage of development people whose morality depends on very general rules, and of neglecting the special relations (especially of caring) that we ought to have with particular people. But there is nothing in the universalizability of moral judgements to prevent our being guided in our actions by very specific attachments to particular people with whom we have formed caring relations. I would not myself put in the highest moral class people who cannot manage this. I have already spoken about the confusion (that between singular prescriptions and universal relational prescriptions) involved here.

The fault of the advocates of caring, as before, is not that the virtues they emphasize are not virtues. Everyone can agree that caring, and friendship on which Blum lays so much stress, are important features of the morally good life. Helga Kuhse, in an important paper (1993), has pointed out the baffling ambiguity of the notion of caring, which its advocates have not done enough to clear up. She also points out how little guidance the notion, even if clarified, gives to our moral decisions as to what actually to do when faced with difficult choices. But the main fault of the proponents of caring ethics is that they give a completely unfair and unbalanced caricature of the views they are attacking. One would think from the way they write that no philosophers before them had said anything about caring.

Gilligan thinks that the lack of attention to caring is a symptom of male domination of philosophical thought. Peter Singer has a useful discussion of the relation between gender and approaches to philosophy in his new book (1993). It has to be admitted that nearly all famous philosophers until recently have been male; but it is simply not true that they have ignored caring and friendship. People who think they have might start by reading Anthony Price's excellent book *Love and Friendship in Plato and Aristotle* (1989), and looking at the texts he refers to. Aristotle *EN* 1168a 28 - 69b 2 is especially relevant. After that they might go on to what Hume says about sympathy (1739, bk.2, pt. 1, sec. 11). Even Kant thought that we ought to treat the ends of other people as if they were our own. He says that we shall not be treating humanity as an end in itself, 'unless every one endeavours also, so far as in him lies, to further the ends of others' (*Gr.* BA69 = 430). If that is not caring, I do not know what is.

I shall be arguing later that it is quite easy to accommodate caring within a Kantian framework, as I have tried to do. I shall be arguing also, as I have argued elsewhere (H 1993a), that there is no inconsistency between a carefully formulated Kantianism and a carefully formulated utilitarianism. Within such a framework the carers can have all the caring they need or desire; only they must not think (and I do not suggest that they do think) that caring is the whole of morality. Blum in particular is very fair about this; he thinks he is simply redressing the balance; but it needs to be asked whether he is not actually (again in the interests of novelty) tilting it too far in the opposite direction.

This is particularly clear if we consider what the carers say about impartiality. Wishing to stress the importance for the moral life of caring relationships, and recognizing the obvious fact that we cannot have such relationships with everybody, they are in danger of neglecting another important aspect of morality, namely justice and the impartial pursuit of the common good. What are we to say of the doctor who cares so much for his children that he holds back supplies of badly needed drugs in scarce supply so as to have a reserve for them? To this question too I shall return; it will prove not so difficult to answer once we have a balanced account of morality as a whole.

5. The last group of theories I shall have time to consider is that known as 'right-based' or 'rights-based' theories. The best discussion of these that I know is in Mackie 1978. There are many varieties of them, but what is common to them is the thought that we can found the whole of morality on an appeal to people's rights. This kind of theory too grasps one part of the truth but neglects other equally important parts. It is certainly true that rights play a significant part in morality (H 1989b: 79-120). Nobody ought to want to get rid of them. But all the same the appeal to rights has been much abused recently, owing to the idea that one can claim a right without producing any argument to show that one has it. Such right-claims rest in the end on nothing but the claimant's intuitions (some would say 'prejudices'). We have reached a stage at which, if anybody has a mind to something, he will say he has a right to it. Without a secure way of determining who has rights to what, disputes about rights will never end. And it is certainly going to be impossible to base morality on rights, if they themselves are based on nothing but hot air.

Wayne Sumner has written an excellent book about this question (1987), which I recommend to anybody who wishes to understand how to argue for rights. He comes to a conclusion with which I agree almost entirely, that the most satisfactory foundation for rights is a consequentialist one. I would put it by saying that we ought to acknowledge those rights whose recognition and preservation does the best for all those affected, considered impartially. But I shall return later to the details of this suggestion.

6. I have had time to list only a few of the ethical theories that have been popular recently; and my treatment of them has been very cursory. I will now go on to show how they all fall down through ignoring important parts of the truth about morality. After that I shall show how to fill in the whole picture, and thus give the supporters of these theories what they are after, without neglecting the truths which they neglect.

The situation ethicists, with whom I started, say that we have to consider each situation on its merits. But they do not say how we are to judge the merits of situations. In default of some method for judging, everybody will be at liberty to say what they feel like saying. It is hard to see how any method for judging situations can get far without giving reasons for judging them one way rather than another. And any statement of the reasons is bound to bring in principles - not the very simple general principles that the situation ethicists so dislike, but universal principles all the same. If it is a reason for banning a drug from public sale that it could endanger life, then that is because of a principle that drugs which endanger life ought not to be on public sale. Of course reasons can be much more complicated than that; but they will have to state certain features of situations which make it right to do this or that; and these features will always have to be described in universal (though not always highly general) terms.

Even rather general principles, however, have their uses. If we had to scrutinize every situation de novo, we should have no time to make many decisions in the course of our lives. What sensible people do is to form for themselves some fairly general principles to deal with the general run of cases, and reserve their attention for scrutinizing the difficult cases in more detail. But I shall be returning to this point.

Situation ethics does not do much good for bioethics beyond that of deterring us from oversimplification of the issues. Once we get into the really difficult problems, we find ourselves driven to give reasons for our opinions. We have, indeed, to look carefully at particular cases; but after we have done that we shall want to learn from these cases principles that we can apply to other cases. Cases differ from one another, no doubt; but that does not mean that we cannot learn from experience. The salient reasons for one decision may also be important for another decision. So, while avoiding oversimplification and too rigid general rules, we can still, and good medical practitioners do, form for ourselves and others general guidelines for the future. These guidelines have to be to some degree general, or they will apply to only one situation, and be useless for preserving the lessons of experience for later situations. I shall be coming back later to the different roles in bioethics of general principles and the careful examination of particular cases.

7. Virtue ethics, which I mentioned next, falls down for a different reason; it ignores another part of the truth about morality. It shares this fault with a type of ethical theory that in other respects might be thought antagonistic to it, namely that of a typical intuitionist deontologist who believes in the ultimacy of duties. Both of these kinds of theory are exposed to the question, 'How do we decide what are duties or virtues?'. We should most of us agree that there are duties and that there are virtues, and that both are important in morality; but it is no use the moralist saying to us just that we have to acquire virtues or perform our duties; the difficult part of morality is knowing what these are. I have written a lot in other places (H 1981: 10, 1995) about intuitionism and its failings, so I will not repeat it now. I shall be coming back later to my way of meeting this deficiency in both virtue ethics and intuitionist deontology. But it should be obvious already that neither theory is going to do much for bioethics unless it can tell us how to answer what I said is the difficult question. If we do not know what traits of character are virtues, we obviously cannot know what we have to do in order to display them.

There is also another fault in virtue ethics, which, however, may not affect all varieties of it. It does not affect Aristotle, but then that is because he is much more than a virtue ethicist. This is the fault of concentrating attention on the character of the moral agent, and diverting it from the scrutiny of what he actually does. It is possible for very virtuous people to do terrible things - and not necessarily by mistake or inadvertence.

Let me take the example of a very devout Roman Catholic missionary, a saintly man, who accepts wholeheartedly the teaching of his church about contraception. He therefore does all he can to stop the government of the African country in which he works, and in which he has some influence, from encouraging the provision of contraceptives. If successful in this, he will be contributing to the population explosion and to the keeping of women in subjection, which, we may agree, are great evils. But we may still think him a very good, though misguided, man. Devout Roman Catholics will not like this example; but they can easily find others which illustrate the same point.

The point is that very good people sometimes do things which they ought not to do, and we must preserve the possibility of saying this. If I were to confine my moral thinking to the improvement or at least preservation of my own good character, I might sometimes fail to question the morality of my _acts_. Aristotle is immune to this danger, because he explicitly says that nobody would have even a prospect of becoming good by _not_ doing good acts (1105b 11). A person becomes upright by doing upright acts (1105b 9); and this can be taken in two senses; doing upright acts is _part_ of the qualification for being _called_ upright, and doing upright acts is a way of _making_ oneself into an upright person (1103a 32 ff.). It is not the _whole_ of the qualification, for the acts have to be done _because_ one is that sort of person (1105a 30). But for Aristotle, nevertheless, right action is a necessary condition for virtue. Like Kant, and like any balanced moralist, he appreciates the intimate link between character and action in morality. I shall be returning to the nature of this link.

8. The third on my list of ethical theories I called 'caring ethics'. If all that the proponents of such theories did was to encourage us to be more caring, in most of the senses of that ambiguous word, we could applaud them for that. But caring people, like virtuous people of all kinds, can do wrong things. I mentioned earlier the example of a doctor who cares so much for his children that he deprives other doctors' patients of drugs that are in short supply. We might condemn him even if the beneficiaries were not his children but his own patients. If there is in force a fair system for distributing the drugs, we might think that he ought not to try to cheat the system. We should say the same about a nurse who found that she was caring so much for one of her patients that she neglected the others. It is a difficult question, how to reconcile the duties or virtues of caring and justice. Many of the most difficult issues in bioethics hinge on this question, to which I shall be returning.

9. The last class of theories that I mentioned was that of rights-based theories. We have already noticed one of their faults, that they commonly give no way of deciding what rights people have. But, apart from this, it is hard to see how a rights-based theory could cover all that we want to say by way of moral judgements. Some of the aspects of morality that such theories leave out are, indeed, those emphasized by the other theories we have been discussing. For example, it is hard to see how a rights-based theory can give an adequate account of caring or of virtue. A virtuous person is much more than someone who respects other people's rights, and caring for someone is much more than not infringing his (or her) rights. So here again we have a one-sided theory which emphasizes part of the truth about morality to the exclusion of other equally important

parts. An adequate theory, such as I shall be sketching shortly, will cover all these aspects of morality. It is not difficult to do this, once the structure of moral thinking is understood.

A rights-based theory is likely also to give an inadequate account of yet other moral notions besides those emphasized by caring ethics and virtue ethics. It will find it hard to give a full account even of duties. Most moral systems contain duties which are not duties to anybody, and which therefore generate no rights. For example, many people think that we have a duty to develop our appreciation of great art and great music and great literature; but it is extremely strained to say that this is a duty to anybody - for example to ourselves, or to the artists or composers or writers, most of whom are dead. Nobody, therefore, has a right to have us appreciate these things.

The matter becomes even worse when we pass from the narrow notion of duty to the wider notion of what we morally ought to do. To cite a familiar example: if when driving on a dirty night I pass someone who needs a ride and does not look like a criminal, I might think that I ought to pick him up. But I am unlikely to think that I have a duty to him to pick him up, or that he has a right to be picked up. Such acts of kindness are not obligations, but we may all the same commend them morally. So again, something important has been left out.

10. It is time we turned from this fault-finding to something more positive. Is there a theory that can cover all the aspects of morality that these different theories emphasize? I shall argue that a carefully formulated combination of Kantianism and utilitarianism, such as I have advocated in my books, can do this. In case anyone thinks that Kantianism is incompatible with utilitarianism, I can now refer to a paper in which I argue that this is a mistake (H 1993a). Kant was not a utilitarian: he held views which no kind of utilitarian theory could justify (for example about punishment). But it is doubtful whether these views could be justified by his own theory either. If we look simply at his theory of the Categorical Imperative, it can be argued that this is compatible with a carefully formulated version of utilitarianism. What this version is, I have tried to explain elsewhere (H 1981).

The key to an understanding of all these problems is to see that moral thinking takes place at at least two levels. There is, first of all, the day-to-day level at which most of us do most of our moral thinking. I say 'moral thinking'; but a lot of what goes on at this level can hardly be dignified by the name of 'thinking' at all. If we have been well brought up, we often know at once what is right or wrong without doing any thinking. Philosophers call this knowledge of right and wrong that most of us have, 'moral intuition'. What intuitionists say about this intuitive level of moral thinking is mostly correct, except that they think that it is self-supporting, which it is far from being. Most of the difficult problems in moral philosophy arise because intuitions conflict: either the intuitions of one person, or the intuitions of different people. A different level of moral thinking is needed to settle these conflicts.

This higher level of moral thinking can be called the critical level. It cannot appeal to our intuitive sense of right and wrong to settle conflicts between intuitions, because that would obviously be arguing in a circle. The method of thinking to be employed in critical moral thinking is radically different from that appropriate to the intuitive level. Here we have to reason. How we have to reason remains, however, a matter for dispute. My own account of the method of moral reasoning at the critical level draws heavily on both the utilitarians and Kant, and is based on an analysis of moral language and its logical properties. It makes no appeal to moral intuitions at the critical level. However, I do not need to defend my view here, because the mere distinction between the two levels is enough to sort out our present problems, which arise mainly through neglect of the distinction.

The critical level of moral thinking is used, not only to settle conflicts between intuitions at the intuitive level, but to select the moral principles and (which comes, as we have seen, to the same thing) the virtues that we should seek to cultivate in our children and ourselves. On my own account of critical thinking, the selection is done by assessing the acceptance utility of the virtues and principles - that is, by asking what are on the whole the best for society to acknowledge and cultivate. Those who have absorbed these principles and acquired these virtues will have the corresponding intuitions about right and wrong, good and bad, and will also, unless overcome by temptations, follow the principles and display the virtues in practice. If the critical thinking has been well done, and if, therefore, the right virtues and principles have been chosen, the person who has them will be a person of good character, that is, a morally good person.

The structure that I have outlined is therefore able to give an account both of moral virtues and of moral principles. It has to be added, however, that for virtue or goodness of character it is not sufficient to do the right actions. As Aristotle saw, it is necessary that they should be done on the basis of settled dispositions, which constitute a person's character. The distinction between levels was anticipated by Aristotle, and indeed by Socrates and Plato. To have virtue properly so called, it is necessary to do what one ought to do, and to know why it is what one ought to do. In other words, both right actions and good dispositions, and the ability to explain why they are right and good (to give their *logos*) are necessary for virtue. The person who merely knows which actions are right and which dispositions are good, and does not understand why, lacks something, namely the intellectual virtue that Aristotle calls *phronêsis* and Plato and Socrates call *epistêmê* or understanding, as contrasted with mere right opinion. He can do only intuitive, but not critical thinking.

This two-level structure can therefore account adequately for the place of virtues and of principles and of duties in our moral thinking. But among the virtues are those on which caring ethics lays so much stress. To be a caring person is to have the disposition to feel sympathy for other people, especially when they are suffering, and to act accordingly. This is a very important virtue, but not the only one. Justice is also important, but is underemphasized by caring ethics. Sometimes justice requires us to be impartial between people for whom we care and people for whom we do not.

Here the distinction between levels is extremely important. The better of us have principles to be followed, and virtues to be exercised, at the intuitive level that require partiality to those for whom we care. A mother should, we think, give priority to the needs of her own children over those of other people's children. Doctors and nurses should devote themselves to their own patients more than to other peoples' patients. Partiality in caring is required by the intuitive principles that most of us have been taught, and probably these partial principles are sometimes innate. Here again we must avoid the confusion between singular prescriptions and universal relational ones.

However, this is all at the intuitive level. Partial principles at the intuitive level can be justified by impartial thinking at the critical level (H 1979, 1981; 135-40). If we were concerned impartially for the good of all children, we should want mothers to behave partially toward their own children and have feelings which made them behave in this way. We should want this because, if mothers are like this, children will be better looked after than if mothers tried to feel the same about other people's children as about their own. The same applies to doctors and nurses. Thus impartial critical thinking will tell us to cultivate partial virtues and principles. But it will also tell us to cultivate impartiality for certain roles and situations. These obviously include that of judges, but also those of anybody who has to distribute benefits and harms fairly, as doctors do when they have to divide scarce resources between their patients.

Lawrence Blum, whom I have mentioned already, considers the possibility that he can hive off the virtue of impartiality into these particular roles, and thus exclude it from other parts of morality (1980: 46). This is all right at the intuitive level. But, because he seems not to understand the importance of the distinction between the levels, he misses the point that impartiality is required in all thought at the critical level, even though this impartial critical thought will bid us be partial in certain roles at the intuitive level. He does indeed (1980: 59) consider the possibility that rule-utilitarianism (which is a kind of two-level theory) might make a distinction of levels, and thus seek to show that partial virtues should be cultivated because that is for the best for all considered impartially. But his book was published before my own book *Moral Thinking* (H 1981), and he probably had not come across earlier writings of mine in which I sketched a two-level theory that escapes the faults he finds in the cruder two-level theory he discusses (e.g. H 1976).

In that book I gave enormous emphasis to the place in moral thinking of empathy. Indeed, it is one of the crucial elements in the system of moral reasoning that I was constructing. In default of the ability to represent to ourselves fully what it is like to be the other people that our actions affect, we are not making our moral decisions with an adequate understanding of the facts of the situation in which we are acting. To enter fully into their situation, we have to think of them as if they were ourselves. And if we then universalize our prescriptions, we are led to treat their preferences as if they were our own preferences. This gets in all that the carers are asking for.

11. Coming now to rights-based theories: it is extremely easy to find a place for rights in the kind of two-level structure that I have been suggesting, but impossible to base the whole of morality on them. They have a place both at the intuitive level and at the critical level. I can be brief, because I have explained elsewhere (H 1981, ch. 9) what these places are. At the critical level we are constrained only by the formal requirement that we eliminate all individual references from our moral principles. That is, we must not give the fact that any particular person is in a particular position in a situation as a reason for a moral judgement. This has the consequence that we have to treat all individuals on a par - to give them equal concern and respect, as some writers say. None has a greater claim on us *qua* that individual. We could, if we wished, put this in terms of rights, saying that all individuals have a right to equal concern and respect.

However, it has been generally recognized that from this formal requirement no substantial or contentful rights can be derived. We have to reason, in accordance with the formal requirement, counting everybody for one, as Bentham said (cited in Mill 1861, ch. 5), or treating the ends of all others as our own ends, as Kant said (*Gr.* BA69 = 430). And what substantial principles we then select will depend on what ends the others have. For example, since nearly everyone has the end of not being killed, we are likely to have a principle giving them a right not to be killed.

But these substantial principles will all be for use at the intuitive level. They will be defeasible or overridable. For example, if some suffering terminal patient beseeches her doctor, as happened in a recent case in Britain, to end her misery, it would be foolish to base a ban on euthanasia on the right to life of the patient (H 1993b). The right exists because in nearly all cases people want not to be killed; in cases where a patient does want to be killed, can she not voluntarily waive the right, as we can most rights?

It will be found that by keeping substantial moral rights at the intuitive level, while preserving the formal right to equal concern and respect at the critical level, all the problems about conflicts of rights, and conflicts between rights and other duties, can be resolved. But since I have dealt with questions of rights and their place in morality at great length elsewhere (H 1989b: 79-120), I shall not go into any more details now.

12. I come back last to the theory with which I started, situation ethics. It is obvious that a distinction between levels can explain what is right and what is wrong about such a theory. Taken literally, the theory would require us to use critical thinking in all our moral decisions however straightforward. But usually we do not have time for this, nor, always, the necessary information about the consequences of alternative actions. We are also affected by personal bias, which, in spite of what some of the people I have discussed say, is often a source of wrong decisions.

So the sensible thing to do is to form for ourselves principles, and cultivate virtues, which in the general run of straightforward cases will lead us to do the right thing without much thought, and reserve our powers of deep thought for the awkward cases. If we do not have time for this deep thought when the decision confronts us, or if we do not then have the full information needed for a right decision, we can think about it afterwards, and perhaps modify our intuitive principles accordingly. When we do this critical thinking, we have to consider each situation on its merits and in detail, as the situation ethicists say we should. But it would be absurd and impracticable to do this on every occasion.

13. I will end by pointing out how important these considerations, which apply to all moral thinking, are for bioethics in particular. I have attended a lot of classes on medical ethics, such as the best medical and nursing schools make their students take. Often these classes have the form of a discussion of particular awkward cases in which doctors and others have to make agonizing decisions. The reason why they are agonizing is that principles that most of us accept conflict with one another.

For example, there are cases in which we cannot save a patient's life unless we do something to him without his consent, or even contrary to his express wishes. There is the principle requiring informed consent, and there is the principle bidding us save life if we can. Both are sound principles, but they are defeasible or overridable. The right way of handling such decisions is provided by the structure I have outlined. We have to decide what is the right decision *in this case*; and that entails examining the case on its merits and in detail. So far the situation ethicists are right. But what we decide in this case may well, and should, get incorporated into our general body of principles for use in the future. We may decide that one of the competing principles, though sound, has exceptions; and sometimes these exceptions need to be written into the rule as qualifications of it. That is what it is to learn from experience, as I said. The person who has been through such an agonizing decision ought to have learnt something, even though all situations, and all patients, are different.

In very awkward cases, we may have to use critical thinking, though our intuitive principles will probably help us decide what aspects of a case to think about first. But the cases are awkward precisely because they are not like the general run of cases, in which, if we have sound intuitive principles, they will guide us without too much thought.

Some of the cases will be awkward because different rights, whether rights of the same person or of different people, conflict. Because these rights are defeasible or overridable, we shall have to use critical thinking to determine which of them should yield in this particular case. And here again this may add to our wisdom for the future, if we incorporate the lessons of this case into our body of moral principles.

In other cases it may seem that what is required by duty conflicts with what is required by caring, or by the pursuit of some other virtue. These are all conflicts at the intuitive level; at the critical level they can be resolved by the application of the formal or logical requirements for moral thinking, in conjunction with the facts about the particular case, and especially the facts about what those affected by our decision prefer, or what their ends are. To understand these facts fully, empathy is required; otherwise we shall be making our decision in ignorance of what the outcome means for those affected. The caring ethicists do right to stress this.

It is at this higher level that the combination of Kantianism with utilitarianism that I have advocated comes into play. At the lower intuitive level we have to be guided by the sound principles that we have learnt, and by the virtues (including that of caring) that we have acquired. But when these sound principles and admirable virtues conflict in a particular case, we may need to have recourse to critical thinking to sort out the conflict, dangerous and agonizing as this may sometimes be. This thinking may even lead us to qualify one of the principles. If the students in the classes I have attended had known about the distinction between the levels of moral thinking, they would have found it easier to sort out their problems. But nobody had told them.

BIBLIOGRAPHY
Writings of R.M.Hare (preceded by 'H' in text):
1972 'Principles', *Proceedings of Aristotelian Society* 73, 1972/3. Repr. in H 1989a.
1976 'Ethical Theory and Utilitarianism', in *Contemporary British Philosophy 4*, ed. H.D.Lewis. Repr. in H 1989a.
1979 'Utilitarianism and the Vicarious Affects', in *The Philosophy of Nicholas Rescher*, ed. E.Sosa (Dordrecht, Reidel). Repr. in H 1989a.
1981 *Moral Thinking:its Levels, Method and Point* (Oxford, Oxford UP).
1987 'How to Think about Moral Questions rationally', *Critica* 18. Repr. in H 1989a.
1989a *Essays in Ethical Theory* (Oxford, Oxford UP).
1989b *Essays on Political Morality* (Oxford, Oxford UP).
1992 'Universalizability', in *Encyclopedia of Ethics*, ed. L.Becker (New York, Garland).
1993a 'Could Kant have been a Utilitarian?', *Utilitas* 5. Also in *Kant and Critique*, ed. R.M.Dancy (Dordrecht, Kluwer, 1993).
1993b 'Is Medical Ethics Lost?' and letters, *Journal of Medical Ethics* 19.
1995 The Axel Hägerström Lectures (Uppsala, 1991), forthcoming. Original title, *A Taxonomy of Ethical Theories*. Provisional title, *Sorting out Ethics.*

Other Writings
Aristotle, *Nicomachean Ethics (EN)*. Refs. to pages of Bekker edition. Refs are to this work unless otherwise indicated.
------- *Posterior Analytics (An. Post.)*. Refs. to pages of Bekker Edition.

Blum, L. (1980), *Friendship, Altruism and Morality* (London, Routledge).
------- (1988), 'Gilligan and Kohlberg: Implications for Moral Theory', *Ethics* 99.
Gilligan, C. (1982), *In a Different Voice* (Cambridge, Mass. Harvard UP).
Hume, D. (1739), *A Treatise of Human Nature* (London, Noon).
Kant, I. (1785), *Grundlegung zur Metaphysik der Sitten* (*Gr.*). Refs. to pages of original editions and of Royal Prussian Academy edition. Translation by H.Paton, *The Moral Law* (London, Hutchinson, 1948).
------- *Tugendlehre* (*Tgl.*). Translation by M.Gregor, The *Doctrine of Virtue* (New York, 1964).
Kuhse, H. (1993), 'Caring is not enough: reflections on a nursing ethics of care', *Australian Journal of Advanced Nursing* 11.
Mackie, J.L. (1978), 'Can there be a Right-based Ethical Theory?', *Midwest St. in Ph.* 3. Repr. in his *Persons and Values* (Oxford, Oxford UP, 1985).
Mill, J.S. (1861), *Utilitarianism*.
Noddings, N. (1984), *Caring* (Berkeley, California UP).
Price, A. (1989), *Love and Friendship in Plato and Aristotle*, (Oxford, Oxford UP).
Singer, P. (1993), *How are we to live?* (Melbourne, Text Publishing Co.)
Sumner, L.W. (1987), *The Moral Foundation of Rights* (Oxford, Oxford UP).

Part VIII
The Ethics of Care

[23]

Two Perspectives:
On Self, Relationships, and Morality

NONA PLESSNER LYONS
Harvard University

Nona Plessner Lyons offers interview data from female and male children, adolescents, and adults in support of the assertions of Carol Gilligan (HER, 1977) that there are two distinct modes of describing the self in relation to others—separate/objective and connected—as well as two kinds of considerations used by individuals in making moral decisions—justice and care. She then describes a methodology, developed from the data, for systematically and reliably identifying these modes of self-definition and moral judgment through the use of two coding schemes. Finally, an empirical study testing Gilligan's hypotheses of the relationship of gender to self-definition and moral judgment is presented with implications of this work for psychological theory and practice.

Asked in the course of an open-ended interview to respond to the question, "What does morality mean to you?" two adults give different definitions.[1] A man replies:

> Morality is basically having a reason for or a way of knowing what's right, what one ought to do; and, when you are put into a situation where you have to choose from among alternatives, being able to recognize when there is an issue of "ought" at stake and when there is not; and then . . . having some reason for choosing among alternatives.

A woman responds:

> Morality is a type of consciousness, I guess, a sensitivity to humanity, that you can affect someone else's life. You can affect your own life, and you have the responsibility not to endanger other people's lives or to hurt other people. So morality is complex. Morality is realizing that there is a play between self and others and that you are going to have to take responsibility for both of them. It's sort of a consciousness of your influence over what's going on.

---

[1] Responses are taken from interview data of the sample and study described in full beginning on page 137.

In contrast to the man's notion of morality—as "having a reason," "a way of knowing what's right, what one ought to do"—is the woman's sense of morality as a type of "consciousness," "a sensitivity" incorporating an injunction not to endanger or hurt other people. In the first image of an individual alone deciding what ought to be done, morality becomes a discrete moment of rational "choosing." In the second image, of an individual aware, connected, and attending to others, morality becomes a "type of consciousness" which, although rooted in time, is not bound by the single moment. Thus, two distinct ways of making moral choices are revealed.

The representation in psychological theory of these two different images and ideas of making moral choices is the concern of this paper. One view has come to dominate modern moral psychology—the image of the person in a discrete moment of individual choice. The identification of a second image—the individual connected and attending to others—and the systematic description of both views from empirical data are presented in this work. In her critique of moral philosophy, Murdoch (1970), the British novelist and philosopher, indicates the importance of this investigation. She elaborates two issues raised by this second image of the self which apply as well to moral psychology: the need for a conception of self not limited to that of a rational, choosing agent, and a concern for acknowledging a conception of love as central to people and to moral theory.

Describing present-day moral philosophy as "confused," "discredited," and "regarded as unnecessary," Murdoch focuses on philosophy's idea and image of the self. Believing that modern moral philosophy has been "dismantling the old substantial picture of the self," Murdoch sees the moral agent reduced to an "isolated principle of will or burrowing point of consciousness." The self as moral agent, "thin as a needle, appears only in the quick flash of the choosing will" (pp. 47, 53). Murdoch rejects this classic Kantian image of the self as pure, rational agent. For her, moral choice is "as often a mysterious matter, because, what we really are seems much more like an obscure system of energy out of which choices and visible acts of will emerge at intervals in ways that are often unclear and often dependent on the condition of the system in between the moments of choice" (p. 54).

The picture of the self as ever capable of detached objectivity in situations of human choice is thus rejected by Murdoch. Yet this is the image assumed in Kohlberg's (1969, 1981) model of moral development. That model, which is a hierarchically ordered sequence of stages of moral judgment-making based in part on the pioneering work of Piaget (1932/1966), is the dominant model of modern moral psychology. In addition, Murdoch's challenge to philosophy "that we need a moral philosophy in which the concept of love, so rarely mentioned now . . . can once again be made central," can also be directed to moral psychology (1970, p. 46). Murdoch's assumption is that love is a central fact of people's everyday lives and morality. But modern moral psychology, grounded in the concepts of justice and rights, subsumes any notion of care or concern for another we might call love. It was Gilligan (1977) who first revealed this distortion of moral psychological theory.

Gilligan (1977, 1982), listening to women's discussions of their own real-life moral conflicts, recognized a conception of morality not represented in Kohlberg's work. To her, women's concerns centered on care and response to others. Noting too that women often felt caught between caring for themselves and caring for others, and characterized

Two Perspectives
NONA PLESSNER LYONS

their failures to care as failures to be "good" women, Gilligan suggested that conceptions of self and morality might be intricately linked. In sum, Gilligan hypothesized (1) that there are two distinct modes of moral judgment—justice and care—in the thinking of men and women; (2) that these are gender-related; and (3) that modes of moral judgment might be related to modes of self-definition.

The research described here includes the first systematic, empirical test of these hypotheses. This paper reports on the identification, exploration, and description from data of two views of the self and two ways of making moral choices. The translation of these ideas into a methodology made possible the testing of Gilligan's hypotheses.

The empirical data consist of responses of thirty-six individuals to questions asked in open-ended interviews designed to draw out an individual's conception of self and orientation to morality. The data were analyzed first for descriptions of self, then for considerations individuals presented from their own real-life moral conflicts, and finally for correlations between the two.

The first part of this article presents interview data on ways that individual males and females—children, adolescents, and adults—describe themselves. These data reveal two characteristic modes of describing the self-in-relation-to-others: a self separate or objective in its relations to others and a self connected or interdependent in its relations to others. Then, from individuals' discussions of their own real-life moral conflicts, two ways of considering moral issues are distinguished: a morality of rights and justice and a morality of response and care. These data are then used to develop two coding schemes, methodologies for systematically and reliably identifying peoples' modes of self-definition and bases of moral choice. Finally, results of the study designed to test Gilligan's hypotheses and a discussion of the implications of this work for psychological theory and practice are presented. Thus, this article moves between the discursive essay and the research report, to show the evolution of a conceptual framework based on peoples' real-life experiences, and the translation of that framework into a systematic methodology for analyzing data and testing hypotheses.

A social dimension emerges as central in this work: in each of the two images of people making moral choices, there is a distinct way of seeing and being in relation to others. Although Kohlberg has identified a developmental pattern of a morality of justice, he has not elaborated the connection between his conceptualization of moral development and an understanding of relationships. Because this present work assumes that an understanding of relationships is central to a conception of morality, it is not directly parallel to Kohlberg's, yet it does maintain an indebtedness to it.[2] Gilligan and her associates (Gilligan, 1977, 1982; Langdale & Gilligan, Note 1; Lyons, Notes 2, 3) have outlined, but only broadly, the developmental patterns of an orientation to care. What remains then is the task of examining the developmental patterns of a morality of justice and of care within a framework of relationships. This present work supports, modifies, and elaborates Gilligan's ideas and confirms Piaget's central insight that "apart from our relations to other people, there can be no moral necessity" (Piaget, 1932/1966, p. 196).

---

[2] Kohlberg's coding scheme focuses on analyzing moral judgments. It does not analyze the construction, resolution, and evaluation of moral choices, or considerations other than judgments in the resolution of conflict. In addition, it does not deal with real-life data, focusing instead on hypothetical moral dilemma data.

Data

When asked to talk about themselves, individuals differ in how they describe themselves in relation to others. Because these differences became central to the construction of the coding schemes for identifying modes of self-definition and moral choice, it is useful to look closely at the differences in the responses of adolescents, children, and adults. These data reveal two distinct conceptions of relationships, each characterized by a unique perspective toward others.

For two fourteen-year-olds taking part in an open-ended interview, the question was the same: "How would you describe yourself to yourself?" Jack begins:

> What I am? (pause) That's a hard one . . . Well, I ski—I think I'm a pretty good skier. And basketball, I think I'm a pretty good basketball player. I'm a good runner . . . and I think I'm pretty smart. My grades are good . . . I get along with a lot of people, and teachers. And . . . I'm not too fussy, I don't think—easy to satisfy, usually—depending on what it is.

Presenting ways by which he evaluates himself, Jack comments on how he measures up in terms of some ranking of abilities: good skier, basketball player, runner, pretty smart. Talking about his relations with others, Jack continues to focus on his abilities: "I get along with a lot of people and teachers."

Fourteen-year-old Beth's response begins as Jack's did with the activities that engage her; however, she then tells of the network of relations that connect her to others:

> I like to do a lot of things. I like to do activities and ski and stuff. I like people. I like little kids and babies. And I like older people, too, like grandparents and everything; they're real special and stuff. I don't know, I guess I'd say I like myself. I have a lot of stuff going on. I have a lot of friends in the neighborhood. And I laugh a lot.

The interviewer asks, "Why do you like yourself?" and Beth replies:

> I don't know. I think it's the surroundings around me that make my life pretty good. And I have a nice neighborhood and a lot of nice friends and older people. . . . We visit new people everywhere we go. And there's my grandmother, and every time I go to my grandmother's, she makes me see all her friends and stuff. And I think that helps me along the line, 'cause you get to know them, and it makes you more friendly.

The contrast between these two responses may not at first glance seem striking, but there is a difference between the images and ideas of each person's relationships to others. Jack connects himself to others through his abilities. Like his ranking of himself as a "pretty good skier" and a "good runner," Jack's way of relating to others is another measure of his abilities: "I get along with a lot of people and teachers." Jack's perspective toward others is in his own terms, through the self's "I." Beth's connection to others is through the people who make up her "surroundings"—nice friends, older people, little kids, and babies. Her connections *through* others are in turn *to* others: "My grandmother . . . she makes me see all her friends and stuff." Thus, Beth's perspective towards others is to see them in their own terms. She sees, for example, her grandmother with her own friends, in her own context. Further, Beth seems to see a circle of interdependence in these relationships: "And I think that helps me along the line, 'cause you get to know them, and it makes you more friendly." Although both young people discuss re-

Two Perspectives
NONA PLESSNER LYONS

lational topics that sound similar, they reflect different perspectives towards others: seeing others in their own terms, or through the self's perspective.

These different ways of seeing others also emerge in individuals' considerations when talking about moral conflict. When asked, "Have you ever been in a situation where you had to make a decision about what was right but you weren't sure what to do?" Jack relates an experience of being with a group of his peers who wanted to wax windows on Halloween. To an earlier question, "What makes something a moral problem?" Jack had replied, "Somewhere I have to decide . . . whether I should do this or not . . . whether it's right that I should do something or whether it's wrong." Now, talking about his conflicts about that Halloween, he echoes the earlier response: "I knew it wasn't right, but they, the kids, they would think, 'Oh, he's no fun, he doesn't want to do it, he's afraid he's going to get in trouble,' stuff like that." Urged by the interviewer to describe the consequences he considered when making his decision, Jack mentions "getting in trouble,""'my mother and father would have been upset by something like that—they wouldn't like it," and "if I didn't go, some of my friends would think . . . 'Well, he's no fun'." Jack also describes his major consideration in making a decision: "Well, you have to think about what would be right . . . and then . . . are you gonna stand up for what's right and wrong to your friends, or are you gonna let them—get you into going." Revealing that in the end he didn't go with his friends, he elaborates why: "I didn't think it was right . . . and if somebody wanted to wax my windows, I wouldn't like it, so I wasn't going to do that to someone else."

Through reciprocity Jack resolves this moral conflict. Asked if he had made the right decision, Jack replies, "Well . . . my parents would have been pleased that I had not gone. . . . If the kids had gotten into trouble, I would have known that I made the right decision, 'cause I wouldn't have wanted to have been in that group." When challenged, "What if no one knew about it?" Jack resorts again to his "principle" for choice: "I don't think you could think that was the right decision if you were to do that—to wax somebody's windows and go away thinking that was the right thing to do."

For Jack, the moral problem hinges on knowing what is right and acting on that in spite of pressures or taunts from his friends. Solving the problem, then, becomes a matter of thinking about what would be right and standing up to that. His reciprocity-based justification is derived from the self's perspective: "If somebody wanted to wax my windows, I wouldn't like it, so I wasn't going to do that to someone else." Like the measure of self-in-relation-to-others found in his self-description, Jack sees and resolves moral conflict through the self's perspective.

Beth's moral problem arises from a different set of concerns as well as a different perspective towards others. First she narrates the events surrounding her conflict: "I had a decision to give up my paper route. And I had a decision over two people, like two people wanted it. And I didn't know what was the right decision." Asked to describe the conflicts for her in that situation, she says: "Well, some friends of the person that I said could not have the route were going against me and saying that, you know, 'You did it' and 'What a stupid thing to do, to give it to the other person.' The person got kinda upset, and kinda turned against me."

Reconstructing how she thought through the problem, Beth illuminates her way of thinking in choice:

129

> [at first] I was trying to think mostly who I thought was going to do better at it. I don't know, it kinda got me all upset because I didn't want to hurt somebody, one person's feelings by telling them they couldn't have it. And going to the other person and saying you can. I think that's mostly what bothered me. . . . And then it bothered me more when I thought of what person was mostly gonna get it, I was thinking, well, are they really gonna do a good job? . . . I didn't want anybody doing it that was gonna be nasty to anybody. Because I have some older people that I do on the route, and they like to talk to you and everything. And I didn't want to give it to anybody that was gonna walk away. I wanted them to get along. . . . I didn't want anybody getting in fights or anything.

As she envisions the elderly people on her paper route, Beth's decision turns on her considerations of their needs. The moral problem at first hinges on seeing the possible fractures between people and trying to avert them. Caught between wanting someone good for the paper route job and not wanting to hurt the person she had to turn down, Beth's concerns for relationships and for the welfare of others conflict.

Asked, "How did you know that it was the right decision?" Beth tells us how things worked out: "The person that was bad for the job finally realized that the person [chosen] was going to be a good person to do it." She also describes how she evaluates the decision: "I told my friends about it and my parents, and they said, 'Yeah.' And I told my paper route people that there was gonna be a new person, and they said 'Yeah,' they liked that person. And so I thought, 'Well, I think I did a pretty good job, if everybody's happy'." Beth measures the rightness of her choice by how things worked out. Having told her friends, parents, and "my paper route people," and having their concurrence, she finds in the restoration of relationships the validation of her choice.

Although Jack and Beth both wrestle with issues raised by friendships, two different kinds of moral problems concern them. Through two different perspectives—the perspective of self or the perspective of others—different problems arise and different resolutions are sought. These distinctions are found in data from younger children and adults as well.

Two eight-year-olds are asked, "How would you describe yourself to yourself?" Jeffrey answers in the third person, saying that "he's got blond hair" and "has a hard time going to sleep." He also focuses on abilities: "He learns how to do things; when he thinks they're going to be hard, he learns how to do them." Describing his way of relating to others, Jeffrey says, "He bugs everybody and he fights everybody," concluding with, "That's it. I'm lazy."

To the interviewer's question, eight-year-old Karen replies in the first person, "I don't know. I do a lot of things. I like a lot of things." Adding, "I get mad not too easy," she comments that she has "made a lot of new friends" and concludes, "And, um, I don't know if everyone thinks this, but I think I tell the truth most of the time."

Echoing themes of Jack, the adolescent, Jeffrey presents a measure of himself by abilities: "He learns how to do things; when he thinks they're going to be hard, he learns how to do things." Karen's observation that she has "made a lot of new friends" echoes adolescent Beth's self-description of her connection to the people surrounding her. It is in contrast to Jeffrey's "he bugs everybody and he fights everybody."

Themes in the real-life conflicts which the children report repeat those of the adolescents. Jeffrey talks with the interviewer about a real-life conflict. "Like when I really

Two Perspectives
NONA PLESSNER LYONS

want to go to my friends and my mother's cleaning the cellar. I don't know what to do." Urged by the interviewer to say why this is a conflict, Jeffrey elaborates:

> 'Cause it's kinda hard to figure it out. Unless I can go get my friends and they can help me and my mother clean the cellar.
> *Why is it hard to figure it out?*
> 'Cause you haven't thought about it that much.
> *So what do you do in a situation like that?*
> Just figure it out, and do the right thing that I should do.
> *And how do you know what you should do?*
> 'Cause when you think about it a lot, then you know the right thing to do first.
> *How do you know it's the right thing?*
> 'Cause you've been thinking about it a lot.
> *Can you tell me how you think about it?*
> It's really simple if you think about it real quick. I think about my friends and then I think about my mother. And then I think about the right thing to do.

To the interviewer's question, "But how do you know it's the right thing to do?" Jeffrey concludes, "Because usually different things go before other things. Because your mother—even though she might ask you second—it's in your house."

For Jeffrey, having a rule—"different things go before other things"—allows him to resolve the dilemma of choice. Like Jack's use of the Golden Rule, Jeffrey finds a resolution to his conflict in the rule of "some things go first." For both Jack and Jeffrey it is through the self's perspective—the self's rule or standard—that moral conflict is cast and resolved.

Different issues concern eight-year-old Karen. She describes conflicts with friends: "I have a lot of friends and I can't always play with all of them, so I have to take turns. Like, they get mad sometimes when I can't play with them. And then that's how it all starts." Asked what kinds of things she considers when trying to decide with whom to play, Karen replies, "Um, someone all alone, loneliness. Um, even if they are not my friends, not my real friends, I play with them anyways because not too many people do that. . . . They never think of the right person."

Describing the "right person" as someone who is "quiet who . . . doesn't talk too much, who doesn't have any brothers or sisters," Karen, like Beth, tries to connect people to one another, "to make them feel more like at home." Asked to elaborate, Karen responds: "If a person's all alone . . . if that person never has anyone to talk to or anything . . . they are never going to have any friends. Like when they get older they are gonna have to talk. And if they never talk or anything, then nobody's going to know them. . . . If that person always stays alone, she's not going to have any fun."

For Karen, as for Beth, moral conflicts arise from having to maintain connections between people, not wanting people to be isolated, alone, or hurt. For both, resolutions are found by considering the needs of those involved. Like their adolescent counterparts, these two eight-year-olds reflect different perspectives towards others. They see and attend to different things.

These distinguishing characteristics and different ways of seeing others are manifest in adulthood. John, the thirty-six-year-old professional educator quoted at the beginning of this paper, reveals a "logic" consistent with that of Jack and Jeffrey. He describes the decision to fire a colleague as a personal moral conflict. Although believing that the firing breached a prior agreement, he describes his conflict as "lack of confidence in my own judgment . . . feeling like maybe the others were right." His co-workers had decided, after the deadline, to fire the staff member. Describing how he felt in trying to think about what to do, he says: "I felt I had a commitment to live with . . . [we] all had a commitment to honor. . . . But for me it was a serious matter of principles."

Later, reflecting on his decision to offer his resignation in protest, he comments on how he thought about the decision:

> Well, I guess I will never know for sure . . . but I am comfortable with it, in the sense that given the pressures, and given the fact I had to decide and I don't feel I perverted any principle I hold now in making that decision. For me it was a test, in a way it became a symbol, because all this had been weighing on me. In a way the principle was commitment to principle, and I had to decide whether I had it or not, and if I let it go by, then maybe I didn't have the right to ever challenge anybody else.

In childhood and adulthood, a line of thinking in moral choice is revealed in the conflicts expressed by Jack, Jeffrey, and John in which issues of morality hinge on "moments of choice" and "knowing how to decide," thus conjuring up Murdoch's image of the self in the "quick flash of the choosing will."

Answering the question, "How would you describe yourself to yourself?" John goes on to talk explicitly about his own perspective towards others. He acknowledges: "I happen to be a person who likes the world of ideas," who can "delight myself for hours on end reading and thinking, puzzling over things. . . . I am not the sort of person who has a natural outreaching towards other people. That for me is always sort of an effort . . . an effort that I need to be nudged to do." Suggesting the importance of relationships to him, he continues talking about their difficulties and rewards for him personally:

> I am nudged [towards others] in several ways—by other people . . . but also by my convictions that tell me that I have responsibilities to other people; and, once nudged though, the interesting thing is that it is always rewarding. And I am grateful because most of the personal growth I have gone through has been through these other people and not through thinking about the world of ideas and that sort of stuff. But somehow I always retreat into the corner and want to be off by myself. It is a paradox about me, one that I still haven't fully understood. . . . Gregarious people I think can't fully understand sometimes how hard it is for certain people to become involved with people because what they regard as either minor personal risks or non-risks altogether, can strike a person like me sometimes as insurmountable obstacles. So that is one aspect of myself that just happens to come to mind. This is interesting because I had never thought about this much.

John picks up the themes of relating to others from the self's perspective heard earlier in the responses of Jack and Jeffrey. So, too, an adult woman repeats themes found in the concerns of Karen and Beth.

Forty-six-year-old Sarah, a lawyer, who describes herself as "perceptive" and "responsive" to others, tells about a moral dilemma she faced. She discovered in the course of a contested custody case that her client's boyfriend was an illegal alien. Although withholding this information was not technically illegal, she sensed that the information could affect the judge's ruling. She asked herself if telling would really make a difference

Two Perspectives
NONA PLESSNER LYONS

in the long run and decided that it would not, that it would resolve itself one way or the other." She concludes, "nobody is getting particularly hurt by this." Talking about her dilemma in a larger context, she describes the conflict her role creates:

> I think that I run into a dilemma in doing domestic relations work in the sense that I am dealing with a legal system that is dealing with something that it doesn't know how to deal with very well and I get very distressed because it is hard for me to put together exactly what my role is supposed to be . . . you are presiding over some pretty emotional moments in people's lives, and I never know whether I should be sort of, here is the lawbook, and not do anything to try to do whatever kind of counseling, whatever kind of support one might provide for people without costing them a fortune. . . . On the other hand, I think people need something like this. I end up in a dilemma in dealing with custody decisions, which are very messy. And God knows, there is no right and no wrong. It is a question of how can you work out something that is going to be the least painful alternative for all the people involved. . . .

The ultimate principle for resolving moral conflict, for Sarah, seems to be to work out "the least painful alternative for all the people involved."

From these examples, we see that individuals describe different kinds of considerations in moral choice tied to different ways of being with, and seeing, others: to treat others as you would like to be treated or to work out something that is "the least painful alternative for all involved." To treat others as you would be treated demands distance and objectivity. It requires disengaging oneself from a situation to ensure that each person is treated equally. In contrast, to work out the least painful alternative for all those involved means to see the situation in its context, to work within an existential reality and ensure that all persons are understood in their own terms. These two ways of perceiving others and being in relation to them are thus central both to a way of describing the self and to thinking in moral choice.

Development of the Coding Schemes

When moving from data to the conceptual constructs on which a coding scheme is based, a circular interaction occurs: the data account for the constructs and are in turn explained by them. Indeed, as Loevinger (1979) argues, such circularity is necessary to validate the coding schemes and to build the theory of which they are a part. This interactive process is described below to illuminate how ideas about human relationships, identified first in the statements of individuals, were translated into systematic categories of a coding scheme, a methodology for analyzing data.

Many researchers (Broverman, Vogel, Broverman, Clarkson, & Rosenkrantz, 1972; Erikson, 1968; Freud, 1925/1961; Piaget, 1932/1966) have commented on the relational bias of women's conceptions of self and morality. But it was Gilligan (1977) who first suggested that this relational bias might represent a unique construction of social reality. The study discussed below, designed by Gilligan, hypothesized that men and women do think differently about themselves in relation to others. That there is such a difference was supported in an examination of data—such as the comments of those quoted above—and then elaborated conceptually on the basis of that data. In that process two different ideas and ways of experiencing human relationships were revealed that seemed tied to two characteristic ways of seeing others. This distinction was then conceptualized as two perspectives towards others. Table 1 presents schematically the two modes of being-in-relation-to-others, separate/objective and connected, and their respective perspective towards others, reciprocity or response.

Each of these two ideas of relationships with their characteristic perspective towards others implies a set of related ideas. The perspective of the separate/objective self—labeled "reciprocity"—is based on impartiality, objectivity, and the distancing of the self from others. It assumes an ideal relationship of equality. When this is impossible, given the various kinds of obligatory role relationships and the sometimes conflicting claims of individuals in relationships, the best recourse is to fairness as an approximation of equality. This requires the maintenance of distance between oneself and others to allow for the impartial mediation of relationships. To consider others in reciprocity implies considering their situations as if one were in them oneself. Thus, an assumption of this perspective is that others are the same as the self.

The perspective of the connected self—labeled "response"—is based on interdependence and concern for another's well-being. It assumes an ideal relationship of care and responsiveness to others. Relationships can best be maintained and sustained by consid-

TABLE 1
Relationships[a] of Reciprocity and Relationships of Response

The Separate/Objective Self

Relationships are experienced in terms of	mediated through	and grounded in
RECIPROCITY between separate individuals, that is, as a concern for others considering them as one would like to be considered, with objectivity and in fairness;	RULES that maintain fairness and reciprocity in relationships;	ROLES which come from duties of obligation and commitment.

The Connected Self

Relationships are experienced as	mediated through	and grounded in
RESPONSE to OTHERS in THEIR TERMS that is, as a concern for the good of others or for the alleviation of their burdens, hurt, or suffering (physical or psychological);	THE ACTIVITY OF CARE which maintains and sustains caring and connection in relationships;	INTERDEPENDENCE which comes from recognition of the interconnectedness of people.

[a]Relationships—the ways of being with or towards others that all individuals experience but that may be understood in either of two ways.

Two Perspectives
NONA PLESSNER LYONS

ering others in their specific contexts and not always invoking strict equality.³ To be responsive requires seeing others in their own terms, entering into the situations of others in order to know them as the others do, that is, to try to understand how they see their situations. Thus, an assumption of this perspective is that others are different from oneself.

In Table 2 the relationship between these conceptions of self and orientations to morality, as they emerged from the empirical data, are presented schematically. The data revealed that separate/objective individuals tend to use a morality of "justice," while connected individuals use a morality of "care."

The conceptions of morality and the perspectives towards others are constructs, and as such represent ideals containing strengths and weaknesses. Equality is an ideal and a strength of a morality of justice; the consideration of individuals' particular needs—in their own terms—is both an ideal and a strength of a morality of care. On the other hand, an impartial concern for others' rights may not be sufficient to provide for care, and caring for others may leave individuals uncaring of their own needs and rights to care for themselves. In addition, the response perspective may suggest an unqualified and overly emotional concern for meeting the needs of others.⁴ However, the present research suggests a greater complexity of meaning. Response to another is an interactive process in which a developing and changing individual views others as also changing across the life cycle.

Within most psychological models the ability to see another's perspective is considered a cognitive capacity which gradually becomes more objective and abstract (Kohlberg, 1969, 1981; Mead, 1934; Selman, 1980). In contrast, the perspective of response described here emphasizes the particular and the concrete. While it is assumed that this perspective changes over the course of development, the nature of these changes is not yet known. It may be that in "maturity" one generalizes the particular, that is, one always looks at the particular, and this *is* the general principle. This research suggests that our current unitary models of perspective-taking may need revision. Perspective-taking and a "perspective-towards-others" conceptualized here are separate phenomena.

It is important also that the use of the word "response" or "reciprocity" in subjects' re-

---

³ A fourteen-year-old girl suggested the subtlety of the process of considering others in their terms. Asked by the interviewer, in response to a comment she had made, "How do you think about what someone else's reaction is going to be?" she says: "Well, first I look at the person and I think about what they are like and how they have reacted in similar situations and how they react in general and, then, I put myself away from that person and say, 'This is how they would react probably in this situation.' " Asked, "What do you mean when you put yourself away from another person?" she replies, "Um—(pause) I guess maybe I don't put myself away from them, more the opposite. I put myself in that person and try to put together a way that they would feel about this and this and this with the ideas that I have." She continues her explanation, "I guess I put myself away from me for a minute, put myself in their—but I am not relating myself to the subject at all, I am not relating the way that I feel about it, what's important to me—to what I let them think, to what I think that they'll feel." This interview is from a study of adolescent girls currently being conducted with Carol Gilligan at the Emma Willard School (Troy, New York) through the support of the Geraldine R. Dodge Foundation and with the collaboration of Robert Parker, Principal, Trudy Hammer, Associate Principal, and the students and staff.

⁴ In considering the "emotional aspect of concern for another," it is useful to note Blum's work, *Friendship, Altruism and Morality* (1980). Blum argues for a second mode of morality concerned with the good of the other and challenges the dominant Kantian view to argue that altruistic concerns and emotions can be morally good. The work presented here assumes Blum's philosophical argument and demonstrates empirically the psychological phenomenon that individuals do act out of concern for the good of another.

TABLE 2
The Relationship of Conceptions of Self and of Morality to Considerations Made in Real-Life Moral Choice: An Overview

A Morality of Justice

Individuals defined as SEPARATE/OBJECTIVE In RELATION to OTHERS: see others as one would like to be seen by them, in objectivity; and	tend to use a morality of *Justice as Fairness* that rests on an understanding of RELATIONSHIPS as RECIPROCITY between separate individuals, grounded in the duty and obligation of their roles;	moral problems are generally construed as issues, especially decisions, of conflicting claims between self and others (including society); resolved by invoking impartial rules, principles, or standards,	considering: (1) one's role-related obligations, duty, or commitments; or (2) standards, rules, or principles for self, others, or society; including reciprocity, that is, fairness—how one should treat another considering how one would like to be treated if in their place;	and evaluated considering: (1) how decisions are thought about and justified; or (2) whether values, principles, or standards are (were) maintained, especially fairness.

A Morality of Response and Care

Individuals defined as CONNECTED In RELATION to OTHERS: see others in their own situations and contexts; and	tend to use a morality of *Care* that rests on an understanding of RELATIONSHIPS as RESPONSE to ANOTHER in their terms;	moral problems are generally construed as issues of relationships or of response, that is, how to respond to others in their particular terms; resolved through the activity of care;	considering: (1) maintaining relationships and response, that is, the connections of interdependent individuals to one another; or (2) promoting the welfare of others or preventing their harm; or relieving the burdens, hurt, or suffering (physical or psychological) of others;	and evaluated considering: (1) what happened/will happen, or how things worked out; or (2) whether relationships were/are maintained or restored.

sponses not be assumed to indicate automatically the possession of that particular perspective on morality or relationships. For example, an individual using a morality of justice and having a perspective of reciprocity might state, as did fourteen-year-old Jack, "I would not do that because I would not like someone to do that to me." However, an indi-

Two Perspectives
NONA PLESSNER LYONS

vidual using a morality of care and having a perspective of response might use the *word* "reciprocity" but with a different meaning. "I want to reciprocate because they will need that kind of help and I will be able to do that for them." In a perspective of response, the focus is always on the needs of others; it is the welfare or well-being of others in their terms that is important, not strictly what others might do in return or what the principle of fairness might demand or allow.[5]

What follows from these distinctions is that the language of morality must always be scrutinized for differences in underlying meaning. For example, words like "obligation" or "responsibility" cannot be taken at face value. (The moral imperatives of what one is "obliged" to do, "should" do, or what "responsibilities" one has are, in fact, shaped by one's perspective towards others.)

Research is needed to elaborate the conceptualizations presented here—of two perspectives on self, relationship, and morality—across the life cycle, especially attending to the issues of change and development. Research should also address potential interactions, that is, ways in which one orientation to morality may affect or be affected by the other.[6] In addition, individuals' understanding and awareness of their own perspectives of themselves-in-relation-to-others needs to be elaborated. The work presented here shows how the logic of each mode of morality and self-description has been elicited from interview data. The next section will describe how that logic was captured in a methodology, that is, in two coding schemes and used to test a set of hypotheses.

An Empirical Study Testing Gilligan's Hypotheses

In this empirical study,[7] male and female subjects were interviewed in order to ascertain their modes of self-definition and of moral choice, and to explore the connection between self-definition and modes of moral choice. A wider age-range was sampled to help elaborate modes of moral choice and of self-definition previously observed by Gilligan (1977) in a narrower age span of women. Both men and women were included to

---

[5] "Response" is an ancient word in English meaning "an answer, a reply; an action or feeling which answers to some stimulus or influence." "Responsibility"—usually associated with moral accountability and obligation and most frequently with contractual agreements related to a morality of justice—itself carried in its earliest meaning "answering to something." It was only in the nineteenth century that "responsibility" became attached to moral accountability and rational conduct. *(Shorter Oxford English Dictionary,* 3rd ed., s.v. "response," "responsibility.")

For a useful discussion of "responsibility" as a new symbol and image in ethics, see Niebuhr's *The Responsible Self* (1963). Niebuhr makes the interesting argument that "responsibility" as a new image of man—"man the answerer, man engaged in dialogue . . . acting in response to action upon him"—when used of the self as agent, as doer "is usually translated with the aid of older images [of man] as meaning directed toward goals or as ability to be moved by respect for the law." Further, Niebuhr says, "the understanding of ourselves as responsive beings who in all our actions answer to action upon us in accordance with our interpretation of such actions is a fruitful conception, which brings into view aspects of our self-defining conduct that are *obscured* when the older images are exclusively employed" (p. 57). Niebuhr's point is relevant to the argument here. The meaning of "responsibility" in its sense of "responsiveness" is, or may be, obscured by teleological or deontological conceptions of morality.

[6] This interaction is not to be confused with the fact that an individual with a major, or predominant, orientation may call upon considerations within either orientation when dealing with moral choice. But how a major orientation is influenced by the other, or minor, mode in its own sequence of development has not yet been elaborated and requires future work.

[7] The data for this study were originally collected by Carol Gilligan and Michael Murphy in 1978 to test Gilligan's hypotheses of the relations between sex and conceptions of self and between conceptions of self and of morality.

avoid the bias of a single-sex sample and to allow for the exploration of both justice and care orientations across the life-cycle. If—as Gilligan suggested—the absence of women subjects in past research obscured an understanding of the morality of care, the inclusion of men and women within this study may reveal its complexity for both sexes.

A secondary purpose of the study was to explore a suggestion of Kohlberg and Kramer (1969) that when women are engaged professionally outside the home and occupy equivalent educational and social positions as do men, they will reach higher stages of moral development than the typical adult women's stage (stage three—interpersonal mode) of his six stage system of moral judgment-making. Therefore, a sample of professional women was essential. It was also expected that such a sample would provide evidence concerning Gilligan's hypothesis that women consistently demonstrate a morality of care regardless of their profession.

Sample. The sample of thirty-six people consisted of two males and two females at each of the following ages: 8, 11, 14-15, 19, 22, 27, 36, 45, and 60-plus years. The sample was identified through personal contact and recommendation, and all subjects referred met the sampling criteria of high levels of intelligence, education, and social class.

Procedure. The data were collected in a five-part, open-ended interview which was conducted in a clinical manner, a method derived from Piaget (1929/1976). The interview proceeds from structured questions to a more unstructured exploration and clarification of each person's response. (See Appendix A for interview schedule.) Interview questions were developed to illuminate how the individual constructs his or her own reality and meaning, in this case, the experience of self and the domain of morality.

Data Analysis. The data were analyzed first for modes of self-definition, then for the subjects' orientations within considerations[a] of real-life moral conflicts. Finally, they were analyzed for correlations between the two (Lyons, 1982, Note 3).

Considerations of Justice or Care in Moral Conflicts

By examining the considerations individuals present in the construction, resolution, and evaluation of real-life moral dilemmas, the relative predominance of justice or care orientations to morality was determined. Considerations were categorized as either response (care) or rights (justice) (see Coding Scheme, Appendix B), and scored by counting the number of considerations each individual presented within either mode. In addition to identifying the presence of justice or care considerations, predominance of mode within this scoring system was determined by the higher frequency of one or the other mode in a subject's responses. Results were also expressed as percentages indicating the relationship of the dominant mode to all considerations the individual gave.

Intercoder reliability was established by two additional coders for both identification of considerations within real-life dilemmas (Step 1) and categorization of considerations as belonging to response or rights modes within the subjects' construction, resolution, and evaluation of their moral conflict (Step 2). Agreements for Step 1 were 75 and 76 percent, for Step 2, 84 and 78 percent.

Table 3 summarizes the predominance of response and rights considerations in real-life moral dilemmas for both males and females. The table shows that in real-life con-

---

[a] A consideration—the unit of analysis of the coding scheme—is an idea presented by the individual in the framing, resolution, or evaluation of choice.

Two Perspectives
NONA PLESSNER LYONS

TABLE 3
Predominance of Considerations of Response or Rights in Real-Life Dilemmas by Females and Males

Sex	Response Predominating %(N)	Rights Predominating %(N)	Equal Response/ Rights Considerations %(N)
Females (N = 16)	75 (12)	25 (4)	0 (0)
Males (N = 14)	14 (2)	79 (11)	7 (1)

Note: $x^2(2) = 11.63\ p < .001$

flicts, while women use considerations of response more frequently than rights and men use considerations of rights more frequently than response, in some instances the reverse is true.

Table 4 illustrates this pattern in another way, indicating that all the females in this sample presented considerations of response, but 37 percent (6) failed to mention any considerations of rights. Similarly, all the males presented considerations of rights, but 36 percent (6) failed to mention any considerations of response. These findings show that, in real-life moral conflict, individuals in this sample call upon and think about both care and justice considerations but use predominantly one mode which is related to but not defined or confined to an individual by virtue of gender.

TABLE 4
Absence of Considerations of Response or Rights: by Females and Males

Sex	No Considerations of Response %(N)	No Considerations of Rights %(N)
Females (N = 16)	0 (0)	37 (6)
Males (N = 14)	36 (6)	0 (0)

Although this study did not specifically consider developmental changes in moral thinking and self-definition, some results suggest possible developmental issues. It is clear that considerations of both response and rights are found across the life cycle. However, after age 27, women show increased consideration of rights in their conceptualization of moral problems or conflict, although they still use considerations of response more frequently than rights in the resolution of conflict. This may be related to a second finding: the disappearance of the response consideration of "care of the self" at the same age. These findings suggest the possibility of an interaction between the rights and response orientations for women in their late twenties. Another finding with implications for developmental change is the greater persistence of considerations of response among male adolescents. In general, however, across the life cycle men's considerations of rights maintain greater consistency than do women's considerations of response. Taken together, these findings suggest separate developmental shifts for men and women which deserve further study.

Keeping in mind that the sample is small (N = 36), the results reported here support the hypothesis that there are two different orientations to morality—an orientation towards rights and justice, and an orientation towards care and response to others in their own terms. Morality is not unitarily justice and rights, nor are these orientations mutually exclusive: individuals use both kinds of considerations in the construction, resolution, and evaluation of real-life moral conflicts, but usually one mode predominantly. This finding of gender-related differences, however, is not absolute since individual men and women use both types of considerations.

Modes of Self-Definition: Separate/Objective or Connected

This study also tested the hypothesis that individuals use two distinct modes of self-definition. Respondents were asked "How would you describe yourself to yourself?" and responses were analyzed to determine the predominance of one of two modes of self-definition—separate/objective or connected. In a manner similar to that used for the analysis of the moral conflicts data, these self-descriptive responses were categorized according to four components: general and factual; abilities and agency; psychological; and relational (see Coding Scheme, Appendix C). Each individual was scored by counting the number of separate/objective or connected relational characterizations, and then the predominant mode was determined.

Intercoder reliability for the self-description data was established using two independent coders in a two-step coding process which was more rigorous than most correlational reliability procedures. Every statement about self-definition was coded. In Step 1, in which each idea about the self was identified, intercoder reliability was 70 and 71 percent. In Step 2, in which each idea was categorized according to specific aspects within components, intercoder reliability was 74 and 82 percent.

A summary of male and female modes of self-definition is given in Table 5. As the table indicates, women more frequently use characterizations of a connected self, while men more frequently use characterizations of a separate/objective self. Although these different gender-related modalities occur systematically across the life-cycle, they are not absolute; some women and some men define themselves with elements of either mode. In addition, and perhaps most striking, is the finding that both men and women define themselves in relation to others with equal frequency, although their characterizations of these relationships are different.

TABLE 5
Modes of Self-definition: Females and Males

Sex	Predominately Connected	Predominately Separate/ Objective	Equally Connected and Separate	No Relational Component Used
	%(N)	%(N)	%(N)	%(N)
Females (N = 16)	63 (10)	12 (2)	6 (1)	19 (3)
Males (N = 14)	0 (0)	79 (11)	7 (1)	14 (2)

Note: $x^2(3) = 16.3$ p < .001

Two Perspectives
NONA PLESSNER LYONS

Relationship of Definitions of Self to Considerations in Real-Life Moral Choice
Some of the most important results of this study concern the testing of the hypothesis of the relationship between modes of moral choice and modes of self-definition. Table 6 presents these findings. In this sample, regardless of sex, individuals who characterized themselves predominantly in connected terms more frequently used considerations of response in constructing and resolving real-life moral conflicts; and individuals who characterized themselves predominantly in separate/objective terms more frequently used considerations of rights.

TABLE 6
Modes of Self-definition Related to Modes of Moral Choice

Predominant Modes of Moral Choice	Modes of Self-definition: Connected	Separate/ Objective	Other (S/C or none)[a]
Response N = 13 (1M, 12F)	10 (10F)	0	3 (1M, 2F)
Rights N = 16 (12M, 4F)	0	13 (11M, 2F)	3 (1M, 2F)

Note: $x^2(2) = 15.77$ $p < .005$. In order to calculate the x^2 statistic, 1 was added to each cell in order to eliminate 0 cells.
[a]S/C indicates individuals having an equal number of separate/objective and connected characterizations; none indicates an individual having no relational characterizations.

Although these results do not allow us to claim a causal relationship between modes of self-definition and modes of moral choice, we can say an important relationship exists. Further research is needed to see if these results hold over larger samples of a broader socio-economic status. Furthermore, research is needed to test the possibility that patterns of decision-making in areas other than moral choice may also be related to these modes of self-definition.

Implications

The development of the methodologies presented here—the coding schemes for identifying modes of self-definition and moral judgment—made possible the testing of a set of hypotheses important for theories of ego and moral development and for educational and clinical practice as well. Although all of the implications cannot be addressed fully, some of the most important ones are identified as an invitation to others to join in further clarification.

1. Psychological theories of moral development should recognize a morality of care as a systematic, lifelong concern of individuals. It should not be identified solely as a temporary, stage- or level-specific concern, or as subsumed within a morality of justice, as Kohlberg's work posits.

2. Psychological theories of ego and identity development need to consider a relational conception—the self-in-relation-to-others—as central to self-definition. This concern for connection to others should not be considered as present only at particular stages or as issues pertaining only to women. Although men and women tend to un-

derstand and define relationships in different ways, definition of self in relation to others is found *in both sexes* at all ages.
3. Theories of cognitive and social development should recognize that individuals construct, resolve, and evaluate problems in distinctively different ways. These differences are not simply in content, but seem to be related to two different perspectives towards others. Theories of cognitive and social development built on unitary models of social perspective-taking should be reconsidered.
4. Counselors, teachers, and managers, when dealing with conflicts within relationships, need to take into account that the language of morality in everyday speech has different meanings for people and that these may carry behavioral implications. For example, what people feel obliged to do or what their responsibilities to others are may be defined and understood differently.
5. Designs for psychological research need to reflect in their subjects of study the centrality of interpersonal interactions. This means research should focus not just on the individual but on both members of an interacting unit—husband and wife, friends, mother and child, teacher and student, manager and staff, and so forth.
6. Sex as a variable for study ought to be included in research designs and methodologies as a matter of course. This paper suggests both the difficulty in understanding sex differences and their importance to an improved understanding of theory and practice.

To accommodate the problems of modern moral philosophy, Murdoch (1970) has called for psychology and philosophy to join in creating a "new working philosophical psychology" (p. 46). This paper offers to psychologists and philosophers alike some new premises and methodologies by which to explore further the meaning of morality in our lives.

I wish to thank Carol Gilligan for her continuing support and encouragement, and Jane Attanucci, Miriam Clasby, Maxine Greene, Kay Johnston, Lawrence Kohlberg, Sharry Langdale, Jane Martin, Michael Murphy, Erin Phelps, Sharon Rich, Linda Stuart, Sheldon White, Bea Whiting, and Robert Lyons for their help and insights in the development of this work. I want to acknowledge, too, the support and personal encouragement of Marilyn Hoffman. The National Institute of Education funded the research reported here. The Geraldine R. Dodge Foundation is supporting a study of adolescent girls, part of which is also reported.

Reference Notes

1. Langdale, C., & Gilligan, C. *The contribution of women's thought to developmental theory (Interim Report to the National Institute of Education)*. Cambridge, Mass.: Harvard University, 1980.
2. Lyons, N. *Seeing the consequences*. Unpublished qualifying paper, Harvard University, 1980.
3. Lyons, N. *Manual for coding responses to the question: How would you describe yourself to yourself?* Unpublished manuscript, Harvard University, 1981.
4. Gilligan, C., Langdale, S., Lyons, N., & Murphy, J. M. *The contribution of women's thought to developmental theory (Final Report to the National Institute of Education)*. Cambridge, Mass.: Harvard University, 1982.

References

Blum, L. *Friendship, altruism and morality*. Boston: Routledge & Kegan Paul, 1980.
Broverman, I., Vogel, S., Broverman, D., Clarkson, F., & Rosenkrantz, P. Sex-role stereotypes: A current appraisal. *Journal of Social Issues*, 1972, 28, 58-78.
Erikson, E. *Identity: Youth and crisis*. New York: Norton, 1968.

Two Perspectives
NONA PLESSNER LYONS

Freud, S. [Some psychical consequences of the anatomical distinction between the sexes.] In J. Strachey (Ed. and trans.), *Standard Edition 19*. London: Hogarth Press, 1961. (Originally published, 1925.)

Gilligan, C. In a different voice: Women's conceptions of the self and of morality. *Harvard Educational Review*, 1977, 47, 481-517.

Gilligan, C. *In a different voice*. Cambridge, Mass.: Harvard University Press, 1982.

Kohlberg, L. Stage and sequence: The cognitive developmental approach to socialization. In D. Goslin (Ed.), *The handbook of socialization theory and research*. Chicago: Rand McNally, 1969.

Kohlberg, L. *The philosophy of moral development: Moral stages and the idea of justice*. San Francisco: Harper & Row, 1981.

Kohlberg, L., & Kramer, R. Continuities and discontinuities in childhood and adult moral development. *Human Development*, 1969, 12, 93-120.

Loevinger, J. *Scientific ways in the study of ego development*. Worcester, Mass.: Clark University Press, 1979.

Lyons, N. *Conceptions of self and morality and modes of moral choice*. Unpublished doctoral dissertation, Harvard University, 1982.

Mead, G. H. *Mind, self, and society*. Chicago: University of Chicago Press, 1934.

Murdoch, I. *The sovereignty of good*. Boston and London: Routledge & Kegan Paul, 1970.

Niebuhr, H. R. *The responsible self*. New York: Harper & Row, 1963.

Perry, W. *Forms of intellectual and ethical development in the college years*. New York: Holt, Rinehart & Winston, 1968.

Piaget, J. *The moral judgment of the child*. New York: Free Press, 1966. (Originally published, 1932.)

Piaget, J. *The child's conception of the world*. Totowa, N.J.: Littlefield, Adams, 1976. (Originally published, 1929.)

Selman, R. L. *The growth of interpersonal understanding: Developmental and clinical analyses*. New York: Academic Press, 1980.

Appendix A

Interview Schedule

1. A general introductory question: "Looking back over the past year/five years, what stands out for you?" (from Perry, 1968).

2. Hypothetical, moral dilemma questions: the classic Kohlberg justice dilemma, the "Heinz dilemma," and a "responsibility," or caring, dilemma developed from Gilligan's research.

3. Discussion of a real-life dilemma generated by questions about personal moral conflict and choice asked in several ways: "Have you ever been in a situation where you weren't sure what was the right thing to do?" or, "Have you ever had a moral conflict?" or, "Could you describe a moral conflict?" These were followed by a more consistent set of questions: "Could you describe the situation?" "What were the conflicts for you in that situation?" "What did you do?" "Did you think it was the right thing to do?" "How did you know it was the right thing to do?"

4. A set of self-description questions: "How would you describe yourself to yourself?" "Is the way you see yourself now different from the way you saw yourself in the past?" "What led to the change?"

5. General questions: "What does morality mean to you?" "What makes something a moral problem to you?" "What does responsibility mean to you?" "When responsibility to self and responsibility to others conflict, how should one choose?" (Gilligan, Langdale, Lyons, & Murphy, Note 4).

Appendix B

Morality as Care and Morality as Justice: A Scheme for Coding Considerations of Response and Considerations of Rights

I. The Construction of the Problem
  A. Considerations of Response (Care)
    1. General effects to others (unelaborated)
    2. Maintenance or restoration of relationships; or response to another considering interdependence
    3. Welfare/well-being of another or the avoidance of conflict; or, the alleviation of another's burden/hurt/suffering (physical or psychological)
    4. Considers the "situation vs./over the principle"
    5. Considers care of self; care of self vs. care of others

  B. Considerations of Rights (Justice)
    1. General effects to the self (unelaborated including "trouble" "how decide")
    2. Obligations, duty or commitments
    3. Standards, rules or principles for self or society; or, considers fairness, that is, how one would like to be treated if in other's place
    4. Considers the "principle vs./over the situation"
    5. Considers that others have their own contexts

II. The Resolution of the Problem/Conflict
  [same as part I]

III. The Evaluation of the Resolution
  A. Considerations of Response (Care)
    1. What happened/how worked out
    2. Whether relationships maintained/restored

  B. Considerations of Rights (Justice)
    1. How decided/thought about/justified
    2. Whether values/standards/principles maintained

© 1981 by Nona Lyons

Two Perspectives
NONA PLESSNER LYONS

Appendix C

A Scheme for Coding Responses to the "Describe Yourself" Question

I. *General and Factual*
   A. General factual
   B. Physical characteristics
   C. Identifying activities
   D. Identifying possessions
   E. Social status

II. *Abilities and Agency*
   A. General ability
   B. Agency
   C. Physical abilities
   D. Intellectual abilities

III. *Psychological*
   A. Interests (likes/dislikes)
   B. Traits/dispositions
   C. Beliefs, values
   D. Preoccupations

IV. *Relational Component*
   A. Connected in relation to others:
      1. Have relationships: (relationships are there)
      2. Abilities in relationships: (make, sustain; to care, to do things for others)
      3. Traits/dispositions in relationships: (help others)
      4. Concern: for the good of another in *their* terms
      5. Preoccupations: with doing good for another; with *how* to do good

   B. Separate/objective in relation to others
      1. Have relationships: (relationships part of obligations/commitments; instrumental)
      2. Abilities in relationships: (skill in interacting with others)
      3. Traits/dispositions in relationships: (act in reciprocity; live up to duty/obligations; commitment; fairness)
      4. Concern: for others in light of principles, values, beliefs or general good of society)
      5. Preoccupations: with doing good for society; with *whether* to do good for others)

V. *Summary Statements*

VI. *Self-evaluating Commentary*
   A. In self's terms
   B. In self in relation to others
      1. Connected self
      2. Separate self

© 1981 by Nona Lyons

[24]
The Role of Caring in a Theory of Nursing Ethics

SARA T. FRY

The development of nursing ethics as a field of inquiry has largely relied on theories of medical ethics that use autonomy, beneficence, and/or justice as foundational ethical principles. Such theories espouse a masculine approach to moral decision-making and ethical analysis. This paper challenges the presumption of medical ethics and its associated system of moral justification as an appropriate model for nursing ethics. It argues that the value foundations of nursing ethics are located within the existential phenomenon of human caring within the nurse/patient relationship instead of in models of patient good or rights-based notions of autonomy as articulated in prominent theories of medical ethics. Models of caring are analyzed and a moral-point-of-view (MPV) theory with caring as a fundamental value is proposed for the development of a theory of nursing ethics. This type of theory is supportive to feminist medical ethics because it focuses on the subscription to, and not merely the acceptance of, a particular view of morality.

INTRODUCTION

During the past ten years, a number of books on ethics in nursing practice have appeared (Benjamin and Curtis 1986; Davis and Aroskar 1983; Jameton 1984; Muyskens 1982; Thompson and Thompson 1985; Veatch and Fry 1987). Unlike earlier writings that viewed ethics in nursing as primarily feminine etiquette (Aikens 1916; Gladwin 1937; Robb 1900), these books view nursing ethics as a subset of contemporary medical ethics. Accordingly, they apply medical ethics to the practice of nursing using frameworks from bioethical theory (Beauchamp and Childress 1983), theologically-based contract theory (Veatch 1981), pluralistic secular-based theory of human rights (Engelhardt 1986), and a well-known, liberal theory of justice (Rawls 1971).

This influence on the development of nursing ethics has been quite extensive. Current nursing ethics discussions tend to revolve around deontological versus utilitarian theories, the weight of medical ethical principles and rules in nurses' decision-making, and the relative importance of nursing's contract with society and individual patients. Empirical studies in nursing ethics have almost exclusively used justice-based theories of moral reasoning from cognitive psychology to interpret their findings on nurses' moral behavior, moral judgment, and moral reasoning (Crisham 1981; Ketefian 1981a, 1981b, 1985; Munhall 1980; Murphy 1976). In addition, medical ethical frameworks guide the majority of normative discussions of ethics in nursing (Cooper 1988; Silva 1984; Stenberg 1978). The result is a trend in nursing ethics that does not take into consideration the role of nurses in health care, the social significance of nursing in contemporary society, or the value standards for nursing practice. By focusing on the terms of justification, gender-biased considerations of justice, and the language of principles and rules, nursing ethics has seemingly adopted the "language of the father," to use Noddings's apt terminology (1984, 1).

This paper challenges the presumption of medical ethics, especially a "masculine" medical ethics, as an appropriate model for nursing ethics. By a "masculine" medical ethics, I mean ethical theorizing and associated argumentation that proceeds as if it were governed by an implicit, logical necessity between hierarchically arranged levels of ethical principles, rules, and actions. Often called "the engineering model" of medical ethics (Caplan 1982, 1983), this type of theorizing has been criticized by bioethicists for a number of years (Ackerman 1980, 1983; Basson 1983; Toulmin 1981). Medical ethics based on this type of theorizing often relies on a lexical ordering of principles (Toulmin 1981) or the context of justification for ethical decision-making rather than the context within which such decision-making takes place (Noddings 1984) or the kinds of reasons that are regarded appropriate to the making of moral judgments (Frankena, 1983).

Drawing on the results of empirical studies on physician and nurse decision-making as well as philosophical discussions of nursing ethics, I show that the theoretical and methodologic foundations of nursing ethics have been largely derived from "masculine" forms of medical ethics. I argue that caring ought to be the foundational value for any theory of nursing ethics. In addition, caring must be grounded within a moral-point-of-view of persons rather than any idealized conception of moral action, moral behavior, or system of moral justification.

If successful, my argument might be significant in two respects. First, it just might be supportive to a feminist medical ethic. While we might agree that medical ethics, in general, ought to be cpale ofbeing practiced by both males and females, surely feminist medical ethics necessarily must be capable of being practiced by females. Since the nursing profession, the largest group of health care providers in the United States, has already articulated caring as an important value (Fry 1988; Gadow 1985; Watson 1985) and nursing is usually practiced by females, this means that caring and the type of functions that are usually associated with the practice of nursing are related to one another—at least in the minds of a significant portion of individuals in the health care arena. Hence, the connections between the value of caring and feminism cannot be easily denied. Since the phenomenon of human caring need not be gnder related, any claim to feminist medical ethics must demonstrate that it has broader applications than either just to medical practice or just to females. After all, patients are cared for by individuals other than physicians, and those who do this caring are not always females. A nursing ethic with caring as a foundational value might be an important asset to the perceived need to articulate a feminist medical ethic.

Second, since articulation of the phenomenon of human caring has already challenged justice based theories of moral development and moral judgment (Gilligan 1982, 1987) and theories of ethics and moral education (Noddings 1984), a theory of nursing ethics with a moral-point-of-view of caring as a central value might also challenge any theory of medical ethics that utilizes traditional ethical principles or that depends on the context of justification for determining what is morally right and/or wrong in medical practice. Given the present dissatisfaction with traditional foundations of biomedical ethics, moral-point-of-view theories as well as a caring-based ethic might prove very attractive as the discipline of bioethics moves into the 21st century and faces new tests for its moral foundations and traditional arguments.

TRADITIONAL VALUE FOUNDATIONS OF NURSING ETHICS

Several interesting approaches have been used to identify the moral foundations of nursing and the central value(s) of the nursing ethic. For example, empirical studies of the clinical decision-making of nurses have pinpointed autonomy as a fundamental value affecting moral dimensions of nursing practice (Alexander, Weisman, and Chase 1982; Prescott, Dennis, and Jacox 1987). The results of one other study have suggested that subjective values, such as producing the greatest good for the greatest number, are foundational to nurses' ethical decision-making (Self 1987). Unfortunately, the results of these studies were interpreted in terms of these values as predetermined ideologies for nursing practice. In other words, autonomy and producing good were categories that the researchers expected to find because autonomy and producing good are prominent features of medical ethics. What was assumed to be the case in medical ethics was assumed to be the case in nursing ethics, as well.

This should not surprise us. Both of these values—autonomy and producing good—are prominent features of theories of medical ethics. Engelhardt (1986), for example, posits autonomy as the foundational value of secular bioethics while Pellegrino and Thomasma (1981, 1988) urge the restoration of beneficence as the fundamental principle of medical ethics. As used in these theories, autonomy and roducing good constitute idealized value components of a social ethic for the practice of medicine and function within a structured framework of ethical principles and rules for physician decision-making. Both theories rely on traditional interpretations of their central principles and utilize traditional patterns of moral justification as articulated by leading bioethicists. The same views of autonomy and beneficence have even been claimed by some nurses as the moral basis for needed socialreform on the institutional setting in which nursing is practiced (Yarling and McElmurry 1986). However, there is no good reason to assume that autonomy and producing good are, *de facto*, the appropriate value foundations for the practice of nursing simply because they are accepted for the practice of medicine. While no one would dispute that autonomy and producing good are related to the practice of nursing, neither of these values, derived from theories of medical ethics, have been convincingly argued to be the primary moral foundation(s) of the nursing ethic.

Other approaches to identifying the moral foundations of nursing or the fundamental value of the nursing ethic have been both analytical and normative. For example, Stenberg (1979) analyzes value concepts of several theoretical frameworks in medical ethics for their relevance to the practice of nursing. She analyzes the concepts of code, contract, and context as discussed in the works of May (1975) and Fletcher (1966) and finds them inadequate bases for the nursing ethic. However, the concept of covenant as discussed in the medical ethical works of Ramsey (1970) and May (1975) is adequate as an "inclusive and satisfying model for nursing ethics" (Stenberg 1979, 21). Viewing covenant as the foundational value for such health worker actions as fidelity, promise-keeping, and truth-telling in patient care, Stenberg adopts it without alteration. Because covenant is a moral foundation for the physician/patient relationship, Stenberg considers it valid for the nurse/patient relationship, as well. This tendency to adopt medical ethical frameworks as valid moral foundations for the practice of nursing is repeated in more recent analyses of the moral foundations of the nursing ethic (Bishop and Scudder 1987; Cooper 1988).

Again, what is appropriate to the practice of medicine or is argued as a moral foundation for the physician/patient relationship is not necessarily the case for the practice of nursing or the nurse/patient relationship.

THE MORAL VALUE OF CARING AS A FOUNDATION FOR NURSING ETHICS

Foregoing recourse to medical ethics, a few nurses have attempted to articulate other foundational values for the moral practice of nursing. Sally Gadow (1985), for example, argues that the value of caring provides a foundation for a nursing ethic that will protect and enhance the human dignity of patients receiving health care. Viewing caring in the nurse/patient relationship as a commitment to certain ends for the patient, Gadow analyzes existential caring as demonstrated in the nursing actions of truth-telling and touch. Through truth-telling, the nurse assists the patient to assess the subjective as well as objective realities in illness and to make choices based on the unique meaning of the illness experience. Through touch, the nurse assists the patient in overcoming the objectness that often characterizes a patient's experience in the health care setting. To touch the patient is to affirm the patient as a person rather than an object and to communicate the value of caring as the basis for nursing actions. This approach identifies a moral foundation for nursing ethics based on the reality of the nurse/patient encounter in health care. It has also been supported by others who wish to articulate caring as a foundation of the nurse/patient relationship and its meaning (Griffin 1983; Huggins and Scalzi 1988; Packard and Ferrara 1988).

Building on the ideas of Gadow, Jean Watson (1985) proposes a slightly different view of caring as the foundation of "nursing as a human science" (13). Viewing nursing as a means to the preservation of humanity within society, Watson posits caring as a human value that involves "a will and a commitment to care, knowledge, caring actions, and consequences" (1985, 29). Such a view of caring requires a commitment toward protecting human dignity and preserving humanity on the part of the nurse. Caring becomes a professional ideal when the notion of caring transcends the act of caring between nurse and patient to influence collective acts of the nursing profession with important implications for human civilization. Like Gadow, Watson views caring as a moral ideal that is rooted in our notions of human dignity. However, unlike Gadow, Watson's human caring constitutes a philosophy of action with many unexplained metaphysical and spiritual dimensions. As such, her view of caring supports her abstract philosophy of nursing but does *not* adequately support caring as a moral value that ought to be a foundation for the nursing ethic. The value of caring remains an ideal rather than an operationalized aspect of nursing judgments and/or actions.

Like Gadow (1985) and Watson (1985), Griffin (1983) posits caring as a central value in the nurse/patient relationship. She considers caring to be, first, a mode of being. A natural state of human existence, it is one way that individuals relate to the world and to other human beings. This is not unlike Heidegger's (1962) notion of care as a fundamental way that humans exist in the world and Noddings' (1984) view of caring as a natural sentiment of being human. As a mode of being, caring is natural—a feeling or an internal sense made universal in the whole species; it is neither moral nor non-moral.

Second, caring is considered a precondition for the care of specific entities—other things, others, or oneself (Griffin 1983). This means that a conceptual *idea* about caring exists as a structural feature of human growth and development prior to the point at which the process of caring actually commences.

Third, caring is identified with social and moral ideals. For example, Watson views caring as occurring in society in order to serve human needs such as protection from the elements or the need for love. Gadow views caring as a means to protect the human dignity of patients while their health care needs are met. Thus, caring, a phenomenon of human existence, gains moral significance because it is consistently reinforced as an ideal by those who have responsibility to serve the needs of others (Griffin 1983). Since the practice of nursing is socially mandated to assist the health needs of individuals (American Nurses' Association 1980) and the nurse/patient relationship has undeniably moral dimensions, caring becomes strongly linked to the social and moral ideals of nursing as a profession.

THREE MODELS OF CARING RELEVANT TO NURSING ETHICS

Given these attributes of caring as defined by accounts of the nurse/patient relationship, at least three models are relevant for a theory of nursing ethics which posits caring as a foundational value.

NODDINGS'S MODEL OF CARING

The first model is found in the work of Nel Noddings (1984) and is theoretically based on ethics and social psychology. Building on the work of Carol Gilligan (1977, 1979, 1982), Noddings has combined knowledge of ethics with perspectives on moral development in women. She states her purpose to be "feminine in the deep classical sense, rooted in receptivity, relatedness, and responsiveness" (Noddings 1984, 2), yet she is careful to develop her notion of caring to be applicable to both females and males.

Caring is a feminine value in that the attitude of caring expresses our earliest memories of being cared for—one's store of memories of both caring and being cared for is associated with the mother figure. However, caring is also masculine in that it involves behaviors that have moral content and that can be adopted and embraced by men, even though it is not in their natural tendencies to adopt such notions. In defining care, Noddings states, ". . . to care may mean to be charged with the protection, welfare, or maintenance of something or someone" (1984, 9). Rather than an attitude that begins with moral reasoning, it represents the attitude of being moral or the "longing for goodness" (Noddings 1984, 2). Rather than an outcome of behavior, Noddings's view of caring is ethics itself. As such, it is not necessarily gender-dependent but is gender-relevant.

Central to this view of caring are the notions of receptivity, relatedness, and responsiveness: the acceptance or confirmation by the one-caring of one who is the cared-for (receptivity), the relation of the one-caring to one who is cared-for as a fact of human existence (relatedness), and commitment from one-caring to one who is cared-for (responsiveness). Ethical caring is simply the relation in which we meet another morally. Motivated by the ideal of caring in which we are a partner in human relationships, we are guided not by ethical principles but by the strength of the ideal of caring itself, claims Noddings. Thus, instead of the notions inherent in conditions for traditional moral justification (Beauchamp 1982), Noddings's ethic of caring depends on "the maintenance of conditions that will permit caring to flourish" (1984, 5). It is a person-to-person encounter that ultimately results in joy as a basic human affect within relationships bound by ethical caring.

Scholarship on the caring phenomenon, in general, has been strongly influenced by Noddings's model of caring. Her view has stressed the ethics and morality of caring from a perspective that is definitely gender-related although Noddings herself would undoubtedly deny that she is advocating a "feminist model." Yet, the model's relevance to the practice of nursing remains largely unexplored. For those who recognize the limitations of the bioethical model of ethical decision-making, however, Noddings's model is a rich ground for the future discussion of nursing ethics. It may also prove to be an acceptable model for the descriptive study of ethical decision-making in nursing practice. While its focus on the ethic of caring as feminine might not be attractive to nurses who are not also female, its foundations in the notions of receptivity, relatedness, and responsiveness between the one-caring and the one who is cared-for make it a viable framework for the realistic nature of the nurse/patient relationship.

PELLEGRINO'S MORAL OBLIGATION MODEL OF CARING

Edmund Pellegrino, a humanist and physician, has written extensively on caring as a derivative value of the physician's obligation to do good (1985; Pellegrino and Thomasma 1988). When discussing the role of the physician to the patient, Pellegrino notes that there are at least four senses in which the word "care" is understood by the practice of medicine (1985). The first sense is "care as compassion" or being concerned for another person. This is a feling, a sharing of someone's experience of illness and pain, or just being touched by the plight of another person. To care in this sense, according to Pellegrino, is "to see the person who is ill" as more than the object of our ministrations (1985, 11). He or she is "a fellow human whose experiences we cannot penetrate fully but which we can be touched by simply because we share the same humanity" (Pellegrino 1985, 11).

The second sense of caring is "doing for others" what they cannot do for themselves (1985). This entails assisting others with the activities of daily living that are compromised by illness (for example, feeding, bathing, clothing, and meeting personal needs). Pellegrino recognizes that physicians do little of this type of caring but that nurses and nurses' assistants do a great deal.

The third sense of caring discussed by Pellegrino is caring for the medical problem experienced by the patient (1985). It includes: (1) inviting the patient to transfer responsibility and anxiety about what is wrong to the physician, (2) assuring that knowledge and skill will be directed to the patient's problem, and (3) recognizing that the patient's anxiety needs a specialized type of caring that is presumed available from a physician.

Pellegrino's fourth sense of caring is to "take care" (1985, 12). This means to carry out all the neessary procedures (personal and technical) in patient care with conscientious attention to detail and with perfection. He finds this a corollary of the third sense of care but argues that it is differentiated from the third sense by its emphasis on the craftmanship of medicine. Together, the third and fourth senses of caring comprise what most physicians understand as *competence*.

Pellegrino does not find these four senses of caring separable in clinical practice. Care that satisfies the four senses that he has defined is called "integral care" (1985). This type of care is, for Pellegrino, a moral obligation of health professionals. It is not an option that can be exercised or interpreted "in terms of some idiosyncratic definition of professional responsibility" (1985, 13). The moral obligation to care in this manner is created by the special human relationship that brings together the one who is ill and the one who offers to help (1985).

In assessing whether the caring model is foundational for medical practice, Pellegrino reexamines the roles of physicians to their patients and concludes that "to care for the patient in the full and integral sense, requires a reconstruction of medical ethics" (1985, 17). What is needed, he claims, is an ethic that attends to the concept of care in its broadest sense and that makes caring a strong moral obligation between patient and professional. Instead of a relationship of curing between physician and patient, a relation of caring is needed to express the nature of the obligation between physician and patient.

Underlying Pellegrino's notion of care is the good of the individual, a complex notion that has at least three components. For Pellegrino, "a morally good clinical decision should attend to all three senses of patient good and satisfactorily resolve conflicts among them" (1985, 20).

The first sense of good is "biomedical good"—the good a medical intervention can offer by modifying the natural history of disease in a patient. It takes into consideration the craftsmanship of physicians (and presumably, nurses), of science, and the medical indication for treatment (1985, 21).

The second sense of good is the patient's concept of his or her own good. It takes into consideration what patients consider worthwhile, or in their best interests, and can be designated to surrogate decision-makers (1985, 21).

The third sense of patient good is "the good most proper to being human" (1985, 22). For Pellegrino, this is the capacity to make choices, to set up a life plan, and to determine one's goals for a satisfactory life. It is whatever fulfills our potentialities as individuals of a rational nature, respects patient dignity, and expresses human freedom.

In comparing these three senses of patient good to one another and to our ideas of social good, Pellegrino argues that patient good is prior to any other notion of good within the practice of medicine. Within a human obligation model of caring, patient good ultimately guides a physician's decision-making where a patient's health and illness are concerned. Hence, while the senses of caring engender desirable physician behaviors with the patient, the physician's decision-making is primarily guided by the notions of patient good. In the final analysis, Pellegrino's "integral caring" is reduced to a derivative value of patient good. It succumbs to typical medical ethical frameworks by utilizing a more general (and traditional) value as the foundational value for a theory of medical ethics. Rather than a theory of caring, Pellegrino actually proposes a theory of patient good that simply uses caring to operationalize patient good.

While Pellegrino's ideas about caring, in general, fit in with the practical sense of nursing practice, caring's subordinate role within his theory of medical ethics makes it problematic for nursing ethics. For nursing, caring seems to be more than a mere behavior between nurse and patient and might not always be derived from a notion of patient good. For example, even when the good of the patient is undecided or unknown, the nurse carries out interventions designed to care for the patient (as in emergency situations). Conversely, even when the patient's good has been made evident, nursing interventions may be carried out that do not, in fact, contribute to this sense of patient good (for example, when the physician's interpretation of the patient's good is not accepted by those planning and administering nursing care for the patient). The value of caring, for the nurse, extends beyond the notion of patient good as conceived by Pellegrino because nurse caring relates to the patient's status as a human being (Gadow 1985; Griffin 1983). For this reason, Pellegrino's moral obligation model of caring is not truly appropriate to the practice of nursing.

FRANKENA'S MORAL-POINT-OF-VIEW THEORY ON CARING

The third and final model of caring relevant to the development of nursing ethics is the moral-point-of-view (MPV) version. It is largely discussed by William Frankena in his critique of other MPV theories (1983) and entails adopting a certain point of view by defining its moral principle or central moral value. The result is a type of ethical theory (MPVT) for which Frankena seems to be a major spokesman.

In essence, one takes a moral-point-of-view by (1) subscribing to a particular substantive moral principle (or value) and (2) taking a general approach, perspective, stance or vantage point from which to proceed. While most MPV theories contain views about moral judgments and principles, about the differences between them and nonmoral principles, and views about the general nature of their justification, taking the MPV, by itself, simply means to adopt a moral principle (or value) and one's methodology to argue for that principle. It entails endorsing a general outlook or method by someone seeking to reach conclusions in a particular field (Frankena 1983).

According to Frankena, various moral principles have served as the central principles (or values) of MPV theories. Mill, for example, accepts a principle of utility that is pivotal to his MPV theory—that of utilitarianism (1863). Mill starts with a particular outlook (his moral point of view) and adopts the principle of utility as *the* moral principle that indicates the kinds of facts that one would make moral judgments about. Frankena, however, argues for taking the MPV more fully than simply accepting a certain view of morality. For him, taking the MPV entails not only acceptance of a particular view of morality but entering the moral arena oneself, "using moral considerations of the kind defined as a basis for evaluative judgments" (Frankena 1983, 70). It means subscribing to a particular view of morality and living that morality in one's life rather than merely accepting a certain view of morality and the conditions for the separation of the moral from the nonmoral.

This is a significant move for Frankena as it establishes the crucial difference between his conception of taking the MPV and the approaches of others who espouse MPVs and their related theories. Like Hume (1751) who espouses sympathy as his "sentiment of humanity," Frankena believes that there is always something that "moves us to approve or disapprove of persons" (1983, 70). This something is an attitude or precondition that is ultimately the source or motivating factor of anyone who takes the MPV. In other words, the setting forth of any particular fact is not so much the reason for deciding what is good and right in taking the MPV as is what generates the setting forth of that particular fact (and not some other fact).

For Frankena, this attitude or precondition concerns the fundamental status of persons and their human dignity. While he never explicitly defines what this attitude or precondition is for his own MPV, he eventually claims that this attitude generates the MPV of Caring or, as he puts it, "a Non-Indifference about what happens to persons and conscious sentient beings *as such*" (1983, 71). Frankena's substantive moral value is the value of caring and takes the form of Kantian respect-for-persons or Christian love. It includes making normative judgments and a concern for being rational in one's judgments but does *not* entail the acceptance or use of any particular test of justifiability, validity, or truth. A judgment based on caring is assumed to be morally justifiable because it "would be agreed to by all who genuinely take the MPV and are clear, logical, and fully knowledgeable about relevant kinds of facts (empirical, metaphysical, or whatever)" (1983, 72).

Frankena's view on caring is quite different from the view of Pellegrino. Where Pellegrino's notion of patient good provides the basis for the physician's evaluative judgments, Frankena posits caring as the basis of human normative judgments, in general. His focus on caring is direct and involves taking the MPV toward caring as a fundamental moral value or principle for normative judgments involving persons rather than the indirect focus on caring (through patient good) that is characteristic of Pellegrino's medical ethics. Like Noddings, Frankena eschews the structures of moral justification that typify traditional medical ethical theorizing and the separation of the conditions for justification from the context of ethical decision-making with persons. Where much of moral philosophy takes the MPV by simply acting on principle or out of duty, Frankena's MPV requires a human response from the one taking the MPV in the form of respect-for-persons or Christian love. It requires an identifiable form of response from the one-caring to the one cared-for, to use Noddings's terminology.

Unfortunately, Frankena makes no attempt to define exactly what he interprets as respect-for-persons and certainly does not discuss his principle of caring in terms relevant to feminist philosophy. However, he does indicate that adopting the MPV of caring is made from an undefined preconditional attitude toward personhood and human dignity. This is not unlike Noddings's notions of receptivity, relatedness, and responsiveness which anchor her view of ethical caring. While it would not be appropriate to interpret Frankena's view of caring as identical or even similar to Noddings's view, certainly his method of arriving at caring as a lived principle for a system of morality (taking the MPV) bears some relevance to Noddings's views and a feminist approach to medical ethics.

CONCLUSIONS

Given the models of caring proposed by Noddings (1984), Pellegrino (1985), and Frankena (1983), and the views on caring that have been developed by nurses (Gadow 1985; Griffin 1983; Watson 1988), several recommendations for the future development of a theory of nursing ethics and any system of feminist medical ethics seem relevant.

First, theories of medical ethics as currently proposed do not seem appropriate to the development of a theory of nursing ethics. The context of nursing practice requires a moral view of persons rather than a theory of moral action or moral behavior or a system of moral justification. Present theories of medical ethics have a tendency to support theoretical and methodological views of ethical argumentation and moral justification that do not fit the practical sense of nurses' decision-making in patient care and, as a result, tend to deplete the moral agency of nursing practice rather than enhance it. Any theory of nursing ethics will need to consider the nature of the nurse/patient relationship within health care contexts and adopt a moral-point-of-view that focuses directly on this relationship rather than on theoretical interpretations of physician decision-making and their associated claims to moral justification for this decision-making. The same might be said for any theory of feminist medical ethics, depending on how the nature of the relationship between the one-caring and the one who is cared-for is perceived.

Second, the value of caring ought to be central to any theory of nursing ethics and any theory of feminist medical ethics, as well. Given the need for nursing care within our society, nursing's perceived social mandate to provide the "diagnosis and treatment of human responses to actual or potential health problems" (American Nurses' Association 1980, 9), and the nature of the nurse/patient relationship, nursing has a significant opportunity to influence the quality of patient care through the acceptance and use of its theories. The profession of nursing has already made substantial commitment to the role of caring in several conceptions of nursing ethics and nursing science. In addition, there appears to be an important link between the value of caring and nursing's views toward persons and human dignity. As proposed by Frankena, there is good reason to subscribe to a MPV that is rooted in an attitude of respect toward persons. If a theory of nursing ethics is to have any purpose, it must necessarily make evident a view of morality that not only truly represents the social role of nursing, as a profession, in the provision of health care but that also promises a moral role for nursing in the care and nurture of individuals who have health care needs. For theory to achieve this purpose, its view of morality ought to turn on a philosophical view that posits caring as a foundational value rather than a derivitive value. The same might also be said for any theory of feminist medical ethics that uses caring as a gender-relevant (but not gender-dependent) moral principle or value.

Third, taking the moral-point-of-view and developing a MPV theory need not necessarily include the acceptance or use of any particular test of moral justification. This means that any theory of nursing ethics need not endorse typical frameworks of justification contained in theories of medical ethics for moral judgments made within its parameters to be regarded as true, valid, or rationally justified. It is true that such judgments must be justified within the MPV and pertain to the sorts of facts considered relevant according to the MPV theory. However, the MPV of the theory of nursing ethics itself is not defined by reference to such a system of justification. This means that feminist models of moral decision-making with similar views about moral justification may have particular relevance to the development of nursing ethics and vice versa.

To the extent that any theory of nursing ethics takes seriously the claims of MPV theorizing and the role of caring as a central value within its framework, there is reason to believe that medical ethics will benefit for such a theory cannot develop apart from the practice of medical ethics or from the evolution of bioethics as an applied ethics discipline. Likewise, claims to feminist medical ethics cannot be made apart from all health care practices (medicine as well as nursing) and necessarily draw on the development of moral thought within bioethical theorizing. Perhaps the links between all three types of theorizing are more important than currently realized.

ACKNOWLEDGEMENTS

The author would like to thank the anonymous reviewers of this journal, and editors Helen Holmes and Laura Purdy for their helpful criticisms on the first drafts of the manuscript. Their comments significantly improved the clarity of my arguments and are gratefully acknowledged.

REFERENCES

Ackerman, Terrance F. 1980. What bioethics should be. *Journal of Medicine and Philosophy* 5:260-275.

Ackerman, Terrance F. 1983. Experimentalism in bioethics research. *Journal of Medicine and Philosophy* 8:169-180.

Aikens, Charlotte A. 1916. *Studies in ethics for nurses*. Philadelphia: W.B. Saunders Company.

Alexander, Cheryl S., Carol S. Weisman and Gary A. Chase. 1982. Determinants of staff nurses' perceptions of autonomy within different clinical contexts. *Nursing Research* 31 (1):48-52.

American Nurses' Association. 1980. *Nursing: A social policy statement*. Kansas City: The Association.

Basson, Marc D. 1983. Bioethical decision-making: A reply to Ackerman. *Journal of Medicine and Philosophy* 8:181-185.

Beauchamp, Tom L. and James F. Childress. 1983. *Principles of biomedical ethics* (2nd. ed.). New York: Oxford University Press.

Benjamin, Martin and Joy Curtis. 1986. *Ethics in nursing*. New York: Oxford University Press.

Bishop, Anne H. and John R. Scudder, Jr. 1987. Nursing ethics in an age of controversy. *Advances in Nursing Science* 9 (3):34-43.

Caplan, Arthur 1982. Applying morality to advances in biomedicine: Can and should this be done? In *New Knowledge in the Biomedical Sciences*. William B. Bondeson, H. Tristram Engelhardt, Stuart F. Spiker and John M. White, eds. Boston: D. Reidel.

Caplan, Arthur. 1983. Can applied ethics be effective in health care and should it strive to be? *Ethics* 93:311-319.

Cooper, C. Carolyn. 1988. Covenantal relationships: Grounding for the nursing ethic. *Advances in Nursing Science* 10 (4):48-59.

Crisham, Patricia. 1981. Measuring moral judgment in nursing dilemmas. *Nursing Research* 30:104-110.

Davis, Anne J. and Mila A. Aroskar. 1983. *Ethical dilemmas and nursing practice.* Norwalk, Conn.: Appleton-Century-Crofts.

Engelhardt, H. Tristram Jr. 1986. *The foundations of bioethics.* New York: Oxford University Press.

Fletcher, Joseph. 1966. *Situation ethics: The new morality.* Philadelphia: Westminister Press.

Frankena, William K. 1983. Moral-point-of-view theories. In *Ethical theory in the last quarter of the twentieth century.* Norman E. Bowie, ed. Indianapolis: Hackett Publishing Company.

Fry, Sara T. 1988. The ethic of caring: Can it survive in nursing? *Nursing Outlook* 36 (1):48.

Gadow, Sally. 1985. Nurse and patient: The caring relationship. In *Caring, curing, coping: Nurse, physician, patient relationships.* Anne H. Bishop and John R. Scudder, Jr., eds. Birmingham, Ala.: University of Alabama Press.

Gilligan, Carol. 1977. In a different voice: Women's conception of self and of morality. *Harvard Educational Review* 47:481-517.

Gilligan, Carol. 1979. Woman's place in man's life cycle. *Harvard Educational Review* 49:431-446.

Gilligan, Carol. 1982. *In a different voice.* Cambridge, Mass.: Harvard University Press.

Gilligan, Carol. 1987. Gender difference and morality: The empirical base. In *Women and moral theory.* E.R. Kittay and D.T. Meyers, eds. Totowa, N.J.: Rowman & Littlefield.

Gladwin, Mary E. 1937. *Ethics: A texbook for nurses.* Philadelphia: W.B. Saunders Company.

Griffin, Anne P. 1983. A philosophical analysis of caring in nursing. *Journal of Advanced Nursing* 8:289-295.

Heidegger, Martin. [1927] 1962. *Being and time.* J. Macquarrie and E. Robinson, trans. New York: Harper & Row.

Huggins, Elizabeth A. and Cynthia C. Sclazi. 1988. Limitations and alternatives: Ethical practice theory in nursing. *Advances in Nursing Science* 10 (4):43-47.

Hume, David. [1751] 1957. *An inquiry concerning the principles of morals.* Indianapolis: Bobbs-Merrill Company.

Jameton, Andrew. 1984. *Nursing practice: The ethical issues.* Englewood Cliffs, N.J.: Prentice-Hall.

Kant, Immanuel. [1785] 1964. *Groundwork of the metaphysic of morals.* H. J. Paton, trans. New York: Harper & Row.

Ketefian, Shake. 1981a. Critical thinking, educational preparation, and development of moral judgment among selected groups of practicing nurses. *Nursing Research* 30:98-103.

Ketefian, Shake. 1981b. Moral reasoning and moral behavior among selected groups of practicing nurses. *Nursing—Research* 30:171-176.
Ketefian, Shake. 1985. Professional and bureaucratic role conceptions and moral behavior among nurses. *Nursing Research* 32:248-253.
May, William F. 1975. Code, covenant, contract, or philanthropy. *Hastings Center Report* 5(1):29-38.
Mill, John S. [1863] 1971. *Utilitarianism*. S. Gorovitz, ed. Indianapolis: Bobbs-Merrill Co., Inc.
Munhall, Patricia. 1980. Moral reasoning levels of nursing students and faculty in a baccaluareate nursing program. *Image* 12(3):57-61.
Murphy, Catherine C. 1976. *Levels of moral reasoning in a selected group of nursing practitioners*. New York, Teachers College, Columbia University (unpublished doctoral dissertation).
Muyskens, James L. 1982. *Moral problems in nursing: A philosophical investigation*. Totowa, NJ: Rowman & Littlefield.
Noddings, Nel. 1984. *Caring: A feminine approach to ethics & moral education*. Berkeley, CA: University of California Press.
Packard, John S. and Mary Ferrara. 1988. In search of the moral foundation of nursing. *Advances in Nursing Science* 10 (4):60-71.
Pellegrino, Edmund D. 1985. The caring ethic: The relation of physician to patient. In *Caring, curing, coping: Nurse, physician, patient relationships*. Anne H. Bishop and John R. Scudder, Jr., eds., Birmingham, Ala.:University of Alabama Press.
Pellegrino, Edmund D. and David C. Thomasma. 1988. *For the patient's good*. New York: Oxford University Press.
Prescott, Patricia A., Karen E. Dennis, and Ada K. Jacox. 1987. Clinical decision making of staff nurses. *Image* 19(2):56-62.
Ramsey, Paul. 1970. *The patient as person*. New Haven: Yale University Press.
Rawls, John. 1971. *A theory of justice*. Cambridge, Mass.: Harvard University Press.
Robb, Isabel H. 1900. *Nursing ethics: For hospital and private use*. Cleveland: E.C. Loeckert.
Self, Donnie J. 1987. A study of the foundations of ethical decision-making of nurses. *Theoretical Medicine* 8:85-95.
Silva, Mary C. 1984. Ethics, scarce resources, and the nurse executive: Perspectives on distributive justice. *Nursing Economics* 2:11-18.
Stenberg, Margorie J. 1979. The search for a conceptual framework as a philosophic basis for nursing ethics: An examination of code, contract, context, and covenant. *Military Medicine* 144:9-22.
Thompson, Joyce B. and Henry O. Thompson. 1985. *Bioethical decision making for nurses*. Norwalk, Conn.: Appleton-Century-Crofts.
Toulmin, Stephen 1981. The tyranny of principles. *The Hastings Center Report* 11 (6):31-39.

Veatch, Robert M. 1981. *A theory of medical ethics*. New York: Basic Books.
Veatch, Robert M. and Sara T. Fry. 1987. *Case studies in nursing ethics*. Phildelphia: J.B. Lippincott Company.
Watson, Jean. 1985. *Nursing: Human science and human care*. Norwalk, Conn.: Appleton-Century-Crofts.
Yarling, Roland B. and Beverly J. McElmurry. 1986. The moral foundation of nursing. *Advances in Nursing Science* 8 (2):63-73.

CLINICAL ETHICS AND NURSING: "YES" TO CARING, BUT "NO" TO A FEMALE ETHICS OF CARE

HELGA KUHSE

ABSTRACT

According to a contemporary school of thought there is a specific female approach to ethics which is based not on abstract "male" ethical principles or rules, but on "care". Nurses have taken a keen interest in these female approaches to ethics. Drawing on the views expounded by Carol Gilligan and Nel Noddings, nurses claim that a female "ethics of care" better captures their moral experiences than a traditional male "ethics of justice". This paper argues that "care" is best understood in a dispositional sense, that is, as sensitivity and responsiveness to the particularities of a situation and the needs of "concrete" others. While "care", in this sense, is necessary for ethics, it is not sufficient. Ethics needs "justice" as well as "care". If women and nurses excessively devalue principles and norms, they will be left without the theoretical tools to condemn some actions or practices, and to defend others. They will, like generations of nurses before them, be condemned to silence.

I INTRODUCTION: ETHICS, PRINCIPLES, WOMEN AND NURSES

Is ethics gendered? Do women and men approach ethics differently? The answer of many thinkers has been "yes".

Rousseau thought that abstract truths and general principles are "beyond a woman's grasp ...; woman observes, man reasons".[1] Schopenhauer bluntly proclaimed: "... the fundamental fault of the female character is that it has *no sense of justice*". This "weakness in their reasoning faculty", Schopenhauer continued, "also explains

[1] Jean-Jacques Rousseau: *Emile*, trans. Barbara Foxley, London: Dent, 1966, pp. 349, 350.

208 CLINICAL ETHICS AND NURSING

why women show more sympathy for the unfortunate than men".[2] Finally, to give just one more example, Freud believed that "for women the level of what is ethically normal is different from what it is in men". Women, he wrote, "show less sense of justice than men".[3]

On these views, then, men and women not only approach ethics differently, but insofar as women were thought to lack a head for abstract principles, and a sense of justice, their ethical approach was also regarded as somewhat defective and inferior to that of men. At the same time, and rather paradoxically, women's traits and moral dispositions were often seen as somewhat purer, and more worthy, than those of men. For Rousseau, for example, women who had developed the distinctively feminine traits of gentleness, tenderness, compassion, self-sacrifice and mental passivity, were only a "little lower than the angels";[4] and the poet Lord Tennyson called women the "interpreters between gods and men".[5]

Nursing has always been a predominantly female profession and there was, and probably still is, a widespread belief that nursing, like few other professions, allows women to develop and express their specific feminine virtues. As one writer put it as recently as 1980:

> [N]urses were ... angels! Angels of mercy! They were with him constantly, these women figures. They were gentle and good. They fixed his pillows. They came when he called for help. They said: "This will make you feel better" and "There, isn't that better?" They touched him with their hands, flesh to flesh. His succor. His life savers. His lifelines.[6]

Mary Wollstonecraft, a contemporary of Rousseau's, saw a firm link between the feminine virtues of gentleness and docility, and the subjection of women. She charged that Rousseau and some other "specious reasoners", consistently recommended "[g]entleness, docility and a spaniel-like affection ... as the cardinal virtues of the sex",

---

[2] Arthur Schopenhauer: "On Women" in Mary Mahowald (ed): *Philosophy of Woman — An Anthology of Classic and Current Concepts*, Indianapolis: Indiana, 1983, p. 231 (emphasis in original).

[3] Sigmund Freud: "Some Psychical Consequences of the Anatomical Distinction Between the Sexes", in *The Standard Edition of the Complete Psychological Works of Sigmund Freud*, trans. and ed. James Strachey, London: The Hogarth Press, 1961, Vol. XIX, pp. 257–58. (I owe this reference to Carol Gilligan: *In a Different Voice*, Cambridge, Mass.: Harvard University Press, 1982, p. 7.)

[4] Jean-Jacques Rousseau: *Emile*, op. cit., p. 359.

[5] Alfred Lord Tennyson: "The Princess". (The poem can be found in various anthologies.)

[6] Martha Lear: *Heartsounds*, New York: Simon and Schuster, 1980, pp. 38–39.

© Blackwell Publishers Ltd. 1995

but ultimately regarded women as "gentle, domestic brutes", incapable of the kind of reason that distinguishes human beings from the beast. "The nature of reason", she said, "must be the same in all".[7]

Many modern feminists still accept Wollstonecraft's basic point that there is but one ethics for women and men. There is, however, also another school of thought which holds that traditional male thinkers, while wrong on much else, were right on at least one point: that women and men do approach ethics differently. This school of thought rejects the idea that women are *incapable* of abstract, principled thinking; rather, and much more fundamentally, it claims that principled ethical thinking is not the only valid (or best) approach to ethics. There is, according to this view, an alternative "female" approach to ethics which is based not on abstract "male" ethical principles or wide generalisations, but on "care", that is, on receptivity and responsiveness to the needs of others.

Nurses have taken a keen interest in these female approaches to ethics. Drawing on the views expounded by Carol Gilligan[8] and Nel Noddings,[9] nurses claim that a female "ethics of care" better captures their moral experiences than a traditional male "ethics of justice".[10] The latter approach, a prominent proponent of a nursing ethics of care proclaims, regards principles as more important than people; nurse-caring, on the other hand, is patient-centered: "it ties us to the people we serve and not to the rules through which we serve them".[11]

The claim that women and men approach ethics differently is not the focus of my paper, although I will briefly return to it at the end of

---

[7] Mary Wollstonecraft: *A Vindication of the Rights of Women*, New York: Norton, 1967, pp. 50, 68, 69.

[8] Carol Gilligan: *In a Different Voice*, Cambridge: Harvard University Press, 1982.

[9] Nel Noddings: *Caring — A Feminine Approach to Ethics and Moral Education*, Berkeley: University of California Press, 1984.

[10] See, for example, the articles in the collection by Jean Watson and Marilyn A. Ray (eds.): *The Ethics of Care and the Ethics of Cure: Synthesis in Chronicity*, New York: National League for Nursing, 1988; Mary Carolyn Cooper: "Gilligan's Different Voice: A Perspective for Nursing", *Journal of Professional Nursing*, Vol. 5, No. 1, 1989, pp. 10–16; Sara T. Fry: "Toward a theory of nursing ethics", *Advances in Nursing Science*, Vol. 11, No. 4, pp. 9–22; Randy Spreen Parker: "Nurses' stories: The search for a relational ethics of care", *Advances in Nursing Science*, Sept. 1990, pp. 32–40; Dena S. Davis: "Nursing: An Ethics of Caring", *Hum. Med.*, 1985, Vol. 2, No. 1, pp. 19–25.

[11] Jean Watson: "An Introduction: An Ethics of Caring/Curing/Nursing" *qua* Nursing: in Jean Watson and Marilyn A. Ray (eds.): *The Ethics of Care ...*, op cit., p. 2. Jean Watson is here citing Nel Noddings: *Caring ...*, op. cit., no page number given.

210 CLINICAL ETHICS AND NURSING

my discussion. I will be addressing the second issue, that is, the claim that nurses should adopt a female ethics of care because this is preferable to the justice approach. Since different writers have distinct ideas about what constitutes a (nursing) ethics of care, all I can do in this paper is introduce and then briefly discuss one common central theme: that a female ethics of care has no use for, and does not need, universal principles or rules.

As my discussion will show, I very much doubt that such an ethics will serve either patients or nurses well. Rather, nurses who decide to conduct their professional lives in accordance with an ethics of care are likely to find themselves in a position where they, like generations of nurses and women before them, may be praised for their caring feminine traits and dispositions, but will be unable to assert their moral claims, or to speak on behalf of those for whom they care.

Let me begin my critique by taking a closer look at the notion of "care".

II CARING AS A MORAL DISPOSITION[12]

"Care" is a rich and highly ambiguous notion. Caring for another person — the notion that will occupy us in the present context — has connotations of concern, compassion, worry, anxiety, and of burden; there are also connotations of inclination, fondness and affection; connotations of carefulness, that is, of attention to detail, of responding sensitively to the situation of the other; and there are connotations of looking after, or providing for, the other.[13]

For the purposes of understanding and evaluating an ethics that has care as its central concept, it would be important to know which understanding of "care" its exponents have in mind. Unfortunately the nursing literature is not of any great help. Nurses use the term "care" in many different and potentially contradictory ways.[14] As Howard Curzer notes, proposals include "presence", "empathy plus expression of feeling", "truth-telling and touch", "showing

---

[12] This section contains some passages drawn from Helga Kuhse: "Against the Stream: Why Nurses Should Say 'No' to a female Ethics of Care", forthcoming in *Revue Internationale de Philosophique*.

[13] On the richness of the notion of "caring", see Nel Noddings: *Caring ...*, op. cit., pp. 9–16.

[14] For a thorough critique of Sara Fry's concept of care (in "The role of caring in a theory of nursing", *Hypatia*. Vol. 4, No. 2, 1989, pp. 88–103) see Howard J. Curzer: "Fry's Concept of Care in Nursing Ethics, *Hypatia*, Vol. 8, No. 3, 1993, pp. 174–183.

concern", and "enabling or assisting".[15] Underlying these different understandings is some general agreement that "care" must involve more than mere caring behaviour; there must also be some empathy, attachment or connectedness, in the sense of "caring about" the patient.

What precisely "caring for/caring about" amounts to is, however, none too clear. Definitions and explanations are imprecise, obscure and sometimes even mystical. One prominent writer in the field, Sally Gadow, for example, defines "care"

> as an end in itself. While it may serve as a means of reaching a further state, it is always and above all a state that itself can be fully inhabited. While it may serve as a vessel for reaching a remote shore, it is at the same time and above all a vessel in which one can live even when — especially when — there is no destination in sight or in mind.[16]

Similarly Jean Watson. Watson holds that true "transpersonal caring" entails that

> the nurse is able to form a union with the other on a level that transcends the physical ... [where] there is a freeing of both persons from their separation and isolation ... .[17]

Other writers speak of nurse-caring as "a feeling of dedication to the extent that it motivates and energizes action to influence life constructively and positively by increasing intimacy and mutual self-actualization";[18] an "interactive process", which is achieved by "a conscious and intuitive opening of self to another, by purposeful trusting and sharing energy, experiences, ideas, techniques and knowledge";[19] or as "the creative, intuitive or cognitive helping process for individuals and groups based upon philosophic, phenomenologic, and objective and subjective experiential feelings and acts of assisting others".[20]

---

[15] Howard J. Curzer: "Fry's Concept of Care ...", ibid., p. 175.

[16] Sally Gadow: "Covenant Without Cure: Letting Go and Holding On in Chronic Illness", in (eds.) Jean Watson and Marilyn A. Ray (eds.): *The Ethics of Care and the Ethics of Cure* ..., op. cit., p. 5—6.

[17] Jean Watson: *Nursing — Human Science and Human Care: A Theory of Nursing*, Norwalk, Conn.: Appleton-Century Crofts, 1985, p. 66.

[18] E.O. Bevis: "Caring: A Life Force", in (ed.) M. Leininger: *Caring: An Essential Human Need*, Thorofare, NJ: Slack, 1981, p. 50.

[19] B. Blattner: *Holistic Nursing*, Englewood Cliffs, NJ: Prentice Hall, 1981, p. 70.

[20] M. Leininger: "Caring: A Central Focus of Nursing and Health Care Services", *Nursing and Health Care*, October 1980, p. 143, as cited by Hilde L. Nelson: "Against Caring", *The Journal of Clinical Ethics*, Vol. 3, No. 1, Spring 1992, p. 9.

212 CLINICAL ETHICS AND NURSING

Writers in the field generally recognize that the notion of "care" is as yet inadequately understood, and that there is as yet no satisfactory ethics of care that can serve as a foundation for nursing.

Despite these inconsistencies and obscurities, and my doubts about the feasibility of building an ethical theory on the concept of care alone, there is value in focusing on care as an important, but often neglected, component of ethics.

A sympathetic reading of the nursing literature will reveal a number of common threads. As also in Nel Noddings' approach,[21] there is emphasis on relationship, on attachment, openness, and on attentiveness and responsiveness to the needs of the cared-for. "Caring" is thus not so much a matter of actions, task, or processes, as a mode of being, a virtue, or a stance or attitude towards the object of one's attention. In other words, in attempting to articulate an ethics of care, writers are not so much trying to answer the traditional ethical question of right action: "What should I do?"; but rather the question: "How should I, the carer, meet the cared-for". I shall refer to this understanding of care as "dispositional care".

Dispositional care presupposes not only commitment and motivation, but also openness and receptivity to the needs of the other — a state that Nel Noddings calls "engrossment". Engrossment entails a putting aside of the self so that the carer can perceive, and then sensitively respond to, the particular and unique experiences and needs of the other.

The ideas of dispositional care and of engrossment are far from unproblematical. Various criticisms have been raised against current articulations of them — that they are, for example, based on an impractical ideal, that they employ a notion of care that, while suited to characterise personal relationships of great intimacy and depth, is ill-suited for the nurse-patient encounter, or that they are potentially exploitative of women.[22] While these criticisms cannot easily be dismissed, I take it as given that there is *some* sense in which our attitudes or dispositions matter and that a caring disposition or stance, loosely understood as sensitive openness and responsiveness

---

[21] Nel Noddings: *Caring* ..., op. cit.

[22] See, for example, Stan van Hooft: "Caring and professional commitment", *The Australian Journal of Advanced Nursing*, Vol. 4, No. 4, 1987, pp. 29–38; Helga Kuhse: "Caring is not enough: reflections on a nursing ethics of care", *The Australian Journal of Advanced Nursing*, Vol. 11, No. 1, 1993, pp. 32–42. Catharine A. MacKinnon: *Feminism Unmodified: Discourses on Life and Law*, Cambridge: Harvard University Press, 1987. Janice G. Raymond: "Reproductive Gifts and Gift Giving: The Altruistic Woman", *Hastings Center Report*, November/December 1990, pp. 7–11.

to the needs of particular others, will contribute to better patient care. It emphasises the importance of receptivity and responsiveness, as well as the uniqueness of particular persons and situations. Health-care professionals who are "dispositional carers" are more likely to be receptive to the needs of patients, where these patients are recognised as *particular others*, that is, as individuals, with special needs, beliefs, desires and wants — rather than, say, as "the cancer" in Ward 4. This entails that dispositional care is not only an appropriate part of nursing ethics, but of medical ethics as well.

When dispositional care is lacking, patients' needs may not be met. This view gets some support from a recently published observational study reporting on the interaction of nurses and doctors with dying patients. The non-participant observer reported one case, where nurses failed to notice that a dying patient was thirsty, that the patient could not reach the drink that was placed before her, and that she could not sit up unaided and would fall back when no support was provided. While many factors other than the lack of dispositional care could also explain why this patient's needs were not met, the case description suggests that the nurses, rather than simply being callous, were not receptive and sensitive enough to recognize that this particular patient needed additional help.[23]

As Lawrence Blum has observed, moral philosophy's traditional preoccupation with action-guiding rules and principles, and focus on such notions as universalizability and impartiality, have masked the importance of what he calls "moral perception and particularity" — that is, the important role that is played by our ability to recognise the morally salient features of a situation. For all the moral principles in the world (and our willingness to employ them) will not help if we lack the kind of "moral perception" necessary to tell us when to employ them.[24]

To sum up, then, it seems that Blum and proponents of a nursing ethics of care are right when they say that such traits as perceptivity, sensitivity and responsiveness are morally significant. Blum is also right, it seems to me, when he says that philosophy's traditional preoccupation with sometimes blunt rules and principles, and with universalizability and impartiality, has resulted in less than adequate attention being paid to this aspect of ethics. Proponents of a care approach do, however, often want to go much further than that. They are saying that care alone should be playing a role — that

---

[23] Mina Mills, Huw T.O. Davies, William A. Macrae: "Care of dying patients in hospital", *British Medical Journal*, Vol. 309, Sept. 3, 1994, pp. 583–586.

[24] Lawrence Blum: "Moral Perception and Particularity", *Ethics*, Vol. 101, July 1991, pp. 701–725.

© Blackwell Publishers Ltd. 1995

214 CLINICAL ETHICS AND NURSING

there is no place, or only a very limited place, in an ethics of care for abstract universal principles or rules.

III THE REJECTION OF PRINCIPLES

Caring is a good thing and everyone, not just nurses, should be more caring. If dispositional care can thus quite properly be regarded as a significant part of ethics, it is, however, not the whole of ethics. Ethics is also, and some would say, primarily, about the justification of actions. This aspect of ethics becomes particularly important in contexts, such as nursing and medicine, where there is frequent moral disagreement about the rightness or wrongness of actions: whether a dying patient should, for example, be kept alive, or allowed to die; told the truth, or be protected from it for her own good.

Proponents of female ethics of care do, however, display a distaste for reasoned argument and justification. In her book *Caring*, Nel Noddings explicitly rejects abstract principles and the requirement of universalizabililty as an appropriate part of ethics. Ethics, she suggests, is not a matter of impartial and abstract principles and rules, but of relationships — of care for family, friends, and the "proximate stranger".[25] But, as Hilde Nelson notes, care is "blind and indiscriminate".[26] It cannot by itself tell us what to do.

The following "personal narrative" by a nurse, Randy Spreen Parker, will illustrate what can happen when the rejection of principles is taken to its logical conclusion.[27] The narrator describes herself as a "seasoned critical care nurse", who had abandoned "[t]he language of rights, duties and obligations" (which she experienced as "alien" and "detached from the experience" of nursing) to "learn the lines of a different script — a script that was written in a universal, relational language" — the language of care.

Parker had cared in what appears to have been an admirable fashion for an aphasic patient, Mike, who had difficulties in speaking and understanding.

Mike was a diabetic. Due to poor blood circulation, it was necessary to perform a hip-disarticulation — a radical amputation of the leg at the hip. He was left with a deteriorating "gaping cavernous wound that extended from his rib cage to his pelvis". The wound

---

[25] Nel Noddings: *Caring* ..., op. cit.

[26] Hilde L. Nelson: "Against Caring", *The Journal of Clinical Ethics*, Vol. 3, No. 1, 1992, p. 9.

[27] A similar description of this case also appears in Helga Kuhse: "Against the Stream ...", op. cit.

needed dressing changes every three hours. This was excruciatingly painful, since Mike, who also had a lung problem, could not be given adequate pain medication.

When it became clear to both patient and nurse that "further medical interventions served no meaningful purpose", Parker spoke to the attending physician and head nurse and told them that she "did not feel" that Mike (who had difficulty speaking coherently) wanted to continue life-sustaining treatment.

Parker asked to remain Mike's primary nurse and to care for him, but, she explained, she could not participate in any further dressing changes or resuscitation measures.

> I tried to explain my rationale but found myself fumbling for the right words. How could I translate my own moral experience into traditional moral language? The scripts were different. After several meetings with the attending physician and other nurse managers, I was removed from intensive care and placed on a medical-surgical unit.

Over the next week, Mike was resuscitated several times, before he died "in pain, frightened and alone".[28]

Parker's realization that her "moral experience" of caring and "traditional moral language" have radically different scripts is of course quite correct. Moral experience is private, traditional moral language is not. One person's raw moral experience holds no persuasive powers for others, and should also be regarded critically by the person herself. After all, at times our feelings and experiences may seriously mislead us. They need testing against some standard that lies outside the experience itself.

When it comes to the justification of particular actions, we need to give reasoned arguments for our views. In the clinical context, such arguments will typically rely on certain universal principles, such as respect for autonomy or a health care professional's *prima facie* duty to act in the patient's best interests. To eschew all moral principles is to withdraw from moral discourse and to retreat into an essentially dumb world of one's own.

Of course, the assumption is that caring, in its sensitive attention to the particularities of the situation can give the right answer. But this is not so. Sensitivity and particularity alone can not guide action. We always must decide which particularities of a situation, which elements of the personal histories of those involved, are of moral significance and which are not.

---

[28] Randy Spreen Parker: "Nurses' Stories ...", op. cit., pp. 31–34.

216 CLINICAL ETHICS AND NURSING

To decide what she should do, the agent must first "abstract" some particularities of the situation — those that she regards as morally significant — as her action guide. These abstractions — for example that Mike was suffering and wanted to die, that there was no hope, and so on — are the kind of stuff that principles are made of. Once stated in principled form (for example: "Patients who are hopelessly ill, who are suffering and want to die, should be allowed to die") these abstractions can be tested, and accepted or rejected, as the case may be. Without principles of some sort — and it is of course an open question what these principles should be — there can be no ethical discourse, no justification — only particularities and unguided feelings; neither will have any persuasive powers for others, nor should they have persuasive power for us.

Caring advocates' distaste for principles follows, of course, from the requirement that the carer should be fully attentive to the circumstances of each individual person, and the nuances of her particular and unique situation. The assumption is that abstraction presupposes sameness, where there is, in fact, uniqueness.

Nel Noddings provides an extensive critique of abstract principles by distinguishing the "approach of the father" from that "of the mother":

> The first moves immediately to abstraction where ... thinking can take place clearly and logically in isolation from the complicating factors of particular persons, places, and circumstances; the second moves to concretization where ... feelings can be modified by the introduction of facts, the feelings of others, and personal histories.[29]

Noddings is correct when she suggests that additional facts, feelings, and personal histories will, and should, often make a difference to our moral evaluation of a situation. Nonetheless, the dichotomy she draws between an "ethics of care" and an "ethics of principle" in terms of the distinction between "concretization" and "abstraction" is a false one.

In the passage just quoted, the contrast between "abstraction" and "concretization" seems to rest, at least in part, on the distinction between "thinking in isolation from complicating factors" and "thinking modified by the introduction of facts ...". But could ethical thinking *ever* proceed in isolation from concrete facts and particular circumstances? Even Kant, rigidly holding that one must

---

[29] Nel Noddings: *Caring* ..., op. cit., pp. 36—37.

never lie, even to a would-be-murderer, needs to refer to the facts: do you really know whether the man's intended victim is in the house? How sure do you have to be that he is there, for the statement "I don't know where he is" to count as a lie?[30]

By the same token, even those who take Noddings' "mother's approach" will have to abstract some details from the infintely many that describe a given situation. Noddings' reference to "feelings" and "personal histories" is already an abstraction of particular aspects of the situation: apparently a person's height, or hair colour can (always? usually?) be left out. But even then, it is simply not possible to take all the feelings, or each aspect of every personal history into account. This means that the question is not *whether* context is relevant, but rather *which* elements of that context ought to be "abstracted" from the overall context as significant for ethical decision-making.[31]

What the morally relevant factors are is perhaps the most central and vexing question in traditional ethics. Those who approach ethics from the perspective of the justice tradition will focus on aspects relevant to the application of certain principles or rules; those who approach ethics from a consequentialist perspective will focus on certain goals — for example, how much pleasure or pain a given action will produce, or how well it satisfies the preferences of all those affected by the action; and those who approach ethics from the care perspective will focus on aspects related to the maintenance of relationships, that is, on care for family, friends, and the "proximate stranger".

This brings us to the next question: Is an ethics that focuses on our responsibilities to those with whom we stand in direct relationships adequate?

Nel Noddings regards concern for those distant from us — for example, those starving in Africa, those who are not our patients, or those who do not belong to our species — as a form of "romantic rationalism".[32] But this response will not do. It entails that a whole range of important ethical issues that go beyond personal human relationships and the lived experience of human care, such as the distribution and redistribution of wealth or the distribution of scarce

---

[30] See I. Kant: "On a supposed right to tell lies from benevolent motives" in *Kant's Critique of Practical Reason and Other Works on the Theory of Ethics*, trans. Thomas Kingsmill Abbott, London: Longman's, Green & Co., 1909, pp. 361–365.

[31] This point is also made by George Sher: "Other Voices, Other Rooms", in (eds.) Eva Federe Kittay and Diana Meyers: *Women and Moral Theory*, United States of America: Rowman and Littlefields Publishers, 1987, p. 180.

[32] Nel Noddings: *Caring* ..., op. cit., p. 3.

health care resources, could not be challenged from within the care perspective.[33]

If women and nurses excessively devalue reasoned argument, if they dismiss ethical principles and norms and hold that notions of impartiality and universalizability have no place in a female ethics of care, then they will be left without the theoretical tools necessary to condemn some actions or practices, and to defend others. Bereft of a universal ethical language, women will be unable to participate in ethical discourse. They will not be able to speak on behalf of the patients for whom they care, nor will they be able to defend their own legitimate claims[34] — and the motto of the first Canadian school of nursing: "I see and I am silent" would have continuing relevance for nurses.[35]

IV CONCLUSION

I began my paper by asking whether women and men approach ethics differently. I myself am dubious about the claim that ethics is gendered and that women are inherently more caring than men. Rather, I am more persuaded by the general idea that social practices and roles give rise to particular moral experiences and visions of "the good". Women have traditionally tended the home, nurtured children, supported husbands, and nursed the sick. Men, on the other hand, have traditionally played more public roles. Their activities did not primarily involve care for "concrete others" but rather dealings with strangers or "abstract others".[36]

Broad ethical principles and rules, notions of rights and justice have an appropriate role to play in the public sphere. Insofar as the public sphere is the realm of strangers, we cannot know the personal histories and particular circumstances of all those affected by our decisions, nor can we care for them in a personal way. But we can, and must, ensure that their rights and claims are protected, and that they are treated fairly.

Care, on the other hand, has a more central role to play in the private sphere, where people can respond to each other as "concrete" others, and where the maintenance of relationships

---

[33] See also Claudia Card: "Caring and Evil", *Hypatia*, Vol. 5, No. 1, Spring 1990, pp. 101–108.

[34] See also L.M. Purdy: "Feminist Healing Ethics" in *Hypatia*, Vol. 4, No. 2, Summer 1989, pp. 9–12.

[35] John O. Goden: "Editorials — No Longer Silent", *Humane Medicine*, Vol. 4, No. 1, May 1988, p. 1.

[36] Jean Grimshaw: "The Idea of a Female Ethic" in Peter Singer: *Companion to Ethics*, Oxford: Blackwell, 1991, pp. 496–499.

requires sensitivity and responsiveness to the particularities of the situation and the needs and desires of those concerned.

Now, if it is the case that traditional ethical theories are based on the experiences of men in the public sphere, then we should not be too surprised to find that the insights of women, derived from their experience in the private sphere have often been ignored.[37] Nursing straddles the public and the private. It is a public enterprise, but "care" is quite properly recognised as the — largely — appropriate mode for the one-to-one encounter between nurses and patients. Patients as a whole would not be well-served if they were regarded as "abstract" individuals, as merely the bearers of certain rights or claims. Such an approach would leave many of their needs unmet. While "care" is thus necessary for good patient care, it is not — as I have suggested above — an adequate foundational concept for a nursing ethics of care. Ethics, and women and nurses, need justice as well.

I started by quoting a number of traditional thinkers. Let me close with a quote from one other philosopher. "Clearly", Aristotle maintained,

> ... moral virtue belongs to all ... but the temperance of a man and of a woman, or the courage and justice of a man and of a woman are not ... the same ... "Silence is a woman's glory", but this is not equally the glory of man.[38]

One way to prove him wrong, is to reject a female (nursing) ethics of care.

Centre for Human Bioethics
Monash University

This paper is part of an on-going project on "Partiality and Impartiality in Medical and Nursing Ethics", awarded to Helga Kuhse and Peter Singer by the Australian Research Council.

---

[37] See also Jean Grimshaw: "The Idea of a Female Ethic", op. cit.
[38] Aristotle: *Politics*, Book I, Chapter 13.

© Blackwell Publishers Ltd. 1995

Part IX
The Case Approach

JOHN D. ARRAS

GETTING DOWN TO CASES: THE REVIVAL OF CASUISTRY IN BIOETHICS

ABSTRACT. This article examines the emergence of casuistical case analysis as a methodological alternative to more theory-driven approaches in bioethics research and education. Focusing on *The Abuse of Casuistry* by A. Jonsen and S. Toulmin, the article articulates the most characteristic features of this modern-day casuistry (e.g., the priority allotted to case interpretation and analogical reasoning over abstract theory, the resemblance of casuistry to common law traditions, the 'open texture' of its principles, etc.) and discusses some problems with casuistry as an 'anti-theoretical' method. It is argued that casuistry so defined is 'theory modest' rather than 'theory free' and that ethical theory can still play a significant role in casuistical analysis; that casuistical analyses will encounter conflicting 'deep' interpretations of our social practices and institutions, and are therefore unlikely sources of increased social consensus on controversial bioethical questions; that its conventionalism raises questions about casuistry's ability to criticize norms embedded in the societal consensus; and that casuistry's emphasis upon analogical reasoning may tend to reinforce the individualistic nature of much bioethical writing. It is concluded that, notwithstanding these problems, casuistry represents a promising alternative to the regnant model of 'applied ethics' (i.e., to the ritualistic invocation of the so-called 'principles of bioethics'). The pedagogical implications of casuistry are addressed throughout the paper and include the following recommendations: (1) use real cases, (2) make them long, richly detailed and comprehensive, (3) present complex sequences of cases, (4) stress the problem of 'moral diagnosis', and (5) be ever mindful of the limits of casuistical analysis.

Key Words: casuistry, interpretation, methodology, pedagogy

THE REVIVAL OF CASUISTRY

Developed in the early Middle Ages as a method of bringing abstract and universal ethico-religious precepts to bear on particular moral situations, casuistry has had a checkered history (Jonsen and Toulmin, 1988). In the hands of expert practitioners during its salad days in the 16th and 17th centuries, casuistry

---

John D. Arras, Ph.D., Division of Legal and Ethical Issues in Health Care, Department of Epidemiology and Social Medicine, Montefiore Medical Center – Albert Einstein College of Medicine, Bronx, New York, New York 10467, U.S.A.

generated a rich and morally sensitive literature devoted to numerous real-life ethical problems, such as truth-telling, usury, and the limits of revenge. By the late 17th century, however, casuistical reasoning had degenerated into a notoriously sordid form of logic-chopping in the service of personal expediency (Pascal, 1981). To this day, the very term 'casuistry' conjures up pejorative images of disingenuous argument and moral laxity.

In spite of casuistry's tarnished reputation, some philosophers have claimed that casuistry, shorn of its unfortunate excesses, has much to teach us about the resolution of moral problems in medicine. Indeed, through the work of Albert Jonsen (1980, 1986a, 1986b, 1988) and Stephen Toulmin (1981; Jonsen and Toulmin, 1988) this 'new casuistry' has emerged as a definite alternative to the hegemony of the so-called 'applied ethics' method of moral analysis that has dominated most bioethical scholarship and teaching since the early 1970s (Beauchamp and Childress, 1989). In stark contrast to methods that begin from 'on high' with the working out of a moral theory and culminate in the deductivistic application of norms to particular factual situations, this new casuistry works from the 'bottom up', emphasizing practical problem-solving by means of nuanced interpretations of individual cases.

This paper will assess the promise of this reborn casuistry for bioethics education. In order to do that, however, it will be necessary to say quite a bit in general about the nature of this form of moral analysis and its strengths and weaknesses as a method of practical thinking. Indeed, a general catalogue of the promise and potential pitfalls of the casuistical method should be directly applicable to the assessment of casuistry in educational settings.

Before we can exhibit the salient features of this rival bioethical methodology, we must first confront an initial ambiguity in the definition of casuistry. As Jonsen describes it, 'casuistry' is the art or skill of applying abstract or general principles to particular cases (1986b). In this context, Jonsen notes that the major monotheistic religions were likely sources for casuistic ethics, since they all combined a strong sense of duty with a definite set of moral precepts couched in universal terms. The pre-eminent task for devout Christians, Jews and Muslims was thus to learn how to apply these universal precepts to particular situations, where their stringency or applicability might well be affected by particular factual conditions.

Defined as the art of applying abstract principles to particular cases, the new casuistry could appropriately be viewed, not so much as a rival to the applied ethics model, but rather as a necessary complement to any and all moral theories that would guide our conduct in specific situations. So long as we take some general principles or maxims to be ethically binding, no matter what their source, we must learn through the casuist's art to fit them to particular cases. But on this gloss of 'casuistry', even the most hidebound adherent of the applied ethics model, someone who held that answers to particular moral dilemmas can be deduced from universal theories and principles, would have to count as a casuist. So defined, casuistry might appear to be little more than the handmaiden of applied ethics.

There is, however, another interpretation of casuistry in the writings of Jonsen and Toulmin that provides a distinct alternative to the applied ethics model. Instead of focusing on the need to fit principles to cases, this interpretation stresses the particular nature, derivation, and function of the principles manipulated by the new casuists. Through this alternative theory of principles, we begin to discern a morality that develops, not from the top down as in most interpretations of Roman law, but rather from case to case (or from the bottom up) as in the common law. What differentiates the new casuistry from applied ethics, then, is not the mere recognition that principles must eventually be applied, but rather a particular account of the logic and derivation of the principles that we deploy in moral discourse.

A 'CASE DRIVEN' METHOD

Contrary to 'theory driven' methodologies, which approach particular situations already equipped with a full complement of moral principles, the new casuistry insists that our moral knowledge must develop incrementally through the analysis of concrete cases. From this perspective, the very notion of 'applied ethics' embodies a redundancy, while the correlative notion of 'theoretical ethics' conveys an illusory and counterproductive ideal for ethical thought.

If ethics is done properly, the new casuists imply, it will already have been immersed in concrete cases from the very start. To be sure, one can always apply the results of previous ethical inquiries to fresh problems, but to the casuists good ethics is always 'applied' in the sense that it grows out of the analysis of individual cases. It's not as though one could or should first develop a pristine ethical theory planing above the world of moral particulars, and then, having put the finishing touches on the theory, point it in the direction of particular cases. Rejecting the idea that there are such things as 'essences' in the domain of ethics, Toulmin (1981), citing Aristotle and Dewey, argues that this pursuit of rigorous theory is unhinged from the realities of the moral life and animated by an illusory quest for moral certainty. Thus, whereas many academic philosophers scorn 'applied ethics' as a pale shadow of the real thing (viz., ethical theory), the new casuists insist that good ethics is always immersed in the messy reality of cases, and that the philosophers' penchant for abstract and rigorous theory is a misleading fetish.

According to both Jonsen and Toulmin, the work of the National Commission for the Protection of Human Subjects of Biomedical and Behavioral Research provides an excellent example of this case driven method in bioethics (1988, pp. 16–19, 264, 305, 338). Although the various commissioners represented different academic, religious and philosophical perspectives, Jonsen and Toulmin (who both served, respectively, as Commissioner and consultant to the Commission) attest that the commissioners could still reach consensus by discussing the issues 'taxonomically'. Bracketing their differences on 'matters of principle', the commissioners would begin with an analysis of paradigmatic cases of harm, cruelty, fairness and generosity, and then branch out to more complex and difficult cases posed by biomedical research. The commissioners thus "triangulate[d] their way across the complex terrain of moral life", (Toulmin, 1981) gradually extending their analysis of relatively straightforward problems to issues requiring a much more delicate balancing of competing values.

Thus, instead of looking for ethical progress in the theoretical equivalent of the Second Coming – i.e., the establishment of *the* correct ethical theory – Jonsen and Toulmin contend that a more realistic and attainable notion of progress is afforded by this notion of moral 'triangulation', an incremental approach to problems whose model can be found in the history of our common law. Just as English-speaking peoples have developed highly complex and sophisticated legal frameworks for thinking about tort liability and criminal guilt without the benefit of pre-established legal principles, so (Jonsen and Toulmin argue) ought we to develop a 'common morality' or 'morisprudence' on the basis of case analysis – without recourse to some pre-established moral theory or moral principles.

THE ROLE OF PRINCIPLES IN THE NEW CASUISTRY

Contrary to common interpretations of Roman law and to deductivist ethical theories, wherein principles are said to preexist the actual cases to which they apply, the new casuistry contends that ethical principles are 'discovered' in the cases themselves, just as common law legal principles are developed in and through judicial decisions on particular legal cases (Jonsen, 1986a). To be sure, common law and 'common law morality' (or 'morisprudence') contain a body of principles too; but the way these principles are derived, articulated, used, and taught is very different from the Roman law and deductivist ethical approach (Pitkin, 1972).

The Derivation and Meaning of Principles

Jonsen and Toulmin have sent mixed messages regarding their views of the derivation of moral maxims and principles. In some places they appear to incline towards a weaker interpretation of casuistry as the art of applying whatever moral maxims happen to be lying around at hand in one's culture. At other places, however, Jonsen and Toulmin suggest a much stronger and more controversial view, according to which moral principles of 'common law morality' are entirely derived from (or abstracted out of) particular cases. Rather than stemming originally from some ethical theory, such as utilitarianism or Rawls's theory of justice, these principles are said to emerge gradually from reflection upon our responses to particular cases.

Whichever view of the derivation of principles modern casuistry ultimately embraces, both are fully compatible with the casuistical thesis that the full articulation of those principles cannot be determined in isolation from particular factual contexts. In order to fully understand any principle or maxim, one has to ask, through a process of interpretation, how it might apply to a variety of situations. Thus, whereas 'privacy' might simply mean an undifferentiated interest in 'liberty' to a theorist unfamiliar with the cases, to the casuist the meaning and scope of personal privacy is delimited and shaped by the features of the cases that have called for a public response. Thus, whether or not consensual sodomy is protected by a moral right of privacy will depend upon how the casuist interprets the features of previous controversial cases dealing with such issues as family life, contraception and abortion.

The Priority of Practice

In the applied ethics model, principles not only 'come before' our practices in the sense of being antecedently derived from theory before being applied to cases; they also have priority over practices in the sense that their function is to justify (or criticize) practices. Indeed, it is precisely through this logical priority of principles over practice that the applied ethics model derives its critical edge. It is just the reverse for the new casuists, who sometimes imply that ethical principles are nothing more than mere *summaries* of meanings already embedded in our actual practices (Toulmin, 1981). Rather than serving as a justification for certain practices, principles within the new casuistry often merely seem to *report* in summary fashion what we have already decided.

This logical priority of practice to principles is clearly evident in Jonsen's and Toulmin's ruminations on the experience of the National Commission for the Protection of Human Subjects. In attempting to carry out the mandate of Congress to develop principles for the ethical conduct of research on humans, the commissioners could have straightforwardly drafted a set of principles and then applied them to problematic cases. Instead, note Jonsen and Toulmin, the commissioners acted like good casuists, plunging immediately into nuanced discussions of cases. Progress in these discussions was achieved, not by applying agreed-upon principles, but rather by seeking agreement on responses to particular cases. Indeed, according to this account, the *Belmont Report* which articulated the Commission's moral principles and serves to this day as a major source of the 'applied ethics' approach to moral reasoning, was written at the end of the Commission's deliberations, long after its members had already reached consensus on the issues (Jonsen, 1986a, p. 71).

The Open Texture of Principles

In contrast to the deductivist method, whose principles glide unsullied over the facts, the principles of the new casuistry are always subject to further revision and articulation in light of new cases. This is true not only because casuistical principles are inextricably enmeshed in their factual surroundings, but also because the determination of the decisive or morally relevant features of this factual web is often a highly uncertain and controversial business.

By way of example, consider the question of withdrawing artificial feeding as presented in the case of Claire Conroy.[1] One of the crucial precedents for this case, both legally and morally, was the Quinlan[2] decision. What were the morally relevant features of Karen Quinlan's situation, and what might they teach us about our responsibilities to Claire Conroy? Was it crucial that Ms. Quinlan was described as being in a persistent vegetative state? Or that she was being maintained by a mechanical respirator? If so, then one might well conclude that Claire Conroy's situation – i.e., that of a patient with severe dementia being maintained by a plastic, nasogastric feeding tube – is sufficiently disanalogous to Quinlan's to compel continued treatment. On the other hand, a re-reading of Quinlan might reveal other features of that case that tell in favor of withdrawing Conroy's feeding tube, such as the unlikelihood of Karen ever recovering sapient life, the bleakness of her prognosis, and the questionable proportion of benefits to burdens derived from the treatment.

Although the Quinlan case may have begun by standing for the patient's right to refuse treatment, subsequent readings of that case in light of later cases have fastened onto other aspects of the case, thereby giving rise to modifications of the original principle, or perhaps even to the wholesale substitution of new principles for the old. The principles of casuistic analysis might thus be said to exhibit an 'open texture' (Hart, 1961, pp. 120ff.). Somewhat in the manner of Thomas Kuhn's 'paradigms' of scientific research (Kuhn, 1970), each significant case in bioethics stands as an object for further articulation and specification under new or more complex conditions. Viewed this way, casuistical analysis might be summarized as a form of reasoning by means of examples that always point beyond themselves. Both the examples and the principles derived from them are always subject to reinterpretation and gradual modification in light of subsequent examples.

Teaching and Learning

In contrast to legal systems derived from Roman law, where jurors are governed by a systematic legal code, common law systems derive from the particular judicial decisions of particular judges. As a result of these radically differing approaches to the nature and derivation of law, common law and Roman law are taught and learned in correspondingly different ways. Students of Roman law need only refer to the code itself, and perhaps to the scholarly literature explicating the meaning of the code's various provisions; whereas students of the common law must refer directly to prior judical opinions. Consequently, the so-called 'case method' of legal study is naturally suited to common law jurisdictions, for it is only through a study of the cases that one can learn the concrete meaning of legal principles and learn to apply them correctly to future cases (Patterson, 1951).

What is true of the common law is equally true of 'common law morality'. According to the casuists, bioethical principles are best learned by the case method, not by appeals to abstract theoretical notions. Indeed, anyone at all experienced in teaching bioethics in clinical settings must know (often by means of painful experience) that physicians, nurses, and other health care providers learn best by means of case discussions. (The best way to put them to sleep, in fact, is to begin one's talk with a recitation of the 'principles of bioethics'). This is explained not simply by the fact that case presentations are intrinsically more gripping than abstract discussions of the moral philosophies of Mill, Kant, and Rawls; they are, in addition, the best vehicle for conveying the concrete meaning and scope of whatever principles and maxims one wishes to teach. Contrary to ethical deductivism and Roman law, whose principles could conceivably be taught in a practical vacuum, casuistry demands a case-driven method of instruction. For casuists, cases are much more than mere illustrated rules or handy mnemonic devices for the 'abstracting impaired'. They are, as Jonsen and Toulmin argue, the very locus of moral meaning and moral certainty.

Although Jonsen and Toulmin have yet to consider the concrete pedagogical implications of their casuistical method, we can venture a few suggestions. First, it would appear that a casuistical approach would encourage the use, whenever possible, of real as opposed to hypothetical cases. This is because hypothetical cases, so beloved of academic philosophers, tend to be theory-driven; that is, they are usually designed to advance some explicitly theoretical point. Real cases, on the other hand, are more likely to display the sort of moral complexity and untidiness that demand the (non-deductive) weighing and balancing of competing moral considerations and the casuistical virtues of discernment and practical judgment (*phronesis*).

Second, a casuistical pedagogy would call for lengthy and richly detailed case studies. If the purpose of moral education is to prepare one for action in the real world, the cases discussed should reflect the degree of complexity, uncertainty, and ambiguity encountered there. If for casuistry moral truth resides 'in the details', if the meaning and scope of moral principles is determined contextually through an interpretation of factual situations in their relationship to paradigm cases, then cases must be presented in rich detail. It won't do, as is so often done in our textbooks and anthologies, to cram the rich moral fabric of cases into a couple of paragraphs.

Third, a casuistical pedagogy would encourage the use, not simply of the occasional isolated case study, but rather of whole sequences of cases bearing on a related principle or theme. Thus, instead of simply 'illustrating' the debate over the termination of life-sustaining treatments with, say, the single case of Karen Quinlan, teachers and students should read and interpret a sequence of cases (including, e.g., Quinlan, Saikewicz, Spring, Conroy, and Cruzan) in order to see just how reasoning by paradigm and analogy takes place and how the so-called 'principles of bioethics' are actually shaped in their effective meaning by the details of successive cases.

Fourth, a casuistically-driven pedagogy will give much more emphasis than currently allotted to what might be called the problem of 'moral diagnosis'. Given any particular controversy, exactly what kind of issues does it raise? What, in other words, is the case really about? As opposed to the anthologies, where each case comes neatly labelled under a discrete rubric, real life does not announce the nature of problems in advance. It requires interpretation, imagination and discernment to figure out what is going on, especially when (as is usually the case) a number of discussable issues are usually extractable from any given controversy.

38   *John D. Arras*

PROBLEMS WITH THE CASUISTICAL METHOD

Since the new casuistry attempts to define itself by turning applied ethics on its head, working from cases to principles rather than vice-versa, it should come as no surprise to find that its strengths correlate perfectly with the weaknesses of applied ethics. Thus, whereas applied ethics, and especially deductivism, are often criticized for their remoteness from clinical realities and for their consequent irrelevance (Fox *et al.*, 1984; Noble, 1982) casuistry prides itself on its concreteness and on its ability to render useful advice to caregivers in the medical trenches. Likewise, if the applied ethics model appears rather narrow in its single-minded emphasis on the application of principles and in its corresponding neglect of moral interpretation and practical discernment, the new casuistry can be viewed as a defense of the Aristotelian virtue of *phronesis* (or sound, practical judgment).

Conversely, it should not be surprising to find certain problems with the casuistical method that correspond to strengths of the applied ethics model. I shall devote the second half of this essay to an inventory of some of these problems. It should be stressed, however, that not all of these problems are unique to casuistry, nor does applied ethics fare much better with regard to some of them.

What Is 'a Case'?

For all of their emphasis upon the interpretation of particular cases, casuists have not said much, if anything, about how to select problems for moral interpretation. What, in other words, gets placed on the 'moral agenda' in the first place, and why? This is a problem because it is quite possible that the current method of selecting agenda items, whatever that may be, systematically ignores genuine issues equally worthy of discussion and debate (O'Neil, 1988).

I think it safe to say that problems currently make it onto the bioethical agenda largely because health practitioners and policy makers put them there. While there is usually nothing problematic in this, and while it always pays to be scrupulously attentive to the expressed concerns of people working in the trenches, practitioners may be bound to conventional ways of thinking and of conceiving problems that tend to filter out other, equally valid experiences and problems. As feminists have recently argued, for example, much of the current bioethics agenda reflects an excessively narrow, professionally driven, and male outlook on the nature of ethics (Carse, 1989). As a result, a whole range of important ethical problems – including the unequal treatment of women in health care settings, sexist occupational roles, personal relationships, and strategies of *avoiding* crisis situations – have been either downplayed or ignored completely (Warren, 1989, pp. 77–82). It is not enough, then, for casuistry to tell us *how* to interpret cases; rather than simply carrying out the agenda dictated by health professionals, all of us (casuists and applied ethicists alike) must begin to think more about the problem of *which* cases ought to be selected for moral scrutiny.

An additional problem, which I can only flag here, concerns not the identification of 'a case' – i.e., what gets placed on the public agenda – but rather the specification of 'the case' – i.e., what description of a case shall count as an adequate and sufficiently complete account of the issues, the participants and the context. One of the problems with many case presentations, especially in the clinical context, is their relative neglect of alternative perspectives on the case held by other participants. Quite often, we get the attending's (or the house officer's) point of view on what constitutes 'the case', while missing out on the perspectives of nurses, social workers and others. Since most cases are complicated and enriched by such alternative medical, psychological and social interpretations, our casuistical analyses will remain incomplete without them. Thus, in addition to being long, the cases that we employ should reflect the usually complementary (but often conflicting) perspectives of all the involved participants.

Is Casuistry Really Theory-Free?

The casuists claim that they make moral progress by moving from one class of cases to another without the benefit of any ethical principles or theoretical apparatus. Solutions generated for obvious or easy categories of cases adumbrate solutions for the more difficult cases. In a manner somewhat reminiscent of pre-Kuhnian philosophers of science clinging to the possibility of 'theory free' factual observations, to a belief in a kind of epistemological 'immaculate perception', the casuists appear to be claiming that the cases simply speak for themselves.

As we have seen, one problem with this suggestion is that it does not acknowledge or account for the way in which different theoretical preconceptions help determine which cases and problems get selected for study in the first place. Another problem is that it does not explain what allows us to group different cases into distinct categories or to proceed from one category to another. In other words, the casuists' account of case analysis fails to supply us with principles of relevance that explain what binds the cases together and how the meaning of one case points beyond itself toward the resolution of subsequent cases. The casuists obviously cannot do without such principles of relevance; they are a necessary condition of any kind of moral taxonomy. Without principles of relevance, the cases would fly apart in all directions, rendering coherent speech, thought, and action about them impossible.

But if the casuists rise to this challenge and convert their implicit principles of relevance into explicit principles, it is certainly reasonable to expect that these will be heavily 'theory laden'. Take, for example, the novel suggestion that anencephalic infants should be used as organ donors for children born with fatal heart defects. What is the relevant line of cases in our developed 'morisprudence' for analyzing this problem? To the proponents of this suggestion, the brain death debates provide the appropriate context of discussion. According to this line of argument, anencephalic infants most closely resemble the brain dead; and since we already harvest vital organs from the latter category, we have a moral warrant for harvesting organs from anencephalics (Harrison, 1986). But to some of those opposed to any change in the status quo, the most relevant line of cases is provided by the literature on fetal experimentation. Our treatment of the anencephalic newborn should, they claim, reflect our practices regarding nonviable fetuses. If we agree with the judgment of the National Commission that research which would shorten the already doomed child's life should not be permitted, then we should oppose the use of equally doomed anencephalic infants as heart donors (Meilaender, 1986).

How ought the casuist to triangulate the moral problem of the anencephalic newborn as organ donor? What principles of relevance will lead him to opt for one line of cases instead of another? Whatever principles he might eventually articulate, they will undoubtedly have something definite to say about such matters as the concept of death, the moral status of fetuses, the meaning and scope of respect, the nature of personhood, and the relative importance of achieving good consequences in the world versus treating other human beings as ends in themselves. Although one's position on such issues perhaps need not implicate any full-blown ethical theory in the strictest sense of the term, they are sufficiently theory-laden to cast grave doubt on the new casuists' ability to move from case to case without recourse to mediating ethical principles or other theoretical notions.

Although the early work of Jonsen and Toulmin can easily be read as advocating a theory-free methodology comprised of mere 'summary principles', their recent work appears to acknowledge the point of the above criticism. Indeed, it would be fair to say that they now seek to articulate a method that is, if not 'theory free', then at least 'theory modest'. Drawing on the approach of the classical casuists, they now concede an indisputably normative role for principles and maxims drawn from a variety of sources, including theology, common law, historical tradition, and ethical theories. Rather than viewing ethical theories as mutually exclusive, reductionistic attempts to provide an apodictic *foundation* for ethical thought, Jonsen and Toulmin now view theories as limited and complementary *perspectives* that might enrich a more pragmatic and pluralistic approach to the ethical life (1988, Chapter 15). They thus appear reconciled to the usefulness, both in research and education, of a severely chastened conception of moral principles and theories.

One lesson of all this for bioethics education is that casuistry, for all its usefulness as a method, is nothing more (and nothing less) than an 'engine of thought' that must receive *direction* from values, concepts and theories outside of itself. Given the important role such 'external' sources of moral direction must play even in the most case-bound approaches, teachers and students need to be self-conscious about which traditions and theories are in effect driving their casuistical interpretations. This means that they need to devote time and energy to studying and criticizing the values, concepts and rank-orderings implicitly or explicitly conveyed by the various traditions and theories from which they derive their overall direction and tools of moral analysis. In short, it means that adopting the casuistical method will not absolve teachers and students from studying and evaluating either ethical theories or the history of ethics.

42   John D. Arras

Indeterminacy and Consensus

One need not believe in the existence of uniquely correct answers to all moral questions to be concerned about the casuistical method's capacity to yield determinate answers to problematical moral questions. Indeed, anyone familiar with Alastair MacIntyre's (1981) disturbing diagnosis of our contemporary moral culture might well tend to greet the casuists' announcement of moral consensus with a good deal of skepticism. According to MacIntyre, our moral culture is in a grave state of disorder: lacking any comprehensive and coherent understanding of morality and human nature, we subsist on scattered shards and remnants of past moral frameworks. It is no wonder, then, according to MacIntyre, that our moral debates and disagreements are often marked by the clash of incommensurable premises derived from disparate moral cultures. Nor is it any wonder that our debates over highly controversial issues such as abortion and affirmative action take the form of a tedious, interminable cycle of assertion and counter-assertion. In this disordered and contentious moral setting, which MacIntyre claims is *our* moral predicament, the casuists' goal of consensus based upon intuitive responses to cases might well appear to be a Panglossian dream.

One need not endorse MacIntyre's pessimistic diagnosis in its entirety to notice that many of our moral practices and policies bear a multiplicity of meanings; they often embody a variety of different, and sometimes conflicting, values. An ethical methodology based exclusively on the casuistical analysis of these practices can reasonably be expected to express these different values in the form of conflicting ethical conclusions.

Political theorist Michael Walzer's remarks on health care in the United States provide an illuminating case in point. Although Walzer might not recognize himself as a modern day casuist, his vigorous anti-theoretical stance and reliance upon established social meanings and norms certainly make him an ally of the methodological approach espoused by Jonsen and Toulmin (Walzer, 1983, 1987). According to Walzer, if we look carefully at our current values and practices regarding health care and its distribution – if we look, in other words, at the choices we as a people have already made, at the programs we have already put into place, etc. – we will conclude that health care services are a crucially important social good, that they should be allocated solely on the basis of need, and that they must be made equally available to all citizens, presumably through something like a national health service (1983, pp. 86ff.).

One could argue, however, that current disparities – both in access to care and in quality of care – between the poor, the middle class and the rich reflect equally 'deep' (or even deeper) political choices that we have made regarding the relative importance of individual freedom, social security, and the health needs of the 'non-deserving' poor. In this vein, one could claim that our collective decisions bearing on Medicaid, Medicare, and access to emergency rooms – the same decisions that Walzer uses to argue for a national health service – are more accurately interpreted as grudging aberrations from our free market ideology. According to this opposing view, our stratified health care system pretty well reflects our values and commitments in this area: a 'decent minimum' (read 'understaffed, ill-equipped, impersonal urban clinics') for the medically indigent; decent health insurance and HMOs for the working middle-class; and first cabin care for the well-to-do (Dworkin, 1983; Warnke, 1989).

Viewed in the light of Walzer's democratic socialist commitments, which I happen to share, this arrangement may indeed look like an 'indefensible triage'; but placed in the context of American history and culture, it could just as easily be viewed as business as usual. Thus, on one reading our current practices point toward the establishment of a thoroughly egalitarian health care system; viewed from a different angle, however, these same 'choices we have already made' justify pervasive inequalities in access to care and quality of care. The problem for the casuistical method is that, barring any and all appeals to abstract principles of justice, it cannot decisively adjudicate between such competing interpretations of our common practices (Dworkin, 1983). When these do not convey a univocal message, or when they carry conflicting messages of more or less equal plausibility, casuistry cannot help us to develop a uniquely correct interpretation upon which a widespread social consensus might be based. Contrary to the assurances of Jonsen and Toulmin, the new casuistry is an unlikely instrument for generating consensus in a moral world fractured by conflicting values and intuitions.

In Jonsen and Toulmin's defense, it should be noted that abstract theories of justice divorced from the conventions of our society are equally unlikely sources of uniquely correct answers. If philosophers cannot agree amongst themselves upon the true nature of abstract justice – indeed, if criticizing our foremost theoretician of justice, John Rawls, has become something of a philosophical national pastime (Daniels, 1989; Arneson, 1998) – it is unclear how their theorizing could decisively resolve the ongoing debate among competing interpretations of our common social practices.

It might also be noted in passing that even Rawls has become increasingly loathe in his recent writings to appeal to an abstract, timeless, and deracinated notion of justice as the ultimate court of appeal from conflicting social interpretations. Eschewing any pretense of having established a theory of justice 'sub specie aeternitatis', Rawls now claims that his theory of 'justice as fairness' is only applicable in modern democracies like our own (Rawls, 1980, p. 318). He claims, moreover, that the justification of his theory is derived, not from neutral data, but from its "congruence with our deeper understanding of ourselves and our aspirations, and our realization that, given our history and the traditions embedded in our public life, it is the most reasonable doctrine for us" (Rawls, 1980, p. 519; see also Rawls, 1985, p. 228). Notwithstanding the many differences that distinguish their respective views, it thus appears that Rawls, Walzer, and Jonsen and Toulmin could all agree that there is no escape from the task of interpreting the meanings embedded in our social practices, institutions and history. Given the complexity and tensions that characterize this moral 'data', the search for uniquely correct interpretations must be seen as misguided. The best we can do, it seems, is to argue for our own determinate but contestable interpretations of who we are as a people and who we want to become. Neither theory nor casuistry is a guarantor of consensus.

Conventionalism and Critique

The stronger, more controversial version of casuistry and its 'summary view' of ethical principles gives rise to worries about the nature of moral truth and justification. Eschewing any theoretical derivation of principles and insisting that the locus of moral certainty is the particular, the casuist asks "What principles best organize and account for what we have already decided?" Viewed from this angle, the casuistic project amounts to nothing more than an elaborate refinement of our intuitions regarding cases. As such, it begins to resemble the kind of relativistic conventionalism recently articulated by Richard Rorty (Rorty, 1989).

Obviously, one problem with this is that our intuitions have often been shown to be wildly wrong, if not downright prejudicial and superstitious. To the extent that this is true of *our own* intuitions about ethical matters, then casuistry will merely refine our prejudices. Any casuistry that modestly restricts itself to interpreting and cataloguing the flickering shadows on the cave wall can easily be accused of lacking a critical edge. If applied ethics might rightly be said to have purchased critical leverage at the expense of the concrete moral situation, then casuistry might be charged with having purchased concreteness and relevance at the expense of philosophical criticism. This charge might take either of two forms. First, one could claim that the casuist is a mere expositor of *established* social meanings and thus lacks the requisite critical distance to formulate telling critiques of regnant social understandings. Second, casuistry could be accused of ignoring the power relations that shape and inform the social meanings that its practitioners interpret.

In response to the issue of critical distance, Jonsen and Toulmin could point out that the social world of established meanings is by no means monolithic and usually harbors alternative values that offer plenty of critical leverage against the regnant social consensus. As Michael Walzer has recently argued, even such thundering social critics as the prophet Amos have usually been fully committed to their societies, rather than 'objective' and detached; and the values to which they appeal are often fundamental to the self-understanding of a people or group (Walzer, 1987). (How else could they accuse their fellows of hypocrisy?) The lesson for casuists here is not to become so identified with the point of view of health care professionals that they lose sight of other important values in our culture.

The second claim, while not necessarily fatal to the casuistical enterprise, is harder to rebut. As Habermas has contended in his longstanding debate with Gadamer, interpretive approaches to ethics [such as casuistry] can articulate our shared social meanings but ignore the economic and power relations that shape social consensus. His point is that the very conversation through which cases, social practices and institutions are interpreted is itself subject to what he calls 'systematically distorted communication' (Habermas, 1980). In order to avoid merely legitimizing social understandings conditioned on power and domination – for example, our conception of the appropriate relationship between nurses and physicians – casuistry will have to supplement its interpretations with a critical theory of social relationships, or with what Paul Ricoeur has called a 'hermeneutics of suspicion'. (Ricoeur, 1986).

Reinforcing the Individualism of Bioethics

Analytical philosophers working as applied ethicists have often been criticized for the ahistorical, reductionist, and excessively individualistic character of their work in bioethics (Fox *et al.*, 1984; Noble, 1982; MacIntyre, 1982). While the casuistical method cannot thus be justly accused of importing a short-sighted individualism into the field of bioethics – that honor already belonging to analytical philosophy – it cannot be said either that casuistry offers anything like a promising remedy for this deficiency. On the contrary, it seems that the casuists' method of reasoning by analogy only promises to exacerbate the individualism and reductionism already characteristic of much bioethical scholarship.

Consider, for example, how a casuist might address the problem of heart transplants. He or she might reason like this: Our society is already deeply committed to paying for all kinds of 'half-way technologies' for those in need. We already pay for renal dialysis and transplantation, chronic ventilatory support for children and adults, expensive open-heart surgery, and many other 'high tech' therapies, some of which might well be even more expensive than heart transplants. Therefore, so long as heart transplants qualify medically as a proven therapy, there is no reason why Medicaid and Medicare should not fund them (Overcast *et al.*, 1985).

Notwithstanding the evident fruitfulness of such analogical reasoning in many contexts of bioethics, and notwithstanding the possibility that these particular examples of it might well prevail against the competing arguments on heart transplantation, it remains true that such contested practices raise troubling questions that tend not to be asked, let alone illuminated, by casuistical reasoning by analogy. The extent of our willingness to fund heart transplantation has great bearing on the kind of society in which we wish to live and on our priorities for spending within (and without) the health care budget. Even if we already fund many high technology procedures that cost as much or more than heart transplants, it is possible that this new round of transplantation could threaten other forms of care that provide greater benefits to more people; and we might therefore wish to draw the line here (Massachusetts Task Force, 1984; Annas, 1985).

The point is that, no matter where we stand on the particular issue of heart transplants, we *might* think it important to raise such 'big questions', depending on the nature of the problem at hand. We might want to ask, to borrow from a recent title, "What kind of life?" (Callahan, 1990). But the kind of reasoning by analogy championed by the new casuists tends to reduce our field of ethical vision down to the proximate moral precedents, and thereby suppresses the important global questions bearing on who we are and what kind of society we want. The result is likely to be a method of moral reasoning that graciously accommodates us to any and all technological innovations, no matter what their potential long-term threat to fundamental and cherished institutions and values.

CONCLUSIONS

The revival of casuistry, both in practice and in Jonsen and Toulmin's (1988) recent defense, is a welcome development in the field of bioethics. Its account of moral reasoning (emphasizing the pivotal role of paradigms, analogical thinking, and the prudential weighing of competing factors) is far superior, both as a description of how we actually think and as a prescription of how we ought to think, to the tiresome invocation of the applied ethics mantra (i.e., the principles of respect for autonomy, beneficence and justice). By insisting on a *modest* role for ethical theory in a pragmatic, non-deductivist approach to ethical interpretation, Jonsen and Toulmin join an important chorus of contemporary thinkers troubled by the reductionism inherent in most analytical ethics (Williams, 1985; Hampshire, 1983; Taylor, 1982).

As for its role in bioethics education, no one needs to tell teachers about the importance of cases in the classroom. It's pretty obvious that discussing cases is fun, interesting, and certainly more memorable than any philosophical theory, which for the average student usually has a half-life of about two weeks. Moreover, a casuistical education gives students the methodological tools they are most likely to need when they later encounter bioethical problems in the 'real world', whether as health care professionals, clergy, lawyers, journalists or informed citizens. For all of the obviousness of these points, however, it remains true that all of us teachers could profit from sound advice on how better to use cases, and some such advice can be extrapolated from the work of Jonsen and Toulmin.

For all its virtues *vis-à-vis* the sclerotic invocation of 'bioethical principles', the casuistical method is not, however, without problems of its own. First, we found that the very principles of relevance that drive the casuistical method need to be made explicit; and we surmised that, once unveiled, these principles will turn out to be heavily theory laden. Second, we showed that the casuistical method is an unlikely source of uniquely correct interpretations of social meanings and therefore an unlikely source of societal consensus. Third, we have seen that, because of the casuists' view of ethical principles as mere summaries of our intuitive responses to paradigmatic cases, their method might suffer from ideological distortions and lack a critical edge. Moreover, relying so heavily on the perceptions and agenda of health care professionals, casuists might tend to ignore the existence of important issues that could be revealed by other theoretical perspecitves, such as feminism. Finally, we saw that casuistry, focusing as it does on analogical resemblances, might tend to ignore certain difficult but inescapable 'big questions' (e.g., "What kind of society do we want?"), and thereby reinforce the individualistic tendencies already at work in contemporary bioethics.

It remains to be seen whether casuistry, as a program in practical ethics, will be able to marshall sufficient internal resources to respond to these criticisms. Whatever the outcome of that attempt, however, an equally promising approach might be to incorporate the insights and tools of casuistry into the methodological approach known as 'reflective equilibrium' (Rawls, 1971; Daniels, 1979). According to this method, the casuistical interpretation of cases, on the one hand, and moral theories, principles and maxims, on the other, exist in a symbiotic relationship. Our intuitions on cases will thus be guided, and perhaps criticized, by theory; while our theories and moral principles will themselves be shaped, and perhaps reformulated, by our responses to paradigmatic moral situations. Whether we attempt to flesh out this method of reflective equilibrium or further develop the casuistical program, it should be clear by now that the methodological issue between theory and cases is not a dichotomous 'either/or' but rather an encompassing 'both-and'.

In closing I would like to gather together my various recommendations, strewn throughout this paper, for the use of casuistry in bioethics education:

1. Use real cases rather than hypotheticals whenever possible.
2. Avoid schematic case presentations. Make them long, richly detailed, messy, and comprehensive. Make sure that the perspectives of all the major players (including nurses and social workers) are represented.
3. Present complex sequences of cases that sharpen students' analogical reasoning skills.
4. Engage students in the process of 'moral diagnosis'.
5. Be mindful of the limits of casuistical analysis. As a mere engine of moral argument, casuistry must be supplemented and guided by appeals to ethical theory, the history of ethics, and moral norms embedded in our traditions and social practices. It must also be supplemented by critical social analyses that unmask the power behind much social consensus and raise larger questions about the kind of society we want and the kind of people we want to be.

ACKNOWLEDGEMENTS

This article is based upon a presentation at a conference on 'Bioethics as an Intellectual Field', sponsored by the University of Texas Medical Branch, Galveston, Texas. The author would like to thank Ronald Carson and Thomas Murray for their encouragement.

NOTES

[1] Matter of Claire C. Conroy, Supreme Court of New Jersey, 486 A. 2d 1209 (1985).
[2] Matter of Quinlan, Supreme Court of New Jersey, 355 A. 2d 647 (1976).

BIBLIOGRAPHY

Annas, G.: 1985, 'Regulating heart and liver transplants in Massachusetts', *Law, Medicine and Health Care* 13(1), 4–7.

Arneson, R.J. (ed.): 1989, 'Symposium on Rawlsian theory of justice: Recent developments', *Ethics* 99 (4), 695–944.

Beauchamp, T.L. and Childress J.F.: 1989, *Principles of Biomedical Ethics*, 3rd edition, Oxford University Press, New York, New York.

Callahan, D.: 1990, *What Kind of Life?*, Simon and Schuster, New York, New York.

Carse, A.L.: 1991, 'The "voice of care", Implications for bioethics education', *Journal of Philosophy and Medicine* 16, 5–28.

Daniels, N.: 1979, 'Wide reflective equilibrium and theory acceptance in ethics', *The Journal of Philosophy* 76, 256–82.

Daniels, N.: 1989, *Reading Rawls*, 2nd edition, Stanford University Press, Stanford, California.

Dworkin, R.: 1983: '*Spheres of Justice*: An exchange', *New York Review of Books*, 30 (12), 44.

Dworkin, R.: 1985, *A Matter of Principle*, Harvard University Press, Cambridge.

Fox, R.C. and Swazey, J.P.: 1984, 'Medical morality is not bioethics – medical ethics in China and the United States', *Perspectives in Biology and Medicine* 27, 336–360.

Habermas, J.: 1980, 'The hermeneutic claim to universality' in J. Bleicher (ed.), *Contemporary Hermeneutics*, Routledge & Kegan Paul, London, pp. 181–211.

Hampshire, S.: 1983, *Morality and Conflict*, Harvard University Press, Cambridge, Massachusetts.

Harrison, M.R.: 1986, 'The anencephalic newborn as organ donor: Commentary', *Hastings Center Report* 16, 21–22.

Hart, H.L.A.: 1961, *The Concept of Law*, Oxford University Press, Oxford, England.

Jonsen, A.R.: 1980, 'Can an ethicist be a consultant?', in V. Abernethy (ed.), *Frontiers in Medical Ethics*, Ballinger Publishing Company, Cambridge, Massuchsetts, pp. 157–171.

Jonsen, A.R.: 1986a, 'Casuistry and clinical ethics', *Theoretical Medicine* 7, 65–74.

Jonsen, A.R.: 1986b, 'Casuistry', in J.F. Childress and J. Macgvarrie (eds.), *Westminster Dictionary of Christian Ethics*, Westminster Press, Philadelphia, Pennsylvania, pp. 78–80.

Jonsen, A.R. and Toulmin, S.: 1988, *The Abuse of Casuistry*, University of California Press, Berkeley, California.

Kuhn, T.: 1970, *The Structure of Scientific Revolutions*, 2nd edition, University of Chicago Press, Chicago, Illinois.

MacIntyre, A.: 1981, *After Virtue*, University of Notre Dame Press, Notre Dame, Indiana.

Massachusetts Task Force on Organ Transplantation: 1984, *Report of the Massachusetts Task Force on Organ Transplantation*, Boston, Massachusetts.

Meilaender, G.: 1986, 'The anencephalic newborn as organ donor: Commentary', *Hastings Center Report* 16, 22–23.

Noble, C.: 1982, 'Ethics and experts', *Hastings Center Report* 12, 7–9.

O'Neill, O.: 1988, 'How can we individuate moral problems?' in D.M. Rosenthal and F. Shehadi (eds.), *Applied Ethics and Ethical Theory*, University of Utah Press, Salt Lake City, pp. 84–99.

Overcast, D. et al.: 1985, 'Technology assessment, public policy and transplantation', *Law, Medicine and Health Care* 13 (3), 106–111.
Pascal, B.: 1981, *Lettres écrites à un provincial*, A. Adam (ed.), Flammarion, Paris.
Patterson, E.W.: 1951, 'The case method in American legal education: Its origins and objectives', *Journal of Legal Education* 4, 1–24.
Pitkin, H.: 1972, *Wittgenstein and Justice*, University of California Press, Berkeley, California.
Rawls, J.: 1971, *A Theory of Justice*, Harvard University Press, Cambridge Massachusetts.
Rawls, J.: 1980, 'Kantian constructivism in moral theory: The Dewey Lectures 1980', *The Journal of Philosophy* 77, 515–572.
Rawls, J.: 1985, 'Justice as fairness: Political not metaphysical', *Philosophy and Public Affairs* 14, 223–251.
Ricoeur, P.: 1986, 'Hermeneutics and the critique of ideology', in B.R. Wachterhauser (ed.), *Hermeneutics and Modern Philosophy*, State University of New York Press, Albany, New York, pp. 300–339.
Rorty, R.: 1989, *Contingency, Irony, and Solidarity*, Cambridge University Press, Cambridge, England.
Taylor, C.: 1982, 'The diversity of goods', in A. Sen and B. Williams (eds.), *Utilitarianism and Beyond*, Cambridge University Press, Cambridge, England, pp. 129–144.
Toulmin, S., 1981: 'The tyranny of principles', *Hastings Center Report* 11, 31–39.
Walzer, M.: 1983, *Spheres of Justice*, Basic Books, New York, New York.
Walzer, M.: 1987, *Interpretation and Social Criticism*, Harvard University Press, Cambridge, Massachusetts.
Warnke, G.: 1989–1990, 'Social interpretation and political theory: Walzer and his critics', *The Philosophical Forum* 21 (1–2), 204–226.
Warren, V.: 1989, 'Feminist directions in medical ethics', *Hypatia* 4, 73–87.
Williams, B.: 1985, *Ethics and the Limits of Philosophy*, Harvard University Press, Cambridge, Massachusetts.

[27]
Albert R. Jonsen

Casuistry:
An Alternative or Complement to Principles?

ABSTRACT. Casuistry is a traditional method of interpreting and resolving moral problems. It focuses on the circumstances of particular cases rather than on the application of ethical theories and principles. After a brief history of casuistry, the method is explained and its relation to theory and principles is discussed.

REDISCOVERING CASUISTRY

THE EPISODE OF intellectual activity designated by the word "casuistry" is a minor moment in the intellectual history of Western culture. It flourished among theologians and canon lawyers from approximately the fourteenth to the seventeenth centuries, and then faded into obscurity. But the general human activity that casuistry is built upon is not so transitory. It takes place daily as persons ruminate about how they ought to act or argue about how others should act or have acted. It rings through the literature of our culture, from Homeric epic to *Schindler's List*. It takes up pages of newsprint and hours of television time. This activity consists of thinking and talking about how the circumstances of this or that case of moral perplexity fit the general norms, rules, standards, and principles of morality. This is casuistry in life.

Strangely enough, the modern moral philosophers only recently have noticed the pervasive casuistry of the moral life. They, like Molière's Bourgeois Gentilhomme, who learned with surprise that he had talked prose all his life (*Bourgeois Gentilhomme* II, iv), have discovered that moral discourse talks cases. From the seventeenth century onward, philosophers constructed elegant edifices of ethical theory to explain how the knowledge of morality differed from knowledge of the natural world. They turned away from the moral perplexities that give rise to daily casuistry and occupied themselves with, as the British and Scottish moral philosophers of the Enlightenment used to say, "the Springs of Morality." Henry Sidgwick, one of the nineteenth century's finest moral philosophers, prefaced his *Method of Ethics* with the remark,

> ...the development of the theory of ethics has been much impeded by the preponderance of practical considerations...it would seem a more complete detachment of the scientific study of right conduct from its practical application is to be desired. (Sidgwick 1877, p. 11)

Today, the classic works of these great moralists appear as vast intellectual constructions, but strangely empty: they consist of grand conceptual chambers without the furniture of cases.

Ethics moved even further from cases when philosophers began to wonder whether ethical words, such as "right," had any meaning at all. Since these words did not refer to empirical facts, they must express only emotion. Yet they were, and are, used to command, advise, reprimand. What could they possibly mean? This question fascinated the philosophers, who saw that almost any answer would bring down the grand edifices of their predecessors. Thus, in the years after World War II, moral philosophers walked away from those ethical edifices and built for themselves a new, very modern, unadorned structure of thought called "metaethics." In this spare building, the only question worth asking was, "what do ethical words mean?" Questions about what was right to do in particular circumstances were hushed up. Cases were banished, unless they were simple enough to illustrate some odd usage of language: a seminar in moral philosophy at Oxford in the 1950s debated the question, "Is wearing the wrong colored tie morally offensive?" (Jonsen and Toulmin 1988, p. 394).

In the 1960s, reality began to overtake moral philosophy, then purveyed almost exclusively as metaethics. "Normative" ethics, long unwelcome in the grand mansion of ethics or in the Bauhaus of metaethics, forced its way in. Multiple genuine ethical dilemmas agitated the life of individuals and society in that decade. The war in Southeast Asia, as public policy and as private agony, could not be ignored by persons who called themselves moral philosophers. Racial discrimination, civil rights, and affirmative action were equally troubling. Abortion, also as public policy and private agony, was openly debated. These concerns slowly slipped into the serene halls of the philosophers. By the early 1970s, the then new journal, *Philosophy and Public Affairs*, had made it respectable for philosophers to discuss

JONSEN • CASUISTRY: AN ALTERNATIVE OR COMPLEMENT TO PRINCIPLES?

racial discrimination, conscientious objection, voting rights, political chicanery, and financial exploitation. Even at the more speculative level, respected philosophers, such as Wittgenstein, Austin, and Habermas, had begun to open common language and life forms to inspection, a move that, while remaining abstract, pointed toward the cases that make up common discourse and ordinary life. Finally, interest in the ethical questions raised by contemporary medical science, an interest that eventually was named "bioethics," plunged into cases, for cases are the substance of medicine. The bioethicists had to take that plunge and, as they did, they wondered just how their philosophical training helped them to stay afloat. It was one thing to find support in theory and principle; it was another to apply and interpret them in the various, complex and changing circumstances of cases.

Stephen Toulmin and I were doing just that when we wondered whether what we were doing was anything like historical casuistry. We were working on the task that Congress had set for the National Commission for the Protection of Human Subjects, namely, to develop recommendations to protect the rights and welfare of human subjects of research and to develop the ethical principles that should govern such research. We noted that while debate over general questions, such as "should children ever be subjects of research," ran on interminably, quick agreement greeted more specific cases, in which the research aims, the estimates of risks, the condition of the child, and the competence of the parents were described. We wondered how these circumstances related to broad principles, such as beneficence and autonomy. Finally, we noted that one task of the Commission, the development of ethical principles to govern research, was performed at the end, rather than the beginning, of the Commission's life, after it had proposed recommendations for many specific cases of research, such as that involving children, the incarcerated, and the mentally disabled.

Taking this experience as our inspiration, we set out to study the history and the philosophy of casuistic moral reasoning. We began work on a book that would attempt to explain the historical rise and fall of casuistic ethics and the forms of reasoning that constitute case analysis. We began with the hypothesis and ended with the thesis that historical casuistry represented a sound way of thinking about moral problems and that its evil reputation arose from an abuse of its methods. We titled our book, *The Abuse of Casuistry: A History of Moral Reasoning* (Jonsen and Toulmin 1988). Our title came from a phrase we found in the last book on the subject, written in 1927, *Conscience and Its Problems*. Its author, Kenneth Kirk, Bishop of Oxford, wrote, "The abuse of casuistry is properly directed, not against all casuistry, but only against its abuse" (Kirk 1927, p. 125).

When Toulmin and I began our book, we wondered whether we should use the word "casuistry" in the title. The word had acquired such odious connotations, being seen as, again in Molière's caustic words, "a science to stretch the strings of conscience according to the different exigencies of the case and to rectify the morality of the action by the purity of our intention" (*Tartuffe* IV, v; Jonsen 1993). The great French playwright clearly had plagiarized the great French philosopher, Pascal, whose satirical *Provincial Letters* (1656) had devastated casuistic moral theology some ten years before Molière wrote *Tartuffe*. Should we devise a word less tainted, Toulmin and I wondered, such as "casuistics," or use a bland phrase, such as "case reasoning." As we worked, we came to love "casuistry" for its history and we are proud to have resuscitated it for use in respectable moral discourse.

CASUISTIC REASONING

In the remainder of this essay, I shall explain the unique features of casuistic reasoning and demonstrate its utility for moral discourse. I will begin with an extended simile: casuistry is like an imaginary building; and I shall explain this simile by recalling an actual imaginary building, used as a pedagogical device for many centuries. This simile and example will briefly take the discussion far from the topic, but I shall return to contemporary casuistry before the end.

The Jesuits, a Catholic religious order founded in 1540, quickly became leading scholars, teachers, and advisors to statesmen in Renaissance Europe. Jesuit moral theologians became the most competent, famous, and subsequently infamous practitioners of casuistry, so much so that the derisive terms "Jesuitry" and "casuistry" appear in dictionary entries as synonyms. One Jesuit, who was neither a casuist nor a theologian, but a poet and mathematician, was the Italian Matteo Ricci (1552-1610). In 1583, Father Ricci entered China as a missionary and during the next 30 years became renowned as a scholar and poet in the Chinese language. The historian Jonathan Spence opens his splendid biography of Ricci with the sentence, "In 1596 Matteo Ricci taught the Chinese how to build a memory palace." Spence entitled the book, *The Memory Palace of Matteo Ricci* (Spence 1984, p. 1).

[240]

JONSEN • CASUISTRY: AN ALTERNATIVE OR COMPLEMENT TO PRINCIPLES?

A "memory palace" is a mental device for storing and recalling images and ideas. From antiquity through the middle ages to the Renaissance, the discipline of rhetoric, which was central to all education, contained a treatise on memory and memorization to instruct the orator in the skill of amassing quotations, arguments, and images. The memory palace was an imaginary building of ample proportions, divided into many rooms, large and small, into which the data of memory were placed like furniture and decoration. In search of an idea, the orator would enter the memory palace, go to the room where certain images were stored and see in the mind's eye this or that abstract idea as a concrete image—a statue, a chair, or a painting. In a world with little access to books, this memory device was an interior library. It was to that era what the computer is to ours. Ricci, who was trained, as were all students of his day, in rhetoric and in its system of memory, wrote a small treatise on memory for his Chinese pupils; it became a classic in his adopted land.

Ricci was a Jesuit, some Jesuits were casuists. The point of this comparison is: the memory palace is a technique of classical rhetoric; casuistry is rhetorical reasoning applied to moral matters. The comparison between rhetoric and casuistry might sound as odious as that between casuistry and Jesuitry, but this is because today we say "rhetoric" only when we are disgusted with the windy words and flashy but false advertising whereby politicians promote themselves. For most of our civilized history, rhetoric was the art of making a persuasive argument in favor of the just, the good, and the right, as its great teachers, Aristotle, Cicero, and Augustine said. Rhetoric was the art of encouraging citizens to decide rightly about civic matters and courts to decide fairly about legal ones. Finally, rhetoric was the art of reasoning with contingent facts and drawing plausible conclusions.

Rhetoric is deeply concerned about the case, for it is cases that citizens and courts deliberate about. A case is a confluence of persons and actions in a time and a place, all of which can be given names and dates. A case, we say, is concrete as distinguished from abstract because it represents the congealing, the coalescence, or the growing together (in Latin, *concrescere*) of many circumstances. Each case is unique in its circumstances, yet each case is similar in type to other cases and can, therefore, be compared and contrasted. Cases can be posed at various levels of concreteness. Some will be composed of quite specific persons, times, and places; others will describe an event or practice in more diffuse terms, such as the "case of the Bosnian war" or the "case of medical experimentation." I refer to cases of the latter sort as "great cases," as I note later in this essay.

The classical rhetoricians were expert in teaching how to talk about cases and in how to make a case, that is, to persuade others to hold an opinion or to judge the case in certain ways (Tallmon 1994). The first move in classical rhetoric was to understand what the rhetoricians called "*topoi*," that is "places" or, as we would say, the topics. These are the forms of argument suited to persuasive discourse either in general or in a particular enterprise. Persuasive discourse in general will always use arguments of a certain sort, invariant in themselves, regardless of what the circumstances are. These are arguments that take the forms of defining, comparing, relating, and testifying, and were called by the rhetoricians "common topics." However, all discourse takes place within particular enterprises, such as government, politics, the law, business, education, or medicine. Here the topics are the defining features of those enterprises: the activities and relationships that make them what they are.

The topics, conceived by the rhetoricians as mental places or spaces, are comparable to the rooms within the memory palace. Different subject matter has different palaces. The palace built for political science, for example, has rooms designated for the recurrent and invariant elements proper to that subject, namely, the form of government, the locus of authority, the common welfare, and the like. The topics of commerce or journalism or education are different. The topics of a particular enterprise are often found as the chapter headings of basic textbooks, but they are, in reality, the recurrent and invariant features that constitute the activity. Arguments in favor of or against a form of government, say, will be built on ideas about authority, public welfare, and the like. Clinical medicine, too, has its topics. In our book, *Clinical Ethics*, Mark Siegler, William Winslade, and I suggest that the special topics of clinical medicine are four: medical indications, patient preferences, quality of life, and contextual features. All arguments about the appropriate course of action in a clinical case are built from those four topics (Jonsen, Siegler, and Winslade 1992). The topics are, as it were, the interior design of the palace: the special rooms and spaces that accommodate some particular activity.

For many years, moral philosophy has neglected the design of the social institutions within which human action takes place. Apart from

[242]

JONSEN • CASUISTRY: AN ALTERNATIVE OR COMPLEMENT TO PRINCIPLES?

the political philosophers who dwell on the best form of society—and, even then, they usually consider only the state—the manifold institutions and practices that constitute a social order have held little interest for moral philosophers. They have been fascinated by the concept of rationality that transcends particular practices of life. As moral philosophy turns increasingly to the practical, becoming interested in the ethics of medicine, of business, of government, and of the environment, it will be forced to specify the topics that constitute those activities.

The second step, after the topics are designated, is to describe and evaluate the circumstances, that is, the particulars, of any case. The circumstances are the furniture and decoration of the rooms of the memory palace. A circumstance is not just an isolated fact, but is rather a fact within a topic, as statues are within a room. The classical rhetoricians listed circumstances as "who, what, why, when, and where." Each of these can be described by proper nouns or by numbers such as dates or length of time or amounts of money or statistics or laboratory data. These can be sorted out into the appropriate topics, so that, in clinical medical ethics, laboratory data falls under medical indications; costs of care under contextual features; and age of the patient, in the sense relative to competence, under patient preference and, in the sense relative to the nature of the disease, under medical indications or quality of life.

"Circumstances make the case," it is sometimes said. We know that when we ponder particularly difficult cases, circumstances often loom large. Was this patient an infant or an elderly person? How large was the dosage of morphine? How long might this patient be expected to live? Exactly how much did the patient know? We realize that often our judgment about a case turns on answers to questions such as these, with their quantitative ring of greater, lesser, longer, briefer, richer, poorer. Yet, strangely enough, moral philosophy pays little attention to the moral relevance of circumstances. As mentioned above, the classical philosophers reflected on the foundations of moral value and judgment and on the universal forms of reasoning suited to moral thinking. Thus, in the recent history of moral philosophy, circumstances have been slighted. As a result, when moral philosophers approach cases, they may bring strong theory—the plans for the architecture of the memory palace—but very little sense or skill in interior decoration.

Do not let the metaphor of the memory palace delude you. The metaphor is appropriate because the spaces for memory and the spaces for argument are both the *topoi* of classical rhetoric. However, casuistry is not simply a method of remembering the facts and figures about an issue; it is a way of assessing them and seeking a resolution to a problem that they may pose. Thus, along with the circumstances that can be sorted into the topics come some arguments that can be made about those circumstances. These arguments, however, are not the extended chains of reasoning that philosophers may use to explicate a thesis. Rather, they are abbreviated arguments, of the sort Aristotle and the classical logicians and rhetoricians named "enthymemes." The arguments have a suppressed premise and attain probable rather than certain conclusions. Arguments will be invoked even more succinctly by maxims, statements that the speaker believes all hearers will accept without dissent.

Thus, within the topic of medical indications, one might find arguments such as "the risk of inflicting harm on a patient must be proportionate to the expected benefit," "no one is obliged to do what is futile," or "the intended effect must be to alleviate pain." The topic, patient preferences, includes arguments such as "consent cannot be obtained from a mentally incapacitated person," "persons have the right to take their own risks," or "coercive situations compromise voluntary consent." When maxims, such as "Do no harm" or "Informed consent is obligatory," are invoked, they represent, as it were, cut-down versions of the major principles relevant to the topic, such as beneficence and autonomy cut down to fit the nature of the topic and the kinds of circumstances that pertain to it.

Each topic is a repository for many such abbreviated arguments. As Quintilian, a classical rhetorician wrote, "the topics are quivers from which arguments, like arrows, are drawn." It should be obvious, however, that these enthymemes and maxims are open to challenges of various sorts. Sometimes the challenge arises from the facts and circumstances of the case. For example, one may answer the maxim, "There is no obligation to perform the futile," with "True, but in this case is resuscitation truly futile?" or with a request for definition, "True, but what is futility?" Sometimes the challenge will come from the logical or philosophical underpinnings of the claim, for example, questioning the logic of the so-called "double effect" argument. In some cases, these challenges can be met within the casuistry itself, as with the question, "Is resuscitation in this case truly futile," but in others, they require an ascent to a more speculative level of moral philosophy, for example, the careful examination of the concepts of efficacy, authority, and probability, that underlie the term "futility" (Schneiderman and Jecker 1995). It is at this point that casuistry contacts moral philosophy proper. It is my belief that the need for this contact arises relatively rarely in ordinary moral discourse, but becomes critical under the pressure of novel or unprecedented problems.

A final step in casuistic thinking is the comparison of cases. No ethical problem is absolutely unprecedented. Regardless how novel, it bears some resemblance to problems that are more familiar. The more familiar ones will often be ones for which resolutions have been offered and sometimes accepted. Thus, one compares the new case with the more familiar one. That comparison almost always involves seeking for the similarities and differences in circumstance. Occasionally, in the more novel cases, one will recognize that the topics under which the moral discussion proceeds are inadequate because the practice or institution has manifestly or subtly changed. In this view, ethical reasoning is primarily reasoning by analogy, seeking to identify cases similar to the one under scrutiny and to discern whether the changed circumstances justify a different judgment in the new case than they did in the former. To return to the simile, ethical reasoning walks back and forth between the rooms of the palace, inspecting with care their content. The ultimate view of the case and its appropriate resolution comes, not from a single principle, nor from a dominant theory, but from the converging impression made by all of the relevant facts and arguments that appear in each of those spaces.

This form of reasoning has not been congenial in philosophy for several centuries. The philosophical ideal has been to approach the mathematical ideal, to move from certain premises to certain conclusions. Hobbes envisioned such an ideal, Spinoza attempted to attain it, and many moral philosophers have been fascinated by it. The admonition of Aristotle, in the beginning of the *Nicomachean Ethics* (1094b20), has been little heeded: "we must be content in speaking about ethics...to reach conclusions that are only for the most part true...for it is the mark of an educated person to look for precision in each class of things just so far as the nature of the subject admits: it is evidently equally foolish to accept probable reasoning from a mathematician and to demand from a rhetorician scientific proof."

In this passage, Aristotle, although he is writing ethics, alludes to rhetoric. Again, the rhetorical nature of moral reasoning is suggested. Casuistry is that form of moral reasoning that, like rhetoric, is confronted with a case in all its particularity and peculiarity and, like rhetoric, seeks to discover persuasive arguments to support a right judgment about the case. In so doing, it must take seriously the nature of the practice or institution that gives rise to the case and it must scrutinize with care the circumstances that make this a particular instance of some activity. This work does not make casuistry a distinct theory of moral reasoning; it merely makes it a necessary adjunct of any moral reasoning that delves into the particular and the concrete.

Casuistry does need moral theory, but only rarely must it have recourse to moral theory for resolution of a particular case. Rather, moral theory can illuminate certain problems that plague casuistry, such as the problem of moral relativity, or its relative weakness as an instrument for radical criticism of social institution, its inability to demonstrate the ultimate foundations of moral principles or of morality itself. These questions hover over all morality and, on occasion, such as the times when a case arises from previously unknown practices (for example, the technology of assisted reproduction), become particularly urgent. Yet the ordinary course of moral judgment—and I mean even the difficult cases that arise within settled practices and institutions—are resolved by casuistry rather than by recourse to theory. And even when theory is appropriately invoked, casuistry has no special theoretical allegiances, proposing instead that one ethical theory might be suited for certain sorts of problems, and another for others.

The title of this article asks a question, "Casuistry: An Alternative or Complement to Principles?" That question has yet to be answered. The metaphor of the memory palace can set us on the road to an answer. First, casuistry is no more an alternative to principles than are walls and foundations to the palace. Casuistry, as I have described it, is a matter of designing and decorating rooms in order to move through the mental spaces of moral argument with ease and enjoyment. Rooms are interior space created by a frame of foundation, walls, and roof, all of which are relatively permanent. In my view, ethical principles are like this frame. Principles, such as respect, beneficence, veracity, and so forth, are invoked necessarily and spontaneously in any serious moral discourse: indeed, it would be difficult to distinguish moral discourse from any other sort of talk without such reference. As I noted above,

JONSEN • CASUISTRY: AN ALTERNATIVE OR COMPLEMENT TO PRINCIPLES?

moral terms and arguments are imbedded in every case, usually in the form of maxims and enthymemes. The more general principles are never far from these maxims and enthymemes and are often explicitly invoked. Thus, casuistry is not an alternative to principles, in the sense that one might be able to perform good casuistry without principles.

In another sense, casuistry is an alterative to principles: they are alternative scholarly activities. A person can choose to do the work of the casuist or the work of the moral philosopher. Traditionally, casuistry was considered a special branch of moral philosophy or moral theology. G. E. Moore, a moral philosopher who did much in recent times to promote interest in ethical theory, writes in the first pages of his influential *Principia Ethica*, "Casuistry forms part of the ideal ethical science: ethics cannot be complete without it...for casuistry is the goal of ethical investigation" (Moore [1902] 1988, p. 5). And one of the leading anti-theorists in ethics, William James, wrote:

> There are three questions in ethics which must be kept apart...the psychological question [which] asks after the historical origin of our moral ideas and judgments; the metaphysical question [which] asks what the very meaning of the words 'good,' 'ill,' and 'obligation' are; the casuistic question [which] asks what is the measure of the various goods and ills which men recognize, so that the philosopher may settle the true order of human obligations. (James [1891] 1977, p. 611)

It is possible, even desirable, that all ethicists ponder the first two questions with intensity. Some will do so exclusively, attempting to sort out of the long literature of moral philosophy the origins and meaning of ethical concepts and claims with as much generality as they can muster. Such is the work of moral philosophy proper. Other ethicists will move from these questions to the casuistical questions: How in this situation do we measure or weigh this value or this principle against some other? In so doing, they are pursuing, as Moore (1902, p. 4) said, "the goal of ethical investigation," which is "to discover which actions are good whenever they occur." All honest casuists must be competent moral philosophers or theologians, else they are nothing more than sophists.

It is a proper question of moral philosophy, then, to ascertain the psychological and metaphysical (and, one might also say, the sociological and anthropological) origins and meaning of principles and their relationship to theory, on the one hand, and to maxims and various sorts of moral argumentation. Thus, when Beauchamp (1995, pp. 191–92) argues that casuists fail to appreciate that principles and value commitments are in some sense prior to cases and in some sense distinct from the facts of cases, he raises a genuine problem of moral philosophy. A moral philosopher with a casuistic bent might tackle this problem from quite a different angle than one with a theoretical bent. The casuistic moral philosopher might question the how and why of "principles...present prior to the decision." Still, however this complex question is settled, the casuist will insist that the relation between principles and moral judgment cannot be properly understood without an appreciation of the place of circumstances as integral constituents of moral argument. The moral philosopher may be the architect of the moral "memory palace" but the casuist is its interior decorator. The palace, constructed of theory and principles, is empty without the interior design, finishing, and furniture of circumstance. These do not merely stand around as neutral items, but are intrinsic features of the edifice, without which interpretation and appreciation are impossible.

Thus, in one sense, casuistry is not an alterative to principles: no sound casuistry can dispense with principles. In another sense, casuistry is an alternative task: It looks not to the origins and meaning of principles, as does moral philosophy proper, but to their complementarity to circumstances. So, yes, casuistry is a complement to principles. Among the many ways that these two complement each other, two might be noted.

First, the circumstances of cases suggest the relevance of principles. Beauchamp (1995, p. 182) remarks that "our set of principles," those stated in *Principles of Biomedical Ethics*, "was developed specifically for biomedical ethics and was never presented as a comprehensive ethical theory." Even though respect for autonomy, nonmaleficence, beneficence, and justice could constitute the total or partial elements of an ethical theory—William Frankena (1963), for example, proposed a theory of obligation consisting of two principles, beneficence, in which he included nonmaleficence, and justice—Beauchamp and Childress crafted their principles for an ethics of health care. The relevance of these principles arises from the circumstances of the institution and practices that constitute health care in twentieth century America, as well as from the long tradition of medicine and physicians' roles. Indeed, the relevance of these principles may reflect something profound about the relationship of one person who engages in helping another, regardless of particular culture and tradition. These are all

JONSEN • CASUISTRY: AN ALTERNATIVE OR COMPLEMENT TO PRINCIPLES?

"circumstances" that make up the "Great Case" of the moral dimensions of health care. The choice of these four principles is unintelligible without reference to these circumstances.

A second complement is the way in which circumstances reveal the suitability or fittingness of a particular specification of a principle. Beauchamp gives the example of the specification of the duties of a physician who might also be a researcher. He suggests that "disclosure" of the dual role might make acceptable an otherwise inappropriate conflict of roles. Again, the moral obligation that would establish a practice of disclosure "fits" only because we are dealing with the helping, medical relationship. Disclosure not only warns the patient that he or she may, at some time, be asked to be a research subject, it also opens the way toward the "identity" between the patient and other future patients that some philosophers, such as Hans Jonas (1970) consider the moral essence of ethical research. It is, then, a most fitting specification of the general obligation of physicians. However, it should be clear that "disclosure" fits here because of the circumstances of the "great case" of biomedical research. If one were dealing with the ethics of spying or even of diplomacy, disclosure would not be a fitting way to specify the general obligations of secret agents or ambassadors.

It should be clear that this casuist, at least, considers casuistry to be complementary to principles. The task of working out exactly what the complement is belongs to moral philosophy (and moral philosophers have been working at it for centuries). The value of casuistry lies in its effort to appreciate more fully the way in which circumstances play an intrinsic role in moral judgment and in its attempt to provide to the one making a judgment a sort of "guided tour" through the complexity of circumstances. It is my opinion that moral philosophy, as it has been done in recent times, provides little guidance through cases. It points to the impressive structure of theory and principle and says to the perplexed, "There it is, explore it and learn from it," just as a tour leader might point to the Louvre or the Metropolitan and say, "Go in and look around. You will learn a lot." Casuistry goes further. It points to the case and says, "You will find this case full of facts and maxims. Here is a plan that will route you through and call attention to the important ones. When you emerge, you will better understand the case and even be able to tell others where to look for the relevant features." Principles and circumstances are complementary in a complex, subtle way. Moral philosophers and casuists can complement each other as they work at understanding the origin and meaning of principles, values, and virtues and at measuring the relevance and importance of circumstances and maxims. Moral philosophers and casuists can also *compliment* each other when they find that the structure of principles that frame a moral problem and the interior design that highlights the concrete features of that problem in a specific instance fit together in ways that allow persons to reach a conclusion about a moral question. They, like the architect and interior designer who create a pleasing and functional edifice, have worked well together and are, as Beauchamp (1995, pp. 190, 193) suggests, "good friends [rather] than hostile rivals."

Some stronger claims for casuistry might be made. One of those claims is that cases are the source of principles: The palace of theory is built of cases, and cases remodel it from time to time. This stronger claim may seem too strong, but I am encouraged that much of the thinking in moral philosophy today appears to creep toward it. The interest in alternative modes of practical reasoning, in narrative, in anti- or nonfoundationalism, and in moral languages all favor, I think, the opinion, modestly proposed, that the case is the base of moral perception, reasoning, and judgment. The palace of moral theory, constantly worn by the daily commerce of cases, may have to be redesigned as a modern edifice, with an open interior design and contemporary furnishings. But that argument remains for another day.

REFERENCES

Beauchamp, Tom L. 1995. Principlism and Its Alleged Competitors. *Kennedy Institute of Ethics Journal* 5: 181–98.

Frankena, William. 1963. *Ethics*. Englewood Cliffs, NJ: Prentice-Hall.

James, William. [1891] 1977. The Moral Philosopher and the Moral Life. In *The Writings of William James*, ed. John J. McDermott, pp. 610-29. Chicago: University of Chicago Press.

Jonas, Hans. 1970. Philosophical Reflections on Experimenting with Human Subjects. In *Experimentation with Human Subjects*, ed. Paul Freund, pp. 1-31. New York: George Braziller.

Jonsen, Albert. 1993. Platonic Insults: Casuistical. *Common Knowledge* 2 (2): 48-66.

———; Siegler, Mark; and Winslade, William. 1992. *Clinical Ethics.* 3d ed. New York: McGraw-Hill.

Jonsen, Albert, and Toulmin, Stephen. 1988. *The Abuse of Casuistry: A History of Moral Reasoning.* Berkeley and Los Angeles: University of California Press.

Kirk, Kenneth. 1927. *Conscience and Its Problems: An Introduction to Casuistry.* London: Longman's Green.

Moore, G. E. [1902] 1988. *Principia Ethica.* Buffalo: Prometheus Books.

Schneiderman, Lawrence, and Jecker, Nancy. 1995. *Wrong Medicine.* Baltimore: Johns Hopkins University Press.

Sidgwick, Henry. 1877. *Method of Ethics.* London: Macmillan.

Spence, Jonathan. 1984. *The Memory Palace of Matteo Ricci.* New York: Viking Press.

Tallmon, James. 1994. How Jonsen Really Views Casuistry: A Note on the Abuse of Father Wildes. *Journal of Medicine and Philosophy* 19: 103-13.

KEVIN WM. WILDES, S. J.

THE PRIESTHOOD OF BIOETHICS AND THE RETURN OF CASUISTRY

ABSTRACT. Several recent attempts to develop models of moral reasoning have attempted to use some form of casuistry as a way to resolve the moral controversies of clinical ethics. One of the best known models of casuistry is that of Jonsen and Toulmin who attempt to transpose a particular model of casuistry, that of Roman Catholic confessional practice, to contemporary moral disputes. This attempt is flawed in that it fails to understand both the history of the model it seeks to transpose and the morally pluralistic context of secular, postmodern society. The practice of casuistry which Jonsen and Toulmin wish to revive is a practice set in the context of a community with a shared set of moral values and structures of moral authority. Without a set of common moral values and rankings, and a moral authority to interpret cases the casuistry of the postmodern age will be pluralistic; that is, there will be many casuistries not just one.

Key Words: casuistry, common morality, kinetics, moral authority, moral pluralism, morphology, paradigm cases, taxonomy

In the mid-seventeenth century, in the midst of great religious controversy throughout the Christian world, Blaise Pascal set out a vitriolic attack on the practice of casuistry in the Roman Catholic Church and its principal practitioners, the Society of Jesus. The heart of Pascal's criticism of Jesuit casuistry was its laxness and hypocrisy. Against the moral standard of a "God Who judges" the casuists gave moral license to subvert the demands of God's moral standard. According to Pascal:

...the license which they have assumed to tamper with the most holy rules of Christian conduct amounts to a total subversion of the law of God (Pascal).

The casuists were hypocrites in that they pretended to be, in the midst of their laxness, something they were not – faithful Christians.

Kevin Wm. Wildes, S. J., Ph.D., Managing Editor, The Journal of Medicine and Philosophy, Center for Ethics, Medicine and Public Issues, Baylor College of Medicine, One Baylor Plaza, Houston, TX, 77030, U.S.A.

34   Kevin Wm. Wildes, S. J.

Pascal's attack on casuistry had devastating effects on the practice as a form of moral reasoning. The term itself came to mean an unfaithful application of principles. Over time casuistry, as a model of moral reasoning, fell out of favor except in a few particular circles, such as Roman Catholicism, Judaism, and some denominations of Protestantism. Other models, more 'theoretical' in structure, became dominant forms of moral reasoning.

In the last thirty years with the emergence of the field of secular bioethics and the prominence of concrete moral dilemmas and controversies in moral philosophy the theoretical models have proven to be inept in resolving such controversies and dilemmas in a secular world. One response to the particular dilemmas of the clinic has been the attempt to develop a casuistry for bioethics (Jonsen and Toulmin; Jonsen; B. A. Brody).[1] The call has arisen as a response to the apparent failure of theoretical models of ethics to resolve moral disputes. It is also driven, in part, as a response to the 'case' orientation of clinical medicine. These proposed models of casuistry are put forth to resolve moral dilemmas in the context of secular moral discussions. One needs to approach casuistical reasoning, however, with a discerning eye in that 'casuistry' is a label which encompasses very different models. Indeed the model of Jonsen and Toulmin is quite different from the model of Baruch Brody.

The principal thesis of this paper is that the model of casuistry proposed by Jonsen and Toulmin is ill-suited to a secular moral context. The hopelessness of deploying this model is obvious if one understands two points: the history of this model and the morally pluralistic nature of contemporary society. In the context of a moral pluralistic society one is faced with moral pluralism which does not admit a single standard of moral goods and judgment such as exists among those who share common moral assumptions and premises. The secular, moral context admits many moral standards, assumptions, and premises. Within such a context it is not possible to adopt the model of casuistry proposed by Jonsen and Toulmin which depended, in part, on a particular moral world view. Roman Catholic casuistry was practiced in a framework which held a certain hierarchy of moral values. This moral world view was, in turn, expressed in a metaphysical view of moral action. Jonsen and Toulmin assume a common morality which functions in the same way. They assume that there are paradigmatic examples of right and wrong as well as widespread commonalities to be found in cultural views of right and wrong (Jonsen and Toulmin, p. 303). This view, however, makes two crucial assumptions. First they make no argument as to why we should think that there is a common morality and second they assume that such a morality should be normative. Many of the moral controversies of bioethics should give one pause in making either assumption.

Even if a common morality exists in the way Jonsen and Toulmin assume, the model of casuistry for which they argue would still be ill-suited for contemporary bioethics. For the casuistry, whose story they tell, was reliant not only upon a moral sense and a metaphysical structure but also upon communal structures of moral authority and interpretation.

Perhaps the proper analogue for secular casuistry is not the casuistry of Roman Catholic moral theology but the casuistry of law courts. Indeed some of their remarks about common morality compare the enterprise of moral casuistry to common law reasoning (p. 330). This analogue, however, does not transfer readily to moral casuistry in a secular world in that the casuistry of the law courts relies on a clearly defined authority to interpret and resolve cases. Moral authority, in the secular world, is vested, primarily, in the moral agent not in the agencies of society.

To make out the difficulties with the model of casuistry proposed by Jonsen and Toulmin, one must first understand how the model is supposed to work. Then one needs to assess the assumptions that the model requires, in the light of contemporary secular society and the history of the model, if it is to be transposed. Finally, in the midst of this assessment one can come to understand how a different model of casuistry might achieve a limited success in a secular context.

CASUISTRY: THE HOPE AND THE MODEL

Bioethics, following the history of modern moral philosophy, has deployed different moral theories to resolve bioethical disputes (e.g., Singer, Veatch, Daniels, Pellegrino & Thomasma). One conceptual difficulty in the use of moral theory is the difficulty of justifying the basis of one theory over and against other approaches (e.g., utilitarianism, deontology) (Brody, 1988). A second conceptual issue is that any theory requires a particular moral commitment or set of moral values in order to reach solutions to the dilemmas (Engelhardt, 1986). Moral theorists have become mired in disputes about both the foundations and values which should be deployed in developing a moral theory.

In the absence of a unified moral theory for resolving dilemmas in applied ethics a number of strategies have emerged to meet the challenges of moral pluralism. The claim has been made that one does not need a unified moral theory to resolve the controversies and dilemmas of bioethics. Perhaps the best known model proposed to circumvent these problems is the appeal to middle-level principles (Beauchamp and Childress).

Another strategy which seeks to avoid the dilemmas of moral theory is the effort by Jonsen and Toulmin to revive the practice of casuistry. Simply understood casuistry is a case oriented model of reasoning. Rather than resolving moral controversies and dilemmas by moving from general principles or theory to cases, the reasoning process is centered on the case. There are, however, numerous ways that one can develop a case based reasoning. Jonsen and Toulmin adopt a particular model of casuistry and they hold out the hope that this model can provide a way of reasoning which can resolve moral disputes in a secular age. They argue for a very strong thesis; that is, that a modern casuistry will resemble its medieval, Catholic counterpart in *both substance and method* (Jonsen and Toulmin, p. 306) and that such a method allows us to sidestep the problems of moral pluralism. The hope for this casuistry is grounded in the work of The National Commission for the Protection of Human Subjects of Biomedical and Behavioral Research which Jonsen and Toulmin assert worked on a casuistical method.

In their book Jonsen and Toulmin offer a history of casuistry and its roots in the West. They argue that moral reasoning is essentially *practical* reasoning; that is, reasoning about cases. This type of reasoning is contrasted with 'theoretical' reasoning which has been central to moral philosophy in the modern age. Reflecting on their work on the National Commission, Jonsen and Toulmin hold that a model of practical case based-reasoning it is possible, in the context of a secular, morally pluralistic society, to resolve moral dilemmas and controversies. They then proceed to give a history of casuistry, and its roots, in the West but they say little about how the model is to work. In a later piece Jonsen puts forth a more specific methodology for casuistry in bioethics (Jonsen).

In his article on methodology Jonsen defines casuistry as

the interpretation of moral issues, using procedures based on paradigms and analogies, leading to the formulation of expert opinion about the existence and stringency of particular moral obligations, framed in terms of rules or maxims that are general but not universal or invariable, since they hold good with certainty only in the typical conditions of the agent and circumstances of action (Jonsen, p. 297).

The article is set up to take the step not taken in the book, namely, to explicitate how casuistry can become a useful technique of practical reasoning for clinical ethicist or ethics consultant (Jonsen, p. 297). In doing this Jonsen develops three categories necessary for a contemporary casuistry: (1) morphology, (2) taxonomy, and (3) kinetics.

1. Morphology:

A "case" is constructed out of the statements about certain persons, places, times, actions and affairs (Jonsen, p. 298). The statements of the circumstances, stand, Jonsen argues, around the core of the case – its center. This core or center is represented by certain maxims, beliefs, or rules which give the moral identity to the case. The morphology of a case reveals the *invariant* structure of the particular case, whatever its contingent features, and also the invariant forms of argument relevant to any case of this sort.

2. Taxonomy:

Central to this model of casuistry is the notion that cases are instances of a "type" (Jonsen, p. 301) and that they can be lined up in a certain order. The taxonomy is a set of paradigm cases which guide moral reasoning. In the article Jonsen uses "Debbie's Case" and the taxonomy of cases in which there is the taking of human life as illustrative of a taxonomy and how it can resolve a moral dilemma. For the analysis of this case Jonsen begins with the paradigm case of the killing a human being by another. He thinks that there would be universal disapproval of the paradigm case. He then 'lines up' the additional cases which fall under the heading of killing (e.g. cases of self-defense). He notes that in evaluating the circumstances one is attempting to resolve of a case one comes to identify where in the taxonomy the case under consideration should fall. In Debbie's case, for example, some might argue that the proper paradigm is not that of killing but an act of mercy. The taxonomy of paradigm cases allows for differences between cases but also makes it clear that cases are not, like the angels, species unto themselves.

The morphology of a case identifies the 'core' of a case while the taxonomy gives different ways a case can be interpreted.

3. Kinetics:

Jonsen borrows the term "kinetics" from classical physics and by it he means "the way in which one case imparts a kind of moral movement to other cases" (Jonsen, p. 303). Thus one can say of the paradigm case, "X is clearly wrong" and of an analogous case "but in Y what was done was justified, or excusable" (303). Jonsen stresses that the kinetics (the application of the taxonomy of paradigms to the morphology of the case at hand) is not mechanical. Borrowing from Aristotle Jonsen stress the importance of *phronesis*. In deciding a case the casuist must be *prudent*. The prudent person need not be imagined, according to Jonsen, as a guru, but rather is a person of 'common sense' who exemplifies the ideals of 'good judgment'. The clinical ethicist must be a prudent person; that is, the ethicist must have knowledge of his field, the cases at hand, and be able to fit cases into a taxonomy.

PARADIGMS, PRUDENCE, AND AUTHORITY

There are several important difficulties which confront the transfer of this model of casuistry to the context of secular bioethics. One way to understand these difficulties is through the history of the model. The second way is to examine the set of assumptions which must be made to create a secular version of the model. In *The Abuse of Casuistry* Jonsen and Toulmin set out the history of casuistical reasoning in the West and focus on the particular history of casuistry in Roman Catholic confessional practice. In the most recent contribution Jonsen has moved beyond the historical background and moved to specify what a contemporary, secular moral casuistry would be like. The different elements he has outlined (morphology, taxonomy, kinetics) redescribe elements which are a part of the Roman Catholic medieval practice of casuistry. There are however, significant conceptual difficulties to the project as a whole and each of its constitutive elements. Within this model there are significant metaphysical and epistemological assumptions which, when explicated, make a secular version of casuistry, based on this model, untenable. The more one understands the history of Roman Catholic casuistry the more one understands the assumptions and structures which the model requires.

1. Paradigm Cases:

Jonsen and Toulmin are correct in pointing out that certain paradigm cases are central to the work of this model. These cases stake out the moral geography. The work of the casuist in this model is to link together the cases at hand with the appropriate paradigm case.

As the work of Thomas Kuhn (Kuhn) illustrates, and others have shown, the term 'paradigm' has a wide variety of meanings (Masterman). There are however, at least five general ways in which a paradigm can function and these different functions give rise to the different senses of 'paradigm': metaphysical paradigms, construct paradigms, sociological paradigms, exemplars of knowledge, and exemplars for action (Masterman). Richard Grandy notes that part of the confusion over paradigms stems from the use of the term to identify both a 'disciplinary matrix' and one specific part of the matrix (Grandy). A 'disciplinary matrix' identifies the web of symbolic, metaphysical, epistemological, axiological, and practical components that shape the research of a scientific discipline. One can argue that Catholic confessional practice, in the Middle Ages, was a disciplinary matrix and the practice of casuistry was embedded within that matrix. If this analysis is correct, it makes no sense to talk of the medieval model of casuistry outside of the disciplinary matrix of Catholic confessional practice absent the axiological system of moral values, the structures of authority which could give the definitive interpretation of cases, or the epistemological assumptions about how values were known.

A central element to the practice of medieval casuistry is the set of cases which functioned as paradigms (exemplars) for moral reasoning. Exemplars are important components of any disciplinary matrix in that they are the shared examples which guide those who use the matrix and they bind together the other elements of the matrix (Grandy, pp. 10–11). Jonsen and Toulmin are correct to argue that paradigmatic cases and taxonomies are crucial to the practice of casuistry in the medieval, Roman Catholic model. However, they do not show how secular paradigms can be established. They simply assert that they can be. Their failure to address the difficulties in establishing secular paradigms is due, in part, to the flaws of their history in which they do not address the links between casuistry, confessional practice, and Catholic moral theology. An examination of such links would show the model of casuistry, for which they argue, to be a *particular* model embedded within a tradition.

They do assert a common morality in which, one assumes, the paradigm cases are embedded. However, in light of arguments made by thinkers as diverse as Alasdair MacIntyre (1981), H. Tristram Engelhardt (1986, 1991), and Jean-Francois Lyotard (1984) it would seem that there should be some argument as to why the existence of common morality should be assumed. Implicit in this assumption about the existence of common morality is the further assumption that a common morality, if it exists, should be normative. John Arras has raised important questions as to whether or nor we should make this assumption in that common morality may well champion what some may view as immorality (Arras). For example, one might think of a common morality which upheld slavery as a moral institution. Similar concerns about the assumed values of common morality have been raised by feminist writers about how the moral agenda is established (Carse; Gilligan).

The model of casuistry emulated by Jonsen and Toulmin did have a common morality and the justification for its normative force rested on God's creation of a natural order and God's revelation. In the model sketched by Jonsen and Toulmin, however, it is not clear how the paradigms are selected. In the past, the moral sense of the Roman Catholic Community played an important role in selecting the paradigms and defining them. At the very least there was a dialectical relationship between the community's moral sense and ranking of moral values and the paradigm cases of casuistry.

2. Description: Morphology and Taxonomy

One can see in medieval confessional practice different elements of a disciplinary matrix. Metaphysical commitments are often implicit in a disciplinary matrix (Grandy, p. 8–9). The casuistry to which Jonsen and Toulmin appeal often expressed the moral view of Catholic moral theology in the language of Aristotelian-Thomistic metaphysics. Aquinas, for example, speaks of action in the language of "substance", "accidents", and "essence" (Aquinas). While it may not always be clear what metaphysical commitments were involved, certainly in the context of the time one can conclude that there were certain realist metaphysics at work in Catholic moral thought and confessional practice.

These assumptions seem to be part of the formative background of Jonsen's notion of 'morphology'. The idea that a case has a 'core' needs further explication. What kind of core is it? It seems as though Jonsen is making a claim about the structure of the world, or at the very least, an assumption about how we know the world. There are strong metaphysical or epistemological assumptions lurking behind the talk of the description of the case when he speaks of a case as having an "invariant structure" (Jonsen, p. 301). Jonsen and Toulmin fail to address the possibility that, even if a 'core' does exist, we may lack the ability to know what that core is or agree on what the correct description of it should be. In a morally pluralistic society some may not even see a moral issue where others do. One thinks, for example, of recent discussions about the use of baboon livers for transplant to humans with Hepatitis B. For some the use of the livers was a moral controversy while others found it difficult to see a moral problem.

The choice of a description of an act not only affects its morphology but also its taxonomy. The use of the taxonomy depended on the description and evaluation of moral dilemma at hand. The description of the case is a crucial evaluative tool. If a case is 'lined up' from a different perspective it may look very different for the evaluative eye. For example, one can evaluate, morally, the management of PVS patients in at least five different ways.[2]

3. Kinetics:

The third element of the structure of casuistry is that of 'kinetics'. Here, as in the book, the Jonsen-Toulmin model addresses the question of how one is to link together the case at hand with the appropriate paradigm case and render a judgment about the dilemma or controversy.

In their history Jonsen and Toulmin have failed to give an adequate account of the important role of confessors in the practice of casuistry; that is, to the role of confessors in selecting and applying paradigms to the cases before them. Lateran IV prescribes:

The priest is to be discerning and careful, so that like a skillful doctor he can apply wine and oil [Lk 10:34] to the wounds of the injured person, diligently asking for the circumstances of the sinner and of the sin, through which he can *prudently* understand what advice he ought to give, and what sort of remedy to apply trying various things to heal the sick person (Denzinger & Schonmetzer, #813, emphasis added).

Jonsen and Toulmin miss the importance of training confessors to be 'prudent' men who will properly select the paradigmatic case that will address the moral problems before them.

'Prudence' has a much different meaning for the medieval Christian than for the person of the modern and contemporary, Western world. The medieval Christian sense of 'prudence' is important to this model of casuistry.

In a contemporary understanding 'prudence' is frequently seen as rational self interest. The medieval understanding of prudence was grounded in the Aristotelian *virtue* of phronesis which was an intellectual virtue required by the other virtues (NE 1144 b17–1145 a6; 1178 a16–19). It was not a moral virtue but the ability to be practically wise (Sorabji, p. 205). However, to be morally virtuous one needed to be practically wise (NE 1144 a22 – b1). Phronesis is the exercise of right choice in particular cases, *in light of more universal knowledge* (Book 6, Ch 1). Cicero translated the Aristotelian term 'phronesis' as 'prudentia' and spoke of it in moral terms (Cicero, I, 43). For St. Thomas prudentia was one of the four cardinal virtues which was "knowledge of what should be done and what avoided" and which guided reasoning about what ought to be done (II–II 47, 5; I–II 47aa. 1–16). The prudent man, in the world of medieval casuistry had a Christian sense about how one ought to act. This concrete, particular moral sense shaped his judgment about which cases should be considered as paradigmatic in analyzing the cases presented and how new dilemmas and controversies should be resolved. This understanding of prudence is not one abstractly concerned with self-interest.

It is interesting to note that for the Jesuits, the most famous practitioners of casuistry, prudence was one of the most admired virtues. Prudence, in the language of St. Ignatius Loyola, was the virtue of 'discerning love'. Ignatius uses the language of "prudens caritas" and "discreta carita" interchangeably in the Constitutions of the Society (Ganss, #582, and footnote #2, pp. 260–261). His usage of 'prudence' and 'discretion' connoted the language of the discernment of spirits developed in the *Spiritual Exercises* (Loyola, No. 176, 328). Prudent agents are guided, in making choices, by discrete charity which impels them to choose the better course after all the circumstances have been considered. The root of this discrete charity is the interior law of charity described by St. Paul in his *Letter to the Romans*.[3] The presence of the Holy Spirit gives the agent the grace to carry out what the law requires (Ganss, #134; Aquinas, I–II, q. 90; 92 a.1).

As one recovers the notion of prudence, as part of the practice of casuistry, one can grasp the centrality of a particular moral vision and sensibility that was and is crucial to the practice of Catholic casuistry. The contextual embeddedness of medieval casuistry raises the question as to whether or not, in a secular age, fragmented by many different moral sense, and which eschews the guidance of the Holy Spirit, casuistry can be practiced on a medieval model.

4. Authority:

In his development of the 'kinetics' of casuistry Jonsen addresses briefly how it is that this model of casuistry deals with cases about which there is divided opinion. He also speaks about 'authorities', 'strict opinion'. Such language raises an important issue about the role of 'authority' in the practice of casuistry.

In the medieval practice of casuistry 'probabalism' emerged as a central way to resolve emerging moral dilemmas.[4] In the development of probabalism there were three central factors: 1) the role of conscience, 2) the role of authority, and 3) their relationship one to the other. In making moral decisions the medieval mind had to reconcile a number of sources of moral authority. There were codes of law and sacred books. There were individuals who *were* authorities, in the sense of experts concerning morality (theologians), and those *in* authority (e.g. confessors, bishops) who had the juridical power to render final judgments about moral controversies (See, Flathman). For example, one can view the discussion of probabalism, so important to medieval casuistry, as a discussion of proper authority. One can also recall the role of juridical authority in the casuistical debates about abortion.[5] The conceptual question for contemporary bioethics and moral philosophy is determining who is the moral authority today. We live in a morally pluralistic society in which moral authority is grounded in individual agents. Jonsen, in the later article, seems to put faith in the notion that there are those who can be considered as authorities (experts). One need not be a "guru" to be the prudent expert according to Jonsen (p. 306). However one does need experience and the "ideals that makes possible good judgment" (p. 306). The confessors of Roman Catholic casuistry possessed both juridical authority and the authority of being experts. The new priesthood of the bioethicist, however, must rely on knowledge alone; that is, he must know the ideals of good judgment.

5. Summary:

The transformation of classical casuistry into a model of secular reasoning requires more than Jonsen and Toulmin seem willing to admit. They must assume that there is a common morality and that it has normative force. In the absence of the interpretative structures of moral authority (confessors, popes, councils), Jonsen and Toulmin must make certain metaphysical and epistemological assumptions about the structure of cases and the ability to know them. Also, this model, like any model, must make initial assumptions about moral rationality; that is, that it is case oriented and that there are certain canonical ideals which allow us to know good judgment from bad (Jonsen, p. 306). Indeed feminist writers, among others, have raised important questions about our understandings of moral reason and the issues that are placed on the moral agenda (Carse; Gilligan).

One is led to wonder if Jonsen and Toulmin have not chosen the wrong analogue for secular casuistry. Perhaps they should have used the casuistry of jurisprudence in which there are structures *in* authority to interpret cases. However, even this analogue fails in that secular morality relies primarily on the authority of moral agents not of the state.

THE POSSIBILITIES OF CASUISTRY IN THE CLINICAL SETTING

In spite of the difficulties with the Jonsen and Toulmin model, a cased based reasoning is still possible for clinical ethics. The shape of such reasoning will be very different from the Catholic casuistry of Jonsen and Toulmin. A secular casuistry for the clinic will also be more limited than that for which Jonsen and Toulmin hope.

To understand the possibilities for secular casuistry one must understand the necessary conditions for a model of case based reasoning. A minimal condition for secular casuistry is that there is some shared moral sense, (both a set of moral values and a common ranking of those values), among moral agents. The model of casuistry which Jonsen and Toulmin seek to transpose to the secular context has an identifiable moral framework with a clear set of moral values. The difficulty for a secular version of this model of casuistry is that in a morally pluralistic culture one cannot assume there exists a coherent set of shared moral values. A practice of casuistry in clinical bioethics will require some common moral sense. Without such a sense it will not be possible to reach a resolution of moral controversies. In fact, without such a sense clinical, secular casuistry will not even be able to *identify* a case.

G. E. M. Anscombe has argued that actions are not "bare particulars" which can have a single description. Rather they are the subject of many descriptions (Anscombe). A physical action of killing can be described morally as 'murder', 'self-defense', 'retribution', or 'unintended side effect'. When people share a common moral framework and ranking of values they share a language for discourse. The potential then exists that cases can be identified and resolved.

The Jonsen and Toulmin approach to casuistry assumes that there is a common morality and, implicitly, that this morality has a normative function. In short they do not take moral pluralism seriously. How one should understand pluralism in one's explanation of morality is a topic that need not be explored at this point. However, it seems that a model of casuistry must take into account the existence of such pluralism for it will serve to test the extent and limits of the paradigms deployed by a secular casuistry.

In examining the possibilities of a secular casuistry one needs to take into account, along with moral pluralism, the nature of 'agreement' and 'disagreement' in moral judgment for not all agreements (or disagreements) are equal. For example, men and women may come to agree on a particular course of treatment for very different reasons. The importance of this observation bears upon the ability of casuistry to generate a structure of paradigm cases. While men and women may reach an agreement about a particular case where all involved agree on that a particular decision should be made.

The strength of the agreement will depend not only on the resolution of the case but the reasons for it. The power of an agreement is limited by the extent to which men and women share the same moral reasons. The ability to generalize beyond a particular case, and develop a taxonomy of paradigm cases, will depend upon the extent to which reasons are shared. Pointing to a phenomenon of agreement, whether on the National Commission or in the clinic, tells us very little about the ability to generate a structure for this model of casuistry. One must look beyond the surface to grasp the strength of the agreement.

An alternative model for a secular casuistry which would prove more helpful is the model suggested by Baruch Brody (Brody, 1988). The virtue of this model of casuistry is that it avoids the implicit metaphysical commitments about cases, and the epistemological commitments about paradigms and analogies which are essential to the Jonsen and Toulmin model. Brody's model of casuistry relies on intuitions we have about particular cases. It attempts to take pluralism seriously and give a general account of how resolutions might be reached in that the model moves to organize these intuitions into a coherent system of beliefs about the moral world (a moral 'theory'). This model allows one to understand why certain judgments are made. The model must still rely on a shared moral sense but it does give a mechanism by which to test the limits of moral judgments and explore the reasons for them. The strength of this model is also its limit. The model of casuistry will work only insofar as men and women share similar moral intuitions and rankings of values. In a context with diverse moral points for view the possibility for successful casuistry will be limited.

CONCLUSION

Priests are authorized to perform certain sacred rites and roles in different religious traditions. In turn they need certain knowledge by which they learn how to perform the sacred rites. In some faiths priesthood is hereditary while in others it is open. In all cases one must learn in order that one perform roles and rituals properly.

Jonsen's later article, which builds on the book, describes the priesthood of bioethics. It is not a hereditary priesthood; rather it is one that is open to all. But, candidates must be trained in the ideals of good judgment; that is, they must have the knowledge of maxims, arguments, and circumstances which allow them to fit each unique case into the taxonomy. This sounds suspiciously like the role of the priest in confessional practice as described earlier in the words of the Fourth Lateran Council. The priest is to be "discerning and careful", "diligently asking for the circumstances of the sinner and of the sin". It is through the circumstances that he can *"prudently* understand what advice he ought to give, and what sort of remedy to apply" (Denzinger & Schonmetzer, #813, emphasis added). This model of secular casuistry not only has a priesthood, but it also has a 'faith' in the metaphysical, moral, and epistemological commitments required to by this model work. However, when such commitments are explicitated the priesthood may find itself with a very small congregation as the faithful may go elsewhere. Yet without these commitments the 'agreements' of case analysis become a 'slight of hand' like the healings of some televangelists.

NOTES

[1] Baruch A. Brody (1988) offers a very different model of casuistry than do Jonsen and Toulmin. The model he offers will be explored in the section on the possibilities of casuistry.

[2] In a recent article Baruch Brody (1992) has been analyzed five different ways that PVS patients have been discussed: 1. As patients who are really dead; 2. PVS patients will die without artificial feeding and hydration. These treatments should be deployed as one would other treatments; 3. As being supported by life-sustaining therapy that is futile; 4. that the standard consensus on surrogate decision making cannot be applied; 5. PVS patients are not persons and should have only a low priority in the allocation of resources (Brody, 1992).

[3] "They show that what the law requires is written on their hearts..." Romans 2:15.

⁴ Probabalism holds that, in a case of practical doubt, a probable opinion may be followed even when the contrary opinion is more probable. It employs the principle that a doubtful law does not oblige.

⁵ There had been lively discussion among the casuists as to whether or not a fetal craniotomy could be preformed if it was therapeutic for the life of the mother. Many had interpreted some of the older casuists to hold the opinion that when the life of the mother was threatened an abortion could be preformed. However in a series of opinions beginning in 1889 the Holy Office of The Inquisition said that it was not "safe" to teach in Catholic schools that a craniotomy necessary to save the mother's life was lawful (Denzinger and Schonmetzer, n. 1889).

REFERENCES

Aristotle: 1984, *Nicomachean Ethics*, W. D. Ross (tr.), in *The Complete Works of Aristotle*, J. Barnes (ed.). Princeton University Press, Princeton.

Arras, J. D.: 1991, 'Getting down to cases: The revival of casuistry in bioethics', *The Journal of Medicine and Philosophy* 16, 29–51.

Anscombe, G. E. M.: 1979, 'Under a description', *Nous* 13, pp. 219–234.

Aquinas, T.: 1948, *Summa Theologica*, Christian Classics, Westminster, Maryland.

Beauchamp, T. and Childress, J.: 1989, *Principles of Biomedical Ethics*, Oxford University Press, New York.

Brody, B. A.: 1988, *Life and Death Decision Making*, Oxford University Press, New York.

Brody, B. A.: 1992, 'Special ethical issues in the management of PVS patients', *Law, Medicine & Health Care*, 20, 104–115.

Carse, A.: 'The 'voice of care': Implications for bioethical education', *The Journal of Medicine and Philosophy*, 16, 5–28.

Cicero: 1913, *De Officiis*, W. Muller (trans.), Cambridge University, London.

Daniels, N.: 1985, *Just Health Care*, Cambridge University Press, New York.

Denzinger, H. and Schonmetzer, A.: 1963, *Enchiridion Symbolorum*, Herder, New York.

Engelhardt, Jr., H. T.: 1986, *The Foundations of Bioethics*, Oxford University Press, New York.

Engelhardt, Jr., H. T.: 1991, *Bioethics and Secular Humanism: The Search for a Common Morality*, SCM Press, London.

Flathman, R. E.: 1982, 'Power, authority, and rights in the practice of medicine' in *Responsibility in Health Care*, George Agich (ed.), D. Reidel Publ. Co., Dordrecht, pp. 105–126.

Ganss, G.: 1970, *The Constitutions of the Society of Jesus*, The Institute of Jesuit Sources, St. Louis, MO.

Gilligan, C.: 1982, *In A Different Voice: Psychological Theory and Women's Development*, Harvard University Press, Cambridge.

Grandy, R.: 1983, 'Incommensurability: Kinds and causes', *Philosophica*, 32, 8.

Jonsen, A. and Toulmin, S.: 1988, *The Abuse of Casuistry*, Oxford University Press, New York.

Jonsen, A.: 1991, 'Casuistry as methodology in clinical ethics', *Theoretical Medicine*, 295–307.

Kuhn, T.: 1970, *The Structures of Scientific Revolutions*, (Second Edition), University of Chicago Press, Chicago.

Loyola, Ignatius: 1976, *The Spiritual Exercises*, Institute of Jesuit Sources, St. Louis, MO.

Lyotard, J. F.: 1984, *The Postmodern Condition: A Report on Knowledge*, G. Bennington and B. Massumi (trs.), Manchester University Press, Manchester.

MacIntyre, A.: 1981, *After Virtue*, University of Notre Dame Press, Notre Dame.

Masterman, M.: 1970, 'The nature of a paradigm', in *Criticism and the Growth of Knowledge*, I. Lakatos and A. Musgrave (eds.) Cambridge University Press, London.

Pascal, B.: *The Provincial Letters*, 'Letter X'.

Pellegrino, E. and Thomasma, D.: *A Philosophical Basis of Medical Practice*, Oxford University Press, 1981.

Singer, P.: 1979, *Practical Ethics*, Cambridge University Press, London.

Sorabji, R.: 1980, 'Aristotle on the role of intellect in virtue', in *Essays on Aristotle's Ethics*, A. Rorty (ed.), University of California Press, Berkeley.

Veatch, R. M.: 1981, *A Theory of Medical Ethics*, Basic Books, New York.

Part X
Cultural Diversity and Bioethics

CAN ETHNOGRAPHY SAVE THE LIFE OF MEDICAL ETHICS?

BARRY HOFFMASTER

Westminster Institute for Ethics and Human Values, 361 Windermere Road, London, Ontario, Canada N6G 2K3

Abstract—Since its inception contemporary medical ethics has been regarded by many of its practitioners as 'applied ethics', that is, the application of philosophical theories to the moral problems that arise in health care. This 'applied ethics' model of medical ethics is, however, beset with internal and external difficulties. The internal difficulties point out that the model is intrinsically flawed. The external difficulties arise because the model does not fit work in the field. Indeed, the strengths of that work are its highly nuanced, particularized analyses of cases and issues and its appreciation of the circumstances and contexts that generate and structure these cases and issues. A shift away from a theory-driven 'applied ethics' to a more situational, contextual approach to medical ethics opens the way for ethnographic studies of moral problems in health care as well as a conception of moral theory that is more responsive to the empirical dimensions of those problems.

Key words—medical ethics, bioethics, ethnography

INTRODUCTION

A decade ago Stephen Toulmin published his well known article, "How Medicine Saved the Life of Ethics" [1], in which he claimed that renewed attention to moral problems in medicine had rejuvenated the moribund discipline of ethics. Even if the correctness of Toulmin's analysis is granted, the salvaging of ethics by medicine has been short-lived because the patient has, regrettably, had a relapse. Two symptoms of the patient's critical condition have been recorded. First, Peterson, in reviewing a recent textbook in medical ethics, tellingly captures the barrenness of its theoretical approach. He describes articles intended to impart an "understanding of underlying ethical principles" and "skill in critical analysis" as lacking "substance" and observes that the introductory section on ethical foundations is "insufficiently related to the rest of the book" [2]. These defects do not reflect a lack of expertise or diligence on the part of the editors; rather, they are unavoidable because they are endemic to the prevailing 'applied ethics' approach to moral problems in medicine.

Second, Baron has observed that "practicing clinicians often feel let down by bioethics" [3]. The enchantment cast by exposure to the concepts and jargon of a new field has dissipated. Yet although the spell of the philosophical incantations has worn off, the problems that confront clinicians stubbornly persist. Baron attributes the disappointment of clinicians in part to their own unrealistic expectations, but adds that it is also a function of

... the extent to which bioethics as a discipline doesn't seem to be in possession of the realities of practice. Bioethicists tend to leave the 'facts' of clinical medicine to the doctors; their task is then to apply elegant and compelling arguments drawn from first principles of ethics... to these undisputed and indisputable facts. Unfortunately, when the relationship between clinical medicine and bioethics is conceived... [in this way], the result is a very sterile discourse [3].

The culprit here, too, is the regnant conception of medical ethics as 'applied' moral philosophy. In moral philosophy factual matters are prescinded in favor of constructing rational defenses of general principles and organizing these principles into a consistent theoretical system. The assumption behind the view that medical ethics is 'applied ethics' is that the resulting moral system can yield determinate solutions for real moral problems. The failure of this assumption is largely responsible for the parlous state of orthodox medical ethics.

The uncritical manner in which 'applied ethics' has been adopted as *the* way of approaching moral problems in medicine and the emerging discomfiture with 'applied ethics' reflect an underlying ambivalence about the function of moral philosophy. On one side is the view that moral philosophy should have something productive to say about actual moral issues. Sidgwick, for example, conceives the aim of a moral philosopher to be "... to do somewhat more than define and formulate the common moral opinions of mankind. His function is to tell men what they ought to think, rather than what they do think...." [4]. Confidence that moral philosophy can in fact provide this kind of practical direction animates the enterprise of 'applied ethics'.

On the other side, though, are those who do not see practical guidance as a proper task for moral philosophy. Why, it can be asked, should moral philosophy be different from any other branch of philosophy? Epistemology does not tell us which of our particular beliefs are true and justified; aesthetics does not tell us how to paint a beautiful landscape [5]; and philosophy of science does not discover new laws of physics. Why, then, should moral philosophy be unique in having putative practical import?

A number of philosophers explicitly disclaim any such function for moral theory. Broad, for example, says:

We can no more learn to act rightly by appealing to the ethical theory of right action than we can play golf well by appealing to the mathematical theory of the flight of the golf-ball. The interest of ethics is... almost wholly theoretical, as is the interest of the mathematical theory of golf or of billiards [6].

Bradley describes as "a strangely erroneous preconception" the view that moral philosophy can answer the question, "How do I get to know in particular what is right and wrong?" [7]. In Bradley's view,

...there cannot be a moral philosophy which will tell us what in particular we are to do, and... it is not the business of philosophy to do so. All philosophy has to do is 'to understand what is,' and moral philosophy has to understand morals which exist, not to make them or give directions for making them [7].

And G. E. Moore agrees: "The direct object of Ethics is knowledge and not practice..." [8]. The weight of philosophical opinion, if anything, seems to be against regarding moral theory as a source or repository of practical directives [9]. But why is it that providing practical guidance is not a proper task for moral philosophy?

PROBLEMS WITH 'APPLIED ETHICS'

Before enumerating its shortcomings, what is meant by 'applied ethics' needs to be clarified. The object of these criticisms is not 'applied ethics' when that term is used in a catch-all way to refer to activities such as ethics rounds and consultations, the workings of ethics committees, and policy formation with respect to moral issues in health care such as the development of guidelines for 'do not resuscitate' orders. The target is not, in other words, all the morally charged activities that occur on the front lines of health care delivery. Rather, the target is 'applied ethics' in the sense of a philosophically based and motivated theory about how that front-line activity ought to be analyzed and conducted and how medical ethics ought to be taught. To put it this way, though, is misleading because it makes it appear as if there is a gulf between the practice of 'applied ethics' and the theory of 'applied ethics', and it suggests that only the theory of 'applied ethics' is awry [10]. The real culprit, however, is a philosophical approach that creates and sustains the impression that moral theory and moral practice are discrete.

An additional qualification is necessary. Work described as 'applied ethics' is not homogeneous in nature or quality. Many philosophers have made valuable contributions to our understanding of practical moral problems in health care as well as to the moral improvement of front-line activities in the delivery of health care. Those contributions are the result of highly nuanced, particularized analyses of cases and problems and an appreciation of the settings in which these cases and problems arise. So it is important to recognize that not everyone who does medical ethics adopts an 'applied ethics' approach and, indeed, that there has been a gradual, but progressive shift away from an 'applied ethics' model. Yet a more situational, contextual approach has not yet displaced the theory-driven conception of what medical ethics is and, more importantly, of how medical ethics is taught. Nor has it yet made medical ethics a more hospitable venue for social scientists. The criticisms that follow consequently should not be construed as an indiscriminate exercise in 'bioethics bashing'. But the movement away from a theory-driven approach to medical ethics needs a further push, one that opens the field to contributions from an even broader array of disciplines.

There are two kinds of criticism that can be levelled against 'applied' moral philosophy—internal criticism and external criticism. Internal criticism [11] aims to show that moral theory cannot succeed on its own terms. External criticism points out that moral theory cannot account for the phenomena of morality. Several familiar internal criticisms will be presented briefly before turning to external criticisms [12].

First of all, the principles standardly regarded as constituting the core of theoretical medical ethics—principles of autonomy, beneficence, non-maleficence and justice, for example [13]—are too general and vague to apply determinately to concrete situations. In any moral controversy the question of whether, and if so, how, a principle is to be brought to bear upon that dispute is itself contentious. As Frohock observes in his study of treatment decisions in neonatal intensive care units:

The cases themselves—their complexity, the severity of the problems—allow reasonable people to apply the same principles in different ways. This discretionary power, rather than disagreement on principle, is the main source of disputes over therapy in the gray zone... of treatment [14].

The substantive moral work occurs in determining how a principle might impinge upon a particular problem, but the resources for addressing that issue are external to the principles themselves.

Disparity between the abstract semantic formulations of principles and the particular empirical circumstances they supposedly govern is a consequence of the inherently general nature of language [15]. One manifestation of this disparity is the existence of 'essentially contested' concepts, that is, concepts "the proper use of which inevitably involves endless disputes about their proper uses on the part of their users" [16]. 'Applied ethics' might be rescued if it had some way of dealing with the 'essentially contested' concepts at its core, such as the notion of autonomy, but all it has to offer in this regard is the technique of conceptual analysis. Analysis can distinguish a number of different senses that a concept can have, and by exposing ambiguity and equivocation, it can make an important, albeit limited, contribution to practical morality. It cannot, however, resolve substantive issues because it cannot establish that one of these senses is what the concept 'really' means. In other words, although conceptual analysis can elevate a concept from the status of being 'radically confused' to the status of being 'essentially contested' [16, p. 180], it cannot go on to resolve the dispute in which that concept figures.

Take, for example, the controversy about whether a market in transplantable human tissues and organs should be permitted. Are bodily tissues and organs the kinds of things that can be owned and therefore bought and sold? Honoré, a legal commentator, points out that an analysis of the concept of 'things' is, in general, an inviting strategy for trying to decide questions of ownership:

> There is, clearly, a close connexion between the idea of ownership and the idea of things owned, as is shown by the use of words such as 'property' to designate both. We ought, apparently, to be able to throw some light on ownership by investigating 'things' [17].

This strategy is ultimately fruitless, though, as Honoré recognizes, because what lies behind the doctrine that one does not own one's body is not a more perspicuous understanding of what 'thing' means but a substantive moral judgment: "... it has been thought undesirable that a person should alienate his body, skill or reputation, as this would be to interfere with human freedom" [17, p. 130]. And, as Honoré also recognizes, conceptual analysis can neither produce nor defend such substantive judgments: "... it is clear that to stare at the meaning of the word 'thing' will not tell us which protected interests are conceived in terms of ownership" [17, p. 130].

Now it might be objected that this example undermines a critique of 'applied ethics' because Honoré's judgment about no ownership of the body rests on an appeal to human freedom, and that is simply to invoke one of the bedrock principles of 'applied ethics', namely, the principle of autonomy. But rather than undermining the critique, the example strengthens it because autonomy is itself an 'essentially contested' concept. Four senses of autonomy have been distinguished in medical ethics—autonomy as free action, autonomy as authenticity, autonomy as effective deliberation, and autonomy as moral reflection [18]. Given the complexity of the concept, how does one decide which senses are appropriate in given situations? Suppose that a patient's decision to refuse life-saving treatment is autonomous in two of the senses—it is, say, free and the result of effective deliberation—but it is not autonomous in the senses of being authentic and the product of moral reflection. What conclusion follows about whether the patient's decision should be respected? The answer to that question must turn on an assessment of underlying substantive considerations, not further refinement of the concept of autonomy.

Another internal difficulty with 'applied ethics' is that a multiplicity of principles are taken to be relevant to moral problems in medicine, but when two or more of these principles conflict, as they inevitably do in any serious moral quandary, 'applied ethics' offers no way of resolving the conflict. When the principle of autonomy is at odds with the principle of beneficence, say, how does one decide which principle prevails? Theoretical 'applied ethics' contains no hierarchical ordering of its principles and no procedure for 'weighing' or 'balancing' these principles against one another. A standard response is to retreat to even more rarefied theoretical air and contend that moral theories, such as utilitarianism or Kantianism, should be invoked when principles 'run out'. But even if such theories could provide determinate outcomes for moral problems, the same difficulty emerges at this level. When 'doing the greatest good for the greatest number' conflicts with 'not treating persons as means alone', how does one decide which theory prevails? Moral philosophy has yet to produce an accepted way of appraising rival moral theories [19].

A third internal difficulty is that 'applied ethics' is not helpful in addressing some crucial moral issues because these issues challenge assumptions upon which the theoretical edifice of 'applied ethics' is erected. Perhaps the most obvious examples are debates about the domain of morality. What moral status, and therefore what moral protection, do entities such as fetuses, anencephalic infants, animals, and the environment [20] have? The fundamentally rationalistic program of philosophical ethics embodies an answer to this question, namely, that morality protects all and only those beings capable of acting as rational agents, which in turn means all and only those beings capable of rational deliberation. This answer is not obviously correct, however. In response to a question about what makes life worth living, for example, one neonatologist interviewed by Frohock cites simply the ability of a child to smile at his or her parents [14, p. 13]. Thus the rationalist position needs to be defended, but there is a problem because whatever practical bite moral philosophy has in this regard is inadvertent—it is the result of how the overall project of doing moral philosophy proceeds, not of attending to the particular moral controversy in question. Inadvertent answers are not, of course, necessarily wrong, but their relevance needs to be established and their plausibility needs to be supported. Moral philosophy seems to have no way of mounting such a defense on its own terms, though. Because the rationalist answer emerges from the assumptions that ground moral theory, any attempt to defend it in terms of that theory would be circular. Some of the most troublesome questions in medical ethics consequently remain 'up for grabs' within the program of rationalist moral philosophy.

Turning to the external criticisms, there are a number of respects in which moral theory is blind to actual moral phenomena. To begin, 'applied ethics' does not appreciate the dynamic character of morality. Because 'applied ethics' takes morality to be an autonomous theoretical system under which the flotsam of human experience is subsumed, it cannot account for the flux in that experience. It therefore cannot answer three questions that are central to our understanding of morality: why only certain issues come to be recognized as *moral* problems; how moral problems get categorized or labelled; and how and why moral change occurs.

With respect to the first, why, for example, is *in vitro* fertilization a hot moral topic but not expensive microsurgery to reconstruct Fallopian tubes? How is it that some issues but not others come to be dubbed moral, and what is the upshot of conferring this appellation upon them? Inattention to this matter contributes to the almost indiscriminate way in which the rubric of morality is now being used. Fox has noted "a certain inflation in the public and professional notice being given to bioethical questions," which has produced "a kind of 'everything is ethics' syndrome" [21]. But when everything becomes ethics, the danger is that ethics becomes nothing.

Second, how is the phenomenon of moral labelling to be understood? The new reproductive technologies, for instance, can be regarded as either therapies for infertility or alternative means of reproduction, and those labels are not neutral because they carry different implications for who should have access to these technologies. Similarly, medically administered hydration and nutrition can be categorized as either basic human care or medical treatment [22], with different ramifications for the obligatoriness of providing artificial sustenance. But how is the appropriateness of such labels ascertained?

Finally, what induces and precipitates moral change? The salient moral issues of today are different from those of a decade ago, let alone a century ago. 'Applied ethics' nevertheless remains impervious to moral change; it will deal with whatever moral problems are brought before it, assuming that the identification and characterization of moral problems themselves raise no difficulties and that moral problems can be dealt with independently of the contexts in which they arise. Yet how, when, and what issues become 'moral' are vitally important questions. Disputes about the moral status of infants and animals, for example, are not new. To cite only one instance, consider Whewell's reaction in 1852 to Bentham's hedonistic theory of value:

I say nothing further of Mr Bentham's assumption... that because a child cannot *yet* take care of itself, and cannot converse with us, its pleasures are therefore of no more import to the moralist than those of a kitten or a puppy. We hold that there is a tie which binds together all human beings, quite different from that which binds them to cats and dogs;—and that a man, at any stage of his being, is to be treated according to his human capacity, not according to his mere animal condition [23].

Now why is it that the animal rights movement, and the charge of speciesism against those who believe in "a tie which binds together all human beings quite different from that which binds them to cats and dogs," has recently gained such currency? The kinds of arguments upon which proponents of animal rights rely have been around for a long time, so what explains their newfound popularity? Answering that question requires a broader conception of morality than the identification of morality with philosophical moral theory, a conception that situates morality in social, cultural, and historical milieus. Even the abortion controversy—perhaps the most intractable of moral disputes—can be illuminated by locating it culturally and historically as Ginsburg's ethnographic study of abortion activists in Fargo, North Dakota admirably does [24]. In sum, charting the ebbs and flows of morality in action would provide important insights into what morality, as it is actually lived, is all about.

In addition, taking medical ethics to be 'applied' moral philosophy simply does not fit the experience of those who have spent time in clinical settings. The reports of moral problem solving by philosophers who have clinical experience, in particular, Caplan's conclusion about two cases he relates—that "ethical theory would have been the wrong place to turn for a solution to the issues under consideration"—raise a daunting challenge to defenders of 'applied ethics' [25]. To skeptics who continue to maintain that reading and thought experiments are adequate substitutes for experience, one can merely reply, "Go and see for yourself." But until they have done that, deference ought to be given to those who have done the reading and acquired the experience.

The only surprise about these criticisms is the steadfastness with which they are ignored. Two factors contribute to that resistance. One is how central the orthodox theoretical approach to morality is to the concerns of contemporary analytic philosophy. The motivation for conceiving of morality as an independent, consistent system of theoretical norms is, as G.E. Moore recognized, the allure of moral knowledge. As long as epistemology continues to dominate philosophy, moral philosophers will pay obeisance to it. Unfortunately, the philosophical project of generating moral knowledge ultimately displaces morality from the experience in which it is grounded. Moreover, how the transformation of practice into theory is supposed to occur and why it is necessary to remain mysterious. Theoretical systematization supposedly transubstantiates the water of moral experience into the wine of moral knowledge. Although this ritual may continue to play a role in the cathedral of academia, it remains peripheral to the outside world. There moral experience retains its primacy, and it is in appreciating the primacy of experience and in providing ways of understanding and guiding that experience that ethnography can be useful.

The other factor is that there remains no enticing alternative to conventional philosophical moral theory and thus to 'applied ethics'. What is needed is a different brand of moral theory, one that is more closely allied with and faithful to real-life moral phenomena. Ethnography has a vital role to play in developing a more empirically grounded theory of morality.

HOW CAN ETHNOGRAPHY HELP?

Ethnographic studies [26] can make important critical and constructive contributions to our understanding of morality. On the critical side, the results of ethnographic investigations challenge both the dogmas that pervade the received view of medical ethics and the underlying philosophical model upon which 'applied ethics' is predicated. On the constructive side, ethnographic work reveals that morality must be understood contextually, and once that broader, more realistic perspective is adopted, it provides a sobering appreciation of the prospects for moral reform. Examples of ethnography's critical contributions will be provided first.

Perhaps the most prominent tenet of orthodox medical ethics is its individualism, manifested by the field's conspicuous preoccupation with the notion of autonomy [27]. Both Bosk's study of the training of surgeons [28] and Frohock's study of treatment decisions in neonatal intensive care units [14] suggest that an individualistic orientation does not capture the realities of clinical practice. Frohock, for example, observes, "Humanness is not assigned to the individual baby but to the family of the baby" [14, p. 98], and Bosk, in commenting on a case presentation by a pediatric surgeon, notes, "Interesting here is the surgeon's definition of his client as the entire family network" [28, p. 134].

In the same vein Frohock contends that the language of rights, the rhetoric of individualism, does not fit a neonatal intensive care unit: "...contemporary moral terms like rights are inappropriate in a neonatal nursery. The new and, in many cases, unique medical events require a different moral vocabulary. The introduction of harm in place of rights is a reconstruction of the language of medical staffs" [14, p. x]. Not only does the language of harm more accurately portray the moral ethos of neonatal intensive care units, it also is superior because it is responsive to situational particularities:

The proposition that harm is to be avoided whenever possible can constrain actions, and because of its contextual qualities it can do so more credibly than a right-to-life shield. Not claiming the identify of all life forms when none can be established, a harm constraint can instead be concerned to disclose how particular forms of life are harmed and to draw constraints on action that are sensitive to differences among life forms [14, p. 205].

'Life forms' does not refer to aliens from outer space, but to embryos, fetuses, anencephalic newborns, and infants who are profoundly neurologically impaired—entities whose moral status remains problematic. What is objectionable about a rights-based approach is that it crudely assimilates these various 'life forms' to a single moral category and treats them uniformly regardless of significant differences that might exist [29]. A harm-based approach, in contrast, can respond to relevant differences among these 'life forms', differences that, moreover, cannot be exhaustively stipulated in advance or identified theoretically (as proposed definitions of 'humanhood' try to do [30]) but can only be discovered through experience.

In addition to disputing some of the substantive claims of 'applied ethics', social science investigations challenge its underlying philosophical model in two ways. On the one hand, they call into question the existence of a rational method for moral decision making, and on the other hand, they raise doubts about the independence of morality.

The assumption that there is a rational method of moral decision making is, for example, belied by the research of Lippman and Fraser on the decision making of women after genetic counseling [31]. Lippman and Fraser set out believing that women would make decisions about whether to run the risk of conceiving a defective child by being good utility maximizers. Women would, that is, meld the probabilities communicated to them by genetic counselors with their own assessments of the value of likely consequences and then adopt the course of action that maximized expected utility. The work of Lippman and Fraser was, in other words, designed to assess the adequacy of genetic counseling in terms of an influential philosophical method of moral decision making. What they discovered, to their surprise, is that women uniformly ignore the probabilities of alternative outcomes. They reduce the problem to two results—either I will have a defective child or I will not have a defective child. They then construct scenarios of what it would be like to live with a defective child, and if they think they could cope with the worst of these scenarios, they run the risk of conceiving a child who might be handicapped. Women who think they could not cope do not undertake that risk, and women who cannot make up their minds engage in 'reproductive roulette', that is, they have sexual intercourse using methods of contraception they know are insufficient.

What this research reveals is that actual moral decision making is situational—it is tailored to the demands of particular circumstances as well as the capacities and limitations of the persons enmeshed in those circumstances. Yet the decision making of these women appears to be an eminently reasonable way of responding to the pervasive uncertainties that confronted them, even if it does not conform to the dictates of an influential philosophical model [32].

Another example of the adaptability and flexibility of moral practice occurs in neonatal intensive care units when a seriously ill baby is allowed to 'declare itself': "The child declares himself one way or the other (makes the decision for the doctor by taking a dramatic turn for the worse and dying, or by showing signs of improvement that clearly justify aggressive therapy)" [14, p. 62, 33]. Here health care professionals and parents defer to the baby, who, of course, is in no position whatsoever to 'decide'. But again, such temporizing seems perfectly reasonable in the necessitous and uncertain circumstances in which it is used.

Frohock's study also provides examples of how the momentous decision of whether to treat aggressively or allow to die can be replaced by smaller, incremental decisions. A physician might decide not to increase the settings on a ventilator, to use a more 'gentle' antibiotic, or not to check some laboratory values, for instance [14, pp. 48–49]. A theoretically-oriented 'applied ethics', though, tends to focus on 'big' decisions and portray them in binary terms. By doing so, it ignores pragmatic strategies for responding to moral problems such as biding time, compromising, or cycling through competing values [34].

What these examples suggest is that moral decision making is a search for a feasible, appropriate response to a particular situation, not the application of a method that in virtue of its extreme generality is insensitive to the particularities that structure the situation. There is no homogeneous, unifying conception of rationality in morality or anywhere else for that matter, including that veritable paragon of rationality—science. The theoretical disposition of 'applied ethics' renders it insensitive to the flexible ways in which human beings actually handle moral problems. Moral decision making is more a matter of coming up with creative, responsive solutions than it is trying to apply a philosophical formula. Moral rationality consequently assumes diverse, sometimes protean forms. By investigating how moral problems are perceived and constructed by those whom they affect and how these individuals handle those problems, and by assessing these attempted resolutions, ethnographic studies can discover the disparate forms of moral rationality and stake out, in at least a provisional way, the limits of those forms.

Ethnographic studies also suggest that the widespread concern to demarcate morality—to provide criteria that will distinguish morality from, say, prudence, etiquette, and law—is misplaced. Positivist philosophers of science have thought it important to distinguish 'genuine' science from pseudo-science—alchemy, for instance—in the hope that the resulting criteria would have something of consequence to say about dubious pretenders to the mantle of science such as psychoanalysis. This concern with demarcation has infected philosophical morality and impels the repeated and persistent, but ultimately futile, attempts to define morality [35]. The concern also pervades 'applied ethics' and surfaces every time someone insists on addressing only the ethical issues and not the associated economic, legal, social, or policy issues in an area.

The attempt to delimit morality assumes that morality can be isolated in two ways. One is that morality can be detached from practice and exhaustively represented in a consistent theoretical system. The other is that the discrete theoretical system of morality is independent of other discrete theoretical systems such as the law. The work of Bosk and Frohock casts doubt on both independence assumptions. Bosk concludes with respect to the inculcation of norms in young surgeons, "The moral and ethical dimensions of training are not bracketed from all other concerns but are instead built into everyday clinical life" [28, p. 190]. In a hospital or out of a hospital, morality is part-and-parcel of everyday life. Even if the thread of morality could be extracted intact from the fabric of experience, examining that naked thread would produce an incomplete and distorted impression of morality. What needs to be understood is how morality is woven into the experiences and the lives it helps to constitute.

Frohock's comment about the impact of difficult moral decisions is equally telling: "Pain and guilt, rather than immorality and irrationality, plague therapy decisions" [14, p. 115]. Parents of a seriously impaired newborn, in other words, do not see the problems they have to wrestle with as paradigmatically moral or search for distinctive moral reasons to support their decisions. They know they have a hard, perhaps tragic, decision to make, and they want to do the best or the right thing (not the *morally* right thing). They agonize over these decisions, but they do not ask themselves whether a proposed course of action would be immoral or irrational, or whether a reason that appears persuasive to them is really a valid *moral* reason. The philosophical desire to portray such decisions as exclusively and prototypically moral is not faithful to the phenomena. Rather than trying to impose an *a priori* conception of morality on these decisions, theorists should pay more careful attention to how parents themselves perceive the problem and work their way through it. Recognizing the artificiality of the borders of 'applied ethics' leads to worries about the separation of the moral, on the one hand, from the social, the cultural, and the political, on the other. As Fox points out, the circumscription of the moral is most evident in discussions of neonatal intensive care units:

> Bioethical attention has been riveted on the justifiability of nontreatment decisions. Relatively little attention has been paid to the fact that a disproportionately high number of the extremely premature, very low birth weight infants, many with severe congenital abnormalities, cared for in NICUs are babies born to poor, disadvantaged mothers, many of whom are single nonwhite teenagers. Bioethics has been disinclined to regard the deprived conditions out of which such infants and mothers come as falling within its purview. These are defined as *social* rather than ethical problems... [21, p. 231; emphasis in original].

But why is it that ethics stops at the door of the neonatal intensive care unit? What, other than a concern for the theoretical purity of the discipline or an ideological commitment to the individual, prevents a genuine *moral* questioning of the conditions that contribute to the need for neonatal intensive care units?

Ethnographic studies thus reveal *prima facie* tensions between the realities of clinical practice and the dictates of philosophical medical ethics. On which side does the burden of proof reside? The burden, it seems to me, falls to philosophers, who themselves acknowledge it in their recognition that moral theory begins in and ultimately must be tested by practice. It is hard to find a philosopher for whom practice does not remain the touchstone of the adequacy of moral theory. Aristotle provides the clearest statement of this position, but it is prominent in many others, including Sidgwick, the arch-proponent of philosophical moral theory [36]. The Kantian stream in moral philosophy might be regarded as an exception, but even Kant insisted that his view merely elaborated common moral opinions. The methodology of moral philosophy itself recognizes a presumption in favor of the legitimacy of moral practice; departures from moral practice, therefore, need to be vindicated on more than the *a priori* grounds provided by 'applied ethics'.

Another advantage of paying attention to moral practice is the appreciation of context that results. Moral philosophy and its adjunct 'applied ethics' movement run into trouble because they remain stubbornly acontextual. To borrow an example from Toulmin, who in turn borrows it from John Wisdom, the question, "Is a flying boat a ship or an airplane?" is, in the abstract, hopelessly sterile [37]. When a context is supplied—ought the captain of a flying boat to have an airline pilot's license, a master mariner's certificate, or both?—the issue comes into focus and pertinent arguments can be advanced. Reading books and engaging in arm-chair speculation do not supply contexts, however. The contexts in which the moral problems of medicine arise can be appreciated only by becoming immersed in clinical settings, as ethnographers do.

In fact, the most important constructive contribution of ethnographic studies is that they give content to the vague notion of 'putting moral problems into context'. One of the best illustrations is Anspach's study of a neonatal intensive care unit [38]. Anspach found that consensus around moral principles does not remove controversy about the treatment of seriously ill newborns because doctors and nurses frequently disagree about the prognoses for these infants. Her work is an investigation of the forces that shape these discrepant prognostic judgments.

Anspach shows that prognostic conflicts result from the different 'modes of knowing' that doctors and nurses have. Doctors, who spend relatively little time with these infants, base their conclusions on physical findings, the results of diagnostic tests, and the literature of medical research. Nurses, who spend concentrated and extended periods of time with these infants, rely on their personal and social interactions with the infants. There is, as a result, a clash between what Anspach calls "the perspectives of engagement and detachment" [38, p. 227].

What comes out of Anspach's study for our purposes is the recognition that a contextual understanding of morality has at least three facets. One facet concerns individual particularities. A decision about treatment must take into account, obviously, the idiosyncracies of an infant's condition—factors such as this specific infant's diagnosis, medical history, and family situation.

Institutional structure is a second facet. Institutional structure has two main impacts in a neonatal intensive care unit. On the one hand, decisions about treatment can be affected by considerations such as how long an infant has been in the unit and whether infants with similar problems have been in the unit recently and if so, what the outcomes for them were. On the other hand, as Anspach discovered, how work is divided and organized within a neonatal intensive care unit can influence how issues are perceived and how judgments are made. Because, for instance, attending physicians visit the unit for short periods of time, because house staff rotate through the unit on short cycles, and because physicians in tertiary care institutions often have research interests, doctors are both organizationally and personally detached from these infants and their parents. The information they rely on to formulate a problem and resolve it is the technical and, in the case of research findings, general information they possess and value. Because nurses, in contrast, are intimately and continuously involved with these infants, they are organizationally and personally attached to them. Their perceptions of problems and their responses to them consequently are a function of their social interactions with the infants for whom they care.

A third facet emerges when it is pointed out, as Anspach does, that the 'technological cues' of the doctors and the 'interactive cues' of the nurses are not valued equally: "... the interactive cues noted by the nurses are *devalued data*" [38, p. 229; emphasis in original]. Why is that? There are several components to the answer, but the point for our purposes is that all the answers are embedded in the social and cultural background that structures the definition and delivery of health care. One obvious answer ties the devaluation of the nurses' data to prevailing gender roles in society. Another answer, given by Anspach, does not roam quite so far. It appeals to the history of diagnostic technology and locates newborn intensive care in a 'postclinical' medical culture, that is, a culture in which the science of medicine has displaced the art of medicine. In such a scientistic culture, the 'subjective' information of the nurses is no match for the hard, 'objective', technical data of the doctors.

Understanding the problem posed by life-and-death decision making in neonatal intensive care units requires an appreciation of all three facets. Morality cannot be severed from the social, cultural, and historical milieus in which this decision making occurs; nor can morality be identified with any single facet [39]. Morality suffuses this context, and the philosophical attempt to isolate it and treat it as an autonomous, independent theoretical system simply fosters a picture of morality that is artificial, distorted, and ultimately desiccated.

A contextual understanding of morality does not mean that there is no room for moral theory or philosophizing about morality, simply that the nature of that theory must be different. Anspach's research poses obvious and difficult epistemological questions, in particular, the question of whether it is possible to integrate or synthesize the "partial and selective visions of reality" [38, p. 230] possessed by the nurses and doctors. Moral theory needs to take a new turn, however, and be responsive to the issues posed by morality in context.

One of these issues is that, once morality is understood contextually, impediments to moral reform loom large. As Anspach recognizes, any attempt to improve the quality of life-and-death decisions about seriously ill newborns must recognize that "to the extent that decisions cannot be extricated from the social organization of the intensive care nursery, broader changes in that organization may be necessary" [38, p. 230]. Jennings, commenting on the relationship between ethics and ethnography, explains why a recognition of the institutional and structural constraints on behavior should make one less sanguine about the prospects for reform:

Bioethics generally has a simple, not to say simpleminded, notion of what can be done to bring about social change—in most cases to reform professional practice to bring it more into line with established ethical obligations and principled responsibilities. The strategy is: argument, agreement through rational persuasion, and education. The commitment to this polis model runs very deeply in philosophy, and the applied ethics movement of the past twenty years has been premised on the belief that it can be brought out of the confines of the academy and introduced into the conduct of public and professional life.... But what social scientific studies have done, and neonatal ethnography is particularly insistent in this regard, is to force ethicists to pay more attention to the cultural, institutional, and psychological preconditions for social and behavioral change [40].

If moral theory is to be truly practical, it must come to grips with realities that its theoretical preoccupation has so far caused it to steadfastly ignore.

OBJECTIONS

Philosophers have, in the past, been tempted by ethnography but have not succumbed to it. Toulmin cites Descartes' repudiation of his own fascination with history and ethnography on the ground that "[h]istory is like foreign travel. It broadens the mind, but it does not deepen it" [37, p. 340, 41]. Whereas ethnographers and historians collect facts that fascinate and titillate, philosophers, in Descartes' view, do the real work of extracting the general principles behind these facts. This sharp division of labor that consigns ethnographers and historians to the menial task of assembling raw material for philosophers begs the question, however, because it assumes the correctness of the philosophical model of morality that drives 'applied ethics'.

Understood differently, though, there is something to Descartes' objection. Bosk appreciates the danger it points to: "...ethnography...runs the risk of being dismissed as 'merely description'... [but] doing ethnography is always both a theoretic and a theoretically motivated activity..." [28, p. 17]. The challenge this objection raises is to account for the theoretical side of ethnography. If one sees theory in purely formal, *a priori* terms, that, of course, is a hopeless task, and it is no surprise that 'merely' empirical enquiries are deprecated. But once such a narrow conception of rational inquiry is abandoned, the way is open for alternative understandings of theory.

One aim of a critique of 'applied ethics' is precisely to clear the field for new understandings of theory and practice, in particular, understandings that locate theories *in* our practices rather than *underlying* them [42]. What might this involve? A review of a recent study of crime notes the author's ethnographic approach of "turn[ing] away from enquiry after alleged 'background' causes to look at the surface, the 'foreground,' 'the lived experience' of crime," focusing on "many individual human beings," and "cast[ing] doubt on reconstructions of aggregates" [43]. The reviewer points out that the author

...sets out to ask not, 'Why did you do it?' but 'How?' As he says, 'The social science contains only scattered evidence of what it means, feels, sounds, tastes, or looks like to commit a particular crime.' The evidence he has gathered gives some of the answers, after all, to the question 'Why?' [43].

Accounting for the theoretical side of ethnography requires an understanding of this transition from 'How?' to 'Why?' That understanding will not be arrived at in global, *a priori* terms. Rather, it will be embedded in and relative to particular domains of inquiry and particular contexts. The tasks that ethnography poses for philosophers and social scientists, therefore, are twofold: to do moral ethnography and thereby to make more productive contributions to practical ethics; and to develop the moral theory implicit in ethnographic studies.

But, it might be objected, there are daunting practical barriers to that kind of genuinely interdisciplinary work. Just as one must be cognizant of the structural and institutional constraints within neonatal intensive care units, so one must be cognizant of the structural and institutional factors that separate ethnography and ethics. Even if ethnography could save the life of medical ethics, ethnographers have little incentive to do so, particularly if they work in research-oriented universities that prize mainstream contributions to their disciplines. Matters such as degree and licensing requirements, employment prospects, research funding opportunities, tenure and promotion criteria, and formal and informal reward systems militate against research that is non-traditional, innovative, and risky. Although less so in anthropology, ethnography is already marginal enough in sociology. An ethnography that contributed to ethics or bioethics rather than sociology would most likely be ignored if not resisted. On the philosophical side, the opportunities and incentives for rigorous, empirically informed research are equally meager. So who actually would do this work?

In addition, it could be argued that there is a fundamental, and ultimately fruitful, opposition between the humanities and the social sciences. To train philosophers to be good ethnographers could make them bad philosophers; to train ethnographers to be good philosophers could, in turn, make them bad ethnographers.

The latter worry assumes the legitimacy of the disciplinary boundaries, as well as the exaggerated demarcation between facts and values that helps to sustain those boundaries, that is being challenged here. Once philosophy is disabused of its preoccupation with the *a priori* and the pristinely rational, there is no reason to regard philosophy and ethnography as incompatible. And once ethnography finally sheds its vestigial pretension to 'positivist' science, it can become comfortable with investigating the values and the moralities that inform and guide so much of human experience and that make life meaningful. As they exist today, ethics and ethnography probably are at odds. But reconceived in ways that are responsive to the lives and problems they study, ethics and ethnography are not only complementary, they are indispensable to one another.

The practical impediments to this kind of work are, nevertheless, real and should not be underestimated. The way to begin removing them, though, is to make a case for the importance of the work and to recognize its practical value. How to do the research will have to be learned through experience. Bosk describes himself as "a medical sociologist, an ethnographer of medical action," and he admits, "As such, my primary research techniques in this highly technological world are primitive" [44]. That might be all that can be expected now, but approaches will mature as this kind of work evolves and develops. As well, it might be prudent at present for only those with security to embark on such risky research ventures. But a caution appropriate to individuals should not be extended to a general domain of inquiry. What must be offered are support for and recognition of the work that has been done, and encouragement to continue and develop this line of research. The need for and the merits of the results ultimately will dismantle the barriers. To expect deeply engrained, long entrenched obstacles to disappear before the work is undertaken is no more than the counsel of despair.

CONCLUSION

It is time to admit the terminal condition of 'applied ethics'. As Hare has conceded,

... if the moral philosopher *cannot* help with the problems of medical ethics, he ought to shut up shop. The problems of medical ethics are so typical of the moral problems that moral philosophy is supposed to be able to help with, that a failure here would be a sign either of the uselessness of the discipline or of the incompetence of the particular practitioner [45].

It would be rash to suggest that all practitioners of 'applied ethics' are incompetent. So what's a moral philosopher with practical leanings to do? If ethnography is simply incorporated into the prevailing 'theory-centered' [37, pp. 338–341, 41, p. 11] approach to philosophy, that is, the concentration on "abstract, timeless methods of deriving general solutions to universal problems" [37, p. 341], the attempt to rescue medical ethics with ethnography will be futile. Ethnography needs to be integrated into a revivified practical philosophy [46] that, in the words of Toulmin, is interested in the 'oral', the 'particular', the 'local' and the 'timely' [37, pp. 338–341, 41, pp. 186–192].

In a union of ethnography and 'theory-centered' philosophy, social scientists could continue to be no more than servants to philosophers—collectors of the facts that philosophers need to 'apply' their theories. And as long as medical ethics remains 'theory centered', philosophers working in the field will continue to do what the Chinese, in a marvelously apt phrase, call "playing with emptiness" [27, p. 339]. A more viable approach to medical ethics, and a more robust and productive role for both social scientists and philosophers, depends upon the alignment of ethnography with a 'recovered' practical philosophy, that is, a conception of the discipline that recognizes that contributions to "the reflective resolution of quandaries that face us in enterprises with high stakes" [37, p. 352] are not 'applied philosophy' but philosophy itself [37, p. 345, 41, p. 190]. But unless that happens, moral philosophers should heed the advice of Hare and shut up their clinical shops.

Acknowledgements—This paper began as a presentation to the Medical Sociology Section of the American Sociological Association. Later versions were read to the Canadian Humanities Association and the Canadian Philosophical Association and at a conference on "Moral Philosophy in the Public Domain," sponsored by the University of British Columbia. I would like to thank all those who reacted to it on these occasions. I am particularly grateful for the comments I received from Valerie Alia, John Arras, Paula Chidwick, Peter Conrad, Sharon Kaufman, Judith Swazey, Michael Yeo, and anonymous referees for the Canadian Philosophical Association and this journal.

REFERENCES

1. Toulmin S. How medicine saved the life of ethics. *Per. Bio. Med.* **25**, 740, 1982.
2. Peterson L. Review of *Bioethics* (Edited by Edwards R. B. and Graber G. C.). *N. Engl. J. Med.* **318**, 1546–1547, 1988.
3. Baron R. J. Dogmatics, empirics, and moral medicine. *Hastings Center Rep.* **19**, (1) 41, 1989.
4. Sidgwick H. *The Methods of Ethics*, 7th edn, p. 373. Dover Publications, New York, 1966. The seventh edition was originally published in 1907.
5. Philosophers have, however, recently begun talking about 'applied aesthetics'. The assumption apparently is that philosophers of art can have, *qua* philosophers of art, something meaningful to say about issues such as works of art should be purchased with public funds or what parts of the environment should be preserved for distinctly aesthetic reasons. See, e.g. Eaton M. *Basic Issues in Aesthetics*. Wadsworth, Belmont, CA, 1988.
6. Broad C. D. *Five Types of Ethical Theory*, p. 285. Routledge & Kegan Paul, London, 1930. Broad does concede, however, that moral theory may have "a certain slight practical application" insofar as "it may lead us to look out for certain systematic faults which we should not otherwise have suspected...."
7. Bradley F. H. My station and its duties. In *Ethical Studies*, p. 128. Liberal Arts Press, New York, 1951.
8. Moore G. E. *Principia Ethica*, p. 20. Cambridge University Press, Cambridge, 1903.
9. William James falls into this camp, too. Of the choice between life and good, on the one hand, and death and evil, on the other, James says, "From this unsparing practical ordeal no professor's lectures and no array of books can save us." In James' view a moral philosopher has no advantage in making practical decisions: "The ethical philosopher..., whenever he ventures to say which course of action is the best, is on no essentially different level from the common man." James W. The moral philosopher and the moral life. In *The Writings of William James* (Edited by McDermott J. J.), p. 629. The Modern Library, New York, 1967. Melden's comment that "it would be a mistake...to identify the moralist with the moral philosopher" likewise separates the moralist's practical task of giving advice from the philosopher's theoretical interest in exploring the question of what counts as a good moral reason. Melden A. I. On the nature and problems of ethics. In *Ethical Theories*, 2nd edn, p. 2. Prentice-Hall, Englewood Cliffs, NJ, 1967.
10. A distinction between theory and practice and the concomitant gulf that emerges when theory is understood as it has been in medical ethics exist in other 'applied ethics' bailiwicks as well. A review of a recent book in environmental ethics, for example, distinguishes between 'mainline' environmental ethics and 'nonprofessional' environmental ethics and says that elements of the latter, the deep ecology movement and the Earth First! movement, for instance, "are playing a major role at the practical level, where professional writing in the field is currently having little or no impact". Hargrove E. C. Review of Roderick Frazier Nash. *The Rights of Nature: A History of Environmental Ethics. Can. Phil. Rev.* **9**, 457, 1989. And a recent article on the role of theory in business ethics surveys the plethora of theoretical approaches in that discipline and concludes that "there is a serious lack of clarity about how to apply the theories to cases and a persistent unwillingness to grapple with tensions between theories of ethical reasoning." Derry R. and Green R. M. Ethical theory in business ethics: a critical assessment. *J. Bus. Ethics* **8**, 521, 1989.
11. The notion of 'internal criticism' is borrowed from the Critical Legal Studies Movement. Singer describes it as follows: "Internal criticism—criticism that uses a paradigm's criteria against the paradigm itself—merely shows that a certain theory does not do what it purports to do." Singer J. W. The player and the cards: nihilism and legal theory. *Yale Law J.* **94**, 60, 1984.
12. For a more extended criticism of the philosophical underpinnings of 'applied ethics', see Hoffmaster B. Morality and the social sciences. In *Social Science Perspectives on Medical Ethics* (Edited by Weisz G.), pp. 241–260. Kluwer Academic, Boston, 1990.
13. See, e.g. Beauchamp T. L. and Childress J. F. *Principles of Biomedical Ethics*, 2nd edn, Oxford University Press, New York, 1983.
14. Frohock F. M. *Special Care*, p. 51. University of Chicago Press, Chicago, 1986.
15. For a beautiful example of the limited and crude capacity of language to capture particular objects and experiences, see the discussion of Libanius' description of a picture in the Council House at Antioch in Baxandall M. *Patterns of Intention*, pp. 2–5. Yale University Press, New Haven, 1985.
16. Gallie W. B. Essentially contested concepts. *Proceed. Aristotelian Soc.* **56**, 169, 1955–56.
17. Honoré A. M. Ownership. In *Oxford Essays in Jurisprudence*, First Series (Edited by Guest A. G.), p. 128. Clarendon Press, Oxford, 1961.
18. Miller B. L. Autonomy and the refusal of lifesaving treatment. *Hastings Center Rep.* **11**, (4), 22, 1981.
19. The most recent and most influential candidate for such a method is Rawls' notion of reflective equilibrium. Rawls J. *A Theory of Justice*, Harvard University Press, Cambridge, 1971. The attraction of reflective equilibrium is easy to understand because it seemingly allows moral philosophers to have their cake and eat it, too. In theory, principles are revised in light of 'considered judgments' and 'considered judgments' are amended in light of principles until an equilibrium is attained. But close examination reveals, I think, that principles are an idle cog in this justificatory process. Elsewhere [12] I have tried to show that it is the considered judgments, not the principles, that do the work in reflective equilibrium.
20. For a discussion of this issue with respect to the environment, see Stone C. D. *Earth and Other Ethics*. Harper and Row, New York, 1987.
21. Fox R. C. *The Sociology of Medicine*, p. 229. Prentice-Hall, Englewood Cliffs, NJ, 1989.
22. Mirale E. D. Withholding nutrition from seriously ill newborn infants: a parent's perspective. *J. Pediat.* **113**, 262, 1988.
23. Whewell W. *Lectures on the History of Moral Philosophy in England*, p. 226. Parker, London, 1852. (Emphasis in original.)
24. Ginsburg F. D. *Contested Lives*. University of California Press, Berkeley, 1989.
25. Caplan A. L. Can applied ethics be effective in health care and should it strive to be? *Ethics* **93**, 312, 1983. See also Morreim E. H. Philosophy lessons from the clinical setting: seven sayings that used to annoy me. *Theor. Med.* **7**, 47, 1986.
26. Ethnography is not easy to define, but the following characterization fits the studies discussed in this paper: "The data of cultural anthropology derive ultimately from the direct observation of customary behavior in particular societies. Making, reporting, and evaluating such observations are the tasks of ethnography.... An ethnographer is an anthropologist who attempts...to record and describe the culturally significant behaviors of a particular society. Ideally, this description...requires a long period of intimate study and residence in a small, well defined community, knowledge

of the spoken language, and the employment of a wide range of observational techniques including prolonged face-to-face contacts with members of the local group, direct participation in some of the group's activities, and a greater emphasis on intensive work with informants than on the use of documentary or survey data." Conklin H. C. Ethnography. *Int. Ency. Soc. Sci.* **5**, 172, 1968. The term 'ethnography' is, as this account makes clear, closely allied with anthropology. Comparable research in sociology goes by many names, including 'fieldwork' and 'qualitative social research.' See Lofland J. and Lofland L. H. *Analyzing Social Settings*, 2nd edn, p. 3. Wadsworth, Belmont, CA, 1984.

27. For a powerful criticism of this preoccupation with individualism and autonomy, see Fox R. C. and Swazey J. P. Medical morality is not bioethics—medical ethics in China and the United States. *Per. Bio. Med.* **27**, 336, 1984.

28. Bosk C. L. *Forgive and Remember.* University of Chicago Press, Chicago, 1979.

29. One is reminded here of the lawyers' refrain that 'the law is a blunt instrument'. One important difference between law and morality is that morality should escape this objection.

30. For one notorious attempt, see Fletcher J. Indicators of humanhood: a tentative profile of man. *Hastings Center Rep.* **2**, (5), 1, 1972.

31. Lippman-Hand A. and Fraser F. C. Genetic counseling: parents' responses to uncertainty. *Birth Defects: Original Article Series* **15**, (5C), 325, 1979. This is an interview study. Lofland and Lofland include 'intensive interviewing' of the sort used by Lippman and Fraser as one of the methods of qualitative social research. They define 'intensive interviewing' as "a guided conversation whose goal is to elicit from the interviewee rich, detailed materials that can be used in qualitative analysis" [26, p. 12]. Those are the kinds of materials Lippman and Fraser obtained, and their analysis of them was qualitative. For a longer discussion of the moral implications of the work of Lippman and Fraser, see Hoffmaster B. The theory and practice of applied ethics. *Dialogue* **30**, 213, 1991.

32. Lippman and Fraser would, I think, agree with this claim despite their repeated description of the decision making of these couples as non-rational or arational. They say: "...their [the couples'] behavior and their ways of formulating the other issues relevant to childbearing do follow logically when viewed as an attempt to limit or neutralize...uncertainty [31, p. 333].

33. For another description of this phenomenon, see Carlton W. *"In Our Professional Opinion..." The Primacy of Clinical Judgment Over Moral Choice*, p. 68. University of Notre Dame Press, Notre Dame, 1978.

34. For a discussion of the cycling strategy, see Calabresi G. and Bobbitt P. *Tragic Choices.* W. W. Norton, New York, 1978.

35. Wallace G. and Walker A. D. M. (Eds) *The Definition of Morality.* Methuen, London, 1970.

36. Sidgwick says: "I should...rely less confidently on the conclusions set forth in the preceding section, if they did not appear to me to be in substantial agreement—in spite of superficial differences—with the doctrines of those moralists who have been most in earnest in seeking among commonly received moral rules for genuine intuitions of the Practical Reason" [4, p. 384].

37. Toulmin S. The recovery of practical philosophy. *Am. Scholar* **57**, 349, 1988.

38. Anspach R. R. Prognostic conflict in life-and-death decisions: the organization as an ecology of knowledge. *J. Hlth soc. Behav.* **28**, 215, 1987.

39. The danger of a case-oriented approach to 'applied ethics' is that it becomes absorbed with the particularities of individual situations and thus never gets beyond the first facet. This danger is, for the most part, realized in the discussions of cases in Jonsen A. R. and Toulmin S. *The Abuse of Casuistry.* University of California Press, Berkeley, 1988. Broader background considerations are introduced in only their analysis of usury.

40. Jennings B. Ethics and ethnography in neonatal intensive care. In *Social Science Perspectives on Medical Ethics* (Edited by Weisz G.), pp. 270–271. Kluwer Academic, Boston, 1990.

41. Toulmin S. *Cosmopolis*, p. 33. Free Press, New York, 1990.

42. Levinson makes this point with respect to theories of constitutional law. See Levinson S. Law as literature. *Texas Law Rev.* **60**, 391, 1982.

43. Owen G. The pleasures of crime. *The Idler* **23**, 52, 1989, reviewing Katz J. *Seductions of Crime.* Basic Books, New York, 1988.

44. Bosk C. The fieldworker as watcher and witness. *Hastings Center Rep.* **15**, (3), 10, 1985.

45. Hare R. M. Medical ethics: can the moral philosopher help? In *Philosophical Medical Ethics: Its Nature and Significance* (Edited by Spicker S. F. and Engelhardt H. T. Jr), p. 49. Reidel, Dordrecht, 1977. Emphasis in original.

46. Dewey J. *Reconstruction in Philosophy.* Henry Holt, New York, 1920.

[30]

Intersections of Western Biomedical Ethics and World Culture: Problematic and Possibility

EDMUND D. PELLEGRINO

Culture and ethics are inextricably bound to each other. Culture provides the moral presuppositions and ethics the formal normative framework for our moral choices. Every ethical system, therefore, is ultimately a synthesis of intuitive and rational assertions, the proportions of each varying from culture to culture. There is also in every culture an admixture of the ethnocentric and the universal that is indissolubly bound to a particular geography, history, language, and ethic strain and is common to all humans as humans.

These shaping forces, the intuitive and rational, the ethnocentric and the universal, are in constant flux within cultures. The specific point at which a balance is struck will vary from culture to culture. When cultures interact, these moral balance points are disturbed. A complex matrix of value intersections results. Where these balance points will be reset in any particular culture is difficult to predict.

This is precisely the situation in contemporary biomedical ethics. In a world contracted in time and space by modern communications technologies, no people, however isolated or underdeveloped, can remain impervious to medical knowledge. Each culture is compelled to respond to both the potential advantages and the accompanying challenges to traditional values posed by humanity's new-found power over life, death, and procreation.

Whereas premature acceptance of these new technologies can threaten a culture's self-identity, premature rejection can deprive a culture of badly needed medical benefits. Each culture must decide how—and whether—to reconcile its own ethical system with what might be required to adapt to new medical technologies. This adaptation requires choosing what is congruent and rejecting what is incongruent with deeply held beliefs about the nature, meaning, and purpose of human life.

In biomedical ethics, this transcultural challenge is vastly complicated because medical science and technology, as well as the ethics designed to deal with its impact, currently are Western in origin. They are deeply ingrained with three sets of values distinctly Western—the values of empirical science, principle-based ethics, and the democratic political philosophy. Such values are often alien, and even antipathetic, to many non-Western world views.

The dominant characteristics of Western science, ethics, and politics are mutually supportive: Western science is empirical and experimental, pursuing objectivity and quantification of experience. Ultimately, it attempts to control nature to the greatest extent possible. Western ethics is analytical, rationalistic, dialectical, and often secular in spirit. Western politics is liberal, democratic, and individualistic and governed by law. Western science, ethics, and politics provide an environment that gives rise to and sustains the use of complex medical technol-

Edmund D. Pellegrino

ogies. As a result, it is difficult to divorce medical knowledge and the benefits it offers from the Western cultural and ethical milieu that support and sustain them.

Western values, however, may be strongly at odds with world views held by billions of other human beings. Those billions may be less inclined to an aggressive uncovering of the mysteries of nature and less obsessed with the need for experimental verification. Instead, they may be drawn more strongly by the spiritual and qualitative dimensions of life. Their ethical systems may be less dialectical, logical, or linguistic in character; less analytical, more synthetic, or more sensitive to family or community consensus than to individual autonomy; and more virtue based than principle based. In turn, their political systems may be more attuned to authority, tradition, ritual, and religion; more comfortable with and more responsive to the centralization of decision making; and more tolerant of social stratification and inequality.

Such divergences in value systems are often irreconcilable. Yet, as the power and influence of medical science and technology grow, these conflicting systems of belief will be drawn into more acute confrontation and conflict with each other. Only by dealing constructively with these conflicts can a nation enjoy the benefits of medical progress. Even more important, only in this way can we effect the transnational, transcultural cooperation necessary for the improvement of world health as a whole.

Such confrontations are visible at many technological, ethical, and cultural intersections. Some of these confrontations are more easily dismissed or neglected than others. In medicine, however, the issues are more urgent, less easily avoided, and more explicit than in other arenas. Moreover, disease has no respect for geographic or cultural boundaries. As the biosphere expands to embrace the whole globe, every nation has a stake in every other nation's health. For these reasons, the practical and conceptual questions of transcultural biomedical ethics are more sharply defined than in some other domains of knowledge.

The central problematic is the moral status of cultural autonomy. There would seem to be a prima facie obligation to respect cultural values that may differ from our own. Given even that prima facie obligation, we must nevertheless ask ourselves: What are the limits of cultural autonomy? Is the limit reached only when one culture forcibly imposes its values upon another? Is cultural ethical relativism the only valid moral posture? Are there morally valid and morally invalid cultures? Is there any foundation for a common morality by which different ethical systems may be judged and through which transcultural cooperative efforts can be transacted? Or does it follow, as some would argue, that the quest for a common substantive ethics is futile in a pluralist world society? Are conceptual clarity and procedural guidelines all that ethics can be expected to provide? Does it then follow that medical and biomedical ethics are, themselves, purely cultural artifacts and that there should be as many medical ethical systems as there are cultures?

A strong case can be made for cultural autonomy and the obligation to respect ethical systems alien to our own. Culture is a complex whole that summates the most fundamental beliefs of a people in art, language, literature, custom, and law. Culture is gradually assimilated into every individual's personal identity from the moment that person begins to become aware of his or her cultural milieu. Even if we reject or are rejected by the culture in which we are born and raised, interaction with that culture will mold our deepest beliefs about the meaning and purpose of our political, communal, social, and individual lives. To violate a person's

Western Biomedical Ethics and World Culture

cultural beliefs and practices is tantamount to assaulting his or her very humanity. To impose alien beliefs and practices on an individual or an entire society is to violate their humanity. Such violations are immoral. Human beings, whether as individuals or aggregates, are inherently entitled to respect; they possess an inviolable dignity.

To grant this premise, however, is not to sanction the absolutization of either personal or cultural autonomy. Although autonomy is to be respected, we must also recognize our interdependence—as individuals, cultures, societies, and states. The impact of medical technology cannot be contained within geographical or cultural boundaries. For that reason, absolutization of cultural autonomy is particularly dangerous in our use of medical knowledge. The impact of medical technology cannot be contained within geographic or cultural boundaries. Our capacities to prevent and cure illness, to forestall death, to control procreation, to modify genes, to improve the lifespan, and to ease disability have an enormous economic, political, and social impact on our world society.

Medical knowledge, like communication technology, makes the "global village" a reality. The central medical ethical issues we now face as individual countries are, or will shortly be, common problems. All countries want to take advantage of some feature of Western technology. Each will want to do so without compromising its own fundamental moral values. Yet what is accepted and what is rejected by one country has unavoidable effects on others. Cultural and ethical autonomy, therefore, must know some limit in the interest of world welfare.

The eradication of smallpox, for example, was not a Western but a world accomplishment. The science was Western. But if all nations had not cooperated in the massive vaccination of large populations, all would have continued to be at risk, just as all are at risk, even today, whenever a contagious disease appears anywhere in the world. In the same way, responses to ethical issues in one part of the world are felt elsewhere: Effective but expensive life-saving treatments are not given equal moral weight from one nation to another. "Salvageable birth weight" varies enormously among countries, as do such practices as infanticide, sterilization, and concern for the aged, infants, and children. Wealthy, organ-hungry countries can drain the organ supply of poorer countries by paying for organs. Wealthy nations can pursue clinical experimentation not permitted within their own borders by setting up camp in countries with less rigorous surveillance. Confidentiality, patient autonomy, and distributive justice are all interpreted differently in the professional mores of the world's physicians.

As we survey the spectrum of the world's moral perspectives depicted in this volume, we are struck simultaneously by the similarities and dissimilarities. The temptation is to concentrate on the extremes—emphasizing differences, which often fosters claims to cultural superiority, or emphasizing similarities, which sacrifices moral integrity to ethical relativism. These extremes must be resisted. It is essential to seek the middle ground in which some values overlap. In this "middle ground," we must seek compromises that can be made without losing the whole of one's cultural identity.

There is reason to expect that such a shared moral ground may be found on some of the issues confronting contemporary biomedical ethics. We may take some solace in the historical fact that all major ancient cultures have had guidelines for the use of medical knowledge. Hippocratic, Chinese, Arabic, and Indian physicians shared an ethic based in the primacy of the patient's welfare. Each recognized that medical knowledge is not proprietary like other commodities, that

Edmund D. Pellegrino

those who possess it have moral obligations of a special kind, and that some suppression of self-interest in the interest of the sick person is a moral requirement of ethical practice.

These ancient premises have a continuing influence today. They find concrete expression in the ethical precepts of the Declarations of Helsinki and Geneva, the Ethical Codes of the World Medical Association, the International Code of Medical Ethics, and the United Nations Principles of Medical Ethics, to name a few examples. Because they are shared across cultural systems, medicine and a concern for health are among the more accessible pathways for intercultural and transcultural discourse and cooperation. Physicians and other healthcare professionals can communicate in a common language across sociopolitical, historical, and cultural barriers that often isolate peoples from one another because all healthcare professionals have experience in the ways in which medical knowledge may impinge on deeply ingrained cultural beliefs. They can also recognize ways in which traditional medical mores can be subverted by political and economic philosophy.

Despite the fact that, in many cultures, the physician's authority remains largely undisputed, patient autonomy is slowly becoming a reality. The growth and expansion of political democracy, education, and economic power are eroding the benign authoritarianism that was for so long the hallmark of professional medical ethics worldwide. In more cultures than ever before, there is recognition of the moral rights of patients to participate in decisions that affect them, to protection of confidentiality, to humane treatment, and to access to healthcare. There is a long way to go before unanimity on these matters is achieved, but it is clear that older models of physician-dominated relationships are under scrutiny everywhere.

What emerges from the intersection of systems of medical ethics across cultural lines is a recognition of the need for and the possibility of some form of metacultural ethic that can ameliorate cultural relativism. In medical ethics, all ethical positions are not of equal moral status—regardless of how tightly bound they may be to a particular culture; for example, consider the nearly universal approbation for cooperative efforts of physicians who oppose the use of nuclear weapons and the condemnation of physicians who torture or experiment with prisoners of war. Even if violations of patient rights are tolerated in certain social and cultural settings, they are not tolerable in any common ethic of medicine. Growing recognition of the moral rights of patients, their special vulnerability as sick persons, and their dependency on the physician's knowledge constitute the empirical foundation of a morally defensible ethic of medicine. Those cultural systems that violate such norms cannot be given equal moral standing with systems that respect these norms, not because the cultural systems that support human and patients' rights are per se superior but because the protection of human rights is grounded in something more fundamental than culture—the deference owed to all human beings qua human beings. This is a norm by which every culture may be judged.

To be sure, the present idea of respect for the self-determination of patients originated in contemporary bioethics, which in its present form is a product of Western (largely American) conceptions of ethics. However, we must not forget that it has been only two decades since even Western medical ethics abandoned the stance of medical authoritarianism. It did so because it recognized that the duty of respect for the moral right of patient autonomy is grounded in the rights and moral claims all human beings have on one another. Patient self-determination

Western Biomedical Ethics and World Culture

happens to have been first emphasized by "Western" medical ethics, but it should be universally recognized because of its metacultural justification, not its propagation by Western medicine. The dignity of the human person is not something that can be continually asserted or denied. It transcends culture because it resides inalienably in what it is to be a human being.

Indeed, the problem in the West is now becoming how to mitigate the absolutization of patient autonomy. Some bioethicists now argue that the physician is a mere instrument in the hands of the patient, that the physician's personal moral beliefs should be divorced from his or her professional life, and that the patient's wishes must be respected. This idea applies to such cases as active euthanasia, assisted suicide, abortion, purchase of organs for transplantation, all forms of reproductive technology and surrogate parenthood, preservation of confidentiality, or the use of public sources of healthcare funding. This form of absolute ethical individualism ignores the duties we owe others as members of the human community. Left unchecked, it will destroy any sense of communitarian ethics, and it will subvert the conscience of the physicians in morally dangerous ways.

Clearly, the Western—particularly the American—form of biomedical ethics must resist the forces within its own culture driving it to absolute individualism and moral atomism of a socially destructive kind. It must go beyond the tendencies within its own cultural milieu and seek something morally more fundamental. It must sift through the conflicting values within democratic liberalism itself to identify those that have a morally valid foundation and those that do not. The physician must be recognized as a moral agent, as is the patient. The physician's moral beliefs cannot simply be set aside to satisfy the patient's demands. This question of balancing autonomy is a necessary part of any transcultural dialogue in medical ethics.

The ethics of medicine offers a fruitful point for beginning a larger cultural dialogue between and among the world's major cultures. The ends of medicine are more easily defined than the ends of human life. The functions of medicine derive from the needs of the sick person. These are easier to delineate than the more general needs of human beings as such for happiness or fulfillment. We cannot yet agree worldwide on a philosophical anthropology, but we probably can eventually agree on some philosophy of medicine and medical ethics suitable for resolving the dilemmas of medical progress if the dialogue is sustained and conducted with goodwill.

The ethical system of any culture is morally defensible because it is grounded in truths that transcend that culture; it is not morally defensible simply because it is the product of a particular culture. Respect for culture and ethics other than our own is the beginning of any intercultural dialogue, not its ending. The fact of cultural difference does not, as too many anthropologists have argued, necessitate absolute cultural relativism. Rather, it energizes the search for those ethical elements that transcend particular cultures.

Medical technology—and, parenthetically, political democracy—are reshaping the ancient edifice of medical ethics. As technology and democracy come into closer contact with other world cultural and ethical systems, they engender a dialectic and dialogue that is essential to the humane uses of medical knowledge. The wide variety of extant cultures and ethical systems notwithstanding, the emergence of a medical ethics based in certain features of our common humanity is possible and even likely.

As the transcultural dialogue in medical ethics continues, it should serve as an

Edmund D. Pellegrino

encouraging prototype for the larger dialogue between and among all cultural and ethical systems. This dialogue is needed if we are to find some metacultural set of moral values to which all may subscribe. This metacultural set of values mean the triumph of some "superior culture." Its validity will be based in what it is to be a human being—over and above the particular language, art, custom, or history of any one people.

The need to use medical knowledge humanely and within strict constraint can move us closer together or divide us further. Let us hope the dialogue continues and that medical ethics will serve to reemphasize our shared fate as human beings who are different yet similar.

Hastings Center Report, May-June 1996

Judging the Other
Responding to Traditional Female Genital Surgeries

by Sandra D. Lane and Robert A. Rubinstein

Western feminists, physicians, and ethicists condemn the traditional genital surgeries performed on women in some non-Western cultures. But coming to moral judgment is not the end of the story; we must also decide what to do about our judgments. We must learn to work respectfully with, not independently of, local resources for cultural self-examination and change.

Traditional female genital surgeries, often referred to as female circumcision, have been the source of enormous and bitter international controversy since the late 1970s. The debate often reaches an impasse between two well-meaning but seemingly irreconcilable positions: cultural relativism and universalism. The clash between these two approaches is an implicit obstacle in a great number of issues in bioethics, human rights, and social theory. In this paper we use female circumcision as a case study to examine how it may be possible to move beyond the current impasse.

Recent developments in bioethical theory have challenged the deductive model of ethical reasoning, which proceeds from abstract principles (as do both cultural relativism and universalism) to moral judgments. Casuistry, or contextual, case-based reasoning may consider moral principles, but does not proceed from them alone in a deductive process. Rather, contextual elements like historical and cultural issues, power relations, and responsibility are important factors to consider. It is in this regard that cultural relativism, at least descriptive relativism as explicated by Melford Spiro,[1] legitimates the examination of cultural data as an aid to understanding the practice of female circumcision. In this paper we argue that cultural relativism, even at its inception, did not mean an absolute refusal to engage moral questions and was, in fact, a moral response to the devaluation of non-European cultures by nineteenth century "Social Darwinists." As anthropologists we also argue that a critically important question in any moral debate is: Why is this issue the central question that bioethicists, feminists, and others are concerned with now? Female circumcision—like any issue subject to ethical debate—has, in addition to the fact of its practice, layers of symbolic meaning that lend heat to the debate.

Cultural Relativism and Moral Universals

The two apparently irreconcilable positions of ethical universalism and cultural relativism frame the debate about traditional female genital surgeries. The consequence of this framing is often an ideological impasse. Both ethical relativism and cultural relativism embrace the notion that groups and individuals hold different sets of values that must be respected. The two approaches derive, however, from different bodies of theory and from distinct historical roots.

Cultural relativism is complex, encompassing, on the one hand, questions of how much we can actually understand of other culturally based realities, and on the other hand, prescriptions for appreciating those diverse realities.[2] Spiro's typology of three types of cultural relativism—descriptive, normative, and epistemological—reflects this complexity and helps clarify why discussions of relativism are often frustrating.[3] On Spiro's account descriptive relativism simply implies an acknowledgement of the diversity of beliefs and behaviors across cultures; normative relativism implies an acceptance of each culture's moral judgments as reasonable for that culture; and epistemological relativism questions how one can even comprehend the "Other's" reality sufficiently to make an evaluative judgment. Cultural relativism as understood by contemporary American social theory began as a rejection of nineteenth century Social Darwinist theories that held European culture to be the pinnacle of evolution, and other cultures (especially pre-literate, so-called "primitive" cultures) to be examples of Europeans' living ancestors. The social milieu in the United States at the time was profoundly xenophobic, with waves of immigrants passing through Ellis Island. In this context, cultural relativism, as espoused by Franz Boas and his students Ruth Benedict, Margaret Mead, and Melville Herskovits, was a moral force for tolerance.[4] By insisting that cultural values and beliefs have meaning and must be understood within

---

Sandra D. Lane and Robert A. Rubinstein, "Judging the Other: Responding to Traditional Female Genital Surgeries," *Hastings Center Report* 26, no. 3 (1996): 31-40.

the context of each culture, it promoted a respect for diversity.

The American Anthropological Association maintained its official stance of relativism even in the face of the atrocities of the second World War and international political support for the doctrine of universal human rights. In 1947 the association's statement in response to the United Nations Declaration of Human Rights asserted, "Man in the Twentieth Century cannot be circumscribed by the standards of any single culture."[5] Although most anthropologists at the time appeared to consent to this cultural relativism, some rejected it. Julian Steward, a leading anthropologist of this period, wrote in the *American Anthropologist*,

> Either we tolerate everything, and keep hands off, or we fight intolerance and conquest . . . As human beings, we unanimously opposed the brutal treatment of Jews in Hitler Germany, but what stand shall be taken on the thousands of other kinds of racial and cultural discrimination, unfair practices, and inconsiderate attitudes found throughout the world?[6]

More recent theoretical developments in anthropology, including interpretive and postmodernist theory, have called attention to the epistemological issues involved in cross-cultural understanding. By focusing on the preeminence of culture in shaping perceived reality,[7] on the role of Western value judgments in contemporary social science,[8] and on the nature of power relations and resistance in everyday acts,[9] contemporary anthropologists have underscored the difficulties involved in developing adequate cross-cultural understanding. Such questioning can help us develop deeper, more nuanced understandings of cultural practices that are now the focus of ethical, legal, and moral debate.

Traditional female genital surgeries are one such locus of debate, in which the impasse between respecting cultural diversity and protecting basic human rights has become especially acute. Of the growing number of analyses by both philosophers and anthropologists, most conclude by calling for an end to the practice on the grounds that it is ethically wrong, though they may differ in what they understand the ethical failing to be.[10] The human rights scholar Alison Slack, for example, identifies two major opposing concerns: the absolute right of "cultural self-determination" and the right of the individual not to be subjected to a tradition or practice that might be harmful or fatal.[11] Slack's argument rests on the issue of consent, noting that the surgeries are performed on children who "have no say in the matter" (p. 470). And indeed because of low rates of education even adult women who voluntarily undergo the procedure cannot be considered truly informed about the deleterious complications of the custom. Anthropologist Robert Edgerton calls his colleagues to task for romanticizing pre-literate and peasant societies.[12] And Daniel Gordon argues that anthropology has failed professionally because it has not adopted a position of moral advocacy against female circumcision.[13]

Female Circumcision

Female circumcision denotes a set of traditional surgeries, usually performed in childhood, that remove part or all of the external genitalia and are conducted primarily on African and some Middle Eastern and Asian women. Most researchers of the custom have followed a typology that categorizes traditional female genital surgeries as circumcision, excision, and infibulation. *Circumcision proper* involves removal of the prepuce, which is also known in some Muslim countries as *sunna* circumcision. Removal of only the clitoral prepuce is very uncommon.[14] Even if the practitioner attempts to remove only the prepuce, careful surgical dissection of the prepuce from the glans clitoris is difficult, if not impossible, especially when many of these operations are performed on nonanesthetized children. *Excision* involves removal of part or all the clitoris and in some cases the adjacent parts of the labia minora; in *infibulation* or *Pharaonic circumcision* the clitoris and labia minora are removed and the anterior portion or more of the labia majora are removed and sutured together, covering the vagina except for a small opening. Robert Cook and a number of other authors have further adapted this system to add *introcision*, an operation to enlarge the vaginal opening that has been reported among Aboriginal Australian groups who also enlarge the male's penis with the practice of subincision.[15] While introcision and subincision certainly pose health risks, they differ considerably from the types of procedures found in many African and some Asian societies that are the topic of this paper.

Nahid Toubia, a Sudanese feminist and physician, suggests a clearer two-part scheme of classification that divides the procedures into reduction and covering operations.[16] Reduction operations include partial or total clitoridectomy, in some cases with excision of the labia minora. Covering operations (infibulation or Pharaonic circumcision) involve clitoridectomy, excision of the labia minora, removal of part of the labia majora, and approximation of the wound edges of the remaining labia majora, which heal to form a sheet of skin and scar tissue. The wound edges are held together while healing by suturing (often with indigenous thorn sutures) or by binding the girl's legs together for up to forty days. In some cases, an object such as a thorn is placed in the wound to maintain a small opening for the flow of urine and menstrual blood. The resulting "hood of skin" covers the urinary meatus and most of the vagina. Depending on the resulting size, the vaginal opening may need to be widened after marriage to allow sexual intercourse. Deinfibulation, or anterior episiotomy, to release the scar must be performed for childbirth. Women are then reinfibulated, or resutured, after childbirth.[17]

Epidemiology. Female circumcision is performed on an estimated 80 to 114 million women in twenty-seven Eastern and Western African countries, parts of Yemen, and scattered groups in India and Malaysia.[18] However, female circumcision has not been unique to Africa and Asia. To "cure" female nervousness and masturbation, clitoridectomy was performed on European and American women and girls during the nineteenth century and as recently as the 1940s.[19] The procedure has also been reported among African immigrants to Western countries.

Available data show that 85 percent of female circumcision worldwide involves clitoridectomy, while infibulation accounts for about 15 percent of all procedures.[20] Gordon suggested that female circumcision is decreasing in Egypt,[21] but this decrease appears to be restricted to the educated middle and upper classes. Studies conducted in Egypt in the late 1980s and early 1990s indicate that 99 percent of rural and lower-income urban women in and around Alexandria,[22] and over 80 percent of high school girls in Alexandria are circumcised.[23] In Sudan the 1989-90 Demographic Health Survey, which covered northern Sudan, reported 89 percent of women aged fifteen to forty-nine were circumcised: 82 percent by infibulation and the remainder by "intermediate," which is a modified form of infibulation, or by reduction operations.[24]

Health Effects. In a great number of cases the surgery is performed without anesthesia and without sterile instruments. The immediate adverse health effects include hemorrhaging, shock, infection, pain, urinary retention, and damage to the urethra or anus. Septicaemia, tetanus, and urinary infections result from the use of unsterilized instruments and/or unhygienic salves in treating wounds. Acute urinary retention may result due to fear of the pain of urinating through the open wound.

The range of long-term physical complications and health effects due to the procedures are considerably more severe with covering operations than with reduction operations, and include repeated urinary tract infections, urethral or bladder stones, excessive scar tissue formation, dermoid cysts, and obstructed labor. After infibulation the urinary meatus is covered by the "hood" of skin, making urination occur more slowly, which makes a woman more prone to urinary tract infection and to the formation of stones. Among infibulated women scarring and the need for an anterior episiotomy for childbirth, and frequently resulting tears, fistulae, and chronic pelvic infections, are likely contributors to infertility and the very high rates of maternal mortality in Sudan and Somalia.[25] Sexual and psychological problems include painful intercourse, diminished sexual response, depression, and anxiety.

Pelvic inflammatory disease from chronic infection and blockage of the fallopian tubes by scar tissue can cause infertility. In a study conducted in Khartoum Hospital, Hamid Rushwan found that infibulation is an important cause of pelvic inflammatory infection in northern Sudan.[26] Vesicovaginal fistulae and rectovaginal fistulae are disabling consequences of childbirth among Sudanese women.[27] These fistulae most often result from prolonged obstructed labor, in part due to the extensive scar tissue caused by infibulation.

Culture, Religion, Social Change, and Female Circumcision. Female circumcision is usually controlled by mothers, grandmothers, and other female kin; fathers and male relatives do not traditionally take part in the decision to circumcise or in the performance of the procedure. Circumcision is often cited as a necessary prerequisite for marriage, and there are numerous additional explanations for the practice. Many rural and poor urban Egyptians, for instance, say that if a girl is not circumcised her clitoris will grow long like a penis and thus removal of this potentially masculine organ makes a girl more completely female.[28] Perhaps the most important rationale for female circumcision is that because it is such an ancient and commonly practiced tradition, reduced or infibulated genitals are simply considered normal. Indeed, when Sudanese or Egyptian villagers have discussed the custom with female Western researchers, they have been shocked to discover that the female researchers have not themselves been circumcised.[29]

In areas where different ethnic groups live in close proximity, the tradition can be an important marker of group identity. Ellen Gruenbaum gives one such example in the Sudan,

---

Perhaps the most important rationale for female circumcision is that because it is such an ancient and commonly practiced tradition, reduced or infibulated genitals are simply considered normal.

---

where two Muslim ethnic groups, the Arabic-speaking Kenana and West African-origin Zabarma, live side-by-side in the Rahad Development Scheme.[30] Both groups acknowledge the Kenana's ethnic superiority, which is based on their Arab identity and on extensive infibulation that they practice. Although Zabarma undergo clitoridectomy, the Kenana refer derisively to them as "uncircumcised." As a result of this close contact, some Zabarma have begun to undergo infibulation rather than clitoridectomies, employing the Kenana midwife to perform the procedures.

Concerns with virginity, marriageability, and the husband's sexual pleasure are also commonly stated reasons for performing traditional female genital surgeries.[31] Infibulation provides physical evidence of virginity, and the diminution of a woman's sexual response caused by removal of clitoris and labia minora is valued because it is believed that she will then be much less likely to act in a manner that would compromise her family's honor. In contrast to the limiting effect of female circumcision on a woman's sexual response, the infibulated vaginal opening is believed to offer greater friction for the husband during sexual intercourse and is considered an enhancement to male sexual response.[32]

Also common is the belief that female circumcision is required by religion. The practice of female circumcision predates the advent of both Christianity and Islam as evidenced by a reference to it in a Greek papyrus in Egypt, circa 163 B.C.E.[33] In Egypt and Sudan, both Christians and Muslims,[34] and in Ethiopia, the Falashas, a Jewish group, have all circumcised young girls.[35]

Removal of the prepuce is a religious requirement for all Muslim male children, but is not deemed a requirement for female children by most Islamic scholars. Although it is not a practice of the majority of Muslims in the world, among those who do practice it female circumcision is nonetheless often considered to be legitimated by religion. Islamic law is based on the *Qur'an*, which Muslims believe to be the exact words of God as revealed to the Prophet Muhammad; the *Hadith*, which are the sayings and actions of the Prophet during his lifetime; and on the body of religious commentary, which in Sunni Islam has been elaborated in four schools of jurisprudence, *Shafi*, *Hanbali*, *Maliki*, and *Hanafi*. Female circumcision is not mentioned at all in the *Qur'an*. According to some scholars of *Hadith*, the Prophet Muhammad is reported to have said, "When you perform excision do not exhaust [do not remove the clitoris completely], for this is good for women and liked by husbands."[36] Yet the Prophet's reported advice on excision is based on a so-called "defective chain of narrators" in the oral tradition and is therefore considered by many scholars unreliable as evidence of the Prophet's statement. Despite this, in the writings of all of the schools of Sunni Islamic jurisprudence the notion that female circumcision is *religiously recommended* receives some support from scholars who base their opinions largely on custom and beliefs about the need to control female sexuality, rather than on the authority of the *Qur'an* or *Hadith*.

In Islam as practiced in everyday life, the association of religious ideas with female circumcision is evident in the colloquial terms used to describe the custom. The use of the term *sunna* (meaning to follow the tradition of the Prophet), implies that the custom is religiously ordained. Similarly, although the classical Arabic term for female circumcision is *khifad* (literally "reduction"), in colloquial Arabic it is popularly called *tahara*, referring to a ritual state of purity that is required for Islamic prayer.[37] In the bipolar opposition implied by the term *tahara*, genitals in their natural state—unexcised or uninfibulated—are ritually impure. In fact, in Egypt to ask if a woman is circumcised one asks, "*Inti mutahara?*" "Are you purified?" More recent Islamic developments in Sudan, however, may eventually decrease the practice of infibulation, or at least lead to less severe types of surgeries. Gruenbaum, for example, found that because of their belief that infibulation is not an Islamic requirement, Sudanese Islamic movement members advocate less severe forms of the procedure or even abandoning the practice entirely.[38]

In previous centuries Christian doctrine in Egypt also became concerned with female circumcision. Early in the seventeenth century, when Roman Catholic missionaries settled in Egypt, the Roman Catholic priests forbade female circumcision on the mistaken grounds that it was a Jewish custom.[39]

Some parents explained that now that the husbands become migrant laborers for years-long periods female circumcision is a protection against dishonor, since it is believed to calm women's sexual needs.

However, when the female children of the Roman Catholic converts grew up their male coreligionists refused to marry them, choosing instead non-Catholic wives. The College of Cardinals in Rome was forced to rescind its decision and allow traditional genital surgeries among Egyptian Catholics.

Recent social changes associated with development, particularly changes whose impact on women's lives has not been taken into account, have not always resulted in a decrease in the practice. Gruenbaum describes how economic changes associated with development increased women's economic dependency on men, which caused them to focus on maintaining "their marriageability and to prevent divorce by keeping husbands sexually and reproductively satisfied."[40] The resulting economic insecurity made it extremely unlikely that parents would risk leaving their daughters uncircumcised. Interviews conducted by Sandra Lane in rural areas near Alexandria, in Alexandria itself, and in Cairo indicate that the practice of female circumcision is being modernized, but not necessarily abandoned. Many parents who can afford to are choosing to have their daughters' surgeries performed by physicians, with local anesthesia and less risk of infection. Some parents explained that now that the husbands become migrant laborers for years-long periods female circumcision is a protection against dishonor, since it is believed to calm women's sexual needs. Similar reasoning was offered by parents who pointed out that now girls stay longer in school and that women are forced by economic circumstances to work outside the home. These developments make complete chaperonage impossible and thus female circumcision is thought to offer protection.

The Debate Historically

Colonial governments unsuccessfully opposed female circumcision in Kenya during the 1930s and in Sudan during the 1940s. Yet the worldwide debate on the custom did not really begin until the 1970s. Traditional genital surgeries were known and had been widely studied in anthropology at least since Bruno Bettelheim's 1955 psychoanalytic analysis of the indigenous genital alterations. Yet even in the 1960s such surgeries were studied in the context of cultural relativism, with no moral judgment attached to their analysis. A number of developments—unrelated to female circumcision—in Europe and the United States in the late 1960s and early 1970s imbued the debate with its current passion, at least from the Western perspective. African and Arab women have found much of this Western discourse denigrating and reflective of Eurocentric preoccupations with sex, individualism, and other concerns valued in Western societies.

One of the first developments was Masters and Johnson's 1966 publication of *Human Sexual Response*, establishing the centrality of the clitoris in female orgasm and debunking Freud's notion of the mature vaginal orgasm. Feminists, particularly in the United States, linked their aspirations for autonomy and self-determination with control over their sexuality, and rejected notions that women's genitals were shameful, ugly, and dirty: at a National Organization for Women conference in 1973, for example, Betty Dodson's slide show consisting of close-up photographs of women's vulvas received a standing ovation. The artist Judy Chicago created *The Dinner Party*, which consisted of thirty-nine ceramic plates depicting her artist's rendering of the genitals of famous women throughout history. It is not an exaggeration to say that by the late 1970s the clitoris became a metaphor for women's power and self-determination.

As with many social movements, the anti-circumcision crusade has had a charismatic leader. Fran Hosken was traveling in Africa during 1973 when a chance remark about female circumcision literally changed the direction of her life. She writes, "When I began to realize the magnitude and the horror of the problems I was dealing with, I could not stop, or I would not be able to live with myself."[41] Subsequent to this epiphany, Hosken began lobbying the World Health Organization and numerous other international agencies, wrote extensively about the custom for scientific and popular journals, and began a newsletter that she continues to publish.

She is to be credited for compiling much of what is known about the epidemiology of female circumcision around the world. Largely as a result of Hosken's efforts, in 1979 the World Health Organization and the Sudanese government cosponsored an international seminar, "Traditional Practices Affecting the Health of Women and Children," which was concerned predominantly with female circumcision. Unfortunately, the way Hosken characterizes the cultures and the people who practice female circumcision, which she calls mutilation, is often seen as intolerant and insensitive by the very people whom she has sought to help. Thus, Hosken has been a catalyst for both awareness and polarization.

Hosken has had a critical impact on the semantics of the debate. Traditional female genital surgeries have often been referred to in English as "female circumcision," a term that we use in this paper. As Hosken and later activists argue, in the sense of being analogous to male circumcision, this is inappropriate. The anatomical structures removed in female circumcision are much more extensive than those removed in male circumcision. Because mutilation implies removal or destruction without medical necessity, persons working toward abolishing these traditional operations refer to them as "female genital mutilation."

By the 1980s female circumcision was condemned widely in the Western popular and scholarly press, variously labeled as a "crime of gender," "torture," "barbarism," "ritualized torturous abuse," etc. Reports of female circumcision being practiced among African and Asian immigrants to Western countries have led to a variety of legislative and legal responses. Parliaments in the United Kingdom, Sweden, and the Netherlands have passed legislation prohibiting female circumcision.[42] In France, traditional practitioners and parents from eighteen immigrant families have been brought to trial as a result of performing traditional female genital surgeries.[43] In October 1993, Representative Patricia Schroeder introduced a bill before the U.S. Congress to ban female circumcision in the United States (H.R. 3247). The Canadian College of Physicians and Surgeons drafted a policy statement barring Ontario doctors from performing female circumcision.[44] In both the United States and France, women from Nigeria and Mali have requested political asylum to avoid forced circumcision for themselves or their daughters.[45]

Arab and African Women Respond

An important caveat, however, is that many members of societies that practice traditional female genital surgeries do not view the result as mutilation. Among these groups, in fact, the resulting appearance is considered an improvement over female genitalia in their natural state. Indeed, to call a woman uncircumcised, or to call a man the son of an uncircumcised mother, is a terrible insult and noncircumcised adult female genitalia are often considered disgusting.

In interviews we conducted in rural and urban Egypt and in studies conducted by faculty of the High Institute of Nursing, Zagazig University, Egypt, the overwhelming majority of circumcised women planned to have the procedure performed on their daughters.[46] In discussions with some fifty women we found only two who resent and are angry at having been circumcised. Even these women, however, do not think that female circumcision is one of the most critical problems facing Egyptian women and girls. In the rural Egyptian hamlet where we have conducted fieldwork some women were not familiar with groups that did not circumcise their girls. When they learned that the female researcher was not circumcised their response was disgust mixed with joking laughter. They wondered how she could have thus gotten married and questioned how her mother could have neglected such an important part of her preparation for womanhood. It was clearly unthinkable to them for a woman not to be circumcised. Although all of the urban women and men with whom we spoke were aware that in other countries women were not circumcised, many lower class urban women expressed puzzlement that Westerners consider female circumcision so traumatic. One asked, "Why do you think that is such a problem? That happened a long time ago and hurt for a short while. My husband's beatings are a much greater problem."

By the mid-1980s many Arab and African women wanted Western women barred from participating in public discussions of female circumcision. Nahid Toubia, herself an activist against the practice, has argued, for example:

> The West has acted as though they have suddenly discovered a dangerous epidemic which they then sensationalized in international women's forums creating a backlash of over-sensitivity in the concerned communities. They have portrayed it as irrefutable evidence of the barbarism and vulgarity of underdeveloped countries . . . It became a conclusive validation to the view of the primitiveness of Arabs, Muslims and Africans all in one blow.[47]

Similarly, Soheir Morsy argues that Western interest in the topic is a "paternalistic" reminder of a "bygone era of colonial domination."[48] And in a critique of Alice Walker's film on circumcision, *Warrior Marks*, Seble Dawit and Salem Mekuria, activists against the custom, claim that Walker portrays "respected elder women of the village's secret society . . . [as] slit-eyed murderers wielding rusted weapons with which to butcher children."[49]

Between 1988 and 1992 we spoke with a number of Egyptian and Sudanese feminists regarding female circumcision, many of whom argued that female circumcision should be seen within the context of women's lives, in which they face numerous gender-linked health risks. Many of these feminists noted that, from their point of view, women in Europe and North America face serious discrimination as well, and they were critical

---

Many feminists from Egypt and Sudan noted that, from their point of view, women in Europe and North America face serious discrimination as well, and they were critical of Western feminists' failure to link female circumcision with violence against women, child prostitution, breast enlargement surgery, and rape.

---

of Western feminists' failure to link female circumcision with violence against women, child prostitution, breast enlargement surgery, and rape.

An active feminist movement has existed in Egypt since early this century. Even in the beginning of the Egyptian feminist movement, however, Egyptian feminists felt that their contact with American feminists was one-sided, with the American women patronizingly trying to dictate the "correct" agenda. Just after the first World War, for example, American feminists were almost entirely concerned with suffrage and did not understand the importance to Egyptian feminists of their country's struggle against British colonialism.[50] An analogous misunderstanding occurs today. Western feminists make female circumcision a preeminent concern, with little or no regard for the priorities of Arab and African feminists. In fact, a few contemporary feminist groups in Egypt, notably the "New Women Centre," do focus on female circumcision as a substantial part of their activities, but most groups have deemed other issues more pressing. A great deal of activist work has focused, for example, on revising the personal status laws covering divorce and inheritance, on passage of the United Nations Convention to End All Forms of Discrimination Against Women, on women's education and professional attainment, and on helping women to understand their legal rights.

There are nevertheless indigenous individuals and groups who seek to abolish female circumcision, many of whom do so within a framework of women's health rather than women's rights. Egyptian author Youssef Al-Masry, for example, has written that female circumcision "is a wicked mutilation of nature, and because it is against nature, it is an evil, which under all circumstances must be abolished."[51] In 1980 in *The Hidden Face of Eve* Nawal El-Saadawy revealed that she had been circumcised as a child in rural Egypt and described the trauma and medical complications from female circumcision that she had later observed as a physician.[52] Marie Assaad's work on female circumcision in Egypt and Nahid Toubia's in Sudan focus explicitly on how the practice of female circumcision might be ended. In Egypt, a Committee Against Female Circumcision has been organized by Aziza Hussein and other members of the Cairo Family Planning Association specifically to work on ending the practice. The committee's activities include health education and outreach to women around the country with information about the harmful aspects of the custom.[53]

In 1959 the practice was banned by decree in Egypt in all Ministry of Health hospitals and clinics. At the United Nations International Conference on Population and Development (ICPD) held in September 1994 in Cairo, Aziza Hussein organized a presentation on female circumcision and at that time Population Minister Maher Mahran and members of the People's Assembly (Egypt's parliament) spoke publicly in favor of passing legislation to criminalize the practice.[54] Then, during the ICPD, the television network CNN aired a segment on female circumcision that showed an actual operation being conducted by a traditional practitioner on a young Egyptian girl. The broadcast raised a furor among the Egyptian public. In the few-minutes-long segment a small part of Egyptian culture was displayed that seriously angered and "shamed" Egypt before the international community.[55]

Following the ICPD the Grand Shaikh of Al Azhar Gad el-Haq, one of the country's most prominent religious leaders, issued a *fatwa* (religious opinion) that female circumcision is "an Islamic duty to which all Muslim women should adhere."[56] The Minister of Health, Ali Abdel-Fattah then rescinded the 1959 ban by issuing a policy statement allowing the procedure to be performed in governmental health facilities, a move that has resulted, according to the Egyptian Organization for Human Rights, in "big fights among gynaecologists, plastic surgeons, and paediatricians, [who are] competing to operate and get money from the girls' parents."[57]

Can We Move Beyond the Impasse?

The debate about traditional female genital surgeries is a particular instance of the more general class of problems involved in intercultural reasoning in relation to intervention. It is useful in dealing with these problems to keep in mind three characteristics of working with cultural materials, which we briefly consider before suggesting how it may be possible to move beyond the impasse at which the debate about traditional female genital surgeries has stalled.

Intervention always involves claims about legitimacy, standing, and authority that are socially constructed and culturally mediated. In the act of intervention, whether verbal or physical, the intervenor always maintains a perspective on the issue at hand and defends an interest. Further, either implicit or explicit to all interventions are assertions of legitimacy (what actions are appropriate), standing (who has the appropriate status to carry out an intervention), and authority (who has the power to intervene). Despite appeals to impartial standards by intervenors, how people organize themselves in relation to an intervention and the meaning that they both give and take from the intervention result in large measure from social and cultural dynamics.

Colonial relationships, for example, lead to the perception by colonizers and colonials of very different senses of privilege. This sense, in turn may lead to diametrically opposed understanding of the status, roles, and power dynamics involved in interventions, like those directed from the West at eliminating traditional practices. Where the residue (if not the actual sense) of colonial privilege may contribute to a Western intervenor's expectation that her actions will be viewed as appropriate and authoritative, former colonial subjects may take precisely the opposite view. Indeed, this dynamic contributes to the impasses about traditional female genital surgeries.

By calling attention to the social and cultural construction of legitimacy, standing, and authority, we do not mean to suggest an extreme relativist position wherein all practices, regardless of how damaging they may be, are accepted as equally legitimate within the context of the cultures from which they come. Rather, taking account of contemporary and historical relationships of power and privilege are essential first steps toward arriving at a sensitive and nuanced approach to engagement.

Cultural knowledge is dynamic and contingent. Descriptions of cultural practices, values, and beliefs convey the data, and understandings of those data, collected by a researcher in a specific temporal and spatial context. Such characterizations can be useful if their use is strictly anchored in specific circumstances. But it always is misguided to treat such characterizations as stable and unchanging in any significant degree. Doing so commits what Robert Rubinstein has elsewhere called the "fallacy of detachable cultural descriptions."[58] Especially when such detached descriptions are used to form the basis for analyses that cross social and cultural boundaries, they become simplified, dehumanizing stereotypes of complex, deeply human phenomena. Middle Eastern and African women frequently claim, for instance, that traditional female genital surgeries are discussed out of context and in ways that deny their humanity.

Human social and cultural life is dynamic. Moreover, not all members of a society hold or behave according to a single set of norms, which in any event are constantly affected by social, political, and economic changes.

Cultural descriptions also are always made within a specific context and for a particular purpose. Thus, even if well described in relation to a particular context, the unanchored use of cultural descriptions creates a sense of knowledge of the "Other" to which a false precision and completeness too often is attached. The result is that knowledge of other cultures is always contingent, tentative, and incomplete.

The further even a superb analysis is moved from the original investigatory question, the more damage is done by committing the fallacy of detachable cultural descriptions. The quest for stable, generally applicable (universalizable) understandings appears to be an aspect of human cognition, one that works to direct attention away from evidence contradictory to the model.

Effective intervention takes place within a complex communicative web. Too often interventions intended to bring about one result produce quite the opposite effect. In many cases, the paradoxical result of intervention derives in large measure from failing to analyze adequately the potential pitfalls of the intervention. But in what essential way would intervention that avoids these hazards be different?

Culturally responsive efforts to address problematic practices necessarily involve constructing the analysis and subsequent intervention in ways that are at once honest and respectful. In large measure, this leads to acknowledging that what and how we speak about the practice in question makes a real difference. Culturally responsive intervention is made in a voice that engages the "Other" as an equal interlocutor. Finding such a voice does not depend upon having an approach and method that can be applied equally well in a variety of cultural contexts. Methods that are taken to be applicable in this transportable manner inevitably lead to the privileging of the analysts' perspective and interests. In place of such generalizable effort, sensitive cultural analyses depend upon the recognition of the contingent and fluid nature of social relations. Thus, finding a voice requires a more modest sense of how and what can be said with certainty and to whom and, most importantly, listening to and valuing the perspectives of the "Other."

Thus, while we agree with Toubia, who writes, "No ethical defense can be made for preserving a cultural practice that damages women's health and interferes with their sexuality,"[69] ter quite bluntly, if we care about the genitals of the women in those cultures, we need also to care about their feelings.

These procedures have been compared to torture and child abuse. We argue that they are not torture, but sic to the group's now threatened identity.

It is clear that female circumcision, especially the more extensive procedures and especially those that are performed without asepsis or anesthesia, are physically harmful. The procedures are increasingly being performed by physicians, who often claim that they are minimizing the harm that would potentially result if the procedure were performed by traditional operators. Arab and African feminists strongly condemn the medicalization of female circumcision, which they believe will promote its continuation rather than its abandonment. Physicians and nurses in the United States may encounter immigrant parents who request the procedure for their daughters or infibulated women in need of obstetrical services. American health care personnel working abroad may be asked by traditional practitioners or families for their help with the procedures. We therefore urge medical and nursing schools to include information about female circumcision in their curricula. This material should cover both the mechanics of how to care for circumcised women and the legal, ethical, and cultural aspects of the custom.

> When Western authors call for the practice to be eradicated in Africa or Asia it is too often perceived by members of the involved societies as cultural imperialism.

this complex cross-cultural issue cannot be adequately dealt with by a simple condemnation.

Western authors have identified female circumcision as a custom that should be eradicated. The public health language of "eradication" is most often associated with germ theory and worldwide campaigns against infectious diseases like smallpox, malaria, and polio. Female circumcision, however, is not an organism to be rooted out and killed with antibiotics, prevented through immunization, or managed with vector control, and it is especially important that we proceed with high regard for the beliefs and concerns of the cultures where it is practiced.

Enormous damage can be done by inappropriate choice of language. For this reason, although many concerned individuals call the procedure "female genital mutilation" we prefer less inflammatory language. Members of the Arab and African cultures who practice female circumcision have experienced colonialism and other types of continued imperialism by Western governments. They experienced and continue to experience racism and various forms of discrimination. The extreme language used by Western authors to describe female circumcision is perceived by Arab and African people as a continued devaluation of themselves and their entire cultures. To put the matter are arranged and paid for by loving parents who deeply believe that the surgeries are for their daughters' welfare. Parents fear, with much justification, that leaving their daughters uncircumcised will make them unmarriageable. Parents worry about their daughters during the procedures and care for their wounds afterward to help them recover. Even if we disagree with the practice of female circumcision, we must remember that the parents who do this are not monsters, but are ordinary, decent, caring persons.

Regarding legal or policy interventions, we think it is appropriate to legislate against the practice in our own society, and we endorse Representative Patricia Schroeder's bill before the U.S. Congress that would prohibit female circumcision. When Western authors call for the practice to be eradicated in Africa or Asia, however, it is too often perceived by members of the involved societies as cultural imperialism.[6] This perception is strengthened when Western authors fail to acknowledge the important work of indigenous activists who advocate against female circumcision. Pragmatically, moreover, indigenous activists may more correctly judge when a given strategy will succeed. Western efforts, unguided by detailed cultural knowledge, may, like the CNN broadcast, inspire a backlash in which the custom is viewed as intrinsic to the group's now threatened identity.

The search for a way to successfully confront female circumcision and to move beyond the impasse of the confrontation of universalism and cultural relativism depends upon finding a language and constructing an approach respectful of diverse cultural concerns. To that end we conclude with a policy statement that we drafted for discussion by members of the Society for Health and Human Values:

> In recent years it has been recognized that women and girls suffer discrimination in many societies. In many parts of the world women and girls receive less food and medical care than men and boys; in areas of civil conflict women and girls are raped as an intentional strategy of war; in some countries domestic violence causes substantial injury, disability and death; in some areas girls are subject to traditional genital surgeries that cause

long-lasting and severe health consequences; and in other areas cosmetic surgeries and pressures to attain a slender physical ideal also have negative health consequences.

While we respect the beliefs and practices of all cultures, we recognize that, in some cases, traditions that have expressed cherished ideals must be viewed in a new light. We believe that female genital operations, including clitoridectomy, excision of the labia minora, and infibulation, are such traditions. Physicians and other health care specialists world wide have acknowledged the degree of immediate and long-term damage these surgeries cause to the health of women and girls. In light of this medical information, we urge that these procedures be abandoned.

We recognize the efforts of numerous individuals and groups, in the countries where female genital surgeries are common, who have sought to abolish their practice through education and policy change. We endorse and support the efforts of these groups.[61]

Acknowledgments

Earlier versions of this paper were presented at the 1993 annual meeting of the American Public Health Association, San Francisco, California, 28 October, and as a Conversation in Bioethics at the Center for Bioethics, Case Western Reserve University in January 1994. We thank Maha Abou el Saud, Anita Faboš, and Stephanie Maurer for research assistance. We appreciate the helpful comments made on earlier drafts of this paper by Rebecca Dresser, M. Margaret Clark, Jill Korbin, Carol McClean, Thomas Murray, Patricia Marshall, and Deborah Pellow.

References

1. Melford Spiro, "Cultural Relativism and the Future of Anthropology," *Cultural Anthropology* 1 (1986): 259-86.
2. Alison D. Renteln, "Relativism and the Search for Human Rights," *American Anthropologist* 90 (1988): 56-72.
3. Spiro, "Cultural Relativism."
4. Wilcomb E. Washburn, "Cultural Relativism, Human Rights, and the AAA," *American Anthropologist* 89 (1987): 939-43; Renteln, "Relativism."
5. Washburn, "Cultural Relativism," p. 940.
6. Julian Steward, "On Science and Human Rights," *American Anthropologist* 50 (1948): 352-55, at p. 352.
7. Clifford Geertz, "Anti Anti-relativism," *American Anthropologist* 86 (1984): 263-78.
8. Paul Rabinow, "Humanism as Nihilism: The Bracketing of Truth and Seriousness in American Cultural Anthropology," in *Social Science as Moral Inquiry*, ed. Norma Haan, Robert N. Bellah, Paul Rabinow, and William M. Sullivan (New York: Columbia University Press, 1983), pp. 52-75.
9. James Scott, *Weapons of the Weak: Resistance in Everyday Life* (New Haven: Yale University Press, 1991).
10. Eike-Henner Kluge, "Female Circumcision: When Medical Ethics Confronts Cultural Values," *Canadian Medical Association Journal* 148, no. 2 (1993): 288-89; Stephen A. James, "Reconciling International Human Rights and Cultural Relativism: The Case of Female Circumcision," *Bioethics* 8, no. 1 (1994): 1-26; Loretta M. Kopelman, "Female Circumcision/Genital Mutilation and Ethical Relativism," *Second Opinion* 20, no. 2 (1994): 55-71.
11. Alison T. Slack, "Female Circumcision: A Critical Appraisal," *Human Rights Quarterly* 10 (1988): 437-86.
12. Robert Edgerton, *Sick Societies: Challenging the Myth of Primitive Harmony* (New York: The Free Press, 1992).
13. Daniel Gordon, "Female Circumcision and Genital Operations in Egypt and the Sudan: A Dilemma for Medical Anthropology," *Medical Anthropology Quarterly* 5, no. 1 (1991): 3-14.
14. Nahid Toubia, *Female Genital Mutilation: A Call for Global Action* (New York: Women Ink, 1993); "Female Circumcision as Public Health Issue," *NEJM* 331 (1994): 712-16.
15. Robert Cook, "Damage to Physical Health from Pharaonic Circumcision (Infibulation) of Females: A Review of the Medical Literature," in *Traditional Practices Affecting the Health of Women and Children. Female Circumcision, Childhood Marriage, Nutritional Taboos, etc. Report of a Seminar, Khartoum, 10-15 February 1979*, ed. World Health Organization (Alexandria, Egypt: WHO, Regional Office for the Eastern Mediterranean, 1981), pp. 53-69.
16. Toubia, *Female Genital Mutilation*.
17. Asma El Dareer, *Woman, Why Do You Weep?* (London: Zed Press, 1982).
18. Leonard J. Kouba and Judith Muasher, "Female Circumcision in Africa: An Overview," *African Studies Review* 28, no. 1 (1985): 95-110; Minority Rights Group International, *Female Genital Mutilation: Proposal for Change* (London: Minority Rights Group International, 1992); Toubia, *Female Genital Mutilation*.
19. Elizabeth Sheehan, "Victorian Clitoridectomy," *Medical Anthropology Newsletter* 12 (1981): 10-15.
20. Toubia, *Female Genital Mutilation*, p. 10.
21. Gordon, "Female Circumcision and Genital Operations."
22. Sanna A. Nour and Tessby M. Rashad, "Epidemiology of Female Circumcision in Sharkia Egypt," *The Bulletin of the High Institute of Public Health* 18, no. 1 (1988): 89-103.
23. B. Zeitoon, "Circumcision of Girls," (in Arabic) *October* 730 (1990): 48.
24. *Sudan Demographic and Health Survey 1989/1990* (Khartoum, Sudan, and Columbia, Md.: Ministry of Economic and National Planning, and Institute for Resource Development, 1991).
25. Nahid Toubia, "The Social and Political Implications of Female Circumcision: The Case of Sudan." In *Women and the Family in the Middle East*, ed. Elizabeth Fernea (Austin: University of Texas Press, 1985), pp. 148-59.
26. Hamid Rushwan, "Etiological Factors in Pelvic Inflammatory Disease in Sudanese Women," *American Journal of Obstetrics and Gynecology* 138, no. 7 (1980): 877-79.
27. Carla AbouZahr and Erica Royston, *Maternal Mortality: A Global Factbook* (Geneva: World Health Organization, 1991).
28. Evelyn A. Early, *Baladi Women of Cairo: Playing with an Egg and a Stone* (Boulder, Colo.: Lynne Rienner Publishers, 1993), pp. 102-106.
29. Ellen Gruenbaum, "The Movement Against Clitoridectomy and Infibulation in Sudan: Public Health and the Women's Movement," *Medical Anthropology Newsletter* 13, no. 2 (1982): 4-12; Sandra D. Lane, "A Biocultural Study of Trachoma in an Egyptian Hamlet." Unpublished doctoral dissertation, University of California, San Francisco with University of California, Berkeley, 1987.
30. Ellen Gruenbaum, "The Islamic Movement, Development, and Health Education: Recent Changes in the Health of Rural Women in Central Sudan," *Social Science and Medicine* 33 (1987): 637-45.
31. *Sudan Demographic and Health Survey 1989/1990*.
32. El Dareer, *Woman, Why Do You Weep?*
33. Otto Meinardu, "Mythological, Historical and Sociological Aspects of the Practice of Female Circumcision among the Egyptians," *Acta Ethnographica Academiae Scientiarum Hungaricae* 16 (1967): 387-97.
34. Marie B. Assaad, "Female Circumcision in Egypt: Social Implications, Current Research, and Prospects for Change," *Studies in Family Planning* 11, no. 1 (1980): 3-16; *Sudan Demographic and Health Survey 1989/1990*.

35. Toubia, *Female Genital Mutilation.*
36. Abdel Rahman Al Naggar, *Islam and Female Circumcision* (Cairo: Cairo Family Planning Association, 1985).
37. Jamal A. Badawi, *At Taharah: Purity and State of Undefilement* (Indianapolis, Ind.: Islamic Teaching Center, 1979).
38. Gruenbaum, "The Islamic Movement."
39. Meinardu, "Mythological, Historical and Sociological Aspects."
40. Gruenbaum, "The Islamic Movement."
41. Fran P. Hosken, *The Hosken Report: Genital and Sexual Mutilation of Females,* 3rd rev. ed. (Lexington, Mass.: Women's International Network News, 1982), p. 24.
42. Elise Sochart, "Agenda Setting, the Role of Groups and the Legislative Process: The Prohibition of Female Circumcision in Britain," in *Parliamentary Affairs* (Oxford: Oxford University Press, 1988), pp. 508-26; Minority Rights Group International, "Female Genital Mutilation."
43. Marlise Simons, "French Court Jails Mother for Girl's Ritual Mutilation," *New York Times,* 17 January 1993.
44. "Canada: Policy on Female Genital Mutilation," *WIN News* 18, no. 2 (1992): 45.
45. Anna L. Bardach, "Tearing Off the Veil," *Vanity Fair* 56, no. 8 (1993):122-26, 154-58; Sophronia S. Gregory, "At Risk of Mutilation," *Time,* 21 March 1994, pp. 45-46.
46. Nour and Rashad, "Epidemiology of Female Circumcision."
47. Nahid Toubia, "Women and Health in Sudan," in *Women of the Arab World: The Coming Challenge,* ed. Nahid Toubia (London: Zed Books, 1988), pp. 98-109.
48. Soheir Morsey, "Safeguarding Women's Bodies: The White Man's Burden Medicalized," *Medical Anthropological Quarterly* 5, no. 1 (1991): 19-23, at p. 19.
49. Seble Dawit and Salem Mekuria, "The West Just Doesn't Get It," *New York Times,* 7 December 1993.
50. Margot Badran, *Feminists, Islam, and Nation: Gender and the Making of Modern Egypt* (Princeton: Princeton University Press, 1995).
51. Quoted in Meinardu, "Mythological, Historical, and Sociological Aspects," p. 395.
52. Nawal El-Saadawy, *The Hidden Face of Eve* (Boston: Beacon Press, 1980).
53. Cairo Family Planning Association, *Do You Know the Results of Female Circumcision?* (Cairo: Women and Child Health Project, Cairo Family Planning Association, 1990).
54. Dina Ezzat, "Grappling with Conservatism," *Al-Ahram Weekly,* 2-8 June 1994; "In the Interest of the Masses, *Al-Ahram Weekly,* 1-7 September 1994; "Out of Harm's Way," *Al-Ahram Weekly,* 29 September-5 October 1994.
55. Saad E. Ibrahim, "Circumcision of the Egyptian Mind: Guilt or Shame?" *Civil Society: Democratic Transformation in the Arab World* 3, no. 31 (1994): 3.
56. Dina Ezzat, "Battling Mutilation Ritual," *Al-Ahram Weekly,* 30 March-5 April 1995.
57. Dina Ezzat, "Female 'Circumcision' Contested Again," *Al-Ahram Weekly,* 20-26 April 1995.
58. Robert A. Rubinstein, "Culture and Negotiation," in *The Struggle for Peace: Israelis and Palestinians,* ed. Elizabeth W. Fernea and Mary E. Hocking (Austin: University of Texas Press, 1992), pp. 116-29.
59. Toubia, "Female Circumcision as Public Health Issue," p. 714.
60. Ellen Gruenbaum, "Women's Rights and Cultural Self-Determination in the Female Genital Mutilation Controversy," *Anthropology Newsletter* (May 1995): 14-15.
61. Sandra D. Lane and Robert A. Rubinstein, "A Response [to 'On Condemning Female Genital Mutilation']," *Of Value* 24, no. 3 (1994): 3-4.

Part XI
Sociology and Medical Ethics

[32]
The Contributions of Sociology to Medical Ethics

by ROBERT ZUSSMAN

Medical ethics has not always been friendly territory for the social sciences; at least a few sociologists who have wandered across disciplinary borders for a tour report back on unfriendly natives.[1] I should acknowledge, from the first, that I am not among the unhappy visitors. This is not, however, so much because my own brief trips into medical ethics have been met with particularly friendly receptions as because I have been something of an accidental tourist without any great expectations that I would find the comforts of home in foreign territory.

Medical ethics—or, more precisely, what might be called philosophical approaches to medical ethics—and social science approaches to medical ethics are characterized by very different purposes. In the first instance, medical ethics is an applied discipline. The social sciences, including, not least, sociology, are primarily academic disciplines. In making this claim, I am aware of its irony. Certainly, philosophical medical ethics, as it has been practiced in the United States, is given to frequent flights of fancy—grand abstractions and frank speculations—that seem far removed from any immediate application. Equally certainly, empirical sociology, particularly in its ethnographic mode, is marked by a preoccupation with the grubby details of life in hospitals and doctors' offices that often seems far removed from any higher analytic issues.[2]

Nonetheless, philosophical medical ethics is fairly explicitly a branch of applied philosophy, and even its grandest abstractions are put to the service of formulating procedures and policies useful to "problems of therapeutic practice, health care delivery, and medical and biological research."[3] And it is very much in this spirit that medical ethicists have generated a great number of proposals, many later adopted, for the regulation of experimentation with human subjects, of procedures for allocating scarce organs, for allowing the termination of treatments, for ensuring informed consent, and much more. In contrast, sociologists tend to use even grubby details as a route to more analytic observations. Thus many of the sociologists who have dabbled in areas relevant to medical ethics have often disavowed any interest in the application of their researches to procedures and policies, stressing instead their implications for such abstruse matters as the sociology of the professions, "theories" of organizations, or the social organization of cognition. Ironically, then, it is the medical ethicists, trained in philosophy and theology and given to abstraction, who are often worldly, and it is the sociologists of medical ethics who are often curiously otherworldly.

There is, of course, another, probably more conventional distinction between philosophical and social science approaches to medical ethics—that one is normative and the other empirical. But I am not entirely comfortable with this distinction. To be sure, philosophical approaches to medical ethics are

The conventional contrast between "normative" philosophical approaches and "empirical" social science perspectives on medical ethics draws too bright a distinction. One need not be a philosopher to raise normative issues or a sociologist to practice empirical research. The best work in both disciplines should recognize the different ways in which they each join normative reflection and empirical description.

Robert Zussman, "The Contributions of Sociology to Medical Ethics," *Hastings Center Report* 30, no. 1 (2000): 7-11.

typically more *explicitly* normative than are social science approaches. Similarly, social science approaches are typically far more explicitly empirical. Nonetheless, philosophical medical ethicists not only often incorporate empirical material into their analyses but have recently shown a growing inclination to do so. And while sociologists often seem almost embarrassed about acknowledging the normative aspects of their work, nonetheless, for those sociologists who study medical ethics, the normative implications of their work are often unavoidable, even if it is others who make them explicit.

The difference between philosophical and social science approaches to medical ethics is somewhat subtler then than a stark contrast between the normative and the empirical would suggest. To be sure, the philosophers are generally less systematic on matters empirical than the social scientists. For the philosophers it is typically enough to know that a phenomenon exists, regardless of the distributions that often obsessively occupy the social scientists. Similarly, social scientists seem capable of only a fairly limited range of normative claims: deontological arguments, based on judgments about the moral character of an act, are almost entirely absent from social scientific thought. Instead, social scientists interested in medical ethics seem comfortable only with the kind of consequentialist arguments (often implicit, at that) that seem to draw on the kind of causal argument that is their stock-in-trade.

These are significant differences. But they imply no deep incompatibility between philosophical and social science approaches to medical ethics. Quite the reverse, they suggest a fundamental complementarity. None of this is to say that social scientists have made the sort of contribution to the study of medical ethics that they might: compared to the large numbers of scholars and practitioners of medical ethics trained in philosophy and theology, the number of social

> Whether we are reading about informed consent, or reproductive rights, or managed care, suddenly arguments turn out to hinge in large part on empirical propositions.

scientists concerned with medical ethics is slight. Moreover, burdened by the requirements of research, they have typically trailed the philosophers, turning their attention to such matters as informed consent or organ transplantation or the termination of treatment only after those at the cutting edge of medical ethics have already begun to turn their attention elsewhere. As a result, I mean the remainder of this essay not so much as a celebration of the contributions sociologists have made to medical ethics than as a series of suggestions for what those contributions might be. In this sense, the remainder of this essay is less a review and more a statement of intention and possibility.

Consequentialist Arguments

For a sociologist, opening a textbook of medical ethics is a bit like a flight into Never Never Land. We are the Lost Boys in the world of pirates, Indians, and mermaids. Here, however, the fantastical creatures take the altogether extraordinary form of erudite discussions of Kantian or utilitarian ethics that grow even more astonishing with every additional distinction. Yet when we pass beyond the first chapter or two and get down to cases, as even the most insistent practitioner of an applied ethics model does, the world grows suddenly more familiar. Whether we are reading about informed consent, or reproductive rights, or managed care, suddenly arguments turn out to hinge in large part—I would not care to hazard a guess as to the proportion—on empirical propositions.

Let me take as an example one recent and influential discussion of managed care plans. In their excellent discussion of the fate of the "fiduciary ethic" in such plans, Ezekiel Emanuel and Nancy Dubler argue:

> Attending to the well-being of one patient may conflict with caring for another patient. Similarly, it is well recognized that caring for a patient may conflict with—and even be superseded by—the need to protect the interests of a third party.... Managed care plans have already tried various mechanisms to try to reduce physician use of health care resources for their patients, including providing bonuses to physicians who order few tests and basing a percentage of physicians' salaries on volume and test ordering standards. Such conflicts of interest may proliferate with increased price competition, the need for managed care plans to reduce costs, and the absence of government regulation.[4]

The argument they make is for the most part consequentialist. In this sense, although formulated in somewhat different terms, it is fundamentally empirical. To be sure, Emanuel and Dubler take as more or less a given that it is important for physicians to maintain a primary commitment to the well-being of individual patients. (I might add, however, that this, too, is subject to empirical investigation: we might want to know—as we do not—what the consequences would be of an abandonment of that commitment.) More specifically, Emanuel and Dubler's argument hinges on three claims:

1) that there is a conflict between caring for one patient and obligations to both other patients and third parties;

2) that pressures to reduce the use of resources—particularly financial pressures—interfere with the realization of a fiduciary ethic; and

3) that these pressures are likely to increase with increased price competition, increased pressure to reduce costs, and in the absence of government regulation.

These are important claims. The third seems to me unambiguously true and the first and second, roughly true. But there is surprisingly little evidence to support them and the evidence that is available suggests that each needs at least slight modification.

We do not know, for example, very much about how physicians handle conflicts arising from commitments to more than one patient. My own research in two intensive care units suggested that the problems associated with a commitment to a collective mission—the delivery of care by a group of physicians to a group of patients—were perhaps surprisingly slight. On occasions when beds were in short supply—precisely the sort of "lifeboat ethics" situation that might lead to subordinating the needs of one patient to another—the physicians I observed were remarkably inventive in finding ways to expand temporarily the "lifeboat": They kept patients in the emergency room a little longer, found extra nurses, moved ventilators. As long as a utilitarian ethic, in which the needs of different patients were balanced against each other, was applied consistently, neither physicians nor patients nor patient's families seemed much concerned about the abandonment of a fiduciary ethic.[5]

My findings, however, do not generalize easily to managed care. Although the underlying issues are likely similar, the structures are different, both between intensive care and managed care and within managed care organizations themselves. But the findings do raise questions about the sort of ethical issues an empirical study of managed care might address: How intense and how frequent are the conflicts between caring for an individual patient and responsibility to a group of patients? What form do these conflicts take? What sorts of organizational arrangements intensify these conflicts? What sorts of organizational arrangements deflect such conflicts? How do physicians and other health care providers handle such conflicts when they arise? Moreover, beyond this long list of questions about potential conflicts between responsibility to individual patients and responsibility to groups of patients is an equally long list of questions about the potential for conflict between responsibility to individual patients and responsibility to third parties, including insurers and managed care organizations themselves. That I can barely hazard a guess as to the answers to any of these questions is precisely to the point: empirical research would effectively inform any substantive discussion of the ethical issues around managed care.

We do know slightly more, although still not a great deal, about how physicians respond to financial pressures to reduce the use of resources. But what we know suggests that financial pressures may not constitute so immediate a threat to the fiduciary ethic as Emanuel and Dubler fear. Bradford Gray, for example, in a major study of the profit motive in health care, did not find a great deal of difference in the behavior of for profit and not for profit organizations.[6] Moreover, there is at least scattered evidence that financial incentives do not directly affect physician behavior. For example, Alan Hillman and colleagues found that financial incentives are more powerful in group model HMOs than in independent physician associations.[7] So, too, a group headed by David Hemenway found that "substantial monetary incentives" induced groups of physicians to intensify their practices even though not all of them benefited individually from those incentives.[8] In a slightly different context, Mark Notman and his colleagues found that physicians reduced lengths of stay in response to the introduction of diagnostic related groups despite both a hostility to financial considerations and a lack of detailed knowledge of DRGs.[9]

These findings are only suggestive, of course, but the suggestions are interesting ones. I read all three of these studies as suggesting that physicians do not, at least for the most part, act as the profit-maximizing individuals beloved in classical economic theory. Rather, financial incentives, both direct and indirect, become important only within a collective context as networks of physicians elaborate those incentives into a culture of practice. Financial incentives seem, curiously enough, to operate more as a means of institutionalizing ideas and beliefs about what constitutes appropriate practice than as a purely economic phenomenon. What becomes critical, then, to understanding the ethical implications of managed care is not so much an understanding of the intricacies of payment schemes as an understanding of the social context in which physicians make sense of and evaluate those schemes.

Let me summarize a bit more analytically. A good deal of medical ethics is based on consequentialist claims that social scientists are well equipped to assess. If an ethical claim is based on the assertion that a practice or arrangement is ethically questionable because it results in a particular outcome, then that claim is empirically testable. Philosophical medical ethicists rarely mount those tests themselves. Social scientists, whether using ethnographic methods, reviews of records, or survey instruments, can test those claims. There is a sufficient body of social science research, bearing on informed consent, organ transplantation, end of life treatment, and any other number of issues as well as managed care, to suggest that some of the consequentialist claims will be confirmed, that others will not, and that confirmation of some will modify others. But social scientists have by no means provided all the research they might. In many areas, including managed care very prominently, the social science research is suggestive rather than definitive and episodic rather than systematic. Even if the only task for social science in medical ethics is that of testing consequentialist claims, there is a great deal left to be done.

Generating the Normative

The notion that the task for social scientists interested in medical ethics is to test consequentialist claims leaves the sociology of medical ethics in an uncomfortable position. It makes the social scientist a junior partner to the philosopher, someone who responds to ideas generated elsewhere but who generates few if any ideas on his or her own. The sociologist becomes a technician and little more. At least a few observers have suggested, however, that there is a much bigger role for social scientists to play in medical ethics. Barry Hoffmaster, a Canadian philosopher, has made an especially eloquent argument that "moral theory begins in practice."[10] According to Hoffmaster:

> moral decision making is a search for a feasible, appropriate response to a particular situation, not the application of a method that in virtue of its extreme generality is insensitive to the particularities that structure the situation. . . . Moral decision making is more a matter of coming up with creative, responsive solutions than it is trying to apply a philosophical formula. . . . By investigating how moral problems are perceived and constructed by those whom they affect and how these individuals handle those problems, and by assessing these attempted resolutions, ethnographic studies can

In many areas, including managed care very prominently, the social science research is suggestive rather than definitive and episodic rather than systematic.

discover the disparate forms of moral rationality and stake out, in at least a provisional way, the limits of those forms.

Hoffmaster's argument constitutes a virtual manifesto for a sociology of medical ethics and deserves extended consideration.

At the center of his argument is a critique of an "applied ethics" model. Rather than a style of ethics that begins with a few basic principles and then attempts to apply them across a wide range of circumstances, Hoffmaster is suggesting a style of ethical reasoning that works from the ground up, based in dense, local knowledge of particular situations. Moreover, unlike the model of social science testing, which privileges no one research method over any other, Hoffmaster assigns a special place to ethnography. Indeed, if we were to take Hoffmaster's suggestions seriously, medical ethics would become a very different enterprise: The boundaries between social science and philosophy, between the normative and the empirical, would come close to disappearing.

Interesting though Hoffmaster's suggestions may be, I find them disquieting on at least two grounds.

First, I think Hoffmaster is unduly critical of the applied ethics model and underestimates its power. An ethics from the ground up, based on ethnography, attempting to discover "the disparate forms of moral rationality," could have a distinctly conservative feel. Good ethnography may end elsewhere, but it typically begins with sympathy for those the ethnographer studies. If applied ethics has sometimes seemed insensitive to the "lived experience" of physicians, nurses, and hospital administrators, an ethnographic medical ethics would suffer from the opposite defect of too great a sensitivity. It might do little more than reproduce, in different language, the moral standards native to medicine. As a result, it would run the risk of losing what is probably the most important contribution of medical ethics over the last quarter century: precisely the ability to import into medicine a set of ethical standards that are not native to the occupational and organizational cultures of medicine itself.

Second, I suspect that Hoffmaster underestimates the extent to which ethnographers have themselves been driven by an applied ethics model. Ethnographers of medicine, I would suggest, have been far more successful in generating moral concerns when their research has strayed farther from the conventional realms of medical ethics—in, for example, their investigations of the power of physicians, the assaults of organized medicine on conceptions of the self, or the relationship between markets and the delivery of care. In contrast, those of us who have been more or less self-conscious ethnographers of medical ethics—I can speak confidently about myself, more speculatively about others—have typically taken their agenda from that set by the philosophers. If the more philosophically minded medical ethicists have seen problems in the treatment of fetuses and neonates, the ways organs are allocated, the ways consent is obtained, we have for the most part simply followed their lead.

These caveats aside, however, Hoffmaster does raise the important question of how ethical issues are generated. There is certainly one model—that of the ethicist as consultant—in which the ethicist simply responds to issues raised by practitioners. There is equally certainly another model of the ethicist as a gadfly, a lone scholar, reading books, thinking thoughts, and then asking pesky questions that make practitioners uncomfortable. Both of these are viable models. (And I suppose it is to the point that I know of no one who has studied how ethicists do, in fact, generate the issues they raise.) Hoffmaster raises a third possibility—a model of the ethnographic researcher sensitive to normative issues, of the normatively driven scholar immersed in practice. And so long as we do not imagine that this is the only model of either ethics or of social science contributions to ethics, it is a valuable model.

Both/And

Sociology will not and cannot save medical ethics. Indeed, medical ethics seems to have done quite well without sociology. But sociology—and the social sciences more generally—can make medical ethics better. Many of the empirical claims on which much of medical ethics hinges are fairly simple to assess and do not require the methods of social sciences, either quantitative or ethnographic. But some do. The social sciences—and sociology in particular—can lend a bit of reality to the flights of fancy that sometimes characterize the more speculative versions of philosophical medical ethics. Sociology, particularly in its ethnographic mode, may provide a method of discovery that has been slighted elsewhere. Not alone, but in combination with an applied ethics model, ethnography may prove an important method of raising new issues.

Of course, one need not be a sociologist to practice empirical research. It is belaboring the obvious to point out that many physicians, nurses, and health administrators are deeply immersed in the everyday practice of medicine: if they do not need to do ethnographic research, it is because they are already natives. So too at least a few philosophical medical ethicists enjoy a deep, first-hand knowledge of medical practice and at least approach the position of native. But neither does one need to be a philosopher to raise normative issues. Few sociologists—or anthropologists or empirical political scientists or historians—are trained in or comfortable with the kind of rigorous moral reasoning that is the philosophers' stock-in-trade. But the self-conscious disavowal of normative concerns, a style of ersatz hard-boiled realism, probably does not serve sociology well. Just as the philosophical medical ethicists might do well to acknowledge the underlying empirical grounds of their claims, sociologists would do well to acknowledge the normative components of theirs.

Acknowledgment

A version of this paper was presented to the Hastings Center project "Value Perceptions and Realities within Managed Health Care."

References

1. The most prominent of these reports is in R. Fox, *The Sociology of Medicine* (Englewood Cliffs, N.J.: Prentice Hall, 1989).
2. For examples of the kind of work I have in mind, see R. Anspach, *Deciding Who Lives: Fateful Choices in the Intensive-Care Nursery* (Berkeley: University of California Press, 1993); C. Bosk, *All God's Mistakes: Genetic Counselling in a Pediatric Hospital* (Chicago: University of Chicago Press, 1992); D. Chambliss, *Beyond Caring: Hospitals, Nurses and the Social Organization of Ethics* (Chicago: University of Chicago Press, 1996); R. Fox and J. Swazey, *Spare Parts: Organ Replacement in American Society* (New York: Oxford University Press, 1992); C. Lidz et al., "Barriers to Informed Consent," *Annals of Internal Medicine* 99 (1983):539-43; R. Zussman, *Intensive Care: Medical Ethics and the Medical Profession* (Chicago: University of Chicago Press, 1992).
3. T. Beauchamp and J. Childress, *Principles of Biomedical Ethics* (New York: Oxford University Press, 1979), p. vi.
4. E. Emanuel and N. Dubler, "Preserving the Physician-Patient Relationship in the Era of Managed Care," *JAMA* 273 (1995): 328. See also E. H. Morreim, *Balancing Act: The New Medical Ethics of Medicine's New Economics* (Boston: Kluwer Academic Press, 1991) and M. Rodwin, *Medicine, Money, and Morals: Physicians' Conflicts of Interest* (New York: Oxford University Press, 1993). Of the 94 items Emanuel and Dubler cite, roughly one-quarter to one-third could fairly be characterized as reports of systematic empirical research. However, they also point out that in regard to their central claim, "while there has been significant attention on conflict of interest in fee-for-service practice, there has been much less effort to investigate and address conflict of interest in managed care" (p. 328). Both their willingness to cite social science research and their difficulty finding research relevant to their claims seem to me altogether compatible with the position I am taking here.
5. See ref. 2, Zussman, *Intensive Care*. See also W. Finlay et al., "Queues and Care: How Medical Residents Organize Their Work in a Busy Clinic," *Journal of Health and Social Behavior* 31 (1990): 292-305.
6. B. Gray, *The Profit Motive and Patient Care: The Changing Accountability of Doctors and Hospitals* (Cambridge, Harvard University Press, 1993).
7. A. Hillman et al., "How Do Financial Incentives Affect Physicians' Clinical Decisions and the Financial Performance of Health Maintenance Organizations?" *NEJM* 321 (1989): 86-92.
8. D. Hemenway et al., "Physicians' Responses to Financial Incentives: Evidence from a For-Profit Ambulatory Care Center," *NEJM* 322 (1990): 1059-63.
9. M. Notman et al., "Social Policy and Professional Self-Interest: Physician Responses to DRGs," *Social Science and Medicine* 25 (1987): 1259-67.
10. B. Hoffmaster, "Can Ethnography Save the Life of Medical Ethics?" *Social Science & Medicine* 35 (1992): 1421-31. See also B. Crigger, "Bioethnography: Fieldwork in the Lands of Medical Ethics," *Medical Anthropology Quarterly* 9 (1995): 400-417 and R. DeVries and P. Conrad, "Why Bioethics Needs Sociology" in R. DeVries and J. Subedi, eds., *Bioethics and Society* (Upper Saddle River, N.J.: Prentice-Hall, 1998).

[33]
Moral Teachings from Unexpected Quarters
Lessons for Bioethics from the Social Sciences and Managed Care

by JAMES LINDEMANN NELSON

On the usual account of moral reasoning, social science is often seen as able to provide "just the facts," while philosophy attends to moral values and conceptual clarity and builds formally valid arguments. Yet disciplines are informed by epistemic values—and bioethics might do well to see social scientific practices and their attendant normative understandings about what is humanly important as a significant part of ethics generally.

Consider the following sketch of how bioethics relates to health care, its major object of study, and to the social sciences, one of its chief allies. Bioethics's job is to assess in what respects prevailing or proposed health care practices, policies, and institutions are morally defensible. To make these assessments, it draws on an interdisciplinary set of resources, crucial among which are those provided by the social sciences. Yet because it is a normative inquiry, its definitive tools are, broadly speaking, philosophical—theories of morality and of practical rationality, analyses of moral concepts, and so forth. These modules of bioethical analysis—the normative core, the empirical auxiliary, the practice that serves as the target—keep distinct characters, and the flow of thought among them is largely linear. Moral theories, informed by facts, judge practices.

There's no lack of sniping at various aspects of this picture, but I want to explore here what might be gained by standing it more or less on its head. The social sciences, that is, will not merely be seen as sources of the facts that bioethics grinds fine in its normative mill, but of more or less distinctive and potentially unsettling values. Health care—and for my present purposes, managed health care—will not be portrayed solely as an object of bioethics's judgmental gaze, but as a repository of moral understandings of its own. My belief is that inverting common wisdom about the relations between the normative and the descriptive, and between a study and its object, will yield interesting results both methodologically and substantially.

To make this thought plausible, I will first smooth out the rough sketch of the orthodox model of the social sciences-bioethics relationship just given, provide some reasons for being dubious about it, and then describe a more heterodox model, one that sees the interaction among the elements in a more complicated way. From this second model I extract a lesson for how bioethics should go about its work, illustrated by a similarly heterodox discussion of the moral dimensions of managed care. These points suggest yet a third model for the role of social scientific inquiry in bioethical thinking, one that tries to resurrect some of bioethics's formative impulses.

James Lindemann Nelson, "Moral Teachings from Unexpected Quarters: Lessons for Bioethics from the Social Sciences and Managed Care," *Hastings Center Report* 30, no. 1 (2000): 12-17.

Some caveats: the point of this exercise is not exhaustively to delineate the possible jobs that social science methodologies, results, or sensibilities have performed or might perform in association with or as a part of bioethics. Nor do I discuss even a representative sample of views on this topic that already exist in the literature; the scholarly ambitions of this essay are modest. My hope, rather, is to press beyond what I think are fairly common and too simple notions of what the social sciences, and medical practice as well, hold out to bioethics, and to enter a brief for the attractiveness of some more complex ideas. The strategy is to highlight how those ideas make more accessible some promising yet underexplored directions for thinking about bioethics and about ethics *tout court*.

"Just the Facts, Ma'am"

The common picture of the relationship between bioethics and the social sciences assigns responsibility for accurately gathering the pertinent facts to epidemiologists, sociologists, anthropologists, and their kin, and for assessing those facts to bioethicists wielding explicitly normative techniques. We can track this image down to a standard lesson taught in many an undergraduate class in ethics, where good moral reasoning is said to involve the following components: (1) accurate empirical beliefs, (2) defensible moral values, (3) clarity about relevant concepts, and (4) formally valid argumentation.

The first component is where the social sciences would most naturally operate; responsibility for the rest of these elements falls to the lot of other disciplines. Moral philosophy, moral theology, and perhaps other humanities have a good deal to say about articulating and defending moral values. Philosophy in general (in its guise as the guardian of conceptual analysis) and logic take care of conceptual clarity and formal validity.

The sciences, then, both natural and social, provide bioethics with the empirical information relevant to its concerns. How many people are willing to make out advance directives? How do chronically ill people experience their illnesses? What impact does shifting a state's Medicaid population to managed care have on health outcomes overall? And so on.

That any such facts are relevant at all, and how they are to be employed in deliberations that lead to action and policy formation, is determined by the moral values, principles, or virtues identified and justified in component (2). For example, a bioethical analysis of the importance of the impact of Medicaid managed care on participants' health might proceed via consideration of such principles as justice and beneficence. Who is and who is not using advance directives assumes importance against a background moral commitment to the importance of respect for autonomy—and so forth.

There is something rather appealing about this linear view. At least in outline, it is simple, straightforward, and has the virtue of not raising anxieties about committing naturalistic fallacies: "is" and "ought" remain on their respective sides of the fence. Scrupulously observing these distinctions provides another kind of comfort as well: at least part of practical moral reasoning seems disciplined by considerations that resist the influence of parties with a particular stake in various outcomes—the facts, after all, are as they are.

Yet taking too much comfort in this consideration may be naive. Empirical inquiry is itself sensitive to the schedules of value endorsed by those directing such work, and the social sciences are far from immune to this tendency. The notion that the salient facts about the natural world, or about patterns of social interaction, or economic trends, or the phenomenology of chronic illness, are just there, waiting to be scooped up by neutral forms of inquiry, is hotly contested, and not just by critics of a relativist temperament. Indeed, a belief that objective knowledge is a coherent and obtainable goal may be a particularly strong motivation for careful attention to the impact of histories and passions on what and how we see.

Social scientists, then, may well be skeptical about the linear model, as indeed are many students of ethical theory. They regard the four-step approach to moral reasoning displayed above as oversimplifying the relationships among the moral, the empirical, and the conceptual. The interchanges among these categories flow in more than one direction.

From Moral to Epistemic Values—and Back Again

A problem for those skeptical about the linear view is how the normative tints coloring "fact-gathering" enterprises can be acknowledged without thereby undermining moral arguments that draw on them. How can the value-laden character of empirical inquiry be taken up into a more adequate notion of how bioethics ought to go on? The response I wish to press is that we regard the values bound up within the scientist's activities not as essentially distorting

Conceived of as embodying loose "normative traditions" as well as methodologies and facts, the said sciences might also challenge bioethicists.

the bioethicist's access to what is actually going on in the world, but rather as potentially enriching the store of normative understandings from which she constructs the moral convictions she puts into play in her own arguments and analyses.

This might seem to beg the question, and as if that were not bad enough, to involve us in a nasty circularity. After all, would not getting clearer about how values work in empirical disciplines itself be an empirical task? Would it not therefore itself be undermined by distortions introduced by the values we bring to *that* enterprise?

But anxieties about whether acknowledging the role of values in how we form beliefs about the world turns science into propaganda come not from the reasonable reminder that science is done by real human beings in concrete historical settings. A much more ambitious kind of skepticism is operating here, one that holds out a vision of knowledge as an unmediated encounter with states of affairs as they are in themselves, and scolds all existing knowledge claims for not being thus pristine. Skepticism of that sort has been curiously persistent but not plausible. Indeed, it seems to dangle from its own petard—after all, it makes fairly ambitious knowledge claims itself, concerning what knowledge is and what's wrong with all efforts to establish any.

In any event, such hypertrophied skepticism is not what's driving the doubts about the "just the facts" model. Allowing that scientific inquiry incorporates values is not to say that it is self-defeating, but rather to alert us to its complexity. Nothing prevents bioethicists from trying to get clearer about the norms at play in accounts of the facts they need to do their job. Nor does anything preclude the possibility that tracking those norms might, as I suggest above, not only increase the credibility of those accounts but enrich our understanding of values as well.

Here's how this might work: Suppose that the values operating within the ordinary practice of various social sciences tend to cluster into more or less characteristic forms of moral understanding.[1] Consider, for example, the persistent tendency of sociologists to be suspicious about the self-professed benevolence of the professions, and contrast that suspicion with the notable lack of any even roughly similar doubts shared among bioethicists. Should the canny bioethicist who finds herself in need of social science data concerning health care professionals just factor in a "hostility discount" when reading the work of her social scientist colleagues? Or might she be better advised to wonder who actually better understands the moral character of the professions? Perhaps even more significantly, she might wonder why there seems to be a discipline-specific shape to that understanding.

Rather than just supplying bioethicists with accounts of the facts, then, the social sciences, conceived of as embodying loose "normative traditions" as well as methodologies and facts, might also challenge such matters as what bioethicists think it worth their while to attend to, and even whose interests they think it appropriate to serve.

Yet the problem with this idea is patent. How plausible is it to think that the social sciences do embody normative traditions? Even if there is a tendency on the part of sociologists to raise their eyebrows at protestations about the disinterestedness of the professions, it hardly follows that social scientists can be distinguished from other intellectuals with respect to their political and ethical affiliations consistently enough to see their fields as sources of distinct moral views on features of medicine or any other aspect of society. Some social scientists are on the left, some on the right, some in the middle. They scarcely present a morally united front.

Yet it may not do to give up on the spirit behind this notion too quickly; there might still be something to the idea that survives moral and political plurality among sociologists and social scientists generally. Consider that while all the sciences value such ends as truth and such investigator virtues as honesty and trustworthiness, values more particular to each science play a role in individuating the domains of research and determining the methodological orientations that pertain to one discipline rather than another. Such *epistemic values* will be involved in setting investigators' sensitivities to what perceptions count as salient, what forms of argument seem promising, which questions seem settled, and which issues still very much alive. Arguably, many of the epistemic values most vigorously at play in sociology rank highly the heuristic force of accounts of human behavior that rely on group membership. Psychology, for its part, might be said to favor in general a more causally oriented, perhaps more individualist take, often focusing in its explanations on underlying mechanisms rather than patterns of group behavior. Anthropology is particularly keen on diversity among groups.

It is perhaps somewhat ironic that something close to social science's epistemic values—what Renée Fox has called the "ethos of the social science"—has been invoked to explain the disengagement between bioethics and these fields. The medical anthropologist Patricia Marshall, for example, has cited her discipline's focus on the culturally relative, the non-Western, and on perceiving people as parts of a community rather than as autonomous agents, as explaining why anthropology has tended to neglect bioethics.[2]

It seems to me not improbable that these different epistemic values reflect different ensembles of views about what is humanly important, and do so at a more fundamental level than political affiliations may signal. If so, the sociologist's special attention to groups and group participation, or the anthropologist's carefully honed sensitivity to the many different forms human communities can take, themselves highlight features of human life and thought that are normatively significant and yet not foregrounded by other disciplines—including those explicitly concerned with value, such as ethics and its various "applied" branches.

If distinguishable epistemic values do help form distinguishable disciplines, we have reason to see the social sciences as constituting normative traditions, despite the many different moral commitments held by individual social scientists.

But are normative traditions shaped around epistemic values of any ethical interest? It is certainly possible that there is something of a slide between epistemic and ethical values, and that what strikes social scientists as good ways to think about people scientifically will influence what they take to be good ways to think about people morally. Yet whether or not this is right is itself an empirical question. Anthropologists may on examination turn out to be no more *morally* respectful of human diversity than is in general the case, sociologists no less individualistic. But bioethics is surely free to look to the characteristic heuristic interests and procedures of the social sciences for different ways of understanding selves, communities, relationships, responsibilities—to look, in short, for the ethical messages that may be latent there.

It is also free to look to its own procedures and agendas in order to become clearer about the tacit values there, as well as about the tacit effects of explicit values. If examination reveals distinct value orientations characterizing bioethics on the one hand and the several social sciences on the other hand, what are they and how do they figure in analysis and assessment? Why do those orientations take the shapes they do? What considerations of history, disciplinary influence, individual idiosyncracy result in certain values coming to be crucial in the distinctive ways a field looks at the world?

Extracting the ethical lessons from social science's epistemic values and putting bioethics itself under a social scientific gaze might exert fruitful pressure on some of bioethics's own favorite values. It might be interesting to ask, for example, why the chief values of mainstream bioethics—most conspicuously the pride of place given to respect for autonomy—have remained relatively firmly fixed despite countervailing theoretical ferment in other areas of ethics and even in the light of what seems to be rather disturbing empirical findings.

Consider, for example, the indication emerging from the SUPPORT study that promoting patient or surrogate involvement in determining treatment limitations is not typically highly valued by health care professionals, and their lack of involvement seems little regretted by patients and families.[3] The social sciences might make a contribution to bioethics by helping the field's practitioners understand better what's behind its deeply installed respect for individual autonomy and whether it has assumed more the character of an ideology than a moral philosophy.

SUPPORT and similar applications of social science techniques to the ethics of health care promise further lessons for how different moral understandings might come to be installed or resisted in patterns of practice. Bioethical interventions into health care practice have tended to rely on rational persuasion based on arguments about values—that is to say, on the kind of educative models familiar in university settings, addressed in the main to individuals. Bioethical pedagogy thus chimes with the individualist approach that characterizes so much of mainstream ethics. An approach to both analysis and action that looks less at individuals, and more at the characteristics of institutions and how they shape human response, surely seems worth trying in SUPPORT's wake. If bioethicists can better understand how various moral understandings become practically effective, either in the world of medical practice or within the field itself, they clearly are in a better position to have the kinds of

> Extracting the ethical lessons from social science's epistemic values and putting bioethics itself under a social scientific gaze might exert fruitful pressure on some of bioethics's own favorite values.

In the end, the contribution of the social sciences to bioethics may be to complete a trend in this interdisciplinary field—that is, to tear down the hold on our imaginations of the notion that the world breaks down along just the lines that intellectual disciplines do.

influence that they want. But there is a dialectical character to this point as well. Bioethicists more attuned to learning lessons from the epistemic values of the social sciences also may be in a position to be influenced in the kind of way they (should) want—for instance, by better understanding the moral significance of structural shifts within health care.

Managed Care as a Moral Teacher

Thus far, I've contrasted a rather linear model of the relationship of bioethics and the social sciences to an interactive model, finding many more interesting suggestions for the future of the field hiding out in the second image. Here, I want to continue in this vein, asking whether the standard conception that bioethicists often have of health care is not also too linear. My particular focus will be on managed health care.

What are the normative understandings built into managed care? Bioethicists not infrequently look somewhat askance at managed care, skeptical about whether it provides a context hospitable to special moral characteristics of the doctor-patient relationship—the physician's commitment to her patient's health needs, the importance of maintaining and extending the range of patient autonomy, the significance of lasting doctor-patient dyads. Bioethical analysis of managed care tends to take the value of these traditional features of medical practice largely as given, conclusively established by moral arguments not themselves called into question by the confrontation with managed care. Managed care arrangements are then assessed according to how they maintain their allegiance to these values. But this approach excludes the possibility that managed care incorporates, or in any event can and sometimes does incorporate, a set of moral understandings that may be quite defensible in their own right, quite apart from their relationship to a differently populated or ranked set of values.

Suppose, for example, that some forms of managed care are seen as embodying or at least inviting a distinctive kind of ethic—a "capitalist collectivist" view of how to strike the appropriate balance among efficiency, access, and quality. Managed care is capitalist in that it draws on marketplace disciplines to keep costs in order. Plans compete in ways that are reflected financially, and this competition is apparent to consumers, both corporate and individual. Yet at the same time, some managed care arrangements—particularly health maintenance organizations—might be considered morally collectivist: there is a sense in which the members of such groups as a whole are affected by health care decisions made for individual members. Members face limitations on easy availability of resources, particularly those whose effectiveness is in question. In general, individualistic prerogatives are to be weighed against collective concerns. The doctor-patient relationship is not sacrosanct; the ethic of rescue is less prominent.

This constitutes an interesting division of moral labor: at the economic level, managed care relies on the notion of the person as a consumer, as a savvy bargainer in the marketplace. But at the level of service provision, managed care—particularly when it takes the form of an HMO—suggests that people can be responsive to other, less individualist concerns, that they are willing to subordinate some of their own interests to ensure the viability and flourishing of the whole.

Some of the difficulties with and incoherence within managed care may come from a clash between these perspectives; perhaps they cannot peacefully coexist over the long term. But the clashes may not necessarily be evidence that the perspectives must exclude each other: in other contexts, people seem to be able to live with mixed identities as consumers and members of a commonwealth.[4] Perhaps what is needed is for the *sub voce* reliance on a ethic of solidarity within some managed care settings to announce itself explicitly, and for consumers and professionals to be provided with some education about what it means morally, not merely fiscally, to become a participant in managed care.

What might the social sciences contribute to our understanding of the ethical culture of managed care? What, to ask it another way, are the structural features of managed care, of professionalism and the ethics of professionalism, to which bioethicists ought to attend in order to understand the moral problems and the moral possibilities in managed care arrangements? It is fairly patent that an appreciation of the character of social structures, of the "cultures" that operate within them, and of their relationship to broader aspects of society are bioethically pertinent matters for which the tools of social scientific inquiry are key. However, the values and sensibilities that are prevalent in the social sciences may make an even bigger contribution. For example, seeing potential moral interest and perhaps even insight in at least some forms of managed care might well be easier for bioethicists if their assessment of fee-for-service financing was tempered with the kind of suspicion about professions that have been an important part of sociology. One's willingness to see collectivist approaches as in principle at least on a par with individualist assessments of medical ethics might also be easier to achieve if one better appreciated the moral significance of social and group relations as social scientists not infrequently do.

The Oppenheimer View of Bioethics

The attractiveness of an interactive understanding of bioethics and the social sciences can be pressed a step further. Robert Oppenheimer, it is reported, once said that he was attracted to physics because, in the early 20th century, physics was the best way to do philosophy. I suspect that one of the considerations that got a good many philosophers engaged with biomedicine in the late 20th century was a similar feeling: reflecting on developments in health care provided the best way—or at least, a very good way—of doing philosophy. Something similar I think might be said of other of bioethics's contributing disciplines.

Unfortunately, the relative success of bioethics in forging links with clinical practice has sometimes made it difficult to hang on to the Oppenheimer Insight. Is bioethics solely about giving good advice to docs (policy people, managers, patients, payers, etc.)? Or is it about ethics—about how we ought to understand morally relevant ideas (the nature and point of ethical reasoning; the assigning, shouldering, and deflecting of responsibility; the persistence of identity; the significance of human agency and of human relationships in its maintenance; and so forth), such that by thinking about the issues involved in clinical or research or policy contexts, we might better grasp features of these ideas not well understood in other ways?

Suppose that there is something to this view, and suppose that some form of connection with the social sciences is going to be important to achieving these better understandings. What seems suggested by this connection of ideas is that social scientific practices and the attending normative understandings should be regarded as a significant part of ethics considered quite generally.

There are some signs that moral philosophers are taking this possibility seriously. Kathryn Pyne Addleson and Margaret Urban Walker, to mention but two examples, have called for and themselves modeled approaches to ethics that rely importantly on sophisticated, empirically saturated understandings of social life.[5] Addleson's work relies on well-developed ethnographies in order to make evident the class biases at work in authoritative writers who are regarded as doing "pure theory," such as Rawls. And Walker develops a picture of moral deliberation, the "expressive-collaborative" concept, which she contrasts with the regnant "theoretical-juridical" view. Whereas the theoretical-juridical view rests largely on armchair assumptions about "our" moral intuitions, molded into a "logic of justification" that derives from work in the philosophy of science, Walker's alternative underscores the variety of human motivations, arrangements, and forms of life and sees ethics largely as the effort collectively to build and renew social practices that make the ways in which responsibilities and rewards are distributed through societies as clear as possible.

In the end, the contribution of the social sciences to bioethics may be to complete the trend that has played an important role in this interdisciplinary field from the start—that is, to tear down the hold on our imaginations of the notion that, considered normatively or descriptively, the world breaks down along just the lines that intellectual disciplines do. If bioethics could model a way of understanding and resolving human problems that exhibited both a deep engagement with intellectual disciplines and a freedom from their territorial constraints, that might be among its most profound contributions to its culture.

Acknowledgments

A version of this paper was presented to the Hastings Center project "Value Perceptions and Realities within Managed Health Care." I am grateful to all the participants in the ensuing discussion for their thoughtful comments, particularly for those of Bob Zussman. Jonathan Kaplan and Hilde Lindemann Nelson were kind enough to read later drafts.

References

1. This possibility was suggested to me by remarks of Robert Zussman, made at The Hastings Center in November of 1996; it does not represent his own position.

2. See R. Fox, "The Evolution of American Bioethics: A Sociological Perspective," in *Social Science Perspectives in Medical Ethics*, ed. G. Weisz (Boston: Kluwer, 1990); and P. Marshall, "Anthropology and Bioethics," *Medical Anthropology Quarterly* 6 (1992): 49-73. My attention was drawn to these pieces by the discussion in D. Joralemon, *Exploring Medical Anthropology* (Boston: Allyn & Bacon, 1999), p. 110.

3. See the articles in "Dying Well in the Hospital: The Lessons of SUPPORT [Special Supplement]," *Hastings Center Report* 25, no. 6 (1995): S3-S36.

4. See M. Sagoff, "At the Shrine of Our Lady of Fatima," in M. Sagoff, *The Economy of the Earth* (Cambridge: Cambridge University Press, 1988).

5. K. P. Addleson, *Moral Passages* (New York: Routledge, 1994); M. U. Walker, *Moral Understandings: A Feminist Study in Ethics* (New York: Routledge, 1998).

Name Index

Abdel-Fattah, Ali 547
Ackerman, Terrance F. 432
Adams, John Bodkin xvii
Addleson, Kathryn P. 564
Al Azhar Gad el-Haq, Grand Shaikh 547
Albert of Bologna 35
Alexander, Cheryl S. 433
Alexander, Leo 341–2
Al-Masry, Youssef 546
al-Razi xv
Annas, G. 481
Anscombe, G.E.M. xxi, xxiii, 223–36, 240, 242, 249, 315, 515
Anspach, R.R. 529, 530
Aquinas, Thomas xv, xvi, 194, 235, 236, 248, 511, 512, 513
Arderne, John 35
Arimathaeus 34
Aristotle xvi, 132, 135, 145, 171, 172, 199, 200, 224, 320, 327, 377, 396, 397, 400, 402, 466, 491, 494, 495, 508
Aroskar, Mila A. 431
Arras, John D. xx, xxv, xxvi, 99–130, 137, 138, 463–85, 510
Asclepius xv
Assaad, Marie 546
Augustine, St xv, 491
Austen, Jane 197
Austin, John 195, 489

Baby Alexandra xxv
Baby Cotton xvi
Baby Doe 161, 185
Baby M xvi, 117
Baier, A. 131, 134
Barnard, Christiaan xvi
Baron, R.J. 523
Basson, Marc D. 432
Beauchamp, Tom L. xix, xx, 102, 108, 109, 129, 132, 138, 140–42 passim, 144, 148, 153, 204, 210–16 passim, 218, 219, 437, 464, 497, 498, 506
Bede, St 15
Beecher, Henry K. xvii, 3–9
Benedict, Ruth 541
Benjamin, Martin 431–46
Bentham, Jeremy xxii, 77

Bernardin, Joseph C. 86, 87
Bettelheim, Bruno 544
Bishop, Anne H. 434
Bleich, J. David xviii, 90
Blum, Lawrence 397, 398, 403, 453
Boas, Frank 541
Bosk, C.L. 527, 530
Boyes, Lilian xxiv
Boyle, Joseph xxi, xxii, 237–56, 257–69 passim
Bradley, F.H. 184, 524
Brandt, Richard B. 150, 318
Broad, C.D. 524
Brock, D.W. 147
Brody, Baruch A. 132, 140, 252, 253, 267, 504, 505, 516
Broverman, D. 417
Broverman, I. 417
Brown, Louise xvi
Browning, Don S. 94
Burt, Robert A. 114

Cahill, Lisa S. xviii, 83
Callahan, Daniel xviii, xxvii, 71–3, 94, 481
Campbell, A.G.M. xvii
Campbell, Courtney S. xviii, 75–81
Camus, Albert 79
Caplan, Arthur L. 432, 526
Carse, A.L. 473, 510, 514
Carter, Jimmy 94
Cassiodorus 14, 15, 17
Chase, Gary A. 433
Chicago, Judy 545
Childress, James F. xix, xx, 102, 108, 109, 132, 138, 140–42 passim, 144, 148, 153, 204, 210–16 passim, 218, 219, 464, 498, 506
Chisholm, R. 241
Christ, Jesus 95
Cicero 195, 491, 512
Clarkson, F. 417
Clough, A.H. 266
Clouser, K. Danner xix, xx, 112, 132, 139, 142, 203–20
Conroy, Claire 117, 469, 471
Constantine, Emperor 195, 196
Constantine the African 36–7
Cooper, C. Carolyn 432, 434
Cox, Nigel xxiv

Crisham, Patricia 432
Cruzan, Nancy 117
Curran, Charles 72
Curtis, Joy 431
Curzer, Howard 450
Curzon 471

Daniels, N. 150, 482, 505
Davidson, Donald 223, 224
Davis, Anne J. 431
Dawit, Seble 546
DeGrazia, David xx, 112, 113, 131–59
De Renzi, S. 18, 34
Dickens, Charles 195
Dennis, Karen E. 433
Denziger, H. 512, 517
Descartes, Réné 530
Devlin, Lord Patrick xvii, 51
Dewey, John 173, 199, 466
Dodson, Betty 545
Donagan, Alan xxi, 240, 244, 245, 250, 257–71
Douglass, Frederick 197
Downie, R.S. xx
Dubler, Nancy 104, 554–5
Duff, R.S. xvii
Dworkin, Ronald 92, 477

Edelstein, Ludwig 12
Edgerton, Robert 542
Eichmann, Adolf 366
Einstein, Albert 322
Elliott, Carl xxvi
El-Saadawy, Nawal 546
Emanuel, Ezekiel J. xix, 554–5
Englehardt, H. Tristram jr xix, xx, 431, 433, 506, 510
Epicurus 26, 28
Erasistratus 24
Erikson, E. 417
Etziony, M.B. xv

Feinberg, Joel 355
Feldman, David 72, 90
Ferrara, Mary 435
Finnis, John M. xxi, 239, 249
Fisher, Berenice xxiv
Flathman, R.E. 514
Fletcher, Joseph xviii, xix, 72, 434
Foot, Philippa xxiii, 241, 243, 258, 315, 317, 319, 320, 332–3 passim, 341–68
Fox, Renee C. 94, 472, 480, 526, 528
Frankena, William K. 138, 205, 207–10 passim, 219, 432, 439–41 passim, 498
Fraser, F.C. 527

Freud, Sigmund 417
Frohock, F.M. 524, 525, 527, 528
Frost, Robert 199
Fry, Sara T. 431–46
Fuchs, Joseph 86, 87
Fuller, Lon L. xxv

Gadamer, A. 479
Gadow, Sally 432, 434, 435, 439, 441, 451
Ganss, G. 513
Garrison, Fielding 17
Gaskell, Mrs 196
Gert, Bernard xix, xx, 112, 132, 139, 142, 152, 203–20
Gilligan, Carol xx, xxiv, 397, 409, 410–11 passim, 417, 421, 422, 433, 436, 447, 449, 510, 514
Ginsburg, F.D. 526
Glendon, Mary A. 111
Grandy, R. 509, 510, 511
Gray, Bradford 555
Green, R.M. 132
Gregory, John xvi
Gregory I, Pope 15
Griffin, Anne P. 435, 436, 439, 441
Griffin, James 327–8
Grisez, Germain xxi, 239
Gruenbaum, Ellen 543
Gustafson, James M. 84, 85, 87
Guy of Chauliac 35

Habermas, Jürgen 479, 489
Hampshire, S. 481
Hare, R.M. xxiii, 150, 151, 318, 325, 393–406, 531
Harris, John xxii, xxvii, 275–98 passim, 299–311
Harrison, M.R. 474
Hart, H.L.A. 50, 241, 242, 469
Hart, Roisin xxiv
Hauerwas, Stanley 77, 85–6, 94
Heidegger, Martin 435
Hemenway, David 555
Henry of Mondeville 35
Herman, Barbara 317
Herskovits, Melville 541
Hillman, Alan 555
Hippocrates xv, 12, 15, 16, 17, 21, 26, 33–4, 41
Hirsch, Samson R. 90
Hirschfeld 18
Hitler, Adolf 341, 366, 542
Hobbes, Thomas 495
Hoffmaster, Barry xxvii, 523–33, 556, 557
Honoré, A.M. 525
Hosken, Fran P. 545

Huggins, Elizabeth A. 435
Hume, David 353, 397, 440
Hurka, Thomas 335
Hursthouse, Rosalind xxiii, 317, 369–92
Hussein, Aziza 546

Isodore of Seville 15, 25

Jacox, Ada K. 433
Jakobovits, Immanuel xviii, 91
James, Henry 121, 123
James, William 497
Jameton, Andrew 431
Jecker, Nancy 495
Jennings, B. 530
Jerome, St 13–14 *passim*, 15
John, XXIII, Pope 86
Johnson, Virginia E. 545
Jonas, Hans 499
Jones, W.H.S. 11, 38
Johnson, Samuel 322
Jonsen, Albert R. xxvi, 132, 135–6 *passim*, 463–8 *passim*, 470, 475, 477, 478, 481, 482, 487–501, 503, 504–12 *passim*, 513–15 *passim*, 517

Kamm, F.M. 296
Kant, Immanuel 80, 100, 105, 174, 175, 187, 207, 216, 217, 219, 263, 264, 319, 345, 396, 397, 400, 401, 403, 456, 470, 529
Kass, Leon 76, 77, 78
Kaufman, Herbert 198
Ketefian, Shake 432
Kibre, Pearl 13
Kirk, Kenneth 490
Kleinman, Arthur 94
Kohlberg, L. 397, 410, 411, 419, 422
Kopelman, Loretta xxvi
Kramer, R. 422
Kuhse, Helga xxiv, xxv, 397, 447–59
Kuhn, Thomas 128, 469, 509

Lane, Sandra D. xxvii, 541–50
Langdale 411
Laux 18
Levi-Strauss, Claude 84
Lippman, A. 527
Locke, John 105
Loevinger, J. 417
Lyola, St Ignatius 513
Lyons, Nona P. xxiv, 409–29
Lyotard, Jean-François 510

McCormick, Richard xviii, 72, 83, 233

McElmurry, Beverly J. 434
MacIntyre, Alasdair C. 119, 131, 315, 321, 476, 480, 510
MacKinney, Loren C. xv, xvii, 11–41
Mahran, Maher 546
Maimonides, Moses xv
Maine, Sir Henry 195
Mangan, J. 237
Manning, Rita C. xxiv, xxv
Marshall, Patricia 562
Masterman, M. 509
Masters, William H. 545
May, William F. 434
Mead, George H. 419
Mead, Margaret 541
Meeks, Wayne 85
Meilaender, G. 474
Mekuria, Salem 546
Midgely, Mary 95
Mill, John Stuart 100, 105, 205, 207, 216, 220, 403, 440, 470
Mohammed, Prophet 95, 544
Molière, Jean-Baptiste P. 487, 490
Moore, G.E. 497, 524, 526
Morgenstern, O. 168
Morsy, Soheir 546
Moses 95
Munhall, Patricia 432
Murdoch, Iris 410, 426
Murphy, Catherine C. 432
Muyskens, James L. 431

Nagel, Thomas 73, 106, 241, 243, 245, 345
Navarrus xv
Nelson, Hilde 454
Nelson, Horatio 396
Nelson, James L. xxvii, 559–64
Neumann 168
Noble, C. 472, 480
Noddings, Nel xxiv, 397, 432, 433, 435, 436–7 *passim*, 441, 447, 449, 452, 454, 456–7 *passim*
Nonet, P. 67
Notman, Mark 555
Novak, David 89–92
Nussbaum, Martha C. 119, 121–2, 123

Oakley, Justin xxiii, 315–40
O'Neil, O. 472
Oppenheimer, Robert 564
Overcast, D. 480

Packard, John S. 435
Panin, Dmitri 344, 346, 351

Parfit, Derek 285, 289, 291, 296
Parker, Randy S. 454–5 passim
Pascal, Blaise 200, 464, 503
Patterson, E.W. 470
Paul, St 513
Pellegrino, Edmund D. 433, 437–9 passim, 440, 441, 505, 535–40
Percival, Thomas xvi
Paterson, L. 523
Piaget, Jean 411, 417, 422
Pitkin, H. 467
Pius IX, Pope xvi
Pius XII, Pope 3
Plato 402
Platt, Sir Robert 4
Porter, Roy xv
Prescott, Patricia A. 433
Price, Anthony 397

Quill, Timothy 120, 121
Quinlan, Karen A. xvii, 117, 342, 367, 469, 471
Quinn, Warren 239, 242, 243, 245–8 passim, 258
Quintilian 494

Rabanus Maurus 20
Rachels, James 359
Railton, Peter 318, 318
Ramsey, Paul xviii, 72, 79, 83, 434
Rawls, John 92, 101, 108, 109, 154, 197, 205, 206, 207, 212, 216, 431, 467, 470, 478, 482, 564
Ricci, Matteo 490, 491
Richardson, Henry S. xix, 112, 132, 142, 144–8 passim, 153, 161–92
Ricoeur, Paul 480
Rorty, Richard 479
Rose 18
Rosenkrantz, P. 417
Rosner, Fred 91
Ross, W.D. 138, 170–72 passim, 184, 191, 192
Rousseau, Jean-Jacques 447, 448
Rubinstein, Robert A. xxvii, 541–50, 547

Saikewitz 471
Sartre, Jean-Paul 100
Savulescu, Julian xxii, 275–98, 299–311 passim
Scalzi, Cynthia C. 435
Scanlon, T.M. 175
Schneider, Carl xviii
Schneiderman, Lawrence 495
Schonmetzer, A. 512, 517
Schopenhauer, Arthur 447–8
Schroeder, Patricia 545, 548

Schüklenk, Udo xxvii
Scudder, John R. 434
Self, Donnie J. 433
Selman, R.L. 419
Selznick, Philip 67
Sen, Amartya xxii
Sidgwick, Henry 393, 488, 523, 529
Siegel, Seymour 72
Siegler, Mark 492
Sigerist, Henry E. 11, 18, 19
Silva, Mary C. 432
Singer, Peter 150, 397, 459, 505
Slack, Alison T. 542
Slote, Michael 321, 336–7 passim
Socrates 402
Sorabji, R. 512
Soranus 31–2
Spence, Jonathan 490
Spinoza, Benedict 495
Spiro, Melford 541
Spring 471
Stein, Peter 195
Stenberg, Margorie J. 432, 434
Steward, Julian 542
Stout, Jeffrey 73, 84, 87, 95
Styron, William 260
Sullivan, T. 241
Sumner, Wayne 398

Tallmon, James 492
Taurek, J.M. 289
Taylor, Charles 106, 481
Temkin, Oswei 11, 13
Tendler, Moses 91
Tennyson, Lord 448
Theresa, Mother 322
Theron, Stephen 258, 259
Thomasma, David C. 433, 437, 505
Thomson, Judith J. 380
Thompson, Henry O. 431
Thompson, Joyce B. 431
Tolstoy, Leo 196–7 passim, 200
Toubia, Nahid 546, 548
Toulmin, Stephen xx, xxv, 95, 132, 135–6 passim, 193–201, 432, 463–8 passim, 470, 475, 477, 478, 481, 482, 488, 489, 503, 504–6 passim, 509–12 passim, 514–15 passim, 523, 529, 531
Tronto, Joan xxiv

Van der Burg, Wibren xvii, 45–68
Veatch, Robert M. xix, xx, xxiii, 324–5, 431, 505
Verhay, Allen 85, 86, 87
Vogel, S. 417